Free Soil,
Free Labor,
Free Men:

THE IDEOLOGY OF THE REPUBLICAN PARTY
BEFORE THE CIVIL WAR

1. elements of Northern
free labor ideology

2. Repub. critique of South, SH

3. Repub. racial views
include nativism

Free Soil,
Free Labor,
Free Men:

THE IDEOLOGY OF THE REPUBLICAN PARTY
BEFORE THE CIVIL WAR

Eric Foner

With a New Introductory Essay

OXFORD UNIVERSITY PRESS

OXFORD   NEW YORK

1995

Oxford University Press

Oxford   New York
Athens   Auckland   Bangkok   Bombay
Calcutta   Cape Town   Dar es Salaam   Delhi
Florence   Hong Kong   Istanbul   Karachi
Kuala Lumpur   Madras   Madrid   Melbourne
Mexico City   Nairobi   Paris   Singapore
Taipei   Tokyo   Toronto

and associated companies in
Berlin   Ibadan

Published by Oxford University Press, Inc.,
198 Madison Avenue, New York, New York 10016-4314

Oxford is a registered trademark of Oxford University Press

Library of Congress Cataloging-in-Publication Data
Foner, Eric.
Free soil, free labor, free men : the ideology of the
Republican Party before the Civil War / Eric Foner.
p. cm.
Includes bibliographical references and index.
ISBN 0-19-509981-8   ISBN 0-19-509497-2 (pbk)   ꙮ
1. United States—Politics and government—1849-1861. 2. United
States—History—Civil War, 1861-1865—Causes. 3. Republican Party
(U.S. : 1854-   )   I. Title.
E436.F6   1995   973.6—dc20   94-19304

9 8

Printed in the United States of America

for Naomi

Preface

My interest in the ante-bellum period began nine years ago, when as a junior in Columbia College, I was fortunate enough to take Professor James P. Shenton's seminar on the era of disunion and reunion. Since then, Professor Shenton's deep knowledge of the period has aided my work at every stage of its development. As well as being an academic adviser he has become a close and loyal friend. The original version of this work was a doctoral dissertation at Columbia University, supervised by Professor Richard Hofstadter. Professor Hofstadter's keen historical insight helped me clarify my own thoughts at every point, and his own work set an example of the level that historical scholarship can attain. Professor Eric McKitrick was especially generous with his time, interest, and advice. My judgments about the ante-bellum period were refined in the course of many long conversations in his office. His careful reading of a first draft of this work saved me from many an imprecision of style and thought, and his good-humored encouragement made the task of revising the manuscript for publication much easier.

In preparing this work for publication, I was fortunate to receive advice from several outstanding scholars: Eugene D. Genovese, William H. Freehling, Stuart Bruchey, and Allan Silver. All read the manuscript with great care and made many valuable suggestions. I would also like to thank Sheldon Meyer of Oxford University Press for his advice and encouragement. My friend Michael Wallace, a graduate student at Columbia University, gave the manuscript a thorough reading and discussed the subject with me at some length. This work has benefited enormously from the interest, encouragement, and criticisms of all these scholars.

I would also like to thank the librarians of the Columbia University Libraries for their competent and professional assistance, and the staffs of the other libraries I visited, especially the manuscript librarians of the Rush Rhees Library, University of Rochester.

Lastly, I want to thank Naomi, for everything.

The Idea of Free Labor in
Nineteenth-Century America

It is a discomfiting thought—for the author at least—that a quarter of a century has passed since the publication of my first book, *Free Soil, Free Labor, Free Men*. That the book remains in print, and is still assigned in history courses in the United States, is extremely gratifying, although I must admit that its initial impact derived in part from the good fortune of appearing at the very moment when American historians were rediscovering the concept of ideology. The book argued, in brief, that the Republican party before the Civil War was united by a commitment to a "free labor ideology," grounded in the precepts that free labor was economically and socially superior to slave labor and that the distinctive quality of Northern society was the opportunity it offered wage earners to rise to property-owning independence. From this creed flowed Republicans' determination to arrest the expansion of slavery and place the institution on what Lincoln called the road to "ultimate extinction."[1]

Twenty-five years establishes enough distance to reflect not only on a book's longevity, but also its limitations. On re-reading, it is clear that *Free Soil, Free Labor, Free Men* took the free labor ideology as a given, making little effort to trace its ideological origins, social roots, or evolution over time. "Free labor," moreover, was presented as a straight-

1. Eric Foner, *Free Soil, Free Labor, Free Men: The Ideology of the Republican Party Before the Civil War* (New York, 1970).

An earlier version of this essay was delivered as the Commonwealth Fund Lecture at University College London, in February 1994. I wish to thank participants in the subsequent discussion for their valuable criticisms and suggestions.

forward, unitary concept, with little sense of how different Americans
might have infused it with substantially different meanings.

My purpose in this new introduction, however, is not to review my
own book, but to suggest how the transformation of historical scholarship during the past quarter-century enables us to better understand
the idea of free labor and the society in which it flourished. Written,
as it were, on the threshold separating two generations of historical
scholarship, *Free Soil, Free Labor, Free Men* lacked the benefit of the
"new histories" that have matured since 1969: the new concepts and
methodologies that scholars have applied to the study of labor, gender, the law, and political langauge itself. These make it possible to
take a fresh look at the idea of free labor, in the hope of describing it
in greater complexity and situating it more fully in nineteenth-century
American history.

When *Free Soil* was published, historians were just emerging from
what in retrospect appears as a fairly sterile debate over whether
"consensus" or "conflict" characterized the American past. It is now
clear that if nineteenth-century Americans shared a common language of politics, the very universality of that rhetoric camouflaged
a host of divergent connotations and emphases. Concepts central to
the era's political culture—independence, equality, citizenship, freedom—were subject to constant challenge and redefinition, their substance changing over time as different groups sought to redraw their
boundaries and reshape their meanings. Such concepts, moreover,
were generally defined and redefined through the construction of
binary oppositions that ordered Americans' understanding of social
reality, simultaneously illuminating some parts of that reality and
obscuring or glossing over others.[2] Just as freedom and slavery were
joined in the actual development of the New World, the definition of
free labor depended on juxtaposition with its ideological opposite,
slave labor. Under the rubric of free labor, Northerners of diverse
backgrounds and interests could rally in defense of the superiority of
their own society, even as other voices questioned whether the contrast with slavery did not disguise the forms of compulsion to which
free laborers were themselves subjected. The dichotomy between
slave and free labor masked the fact that "free labor" itself referred to

2. See Leon Fink, "Labor, Liberty, and the Law: Trade Unionism and the Problem of
the American Constitutional Order," *Journal of American History,* 74 (December 1987),
907; Joan W. Scott, *Gender and the Politics of History* (New York, 1988), 5–7.

two distinct economic conditions—the wage laborer seeking employment in the marketplace, and the property-owning small producer enjoying a modicum of economic independence. Despite large differences in their economic status, these groups had in common the fact that they were not slaves, that the economic relationships into which they entered were understood as "voluntary" rather than arising from personal dependence.

To think of free labor as coexisting in ideological tension with slave labor (real or imagined, contemporary or, after the Civil War, remembered) suggests that the free labor ideology could not develop without a sharpening of the actual dichotomy between slavery and freedom. It is sometimes forgotten how many varieties of partial freedom coexisted in colonial America, including indentured servants, apprentices, domestic laborers paid largely in kind, as well as sailors impressed into service in the British navy and, in a few areas, tenant farmers. (I leave to one side, for the moment, the quasi-free status of colonial women, whose labor legally belonged to their fathers or husbands.) Indentured servitude, a form of voluntary unfreedom, comprised a major part of the non-slave labor force throughout the colonial era. As late as the early 1770s, nearly half the immigrants who arrived in America from England and Scotland had entered into contracts for a fixed period of labor in exchange for passage. Although not slaves, indentured servants could be bought and sold, were subject to corporal punishment, and their obligation to fulfil their duties ("specific performance" in legal terminology) was enforced by the courts. They occupied, a Pennsylvania judge remarked in 1793, "a middle rank between slaves and freemen."[3]

Of the two kinds of free labor—wage work and independent proprietorship—the latter predominated in colonial America. By the time of the Revolution the majority of the nonslave population were farmers who owned their own land and worked it by family labor, supplemented in many areas by indentured servants and slaves. Recourse to wage labor on the farm was quite rare, and hired workers

3. Robert J. Steinfeld, *The Invention of Free Labor: The Employment Relation in English and American Law and Culture, 1350–1870* (Chapel Hill, 1991), 3–5, 46, 101–2; Linda G. DePauw, "Land of the Unfree: Legal Limitations on Liberty in Pre-revolutionary America," *Maryland Historical Magazine*, 68 (Winter 1973), 355–68; Elizabeth Blackmar, *Manhattan for Rent, 1785–1850* (Ithaca, 1989), 5; Bernard Bailyn, *Voyagers to the West: A Passage in the Peopling of America on the Eve of the Revolution* (New York, 1986), 166; Gordon S. Wood, *The Radicalism of the American Revolution* (New York, 1992), 51–55.

tended to be youths who could expect to acquire property in the future. In colonial cities, wage labor was more prevalent, although the unfree formed a crucial part of the labor force, even outside the South. Until at least the mid-eighteenth century, large numbers of artisans and merchants, North as well as South, owned slaves and employed indentured servants and apprentices. After 1750, the ranks of wage earners began to grow, their numbers augmented by population growth, declining access to land in rural areas, and the completion of the terms of indentured servants. The economic depression of the 1760s seems to have persuaded many employers that the flexibility of wage labor, which could be hired and fired at will, made it economically preferable to investment in slaves or servants. But the market in wage labor remained extremely unpredictable, and employers were bedeviled by frequent shortages of workers.[4]

If colonial Americans were familiar with a broad range of degrees of unfreedom, they viewed dependence itself as degrading. It was an axiom of eighteenth-century political thought that dependents lacked a will of their own, and thus did not deserve a role in public affairs. "Freedom and dependence," wrote James Wilson, were "opposite and irreconcilable terms," and Thomas Jefferson insisted in his *Notes on the State of Virginia* that dependence "begets subservience and venality, suffocates the germ of virtue, and prepares fit tools for the designs of ambition." Representative government could only rest on a citizenry enjoying the personal autonomy that arose from ownership of productive property and was thus able to subordinate self-interest to the public good. Not only personal dependence, as in the case of a domestic servant, but working for wages itself were widely viewed as disreputable. This belief had a long lineage. In seventeenth-century England, wage labor had been associated with servility and loss of freedom. Wage laborers (especially sailors, perhaps the largest group

4. Allan Kulikoff, *The Agrarian Origins of American Capitalism* (Charlottesville, 1992), 7; John L. Brooke, *The Heart of the Commonwealth: Society and Political Culture in Worcester County, Massachusetts, 1713–1861* (New York, 1989), 42–44; Stephen L. Innes, ed., *Work and Labor in Early America* (Chapel Hill, 1988), 18–32; David W. Galenson, "Labor Market Behavior in Colonial America: Servitude, Slavery, and Free Labor," in *Markets in History: Economic Studies of the Past*, ed. David W. Galenson (New York, 1989), 84–93; Sharon W. Salinger, *"To Serve Well and Faithfully": Labor and Indentured Servants in Pennsylvania, 1682–1800* (New York, 1987), 15–17, 62–69, 137–38, 156–70; Peter Way, *Common Labour: Workers and the Digging of North American Canals* (New York, 1993), 25–28.

of wage earners in port cities) were deemed a volatile, dangerous group in the Atlantic world of the eighteenth century.[5]

The abhorrence of the consequences of personal dependence and equation of political identity with economic autonomy have been taken to illustrate the influence of republican thought on American political culture. These beliefs sank deep roots in eighteenth- and nineteenth-century America, not simply as part of an ideological inheritance, however, but because they accorded with the wide distribution of productive property that made a modicum of economic autonomy part of the lived experience of millions. From the earliest days of settlement, migrants from Europe held the promise of the New World to be liberation from the economic inequalities and widespread economic dependence of the Old. John Smith had barely landed at Jamestown when he observed that in America, "every man may be master and owner of his owne labour and land," and during the whole of the colonial era promotional literature that sought to lure settlers to America publicized the image of the New World as a place of exceptional opportunity for social mobility and the acquisition of property. Throughout the nineteenth century, the "small producer ideology," resting on such tenets as equal citizenship, pride in craft, and the benefits of economic autonomy, underpinned a widespread hostility to wage labor, as well as to "non-producers" who prospered from the labor of others. The ideology of free labor would emerge, in part, from this vision of America as a producer's republic.[6]

In the generation after the American Revolution, with the rapid decline of indentured servitude and apprenticeship, the disappearance of journeymen residing in their employers' homes, and the identification of paid domestic service as an occupation for blacks and white females, the contrast between free and slave labor grew ever

5. Wood, *Radicalism*, 56; Thomas Jefferson, *Notes on the State of Virginia* (New York, 1964), 157; Richard L. Bushman, "'This New Man': Dependence and Independence, 1776," in *Uprooted Americans: Essays in Honor of Oscar Handlin*, ed. Richard L. Bushman, *et al.* (Boston, 1979), 77–96; Christopher Hill, *Change and Continuity in Seventeenth-Century England* (London, 1974), 219–24; Peter Linebaugh, "All the Atlantic Mountains Shook," *Labour/Le Travailleur*, 10 (Autumn 1982), 87–121.
6. Philip L. Barbour, ed., *The Complete Works of Captain John Smith (1530–1631)* (3 vols.: Chapel Hill, 1986), I, 332; Jack P. Greene, *The Intellectual Construction of America: Exceptionalism and Identity From 1492 to 1800* (Chapel Hill, 1993), 75, 104; Ronald Schultz, *The Republic of Labor: Philadelphia Artisans and the Politics of Class, 1720–1830* (New York, 1993), 4–13, 154–58; Christopher Clark, *The Roots of Rural Capitalism: Western Massachusetts, 1780–1860* (Ithaca, 1990), 16, 22–23.

sharper. The growing availability of wage earners, the sense that servitude of any kind was incompatible with revolutionary ideology, and
the actions of servants and apprentices themselves (many of whom
took advantage of the turmoil of the Revolution to abscond from their
masters), hastened the decline of the halfway houses between slavery
and freedom. The waning of indentured servitude transformed the
very meaning of the word "servant." In the North, deemed an affront
to personal liberty, it fell into disuse (superseded, for domestic
workers, by "help"); in the South, no longer applied to bound white
labor, "servant" became a euphemism for slave. At the same time, the
abolition of slavery in the North drew a geographical line across the
country, separating slave and free states. Thus, the stage was set for
the development of an ideology that identified the North as the home
of "free labor."[7]

These changes were only a harbinger of the economic revolution
that swept over the United States in the first half of the nineteenth
century. Thanks to the work of a generation of social historians, the
complex consequences of the market revolution are now familiar.
Changes in transportation linked yeoman farmers to national and
international markets and, at least in the North, made them major
consumers of manufactured goods. Family labor, however, remained
the norm, even as the outwork system associated with early industrialization expanded the scope of family labor to include wage work in
many rural homes. "Don't hire when you can do the work yourself,"
read a maxim in an 1830 almanac, and hired agricultural labor remained seasonal and temporary. Not until the 1850s did the decline in
the Northern birthrate and the increased availability of immigrant
labor combine to make wage work on the farm both necessary and
available.[8]

Of course, no household could be truly independent in the age of

7. Salinger, "To Serve," 142–53; Shane White, Somewhat More Independent: The End of
Slavery in New York City, 1770–1810 (Athens, Ga., 1991), 25–36; Bernard Elbaum,
"Why Apprenticeship Persisted in Britain But Not in the United States," Journal of
Economic History, 49 (June 1989), 346; Steinfeld, Free Labor, 122–33; Albert Matthews,
"Hired Man and Help," Publications of the Colonial Society of Massachusetts, 5 (March
1898), 225–56.
8. Clark, Roots, 16–17, 105, 194–95, 252–60, 305; Jeremy Atack and Fred Bateman, To
Their Own Soil: Agriculture in the Antebellum North (Ames, Iowa, 1987), 186; John M.
Faragher, "History From the Inside Out: Writing the History of Women in Rural
America," American Quarterly, 33 (Winter 1981), 546.

the market revolution. Property-owning small producers, however, retained considerable choice as to the extent of market participation, and a degree of shelter from the vicissitudes of commerce. In general, they pursued a "safety first" economic strategy that concentrated on providing for family needs and only then took advantage of the benefits of market involvement. So long as yeoman families retained control of productive property and had the realistic prospect of passing it on to their children, the ideal of autonomy retained social authenticity. "Proprietorship," concludes Randolph A. Roth's study of Vermont's Connecticut River valley, an area fully integrated into the capitalist marketplace by 1860, "remained the ideal and was still a possibility for most citizens." The opening for settlement of land in the West made the goal of farm ownership even more realistic for small farmers and their descendants.[9]

Far different were the consequences of capitalism's development in the nation's commercial and manufacturing cities, especially in the Northeast. Here, the increased scale of production, undermining of traditional crafts, and dwindling of opportunities for journeymen to rise to the status of independent master, combined to make wage labor rather than ownership of productive property the economic basis of family survival. As the centrality of the household to production waned, many male home owners were transformed into wage earners; they occupied simultaneously the positions of property owner and dependent employee, even as the spread of outwork mobilized tens of thousands of poor women for paid labor in their homes. After 1830, the rapid increase of immigration swelled the bottom ranks of the labor force, the "army of wage workers" who dug America's canals, built the railroads, and loaded and unloaded ships in port cities. These developments came later to Western cities; in Cincinnati, for example, most workers at midcentury were still employed in small unmechanized workshops, and the putting out system had made little impact except in textile production. Nonetheless, in 1850 the number

9. Lacy K. Ford, *Origins of Southern Radicalism: The South Carolina Upcountry 1800–1860* (New York, 1988), 56; Kulikoff, *Agrarian Origins*, 27–29, 35–47; Jonathan Prude, "Town-Country Conflicts in Antebellum Rural Massachusetts," in *The Countryside in the Age of Capitalist Transformation: Essays in the Social History of Rural America*, ed. Steven Hahn and Jonathan Prude (Chapel Hill, 1985), 75–76; John M. Faragher, "Open-Country Community," *ibid.*, 245–47; Randolph A. Roth, *The Democratic Dilemma: Religion, Reform, and the Social Order in the Connecticut River Valley of Vermont, 1791–1850* (New York, 1987), 297.

of wage earners in America for the first time exceeded the number of slaves, and ten years later, according to one estimate, wage laborers outnumbered self-employed members of the labor force.[10]

Although nineteenth-century liberalism defined the labor market as inhabiting a private sphere that existed outside the legitimate purview of government, in fact changes in the law and its enforcement helped to institutionalize the wage relationship and legitimize it as an authentic expression of freedom. During the first half of the nineteenth century, American law adopted the definition of wage labor as the product of a voluntary agreement between autonomous individuals. The freedom of free labor arose from the noncoerced nature of the contract itself, not whether the laborer enjoyed economic autonomy. This legal transformation both reflected and reinforced the shift in economic power toward entrepreneurs and investors, while in some ways limiting the actual liberty of wage earners. Court-ordered specific performance of a labor contract fell into abeyance, no longer deemed compatible with the autonomy of the free laborer; but by the same token, the legal doctrine of "employment at will" also relieved employers of any obligation to retain laborers longer than economically necessary. If the right to quit helped define the difference between the free laborer and the slave, along with it came lack of recourse against being fired. While labor itself was not legally enforceable, the labor contract was held to clothe employers with full authority over the workplace. Thus, work rules that seemed extremely arbitrary to employees had the force of law behind them, and any who refused to follow reasonable commands could legally be dismissed without payment of wages due. Judges invoked the definition of the laborer as an autonomous individual to impede workers, via conspiracy laws, from organizing collectively to seek higher wages, and to prevent them from obtaining compensation from employers for injuries on the job (as free individuals, they were presumed to have knowingly assumed the risks of employment). "Free labor" did not, in other

10. Sean Wilentz, "The Rise of the American Working Class, 1776–1877," in *Perspectives on American Labor History*, ed. J. Carroll Moody and Alice Kessler-Harris (DeKalb, 1989), 83–151; Blackmar, *Manhattan*, 125; Amy Bridges, *A City in the Republic: Antebellum New York and the Origins of Machine Politics* (New York, 1984), 46–58; Way, *Common Labour*, 6–7; Steven J. Ross, *Workers on the Edge: Work, Leisure, and Politics in Industrializing Cincinnati, 1788–1890* (New York, 1985), 25–63; U.S. Department of Commerce, Bureau of the Census, *Historical Statistics of the United States* (2 vols.: Washington, 1975), I, 139; Stanley Lebergott, "The Pattern of Employment Since 1800," in *American Economic History*, ed. Seymour E. Harris (New York, 1961), 290–91.

words, contradict severe inequalities of power within either the workplace or labor market.[11]

The rise of wage labor, and its institutionalization in the law, posed a profound challenge for the ethos that defined economic dependence as incompatible with freedom. The market revolution, Thomas Haskell has argued, encouraged a humanitarian sensibility by promoting a sense of individual control over one's own future, and responsibility for the fate of others. But many Americans experienced the expansion of capitalism not as an enhancement of the power to shape their world, but as a loss of control over their own lives. Invigorated with a leaven of Ricardian economics, which identified labor as the source of all wealth and the worker as entitled to the full fruits of his labor, the ideal of the autonomous small producer reemerged in Jacksonian America as a full-fledged critique of early capitalism and its inexorable transformation of free labor into a commodity.[12]

The metaphor that crystallized this discontent—"wage slavery"—implicitly challenged the contrast between free and slave labor. There was nothing new, or uniquely American, in the rhetorical mobilization of chattel slavery to criticize labor relations under capitalism. In Britain, descriptions of wage laborers as subject to coercion akin to slavery dated back to the eighteenth century, and even as the Jacksonian labor movement adopted this rhetoric in the 1830s and 1840s, the Chartist press was carrying articles on "The White Slaves of Great Britain," and Engels was employing much the same language in his critique of the conditions of the working class. But this vocabulary took on special power in America, where slavery was an immediate reality, not a distant symbol, the small producer still a powerful element in the social order, and the idea widespread that the wage earner was somehow less than fully free.[13]

11. Christopher L. Tomlins, *Labor, Law, and Ideology in the Early American Republic* (New York, 1993); Steinfeld, *Free Labor*, 144–60; Jay M. Feinman, "The Development of the Employment at Will Rule," *American Journal of Legal History*, 20 (April 1976), 118–35; David Montgomery, *Citizen Worker: The Experience of Workers in the United States with Democracy and the Free Market During the Nineteenth Century* (New York, 1993), 13–53.
12. Thomas L. Haskell, "Capitalism and the Origins of the Humanitarian Sensibility," *American Historical Review*, 90 (1985), 339–61, 547–66; Sean Wilentz, *Chants Democratic: New York City and the Rise of the American Working Class, 1788–1850* (New York, 1984), 63–103; Schultz, *Republic of Labor*, 206–29.
13. David B. Davis, *The Problem of Slavery in the Age of Revolution, 1770–1823* (Ithaca, 1975), 462; David Turley, *The Culture of English Antislavery, 1780–1860* (London, 1991), 182–84.

The metaphor of wage slavery (or, in New England, its first cousin, "factory slavery") drew on immediate grievances, such as low wages, irregular employment, the elaborate and arbitrary work rules of the early factories, and the inadequacy of contract theory to describe the actual workings of the labor market. But at its heart lay a critique of economic dependence. Workers, wrote one labor leader, "do not complain of wages slavery *solely* on account of the poverty it occasions . . . They oppose it because it holds the laboring classes in a state of abject dependence upon capitalists." In perhaps the most influential statement of the "wage slavery" argument, Orestes Brownson described wages as "a cunning device of the devil for the benefit of tender consciences who would retain all the advantages of the slave system without the expense, trouble, and odium of being slaveholders." His essay, Brownson later recalled, elicited "one universal scream of horror" from respectable opinion. But the idea that permanent wage labor bore some resemblance to slavery was not confined to labor radicals or disaffected intellectuals. Within the Jacksonian Democratic party, from the colorful Mike Walsh (who told New York workingmen, "You are slaves, and none are better aware of the fact than the heathenish dogs who call you freemen") to less demagogic politicos like Amos Kendall, it remained axiomatic that the ideal citizen was a farmer or independent mechanic, and that the factory system and merchant-dominated craft workshop were introducing to America a system of despotism akin to slavery.[14]

Northern laborers and Jacksonian politicians were not alone in employing the concept of wage slavery as a critique of free labor. Southern defenders of slavery like John C. Calhoun, Thomas R. Dew, and George Fitzhugh insisted that the freedom of the Northern wage earner amounted to little more than the opportunity either to be exploited or starve. The free laborer was "the slave of the *community*," a situation far more oppressive than to be owned by an individual master, shielded from the exploitation of the competitive marketplace. The very idea of free labor, they claimed, was a "brutal fiction,"

14. Barry Goldberg, "Slavery, Race and the Languages of Class: 'Wage Slaves' and White 'Niggers,'" *New Politics*, n. s., 3 (Summer 1991), 64–70; *Liberator*, September 25, 1846; David A. Zonderman, *Aspirations and Anxieties: New England Workers and the Mechanized Factory System 1815–1850* (New York, 1992), 113–15; Joseph L. Blau, ed., *Social Theories of Jacksonian Democracy* (Indianapolis, 1954), 306–10; Christopher Lasch, *The True and Only Heaven: Progress and Its Critics* (New York, 1991), 191n.; John Ashworth, *"Agrarians" and "Aristocrats": Party Political Ideology in the United States, 1837–1846* (London, 1983), 31.

which allowed the propertied classes to escape a sense of responsibility for the wellbeing of social inferiors. The elevation of free labor depended on slavery, insisted Senator David S. Reid of North Carolina, for slavery liberated white men from the degrading "low, menial" jobs, like factory labor and domestic service, performed by wage laborers in the North.[15]

It has recently been argued that North as well as South, the rhetoric of wage slavery implicitly rested on a racist underpinning. Slavery was meant for blacks, freedom for whites, and what was degrading in wage labor was reducing white men to the same level as African-Americans. The obvious elements of exaggeration in the idea of wage slavery (sometimes magnified to the point where Northern laborers were said to work in more oppressive conditions than Southern slaves) lend credence to this argument, as does the overt racism of Mike Walsh and other Jacksonians who employed wage slavery language. (Walsh and his fellow New York City Democrats linked to the labor movement even supported Calhoun's quixotic quest for the Presidency in 1844.) On the other hand, artisans and factory workers were, in general, hardly known as defenders of slavery, and many who employed the language of "wage slavery" assumed that, as a Lynn, Massachusetts, labor paper put it, "all kinds of slavery" should be "buried . . . forever." However employed, wage slavery, as David Brion Davis has written, was a blunt instrument for describing the range of subtle coercions operating in the capitalist marketplace; indeed, Davis suggests, analogies with chattel slavery may well have "retarded the development of a vocabulary" more appropriate to market society. Yet at a time when British labor radicalism remained locked within a fundamentally political analysis of the causes of poverty and inequality, the idea of wage slavery provided American labor and its allies with a critique of emerging capitalism in which workplace exploitation, not control of the government by placemen and non-producers, took center stage. In effect, the idea of wage slavery suggested the superiority of a very different conception of labor relations than that embodied in contract thought. It embodied values deeply rooted in nineteenth-century America—that the nation's destiny was liberation from the

15. Marcus Cunliffe, *Chattel Slavery and Wage Slavery: The Anglo-American Context 1830–1860* (Athens, Ga., 1979), 4–7; Eugene D. Genovese, *The Slaveholders' Dilemma: Freedom and Progress in Southern Conservative Thought, 1820–1860* (Columbia, S.C., 1992), 33–34, 48; Jonathan A. Glickstein, *Concepts of Free Labor in Antebellum America* (New Haven, 1991), 35–37, 154–56.

inequalities of Europe, that avarice, class conflict, and economic inequality endangered the republic.[16]

I have dwelled on the idea of wage slavery because in many ways the forthright articulation of an ideology of free labor emerged as a response to this critique of Northern wage labor. This is not to say that "free labor" was cynically calculated as a defense of labor exploitation; rather, in a society of rapidly expanding capitalism, the analogy between free worker and slave inevitably called forth a response celebrating the benefits of the marketplace and the laborer's juridical freedom. One source of the free labor ideology lay in the effort of antebellum economists to reconcile belief in economic progress with the rise of a large number of wage earners. To do so, they turned to Adam Smith and other exponents of eighteenth-century liberalism who had insisted that slavery was a far more costly and inefficient means of obtaining labor than the payment of wages, since it prevented the laborer's self-interest from being harnessed to the public good. "No conclusion seems more certain than this," Smith's compatriot John Millar had written in 1771, "that men will commonly exert more activity when they work for their own benefit than when they are compelled to labor for another." The ever-expanding wants stimulated by participation in the marketplace offered the most effective incentive for productive labor. While lamenting the effects of the division of labor upon workmen consigned to mindless, repetitive tasks, Smith nonetheless insisted that in a commercial society, wage laborers were genuinely "independent" since the impersonal law of supply and demand rather than the decision of a paternalistic master determined their remuneration and they could dispose of their earnings as they saw fit.

In the 1850s, the Republican party would hammer home Smith's anti-slavery message: freedom meant prosperity and slavery retarded economic growth. A generation earlier, however, it was not Smith's

---

16. David A. Roediger, *The Wages of Whiteness: Race and the Making of the American Working Class* (New York, 1991), 7–14, 68–77; Michael A. Bernstein, "Northern Labor Finds a Southern Champion: A Note on the Radical Democracy, 1833–1849," in *New York and the Rise of American Capitalism: Economic Development and the Social and Political History of an American State, 1780–1870*, ed. William Pencak and Conrad E. Wright (New York, 1989), 147–67; Teresa A. Murphy, *Ten Hours Labor: Religion, Reform, and Gender in Early New England* (Ithaca, 1992), 183; Thomas Bender, ed., *The Antislavery Debate* (Berkeley, 1992), 175; Zonderman, *Aspirations and Anxieties*, 116; Bridges, *City in the Republic*, 121–23; Gareth Stedman Jones, *Languages of Class: Studies in English Working Class History 1832–1982* (Cambridge, Eng., 1983), 90–178.

hostility to slavery that appealed to defenders of Northern labor relations, as much as his contention that the transformation of labor into a marketable commodity did not contradict the autonomy of free labor. But Smith's American disciples added a new wrinkle to the argument, one in keeping with the vitality of small producer ideals in America. Smith had seen intractable class divisions as an inevitable consequence of economic development; American economists sought to reconcile wage labor with the idea of the New World as a classless utopia by insisting that in the United States, industrious and frugal laborers could save money, purchase their own homes, and eventually acquire a farm or shop, thereby escaping the status of wage labor and assimilating into the republic of property holders.[17]

This effort to counteract labor's gloomy portrait of the conditions of the wage laborer overlapped with and reinforced another source of the free labor ideology—the effort of craft employers and factory owners to reaffirm the harmony of interests of all engaged in productive enterprise. Just as the master artisan had claimed to embody the interests of the entire craft including those of his journeymen and apprentices as craftsmen of the future, so capitalist entrepreneurs professed a common interest with wage laborers in promoting the economic progress that would enable employees to become proprietors themselves. Via the Whig party, this defense of capitalism and entrepreneurship in the name of equal opportunity entered the political discourse of Jacksonian America. Labor and capital were partners, who must prosper or decline together, argued Whig economic thinkers like Henry C. Carey. The Democrats' rhetoric of class conflict, Whigs insisted, was a European import irrelevant to a society of "self-made men" where the vast majority of the population either owned productive property or had a reasonable expectation of acquiring it. In America, wage labor was a temporary status, and "laborers for hire do not exist as a class."[18]

17. Robin Blackburn, *The Overthrow of Colonial Slavery 1776–1848* (London, 1988), 51–52; Istvan Hont and Michael Ignatieff, "Needs and Justice in the *Wealth of Nations:* An Introductory Essay," in *Wealth and Virtue: The Shaping of Political Economy of the Scottish Enlightenment,* ed. Istvan Hont and Michael Ignatieff (Cambridge, Eng., 1983), 13–15; William B. Scott, *In Pursuit of Happiness: American Conceptions of Property from the Seventeenth to the Twentieth Century* (Bloomington, 1977), 87–93.
18. Wilentz, *Chants Democratic,* 271–86, 303–4; Sean Wilentz, "Many Democracies: On Tocqueville and Jacksonian America," in *Reconsidering Tocqueville's "Democracy in America,"* ed. Abraham S. Eisenstadt (New Brunswick, 1988), 218–19; Anthony F. C. Wallace, *Rockdale* (New York, 1980), 394–97; Ashworth, "*Agrarians,*" 68.

As an intersectional party, the Whigs were understandably reluctant explicitly to contrast free labor with slavery. That task, so essential to the development of a mature free labor ideology, emerged from a different quarter in Jacksonian America—the crusade against slavery. By and large, the defense of free labor was a minor strand in abolition-ist thought—morality, not economics, was always paramount in their minds. Nonetheless, abolitionists, quite naturally, resented equations of Northern labor with Southern bondage. In affirming the unique-ness of the evil of slavery, abolitionists helped to popularize the sharp dichotomy between slavery's illegitimate coercions and the condition of labor in the North, and the related concept that freedom was a matter not of the ownership of productive property, but property in one's self. Slavery's denial of self-ownership, including ownership of one's labor and the right to dispose of it as one saw fit, differentiated it from freedom. "Self-right is the *foundation* right," insisted Theodore Weld, the basis of all other rights in society.[19]

On those occasions when they sought to imagine a post-emancipa-tion world, abolitionists generally envisioned slaves as becoming wage workers, with no stigma attaching to this condition. In 1833, the New England Anti-Slavery Society defined immediate abolition via recog-nition of blacks' family rights, access to education, and "that the planters shall employ their slaves as free laborers, and pay them just wages." Abolitionists vociferously rejected the idea that Northern laborers could accurately be described as wage slaves, a terminology, they insisted, that deflected moral attention from the singular evil of bondage. There was no analogy between the status of labor North and South, insisted Edmund Quincy, because the free laborer had the right to "choose his employer," "contract for wages," and leave his job if he became dissatisfied. To black abolitionists, the wage slavery anal-ogy seemed particularly spurious. When Frederick Douglass, soon after escaping from slavery, took his first paying job in New Bedford, he did not consider himself a wage slave; instead, the wage seemed an emblem of freedom: "I was now my own master . . . [in] a state of independence." Thus, by sharpening the ideological contrast between free labor and slave labor, the abolitionist movement helped to legiti-

19. Eric Foner, *Politics and Ideology in the Age of the Civil War* (New York, 1980), 65; Jonathan A. Glickstein, "'Poverty is Not Slavery': American Abolitionists and the Com-petitive Labor Market," in *Antislavery Reconsidered: New Perspectives on the Abolitionists,* ed. Lewis Perry and Michael Fellman (Baton Rouge, 1979), 207–11; Ronald G. Walters, "The Boundaries of Abolitionism," *ibid.,* 9.

mize the wage relationship even as it was coming under bitter attack. Wage slavery, wrote William Lloyd Garrison, was an "abuse of language." "We cannot see that it is wrong to give or receive wages."[20]

Despite the widespread popularity of the rhetoric of wage slavery, it would be wrong to assume that the emerging ideology of free labor had no appeal among Northern workers. Indeed, another root of the free labor ideology lay in the divided mind of labor itself, which celebrated the independence and equal rights of working men, even as it insisted workers were reduced to wage slavery if forced to market their labor as a commodity. Ironically, the very struggles to incorporate propertyless men into political democracy reenforced the market definition of self-ownership as the foundation of freedom. Beginning with demands for the right to vote by lesser artisans, journeymen, and wage laborers during the American Revolution, insistent pressure from below for an expansion of the suffrage did much to democratize American society. Political enfranchisement, however, subtly contradicted the rhetorical image of the worker as a wage slave and greatly expanded the traditional definition of personal independence. Every man had a property in his own labor. Political virtue was not confined to property holders, said one delegate to the Massachusetts Constitutional Convention of 1820, for men who supported their families "with their daily earnings" had as much "regard for country" as the wealthiest entrepreneur.[21]

The decades after the Revolution witnessed what Gordon Wood has called a transvaluation of labor. Political thinkers as far back as the ancient world had insisted that the progress of civilization depended on a leisured class: freedom *from* labor was far more desirable than freedom *to* labor. Now, except in the South, idleness, not labor, came to be viewed as disreputable, an outlook that drew on sources as diverse as Protestant Christianity, the democratization of politics, and the small producer ideology. The glorification of labor of all kinds as dignified and not degraded—a standard element of political rhetoric by the 1830s—had its appeal to working people. Earning an honest

20. William H. Pease and Jane H. Pease, eds., *The Antislavery Argument* (Indianapolis, 1965), 61; *Liberator*, October 1, 1847; Judith N. Shklar, *American Citizenship: The Quest for Inclusion* (Cambridge, Mass., 1991), 83; Foner, *Politics and Ideology*, 70–71.
21. Robert J. Steinfeld, "Property and Suffrage in the Early American Republic," *Stanford Law Review*, 41 (January 1989), 335–76; Rowland Berthoff, "Independence and Attachment, Virtue and Interest: From Republican Citizen to Free Enterpriser, 1787–1837," in *Uprooted Americans*, ed. Bushman, 115–16.

living could appear as part of the definition of social independence, setting Northern laborers off from both Southern slaves and aristocratic nonproducers. Many journeymen and apprentices may well have found the wage relationship—and the definition of worker and employer as equals in the eyes of both law and marketplace—liberating when contrasted with the traditional hierarchy of the artisan shop and the stigma of subservience that had long attached to manual labor. Indeed, at a time of rapid economic fluctuations, a good wage might offer more genuine independence than the uncertain prospects of operating one's own business, especially in those forms of artisinal and early industrial labor where skilled employees retained considerable control over the work process and among the salaried clerks, managers, and other white collar workers whose numbers grew rapidly with the expansion of trade. The contrast between the slave bound to an owner and the free worker able to leave his job was more than mere rhetoric—it defined a central reality of social life in antebellum America. "No one who enters the factory," said a Waltham worker, "thinks of remaining there his whole life-time." Turnover rates were extremely high, and for many laborers physical mobility—"freedom to move"—served as a means of obtaining leverage in the labor market, an essential element of strategies for survival and possible advancement in a market society.[22]

One further element flowed into the free labor ideology as it emerged in mature form in the 1850s. This was the movement for free soil that emerged in the aftermath of the depression of 1837–42, and which identified access to land as the route to economic independence. Of course, Americans' ideas about freedom have long been tied up with the promise of the West. At the Constitutional Convention, Madison had suggested that territorial expansion would enable the republic to avoid the dangerous rise of a large class of permanently poor citizens. For years, the Democratic party had advocated a policy of easy access to government land, "to afford every American citizen of enterprise," as President Andrew Jackson put it, "the oppor-

22. Wood, *Radicalism*, 277; New York *Tribune*, November 11, 1857; Shklar, *American Citizenship*, 64–67; Gary J. Kornblith, "The Artisinal Response to Capitalist Transformation," *Journal of the Early Republic*, 10 (Fall 1990), 318–20; Zonderman, *Aspirations and Anxieties*, 288; Charles Stephenson, "'There's Plenty Waitin' at the Gates': Mobility, Opportunity, and the American Worker," in *Life and Labor: Dimensions of Working-Class History* (Albany, 1986), 72–91; Jonathan Prude, *The Coming of Industrial Order: Town and Factory Life in Rural Massachusetts, 1810–1860* (New York, 1983), 114–15; Clark, *Roots*, 313.

tunity of securing an independent freehold." But in the 1840s, it was veterans of the Jacksonian labor movement like newspaper editor George Henry Evans and the iconoclastic Horace Greeley, a Whig sympathetic, at this point in his career, to communitarian socialism, who popularized the idea that free homesteads in the West provided the antidote to wage slavery. "Freedom of the soil," Evans insisted, offered the only alternative to permanent dependence for laboring Americans. Indeed, he added, in a preview of Reconstruction debates, if not combined with access to land, the abolition of slavery would leave blacks with no alternative but to be "ground down by the competition in the labor market." Land reform was a persistent, if still neglected, strand in nineteenth-century reform politics, its lineage running from Tom Paine's *Agrarian Justice* through Evans and Greeley, and on to demands for land distribution during Reconstruction, Henry George, the Knights of Labor, and Populism. As the nation's political system began to dissolve under the impact of the question of the expansion of slavery, the idea of free labor was yoked ever more tightly to free soil, as access to Western land came to be seen as the necessary condition for avoiding the further growth of wage slavery in the North.[23]

Thus, numerous ideological currents came together in the free labor ideology of the 1850s. The glue was provided by the party's condemnation of the slave society of the South and glorification of the progress, opportunity, and individual freedom embodied in the "free society" of the North. In constructing the rhetorical image of slave society as the antithesis of free, Republicans consolidated the free labor ideology and gave it its deepest meaning. Republicans were far more sympathetic than most abolitionists had been to the aspirations of Northern laborers for independence, but they identified slavery and the threat of its expansion, not the inner logic of capitalism, as the force that threatened Northern workers' right to the fruits of their toil. The two definitions of free labor that had emerged in the first half of the nineteenth century—the laborer as small producer and as freely contracting wage earner—coexisted in uneasy tension within the free labor ideology, only partly reconciled by the insistence that free soci-

23. Peter S. Onuf, "Liberty, Development, and Union: Visions of the West in the 1780s," *William and Mary Quarterly*, 3 ser., 43 (April 1986), 202–3; Drew R. McCoy, *The Elusive Republic: Political Economy in Jeffersonian America* (Chapel Hill, 1980), 203–4, 237; Scott, *In Pursuit*, 59; Bernard Mandel, *Labor: Free and Slave* (New York, 1955), 85; Foner, *Politics and Ideology*, 70.

ety offered every industrious wage earner the opportunity to achieve economic independence.

Nowhere was the broad appeal of the free labor ideology more apparent or its internal tensions more evident than in the speeches and writings of Abraham Lincoln, whose own life embodied the opportunities Northern society ostensibly offered to all laboring men. Even though, by the 1850s, he lived in a society firmly in the grasp of the market revolution (and he himself served as attorney for the Illinois Central Railroad, one of the nation's largest corporations), Lincoln's America was the world of the small producer. Lincoln was fascinated and disturbed by the writings of proslavery writers like George Fitzhugh. The Southern critique of wage slavery catalyzed in Lincoln a defense of free society. Most Northerners, he insisted, were "neither *hirers* nor *hired*," but worked "for themselves, on their farms, in their houses, and in their shops, taking the whole product to themselves, and asking no favors of capital on the one hand, nor hirelings or slaves on the other." Wage earners were generally young "beginners" hired "by their own consent"; contrary to Southern charges, they were not "fatally fixed in that condition for life." For Lincoln, unlike his Whig predecessors a generation earlier, this vision of Northern society led inexorably to an indictment of slavery. The slave, put simply, was an individual illegitimately deprived of the fruits of his labor and denied the social opportunity that should be the right of all Americans. Yet even Lincoln's eloquent exposition could not escape free labor's inherent ambiguities. Was wage labor a normal acceptable part of the Northern social order or a temporary aberration, still associated with lack of genuine freedom? To some extent, the answer depended on which laborers one was talking about.[24]

For Lincoln, as for most Republicans in the 1850s, the idea of free labor rested on universalistic assumptions. Human nature itself, which responded more favorably to incentive than coercion, explained why free society outstripped slave in economic progress. When, in his debates with Stephen A. Douglas, Lincoln insisted that the right to the fruits of one's labor was a natural right, not confined to any particular set of persons, he drove home the point by choosing as his example a black woman. Like any ideology, however, free labor was defined, in

24. Foner, *Free Soil*, 11–39; Yehoshua Arieli, *Individualism and Nationalism in American Ideology* (Cambridge, Mass., 1964), 315–17; Roy F. Basler, ed., *The Collected Works of Abraham Lincoln* (9 vols.: New Brunswick, 1953–55), II, 405, III, 462, 477–79.

part, by boundaries, lines of exclusion understood as arising from the natural order of things and therefore not really seen as exclusions at all. Lincoln himself hinted at these boundaries when he remarked that only those with a "dependent nature" did not take advantage of the opportunity to escape the status of wage earner.[25] Who were those "dependent" by nature and hence outside the boundaries of free labor thought? The answer was provided by the course of development of American society itself. In a nation in which slavery was a recent memory in the North and an overwhelming presence in the South; whose westward expansion (the guarantee of equal opportunity) required the removal of Indians and the conquest of lands held by Mexicans, it was inevitable that the language of politics—such concepts as citizenship, democracy, and free labor itself—would come to be defined in racial terms. And in an economy where labor increasingly meant work that produced monetary value, it became increasingly difficult to think of free labor as encompassing anyone but men.

Despite its universalistic vocabulary, the idea of free labor had little bearing on the actual conditions of nonwhites in nineteenth-century America. Four million African-Americans, of course, toiled as slaves; in addition, neither free blacks nor members of other racial minorities could easily be assimilated into the rigid compartmentalization of labor systems as either "free" or "slave." Among them, the halfway houses of semifree labor, which disappeared for whites by the early nineteenth century, endured. The West, imagined (and often experienced) by white laborers as a land of economic independence, simultaneously harbored indentured Indian labor, Mexican-American peonage, and work under long-term contracts for Chinese immigrants. These labor systems persisted well past midcentury; indeed, they were reinvigorated by the expansion into the West of market-oriented, labor intensive enterprises in mining, manufacturing, and commercial agriculture. In the older states, free blacks were the last group to experience indentured servitude, for emancipation generally required children of slave mothers to labor for their owners for a number of years before being freed (twenty-eight years in Pennsylvania, far longer than had been customary for white indentured servants). Indeed, the growing identification of indentured servitude

25. Basler, ed., *Lincoln Works*, II, 405, III, 479; Uday S. Mehta, "Liberal Strategies of Exclusion," *Politics and Society*, 18 (December 1990), 427–30.

with blacks made it all the more offensive a status in the eyes of whites.[26]

If any group in American society could be identified as wage slaves, it was free blacks in the antebellum North. Until the beginning of large-scale immigration, African-Americans formed a significant portion of the region's wage-earning proletariat. While the free labor ideology celebrated social advancement, blacks' actual experience was downward mobility. At the time of abolition, because of widespread slave ownership among eighteenth-century artisans, a considerable number of Northern blacks were skilled craft workers. Many artisans were critics of Southern slavery, but few viewed the free black as anything but a low-wage competitor who should be barred from skilled employment. "They are leaders in the cause of equal rights for themselves," a black editor commented of New York City's radical artisans in the 1830s. Hostility from white craftsmen, however, was only one among many obstacles that kept blacks confined to the lowest ranks of the labor market, for white employers refused to hire them and white customers did not wish to be served by them. The result was a rapid decline in economic status, until by mid-century, the vast majority of Northern blacks labored for wages in unskilled jobs and personal service. The goal of economic independence held as much appeal to free blacks as white Americans. But in fact it was almost unimaginably remote. Free blacks, in effect, were excluded from the twin definitions of American identity in the antebellum North—free labor and citizenship (for almost none could vote by the 1830s). The rigid dichotomy between slavery and freedom proved wholly inadequate as a way of describing their circumstances.[27]

Women were another group whose "nature" ostensibly excluded them from the opportunities of free society. For men, control over a household of family dependents offered visible testimony to their own

26. Howard Lamar, "From Bondage to Contract: Ethnic Labor in the American West," in *The Countryside*, ed. Hahn and Prude, 293–326; Alexander Saxton, *The Indispensable Enemy: Labor and the Anti-Chinese Movement in California* (Berkeley, 1971), 3–8; Gary B. Nash and Jean R. Soderlund, *Freedom by Degrees: Emancipation in Pennsylvania and Its Aftermath* (New York, 1991), 173–77.

27. Gary B. Nash, *Forging Freedom: The Formation of Philadelphia's Black Community 1720–1840* (Cambridge, Mass., 1988), 146; Graham R. Hodges, *New York City Cartmen, 1667–1850* (New York, 1986), 158–59; Leonard P. Curry, *The Free Black in Urban America 1800–1850* (Chicago, 1981), 260; *An Address to the Three Thousand Colored Citizens of New-York Who Are the Owners of One Hundred and Twenty Thousand Acres of Land . . .* (New York, 1846), 10.

independence. For women, opportunities for independence barely existed. Women could not compete freely for employment, since only a few low-paying jobs were available to them. Nor could they be considered freely contracting wage workers. According to common law, married women could not sign independent contracts, and not until after the Civil War did the states accord them control over the wages they earned. Even then, the husband retained a proprietary claim to his wife's person and domestic labor. Thus, just as the republican citizen was indisputably male, so too was the ideologically constructed free laborer in antebellum America.[28]

The prevailing definition of the proper roles of men and women, known to historians as the ideology of separate spheres, defined women as existing outside the labor market altogether. Domesticity described woman's place; working for wages was not simply demeaning, as for men, but fundamentally alien to her nature. The proper woman entered the market as a consumer, not a laborer. A reflection of the growing separation of productive labor from the household (at least in the North), the ideology of separate spheres never described the actual lives of most American women. But by identifying the workplace as the world outside the home, it had the effect of rendering women's actual labor virtually invisible. As early as the 1790s, one supporter of Alexander Hamilton's program of economic development insisted that factory work would benefit women, "who otherwise would have little or nothing to do."[29]

It hardly seems necessary to point out that women, in fact, had a great deal to do. The widely accepted distinction between productive and domestic work was ideological rather than economic. Far more

28. Stephanie McCurry, "The Politics of Yeoman Households in South Carolina," in *Divided Houses: Gender and the Civil War*, ed. Catherine Clinton and Nina Silber (New York, 1992), 31; Alice Kessler-Harris, *A Woman's Wage: Historical Meanings and Social Consequences* (Lexington, 1990), 36; Norma Basch, *In the Eyes of the Law: Women, Marriage, and Property in Nineteenth-Century New York* (Ithaca, 1982), 17–26; Joan R. Gunderson, "Independence, Citizenship, and the American Revolution," *Signs*, 13 (Autumn 1987), 59–77; Amy Stanley, "Conjugal Bonds and Wage Labor: Rights of Contract in the Age of Emancipation," *Journal of American History*, 75 (September 1988), 482–99; Blackmar, *Manhattan*, 125.

29. Kessler-Harris, *A Woman's Wage*, 59–63; Linda K. Kerber, *et al.*, "Beyond Roles, Beyond Spheres: Thinking About Gender in the Early Republic," *William and Mary Quarterly*, 3 ser., 46 (July 1989), 565–68; Nancy Osterud, *Bonds of Community: The Lives of Farm Women in Nineteenth-Century New York* (Ithaca, 1991), 5–7; Jeanne Boydston, *Home and Work: Housework, Wages, and the Ideology of Labor in the Early Republic* (New York, 1990), 18–27, 45–47; Berthoff, "Independence," 124.

accurate was the time-honored adage, "woman's work is never done." As Elizabeth Cady Stanton observed, women's work in the home differed from the work of men only because it was "unpaid, unsocialized, and unrelenting." On small farms, North and South, men's work ebbed and flowed with the seasons; women's—including labor in the fields, childrearing, cleaning, cooking, laundering, producing clothing and other items for use at home and others for sale—was constant. By reducing the need to turn to the marketplace for the necessities of life, the food and clothing produced by women at home proved essential to the independence of the yeoman household. Early industrialization enhanced the importance of women's work in the North, as the spread of the putting out system in such industries as shoemaking, hatmaking, and clothing manufacture allowed women working at home to contribute to family income even as they retained responsibility for domestic chores. At the same time, the early factories offered new employment opportunities for the young daughters of farm families. In either case, the vaunted independence of the yeoman household depended in considerable measure on the labor of women—whether unremunerated within the household, or paid wages at home or outside. So too did the free time that enabled men to participate as citizens in the public arena. Thus, free labor embodied a contradiction akin in some ways to slavery's—since no one could remain independent without enlisting uncompensated labor, free labor for some rested on dependent labor for others.[30]

The idealization of the home as a refuge from the marketplace was, of course, a middle-class ideology, and the "idle" housewife, supported by her husband, a token of bourgeois respectability. Even for the middle class, the cult of domesticity concealed the fact that the home was, in fact, a place of work. Not only did middle-class women have many arduous domestic tasks, but through servants—the largest

30. Nancy Folbe, "The Unproductive Housewife: Her Evolution in Nineteenth-Century Economic Thought," *Signs*, 16 (Spring 1991), 464–65, 477; Stephanie McCurry, *Masters of Small Worlds: Yeoman Households, Gender Relations, and the Political Culture of the Antebellum South Carolina Low Country* (New York, forthcoming), ch. 2; Clark, *Roots*, 132–46; John M. Faragher, *Sugar Creek: Life on the Illinois Prairie* (New Haven, 1986), 101–9, 179–80; Mary Blewett, *Men, Women, and Work: Class, Gender, and Protest in the New England Shoe Industry, 1780–1910* (Urbana, 1988), 14–19, 45–61, 103–10; Thomas Dublin, "Women and Outwork in a Nineteenth-Century New England Town," in *The Countryside*, ed. Hahn and Prude, 51–66; Claudia Goldin and Kenneth Sokoloff, "Women, Children, and Industrialization in the Early Republic: Evidence from the Manufacturing Censuses," *Journal of Economic History*, 42 (December 1982), 741–74; Boydston, *Home and Work*, 40, 59, 76–93.

employment category for women in the nineteenth century and a ubiquitous emblem of the bourgeois standard of living—wage labor itself entered the middle-class home (even though relations with servants were generally understood as problems in morality and discipline rather than labor relations). There were 32,000 women working as domestics in New York City in 1855, but this labor was essentially invisible when contemporaries spoke of the rights and wrongs of free labor.[31]

Among urban artisans and wage laborers, women's work often spelled the difference between independence and dependence, and even outright survival. Their homes, too, sheltered paid labor by women—especially the sweated labor of outworkers toiling at subsistence wages. Like domestic servants, the army of female outworkers was rarely mentioned when contemporaries spoke of free labor, except as another indication of how the spread of capitalism was degrading men. The idea that the male head of household should command a "family wage" enabling him to support his wife and children had as powerful a hold on working-class culture as among middle-class upholders of the domestic ideal. Capitalism, said labor leader P. J. McGuire in the 1870s, "tore the woman from her true duties as mother and nurse of the human race," subjecting her to wage slavery while undermining the natural order of the household and the independence and authority of its male head. The fight for a family wage mobilized successive generations of labor organizations, embodying not only a call for substantive justice for wage earners, and resistance to employers' assuming control over important aspects of a family's life, but the ideal of a social order in which men supported their families and women remained at home. Male laborers before the Civil War sometimes supported the demands for higher wages and better working conditions of factory girls and urban seamstresses (often members of the same families as unionists) but their organizations excluded women from membership and generally viewed women workers as threats to craft skill and male wages. Indeed, the contrast between a "family wage" or a "man's wage" (increasingly a badge of honor) and a "woman's wage" (a term of opprobrium) helped to legiti-

31. Blackmar, *Manhattan*, 112–21; Nancy Fraser, "What's Critical About Critical Theory? The Case of Habermas and Gender," in *Feminism as Critique*, ed. Seyla Benhabib and Drucilla Cornell (Minneapolis, 1987), 36–38; Linda K. Kerber, "Separate Spheres, Female Worlds, Woman's Place: The Rhetoric of Women's History," *Journal of American History*, 75 (June 1988), 9–39.

mate the idea that wage labor, if equitably rewarded, was an appropriate status for American men.[32]

Not all women workers, however, agreed that wage labor was inherently oppressive, or that a woman's dignity arose from her status in the family rather than the ability to earn a living. If blacks saw wage labor as a definite improvement over slavery, many nineteenth-century women found in working for wages an escape from the paternalistic bonds and personal dependence of the household. As Harriet Hanson Robinson later recalled her time in the Lowell mills, working for wages offered women autonomy: for the first time "they could earn money, and spend it as they pleased . . . For the first time in this country a woman's labor had a money value." Equal opportunity to enter the labor market was a persistent demand of the early movement for women's rights, which utterly rejected the domestic ideology's celebration of the "idle" housewife. Isolated within the home, cut off from the opportunity to earn wages, economically dependent women, argued nineteenth-century feminists from Susan B. Anthony to Charlotte Perkins Gilman, could make no significant contribution to society. Women, wrote Pauline Davis in 1853, "must go *to work*" to emancipate themselves from "bondage."[33]

The triumph of a party dedicated to the ideology of free labor, of course, precipitated Southern secession and the onset of Civil War. And the destruction of slavery posed in the most concrete way the issue of how Americans would henceforth understand free labor. Northern Republicans to a large extent viewed the transition from slavery to freedom through the prism of free labor. The sheer drama of the triumph of the Union and the destruction of slavery fixed the free labor ideology in the popular mind even more firmly than before

32. Christine Stansell, *City of Women: Sex and Class in New York, 1789–1860* (New York, 1986); Wilentz, *Chants Democratic*, 51, 249; Murphy, *Ten Hours*, 47–49; Blewett, *Men, Women, and Work*, 69–85; Fraser, "What's Critical," 42–43; David N. Lyon, "The World of P. J. McGuire; A Study of the American Labor Movement" (unpub. diss., University of Minnesota, 1972), 55; Kessler-Harris, *A Woman's Wage*, 3–10.

33. Kessler-Harris, *A Woman's Wage*, 27–28; Blewett, *Men, Women, and Work*, 321–33; Harriet H. Robinson, *Loom and Spindle; or Life Among the Early Mill Girls* (New York, 1898), 69; Ellen C. DuBois, "Outgrowing the Compact of the Fathers: Equal Rights, Woman Suffrage, and the United States Constitution, 1820–1878," *Journal of American History*, 74 (December 1987), 847; Daniel T. Rodgers, *The Work Ethic in Industrial America 1850–1920* (Chicago, 1978), 183–90; Jean Matthews, "Race, Sex, and the Dimensions of Liberty in Antebellum America," *Journal of the Early Republic*, 6 (Fall 1986), 282.

the Civil War. Efforts by white Southerners to restrict the freedom of the former slaves in ways that violated fundamental free labor premises had much to do with the unraveling of President Andrew Johnson's postwar policies and the coming of Radical Reconstruction. The Reconstruction period saw the embodiment of free labor principles in federal law, and a redrawing of the boundaries of the free labor ideology to encompass black Americans (although women remained outside its purview). Yet even as the war vindicated the free labor ideology, it strengthened tendencies that inexorably transformed the society of small producers from which that ideology had sprung. At the very moment of its triumph were revealed more fully than ever the contradictions inherent in the concept of free labor.[34]

The Civil War, wrote Republican leader and textile manufacturer Edward Atkinson of Massachusetts, was "a war for the establishment of free labor, call it by whatever name you will." In the vision of a reconstructed South that emerged from the war, blacks were absorbed into the definition of universal human nature at the heart of free labor thought. Enjoying the same opportunities as Northern workers, motivated by the same quest for self-improvement, and capable of the same market discipline, they would labor more productively than as slaves. Meanwhile, Northern capital and immigrants would energize the economy, and eventually the South would come to resemble the free labor image of the North—a society of small towns and independent producers. Unified on the basis of free labor, proclaimed Carl Schurz, America would become "a republic, greater, more populous, freer, more prosperous, and more powerful, than any state history tells us of." Free labor, in sum, was central to the vision of a triumphant national state that emerged from the war.[35]

Proclaiming the superiority of free labor was easy; implementing that vision proved more troublesome. Even as the war drew to a close, the Republican Congress, in debates over the Thirteenth Amendment, struggled to define precisely the repercussions of the destruction of slavery. All agreed that property rights in man must be abrogated, contractual relations substituted for the discipline of the lash,

34. Eric Foner, *Reconstruction: America's Unfinished Revolution 1863–1877* (New York, 1988); William E. Forbath, "The Ambiguities of Free Labor: Labor and the Law in the Gilded Age," *Wisconsin Law Review*, 1985, 778.
35. Foner, *Reconstruction*, 155–56, 225; Carl Schurz, *For the Great Empire of Liberty, Forward!* (New York, 1864).

and the master's patriarchal authority over the lives of the former slaves abolished. The phrase most often repeated in the debates—the "right to the fruits of his labor"—was thought to embody the distinction between slavery and freedom. These debates also made clear what was not implied by emancipation. Several Congressmen expressed concern that the Amendment's abolition of "involuntary servitude" might be construed to apply to relations within the family. "A husband has a right of property in the service of his wife," said one Congressman. But the Thirteenth Amendment was hardly intended to touch power relations within the family. Indeed, slavery's destruction of family life (including the husband's role as patriarch and breadwinner) had been one of abolitionism's most devastating criticisms of the peculiar institution. Republicans assumed emancipation would restore to blacks the natural right to family life, with women assuming the roles of daughters, wives, and mothers within the domestic sphere. Thus, even as they rejected the racialized definition of free labor that had emerged in the first half of the nineteenth century (an accomplishment whose importance ought not to be underestimated), Republicans still clung to the sentiment that the female laborer was an anomaly, not really a free laborer at all.[36]

Southern whites, particularly the planter class devastated by wartime destruction and the loss of their slave property, had, of course, a very different definition of a free labor South. The destiny of the former slaves, said a Southern newspaper, was "subordination to the white race." To enforce this understanding of black freedom, the governments of Presidential Reconstruction enacted the notorious Black Codes, seeking, through mandatory year-long contracts, vagrancy laws, coercive apprenticeship regulations, and criminal penalties for breach of contract, to force the former slaves back to work on plantations. Resurrecting forms of labor coercion familiar in the eighteenth century but which had subsequently fallen into disuse, these measures seemed to make a mockery of essential free labor values—contracts should be free and voluntary agreements, arrived at by mutual consent, workers should be able to choose their employment and

36. Lea S. VanderVelde, "The Labor Vision of the Thirteenth Amendment," *University of Pennsylvania Law Review*, 138 (December 1989), 437–504; *Congressional Globe*, 38th Congress, 2d Session, 215; Ira Berlin, *et al.*, ed., *The Wartime Genesis of Free Labor* (New York, 1990), 15; Leslie Ann Schwalm, "The Meaning of Freedom: African-American Women and Their Transition from Slavery to Freedom in Lowcountry South Carolina" (unpub. diss., University of Wisconsin, 1991), 290–324.

leave at will, and the state should not enforce specific performance of contractual obligations to labor.[37]

The Civil Rights Act of 1866, in part a response to Southern Black Codes that severely limited the liberty of the former slaves, enshrined free labor values as part of the definition of American citizenship. Contract was central to the bill—no state could deprive any citizen of the right to make contracts, bring lawsuits, or enjoy equal protection of the rights of the security of person and property. The law, one Congressman declared, proposed "to secure to a poor, weak class of laborers the right to make contracts for their labor, the power to enforce the payment of their wages, and the means of holding and enjoying the proceeds of their toil." One year later, the Peonage Act outlawed "voluntary or involuntary servitude" throughout the country, and barred states from criminally punishing breaches of labor contracts, another embodiment of free labor ideas in federal law.[38]

Thus, Reconstruction legislation rejected efforts to reimpose a system of legal coercion of labor in the postwar South. But what of the coercions embedded in the free labor market itself? Ostensibly, it was the opportunity to escape wage labor altogether that provided free labor's answer. But, as the radical New Orleans *Tribune* repeatedly pointed out, the realities confronting the former slaves rendered this free labor assumption utterly unrealistic. Lacking land, and encountering not social harmony but unrelenting hostility on the part of the white community, they "cannot rise . . . they must be servants to others, with no hope of bettering their conditions." When General William T. Sherman met with a group of black ministers in the famous Colloquy of January 1865, their spokesman, Garrison Frazier, offered a pithy definition of slavery and freedom as defined by those who had known bondage. Slavery, he said, was "receiving . . . the work of another man, and not by his consent." Freedom meant "placing us where we could reap the fruit of our own labor." For most former slaves, this meant ownership of land. In their own way, the freed people reaffirmed the small producer ideal that equated free labor with ownership of productive property.[39]

As is well known, efforts to give the former slaves land, rather than establishing the conditions that would enable them to acquire it after

37. Foner, *Reconstruction*, 129–35, 199–201; VanderVelde, "Labor Vision," 487–90.
38. Foner, *Reconstruction*, 243–45; Steinfeld, *Free Labor*, 184.
39. Foner, *Reconstruction*, 70, 378–79.

working for wages, failed to receive Congressional approval. Failure to redistribute land, warned Radical Republican George W. Julian, would reduce the freepeople to "a system of wages slavery . . . more galling than slavery itself." Most Republicans, however, believed such "gifts" would deaden the very spirit of enterprise and ambition for material advancement that animated free labor, white or black.[40] In retrospect, Reconstruction may be seen as a decisive moment in fixing the dominant understanding of free labor as freedom of contract in the labor market, rather than ownership of productive property. Even as the overthrow of slavery reinforced the definition of the contract as the very opposite of the master-slave relationship, the policy of awarding black men the right to vote while denying them the benefits of land reform powerfully fortified the idea that the free citizen could be a dependent laborer.

The massive economic changes that followed Reconstruction, as the United States matured into an industrial economy and the "labor question" replaced the struggle over slavery as the dominant focus of public life, further undermined the vision of the small producers' republic. By the late nineteenth century, it became increasingly difficult to maintain that wage labor was a temporary condition on the road to economic independence, or to deny that what *The Nation* called "the great curse of the Old World—the division of society into classes" had become a permanent feature of American life. Increasingly, the contract definition of free labor was enshrined in orthodox economic thought and the emerging social sciences. Severed from empathy for the aspirations of the upwardly mobile poor, this understanding of free labor became part of a doctrinaire laissez-faire ideology. The man born a laborer, announced economist David A. Wells in 1877, would "never be anything but a laborer," and government could do nothing to alter this situation. To liberal thinkers, the right to the fruits of one's labor and the promise of upward mobility seemed quaint anachronisms, irrelevant at a time when the modern corporation had replaced the independent producer as the driving force of economic progress.[41]

40. *Ibid.*, 68, 236–37.
41. *The Nation*, June 27, 1868: Rodgers, *Work Ethic*, 35; John G. Sproat, *"The Best Men": Liberal Reformers in the Gilded Age* (New York, 1968), 145–46; James L. Hutson, "The American Revolutionaries, the Political Economy of Aristocracy, and the American Concept of the Distribution of Wealth, 1765–1900," *American Historical Review*, 98 (October 1993), 1103.

The identification of freedom of labor with freedom of contract was enshrined in successive decisions of state and federal courts, which struck down state laws regulating economic enterprise as an interference with the right of the free laborer to choose his employment, and agree to whatever working conditions he saw fit. This line of thinking was pioneered by Justice Stephen A. Field's famous 1873 dissent in the *Slaughter-House Cases,* which insisted that a butchering monopoly established by Louisiana violated the "the right of free labor" now enshrined in federal law. Essentially, according to Field, this right encompassed the ability to pursue any lawful employment without state interference, and to enjoy the fruits of one's labor. *Slaughter-House,* of course, formed a key step in the Court's abandonment of Reconstruction. But Field's dissent also pointed the way to subsequent decisions that would offer entrepreneurs (if not former slaves) federal protection for the rights secured by the Civil War. "Liberty of contract," not equal protection of the laws for blacks, came to be defined as the essence of the Fourteenth Amendment. By the 1880s, the Court consistently ruled that state regulation of business enterprise, including laws establishing maximum hours of work or ensuring safe working conditions, were a remnant of older paternalism, which deprived the worker of the right to dispose freely of his labor. (Field's belief that freedom involved the right to the fruits of one's labor was by now lost sight of.) Free labor, declared the West Virginia Supreme Court in 1889, meant "not only freedom from servitude . . . but the right of one . . . to pursue any lawful trade or avocation," and no state law could restrict this liberty. Although this court used the gender-neutral term "one," this principle still did not apply to women. They were not independent free laborers, and the Supreme Court proved willing to sanction restrictions on their choice of occupation (upholding, for example, in *Bradwell v. Illinois,* a state law barring women from practicing law).[42]

The dichotomy between free labor and ghost of slavery continued to shape discourse on American labor relations to the turn of the century and beyond. Like former slaves, many wage laborers in the

---

42. Forbath, "Ambiguities of Free Labor," 767–817; Charles W. McCurdy, "Justice Field and the Jurisprudence of Government-Business Relations: Some Parameters of Laissez-Faire Constitutionalism, 1863–1897," *Journal of American History,* 61 (March 1975), 970–1005; Kessler-Harris, *A Woman's Wage,* 37–47; Lea S. VanderVelde, "The Gendered Origins of the Lumley Doctrine: Binding Men's Consciences and Women's Fidelity," *Yale Law Review,* 101 (January 1992), 830.

Gilded Age contested the definition of free labor as personal liberty to sign labor contracts. Even as the courts and middle-class opinion invoked the struggle against slavery to clothe the interests of capitalist entrepreneurs with the mantle of free labor, the labor movement responded that coercion was as inherent in industrial capitalism as it had been under slavery. "Slavery declared to be liberty" was one labor journal's pithy response to the New York Court of Appeals' decision in 1885 striking down a state law prohibiting cigar-making in tenement houses as a violation of freedom of contract. Reaching back across the divide of the Civil War, labor defined employers as a new "slave power," called for the "emancipation and enfranchisement of all who labor," and resurrected for one last time the metaphor of wage slavery as a critique of the plight of workers in the Gilded Age. Through the 1880s, "the abolition of the wage system" remained the stated goal of labor organizations. So widespread, on both sides of the Atlantic, was the rhetoric of wage slavery in the late nineteenth century that when he published his *History of Slavery and Serfdom* in 1895, the English economic historian John K. Ingram felt compelled to include an appendix on the "lax" uses of the word "slavery" among his contemporaries.[43]

Only with the rise of the American Federation of Labor in the 1890s did the dominant organization among American workers frankly accept the fact that class divisions and the wage labor system were intrinsic to capitalism. Free labor was wage labor, insisted Samuel Gompers, and should organize as such, seeking security of employment and favorable wages and working conditions, not the utopian dream of economic autonomy. "Independence" for the worker meant not self-employment but a degree of control over the work process (a control still enjoyed by considerable numbers of skilled industrial workers among whom the AF of L organized).[44]

By the twentieth century, as the promise of economic abundance blunted hostility to the wage system, "slave wages" replaced "wage

43. Eileen Boris, "'A Man's Dwelling House is His Castle': Tenement House Cigarmaking and the Judicial Imperative," in *Work Engendered: Toward a New History of American Labor*, ed. Ava Baron (Ithaca, 1991), 114–41; Christopher L. Tomlins, *The State and the Unions: Labor Relations, Law, and the Organized Labor Movement in America, 1880–1960* (New York, 1985), 49–51; Leon Fink, "Labor, Liberty, and the Law," 912; Goldberg, "Slavery, Race and the Languages of Class," 71–77; John K. Ingram, *A History of Slavery and Serfdom* (London, 1895), 261.
44. Boris, "Dwelling House," 134–35; Lasch, *True and Only Heaven*, 207–8; Montgomery, *Fall of the House of Labor*, 13.

slavery" as a mark of servitude, and a family's level of consumption—the so-called American standard of living—came to define the essence of the American dream. The free American was the citizen able to consume some of the cornucopia of goods created by industrial capitalism. Here, we enter the realm of twentieth-century consumer culture, in which the focus of life shifted over time from work to leisure, production to consumption.[45] Elements of free labor language endure to this day; for example, in anti-union legislation known, in a throwback to the 1880s, as "right to work" laws, or in demands of professional athletes (perhaps the last group denied the right to change employers at will) for "free agency." But these are shards of an ideology that has long since lost its social relevance. For historians of the nineteenth century, however, free labor, despite its contradictions and ambiguities, blind spots and exclusions, continues to offer a valuable window on the consequences of capitalism's expansion, and the divergent ways Americans responded to them.

45. Lawrence Glickman, "Inventing the 'American Standard of Living': Gender, Race, and Working Class Identity, 1880–1925," Labor History, 34 (Spring–Summer 1993), 221–35; David Horowitz, "Consumption and Its Discontents: Simon N. Patten, Thorstein Veblen, and George Gunton," Journal of American History, 67 (September 1980), 301–17; Lasch, True and Only Heaven, 302; John Alt, "Beyond Class: The Decline of Industrial Labor and Leisure," Telos, 28 (Summer 1976), 55–80.

Contents

Abbreviations used in Footnotes and Bibliography

AgH	*Agricultural History*
AHA	American Historical Association
AHR	*American Historical Review*
AmQ	*American Quarterly*
ChicHS	Chicago Historical Society
CWH	*Civil War History*
ConnHS	Connecticut Historical Society
HSPa	Historical Society of Pennsylvania
HEdQ	*History of Education Quarterly*
IllSHS	Illinois State Historical Society
IndMH	*Indiana Magazine of History*
IJH	*Iowa Journal of History*
IJHP	*Iowa Journal of History and Politics*
JAH	Journal of American History
JEcH	*Journal of Economic History*
JNH	Journal of Negro History
JPEc	*Journal of Political Economy*
JSH	Journal of Southern History
LC	Library of Congress
MHS	Massachusetts Historical Society
MinnH	*Minnesota History*
MVHR	*Mississippi Valley Historical Review*
MoHR	*Missouri Historical Review*
NEQ	*New England Quarterly*
NHHS	New Hampshire Historical Society
NYHS	New-York Historical Society

Abbreviations used in Footnotes and Bibliography (continued)

NYHSQ	*New-York Historical Society Quarterly*
NYH	*New York History*
NYPL	New York Public Library
OAHQ	*Ohio Archaeological and Historical Quarterly*
OHQ	*Ohio Historical Quarterly*
OHS	Ohio Historical Society
PaH	*Pennsylvania History*
PaMHB	*Pennsylvania Magazine of History and Biography*
PSQ	*Political Science Quarterly*
POQ	*Public Opinion Quarterly*
SAQ	*South Atlantic Quarterly*
VaMHB	*Virginia Magazine of History and Biography*
WVaH	*West Virginia History*
WRHS	Western Reserve Historical Society
WisHS	State Historical Society of Wisconsin
WisMH	*Wisconsin Magazine of History*

Free Soil, Free Labor, Free Men:

THE IDEOLOGY OF THE REPUBLICAN PARTY BEFORE THE CIVIL WAR

Introduction

Few events in the history of any nation have been the subject of such intense and detailed study as the American Civil War. Yet, surprisingly, while Garrisonian abolitionists have been the subject of a heated historiographical debate, and several recent studies have been devoted to William Lloyd Garrison himself, anti-slavery political parties have received only minimal attention from historians. Recent surveys of the anti-slavery movement by Dwight L. Dumond and Louis Filler deal with political anti-slavery in the most cursory fashion, and there is no modern study of either the Liberty or Free Soil parties.[1] As for the Republicans, there are two excellent studies of that party in the secession crisis, and biographies of such leaders as Charles Sumner and William H. Seward have recently appeared; but the careers of Salmon P. Chase and Gideon Welles, to name only two pivotal figures, still need re-examination.[2] Scores of secondary figures like Governors Kinsley Bingham of Michigan, William Dennison of Ohio, Richard Yates of Illinois, and Alexander Randall of Wisconsin lack scholarly biographies, despite their important roles in the politics of the 1850's.

1. Dwight L. Dumond, *Antislavery, The Crusade for Freedom in America* (Ann Arbor, 1961); Louis Filler. *The Crusade Against Slavery* (New York, 1960); Walter M. Merrill, *Against Wind and Tide* (Cambridge, 1963); John L. Thomas, *The Liberator, William Lloyd Garrison* (Boston, 1963); Aileen S. Kraditor, *Means and Ends in American Abolitionism* (New York, 1969).
2. David Potter, *Lincoln and His Party in the Secession Crisis* (New Haven, 1942); Kenneth Stampp, *And the War Came* (Baton Rouge, 1950); David Donald, *Charles Sumner and the Coming of the Civil War* (New York, 1961); Glyndon G. Van Deusen, *William Henry Seward* (New York, 1967). The best survey of the party's history is George H. Mayer, *The Republican Party, 1854–1966* (New York, 1967 ed.).

and 1860's. And we need badly a full-scale examination of the collapse
of the Whig party and formation of the Republican party between 1854
and 1856.

The absence of a comprehensive study of the politics and ideology
of political anti-slavery is intimately related to the patterns of Civil
War historiography.[3] Aside from histories written by contemporary
participants, which attributed the war to a conspiracy of either slaveholders or abolitionists, interpretations of the war's origins have
generally fallen into two categories: the "irrepressible conflict" school
and the revisionist or "blundering generation" view. Ironically, whatever their differences on other matters, neither of these schools has
had much praise for the Republican party. The belief that the sectional
conflict was irrepressible was presented most persuasively in the 1920's
and 1930's by Charles A. Beard and Arthur C. Cole. In Beard's view,
the war was the inevitable outcome of the struggle between the
planters of the South and an alliance of northern capitalists and
western farmers. Richard Hofstadter has pointed out that as an intellectual child of the Progressive era, Beard played down the moral
and ideological side of the sectional struggle, viewing the arguments
of politicians—particularly those of the Republicans—as merely a cloak
for sectional economic interests. The real aims of the Republican party,
Beard argued, were embodied in the economic program it enacted
during the war years—a high tariff, a centralized banking system,
government aid to internal improvements, and a homestead law. Slavery,
he once wrote, hardly deserved a footnote in the history of the Civil
War. Arthur C. Cole's more extensive treatment of the period, *The
Irrepressible Conflict*, published in 1934, stressed a wider set of social
and intellectual divergences between North and South. Yet he too
agreed that slavery "was scarcely the crux of the sectional issue."[4]

3. In addition to reading the relevant works on the Civil War period, my understanding of the historiographical problems involved has been aided by the following works: David Potter, *The South and the Sectional Conflict* (Baton Rouge,
1968), 87–150; Thomas J. Pressly, *Americans Interpret Their Civil War* (Princeton,
1954); and Thomas N. Bonner, "Civil War Historians and the 'Needless War'
Doctrine," *Journal of the History of Ideas*, XVII (April 1956), 193–216.
4. Charles A. Beard and Mary R. Beard, *The Rise of American Civilization* (2
vols.: New York, 1933 ed.), II, 3–54; Richard Hofstadter, *The Progressive Historians* (New York, 1968), 184, 303, 460; Beard quoted in Nathaniel W. Stephenson, "California and the Compromise of 1850," *Pacific Historical Review*, IV
(June 1935), 115; Arthur C. Cole, *The Irrepressible Conflict* (New York, 1934);
Arthur C. Cole, "Lincoln's Election an Immediate Menace to Slavery in the
States?," *AHR*, XXXVI (July 1931), 766.

Despite their insistence on the inevitability of sectional conflict, Beard and Cole, by removing slavery from the central place it had long held in Civil War intepretation, set the stage for the revisionist writings of the 1930's and 1940's. Avery Craven and James G. Randall, the two leading revisionist historians, insisted that the social and economic differences between the sections were not nearly so important as Beard and Cole had suggested, and were certainly not great enough to lead necessarily to war. Only the inability of political leaders to cope with essentially compromisable problems, and the sectional passions inflamed by irresponsible agitators on both sides, led to a needless war. The Republicans were depicted as inept politicians who used sectional issues to gain political power, and then were unable to resolve the artificial crisis they had created. The war, Craven wrote in 1939, "was the product, not so much of sectional differences as of emotions developed about differences, which by 1861 made it impossible longer to reason, to trust, or to compromise." [5]

The late 1940's witnessed a resurgence of the irrepressible conflict interpretation, but in a very different form from that of Beard and Cole. Historians like Arthur Schlesinger, Jr., and, to a lesser extent, Allan Nevins, again emphasized that sectional differences precluded compromise, although Nevins agreed with the revisionists that the 1850's saw a virtual collapse in creative national political leadership. These historians primarily stressed the moral issue of slavery, with Nevins adding the problem of racial adjustment as well, as the crux of sectional conflict and the primary cause of the war. During the 1950's, the moral emphasis gained wide currency among historians, and was in large measure responsible for the rehabilitation of the abolitionists' historical reputation.[6] But this reassessment did not seem to have much effect on evaluations of the Republicans, who were clearly less concerned with morality than were the abolitionists. Indeed, the 1960's saw a further

5. Avery Craven, *The Repressible Conflict 1830–1861* (Baton Rouge, 1939); Craven, *The Coming of the Civil War* (New York, 1942), esp. 2; J. G. Randall, *Lincoln the President: Springfield to Gettysburg* (2 vols.: New York, 1945); Potter, *The South and the Sectional Conflict*, 92–99; Bonner, "Civil War Historians," 196–97. Recently, Craven has substantially modified his "revisionist" views. See his contribution to *The Crisis of the Union*, ed. George H. Knoles (Baton Rouge, 1963), 60–79.
6. Arthur Schlesinger, Jr., "The Causes of the Civil War: A Note on Historical Sentimentalism," *Partisan Review*, XVI (1949), 968–81; Allan Nevins, *The Emergence of Lincoln* (2 vols.: New York, 1950), II, 462–71. For favorable views of the abolitionists see Martin B. Duberman, ed., *The Antislavery Vanguard* (Princeton, 1965), and the works of Dumond, Filler, and Kraditor previously cited.

decline in the Republicans' historical reputation, as a number of scholars contended that racial prejudice—the desire to prevent blacks, either free or slave, from entering the territories—was at the root of their anti-slavery convictions.[7]

In 1960, David Donald observed that Nevins's magisterial four-volume study of the pre-war decade appeared to be the last effort of historians to investigate in depth the coming of the Civil War. Aside from exercises in historiography, he continued, the war's causes seemed dead as a subject of interest to historians. Recently, however, books have been published on aspects of the 1850's and 1860's that have made important new contributions to our understanding of those years, notably Eugene Genovese's work on the old South, and those of W. R. Brock and David Montgomery on Reconstruction. These books have in common an emphasis on the role of ideology in the conflicts of the 1850's and 1860's.[8] They provide convincing evidence that by studying the ideologies of North and South on the eve of the Civil War it is possible not only to remedy the neglect by historians of political anti-slavery, but also to arrive at a broader understanding of the causes and nature of the entire conflict.

The concept "ideology" has itself been the subject of considerable debate among social scientists. The very term has been confused by a plethora of definitions and made disreputable through its association with fascism and communism, compelling one writer to suggest that it be discarded altogether, in favor of "belief systems."[9] I still prefer the simpler term "ideology," but in this work I shall not use it in the recent sense which implies dogma, a rigid, doctrinaire, black-and-white understanding of the world, but, rather, as the system of beliefs, values, fears, prejudices, reflexes, and commitments—in sum, the social consciousness—of a social group, be it a class, a party, or a section. Genovese uses the term more or less interchangeably with "world view," which also has a certain value (although it hardly conveys the full

7. For example, Eugene H. Berwanger, *The Frontier Against Slavery* (Urbana, 1967), esp. 123–37; Robert F. Durden, "Ambiguities in the Antislavery Crusade of the Republican Party," in *The Antislavery Vanguard*, ed., Duberman, 362–94.
8. David Donald, "American Historians and the Causes of the Civil War," *SAQ*, LIX (Summer 1960), 351–55; Eugene D. Genovese, *The Political Economy of Slavery* (New York, 1965); W. R. Brock, *An American Crisis* (London, 1963); David Montgomery, *Beyond Equality* (New York, 1967).
9. Clifford Geertz, "Ideology as a Cultural System," in *Ideology and Discontent*, ed., David E. Apter (New York, 1964), 47, 50; Philip E. Converse, "The Nature of Belief Systems in Mass Publics," in *Ideology and Discontent*, 207. Cf. Robert E. Lane, *Political Ideology* (New York, 1962), 14.

meaning of the Germanic *Weltanschauung*), because an important aspect of ideology involves the way in which a group perceives itself and its values in relation to the society as a whole. When I speak of the Republican ideology, therefore, I am dealing with the party's perception of what American society, both North and South, was like in the 1850's, and its view of what the nation's future ought to be.

With this concept of ideology, it seems to me, it should be possible to incorporate the most useful aspects of the conflicting theories concerning the origins of the Civil War, while avoiding some of their weaknesses. For instance, historians have generally criticized Beard for posing the economic differences between North and South as a matter of specific legislative policies. As Allan Nevins has observed, the Beardian economic-determinist view of the war is the weakest of all single-cause interpretations.[10] It is easy to show that the Republican commitment to the tariff was by no means definitive in 1860, and that all the economic issues cited by Beard were eminently compromisable. The Republican ideology certainly viewed the South as an obstacle to the material progress of the free states. But the interrelation between the economic structure of a society, its politics, and ideas is much more complex than Beard would have it. Ideology represents much more than the convenient rationalization of material interests. "We may suppose," one sociologist has written, "that a group generally accepts a view of society consonant with its interests; we need not think that ideologies are consciously fashioned to serve those interests or that groups are incapable of acting upon beliefs which appear to contradict those interests." [11]

The irrepressible conflict view is also weak when it centers on the moral issue of slavery, particularly in view of the distaste of the majority of northerners for the Negro and the widespread hostility toward abolitionists. Moral opposition to slavery was certainly one aspect of the Republican ideology, but by no means the only one, and to explain Republicans' actions on simple moral grounds is to miss the full richness of their ideology. And the revisionists can be criticized for denying altogether the urgency of the moral issue, and for drastically underestimating the social and economic differences and conflicts that divided North and South. However, the concept of ideology allows the in-

10. Nevins, *Emergence of Lincoln*, II, 465–66.
11. Norman Birnbaum, "The Sociological Analysis of Ideology (1940–60): A Trend Report and Bibliography," *Current Sociology*, IX (1960), 91.

corporation of their basic insight—that the 1850's was a decade of passion, emotion, and fear, as well as of reasoned debate. Fears and hatreds were essential features of the pre-war situation. Because ideologies deal in fundamental values, they are always susceptible to vivid and exaggerated language rather than cool analysis.[12]

Certain methodological problems which arise in dealing with ideologies should be briefly noted at the outset. One, recently emphasized by Lee Benson, is whether the traditional historical means of gauging public opinion are adequate.[13] Do the opinions of political leaders, that is, accurately reflect mass beliefs. A related problem is that raised by political scientists' studies of voting behavior and voter attitudes over the past twenty years, which conclude that the average voter has a "weak ideological focus." He is not very interested in most political issues and does not usually involve himself in political processes. A small minority of the voters are highly politicized and ideologically oriented, and these—the ones most likely to speak out on public issues, attend political rallies, and write letters to newspapers and Congressmen—represent what might be called visible public opinion.[14]

Some political scientists have tried to extrapolate the information from these voter studies backwards into the 1850's, occasionally with disastrous results.[15] But Walter Dean Burnham has warned against this practice, pointing out that the nineteenth century differed as a "political universe" from the present. And historians of the ante-bellum years agree that politics bulked larger to the average American then than it does today, and that mass participation in politics was much more pronounced. "The pervasive and unremitting popular interest in politics was the most striking feature of Illinois life in the 1850's," according to Don E. Fehrenbacher, and this popular interest was reflected in

12. Geertz, "Ideology," 71.
13. Lee Benson, "Causation and the American Civil War," *History and Theory*, I (1961), 173–74; Lee Benson, "An Approach to the Scientific Study of Past Public Opinion," *POQ*, *XXXI* (Winter, 1967–1968), 555–56. Cf. Joel H. Silbey, *The Shrine of Party* (Pittsburgh, 1967), viii–ix.
14. Angus Campbell, Philip E. Converse, Warren E. Miller, and Donald E. Stokes, *The American Voter* (New York, 1960), 171–74, 187, 197, 249, 543; Converse, "Belief Systems," 212–18, 226; Eugene Burdick, "Political Theory and the Voting Studies," in *American Voting Behavior*, eds., Eugene Burdick and Arthur J. Brodbeck (Glencoe, 1959), 138–40; Robert Axelrod, "The Structure of Public Opinion on Policy Issues," *POQ*, XXXI (Spring 1967), 51–60.
15. For example, Philip E. Converse's article, "The Nature of Belief Systems in Mass Publics," which attempts to prove that the mass of Republican voters were only dimly aware of the slavery issue, shows little understanding of the politics of the 1850's, particularly the differences between abolitionists and Republicans.

voter turnouts which ran as high as 84 per cent for the North in 1860. Allan Nevins writes of political rallies in 1856 which mobilized anywhere from twenty to fifty thousand persons, and Charles Francis Adams addressed one in that year which included nearly a majority of the voting population of Philadelphia. Politics was, in one of its functions, a form of mass entertainment, a spectacle with rallies, parades, and colorful personalities. Leading politicians, moreover, very often served as a focus for popular interests, aspirations, and values.[16] Modern voting studies have shown that many voters tend to take their positions on public issues from political leaders and parties, and contemporaries agreed that shaping public opinion was an important function of political leaders. Lincoln, one of the most astute politicians of his time, remarked in 1858 that Stephen A. Douglas was "a man of vast influence, so great that it is enough for many men to profess to believe anything, when they once find out Judge Douglas professes to believe it." And Wendell Phillips similarly declared of Seward, "Mr. Seward is a power in the state. It is worth while to understand his course. It cannot be caprice. His position decides that of millions." Seward himself recognized that the formation of public opinion was a vital function of political leaders. "In all the slavery debates," he informed the New York editor James Watson Webb in 1858, "I have spoken to the people rather than [to] the Senate." The formation of public opinion and its relation to the ideas of politicians is, of course, a complex process. Seward, Douglas, and Lincoln helped form and express the ideas and values of their constituents, but at the same time if they were to remain effective leaders, their own views could not diverge too sharply from those of the general public.[17]

16. Walter Dean Burnham, "The Changing Shape of the American Political Universe," *American Political Science Review*, LIX (March 1965), 7–28; Don E. Fehrenbacher, *Prelude to Greatness, Lincoln in the 1850's* (New York, 1964 ed.), 14–15; Allan Nevins, *Ordeal of the Union* (2 vols.: New York, 1947), II, 503; Charles Francis Adams Diary, October 9, 1856, Adams Papers, MHS; William N. Chambers, "Party Development and the American Mainstream," in *The American Party Systems* eds., William N. Chambers and Walter D. Burham, (New York, 1967), 11; Richard P. McCormick, "Political Development and the Second Party System," in *The American Party Systems*, 107–8; Logan Esarey, "Elements of Culture in the Old Northwest," *IndMH*, LIII (September 1953), 263.
17. Campbell *et al.*, *American Voter*, 128; Converse, "Belief Systems," 240–41; Benson, "Scientific Study of Past Public Opinion," 550; Herbert M. Hyman, *Political Socialization* (Glencoe, 1959), 75; Roy F. Basler *et al.*, eds., *The Collected Works of Abraham Lincoln* (9 vols.: New Brunswick, 1953–55), III, 27; Wendell Phillips, *Speeches, Lectures, and Letters* (Boston, 1863), 353; William H. Seward to James Watson Webb, May 6, 1858, James Watson Webb Papers, Yale University.

It is, no doubt, safe to assume that the Republican ideology received its most coherent expression from the political leaders whose speeches, letters, and writings form the bulk of the evidence in this study. Yet it would certainly not do to say, as some revisionists have, that the slavery issue and other sectional antagonisms were therefore artificial, having been imposed on an unsuspecting public by agitators. The Republicans' rapid rise to power could never have been achieved had their ideology not incorporated many of the basic values of the northern public. As one historian has written in a somewhat different context, "the very fact that issues could be used for opportunistic purposes by some implies that they served substantive purposes for others. . . . The point is that it would be useless for a politician to make an instrumental use of an issue unless it represented something that a considerable group in the electorate . . . wanted." Moreover, the rate of participation and interest in politics may well have been linked with a greater degree of issue-orientation among the voters than presently exists. Donald Stokes has described the 1850's as the period of American political history with the most pronounced "ideological focus." That focus was provided by the issue of slavery with its range of economic, constitutional, and political consequences.[18]

Political parties today are consciously non-ideological, but in the 1840's and 1850's ideology made its way into the heart of the political system, despite the best efforts of Whigs and Democrats to keep it out. Political sociologists have pointed out that the stable functioning of a political democracy requires a setting in which parties represent broad coalitions of varying interests, and that the peaceful resolution of social conflict takes place most easily when the major parties share fundamental values. Such a view implies, of course, that the peaceful operation of the political system is the highest social value, an implication which, under certain circumstances, may be justly questioned. But it does contain important insights about the normal functioning of the American polity.[19] Government by majority rule, Carl Becker observed

18. William O. Aydelotte, "Voting Patterns in the British House of Commons in the 1840's," *Comparative Stud es n Soc ety and History*, V (January 1963), 154; Donald E. Stokes, "Spatial Models of Party Competition," in *Elections and the Pol tical Order*, eds., Angus Campbell, Philip E. Converse, Warren E. Miller, and Donald E. Stokes (New York, 1966), 170–78.
19. Seymour M. Lipset, "Political Sociology," in *Sociology Today*, eds., Robert K. Merton *et al.* (New York, 1959), 93; Irving L. Horowitz, "Consensus, Conflict, and Cooperation: A Sociological Inventory," *Social Forces*, XLI (December 1962), 177–88.

many years ago, works best when political issues involve superficial problems, rather than deep social divisions. The minority can accept the victory of the majority at the polls, because both share many basic values, and electoral defeat does not imply "a fatal surrender of . . . vital interests." Before the 1850's, the second American party system conformed to this pattern—largely because sectional ideologies and issues were consciously kept out of politics. In this sense, as Richard McCormick points out, the party system had a certain artificial quality. Its divisions rarely corresponded to the basic sectional divisions which were daily becoming more and more pronounced.[20] The two decades before the Civil War witnessed the development of conflicting sectional ideologies, each viewing its own society as fundamentally well-ordered, and the other as both a negation of its most cherished values and a threat to its existence. The development of the two ideologies was in many ways interrelated; each grew in part as a response to the growth of the other. Thus, as southerners were coming more and more consciously to insist on slavery as the very basis of civilized life, and to reject the materialism and lack of cohesion in northern society, northerners came to view slavery as the antithesis of the good society, as well as a threat to their own fundamental values and interests. The existing political system could not contain these two irreconcilable ideologies, and in the 1850's each national party—Whigs, Know-Nothings, and finally Democrats—disintegrated. And in the end the South seceded from the Union rather than accept the victory of a political party whose ideology threatened everything southerners most valued.

At the center of the Republican ideology was the notion of "free labor." This concept involved not merely an attitude toward work, but a justification of ante-bellum northern society, and it led northern Republicans to an extensive critique of southern society, which appeared both different from and inferior to their own. Republicans also believed in the existence of a conspiratorial "Slave Power" which had seized control of the federal government and was attempting to pervert the Constitution for its own purposes. Two profoundly different and antagonistic civilizations, Republicans thus believed, had developed within the nation, and were competing for control

20. Carl Becker, *New Liberties for Old* (New Haven, 1941), 106–7; Richard P. McCormick, *The Second American Party System* (Chapel Hill, 1966), 353. On the relationship of political processes and sectional strife, see also Daniel J. Boorstin, *The Americans: The National Experience* (New York, 1965), 430; Kraditor, *Means and Ends*, 274–76.

of the political system. These central ideas will provide the initial
focus for this study of Republican ideology. The study will then
examine the distinctive ideological contributions of each of the elements which made up the Republican party—radicals, former Democrats, and moderate and conservative Whigs. The attitudes and
opinions of these groups on specific issues will be analyzed, but always
with a view to discovering their basic values and assumptions. Finally,
the Republican response to the competing ideology of nativism will be
discussed, as well as their attitude toward race, an issue which illuminated many of the virtues and shortcomings of the Republican world
view.

Like all ideologies, the Republicans' was more than merely the sum
of its component parts: it must be understood as a total Gestalt, whose
elements blended into and reinforced one another. Indeed, the key
to its widespread acceptance was its multifaceted nature. A profoundly
successful fusion of value and interest, the ideology could appeal in
different ways to various groups within the party, and it gave northerners of divergent social and political backgrounds a basis for collec-
tive action. It provided the moral consensus which allowed the North,
for the first time in history, to mobilize an entire society in modern
warfare.

1

Free Labor:
THE REPUBLICANS AND
NORTHERN SOCIETY

On May 26, 1860, one of the Republican party's leading orators, Carl
Schurz of Wisconsin, addressed a Milwaukee audience which had
gathered to endorse the nomination of Abraham Lincoln. "The Republicans," Schurz declared, "stand before the country, not only as the
anti-slavery party, but emphatically as the party of free labor." Two
weeks later, Richard Yates, the gubernatorial candidate in Illinois,
spoke at a similar rally in Springfield. "The great idea and basis of the
Republican party, as I understand it," he proclaimed, "is free labor.
. . . To make labor honorable is the object and aim of the Republican
party." [1] Such statements, which were reiterated countless times by
Republican orators in the 1850's, were more than mere election-year
appeals for the votes of laboring men. For the concept of "free labor"
lay at the heart of the Republican ideology, and expressed a coherent
social outlook, a model of the good society. Political anti-slavery was
not merely a negative doctrine, an attack on southern slavery and the
society built upon it; it was an affirmation of the superiority of the
social system of the North—a dynamic, expanding capitalist society,
whose achievements and destiny were almost wholly the result of the
dignity and opportunities which it offered the average laboring man.

The dignity of labor was a constant theme of ante-bellum northern
culture and politics. Tocqueville noted that in America, "not only work
itself, but work specifically to gain money," was considered honorable,
and twenty years later, the New York editor Horace Greeley took note

1. Carl Schurz, *Speeches of Carl Schurz* (Philadelphia, 1865), 108; *Speech of
Hon. Richard Yates, Delivered at the Republican Ratification Meeting* . . .
(Springfield, 1860), 6.

of "the usual Fourth-of-July declamation in behalf of the dignity of labor, the nobleness of labor." It was a common idea in both economic treatises and political pronouncements that labor was the source of all value.[2] Lincoln declared in 1859 that "Labor is prior to, and independent of capital . . . in fact, capital is the fruit of labor," and the New York *Tribune* observed that "nothing is more common" than this "style of assertion." Republican orators insisted that labor could take the credit for the North's rapid economic development. Said William Evarts in 1856, "Labor, gentlemen, we of the free States acknowledge to be the source of all our wealth, of all our progress, of all our dignity and value." In a party which saw divisions on political and economic matters between radicals and conservatives, between former Whigs and former Democrats, the glorification of labor provided a much-needed theme of unity. Representatives of all these segments included paeans to free labor in their speeches; even the crusty old conservative Tom Corwin delivered "a eulogy on labor and laboring men" in an 1858 speech.[3]

Belief in the dignity of labor was not, of course, confined to the Republican party or to the ante-bellum years; it has been part of American culture from the very beginning. In large part, it can be traced to the fact that most Americans came from a Protestant background, in which the nobility of labor was an article of faith. One does not need to accept in its entirety Max Weber's association of the "Protestant ethic" with the rise of capitalism in Europe to believe that there is much validity in Weber's insight that the concept of "calling" provided the psychological underpinning for capitalist values. Weber pointed out that in Calvinist theology each man had an occupation or calling to which he was divinely appointed. To achieve success in this calling would serve the glory of God, and also provide visible evidence that an individual was among the few predestined to enter heaven. The

2. Alexis de Tocqueville, *Democracy in America*, eds. J. P. Mayer and Max Lerner (New York, 1966), 552; Horace Greeley, *The Crystal Palace and Its Lessons* (New York, 1852), 28; David Montgomery, *Beyond Equality* (New York, 1967), 253; Arthur M. Schlesinger, Jr., *The Age of Jackson* (Boston, 1945), 314; H. C. Carey, *Principles of Political Economy* (3 vols.: Philadelphia, 1837–40), I, 19; Amasa Walker, *The Nature and Uses of Money and Mixed Currency* (Boston, 1857), 5; *Ohio State Journal*, June 16, 1859; Chicago *Press and Tribune*, August 24, 1859.
3. Roy F. Basler *et al.*, eds., *The Collected Works of Abraham Lincoln* (9 vols.: New Brunswick, 1953–55), III, 478; New York *Tribune*, November 11, 1857; Sherman Evarts, ed., *Arguments and Speeches of William Maxwell Evarts* (3 vols.: New York, 1919), II, 449; Cincinnati *Gazette*, September 2, 1858.

pursuit of wealth thus became a way of serving God on earth, and labor, which had been imposed on fallen man as a curse, was transmuted into a religious value, a Christian duty. And the moral qualities which would ensure success in one's calling—honesty, frugality, diligence, punctuality, and sobriety—became religious obligations. Weber described the Protestant outlook on life as "worldly asceticism," since idleness, waste of time, and conspicuous display or expenditure for personal enjoyment were incompatible with its basic values.[4]

There was more to the Republican idea of free labor, however, than the essentials of the Protestant ethic, to which, presumably, the South had also been exposed, for the relation of that ethic to the idea of social mobility was highly ambiguous. On the one hand, the drive to work zealously in one's calling, the capital accumulation which resulted from frugality, and the stress on economic success as a sign of divine approval, all implied that men would work for an achievement of wealth and advancement in their chosen professions. But if one's calling were divinely ordained, the implication might be that a man should be content with the same occupation for his entire life, although he should strive to grow rich in it. In a static economy, therefore, the concept of "a calling" may be associated with the idea of an hierarchical social order, with more or less fixed classes. But Republicans rejected this image of society. Their outlook was grounded in the Protestant ethic, but in its emphasis on social mobility and economic growth, it reflected an adaptation of that ethic to the dynamic, expansive, capitalist society of the ante-bellum North.

Contemporaries and historians agree that the average American of the ante-bellum years was driven by an inordinate desire to improve his condition in life, and by boundless confidence that he could do so. Economic success was the standard by which men judged their social importance, and many observers were struck by the concentration on work, with the aim of material advancement, which characterized Americans. Tocqueville made the following observation during Jackson's presidency: "The first thing that strikes one in the United States is the innumerable crowd of those striving to escape from their original

4. Max Weber, *The Protestant Ethic and the Spirit of Capitalism* (New York, 1958 ed.), *passim.* Cf. Christopher Hill, "Protestantism and the Rise of Capitalism," in Frederick J. Fisher, ed., *Essays in the Economic and Social History of Tudor and Stuart England* (Cambridge, 1961), 15–39; Stuart Bruchey, *The Roots of American Economic Growth 1607–1861* (New York, 1965), 42–43, 197.

social condition." On the eve of the Civil War, the Cincinnati *Gazette* reported that things had not changed. "Of all the multitude of young men engaged in various employments of this city," it declared, "there is probably not one who does not desire, and even confidently expect, to become rich, and that at an early day." [5] The universal desire for social advancement gave American life an aspect of almost frenetic motion and activity, as men moved from place to place, and occupation to occupation in search of wealth. Even ministers, reported the Cincinnati *Gazette*, "resign the most interesting fields of labor to get higher salaries." The competitive character of northern society was aptly summed up by Lincoln, when he spoke of the "race of life" in the 1850's.[6]

The foremost example of the quest for a better life was the steady stream of settlers who abandoned eastern homes to seek their fortunes in the West. The westward movement reached new heights in the mid-1850's, and it was not primarily the poor who migrated westward, but middle class "business-like farmers," who sold their farms to migrate, or who left the eastern farms of their fathers. "These emigrants," said a leading Republican newspaper of Ohio, "are not needy adventurers, fleeing from the pinchings of penury. They are substantial farmers." [7] Those without means who came to the West were interested in obtaining their own farms as quickly as possible, because to the American of the nineteenth century land was not the bucolic ideal of the pre-capitalist world, but another means for economic advancement. Tocqueville noted that the small farmer of the West was really a landed businessman, an entrepreneur who was prepared to sell his farm and move on, if he could get a good price. What Horace Greeley called "the nomadic tendency" of Americans contributed to the rapid expansion of the western frontier. "The men who are building up the villages of last year's origin on the incipient Railroads of Iowa," said the New York editor, "were last year doing the like in Illinois, and three years since in Ohio." The acquisitive instincts of western settlers were described by Kinsley Bingham, the first Republican governor of Michigan: "Like most new States, ours has been settled by an active,

5. Tocqueville, *Democracy in America*, 603; Cincinnati *Gazette*, June 11, 1860.
6. Marvin Fisher, *Workshops in the Wilderness* (New York, 1967), 65–67; Cincinnati *Gazette*, November 20, 1857; Basler, ed., *Lincoln Works*, IV, 240, 438. Cf. Marvin Meyers, *The Jacksonian Persuasion* (New York, 1960 ed.), 123.
7. Joseph Schafer, "The Yankee and the Teuton in Wisconsin," *WisMH*, VI (1922–23), 135; *Ohio State Journal*, April 6, 1854.

energetic and enterprising class of men, who are desirous of accumulating property rapidly." [8]

The Republican idea of free labor was a product of this expanding, enterprising, competitive society. It is important to recognize that in ante-bellum America, the word "labor" had a meaning far broader than its modern one. Andrew Jackson, for example, defined as "the producing classes" all those whose work was directly involved in the production of goods—farmers, planters, laborers, mechanics, and small businessmen. Only those who profited from the work of others, or whose occupations were largely financial or promotional, such as speculators, bankers, and lawyers, were excluded from this definition. Daniel Webster took a similarly all-embracing view. In his famous speech of March 7, 1850, Webster asked, "Why, who are the laboring people of the North? They are the whole North. They are the people who till their own farms with their own hands; freeholders, educated men, independent men." [9] And the Republican definition, as it emerged in the 1850's, proved equally broad. Some Republicans did exclude commercial enterprise from their idea of labor—the Springfield *Republican*, for example, suggested that three-quarters of the traders in the country should go into some field of "productive labor." In general, however, Republicans would agree with Horace Greeley that labor included "useful doing in any capacity or vocation." They thus drew no distinction between a "laboring class" and what we could call the middle class. With Webster, they considered the farmer, the small businessman, and the independent craftsmen, all as "laborers." [10]

If the Republicans saw "labor" as substantially different from the modern-day notion of the "working class," it was partly because the line between capitalist and worker was to a large extent blurred in the ante-bellum northern economy, which centered on the independent farm and small shop. Moreover, for the Republicans, social mobility

8. Tocqueville, *Democracy in America*, 526; Richard Hofstadter, *The Age of Reform* (New York, 1955), 23–24, 38–43; New York *Tribune*, February 28, 1857; George N. Fuller, ed., *Messages of the Governors of Michigan* (4 vols.: Lansing, 1925–27), II, 315.

9. Meyers, *Jacksonian Persuasion*, 21; Irwin Unger, *The Greenback Era* (Princeton, 1964), 30–31; *The Writings and Speeches of Daniel Webster* (18 vols.: Boston, 1903), X, 92. Cf. Joseph L. Blau, ed., *Social Theories of Jacksonian Democracy* (New York, 1947), 203; Bruchey, *Roots of American Economic Growth*, 207.

10. Springfield *Republican*, January 16, 1858; Horace Greeley, *Hints Towards Reforms* (New York, 1850), 9. Cf. Bernard Mandel, *Labor: Free and Slave* (New York, 1955), 13.

was an essential part of northern society. The ante-bellum Republicans
praised the virtues of the enterprising life, and viewed social mobility
as the glory of northern society. "Our paupers to-day, thanks to free
labor, are our yeomen and merchants of tomorrow," said the New
York *Times*. Lincoln asserted in 1859 that "advancement, improvement in condition—is the order of things in a society of equals," and
he denounced southern insinuations that northern wage earners were
"fatally fixed in that condition for life." The opportunity for social
advancement, in the Republican view, was what set Americans apart
from their European forebears. As one Iowa Republican put it: [11]

> What is it that makes the great mass of American citizens so much
> more enterprising and intelligent than the laboring classes in Eur-
> rope? It is the stimulant held out to them by the character of our
> institutions. The door is thrown open to all, and even the poorest
> and humblest in the land, may, by industry and application, attain
> a position which will entitle him to the respect and confidence of
> his fellow-men.

Many Republican leaders bore witness in their own careers to how far
men could rise from humble beginnings. Lincoln's own experience, of
course, was the classic example, and during the 1860 campaign Republican orators repeatedly referred to him as "the child of labor," who
had proved how "honest industry and toil" were rewarded in the
North.[12] Other Republican leaders like the former indentured servant
Henry Wilson, the "bobbin boy" Nathaniel P. Banks, and the ex-laborer
Hannibal Hamlin also made much of their modest beginnings in
campaign speeches.[13]

In the free labor outlook, the objective of social mobility was not
great wealth, but the middle-class goal of economic independence. For
Republicans, "free labor" meant labor with economic choices, with the

11. New York *Times*, November 18, 1857; Basler, ed., *Lincoln Works*, III, 462,
478; *The Debates of the Constitutional Convention of the State of Iowa* (2 vols.:
Davenport, 1857), I, 193. Cf. *Congressional Globe*, 35 Congress, 1 Session, 1025;
New York *Tribune*, October 25, 1856; Cleveland *Leader*, April 21, 1855; John G.
Palfrey, *Papers on the Slave Power* (Boston, 1846), 53.
12. Schurz, *Speeches*, 113; Chicago *Press and Tribune*, August 1, 1860; William
M. French, ed., *Life, Speeches, State Papers, and Public Services of Gov. Oliver
P. Morton* (Cincinnati, 1866), 117; *Speech of Hon. Richard Yates*, 11; Charles
E. Hamlin, *The Life and Times of Hannibal Hamlin* (Cambridge, 1899), 356–57.
13. Thomas Russell and Elias Nason, *The Life and Public Services of Hon. Henry
Wilson* (Boston, 1872), 17; Fred Harvey Harrington, *Fighting Politician, Major
General N. P. Banks* (Philadelphia, 1948), 1–3; *Congressional Globe*, 35 Congress,
1 Session, 1006; James A. Rawley, *Edwin D. Morgan 1811–1883: Merchant in
Politics* (New York, 1955), 80.

opportunity to quit the wage-earning class. A man who remained all his life dependent on wages for his livelihood appeared almost as un-free as the southern slave.[14] There was nothing wrong, of course, with working for wages for a time, if the aim were to acquire enough money to start one's own farm or business. Zachariah Chandler described in the Senate the cycle of labor which he felt characterized northern society: "A young man goes out to service—to labor, if you please to call it so—for compensation until he acquires money enough to buy a farm . . . and soon he becomes himself the employer of labor." Similarly, a correspondent of the New York *Tribune* wrote in 1854, "Do you say to me, hire some of the thousands and thousands of emigrants coming to the West. Sir, I cannot do it. They come West to labor for themselves, not for me; and instead of laboring for others, they want others to labor for them." The aspirations of the free labor ideology were thus thoroughly middle-class, for the successful laborer was one who achieved self-employment, and owned his own capital—a business, farm, or shop.[15]

The key figure in the Republicans' social outlook was thus the small independent entrepreneur. "Under every form of government having the benefits of civilization," said Congressman Timothy Jenkins of New York, "there is a middle class, neither rich nor poor, in which is concentrated the chief enterprise of the country." Charles Francis Adams agreed that the "middling class . . . equally far removed from the temptations of great wealth and of extreme destitution," provided the surest defense of democratic principles. In a nation as heavily agricultural as the ante-bellum United States, it is not surprising that the yeoman received the greatest praise. "The middling classes who own the soil, and work it with their own hands," declared Thaddeus Stevens, "are the main support of every free government."[16] But the exponents of the development of manufactures also looked to the small capitalist, not the very wealthy, as the agents of economic progress. "The manufacturing industry of this country," said Representative

14. Arnold W. Green, *Henry Charles Carey, Nineteenth Century Sociologist* (Philadelphia, 1951), 118–19; Greeley, *Hints*, 354; *The Address of the Southern and Western Liberty Convention to the People of the United States; the Proceedings and Resolutions of the Convention* . . . (Cincinnati, 1845), 21.

15. *Congressional Globe*, 35 Congress, 1 Session, 1093; New York *Tribune*, November 29, 1854. Cf. Philadelphia *North American and United States Gazette*, September 27, 1856.

16. *Congressional Globe*, 30 Congress, 2 Session, Appendix, 103; Boston *Advertiser*, clipping, Charles Francis Adams Diary, November 2, 1860, Adams Papers, MHS; *Congressional Globe*, 31 Congress, 1 Session, Appendix, 142.

Samuel Blair of Pennsylvania, "must look to men of moderate means for its development—the men of enterprise being, as a class, in such circumstances." In their glorification of the middle class and of economic independence, the Republicans were accurately reflecting the aspirations of northern society. As Carl Schurz later recalled of his first impressions of the United States, "I saw what I might call the middle-class culture in process of formation." [17]

II

The Republicans' glorification of northern labor might have led them to a radical political appeal, in which the rights of workingmen were defended against the prerogatives of the rich and propertied. And there was a substantial body of Republicans—the former Democrats—who came from a political tradition which viewed the interests of capitalists and laborers as being in earnest conflict. As Marvin Meyers points out, the political rhetoric of Jacksonian Democrats involved a series of sharp social antagonisms. They insisted that there existed real class differences between rich and poor, capital and labor, and consciously strove to give their party an anti-wealth persuasion.[18] Democrats traditionally opposed measures like the protective tariff, which they viewed as government aid to the capitalist class, and paper money, which they claimed, robbed the laborer of a portion of his wages by depreciating in value.[19]

Behind the radical rhetoric of the Jacksonians, however, lay a basically middle-class perception of the social order. They believed that the social opportunity inherent in northern society would enable most laborers to achieve ownership of capital, and they were also convinced that the growth of the northern economy would lead to an increasing equalization in the distribution of wealth, rather than merely

17. *Congressional Globe*, 36 Congress, 1 Session, Appendix, 410; Carl Schurz, *Reminiscences of Carl Schurz* (3 vols.: New York, 1907–08), II, 158. Cf. H. C. Carey, *The Past, The Present, and the Future* (Philadelphia 1872 ed.), 323; Philadelphia *North American and United States Gazette*, August 26, 1856.
18. Meyers, *Jacksonian Persuasion*, 10. Cf. Schlesinger, *Age of Jackson*, 168, 306–8; Blau, ed., *Social Theories*, 199–207; Charles T. Congdon, *Reminiscences of a Journalist* (Boston, 1880), 61; William Trimble, "Diverging Tendencies in New York Democracy in the Period of the Locofocos," *AHR*, XXIV (April 1919), 406.
19. *Congressional Globe*, 29 Congress, 1 Session, Appendix, 767–71; Schlesinger, *Age of Jackson*, 115–31; Martin Van Buren to Samuel Medary, February, 1846 (draft), Martin Van Buren Papers, LC.

adding to the holdings of the rich. The primary aim of the Jacksonians was not to redistribute the property of the rich, but to open the avenues of social advancement to all laborers. Several historians have pointed out that, despite their disagreements over such matters of economic policy as tariffs and banks, Democrats and Whigs did not differ on such basic assumptions as the value of economic individualism, the rights of property, and other capitalist virtues. Nor should Jacksonian rhetoric be confused with a lack of enthusiasm for the economic development which most northerners saw as an essential part of social progress. Democrats insisted that their economic policies of free trade and destruction of economic privilege would allow free play to natural economic forces, and actually speed up economic advancement.[20] Salmon P. Chase, for example, condemned the government's aid to the Collins Steamship Line in the 1850's, by arguing that if a real economic necessity existed, steam lines would be established by private enterprise, whether the government subsidized them or not. Similarly, Democratic free-traders like William Cullen Bryant argued that competition with foreign producers would stimulate the growth and progress of American firms, while protection would only encourage sluggishness. Democrats who entered the Republican party in the 1850's thus shared the Whig commitment to the nation's economic growth, even while they differed on the specific economic policies that would facilitate it.[21]

Most Republicans, of course, were former Whigs, and they accepted the economic outlook, expressed by Carey and propagated in the pages of the New York *Tribune*, that there existed no real conflict between the interests of different social classes. Since all classes would benefit from economic expansion, this argument went, all had a stake in the national prosperity. "The interests of the capitalist and the laborer," Carey wrote, "are . . . in perfect harmony with each other, as each derives advantage from every measure that tends to facilitate the growth of capital." During the 1850's, Carey served as a consultant

20. W. R. Brock, *An American Crisis* (London, 1963), 240–41; Joel H. Silbey, *The Shrine of Party* (Pittsburgh, 1967), 27; Richard Hofstadter, *The American Political Tradition* (New York, 1948), viii, 62; Douglas T. Miller, *Jacksonian Aristocracy* (New York, 1967), 36–39.
21. *Congressional Globe*, 33 Congress, 2 Session, Appendix, 303–4; New York *Evening Post*, February 10, 1859. Cf. George Opdyke, *A Treatise on Political Economy* (New York, 1851), 259; William A. Williams, *The Contours of American History* (London, 1961 ed.), 248.

to Greeley on economic matters, and the *Tribune*—the North's "sectional oracle"—reflected his views.[22] Other Republican papers, like the Springfield *Republican*, also stressed the "perfect and equal mutual dependence" which existed between capital and labor. Republicans consistently deplored attempts of labor spokesmen to arouse hostility against the capitalist class. "We are not of the number of those who would array one class of society in hostility to another," the Cincinnati *Gazette* announced during the social dislocations caused by the Panic of 1857. Greeley agreed that "Jacobin ravings in the Park or elsewhere, against the Rich, or the Banks," could in no way alleviate "the distress of the poor." The conservatism implicit in the harmony of interests outlook was reflected in Lincoln's remarks to a delegation of workingmen during the Civil War. Condemning those who advocated a "war on property, or the owners of property," the President insisted that as the fruit of labor, property was desirable; it was "a positive good in the world." That some had wealth merely demonstrated that others could achieve wealth, and the prospect encouraged individual enterprise. "Let not him who is houseless," Lincoln told the workingmen, "pull down the house of another; but let him labor diligently and build one for himself, thus by example assuring that his own shall be safe from violence when built." In other words, the interests of labor and capital were identical, because equality of opportunity in American society generated a social mobility which assured that today's laborer would be tomorrow's capitalist.[23]

The most striking example of the Whig-Republican doctrine of the harmony of interests was the idea, developed in the 1840's and expanded in the next decade, that the protective tariff was designed primarily to advance the interests of labor. Led by Greeley and Webster, Whig spokesmen developed the argument that the tariff was really intended to protect American workingmen against the competition of cheap foreign labor. Unless the tariff was used to increase the prices of foreign manufactures before they entered the American market, according to this argument, the only way for American business-

---

22. Carey, *Political Economy*, I, 339; A. D. H. Kaplan, *Henry Charles Carey* (Baltimore, 1931), 47–52; Glyndon G. Van Deusen, *Horace Greeley, Nineteenth Century Crusader* (Philadelphia, 1953), 83; New York *Tribune*, August 28, 1851, January 17, 1855; Jeter A. Isely, *Horace Greeley and the Republican Party 1853–1861* (Princeton, 1947).
23. Springfield *Republican*, July 15, 1857; Cincinnati *Gazette*, November 2, 1857; New York *Tribune*, January 6, 1855; Basler, ed., *Lincoln Works*, VII, 259–60.

men to compete would be to depress their wage payments to the low
European levels.[24] Republican spokesmen for protection almost uni-
formly made this their major argument in the pre-war decade. "Mr.
Chairman," declared a Pennsylvania Congressman as he opened a
tariff speech in 1860, "I rise to advocate the rights of labor." Republicans also argued that the development of American industry,
fostered by protection, would aid all sectors of the economy, by providing an expanding market for farm produce. Greeley insisted that a
country without a home market for agriculture "can rarely boast a
substantial, intelligent and virtuous yeomanry. . . . It may have
wealthy Capitalists and Merchants, but never a numerous Middle
Class."[25]

In spite of their faith in the harmony of interests and their commitment to economic progress and social mobility, there was a certain
suspicion of wealth within the Republican party. To some extent this
was a natural reaction on the part of those who witnessed the reluctance of what Greeley called the "wealthy, timid, and mercantile
classes" to support anti-slavery. It was well known that in the major
cities of the East the wealthiest citizens placed the preservation of
the Union (and of their markets and business connections in the
South) above agitation of the slavery question. In Massachusetts,
Conscience Whig leaders like Sumner, Wilson, and others had long
condemned the political alliance between "the lords of the loom and
the lords of the lash"—the cotton manufacturers and merchants of
Massachusetts and the southern planters. Even the sedate Springfield
Republican complained that "property . . . has frequently stood in
the way of very necessary reforms, and has thus brought itself into
contempt."[26] Like their Boston counterparts, New York merchants
were notorious for their close economic, political, and personal ties
with the South. "Our greatest obstacle," one Republican wrote William

24. F. W. Taussig, *The Tariff History of the United States* (7th ed., New York,
1923), 63–67; George B. Mangold, *The Labor Argument in the American Protective Tariff Discussion* (Madison, 1906), 90–95; John R. Commons, "Horace
Greeley and the Working Class Origins of the Republican Party," *PSQ*, XXIV
(September 1909), 473–74, 487.
25. *Congr ssional Globe*, 36 Congress, 1 Session, 1844; Greeley, *Hints*, 252–53.
26. Isely, *Greeley*, 265; *The Works of Charles Sumner* (10 vols.: Boston, 1870–
83), II, 81; Mary Peabody Mann, *Life of Horace Mann* (Washington, 1937), 320;
Springfield *Republican*, December 19, 1857. Cf. Charles Sumner to Salmon P.
Chase, November 16, 1848, Salmon P. Chase Papers, LC; Charles Francis Adams
Diary, October 4, 1848, Adams Papers.

Seward in 1856, "is the respectable fashionable well to do class," and
the New York *Tribune* spoke of the "plain tendency to a union between the slave capitalists of the South and the moneyed capitalists
of the North." During the 1856 campaign, Republicans throughout
the North found themselves in difficulty when the wealthiest businessmen refused to contribute money to the party's coffers.[27]

But Republican attacks on "the money capitalists" had deeper roots
than political antagonisms. Many Republicans, of both Democratic
and Whig antecedents, were deeply suspicious of corporations and of
economic concentration. Israel Washburn, a leading Maine Republican,
expressed a common fear when he warned of the danger "that the
money-power will be too much centralized—that the lands and property
of the country, in the course of time may come to be held or controlled
by a comparatively small number of people." To some Republicans
the growth of corporations was a harbinger of just such a development. Amasa Walker, the Massachusetts economist who left the
Democratic party to join the Free Soilers and Republicans, insisted at
the Massachusetts Constitutional Convention of 1853 that "this system
of corporations is nothing more nor less than a moneyed feudalism.
. . . It concentrates masses of wealth, it places immense power in a
few hands. . . ." Walker's objections to corporations reflected the
traditional economic anxieties of the small farmer and independent
artisan:

> Corporations change the relation of man to wealth. When a man
> has his property in his own hands, and manages it himself, he is
> responsible for the manner in which he does it. . . . But when the
> management of property is put into the hands of corporations, the
> many delegate the power of managing it to the few. . . . It ag-
> gregates power, of course, and necessarily all the property of the
> Commonwealth, included in these corporations, must be put into
> the hands of a few men. . . . Hence, the agent of a factory, or a
> corporation of any kind, has absolute control over all persons con-
> nected with that corporation.

At the same convention, the Whig William Schouler, who was soon
to become a leading Republican editor, indicated that he felt corporations were merely devices enabling businessmen to escape responsi-

27. Philip S. Foner, *Business and Slavery* (Chapel Hill, 1941), *passim;* George E.
Baker to Seward, December 20, 1856, Seward Papers; New York *Tribune,* Decem-
ber 28, 1859; James A. Rawley, "Financing the Frémont Campaign," *PaMHB,*
LXXV (January 1951), 25–35.

bility for paying their debts.[28] The Republicans' distrust of corporations typified the ante-bellum American outlook. In an economy in which most mills and factories were still owned by individuals or by unchartered joint-stock companies or partnerships, the corporate form was generally confined to enterprises like banks and transportation companies, which serviced the public at large. Indeed, most were quasi-public in nature.[29]

III

"The middle class," wrote the Catholic social critic Orestes Brownson, "is always a firm champion of equality when it concerns humbling a class above it, but it is its inveterate foe when it concerns elevating a class below it." Brownson's statement can be taken as a critique of the free labor ideology. For while it is true that the Republicans insisted on opening the opportunity for social advancement to all wage earners, it must be borne in mind that as true disciples of the Protestant ethic, they attributed an individual's success or failure in the North's "race of life" to his own abilities or shortcomings. Given the equality of opportunity which the Republicans believed existed in northern society, it followed that economic success was, as Horace Greeley argued, a reflection of the fact that a man had respected the injunctions to frugality, diligent work, and sobriety of the Protestant ethic.[30]

In the North, one Republican declared in 1854, "every man holds his fortune in his own right arm; and his position in society, in life, is to be tested by his own individual character." This belief explains the fact that for all their glorification of labor, Republicans looked down upon those who labored for wages all their lives. "It is not the fault of the system," if a man did not rise above the position of wage earner, Lincoln explained, "but because of either a dependent nature which prefers it, or improvidence, folly, or singular misfortune." Poverty, or even the failure to advance economically, were thus individual, not

28. I. W. [Israel Washburn], "Modern Civilization," *Universalist Quarterly,* XV (January 1858), 23–24; *Official Report of the Debates and Proceedings in the State Convention . . . to Revise and Amend the Constitution of the Commonwealth of Massachusetts* (3 vols.: Boston, 1853), II, 58–62. Cf. *National Era,* February 8, 1849; Cincinnati *Gazette,* November 25, 1857.
29. G. Heberton Evans, *Business Incorporations in the United States 1800–1943* (New York, 1948), 10, 20–21; Louis Hartz, *Economic Policy and Democratic Thought: Pennsylvania, 1776–1860* (Cambridge, 1948), 40, 57.
30. Williams, *Contours,* 274; Greeley, *Hints,* 16.

social failures, the consequence of poor personal habits—laziness, extravagance, and the like. Greeley believed that "chance or 'luck,'" had
"little to do with men's prosperous or adverse fortunes," and he complained that too many men blamed banks, tariffs, and hard times for
their personal failures, while in reality the fault was "their own extravagance and needless ostentation." The Springfield *Republican*
summed up this outlook when it declared in 1858 that there could be
"no oppression of the laborer here which it is not in his power to
remedy, or which does not come from his own inefficiency and lack
of enterprise." [31]

The free labor attitude toward the poor was made doubly clear
in the aftermath of the Panic of 1857, when northern cities were struck
by widespread unemployment and labor unrest. Demonstrations of the
poor—"never before witnessed in the towns of the abundant West"—
occurred all too frequently.[32] As they were to do many times subs-
quently, Republicans blamed the Panic not on impersonal economic
forces, but on the individual shortcomings of Americans, particularly
their speculation in land and stocks which had reached "mania" proportions in the years preceding the crash, and on generally extravagant
living. The Cincinnati *Gazette* defined the basic economic problem
as an overexpansion of the credit system, rooted in too many "great
speculations." But speculation was only one aspect of the problem of
general extravagance. "We have been living too fast," complained the
Gazette. "Individuals, families, have been eagerly trying to outdo each
other in dress, furniture, style and luxury." The Chicago *Press and
Tribune* likewise blamed "ruinous extravagance" and "luxurious living"
for the economic troubles, and both papers urged a return to "republican simplicity," and the frugal, industrious ways of the Protestant
ethic.[33]

This kind of advice infused the Republican answer to the problems
of the poor in the difficult winters of the late 1850's. Republican papers
throughout the North urged the unemployed to tighten their belts and

31. New York *Tribune*, May 15, 1854. May 8, 1858; Basler, ed., *Lincoln Works*,
III, 479; Greeley, *Hints*, 326; Springfield *Republican*, October 20, 1858.
32. Cleveland *Leader*, June 16, 1858; Arthur C. Cole, *The Era of the Civil War*
(Springfield, 1919), 203; Floyd B. Streeter, *Political Parties in Michigan 1837–
1860* (Lansing, 1918), 260–61; Chicago *Press*, October 31, 1857.
33. Chicago *Tribune*, January 14, 1858; Cincinnati *Gazette*, September 30, 1857,
October 8, November 11, 1858; Chicago *Press and Tribune*, July 3, 1858. Cf. New
York *Times*, October 8, 1857; Springfield *Republican*, November 10, 1857.

retrench their expenditures. The Chicago *Press and Tribune* went so far as to say that drunkenness and laziness accounted for nine-tenths of the pauperism in the West, and that the only remedy was "a little wholesome hunger and a salutary fit of chattering by reason of excessive cold." [34] ~~Some Republicans did favor emergency public works to employ those unavoidably out of work, but they tended to oppose public charity, on the grounds that this led to dependence and rendered the recipients unwilling to work in the future.~~[35] And when the poor took to the streets demanding bread and work, Republicans reacted with shock and indignation. The *National Era*, one of the most radical Republican journals on the slavery question, declared that the noisiest demonstrators were those who were poor because of their own faults. "We do not believe," said the *Era*, "that the noisy meetings in our Eastern cities, pretending to be composed of working men, represent the real feelings of the working classes. . . . Their style of proceedings and spirit have a flavor of communism about them; they suggest a foreign origin." The reaction of Republicans to the poverty of the late 1850's revealed the basic deficiency of their middle-class free labor outlook. Even as they demanded equal opportunity for social advancement for all laborers, they also subscribed to an ideology which told them that an almost perfect opportunity for social mobility existed. They could therefore say with Senator Harlan of Iowa that their object was to place the laborer "on a platform of equality—let him labor in the same sphere, with the same chances for success and promotion— let the contest be exactly equal between him and others—and if, in the conflict of mind with mind, he should sink beneath the billow, let him perish." [36]

Of course, the ideology of mobility was never quite so simple that it condemned out of hand all who failed to achieve success. As Stephan Thernstrom has pointed out, many nineteenth-century Americans recognized that environmental and social factors could hinder a man's social advancement. Republicans like Lincoln and Greeley had a genuine compassion for the plight of the poor, and were sincerely

34. Chicago *Press and Tribune*, December 3, 1859. Cf. Chicago *Press*, December 4, 1857; Cleveland *Leader*, June 18, 1855; New York *Times*, December 26, 1854.
35. New York *Evening Post*, October 23, 27, 1857; New York *Times*, October 22, 1857; Springfield *Republican*, November 13, 14, 1857, January 13, 1858; Chicago *Tribune*, January 15, 1857.
36. *National Era*, November 12, 1857; *Congressional Globe*, 34 Congress, 1 Session, Appendix, 276. Cf. New York *Times*, November 10, 11, 23, 1857.

interested in their advancement. They recognized that not all the poverty in the nation's urban centers could be blamed on the character deficiencies of the poor. Thaddeus Stevens, for instance, insisted that it was wrong to blame the unemployed for their plight, for "almost all of them would rather work even at moderate wages, if they could find employment, than to go from house to house and beg." [37]

Yet even the most sympathetic Republicans clung to the free labor ideology, and their prescriptions for the ills of society reflected this. Greeley, for example, used the New York *Tribune* to expose the shocking working conditions in many New York City shops, and, unlike many other Republicans, supported a legislative limit on hours of labor. He even believed that the government had the responsibility to guarantee work for all who wanted it.[38] However, his belief in the harmony of interests made him unable to view laborers as a distinct class with its own interests—rather, they were merely nascent capitalists, whose aim was to acquire capital and achieve economic independence. He therefore strenuously opposed self-conscious working-class actions like strikes, though he agreed that laborers could join unions to peacefully petition for higher wages. But shutting down their employers' businesses, and preventing other laborers from working struck Greeley as intolerable. Strikes were a form of "industrial war," the antithesis of the labor-capital co-operation which Greeley desired. If a worker found his wages inadequate, Greeley wrote, he should not "stand idle" by striking, but should take another job or move to the West. And while Greeley recognized the social barriers to economic advancement in the cities, he also believed that it was primarily in the lowest class "that we encounter intemperance, licentiousness, gambling," and other vices.[39]

Other Republicans shared Greeley's outlook. Those Republicans, like Lincoln, who endorsed the right to strike, usually meant that laborers should be free to leave their jobs and take others, rather than

37. Stephan Thernstrom, *Poverty and Progress* (Cambridge, 1964), 73–75; *Congressional Globe*, 36 Congress, 1 Session, 1956. Cf. Basler, ed., *Lincoln Works*, VII, 466–67; Charles M. Segal, ed., *Conversations with Lincoln* (New York, 1961), 65–67.
38. Van Deusen, *Greeley*, 98; New York *Tribune*, September 21, 1853, May 18, 1854; Greeley, *Crystal Palace*, 31.
39. New York *Tribune*, April 20, 1854, November 3, 1853, March 3, 1854. Cf. Van Deusen, *Greeley*, 72–77; Isely, *Greeley*, 198–200.

that they should shut down the establishments of their employers. The Boston *Atlas and Daily Bee* declared strikes "fundamentally wrong," and the Cincinnati *Gazette*, in criticizing a western railroad strike, observed, "We are not speaking of *leaving* work—that all men have the right to do; but of combining to interrupt and arrest the machinery. The first is a plain, individual right. The last is a conspiracy against the interest, and even the safety of the public." And many Republicans opposed legal limits on working hours, on the grounds that, as Samuel Gridley Howe put it, "It emasculates people to be protected in this way. Let them be used to protecting themselves." [40]

The basic Republican answer to the problem of urban poverty was neither charity, public works, nor strikes, but westward migration of the poor, aided by a homestead act. The safety-valve conception of the public lands, popularized half a century later by Frederick Jackson Turner, was accepted as a reality by ante-bellum Republicans. Nascent labor organizations and workingmen's parties had made free land a political issue in the 1830's, by urging it as a panacea for the ills of eastern urban society. Their simple argument—that encouraging the westward movement of eastern workingmen would reduce labor competition in the East and thereby raise wages, provided one basis for the homestead arguments of the 1840's and 1850's. [41] This was the aspect of the plan which attracted Horace Greeley, who became the homestead's leading propagandist. "The public lands," he wrote, "are the great regulator of the relations of Labor and Capital, the safety valve of our industrial and social engine," and he never wavered in the advice he offered to New York's poor and unemployed: "go straight into the country—go at once!" Greeley also stressed the economic benefits which would accrue to the entire country from the rapid settlement of the West, but the primary aim of his homestead policy was to reduce the excess laboring population of the East. Under his editorship, the New York *Tribune* carried the word of the great opportunities

40. Basler, ed., *Lincoln Works*, IV, 24; Mandel, *Labor: Free and Slave*, 159; Boston *Atlas and Daily Bee*, February 20 1860; Cincinnati *Gazette*, January 7, 1858; Laura E. Richards, ed., *Letters and Journals of Samuel Gridley Howe* (2 vols.: Boston, 1909), II, 385.

41. Joseph G. Rayback, "Land for the Landless, The Contemporary View" (unpublished master's thesis, Western Reserve University, 1936), 14–16; George M. Stephenson, *The Political History of the Public Lands from 1840 to 1862* (Boston, 1917), 103–4; Roy M. Robbins, *Our Landed Heritage, The Public Domain, 1776–1936* (Princeton, 1942), 98–99.

for labor in the West far and wide, and the demand there, not only for farmers, but for skilled craftsmen, artisans, and laborers of all kinds.[42]

It is well known how the homestead issue became increasingly sectional in the 1850's. Republicans believed that the settlement of the western territories by free farmers would prove an effective barrier against the extension of slavery, and this made some eastern anti-slavery men, who feared that free land might set off a migration which would depopulate their states, willing to accept the homestead idea. For the same reason, southerners increasingly opposed any plan for giving free land to settlers.[43] The Republican platform of 1860 gave the homestead plan a ringing endorsement, in a plank which Greeley said he "fixed exactly to my own liking" on the platform committee. The homestead plan played a key role in the Republicans' free labor outlook, for in their view, the measure was essential to keeping open the geographical and social mobility which was the hallmark of northern society. Free land, said Richard Yates, would aid "the poor but industrious laborer," in his search for economic advancement, and the *National Era* agreed that the policy would offer "an equal chance to the poor of all states. . . ."[44] The Panic of 1857 gave a great impetus to the Republicans' support for the homestead idea. They blamed the large-scale urban unemployment on the difficulty workers had in securing land. Too many men, said the Cincinnati *Gazette,* had "crowded into the cities," while there was an "abundance of land to be possessed" further West. Some Republicans saw for the first time the specter of a permanent population of urban poor. "In many of the free states," said Illinois' Orville H. Browning, "population is already pressing hard upon production and subsistence, and new homes must be provided,

---

42. Robbins, *Landed Heritage,* 94; New York *Tribune,* July 1, 1854, April 18, 1856, February 14, July 4, November 7, 1857. Cf. Roy M. Robbins, "Horace Greeley: Land Reform and Unemployment, 1837–1862," *AgH,* VII (January 1933), 18–41.

43. Fred A. Shannon, "The Homestead Act and the Labor Surplus," *AHR,* XLI (July 1936), 642–43; Stephenson, *Public Lands,* 145, 162, 173, 193–96; Rayback, "Land for the Landless," 31–34, 44–45, 62–65; Cincinnati *Gazette,* January 12, 1859; George W. Julian, *Speeches on Political Questions* (New York, 1872), 57; Chicago *Democrat,* August 19, 1854.

44. Kirk H. Porter and Donald B. Johnson, comps., *National Party Platforms 1840–1856* (Urbana, 1956), 33; Horace Greeley to Schuyler Colfax, June 20, 1860, Greeley-Colfax Papers, NYPL; *Congressional Globe,* 33 Congress, 1 Session, 506; *National Era,* November 12, 1857.

or the evils of an overcrowded country encountered." [45] Such over-
crowding would effectively bar eastern workers from sharing in the
economic mobility which was the heritage of free laborers.

As an expression of the free labor mentality, the homestead idea
was defended in middle-class, capitalistic terms. "The friends of land
reform," George Julian assured Congress, "claim no right to interfere
with the laws of property of the several States, or the vested interests
of their citizens. They advocate no *leveling* policy, designed to strip
the rich of their possessions." Richard Yates agreed that "the measure
is not agrarian [that is, socialistic]. It does not take your property and
give it to me. . . . It does not bring down the high, but it raises the
low." [46] What the homestead policy did propose to do was to aid the
poor in achieving economic independence, to raise them into the
middle class. If the policy of free land were adopted, said Greeley's
Tribune, every citizen would have the essential economic alternative
"of working for others or for himself." The homestead policy would
transform the dependent poor of the cities into prosperous yeomen. "It
would," said Schuyler Colfax, "by giving them independent freeholds,
incite them . . . to rear families in habits of industry and frugality,
which form the real elements of national greatness and power." And
Congressman Owen Lovejoy summed up all these arguments with
another whose spirit must have been congenial to all Republicans. The
homestead measure, he declared, "will greatly increase the number
of those who belong to what is called the middle class." [47]

IV

In the eyes of the Republicans, northern society exemplified the best
aspects of the free labor ideology. The ideal of equal opportunity for
social mobility and economic independence seemed to them to be not
dreams but living realities. Lincoln declared that the majority of

45. Cincinnati *Gazette,* October 26, 1857; *Speech of Hon. O. H. Browning, Delivered at the Republican Mass Meeting, Springfield, Ill., August 8th, 1860*
(Quincy, 1860), 10. Cf. Julian, *Speeches,* 60; Cleveland *Leader,* October 24,
1857.
46. Julian, *Speeches,* 51; *Congressional Globe,* 33 Congress, 1 Session, 502. For
the contemporary usage of "agrarian," see "Agrarianism," *Atlantic Monthly,* III
(April 1859), 393–94.
47. New York *Tribune,* February 18, 1854; Hollister, *Colfax,* 161; *Congressional
Globe,* 36 Congress, 1 Session, Appendix, 175.

northerners were neither capitalists nor employees—rather, they worked
for themselves in shops and farms, "taking the whole product to themselves, and asking no favors of capital on the one hand, nor of hirelings
and slaves on the other." To southerners who compared northern
laborers with their own slaves, Lincoln insisted that the North had
no class who "are always to remain laborers." "The man who labored
for another last year," he insisted, "this year labors for himself, and
next year he will hire others to labor for him." To Republicans, northern society was the model of what Henry Wilson called "a progressive,
permanent, Christian civilization," and Republican speeches contained
abundant praise of their social order. Republicans admitted that in
the cities—which were carried by the Democrats anyway—there was
poverty, intemperance, and ignorance, but the Republican areas of the
North represented the best of middle-class America. "Sir," said a
Connecticut Congressman, "a majority of the citizens of my State
occupy that happy social position which is a medium between a
wealthy aristocracy on the one hand, and a poverty, which is generally
wedded to ignorance, on the other." And Henry Wilson extolled the
social order of Massachusetts, where laborers were "more elevated
than can be found in any other portion of the globe," and where "our
soil is divided into small estates," not large plantations.[48]

The same ideal social order characterized the free states of the
West, according to Republican leaders of that section. In rural Ohio,
said Congressman Philemon Bliss, "the farmer works his own farm;
the mechanic labors in his own shop, and the merchant sells his own
goods. True, labor is there sold, but mainly as a temporary expedient
to enable the laborer to acquire a small capital. . . ." According to
Senator James Doolittle, four-fifths of the population of Wisconsin
were economically independent. The superiority, indeed, the all but
perfect character of northern society, was graphically depicted by
Carl Schurz: [49]

> Cast your eyes over that great beehive called the free States. See
> by the railroad and telegraph wire every village, almost every back-

48. Basler, ed., *Lincoln Works*, III, 478, II, 364; New York *Tribune*, October 6,
1856; *Congressional Globe*, 35 Congress, 1 Session, 1356; *How Ought Workingmen to Vote in the Coming Election? Speech of Hon. Henry Wilson, at East
Boston, Oct. 15, 1860* (Boston, 1860), 2; Russell and Nason, *Wilson*, 71.
49. *Congressional Globe*, 35 Congress, 2 Session, Appendix, 241; 1 Session, 982;
Frederic Bancroft, ed., *Speeches, Correspondence, and Political Papers of Carl
Schurz* (4 vols.: New York, 1913), I, 131.

woods cottage, drawn within the immediate reach of progressive civilization . . . look upon our society, where by popular education and continual change of condition the dividing lines between the ranks and classes are almost obliterated; look upon our system of public instruction, which places even the lowliest child of the people upon the high road of progressive civilization.

How accurate was the Republican picture of northern society? On visiting the United States in the 1820's, the German economist Friedrich List was impressed by the fact that "the best work on Political Economy which one can read in that modern land is actual life." The Republicans' concept of free labor was obviously a reflection of their experiences in the economic and social life of the North, particularly the Republican North, whose heartland had a predominantly agricultural population, with small towns and independent farmers. The idea that labor created all value, and that all men could aspire to economic independence, were products of the age of independent craftsmen and yeomen, and up to the Civil War, the northern economy could still be described in these terms.[50] It is true that the industrial sector of the economy was expanding rapidly, especially in the 1850's, and that by 1860, the United States had achieved an industrial status second only to Great Britain's. In New England and some of the middle states the rise of the factory system and large-scale production gave a glimpse of the industrial nation which was to emerge later in the century. But on the eve of the war, large factories and great corporations were the exception, not the rule, even in New England. In the West, manufacturing establishments were widely dispersed, located near raw materials such as flour and lumber, and servicing local markets. The typical enterprise employed only a few workmen and only a small amount of capital, and was owned by an individual or partnership. Throughout the North, manufacturing firms had an average of only ten workmen each, and, as Bernard Mandel points out, even in New England the expansion of so important an industry as boot and shoe production in the 1850's and 1860's was due largely to the establishment of many new small plants, not the expansion of old ones.[51]

50. Kaplan, Carey, 29; Chester McA. Destler, American Radicalism 1865–1901 (New London, 1946), 25–26.
51. Douglass C. North, The Economic Growth of the United States 1790–1860 (New York, 1961), v–vi, 159–63, 204; Oscar and Mary T. Handlin, Commonwealth. A Study of the Role of Government in the American Economy: Massachusetts, 1774–1861 (New York, 1947), 201; Victor S. Clark, History of Manufactures in the United States (3 vols.: New York, 1929), I, 455–56; Harry L.

On the other hand, the Republican image of northern society was already outdated in some respects. The decade of the 1850's, according to George R. Taylor, witnessed "the emergence of the wage earner" —a permanent working class, yet in 1859, Lincoln could state that the wage system "does not embrace more than one-eighth of the labor system of the country." Census statistics for the pre-war period are notoriously inaccurate, but Lincoln's statement was surely in error. David Montgomery estimates that almost 60 per cent of the American labor force was employed in some way, not economically independent, in 1860. And, particularly in the large eastern cities, where large-scale immigration was increasing class stratification and holding down the real wages of all workers, the prospect for rising to self-employment was already receding.[52] Nor did the homestead act provide the safety-valve which Republicans claimed. Many studies have shown that it was eastern farmers, not wage earners from the crowded cities, who were able to take advantage of the offer of free land. Moreover, the 1850's saw the widespread introduction of agricultural machinery in the West, resulting in increased production, but raising the costs of farming and making it more difficult for farm laborers to enter the ranks of independent yeomen. Western farmers were already faced with a loss of their economic independence, as they came to rely on banks for credit. Lincoln could say, "I scarcely ever knew a mammoth farm to sustain itself," but the age of large-scale mechanized farming was fast approaching.[53]

We know today, of course, that in spite of the wide acceptance of

Wilkey, "Infant Industries in Illinois as Illustrated in Quincy, 1836–1856," *Journal of the IllSHS*, XXXII (December 1939), 474–97: Isaac L. pp ncott. *A History of Manufactures in the Ohio Valley to the Year 1860* (New York, 1914), 130–31, 152–59; George R. Taylor, *The Transportation Revolution 1815–1860* (New York, 1951), 247; Mandel, *Labor: Free and Slave*, 16–17.

52. Taylor, *Transportat on Revolution*, 270–300; Basler. ed., *Lincoln Works*, III, 459; Montgomery, *Beyond Equality*, 26–27; George R. Taylor, "The National Economy Before and After the Civil War," in David T. Gilchrist and W. David Lewis, eds., *Economic Change in the Civil War Era* (Greenville, Del., 1965), 15; Miller, *Jacksonian Aristocracy*, 31–33, 81–127, 182. Cf. Bruchey, *Roots of American Economic Growth*, 206.

53. Allan Nevins, *Ordeal of the Union* (2 vols.: New York, 1947), II, 295–96; Henry Nash Smith, *Virgin Land* (Cambridge, 1950), 239–40; Clarence Danhof, "Farm-Making Costs and the Safety-Valve, 1850–1860," *JPEc*, LXIX (June 1941), 317–59; Cole, *Era of the Civil War*, 364; Fred Gerhard, *Illinois As It Is* (Chicago, 1857), 317; Paul W. Gates, *The Farmer's Age: Agriculture 1815–1860* (New York, 1960), 96–97; Basler, ed., *Lincoln Works*, III, 475.

the ideology of social mobility, the years after 1860 saw a steady diminution of the prospects for a worker or farm laborer to achieve economic independence. This does not mean that industrialization and mechanized agriculture ended social mobility—on the contrary, the evidence is that they expanded it. But the mobility of the age of the independent producer, whose aspiration was economic self-sufficiency, was superseded by the mobility of industrial society, in which workers could look forward to a rising standard of living, but not self-employment. On the eve of the Civil War, however, these developments still lay largely in the future. If economic mobility was contracting in northern cities, the old social opportunity was at least close enough in time to lend plausibility to the free labor ideology. And in the rural and small-town North, the Republican picture of northern society corresponded to a large degree with reality. The two decades before the Civil War witnessed a substantial improvement in the level of living of western farmers, the result of the transportation revolution and the rise of eastern markets for their products. Farm tenancy was increasing, but the number of northern farmers was still double that of farm laborers and tenants. The factory system was expanding, undermining the economic independence of the small craftsman and artisan, but western industry was still concentrated in small towns and in small-scale enterprises. And according to Douglass North, the small towns and villages of the Republican heartland "showed every sign of vigorous expansion." [54]

In what Stuart Bruchey has termed "an essentially fluid society," with "broadly egalitarian economic opportunity," the free labor outlook had a strong cultural authenticity.[55] A well-organized, persistent person could expect to achieve economic success, and a skilled wage earner could reasonably look forward to the day he acquired enough capital to start a small business of his own. The free labor ideology became inadequate, of course, when applied to the permanent wage earners and unemployed of ante-bellum northern society, but increasing numbers of these were Irish immigrants who, Republicans believed, lacked the qualities of discipline and sobriety essential for social ad-

54. North, *Economic Growth*, 153–54; Barrington Moore, Jr., *Social Origins of Dictatorship and Democracy* (Boston, 1966), 128–29; Gates, *Farmer's Age*, 272–73; Taylor, "National Economy," 7–8; Bruchey, *Roots of American Economic Growth*, 60.

55. Bruchey, *Roots of American Economic Growth*, 206–07.

vancement. When Republicans extolled the virtues of free labor, they were merely reflecting the experiences of millions of men who had "made it" and millions of others who had a realistic hope of doing so.

When Republicans spoke of their party's basic constituency, it was these successful middle-class northerners they had in mind. Charles Francis Adams declared that the party was composed of "the industrious farmers and mechanics, the independent men in comfortable circumstances in all the various walks of life," while the Democrats drew their support from the very rich and "the most degraded or the least intelligent of the population of the cities." Similarly, Seward, when visiting Great Britain, was struck by the parallel between British and American voting patterns. "All artisans and manufacturers are republicans—all their employees (speaking in general terms) are conservative. How like the United States." (Seward's statement again reminds us that when Republicans referred to themselves as a party of "free labor," they meant that their supporters were primarily middle class, not "employees.") Republicans also insisted that there was a high correlation between education, religion, and hard work—the values of the Protestant ethic—and Republican votes. "Where free schools are regarded as a nuisance," declared the Chicago *Democratic Press* after Buchanan's defeat of Frémont, "where religion is least honored, and lazy unthrift is the rule, there Buchanan has received his strongest support." [56] And an Iowa Republican, comparing the election returns with census data on education, concluded that wherever free schools were most common, the Democrats were in the minority. The image which Republicans had of their party was vividly summarized by the Springfield *Republican:* [57]

> Who form the strength of this party? Precisely those who would most likely be expected to,—the great middling-interest class. The highest class, aristocratically associated and affiliated, timid, afraid of change, . . . and the lowest class . . . those are the forces arrayed against Republicanism as a whole. . . . Those who work with their hands, who live and act independently, who hold the stakes of home and family, of farm and workshop, of education and freedom—these as a mass are enrolled in the Republican ranks.

56. Boston *Advertiser,* clipping, Charles Francis Adams Diary, November 2, 1860, Adams Papers; Frederick W. Seward, ed., *Seward at Washington* (2 vols.: 1891), I, 384; Chicago *Democratic Press,* November 19, 1856. Cf. Springfield *Republican,* November 8, 1856.
57. *Debates of Iowa Constitutional Convention,* II, 702; Springfield *Republican,* November 1, 1856.

> They form the very heart of the nation, as opposed to the two
> extremes of aristocracy and ignorance. . . .

Although a great deal of work needs to be done before the social basis
of the ante-bellum political parties can be established with precision,
it is safe to say that the Republicans were weakest in the large cities
and strong in the North's rural areas and small towns. A Pennsylvania
Congressman described his district—"the most intensely Republican
one of the State"—as follows: [58]

> We find it densely populated, mainly with a rural people. Thickly
> planted, each on its own few acres we behold the unpretentious,
> but neat and comfortable dwellings of free laboring farmers, with
> as many tradesmen, manufacturers, and mechanics, mostly located
> in the villages, as the wants of the region require.

But although Republicans celebrated the rural virtues, they left more
than a little room for those "tradesmen, manufacturers, and mechanics . . . located in the villages." [59] They recognized that economic
development was bound to result in an increase in the urban population, and that a growing nation needed artisans, craftsmen, and
capitalists as much as farmers. John Bigelow of the New York *Evening
Post* pointed out at the height of the Panic of 1857 that it was pre-
posterous to urge the poor to go from urban centers to the country,
because there were as many opportunities for social advancement in
industry and commercial towns as on the farm. Indeed, Bigelow
predicted that the independent yeoman would rapidly lose ground to
the large-scale capitalist farmer, and he urged the urban poor to stick
to "mechanic arts," rather than going into agriculture.[60]

58. *Congressional Globe,* 36 Congress, 2 Session, Appendix, 288–89. W. R. Brock
states that the typical Republican constituency was a rural area with small towns,
where most of the population was middle-class and the capitalist ethic pervaded
the culture. Brock, *American Crisis,* 8–9, 244–45. Cf. Carl N. Degler, "Labor in
the Economy and Politics of New York City, 1850–1860" (unpublished doctoral
dissertation, Columbia University, 1952), 295–96, 329–30; Wilfred E. Binkley,
American Political Parties (New York, 1947 ed.), 214, 221.
59. For Republican glorification of rural virtues, see *Congressional Globe,* 31
Congress, 2 Session, Appendix, 136–37, 36 Congress, 1 Session, 1510, 2 Session,
1018. To a large extent, of course, this kind of talk was political rhetoric, reflecting
the political fact of life summarized in the title of one newspaper's election post-
mortem in 1856: "The Country for Freedom—the Cities for Slavery." *Ohio State
Journal,* November 7, 1856. Cf. Ollinger Crenshaw, "Urban and Rural Voting in
the Election of 1860," in *Historiography and Urbanization,* ed., Eric Goldman
(Baltimore, 1941), 43–66.
60. New York *Evening Post,* December 31, 1857; Margaret Clapp, *Forgotten First
Citizen: John Bigelow* (Boston, 1947), 117–18.

Few Republicans were as pessimistic as Bigelow about the prospects for the family farm, but most were firm advocates of economic development. As Leo Marx points out, Americans eagerly embraced the new technology of their expanding capitalist economy, and the western states cried out for railroads and industry. "Industry," said the Indianapolis *Journal*, "is as essential to the development of a virtuous community as education," and the Chicago *Press and Tribune* declared that the western economy was too dependent on agriculture, and needed manufactures for a balanced economic order. Many western Republicans who supported a protective tariff in the late 1850's had just this view in mind. One Iowa Congressman said he favored protection because he wanted to see the abundant water power of his state "applied to mechanical use. I want to see manufactures spring up there . . . [and] machinery be put up and set in motion throughout every beautiful valley of the State." [61]

Republicans therefore accepted the growth of industry as one part of the nation's economic development, and in the 1850's they took a broad view of the power of the federal government to aid in economic growth, supporting such measures as the tariff, homesteads, and internal improvements. But they also believed that industrial development should take place within the context of the society with which they were familiar, and they emphatically rejected the idea that industrialization and the rise of great cities and large factories necessarily went hand in hand. The idea that the North could remain a society of family farms and small towns, while still experiencing the benefits of industrialization, was put forward most clearly by Henry C. Carey, the Pennsylvania economist. Carey insisted that industrialization would lead to an increase, not a decline, in economic opportunity for the laborer, for it would create a balanced, diversified economy in which many different enterprises competed for the services of labor and thus drove wages upward. Carey's advocacy of the protective tariff was based on precisely this premise—that the growth of industry was essential to the betterment of the worker, for "where all are farmers, there can be no competition for the purchase of labor." [62] His ideal

---

61. Leo Marx, *The Machine in the Garden* (New York, 1964), 207–8; Kenneth Stampp, *Indiana Politics During the Civil War* (Indianapolis, 1949), 11; Chicago *Press and Tribune*, July 29, 1859; *Congressional Globe*, 36 Congress, 1 Session, 2021. Cf. 36 Congress, 1 Session, 2024; *Debates of Iowa Convention*, I, 108.
62. H. C. Carey, *The Slave Trade, Domestic and Foreign* (Philadelphia, 1856), 57. Cf. [Henry C. Carey], *How to Increase Competition for the Purchase of Labor* (np, nd), 4.

was a decentralized economy, centered on the small town, in which artisans, farmers, and small factories all served the needs of a small regional economy. One of his associates, a Pennsylvania Congressman, explained that the aim of protection was not to build up large-scale industries, but to "locate communities around an industrial point." Carey believed that the producer and the consumer should exist side by side, and that long-range transportation—either of western food to the East, or of manufactured goods from Europe or from the East westward—was in large degree a waste of labor and money. "*The nearer* the grist-mill is to the farm," he wrote, "the less will be the labor required for converting wheat into flour, . . . the *nearer* [the farmer] can bring the hatter, the shoemaker, and the tailor, the maker of ploughs and harrows, the less will be the loss in labor in exchanging his wheat for their commodities." [63]

Carey shared the farmer's suspicion of the nation's great commercial centers, which, he wrote, profited from the labor of others, "while producing nothing themselves." He envisioned a society of "little towns and cities," each a local center of manufacturing, serving the surrounding countryside, and providing a market for its industrial produce. The economy of New England approximated his idea most closely, although he and other Republicans were disturbed by the increasing concentration of industry there. One of his economic disciples wrote that he would like to see the large amount of machinery concentrated in the city of Lowell "divided among twenty or thirty little towns." [64]

Of course, Carey's ideas were in a sense romantic, for at the same time that he extolled the virtues of the "little towns and cities" of the North and urged a regional, locally oriented economy, the nation was moving toward an increasingly centralized industrialism and a national market. Yet in Carey's writings we can see the optimism and self-confidence of northern society. For his image for the nation's future involved no fundamental social reorganization--it was basically an extension of the northern present as he saw it.[65] Tocqueville had

63. *Congressional Globe*, 36 Congress, 1 Session. 1848; Carey. *Slave Trade*, 59, 294. Cf. Henry C. Carey, *Financial Crises: Their Causes and Effects* (Philadelphia, 1863).
64. Henry C. Carey, *The Harmony of Interests, Agricultural, Manufacturing, and Commercial* (New York, 1856), 145; Carey, *Past, Present, Future*, 320; E. Pershine Smith to Henry C. Carey, October 3, 1855, Henry C. Carey Papers, HSPa; Cf. Henry C. Carey, *Principles of Social Science* (3 vols.: Philadelphia, 1858–59), I, 44–45, II, 236–37.
65. On this aspect of the idea of progress, see also Rush Welter, "The Idea of Progress in America," *Journal of the History of Ideas*, XVI (June 1955), 404–5.

observed that Americans had a "lively faith in human perfectibility," and that they thought of society as "a body progressing," rather than as a static structure. But in the Republican conception of progress, the North would retain the social order of the 1850's, while making the distribution of income even more equitable, and social mobility even more accessible, through continuing economic development.[66]

V

The contradictions and ambiguities of the free labor ideology, the tension between its conservative aspects and its stress on equality of opportunity and an open society, reflected the world view of the northern middle class. If the social outlook of the Republican party was in many ways conservative, it was not because it defended privilege but because Republicans were satisfied with the economic and social order they perceived in the North. In post-war years, the same cult of the self-made man and of economic success would come to be a justification of every action and privilege of the business class, but in the antebellum world of the Republicans, the promise of economic advancement implied not the rise of big business but the guarantee of mobility to the laborer. Many Republicans insisted that equality of rights and opportunities was a cardinal principle of their party; Seward, for example, stressed that the Republicans stood for "one idea . . . the idea of equality—the equality of all men before human tribunals and human laws." And Lincoln summarized the egalitarian aspects of the free labor outlook when he declared, "In due time the weights should be lifted from the shoulders of all men . . . all should have an equal chance." [67]

To the self-confident society of the North, economic development, increasing social mobility, and the spread of democratic institutions were all interrelated parts of nineteenth century "progress." Each step in the progress of civilization, said Henry Carey, voicing his character-

66. Tocqueville, *Democracy in America*, 343. Cf. *Congressional Globe*, 36 Congress, 1 Session, Appendix, 435; Merle Curti, *The Making of an American Community* (Stanford, 1959), 116.

67. Irwin G. Wylie, *The Self-Made Man in America* (New Brunswick, 1954), 152–59; Baker, ed., *Seward Works*, IV, 302; Basler, ed., *Lincoln Works*, IV, 240. Lincoln used precisely these terms in defining the Union cause in his address to the joint session of Congress in July, 1861: "On the side of the Union, [the Civil War] is a struggle for maintaining in the world, that form and substance of government, whose leading object is, to elevate the condition of men—to lift artificial weights from all shoulders . . . to afford all, an unfettered start, and a fair chance, in the race of life." Basler, ed., *Lincoln Works*, IV, 438.

istic optimism, "is marked by a tendency to equality of physical and intellectual condition, and to the general ownership of wealth." Horace Greeley predicted that the age which had witnessed the invention of railroads, telegraphs, and other marvels could not depart "without having effected or witnessed a vast change for the better, alike in the moral and the physical condition of mankind." The important point was that material and moral developments were but two sides of the same coin. "Good roads and bridges," wrote the New York *Tribune*, "are as necessary an ingredient to the spread of intelligence, social intercourse, and improvement in population, as schools and churches." An Indiana Republican Congressman declared on the eve of the Civil War that throughout the world, manufactures and commerce were "the missionaries of freedom," and William Henry Seward agreed that "popular government follows in the track of the steam-engine and the telegraph." [68] It was but a short step, and one which Republicans took almost unanimously, to the view that for a society as for individuals, economic progress was a measure of moral worth. As Henry Adams later recalled, he was taught in his youth that "bad roads meant bad morals." On this basis, northern society was eminently successful. But when Republicans turned their gaze southward, they encountered a society that seemed to violate all the cherished values of the free labor ideology, and seemed to pose a threat to the very survival of what Republicans called their "free-labor civilization." [69]

68. Carey, *Past, Present, Future*, 415; Greeley, *Hints*, 49; New York *Tribune*, August 22, 1856; *Congressional Globe*, 36 Congress, 2 Session, 1042; Seward, *Seward*, II, 359.
69. [Henry Adams], *The Education of Henry Adams* (Boston, 1918), 47; *Congressional Globe*, 36 Congress, 1 Session, 1914.

2

The Republican Critique of the South

In 1856, William H. Seward told the Senate that he regarded slavery as "morally unjust, politically unwise, and socially pernicious, in some degree, in every community where it exists." For many Republicans, including Seward, who was considered by many "the intellectual leader of the political anti-slavery movement," [1] the third of these reasons was the major basis of their opposition to the spread of slavery. If the free labor outlook gave Republicans a model of the good society, it also provided them with a yardstick for judging other social systems, and by this standard, slave society was found woefully wanting. The most cherished values of the free labor outlook—economic development, social mobility, and political democracy—all appeared to be violated in the South. Instead, the southern economy seemed stagnant to Republicans, the southern class structure an irrevocably fixed hierarchy, and southern society dominated by an aristocracy of slaveholders. To Republicans, the South appeared as an alien and threatening society, whose values and interests were in fundamental conflict with those of the North.

The northern image of the South was not, as some historians appear to believe, based merely on the imagination of abolitionists. Many Republican leaders had first-hand knowledge of economic and social conditions in slave society, and Republican newspapers carried countless reports from travelers to the slave states and the testimony of southern spokesmen themselves. The burden of this evidence was

1. George E. Baker, ed., *The Works of William H. Seward* (5 vols.: Boston, 1853–84), IV, 517; Carl Schurz, *Speeches of Carl Schurz* (Philadelphia, 1865), 108–9. Cf. New York *Times,* February 7, 1855.

always the same—the southern economy was backward and stagnant, and slavery was to blame. William H. Seward, for example, was convinced by his visits to the South in 1835, 1846, and 1857 that aside from all moral considerations, slavery would have to be abolished as an intolerable obstacle to regional and national development. His reaction to his first trip to Virginia was vividly recorded in his journal:

> It was necessary that I should travel in Virginia to have any idea of a slave State. . . . An exhausted soil, old and decaying towns, wretchedly-neglected roads, and, in every respect, an absence of enterprise and improvement, distinguish the region through which we have come, in contrast to that in which we live. Such has been the effect of slavery.

Seward's impressions were reinforced on his subsequent journeys to the South. In 1846 he found that in the Old Dominion "the land was sterile, the fences mean, and a universal impress of poverty [was] stamped on all around me." To his political alter ego Thurlow Weed, Seward described slavery as a serpent, gorging itself on the life-blood of Virginia. Later that year, Seward visited New Orleans, and again he observed how slavery impaired economic development. The geographical situation of the city, he wrote his wife, would seem to ensure its commercial supremacy. "Yet the city is secondary, and the state unimportant. . . . Commerce and political power, as well as military strength, can never permanently reside, on this continent, in a community where slavery exists." [2]

Seward's impressions of the South were so vivid that he wrote the New York abolitionist Gerrit Smith that he had never visited slave society "without wishing that at least one northern man from every town could be with me to see the practical workings of slavery." Other Republicans who visited the South were similarly impressed. "As you travel along, you will see the works of slavery," one of them told the Buffalo Free Soil Convention in 1848. "A worn out soil, dilapidated fences and tenements, and an air of general desolation." Congressman Henry L. Dawes wrote his wife in 1858 that after viewing the Virginia countryside near Washington he was convinced that "if the region were not cursed with slavery it would be the most delightful country

2. Frederick W. Seward, ed., *William H. Seward: An Autobiography* (New York, 1891), 268, 776, 806; William H. Seward to Thurlow Weed, April 22, 26, 1846, Thurlow Weed Papers, Rush Rhees Library, University of Rochester.

in the world." [3] Republicans whose families had once lived in the South told the same story. "It was slavery that drove me from my native state," declared an Iowa Republican. ". . . Slavery withers and blights all it touches . . . slavery is a foul political curse upon the institutions of our country; it is a curse upon the soil of the country, and worse than that, it is a curse upon the poor, free, laboring white man." [4] The indictment of slavery by southern anti-slavery men like Cassius Clay and Hinton Helper was phrased in precisely these terms. Clay had visited New England in his youth, and was struck by the prosperity of the region, despite its poor soil and climate, while his native state of Kentucky, with greater natural resources, languished. "I cannot as a statesman, shut my eyes to the industry, ingenuity, numbers and wealth which are displaying themselves in adjoining states," he told the Kentucky legislature, and during the 1840's and 1850's he addressed countless thousands of northerners on the superiority of free to slave society. [5] Hinton Helper's condemnation of slavery and its effect on the non-slaveholders of the South was also circulated widely in the free states. Helper's points had all been made before, but as Horace Greeley wrote, "Mr. Helper, as an undoubted son of the South, speaking from personal observation and experience, speaks with an authority and a weight which no outsider can have." [6]

During the 1850's, leading northern newspapers sent correspondents into the slave states to give their readers first-hand descriptions of southern life and of the debilitating effects of slavery on the southern economy. Frederick Law Olmsted's series of letters which were published in the New York *Times* and later expanded and reprinted in

3. Seward to Gerrit Smith, March 25, 1847, Gerrit Smith Papers, Syracuse University; *Oliver Dyer's Phonographic Report of the Proceedings of the National Free Soil Convention at Buffalo, N.Y., August 9th and 10th, 1848* (Buffalo, 1848), 11; Henry L. Dawes to Mrs. Ella Dawes, May 21, 1858, Henry L. Dawes Papers, LC. Cf. Harold Schwartz, *Samuel Gridley Howe Social Reformer 1801–1876* (Cambridge, 1956), 154.
4. *The Debates of the Constitutional Convention of the State of Iowa* (2 vols.: Davenport, 1857), II, 681–82.
5. David L. Smiley, *Lion of Whitehall, the Life of Cassius M. Clay* (Madison, 1962), 22–23, 158–59; Horace Greeley, ed., *The Writings of Cassius Marcellus Clay* (New York, 1848), 46, 202–6. Cf. Clay to Chase, March, 1842, Salmon P. Chase Papers, HSPa.
6. Horace Greeley to Edwin S. Morgan, May 3, 1859, Edwin S. Morgan Papers, New York State Library; Hinton R. Helper to Gerrit Smith, October 4, 1856, Smith Papers; *Congressional Globe*, 36 Congress, 1 Session, 16. Cf. 30 Congress, 1 Session, Appendix, 836; Richmond *Republican*, cited in *National Era*, November 25, 1847.

three books, were the most widely read of these reports. Henry J. Raymond called Olmsted's letters the "best report that has ever been made of the industrial condition and prospects" of the South, and endorsed Olmsted's conclusion that without slavery, the wealth of the South would be vastly increased.[7] Olmsted's findings were echoed by the New York *Tribune's* correspondent in a series entitled "The Southerners at Home," published in 1857, and by the Cincinnati *Gazette's* "Letters from the South," which appeared a year later. The *Gazette's* reporter insisted that the natural resources of Kentucky and North Carolina were woefully underdeveloped, and that the substitution of free for slave labor would increase the wealth of these states by millions of dollars and "cause this whole region to become an exceedingly productive one."[8]

The economic superiority of free to slave labor became a major argument of the Republicans in their attempt to win northern votes. The conservative Bostonian, Robert Winthrop, remarked in 1856 that the typical free-soil speech consisted of one-third Missouri Compromise repeal, one-third Kansas outrages, "and one-third disjointed facts, and misapplied figures, and great swelling words of vanity, to prove that the South is, upon the whole, the very poorest, meanest, least productive, and most miserable part of creation. . . ." Elaborate statistical comparisons between northern and southern states were commonplace in Republican speeches and editorials. In one such exercise, the New York *Times* compared the population growth, property values, manufacturing, agriculture, railroads, canals, and commerce of pairs of free and slave states—New York versus Virginia, Ohio versus Kentucky, Michigan versus Arkansas, etc. In every department, the free state was far in the lead.[9] Such comparisons, according to Republican spokesmen, proved that "socially, economically, politically, the slave labor-agricultural system is a failure." And many Republicans believed that such

7. Francis Brown, *Raymond of the "Times"* (New York, 1951), 124; Frederick Law Olmsted, *A Journey in the Seaboard Slave States* (New York, 1856), 138–40, 185; Frederick Law Olmsted, *A Journey in the Back Country* (New York, 1863), 295–96; Frederick Law Olmsted, *A Journey Through Texas* (New York, 1861), xiii.
8. New York *Tribune*, June 10, 1857; Cincinnati *Gazette*, October 5, 1858. Cf. August 19, 27, 1858.
9. Robert C. Winthrop, Jr., *A Memoir of Robert C. Winthrop* (Boston, 1897), 188; New York *Times*, September 5, 1856. Cf. *Congressional Globe*, 33 Congress, 2 Session, Appendix, 321–27, 36 Congress, 1 Session, 1887; New York *Tribune*, February 15, 20, 1854, September 12, 18, December 20, 1856; Cincinnati *Gazette*, August 22, 1855, April 2, 1858, July 28, 1860.

arguments were far more effective politically than mere moralizing about slavery. Seward, for example, as astute a politician as the Republicans had, stressed the economic effects of slavery in speech after speech in the 1850's. The very words and images he used to describe slavery reflected this emphasis. Slavery, Seward declared, wished to lay its "paralyzing hand" on the new territories; it "polluted" the soil; it was a "blight," a "pestilence," and an "element of national debility and decline." [10] The institution had brought upon the South "the calamity of premature and consumptive decline, in the midst of free, vigorous and expanding states." In speeches in 1855 and 1856 he asked New Yorkers to compare the development of New York with that of Virginia, once the Empire State's equal. "Go ask Virginia—go ask even noble Maryland, expending as she is a giant's strength in the serpent's coils, to show you her people, canals, railroads, universities, schools, charities, commerce, cities, and cultivated areas." And on his western campaign tour in 1860, Seward extolled the development of that region, attributing it to the exclusion of slavery. At Lansing, Michigan, he declared that the states which were burdened with slavery had suffered "exhausted soils, sickly states, and fretful and discontented people," and in Kansas he observed that the value of land in a free state averaged three times greater than its value in a slave state. [11]

Despite their persistent use of anti-slavery arguments based on political economy, Republicans did not always make clear what it was in slavery that caused the impoverishment of the South. [12] Often they

10. Cincinnati *Gazette*, November 22, 1858; Baker, ed., *Seward Works*, I, 61; III, 272; IV, 88, 336, 349–50, 470.
11. Baker, ed., *Seward Works*, III, 97; IV, 25–52, 87, 394; *Immigrant White Free Labor, or Imported Black African Slave Labor. Speech of William H. Seward at Oswego, New York, November 3, 1856* (Washington, 1857), 1.
12. Although it is not the purpose of this work to evaluate in economic terms the Republicans' view of the South, it should be noted that economic historians have recently re-examined the question of the relative economic development of the sections before the Civil War. Richard Easterlin has compiled figures showing that per capita income of southern whites was not substantially lower than that for northerners, although southern income did decline relative to the North's between 1840 and 1860. And Stanley Engerman argues that the rate of southern economic growth exceeded the national average. On the other hand, Julius Rubin points out that there was a substantial maldistribution of income within the South, with a small group of wealthy planters and a large subsistence sector of poor white farmers, and Engerman acknowledges that educational facilities in the South were quite deficient compared with the rest of the nation. Moreover, the aggregate figures used by Easterlin and Engerman conceal the great regional differences within the South. The South Atlantic and East South Central states had per capita incomes significantly below the national average, while the high

were content to draw the comparison between free and slave states and let their listeners draw their own conclusions. But when Republicans did explain the economic backwardness of the South, they placed the greatest stress on the effect of slavery upon southern labor—both slave and free. Some Republicans believed, to be sure, that the Negro was by nature wasteful and lazy, and that his labor, therefore, could never be as productive as the white man's; this same argument, moreover, was used by southerners in belittling the statistical arguments of Republican spokesmen. But usually Republicans argued that it was not the Negro himself who was to blame for the South's backwardness; it was rather that the institution of slavery deprived him of both the education and the incentives which made the labor of northern freemen so productive. Slavery, said Seward, reduced the slave to "a brute . . . incompetent to cast a shuttle, to grease or oil a wheel and keep it in motion," and Lincoln charged that southerners believed the ideal laborer was not an educated, skilled freeman, but "a blind horse upon a tread-mill." [13] Such labor had perhaps been unavoidable in the colonial era, when slavery had been introduced to meet a shortage of labor, but it was out of date in the modern world. What a diversified economy needed, Seward insisted, was "no longer the ignorant labor of barbarians, but labor perfected by knowledge and skill, in combination with all the scientific principles of mechanism." Few slaves, he noted, could perform such complicated tasks as lumbering, quarrying, manufacturing, and mining. As long as so much of its labor force was uneducated, the South could never aspire to the diversity of economic pursuits so essential to regional growth.[14]

But even educated slaves would not be as productive as free labor,

---

figure for the West South Central states was, in large measure, the result of Louisiana's profitable sugar industry and the Mississippi River trade. Richard Easterlin, "Regional Income Trends, 1840–1950," in Seymour Harris, ed., *American Economic History* (New York, 1961), 525–47; Stanley Engerman, "The Effects of Slavery Upon the Southern Economy," *Explorations in Entrepreneurial History*, IV (1967), 71–97; and Julius Rubin's contribution to David T. Gilchrist and W. David Lewis, eds., *Economic Change in the Civil War Era* (Greenville, Del., 1965).

13. "The 'Free-State Letter' of Judge George H. Williams," *Oregon Historical Quarterly*, IX (1908), 260–61; Baker, ed., *Seward Works*, IV, 600; Roy F. Basler et al., eds., *The Collected Works of Abraham Lincon* (9 vols.: New Brunswick, 1953–55), IV, 479–80. Cf. *Ohio State Journal*, March 29, 1856; New York *Tribune*, June 2, 1855.

14. Baker, ed., *Seward Works*, IV, 378–79. Cf. III, 13; Richard Hildreth, *Despotism in America* (Boston, 1840), 132; Wellesville *Patriot*, February 7, 1854, clipping, Box 20, Chase Papers, HSPa.

Republicans maintained, because slaves lacked the incentive which inspired free laborers—the hope of improving their social condition and that of their families. "Enslave a man," Horace Greeley explained, "and you destroy his ambition, his enterprise, his capacity. In the constitution of human nature, the desire of bettering one's condition is the mainspring of effort." George Opdyke of New York, a leading merchant and something of an economist, wrote that the slave did as little labor as he could because he had no personal stake in the results of his effort. "He knows that however much of revenue he may produce, his own share will be strictly limited to the necessities of life." The same conclusion was reached by Olmsted after his journeys to the South.[15]

The effects of slavery on the southern economy, however, were not confined to the slave himself. Tocqueville and many other visitors commented upon the contempt in which labor of any kind was held in the South, and Republicans insisted that the South's refusal to honor "the dignity of labor" was another cause of its economic backwardness. According to Olmsted, any kind of work which slaves performed was automatically considered unfit for a southern white man. "Manual agricultural labor is the chief employment of slaves in the South," he reported. "For manual agricultural labor, therefore, the free man looking on, has a contempt. . . ." Martin Van Buren agreed that both slaveowners and poor whites disdained labor—and the latter were themselves held in contempt because they had to work to support themselves. The divergent attitudes of the two sections toward labor were summarized by the conservative former Whig, Thomas Ewing, in 1858. Labor, he declared, "is held honorable by all on one side of the line because it is the vocation of freemen—degrading in the eyes of some on the other side because it is the task of slaves."[16]

Of all the evils of slavery, none seemed to impress Republicans more than the poverty and degradation of the mass of southern non-slave-

15. *Congressional Globe,* 30 Congress, 1 Session, Appendix, 835; George Opdyke, *A Treatise on Political Economy* (New York, 1851), 330; Olmsted, *Seaboard Slave States,* 711; Olmsted, *Back Country,* 305. Cf. John C. Underwood to Henry C. Carey, November 6, 1860, Henry C. Carey Papers, HSPa.
16. Alexis de Tocqueville, *Democracy in America,* eds., J. P. Mayer and Max Lerner (New York, 1966), 318; Olmsted, *Seaboard Slave States,* 712; Olmsted, *Back Country,* 299; John Bigelow, ed., *The Writings and Speeches of Samuel J. Tilden* (2 vols.: New York, 1885), I, 569; C. L. Martzolff, ed., "Address at Marietta, Ohio, 1858. By Hon. Thomas Ewing," *OAHQ,* XXVIII (1919), 194.

holders. Olmsted was shocked by the condition of the poor whites with whom he came in contact in the South, and drew a vivid portrait of their ignorance, poverty, and the utter hopelessness of their situation in slave society. The young British journalist E. L. Godkin likewise visited the South before the Civil War, and reported that he had never met men "in whom hope, energy, and courage to all outward appearance, seemed so utterly extinguished." [17] In describing the poor whites of the South, Republicans seemed to vacillate between outright contempt and compassion. John G. Palfrey, for example, drew a contrast between the independent laborers of the North and "the very different specimen of humanity known as the *mean white man*, the *poor buckra*, in the southern States . . . the poor, shiftless, lazy, uninstructed, cowed non-slaveholder of the South." And George Weston declared that because of slavery three-quarters of the South's white population "retire to the outskirts of civilization, where they live a semi-savage life, sinking deeper and more hopelessly into barbarism with every succeeding generation." [18] Generally, Republicans blamed the lack of educational opportunities and the degradation of labor in slave society for the position of the poor whites. "They are depressed, poor, impoverished, degraded in caste, because labor is disgraceful," Jacob Collamer of Vermont put it in 1856.[19]

The plight of the poor whites was compounded, as Republicans saw it, by their lack of opportunity to rise in the social scale. In the Republican portrait of southern society, there were only two classes of whites—the slaveholding aristocracy and the very poor. "In the slave states," Timothy Jenkins of New York told the House of Representatives, "there is in substance no middle class. Great wealth or hopeless poverty is the settled condition." An Ohio Congressman agreed that the South "builds up no middle class of intelligent farmers, artisans, and mechanics, who constitute the real strength, who make the real

17. Broadus Mitchell, *Frederick Law Olmsted, A Critic of the Old South* (Baltimore, 1924), 102; Olmsted, *Back Country*, 12–13, 297, 303ff.; Olmsted, *Seaboard Slave States*, 537–39; Rollo Ogden, ed., *Life and Letters of Edward Lawrence Godkin* (2 vols.: New York, 1907), I, 29–30. Cf. Cincinnati *Gazette*, October 5, 1858, July 28, 1860; New York *Tribune*, December 1, 1855, June 9, 1856.
18. *Congressional Globe*, 30 Congress, 2 Session, Appendix, 315; George Weston, *The Poor Whites of the South* (Washington, 1856), 5. Cf. Bigelow, ed., *Tilden*, II, 569; *Great Mass Meeting on the Battle Ground of Tippecanoe . . . Speech of General J. Watson Webb* (np, [1856]), 14.
19. *Congressional Globe*, 34 Congress, 3 Session, Appendix, 53. Cf. 31 Congress, 1 Session, Appendix, 142.

wealth, and are justly the pride and glory of the free states." [20] The comparative lack of a middle class effectively blocked any hope of social advancement for the mass of poor whites, for it was all but impossible for a non-slaveholder to rise into the southern aristocracy. "The northern laboring man," Cassius M. Clay told an Ohio audience in 1856, "could, and frequently did, rise above the condition [in] which he was born to the first rank of society and wealth; but [I] never knew such an instance in the South." A Wisconsin Republican journal declared that even Stephen A. Douglas should recognize the superiority of free to slave institutions, because Douglas himself had risen from poverty to national leadership. "Had Douglas been born in a slave state," this newspaper continued, "his inheritance of poverty would have clung to him." And the Chicago *Democratic Press* summed up what Republicans felt was the most salient difference between North and South so far as labor was concerned when it declared in 1854, "Fortunes are frequently inherited at the South—they are rarely made." [21]

In the eyes of many Republicans, slavery's impact upon labor was visible not only in the South but in the areas of the free states settled by southern migrants. The southern parts of the states of the lower West—Ohio, Indiana, Illinois, and Iowa—were inhabited by migrants from the slave states, while the northern areas were settled by easterners. The hostility between the two groups of settlers was proverbial. "In this state," wrote an Indiana politician, "we have various phases of public opinion; the enterprising Yankee of Northern Indiana, despises the sluggish and inaminate [sic] North Carolinian, Virginian, and Kentuckian in the southern part of the State," while the southerners were equally hostile to their northern neighbors.[22] The westerners of northern background, most of whom went into the Republican party, believed that their portion of the Northwest reflected the best aspects of free labor civilization. "One thing is certain," wrote a resident of

20. *Congressional Globe*, 30 Congress, 2 Session, Appendix, 103; 35 Congress, 1 Session, 774. Cf. Chicago *Weekly Democrat*, March 8, 1856; Cincinnati *Gazette*, August 25, 1858.
21. Cincinnati *Gazette*, July 31, 1856; Racine *Weekly Advocate*, March 6, 1854; Chicago *Democratic Press*, August 5, 1854.
22. J. Herman Schauinger, ed., "The Letters of Godlove S. Orth, Hoosier Whig," *IndMH*, XXXIX (December 1943), 367; Don E. Fehrenbacher, *Prelude to Greatness, Lincoln in the 1850's* (New York, 1964 ed.), 6; *Report of the Debates and Proceedings of the Convention for the Revision of the Constitution of the State of Ohio, 1850-51* (2 vols.: Columbus, 1851), II, 637; New York *Tribune*, August 12, 1854.

Illinois in 1850, "that where New England emigrants do not venture, improvements, social, agricultural, mechanic, or scientific, rarely flourish. . . ." In the Western Reserve of northern Ohio, a correspondent of the New York *Tribune* maintained in 1857, there was "a neatness and a *home-ish* look to the farms and villages . . . which are not characteristic of the parts settled by Virginians and Kentuckians." Both these writers could have cited statistics to show that Republican areas of the Northwest tended to be more prosperous, economically progressive, and more literate than Democratic areas, particularly those settled from the South.[23]

To Republicans, the southern Northwest seemed, as George Julian remarked, like parts of slave states transplanted onto free soil. Such an attitude was understandable when one remembers that southern Ohio, for example, with its large farms raising tobacco and its close commercial relations with the South, did reflect much of the southern way of life.[24] When Republicans looked at these areas they were most struck by the ignorance and shiftlessness of the inhabitants. "The Southern portions of the States of Illinois and Indiana," according to one newspaper, "have become proverbial for the intellectual, moral, and political darkness which covers the land." A correspondent of Lyman Trumbull's wrote with disdain of the portion of Illinois' population "which comes directly or indirectly from slave states and which *reads but little*," and it was true that the southern Northwest had the highest illiteracy rate in the section.[25] The southern-born settlers seemed content with their status in life, and appeared to lack the typical northern desire to improve their condition. One traveler in Illinois expressed surprise that southern settlers were content "to shelter their families in a mere

---

23. Arthur C. Cole, *The Era of the Civil War 1848–1870* (Springfield, 1919), 13–14; New York *Tribune*, June 27, 1857; W. R. Brock, *An American Crisis* (London, 1963), 245; Harry E. Pratt, ed., "Illinois as Lincoln Knew It," *Papers in Illinois History*, XLIV (1937), 153, 166–67; Don E. Fehrenbacher, "Illinois Political Attitudes, 1854–1861" (unpublished doctoral dissertation, University of Chicago, 1951), 4; Lois K. Mathews, *The Expansion of New England* (Boston and New York, 1909), 208–9.

24. George W. Julian, *Political Recollections, 1840–1872* (Chicago, 1884); 72; David H. Bradford, "The Background and Formation of the Republican Party in Ohio, 1844–1861" (unpublished doctoral dissertation, University of Chicago, 1947), 33–34; Henry C. Hubbart, " 'Pro-Southern' Influences in the Free West 1840–1865," *MVHR*, XX (June 1933), 47–49.

25. "Egyptian Darkness," unidentified news clipping, Scrapbook, Logan Family Papers, LC; H. Wing to Lyman Trumbull, November 28, 1859, Lyman Trumbull Papers, LC; Henry C. Hubbart, *The Older Middle West 1840–1880* (New York, 1936), 38.

shantee or mud-walled cottages," while Yankees farther north built
neat log cabins, schools, and churches. The air of superiority with
which Republicans looked upon the southern settlers in the free states
was expressed by George Weston, the former Democrat from Maine
who became a prominent Republican editor: [26]

> It is unquestionable that the immigration from the South has
> brought into the free states more ignorance, poverty, and thriftless-
> ness, than an equal amount of European immigration. Where it
> forms a marked feature of the population, as in Southern Illinois,
> a long time must elapse before it is brought up to the general stand-
> ard of intelligence and enterprise in the free States.

The Republican critique of southern society thus focused upon the
degradation of labor—the slave's ignorance and lack of incentive, and
the laboring white's poverty, degradation, and lack of social mobility.
The result was not only regional economic stagnation, but a system
of social ethics entirely different from that of the North. The moral
qualities of free labor, hard work, frugality, and interest in economic
advancement seemed absent in the South. When Republicans visited
the slave states they were struck by the character of the people
even more than the poverty of the region. The Cincinnati *Gazette's*
traveling correspondent reported in 1858 that he was astonished by
the "lack of invention and resource, the clinging to old and now un-
profitable ways" among southern laborers, and he added that there
seemed to be "a sort of sluggish inactivity" throughout slave society.
Compared with the North, this writer declared, the South seemed to
be a "dead society." Samuel Gridley Howe visited the South in the
1840's and commented upon the "inefficiency and irresolution which
characterizes all classes of people," and the broken-down fences, dirty
streets, and unkempt homes whose inhabitants seemed too lazy to
repair them. Henry L. Dawes was similarly impressed by the sluggish
pace of life in the South, by the "sameness of poverty and unthrift" in
the southern landscape. And the New York *Tribune's* correspondent
Bayard Taylor reported from Kentucky in 1855 that despite their
poverty and degradation, people seemed to be "content with things as
they are." [27]

26. John S. Wright, "The Background and Formation of the Republican Party
in Illinois, 1846–1860" (unpublished doctoral dissertation, University of Chicago,
1946), 4; Weston, *Poor Whites*, 7.
27. Cincinnati *Gazette*, August 25, 31, September 3, 1858; Laura E. Richards,
ed., *Letters and Journals of Samuel Gridley Howe* (2 vols.: Boston, 1909), II,

The whole mentality and flavor of southern life thus seemed antithetical to that of the North. Instead of progress, the South represented decadence, instead of enterprise, laziness. "Thus it appears," wrote the anti-slavery writer and historian Richard Hildreth, "that one plain and obvious effect of the slaveholding system is to deaden in every class of society that *spirit of industry* essential to the increase of public wealth." [28] To those with visions of a steadily growing nation, slavery was an intolerable hindrance to national achievement. Seward, who believed that a stable and prosperous American nation could serve as the base for an overseas empire which would spread American ¹nfluence and power throughout the world, saw most clearly the way in which slavery stood in the way of national greatness.[29] Slavery, he declared, was "incompatible with all . . . the elements of the security, welfare, and greatness of nations." It impaired the strength of the entire country and subverted the "intelligence, vigor, and energy" which national growth required. This was why, as early as 1845, Seward declared that abolition was the most important object which could occupy the attention of American statesmen. The question of restricting and ultimately abolishing slavery, he declared, was the question of "whether impartial public councils shall leave the free and vigorous North and West to work out the welfare of the country, and drag the reluctant South up to participate in the same glorious destinies." [30]

II

"The aim of the present black republican organization," the New York *Herald* charged in 1860, "is the destruction of the social system

---

110–11; Henry L. Dawes Journal, June 27, 1852, Dawes Papers; New York *Tribune*, May 24, 1855. Cf. *Congressional Globe*, 36 Congress, 1 Session, 1914.
28. Hildreth, *Despotism*, 115–16. Cf. William Stocking, ed., *Under the Oaks* (Detroit, 1904), 46; Cleveland *Leader*, January 29, 1856; George N. Fuller, ed., *Messages of the Governors of Michigan* (4 vols.: Lansing, 1925–27), II, 293.
29. On Seward's view of empire, see Glyndon G. Van Deusen, *William Henry Seward* (New York, 1967), 206–11; Baker, ed., *Seward Works*, I, 57, 250; III, 12–13, 188; IV, 166–70, 333; Walter La Feber, *The New Empire* (Washington, 1963), 24–32.
30. Baker, ed., *Seward Works*, I, 76, IV, 395; *The Address of the Southern and Western Liberty Convention to the People of the United States; the Proceedings and Resolutions of the Convention* . . . (Cincinnati, 1845), 18; Seward, ed., *Seward Autobiography*, 717. Cf. the statement of the New York *Times*, May 16, 1857: "Whatever impedes the advance or interfers with the prosperity of the nation, of the United States, as a grand consolidated empire, will excite the attention and invite upon itself the indignation of the northern States. . . ."

of the Southern States, without regard to consequences." The *Herald*,
of course, was overstating the case, since many Republicans were more
concerned with preventing the extension of slavery, than undermining
it in the South. And those Republicans interested in fundamental
changes in the southern social order were hardly heedless of the
consequences. They firmly believed that they had the best interests
of the whole nation—including the South—at heart. As George Weston
put it, "to destroy slavery is not to destroy the South, but to change
its social organization for the better," [31] What Republicans like Weston
meant was that through abolition, southern life could come to resemble that of the North. The South, the New York *Tribune* declared
on the eve of the Civil War, would have to take up manufacturing and
"adopt the thrift and industry of the North, bringing the consumer
and producer together on her soil." The Cincinnati *Gazette's* southern
reporter summed up this outlook when he described in August 1858,
the way to regenerate southern society: "It is by the introduction upon
Southern territory of the Northern system of life." [32]

This commitment to the reconstruction of southern society, which
some historians have seen as a characteristic of radical Republicans,[33]
was actually quite common throughout the party in the 1850's. Many
Republicans urged that the reconstruction be accomplished through
the mass migration of northerners into the South. These men would
bring the qualities of industry, thrift, and enterprise so lacking in
southern life, and would begin the economic diversification so essential
if the South were to escape from economic stagnation. "You cannot
expect the advantages of machinery," a New York Congressman informed the slave states in 1860, "until some Yankees go down and
explain the mode and manner of its use." Another Congressman declared that he had seen barren lands in the slave states "converted into
luxuriant clover-fields by the enterprise and industry of Yankee

31. New York *Herald*, April 28, 1860; George M. Weston, *The Progress of Slavery
in the United States* (Washington, 1857), 242. Cf. Joel Benton, ed., *Greeley on
Lincoln with Mr. Greeley's Letters to Charles A. Dana and a Lady Friend* (New
York, 1893), 141.
32. George W. Smith, "Ante-Bellum Attempts of Northern Business Interests to
'Redeem' the Upper South," *JSH*, XI (May 1945), 177–81; Kenneth Stampp,
And the War Came (Baton Rouge, 1950), 258; Cincinnati *Gazette*, August 23,
1858. Cf. *Congressional Globe*, 36 Congress, 1 Session, Appendix, 252.
33. Margaret Shortreed, "The Antislavery Radicals: From Crusade to Revolution
1840–1868," *Past and Present*, XVI (November 1959), 66; Barrington Moore, Jr.,
Social Origins of Dictatorship and Democracy (Boston, 1966), 145.

farmers." And the New York *Tribune* held out the following advice as to how one state could achieve progress: [34]

> It is only by the abolition of slavery and the cessation of slaveholding and the slave trade, followed by an emigration of Northern capitalists, manufacturers, and merchants, that the practical regeneration of Virginia can be effected.

Some Republicans, however, believed that northern emigration did not have to wait until abolition had been accomplished. Indeed, they were convinced that the establishment of free labor settlements in the border states would demonstrate the superiority of free to slave labor, arouse the latent anti-slavery feelings of the southern poor whites, and begin the process of overthrowing slavery. George Weston voiced the confidence of these Republicans when he predicted that since "an inferior civilization must give room to that which is superior," organized emigration could succeed in undermining slavery.[35] The most important plan for the settlement of free labor in the South before the Civil War was the one drawn up by the Massachusetts conservative Republican Eli Thayer, and the New Yorker who had himself settled in Virginia, John C. Underwood. Underwood and Thayer established the North American Emigrant Aid and Homestead Company, and did succeed in creating a settlement in western Virginia in 1857. They had studied Carey's writings well, and hoped to create the locally oriented, diversified economy he idealized, with factories, farms, and small businesses in close interdependence. Many Republican newspapers endorsed this plan to bring "a better civilization" into the South, and a number of prominent New York bankers, merchants, and lawyers became involved, hoping to profit if the economic development of Virginia could be begun. For a variety of reasons, including southern opposition and conflicts among the company's directors, the plan never became a reality, but it did indicate the lines along which many Republicans were thinking.[36] And even those who believed that large-

34. *Congressional Globe*, 36 Congress, 1 Session, 1031, 2 Session, Appendix, 191; New York *Tribune*, August 22, 1856. Cf. George W. Smith, "Some Northern Wartime Attitudes Toward the Post-Civil War South," *JSH*, X (August 1944), 254; *Congressional Globe*, 30 Congress, 1 Session, Appendix, 837.
35. Weston, *Progress*, 33–34. Cf. New York *Tribune*, April 1, 1858; Cincinnati *Gazette*, October 30, November 9, December 20, 27, 1858, January 1, 19, 1859; Washington *Republic*, July 6, 1858.
36. On the Underwood-Thayer plan, see Smith, "Ante-Bellum Attempts," 191–210; Patricia Hickin, "John C. Underwood and the Antislavery Movement in Virginia, 1847–1860," *VaMHB*, LXXIII (April 1965), 161–64; Elizabeth K.

scale migration of free labor would have to wait until abolition had been achieved were convinced that such a flow of population would be necessary "to Northernize the South." "Abolish slavery in Virginia tomorrow," wrote one New York politician, "and the exodus from New England would be tremendous." In the eyes of many Republicans, the South needed not only to abolish slavery but also to adopt the northern way of life, in order to enter the modern world.[37]

If Republicans were anxious to reshape southern society in the image of the North, they were doubly determined that the slave system should not expand beyond its existing borders. It is impossible to understand the intensity of Republican opposition to the expansion of slavery into the West without bearing in mind their image of southern society, as well as their conviction that free land in the West provided an insurance of continuing social mobility in the North. Many historians have suggested that the whole controversy over slavery in the territories was artificial, both because climate barred the institution's expansion, and because the number of slaves in the West in 1860 was miniscule. James G. Randall, for example, insisted in his biography of Lincoln that the specific political disputes of the 1850's "did not touch large questions of slavery at all," and that the problem of "an almost non-existent slave population in the West . . . was magnified into an issue altogether out of scale with its importance." Whether slavery could and would have expanded had the Civil War not intervened is, of course, something historians can never know. But to belittle the question is to betray a lack of understanding of the Republican mind. Most Republicans had no faith in Webster's "law of nature" barring slavery from the West, and fully believed that the institution would expand unless barred by law.[38] And the consequences of such ex-

McClintic, "Credo: An Experiment in Colonization and a Dream of Empire," *West Virginia Review*, XV (1938), 168–90, 198–200, 233–54; New York *Times*, January 21, 1857; Springfield *Republican*, April 14, 1857.

37. E. Pershine Smith to Henry C. Carey, December 19, 1859, Carey Papers. Cf. New York *Times*, May 23, 1855; *National Era*, October 2, 1856; Smith, "Ante-Bellum Attempts," 187–88. C. Vann Woodward develops this point in relation to northern attitudes during Reconstruction in "The Southern Ethic in a Puritan World," *William and Mary Quarterly*, 3 ser., XXV (July 1968), 365–67.

38. J. G. Randall, *Lincoln the President: Springfield to Gettysburg* (2 vols.: New York, 1945), I, 86; Charles R. Hart, "Congressmen and the Expansion of Slavery Into the Territories: A Study in Attitudes, 1846–1861" (unpublished doctoral dissertation, University of Washington, 1965), 41–50, 88–95; Joseph P. Smith, ed., *History of the Republican Party in Ohio* (2 vols.: Chicago, 1898), I, 13.

pansion would be so disastrous for both northern society and the nation's future that Republicans were willing to risk civil war to prevent it.

In the eyes of many Republicans, the development of the West held the key to America's future. "The wealth and political power of the country," wrote Frank Blair in 1854, "will in a little time reside at its Geographical centre . . ." and most Republicans agreed that the sectional contest would be decided by the new states of the West. William Seward, for example, said he looked to the new states "to finally decide whether this is to be a land of slavery or of freedom. The people of the northwest are to be the arbiters of its destiny. . . ."[39] Moreover, as Arthur Bestor points out, Americans of the nineteenth century believed that the character of a society was forged at its birth, and was extremely difficult to alter thereafter. General James Nye expressed this idea when he told the Buffalo Free Soil Convention in 1848 that although legislative errors on such matters as banks and tariffs could be remedied at any time, "if we are wrong on the subject of slavery, it can never be righted." Once slavery entered a territory, it would be extremely difficult to dislodge.[40]

The question of slavery in the territories was thus one of potentialities. Whatever the actual number of slaves involved, the character of institutions which would affect the lives of millions of Americans was being determined. In taking this position, Republicans often compared the territories to children, whose upbringing would determine their future development. "The character of States, like that of individuals," said Kinsley Bingham of Michigan, "is formed while in a state of pupilage," and he added that all the territories in which slavery had been permitted had become slave states, while free states had developed where it had been barred. (Schuyler Colfax advised Lincoln that this latter argument was sure to be well received by campaign audiences.) The future would be vitally affected by present decisions. According to Roger Baldwin of Connecticut, "It is a great question of national policy, involving responsibilities and consequences

39. Francis P. Blair, Jr., to Edward L. Pierce, April 28, 1854, E. L. Pierce Papers, Houghton Library, Harvard University; Baker, ed., *Seward Works*, IV, 346–47. Cf. Henry Nash Smith, *Virgin Land* (Cambridge, 1950), 191–92.
40. Arthur E. Bestor, Jr., "Patent-Office Models of the Good Society: Some Relationships between Social Reform and Westward Expansion," *AHR*, LVIII (April 1953), 513–21; *Free Soil Convention*, 4.

affecting the whole American people, and fixing for all future time the destinies of our immense territorial acquisitions bordering on the Pacific." [41]

What it all came down to was whether the western social order would resemble that of the South or of the North. Countless Republican orators phrased the question just this way. As James Grimes put it: [42]

> Shall populous, thriving villages and cities spring up all over the face of Nebraska, or shall unthrift and sparseness, stand-still and decay, ever characterize that State? Shall unpaid, unwilling toil, inspired by no hope and impelled by no affection, drag its weary, indolent limbs over that State, hurrying the soil to barrenness and leaving the wilderness a wilderness still? . . . Are you not bound by the highest considerations of duty to assist in building up the institutions of [Nebraska] on a substantial and free basis?

A West open to slavery would be marked by the same decadence which characterized the South. But if slavery were excluded and the territories open to free labor, the result would be an entirely different social order. John P. Hale asked a New York audience whether the West should be settled by the same free laborers "as made New York and New England what they are? Shall the hum of busy industry be heard on its hills and in its valleys—shall churches and school houses and academies dot its hills?" The New York *Tribune* took for granted that to bar slavery from the territories was "to give them an opportunity to become what New England is now." In 1860, Salmon P. Chase summarized the benefits which the states of the Northwest had received from the Ordinance of 1787. He also indicated how Republicans felt a free West would differ from the same area under slavery. It would be characterized by "freedom not serfdom; freeholds not tenancies; democracy not despotism; education not ignorance . . . progress, not stagnation or retrogression." [43] Given

---

41. Fuller, ed., *Michigan Governors*, II, 321; Schuyler Colfax to Abraham Lincoln, August 25, 1858, Robert Todd Lincoln Papers, LC; *Congressional Globe*, 30 Congress, 1 Session, Appendix, 709. Cf. New York *Times*, February 20, 1854; Parke Godwin, *Political Essays* (New York, 1856), 289.

42. William Salter, *The Life of James W. Grimes* (New York, 1876), 48. Cf. Charles B. Going, *David Wilmot Free-Soiler* (New York, 1924), 451; Cincinnati *Gazette*, January 10, 1860.

43. New York *Tribune*, February 20, 1854, July 10, 1860, "Mississippi Valley," manuscript address, 1860, Box 17, Chase Papers, HSPa. Cf. *Free Soil Convention*, 26.

such alternatives it was difficult for Republicans not to believe that the issue of slavery in the territories was perhaps the most fundamental one the nation had so far faced.

In 1855, Charles Francis Adams observed that it was a weakness of political anti-slavery that it seemed to many voters to be an abstraction, lacking the immediate impact of "temporal, absorbing self-interest." But the issue of slavery in the territories struck millions of northerners in a way in which abstract discussions of the condition of the slave could not. During the debate on the Kansas-Nebraska Act, Elihu Washburne of Illinois spoke of the "thousands of enterprising and hardy men in my own State who are waiting to emigrate" into the West. And throughout the 1850's, western newspapers carried reports of the flood of migrants who were making their way to the territories. "The rush of emigrants West for the last twelve months has been unprecedented," said the Chicago *Democratic Press* in 1856, attributing it to the universal desire of free laborers to possess land.[44]

To northerners who were moving west, or hoped to, the question of slavery in the territories had a direct personal impact. "We are all personally interested in this question," said Oliver Morton in 1860, "not indirectly and remotely as in a mere political abstraction—but directly, pecuniarily, and selfishly." The reason: "If we do not exclude slavery from the Territories, it will exclude us." Free white laborers of the North would never migrate to a land where labor was held to be disreputable, where social mobility was all but non-existent, and where they would have to labor in close proximity with Negro slaves. "Free labor," the Republican governor of Wisconsin explained in 1860, "languishes and becomes degrading when put in competition with slave labor, and idleness, poverty, and vice, among large classes of non-slaveholders, take the place of industry and thrift and virtue." To bar slavery from the territories was to preserve the territories for the free laborers of the North.[45]

Republican spokesmen also brought home to laborers who had no intention of moving west that their interests were affected by the free

44. Charles Francis Adams, *What Makes Slavery a Question of National Concern?* (Boston, 1855), 30, *Congressional Globe,* 33 Congress, 1 Session, Appendix, 461; Chicago *Democratic Press,* January 11, 1856. Cf. Cleveland *Leader,* June 9, 1857; *Ohio State Journal,* March 6, 1855.

45. William M. French, ed., *Life, Speeches, State Papers, and Public Services of Gov. Oliver P. Morton* (Cincinnati, 1866), 88–89; *Annual Message of Alexander W. Randall. Governor of the State of Wisconsin, and Accompanying Documents* (Madison, 1860), 24.

or slave condition of the territories. For one thing, they argued, to allow slaveholders to dominate the new states of the West would be to make the North a permanent minority in the national government. Whiggish Republicans also insisted that the economic development of the West was a necessary part of the advancing prosperity of the entire nation. Seward argued that East and West were economically interdependent, and that the continued growth of the East required the development of increasing western markets. "Western New York," he told an audience in Oswego in 1856, "needs, I think, a more full conception of its capacity for expansion. . . . It seems never to have entered our thoughts that our commercial and political systems must be extended somewhere, or else the growth of the cities and towns of Western New York must be arrested." And other Republicans warned that the whole safety-valve conception of the West presupposed that the availability of cheap land would provide an avenue of social mobility for those who took it, while easing labor competition for those who remained. If slavery were allowed to enter the territories, and effectively bar the migration of free laborers, the eastern laboring population would rise, wages would fall, and class divisions would become more rigid. One Republican appealed to both nativist prejudices and economic fears by arguing that if the avenues of geographical mobility were closed, "the vast emigration from abroad that is now poured into our midst and outflows westward . . . will fall back upon our free States, giving us a surplus population that we do not want, and which will necessarily interfere with the employment and the wages of our own citizens." [46] The future shape of western society was thus a matter of legitimate concern to all northerners, and not, as the popular sovereignty formula implied, merely a matter to be decided by the settlers who happened to occupy a territory in its formative years.

III

The idea that free labor was degraded by slavery, and the corollary that if slavery were allowed to expand into the territories, northern laborers would be effectively barred from settling there because of the invariable stigma attached to labor in slave society, formed vital

46. *Immigrant Free White Labor*, 1–2; *Judge* [William D.] *Kelley's Speech, At Spring Garden Hall, September 16, 1856* (np, nd), 11; *Congressional Globe*, 34 Congress, 1 Session, Appendix, 413; John Jay, *America Free—Or America Slave* (New York 1856), 11.

parts of the Republican appeal in the 1850's. Republicans insisted that
the slavery controversy involved the white laborers of North and South
as directly as it did the slave himself. There were many political reasons for this emphasis. For one thing, abolitionists had always had
difficulty attracting northern labor to their cause, and Republicans felt
that by couching their appeal in terms of the effect of slavery upon
labor, they stood a better chance of gaining these votes. "Convince
the laboring class that [slavery] is at war with our republican institutions and opposed to their interests," was the advice an Indiana Republican gave George Julian during the 1856 campaign.[47] Some Republicans felt that defining the issue in terms of slavery's effect on
labor would also be a way of attracting the support of immigrants.
"The present political contest," a prominent Maine leader wrote,
"when resolved into its simplest elements is the ever enduring and
never ending warfare between free and servile labor—between labor
and *capital* and that capital in man. In such a contest the whole foreign
labor of the country should of right be with us." [48] Moreover, the free
labor argument provided an appeal on which Republicans of all factions could unite. It was an appeal to the lowest common denominator
of party ideology, allowing Republicans to sidestep both the problem
of race and the effects of slavery upon the enslaved.

The attack on slavery for degrading the white laborer and stunting
the economic development of the South was perhaps the major contribution of the political branch of the anti-slavery movement. As
Stanley Elkins and other writers have made clear, the non-political
abolitionists tended to view slavery in extremely personal terms, centering their analysis on the sin of slaveholding rather than on the
system's institutional character. Although abolitionists sometimes discussed the differences between free and slave labor, they did not
emphasize this in their arguments, insisting that the moral issue be
kept always paramount.[49] Political anti-slavery men, however, added

47. Williston H. Lofton, "Abolition and Labor," *JNH*, XXXIII (July 1948), 249–
83; *National Era*, April 17, 1851; Joseph G. Rayback, "The American Workingman
and the Antislavery Crusade," *JEcH*, III (November 1943), 152–63; N. Field to
George W. Julian, September 19, 1856, Giddings-Julian Papers, LC.
48. John Appleton to William Pitt Fessenden, March 10, 1858, William Pitt
Fessenden Papers, WRHS; Cincinnati *Gazette*, October 10, 1859.
49. Stanley Elkins, *Slavery* (Chicago, 1959), 141–43; 161–70; Arthur Young
Lloyd, *The Slavery Controversy 1831–1860* (Chapel Hill, 1939), 72–83; Howard
R. Floan, *The South in Northern Eyes 1831 to 1861* (Austin, 1958), 5–14, 20–25;
Donald G. Matthews, "The Abolitionists on Slavery: The Critique Behind the
Social Movement," *JSH*, XXXIII (May 1967), 180–81.

other grounds for attacking slavery. The Liberty party platforms written by Salmon P. Chase in the 1840's, which helped develop a uniquely political anti-slavery appeal, included attacks on slavery for impoverishing the southern states, denying southern laborers the right to an education, and degrading and dishonoring laborers generally.[50] An additional dimension was added by the Barnburner Democrats in their campaign for the Wilmot Proviso between 1846 and 1848. The Democratic Free Soilers placed their opposition to the extension of slavery almost exclusively on the grounds that the institution degraded white laborers, and would exclude them from the territories. "We protest against the extension . . . of an institution whose inevitable concomitant is the social and political degradation of the white laborer," said a resolution of the 1847 Herkimer Barnburner Convention. A few months later, the call for the Ohio Free Territory Convention, drafted by Chase, declared that "free labor and free laborers shall be virtually excluded from [the territories] by being subjected to degrading competition with slave labor. . . ."[51]

The anti-slavery Democrats were heirs of the Jacksonian political tradition, and were accustomed to couch their political arguments in terms which would appeal to labor. But there was also a strong undercurrent of racial prejudice in their statements. By insisting, as Wilmot did, that they had "no squeamish sensitiveness upon the subject of slavery, no morbid sympathy for the slave," and that it was the influence of slavery extension upon white labor that concerned them, the Barnburners sought both to turn anti-Negro sentiments to anti-slavery use and to answer the perennial charge that anti-slavery men were concerned solely with the fate of black men.[52] Some Barnburners,

50. "Liberty Address to People of Cincinnati," undated manuscript, Box 17, Chase Papers, HSPa; Wm. G. Lewis, *Biography of Samuel Lewis* (Cincinnati, 1857), 309; Edward C. Reilly, "Politico-Economic Considerations in the Western Reserve's Early Slavery Controversy," *OAHQ*, LII (April–June 1943), 141–44; Albert Mordell, *Quaker Militant, John Greenleaf Whittier* (Boston, 1933), 140–41; Salmon P. Chase and Charles D. Cleveland, *Antislavery Addresses of 1844 and 1845* (London, 1867), 114–15.
51. *Proceedings of the Herkimer Mass Convention of October 26, 1847* (Albany, 1847), 5; Cincinnati *Weekly Herald*, May 17, 1848, clipping, Box 20, Chase Papers, HSPa. Cf. New York *Evening Post*, June 7, 1848; O. C. Gardiner, *The Great Issue* (New York, 1848), 119.
52. *Congressional Globe*, 29 Congress, 2 Session, Appendix, 317, 30 Congress, 1 Session, Appendix, 1079. Cf. 29 Congress, 2 Session, 114–15; "Speech of John Van Buren at Columbia County Democratic Convention," news clipping, April 21, 1848, Scrapbook, Chase Papers, LC; *Herkimer Convention*, 28.

in trying to prove that they were concerned only with the effect of slavery on white laborers, went so far as to deny any knowledge of the condition of southern slaves. "I speak not of the condition of the slave," said George Rathbun. "I do not pretend to know, nor is it necessary that I should express an opinion in this place, whether the effect of slavery is beneficial or injurious to him. I am looking to its effect upon the white man, the free white man of this country." And John Van Buren insisted that the main reason he resisted the extension of slavery was that "you cannot induce the white labouring man to work beside a black slave."[53]

During the 1850's, the free labor argument with its racist tinge was utilized by many Republican spokesmen. The reason why such an argument was effective was explained by the New York *Tribune:*

> There are Republicans who are Abolitionists; there are others who anxiously desire and labor for the good of the slave; but there are many more whose main impulse is a desire to secure the new Territories for Free White Labor, with little or no regard for the interests of negroes, free or slave.

It was in order to appeal to this third group of Republicans that newspapers like the *Ohio State Journal* insisted, "the controversy between the free and slave states is not one affecting simply the negro." Some abolitionists resented the emphasis of many Republicans on the effect of slavery on white labor—William Goodell, for example, complained to Seward about his "apparent omission to advocate the rights and interests of other than *'white'* laborers" in his speeches. But by the same token, the New York *Times* spoke for many Republicans when it chided an abolitionist convention for "the omission of any, even the remotest, allusion to the evil effects of slavery on the white race . . ." in its program and resolutions.[54]

Moderate and conservative Republicans were especially attracted by the argument against slavery based on political economy, because it was a means of diverting attention from what they regarded as the

53. *Proceedings of the Utica Convention of February 16, 1848* . . . (Albany, 1848), 25 Boston *Republican,* September, 1848, news clipping, Scrapbook, Chase Papers, LC.
54. New York *Tribune,* October 15, 1856; *Ohio State Journal,* February 15, 1859; William Goodell to William H. Seward, March 17, 1858, William H. Seward Papers, Rush Rhees Library, University of Rochester; New York *Times,* May 14, 1857.

troublesome and inflammatory moral dimension of the slavery controversy. Thus, when Nathaniel Banks addressed audiences in the conservative commercial strongholds of Boston and New York, he emphasized that slavery was "the foe of all industrial progress and of the highest material prosperity." Similarly, the New York *Times* insisted that the slavery controversy should be considered not a matter of "conscience and religion," but "mainly one of *Social and Industrial Economy*. . . ." [55] Some conservatives insisted that it was less a sin than a disease, and that the South should be pitied rather than feared. "For myself," wrote a western editor, "I am opposed to slavery not because it is a misery to the downtrodden and oppressed [slave], but that it blights and mildews the white man whose lot is toil, and whose capital is his labor." [56] Some Republicans even insisted that the real issue between the parties was not slavery at all but the degradation of labor. Southern attacks on the "Northern mud-sills" and "filthy operatives" were trumpeted throughout the Republican press, and Republicans wrote defenses of free labor into their state platforms.[57] The duty of the government, they insisted, was "to see to it that . . . labor, the primal element of American prosperity, shall be honored, elevated and protected." The Chicago *Press* and *Tribune* summed up this aspect of the anti-slavery argument in 1858 when it declared, "There is but one issue in this prolonged and bitter contest. . . . It is this, *shall labor be degraded?*" [58]

Border state Republicans like Cassius M. Clay and the Blair family made perhaps the most persistent and extensive use of the free labor argument against slavery. As early as 1842, Clay requested that Salmon Chase send him information and statistics about the comparative

55. *The Great Questions of National and State Politics, Speech of Hon. Nathaniel P. Banks* . . . (Boston, 1857), 6; Philip S. Foner, *Business and Slavery* (Chapel Hill, 1941), 188; New York *Times*, April 7, 1854. Cf. New York *Tribune*, July 28, 1857; *Congressional Globe*, 35 Congress, 1 Session, 1251.
56. Rachel Sherman Thorndike, *The Sherman Letters* (New York, 1894), 69–70; *Great Meeting at Tippecanoe*, 3; John Sherman to Lydia Maria Child, February 8, 1860, John Sherman Papers, LC; Charles S. Wilson to Trumbull, May 12, 1858, Trumbull Papers.
57. Mandel, *Labor: Free and Slave*, 131, 148; *Congressional Globe*, 36 Congress, 1 Session, Appendix, 98; New York *Times*, October 16, 1852; Julian, *Political Recollections*, 161; B. Gratz Brown to Orville H. Browning, June 10, 1858, Orville H. Browning Papers, Illinois Historical Library; Smith, *Ohio Republican Party*, I, 71.
58. O. J. Hollister, *Life of Schuyler Colfax* (New York, 1886), 97; Chicago *Press and Tribune*, November 1, 1858.

wealth, population, educational institutions, and arts and sciences of the free and slave states, adding, "These are better arguments than invective." Clay always insisted that his program for ending slavery and promoting the industrial development of the South was designed "to seek the highest welfare of the white, whatever may be the consequences of liberation to the African." And he also emphasized that it was inaccurate to describe the slavery controversy as a struggle between North and South. Actually, he wrote in 1851, the real line of division was between northern free laborers and southern non-slaveholders on the one hand, and northern and southern aristocrats on the other.[59]

The Blair family, whose anti-slavery activities in Missouri and Maryland attained more success than Clay's in the years befor the Civil War, used much the same arguments. They always insisted that their concern was not for the slave, but for the white laborer degraded by slavery and denied the economic and educational opportunities which existed in the North. As the Blairs saw it, the issue of emancipation in the South was entirely a practical, and not a moral question. Which system of labor, they asked, was most productive and most beneficial to the laboring man? Their answer was that free labor was unquestionably superior.[60] After a trip to Illinois, for example, Frank Blair wrote back to a Missouri newspaper that no one from a slave state could pass through "the splendid farms of Sangamon and Morgan, without permitting an envious sigh to escape him at the evident superiority of free labor." Basing anti-slavery on the free labor appeal, the Blairs hoped to transform the Republican party into a replica of the old Jacksonian coalition, pitting the underprivileged against aristocrats, labor against capital. The only way for Republicans to gain support in the slave states, the elder Blair insisted, would be to focus their

59. Clay to Chase, December 21, 1842, Chase Papers, HSPa; Greeley, *Clay*, 174; Smiley, *Clay*, 143–44. Cf. 29–30, 47–50, 68–69; New York *Tribune*, July 23, 1857; Greeley, *Clay*, 187, 346–47; Clay to Chase, December 27, 1847, Chase Papers, HSPa.
60. New York *Tribune*, February 5, 1856, March 4, April 20, 1857, July 24, 1858; Cleveland *Leader*, February 28, 1857; Norma L. Peterson, *Freedom and Franchise, The Political Career of B. Gratz Brown* (Columbia, Mo., 1965), 72; Francis P. Blair, Jr., *Colonization and Commerce* (Cincinnati, 1859), 8; William E. Smith, *The Francis Preston Blair Family in Politics* (2 vols.: New York, 1933), I, 263; Francis P. Blair to H. Beecher, January 15, 1857 (draft), Blair-Lee Papers, Princeton University; F. P. Blair, Jr. to Richard Henry Dana, March 1, 1859, Richard Henry Dana Papers, MHS.

arguments not against the South, or even slavery, but against the slaveholding aristocracy. He took this position in a public letter in 1856, and then explained to his son, Montgomery: [61]

> I wish to make a new issue out of the slave question—giving the chief importance to the mischief inflicted on the poor whites rather than the blacks. In making this issue, the argument of my piece proves, that the contest ought not to be considered a *sectional* one but rather the war of *a class*—the slaveholders—against the laboring people of *all classes*. . . .

Most Republicans agreed with Blair that the poor whites of the South were oppressed by an aristocracy of slaveholders. "One of the peculiar effects of southern slavery," said the Springfield *Republican,* "is to develop in the white race, and more particularly among the proprietors, the aristocratic feeling, and to destroy the American sentiment of social equality." Carl Schurz declared that despite the democratic forms of southern state government, "the despotic spirit of slavery and mastership combined pervades their whole political life like a liquid poison." All political power in the South, Republicans believed, was controlled by the slaveholders, while the poor whites were victimized by political and social oppression. Congressman Henry Waldron of Michigan insisted that in the slave states "a system of espionage prevails which would disgrace the despotism and darkness of the middle ages." And a New York Congressman told the House that "the *slave-owners,* by their property and political privileges, are made the ruling class in those States." [62]

The Republican critique of the southern aristocracy was presented most fully by William Seward, who throughout his political career had been a foe of special privilege. Seward entered public office through the Anti-Masonic party, which, as Lee Benson and other writers have noted, was a radically egalitarian movement opposed to special privi-

61. Walter B. Stevens, "Lincoln and Missouri," *MoHR,* X (January 1916), 68; Francis P. Blair to Montgomery Blair, September 21, 1856, Blair Family Papers, LC. Cf. Peterson, *Brown,* 72; F. P. Blair to James Watson Webb, August 12, 1858, James Watson Webb Papers, Yale University; *Congressional Globe,* 35 Congress, 1 Session, 1284.
62. Springfield *Republican,* January 9, 1857; Schurz, *Speeches,* 11–12; *Congressional Globe,* 36 Congress, 1 Session, 1872, 35 Congress, 1 Session, Appendix, 242. Cf. *Ohio State Journal,* May 5, 1854; "Where Will It End?," *Atlantic Monthly,* I (December 1857), 247.

lege and dedicated to equal opportunity in the competition for social advancement.[63] As governor of New York, Seward worked to expand public education on the grounds that equal educational opportunity would facilitate the attainment of full social equality. Universal education was "the leveller we must use to prevent wealth and power from building up aristocratic institutions, and dividing society into unequal classes." Seward also recognized the democratizing effects of economic growth, particularly of internal improvements, which opened new areas of the state and nation to the prospect of social advancement. "The highest attainable equality," Seward told the New York legislature in 1839, "is to be accomplished by education and internal improvement, as they distribute among the whole community the advantages of knowledge and wealth." [64]

Southern society, with its aristocracy based on slaveholding, seemed to Seward the direct antithesis of the egalitarian ideals of the North. He described the South as a land where the basic freedoms taken for granted in the North were absent. "There is nowhere in any slaveholding state," he charged, "personal safety for a citizen, even of that state itself, who questions the rightful national domination of the slaveholding class." In speeches in 1855 and 1856 which Richard Henry Dana said struck "the keynote of the new party," Seward condemned the "privileged classes" of the South and summarized his conception of them. Speaking of some northerners' expectations that the South would abolish slavery on its own initiative, Seward asked, "Did any property class ever so reform itself? Did the patricians in old Rome, the noblesse or the clergy in France? The landholders in Ireland? The landed aristocracy in England?" He identified slaveholders with the reactionary aristocracies throughout history which had blocked the progress of political and social reform.[65]

63. Lee Benson, *The Concept of Jacksonian Democracy* (Princeton, 1961), 11–12, 17–20; David Brion Davis, "Some Themes of Counter-Subversion: An Analysis of Anti-Masonic, Anti-Catholic, and Anti-Mormon Literature," *MVHR*, XLVII (September 1960), 208; Charles McCarthy, "The Anti-Masonic Party," *Annual Report* of AHA, 1902, I, 444, 545.
64. Baker, ed., *Seward Works*, III, 209–13, 223, 263; Frederick W. Seward, ed., *Seward at Washington* (2 vols.: New York, 1891), I, 368. Cf. Baker, ed., *Seward Works*, I, 197–98, III, 289; Samuel B. Ruggles to Seward, October 20, 1852, Seward Papers.
65. Baker, ed., *Seward Works*, IV, 258, 268, 272, 291; Charles Francis Adams, *Richard Henry Dana* (2 vols.: Boston, 1891), I, 348.

IV

The free labor image of North and South did not, of course, go unchallenged during the 1850's. It was during this period that the activity of the pro-slavery theorists reached its peak, and in fact the Republican defense of the northern social order and their glorification of free labor were in part a response to the attacks of these same writers, especially George Fitzhugh. Many Republican leaders were well versed in the literature of the pro-slavery argument. Lincoln's law partner William Herndon, for example, subscribed to the Charleston *Mercury* and Richmond *Enquirer*, and, according to Fitzhugh's biographer, Lincoln studied *Sociology for the South* very carefully. Republican spokesmen in Congress often quoted from the works of Fitzhugh and from the southern press.[66] The pro-slavery writers insisted that in free society labor and capital were in constant antagonism, and that as a result the laborer was insecure and helpless. They denied that any real social mobility or harmony of interests existed in the North. In his famous "mud-sill" speech, South Carolina's Senator James Hammond declared that in all social systems "there must be a class to do the mean duties, to perform the drudgeries of life," and Fitzhugh divided northern society into four classes: the rich, the highly skilled professionals, the poor thieves, and "the poor hardworking people, who support everybody, and starve themselves." For this last class there was no hope of advancement—not one in a hundred, as South Carolina's Chancellor Harper said, could hope to improve his condition. For all practical purposes, according to pro-slavery writers, slavery existed in the North as well as in the South. As Hammond put it, "Your whole class of manual laborers and operatives, as you call them, are slaves." [67]

The pro-slavery argument was not merely a defense or rationalization of slavery. It was also a critique of northern society, and especially

66. Emanuel Hertz, ed., *The Hidden Lincoln* (New York, 1938), 96–97; Harvey Wish, *George Fitzhugh, Propagandist of the Old South* (Baton Rouge, 1943), 146, 155–57; *Congressional Globe*, 34 Congress, 1 Session, Appendix, 954, 36 Congress, 1 Session, 1873, Appendix, 375; Boston *Commonwealth*, September 9, 1854; *How Ought Workingmen to Vote in the Coming Election? Speech of Hon. Henry Wilson, at East Boston, October 15, 1860* (Boston, 1860), 5.
67. *Congressional Globe*, 35 Congress, 1 Session, 962; George Fitzhugh, *Cannibals All!*, ed., C. Vann Woodward (Cambridge, 1960), 16–20, 32–38; *The Pro-Slavery Argument* (Charleston, 1852), 47. Cf. William S. Jenkins, *Pro-Slavery Thought in the Old South* (Chapel Hill, 1935), 296–97.

of its materialism and individualism. In Fitzhugh's analysis, the cause of the North's social problems was the "whole moral code of Free Society," which he summed up as "every man for himself." Free competition, lauded by the classical economists and advocates of the self-made man, was the means by which capital exercised its mastery over labor. It fostered selfishness and greed, arraying the two classes against one another in unceasing combat. Fitzhugh recognized that the free land of the West did give northern society a respite from the severe social problems faced by European societies as they experienced industrialization, but he argued that this would last only "until the Northwest is peopled." Then a rigidly stratified class society would take shape in the North, in an even more brutal form than existed in Europe, since in the free states "free competition" was "more active than in any other country." In place of the acquisitive materialism of the North, Fitzhugh held up the patriarchal values of the South, with their stress on the responsibilities of the planter to the entire community, as the model of social ethics.[68]

It was relatively easy for Republicans to respond to southern charges that northern laborers had no opportunities for social mobility, and were in reality little better off than slaves. The southern attack on northern materialism was more difficult. Several historians have recently suggested that many ante-bellum northerners were themselves disturbed by the increasing materialism and selfishness of their emergent capitalist society, and turned in admiration to the gentility and ease of the southern aristocracy.[69] There is no question that some Republicans, particularly upper-class conservatives, looked favorably upon the southern character. Richard Henry Dana of Boston, for example, admired the aristocrats of both North and South, and wrote his wife after a visit to Virginia that he had been favorably impressed by the "true gentility" of the slaveholders and the "patriarchal side" of slavery. He even told a Free Soil audience in 1848 that they should avoid expressions of hostility toward the South because "there is much to admire in the Southern character; there are some points in

68. George Fitzhugh, *Sociology for the South: or the Failure of Free Society* (Richmond, 1854), 22–24, 201, 250–51; Fitzhugh, *Cannibals All!*, xxvi, 23, 40; *Pro-Slavery Argument*, 30–31.
69. William R. Taylor, *Cavalier and Yankee* (New York, 1961), 18, 95–97, 146, 333–35; Marvin Meyers, *The Jacksonian Persuasion* (New York, 1960 ed.), 81, 90; Fred Somkin, *Unquiet Eagle: Memory and Desire in the Idea of American Freedom, 1815–1860* (Ithaca, 1967), 21, 24; John C. Cawelti, *Apostles of the Self-Made Man* (Chicago, 1965), 51.

which it is superior to our own." Young John A. Kasson had similar reactions when he visited Virginia in the 1840's, and even William Cullen Bryant wrote friendly reports about southern life in the 1840's, praising the civility and manners of the aristocracy and their genteel charm.[70]

Nevertheless, it is difficult to agree with such writers as William R. Taylor that "everywhere" in the North there were reservations about the rise of capitalism and the materialistic values which went with it, and that as a result northerners indicated their preference for the genteel aristocrat over the predatory businessman. It may be that such intellectuals as Cooper, Paulding, and others felt that economic developments were destroying the spiritual values of the old republic, but this is hardly to say that such fears were shared by the majority of northerners. The very word "aristocracy," the New York *Tribune* observed, had "rather a bad sound" to northerners, and one political observer claimed in 1856 that "the aristocractic element of the slave power is the one that has made us a hundred votes, where the moral question has given us one."[71] The Republicans saw no conflict between personal acquisitiveness and social progress—indeed, they assumed for the most part that the two were intimately related. In the North, said George Boutwell of Massachusetts, "every man is interested in adding as much as possible to his own wealth, and therefore interested in adding as much as possible to the wealth of the community." The Republicans accepted the value-system of their bourgeois culture and viewed the South's aristocrats with a mixture of fear and contempt. "Of what use is your idle aristocracy," Ben Wade asked in 1858. ". . . What does your drone, your refined aristocrat, do in his mind? . . . He consumes the products of labor; he is idle . . . He never invents." In the eyes of Republicans, the morals and manners of slaveholders reflected the fact that they were, as Israel Washburn said, "removed from the necessity to labor," and ruled tyrannically

70. Adams, *Dana*, I, 108–9; Samuel Shapiro, *Richard Henry Dana, Jr. 1815–1882* (East Lansing, 1961), 33–34; Floan, *South*, 76, 149–55; Edward Younger, *John A. Kasson* (Iowa City, 1955), 32–35; Edward Younger, ed., "A Yankee Reports on Virginia, 1842–1843. Letters of John Adam Kasson," *VaMHB*, LV (October 1948), 419–21; Howard R. Floan, "The New York *Evening Post* and the Ante-Bellum South," *AMQ*, VIII (Fall 1956), 246–47; Parke Godwin, *A Biography of William Cullen Bryant* (2 vols.: New York, 1883), I, 407–8.
71. Taylor, *Cavalier and Yankee*, 130; New York *Tribune*, April 29, 1856; Sarah Forbes Hughes, ed., *Reminiscences of John Murray Forbes* (3 vols.: Boston, 1902), II, 69–70. Cf. Sarah Forbes Hughes, ed., *Letters (Supplementary) of John Murray Forbes* (3 vols.: Boston, 1905), I, 168.

over a subject population. Slavery, said George William Curtis, fostered "pride, indolence, luxury, and licentiousness. . . . Manners are fantastic and fierce; brute force supplants moral principle . . . a sensitive vanity is called honor, and cowardly swagger, chivalry." [72] Even Republican conservatives like the Philadelphia writer Sidney G. Fisher, who admired the "ease, enjoyment, and leisure" of the South, believed that the North was superior "in everything that constitutes civilization." Most Republicans probably agreed with the stronger language of a Wisconsin voter who wrote his Congressman, "They are a set of cowards, full of gasconade, and bad liquor, brought up to abuse negroes and despise the north, too lazy to work; they are not above living on the unrewarded labor of others. . . ." [73] Republicans were too committed to the ideals of free labor to have much admiration for men who, as they saw it, had not gained their exalted social and political status through honest work.[74]

V

"By 1860," William R. Taylor has written, "most Americans had come to look upon their society and culture as divided between a North and a South, a democratic, commercial civilization and an aristocratic, agrarian one." The best known statement of the depth and irreconcilability of the differences between northern and southern society was Seward's "Irrepressible Conflict" speech of 1858. After describing the divergent interests of the sections, Seward declared:

> Shall I tell you what this collision means? Those who think that it is accidental, unnecessary, the work of interested or fanatical agitators, and therefore ephemeral, mistake the case altogether. It is an irrepressible conflict between opposing and enduring forces, and it means that the United States must and will, sooner or later, be-

72. George S. Boutwell, *Speeches and Papers Relating to the Rebellion and the Overthrow of Slavery* (Boston, 1867), 52; *Congressional Globe*, 35 Congress, 1 Session, 1113, 34 Congress, 1 Session, Appendix, 636; Charles E. Norton, ed., *Orations and Addresses of George William Curtis* (3 vols.: New York, 1894), I, 15–16. Cf. Hildreth, *Despotism*, 142–57; Greeley, *Clay*, 72–74, 119; Cincinnati *Gazette*, August 14, 17, 1858.
73. [Sidney George Fisher], *Kanzas and the Constitution* (Boston, 1856), 3–4; H. B. Evans to John F. Potter, March 8, 1858, John F. Potter Papers, WisHS. Cf. "The Diaries of Sidney George Fisher, 1844–1849," *PaMHB*, LXXXVI (January 1962), 81.
74. "Where Will it End," 242; Chicago *Democratic Press*, April 5, 1854; *Congressional Globe*, 35 Congress, 1 Session, 1113; Julia Griffiths, ed., *Autographs for Freedom* (2nd series: Auburn, 1854), 195–97.

come either entirely a slave-holding nation, or entirely a free-labor
nation. . . .

Seward gave his speech for compelling political reasons, never imagin-
ing that it would cause a political uproar.[75] "There is nothing in the
speech that he has not been saying substantially for the last 15 years,"
a New York politician wrote, and a veteran political abolitionist agreed
that the idea of an irrepressible conflict "was one of the fundamental
principles of our dear old Liberty party. . . ." James S. Pike had
written in the New York *Tribune* of 1856 of the "two opposing civilizations" within the nation, and an Ohio Congressman declared a few
months before Seward's speech that the sectional struggle was "not
between the North and the South . . . but between systems, between
civilizations." It was also in 1858 that the Boston editor William
Schouler declared that there were "two kinds of civilization in this
country. One is the civilization of freedom, and the other is the
civilization of aristocracy, of slavery." [76]

By 1860, the irrepressible conflict idea was firmly imbedded in the
Republican mind. "I regret the facts," Justin Morrill wrote in December, 1860, "but we must accept the truth that there is an 'irrepressible
conflict' between our systems of civilization." [77] Not only the labor
system of the South and its aristocratic social structure, but its entire
way of life seemed alien to the Republicans. Slavery, Seward said in
1860, "is interwoven with all [the South's] social and political interests,
constitutions and customs," and Israel Washburn declared that the
effects of the peculiar institution could be seen in "the manners,
customs, social codes, and moral standards" of the South. Republicans
who came into contact with the South commented upon the feeling
that they were in an alien land. "Here are scenes and modes of life
with which I am not familiar," wrote the Cincinnati *Gazette's* traveling

75. Taylor, *Cavalier and Yankee*, 15; Baker, ed., *Seward Works*, IV, 292. On the
reasons for the speech, see Seward, ed., *Seward*, I, 353; Seward to Robert Carter,
November 7, 1858, Robert Carter Papers, Houghton Library, Harvard University;
Seward to Webb, November 5, 1858, Webb Papers.
76. E. Pershine Smith to Carey, November 4, 1858, Carey Papers; Samuel Harding
to George Julian, November 18, 1860, Giddings-Julian Papers; New York *Tribune*,
June 3, 1856; *Congressional Globe*, 35 Congress, 1 Session, Appendix, 401; Boston
Daily Traveller, clipping, in Charles Francis Adams Diary, October 28, 1858,
Adams Papers. Cf. New York *Tribune*, June 24, 1856, November 9, 1858; Cincin-
nati *Gazette*, November 3, 1858; Godwin, *Political Essays*, 285.
77. Justin S. Morrill to Ruth Morrill, December 7, 1860, Justin S. Morrill Papers,
LC. Cf. *Speech of Hon. O. H. Browning, Delivered at the Republican Mass
Meeting* . . . (Quincy, 1860), 13; Bancroft, ed., *Schurz*, I, 134.

reporter in 1858, and Aaron Cragin, a New Hampshire Congressman, observed after hearing a southern speech, "this language of feudalism and aristocracy has a strange sound to me." Cragin's use of the word "feudalism" in reference to the South is especially revealing, for to many Republicans the slave states seemed relics from a bygone age. "The world is teeming with improved machinery, the combined development of science and art," declared Cassius Clay in 1840. "To us it is all lost; we are comparatively living in centuries that are gone. . . ." [78]

Whether or not the North and South were in reality so different that the idea of an irrepressible conflict between opposing civilizations has historical validity, is still an open question. Eugene Genovese has recently argued that the South was essentially a pre-capitalist society, while other writers have stressed the capitalistic features of the southern economy. There is no doubt, however, that a prominent strain in the ideology of the ante-bellum South—reflected in the pro-slavery critique of northern capitalism—stressed aristocratic values and the virtues of an ordered, hierarchical society. Even Tocqueville and other foreign observers were struck by the division between the aristocratic character of the South and the bourgeois culture of the North.[79] As for the Republicans, whatever their differences on specific political issues and strategies, they were united in their devotion to the mores and values of northern society, and in their conviction of the superiority of the North's civilization to that of the South. "Which constitutes the happiest, the most intelligent, the most prosperous community?" asked David Dudley Field after comparing Virginia and New York; Republicans of all factions would no doubt have agreed on the answer.[80]

78. Baker, ed., *Seward Works*, I, 86; *Congressional Globe*, 34 Congress, 1 Session, Appendix, 637, 1163; Cincinnati *Gazette*, August 23, 1858; Lewis Tappan, *Address to the Non-Slave-Holders of the South, on the Social and Political Evils of Slavery* (London, 1843), 7.

79. Eugene D. Genovese, *The Political Economy of Slavery* (New York, 1965), *passim;* Moore, *Social Origins*, 121–22. According to Tocqueville, southerners had "the tastes, prejudices, weaknesses, and grandeur of every aristocracy," while northerners had "the good and bad qualities characteristic of the middle classes." Tocqueville, *Democracy in America*, 344–45.

80. New York *Tribune*, September 26, 1856. Cf. the statements of the New York *Times* that the North was "a higher and better state of society" than the South (July 22, 1856), and of Congressman Edward Wade, who called the North "the highest order of civilization known to the human race." (*Congressional Globe*, 33 Congress, 1 Session, Appendix, 664.)

The Republicans saw their anti-slavery program as one part of a world-wide movement from absolutism to democracy, aristocracy to equality, backwardness to modernity, and their conviction that the struggle in the United States had international implications did much to strengthen their resolve. They accepted the characteristic American vision of the United States as an example to the world of the social and political benefits of democracy, yet believed that so long as slavery existed, the national purpose of promoting liberty in other lands could not be fulfilled. Lincoln declared in 1854 that slavery "deprives our republican example of its just influence in the world—enables the enemies of free institutions to taunt us as hypocrites," and Charles Sumner agreed that the institution "degrades our country, and prevents its example from being all-conquering." [81] William Seward believed that the spread of American economic influence would be accompanied by the export of America's egalitarian political institutions. The nation, he wrote, had a mission and responsibility "to renovate the condition of mankind" by proving at home that the "experiment in self-government" could succeed, and by aiding abroad "the universal restoration of power to the governed." Just as slavery stood in the way of achieving the nation's imperial destiny, so it interfered with the nation's mission of spreading democracy.[82] Yet as they looked at the world around them, Republicans could not but be confident that they were on the side of history. Carl Schurz captured this outlook in 1860 when he said:

> Slaveholders of America, I appeal to you. Are you really in earnest when you speak of perpetuating slavery? Shall it never cease? Never? Stop and consider where you are and in what day you live. . . . This is the world of the nineteenth century. . . . You stand against a hopeful world, alone against a great century, fighting your hopeless fight . . . against the onward march of civilization. . . .

The Republicans were confident that in the sectional struggle, which one newspaper summarized as a contest between "Northern Progress and Southern Decadence," southern civilization must give way before the onslaught of the modern world.[83]

81. Basler, ed., *Lincoln Works*, II, 255; Sumner to Francis Bird, September 11, 1857, Francis Bird Papers, Houghton Library, Harvard University.
82. Baker, ed., *Seward Works*, III, 292–93; V, 221, 228. Cf. III, 23, 132, 504.
83. Frederic Bancroft, ed., *Speeches, Correspondence, and Political Papers of Carl Schurz* (6 vols.: New York, 1913), I, 156–58; Chicago *Democratic Press*, May 2, 1857.

3

Salmon P. Chase:

THE CONSTITUTION

AND THE SLAVE POWER

The American anti-slavery movement, which began as a moral crusade, eventually found that it would have to turn to politics to achieve its goals. "The question of slavery in the United States is a political question," an Ohio editor observed in 1837; "Its character is mistaken by most abolitionists. . . ."[1] Although the transition was painful for many anti-slavery men, the movement turned almost entirely to political action in the 1840's and 1850's. No anti-slavery leader was more responsible for the success of this transformation, and none did more to formulate an anti-slavery program in political terms than Salmon P. Chase of Ohio. Chase developed an interpretation of American history which convinced thousands of northerners that anti-slavery was the intended policy of the founders of the nation, and was fully compatible with the Constitution. He helped develop the idea that southern slaveholders, organized politically as a Slave Power, were conspiring to dominate the national government, reverse the policy of the founding fathers, and make slavery the ruling interest of the republic. Even his political enemies agreed that Chase was a tireless political organizer, who commanded the anti-slavery forces in Congress in the early 1850's, and made countless speeches designed for mass consumption outlining his political program.[2] The effect of his views

1. L. Belle Hamlin, ed., "Selections from the Follett Papers," *Quarterly Publications* of the Ohio Historical and Philosophical Society, XI (January–March 1916), 11–15.
2. J. W. Schuckers, *The Life and Public Services of Salmon Portland Chase* (New York, 1874), 164–70n.; "Diary and Correspondence of Salmon P. Chase," *Annual Report* of AHA, 1902, II. 207; F. D. Parish to Chase, November 5, 1855, Salmon P. Chase Papers, HSPa; Edward L. Pierce, *Memoir and Letters of Charles Sumner* (4 vols.: Boston, 1893), III, 352n.; *Ohio State Journal*, July 25, 1848; Sandusky *Journal*, cited in Cincinnati *Gazette*, June 23, 1855.

on northern public opinion was widely acknowledged in the 1850's, and at his death in 1873 the New York *Tribune* observed, "To Mr. Chase more than any other one man belongs the credit of making the anti-slavery feeling, what it had never been before, a power in politics. It had been the sentiment of philanthropists; he made it the inspiration of a great political party." [3]

Chase came to the anti-slavery movement in the 1830's, at a time when the constitutional relations of slavery were becoming a subject of increasing national concern. Reformers like Henry B. Stanton and Theodore Weld were drafting the legal case to support abolitionist demands for an end to slavery in the nation's capital, while southerners adopted the position of John C. Calhoun, that the national government was obliged to defend slavery and that abolition in the District of Columbia would be an intolerable injury to the slave system. Some abolitionists—primarily the Garrisonian group—accepted the southern contention that the Constitution recognized and protected slavery, but Weld, Stanton, William Goodell, Senator Thomas Morris of Ohio, and others insisted that the institution was a creature of local law, which could not exist outside the jurisdiction which had created it. [4] In Cincinnati, where Chase practiced law, James G. Birney elaborated similar ideas in his newspaper, the *Philanthropist*, early in 1836. It was the mob attack on Birney's press later that year which brought Chase into the abolitionist camp. [5] Chase took an active part in the editor's defense, and the two struck up a close personal friendship. According to Birney's son, his father and Chase discussed the constitutional status of slavery many times in 1836 and 1837; when Chase defended a runaway slave, Matilda, in 1837, he based his case on Birney's arguments. His legal position, Chase recalled a few years later, was "treated with ridicule or disregard," but within a decade it had been widely accepted in the anti-slavery movement—and by a number of northern judges. One

3. New York *Tribune*, May 8, 1873.
4. [Theodore D. Weld], *The Power of Congress Over the District of Columbia* (New York, 1838); B. F. Morris, ed., *Life of Thomas Morris* (Cincinnati, 1856), 262, 292; Russel B. Nye, *Fettered Freedom* (East Lansing, 1949), 45–46, 188–91; Arthur H. Rice, "Henry B. Stanton: Political Abolitionist" (unpublished doctoral dissertation, Teachers College, Columbia University, 1967), 89–90; Joshua Giddings, *History of the Rebellion* (New York, 1864), 119ff.; Jacobus tenBroek, *The Antislavery Origins of the Fourteenth Amendment* (Berkeley, 1951), 12–13, 16, 25, 37n.
5. Biographical Sketch, July 10, 1853, Chase to Cincinnati *Gazette*, August 4, 1836, E. W. Chester to Chase, November 9, 1859, Chase Papers, LC; "Cincinnati Mob," Manuscript in Box 17, Chase Papers, HSPa; Schuckers, *Chase*, 39–41.

historian has declared that the anti-slavery interpretation of the Constitution was "a cooperative, evolutionary product," and that Birney deserves the credit for having outlined it most fully in 1836.[6] But after that year it became increasingly identified with Chase because of his greater national prominence, and because of Chase's efforts it eventually came to form the constitutional basis of the Republican party program.

At the core of Chase's interpretation of the Constitution was his description of the founding fathers' intentions regarding slavery.[7] Publicly and privately, Chase insisted, the founders deplored the institution and hoped for its early abolition. They regarded freedom and equality as the natural condition of men, and viewed slavery as a temporary and abnormal state. Chase was able to compile an impressive array of abolitionist statements by the founders, and he included them in countless political addresses in the ante-bellum decades.[8] His most important evidence was the attitude of Thomas Jefferson toward slavery. Jefferson, Chase argued, had set forth the common law and political faith of the United States in the Declaration of Independence, dedicating the new nation to the inviolability of personal liberty. By his anti-slavery activities in Virginia and his authorship of the Northwest Ordinance, which barred slavery from all the original territories of the United States, Jefferson demonstrated his hope that the institution would die out. According to Chase, Jefferson planned to prevent the extension of slavery, to mitigate its excesses, and finally to secure abolition by the action of the individual states.[9]

6. Betty Fladeland, *James Gillespie Birney: Slaveholder to Abolitionist* (Ithaca, 1955), 148–49, 152; William Birney, *James G. Birney and His Times* (New York, 1890), 231–34, 259–60; Chase to Charles D. Cleveland, May 18, 1841, Chase Papers, HSPa; Howard J. Graham, "The Early Antislavery Background of the Fourteenth Amendment," *Wisconsin Law Review*, 1950, 638–41. Cf. Chase to Alvan Stewart, May 24, 1841, Miscellaneous Manuscripts, NYHS.

7. Chase's views on the constitutional relations of slavery remained relatively constant throughout his career. His friendly critic Gerrit Smith observed in 1856, "from first to last, you have held the same opinions in regard to the State and National powers over slavery." Because of his consistency, Chase's opinions are examined here without regard to chronology, drawing on speeches and writings throughout the ante-bellum years. Smith to Chase, March 1, 1856, Chase Papers, HSPa. Cf. Chase to Smith, November 23, 1849, Biographical Sketch, July 10, 1853, Chase Papers, LC; "Diary and Correspondence," 289.

8. Salmon P. Chase and Charles D. Cleveland, *Antislavery Addresses of 1844 and 1845* (London, 1867), 88–94; *Congressional Globe*, 31 Congress, 1 Session, Appendix, 468–80; *Liberty or Slavery? Daniel O'Connell on American Slavery. Reply to O'Connell by S. P. Chase* . . . (Washington, 1863), 12.

9. S. P. Chase, *An Argument for the Defendant, Submitted to the Supreme Court*

In view of their anti-slavery convictions, Chase insisted, the founders would hardly have been likely to incorporate any protection for slavery into the Constitution. On the contrary, "the solemn pledge given in the Declaration of Independence" was freshly remembered by the Convention of 1787, and the framers took great care to omit any mention of slavery from the document they drew up. Even the three-fifths and fugitive slave clauses spoke in terms of "persons," carefully avoiding the word "slave." Viewing slavery as a violation of natural right and common law, they made certain that the federal government would have nothing to do with its support. They did not abolish it altogether, because they wished to limit the powers of the federal government, and they lacked the example of "the splendid West Indian experiment" of 1833 which proved, Chase believed, that speedy emancipation was feasible. Nevertheless, "their policy was one of repression, limitation, discouragement; they anticipated with confidence the auspicious result of universal freedom." [10]

Chase's interpretation of the Constitution was summed up in the first Liberty party address he composed, in December, 1841: "The Constitution found slavery and left it a State institution—the creature and dependent of State law—wholly local in its existence and character. It did not make it a national institution." According to the Constitution, Chase maintained, all men must be treated as "persons" by the federal government. The Fifth Amendment, which barred Congress from depriving any "person" of "life, liberty, or property" without due process of law, was intended, in Chase's view, to prevent the national government from sanctioning slavery anywhere within its exclusive jurisdiction. The federal government "cannot create or continue the relation of master and slave," he insisted, and therefore whenever a slave came into an area of federal authority, he automatically became free. Slavery in the District of Columbia, in the national territories, on the high seas, or anywhere outside the slave states, was unconstitutional because of the Fifth Amendment. Congress could, of course, strengthen its commitment to freedom by abolishing slavery in the District and territories, but it could neither establish nor tolerate slavery there.

of the United States, at the December Term, 1846, in the Case of Wharton Jones vs John Vanzandt (Cincinnati, 1847), 77; Chase to F. W. Bird, et al., March 29, 1859, Chase Papers, HSPa; Schuckers, Chase, 48; Chase and Cleveland, Anti-slavery Addresses, 79.
10. Schuckers, Chase, 48–49; Chase, Vanzandt Argument, 78–79; Liberty or Slavery, 10; "Lecture on Slavery—Delivered in Boston winter 1854-5," Manuscript, Box 17, Chase Papers, HSPa; Inaugural Address of Salmon P. Chase (Columbus, 1856), 10–11.

"The very moment a slave passes beyond the jurisdiction of the state, . . . he ceases to be a slave; not because any law or regulation of the state which he enters confers freedom upon him, but because he *continues* to be a man and *leaves behind* him the law of force, which made him a slave." [11]

If slavery was a creature of local law, and a slave became free when he left the slave states, what became of the constitutional obligation to return "fugitives from labor" to the South? Chase did not take the extreme position of some anti-slavery men that the fugitive slave clause was a violation of natural law and therefore void, but in the numerous cases which he argued as "attorney general for fugitive slaves," he tried to interpret the clause almost out of existence. The section of the Constitution relating to fugitives, Chase pointed out, differed from other clauses in neglecting to delegate to Congress power to enforce it by appropriate legislation. Since all powers not delegated to the federal government were reserved to the states, Chase insisted that the clause was really a compact between the northern and southern states, and that "each State must judge for itself as to the character of the compact, and the extent of the obligation created by it." The laws of 1793 and 1850 involving the federal government in the capture of fugitives were unconstitutional, since Congress had no power to legislate on the subject. [12] Chase acknowledged that the Constitution did impose an obligation on the free states to return fugitive slaves, but he also recognized that many northerners could not fulfill such a duty "without consciousness of participation in wrong." During the secession crisis he suggested that the North might agree to pay compensation for fugitive slaves instead of returning them. [13]

---

11. Schuckers, *Chase*, 48–49; Chase to Lewis Tappan, March 18, 1847, Chase Papers, LC; Chase and Cleveland, *Antislavery Addresses*, 83–87; "Diary and Correspondence," 133; Robert B. Warden, *An Account of the Life and Public Services of Salmon Portland Chase* (Cincinnati, 1874), 298–99; *Politics in Ohio. Senator Chase's Letters to Hon. A. P. Edgerton* (np, 1853), 8; *Congressional Globe*, 33 Congress, 1 Session, 421.

12. *Congressional Globe*, 31 Congress, 1 Session, Appendix, 476–77, 2 Session, Appendix, 309, 32 Congress, 1 Session, Appendix, 1121; Chase, *Vanzandt Argument*, 102–4, 75; Chase to Charles Morehead, May 4, 1856, Chase Papers, LC; *The Address and Reply on the Presentation of a Testimonial to S. P. Chase, by the Colored People of Cincinnati* (Cincinnati, 1845), 4–10; *Speech of Salmon P. Chase, in the Case of the Colored Woman, Matilda* (Cincinnati, 1837), 19–22; Chase to J. F. Morse, December 12, 1850, Chase Papers, LC.

13. L. E. Chittenden, *A Report of the Debates and Proceedings in the Secret Sessions of the Conference Convention . . .* (New York, 1864), 430–31; John Albree ed., *Whittier Correspondence From the Oak Knoll Collection 1830–1892* (Salem, 1911), 137–38; Warden, *Chase*, 367; "Diary and Correspondence," 293.

When Chase joined the Liberty party in 1841, it was composed of only a handful of abolitionists. Founded in 1839 by a group of New York anti-slavery men who recognized that the tactics of moral suasion and questioning candidates of the major parties had failed to produce tangible results, the party polled only 7,000 votes for its first presidential candidate, James G. Birney. Chase himself cast his ballot for William Henry Harrison in 1840. But he soon became disgusted with the major parties' neglect of the slavery issue, and by the end of 1841 he had fully identified himself with the abolition party. When the first Ohio State Liberty Convention met in December, Chase was given the task of writing the platform and address to the citizens of Ohio.[14] But he soon found that his conception of an effective political program differed sharply from that of other Liberty party leaders, particularly those who had organized the party in the East. For the Liberty party had been created more as a religious crusade than as a political party. Its first address, written by the New Yorker Alvan Stewart, denounced slavery in strong religious and moral terms, and demanded its immediate destruction as a crime against man and God. The Bible was the political textbook of the party and its organizers said they intended to bring Christian ethics into government. Throughout the North, ministers played a leading role in spreading the Liberty party faith, Liberty party tickets were often prefaced with quotations from Scripture, and a number of Liberty conventions adopted lengthy resolutions on the Biblical reasons for abolishing slavery. As one western Liberty leader wrote, "the truth is, that most of our leaders and political speakers have been and are *ministers*—not statesmen or politicians." [15]

Chase himself was a deeply religious man. As a youth he had lived for several years with his uncle, the Episcopalian bishop of Ohio. Chase read the Bible and recited psalms every morning before breakfast, attended church regularly, admired chastity and disliked drinking, cursing, and the theater. His biographers agree that religious feeling

14. Ralph V. Harlow, *Gerrit Smith, Philanthropist and Reformer* (New York, 1939), 152; Chase to Charles D. Cleveland, August 29, 1840, May 18, 1841, Chase Papers, HSPa; Biographical Sketch, July 10, 1853, Chase Papers, LC.
15. Luther Marsh, ed., *Writings and Speeches of Alvan Stewart on Slavery* (New York, 1860), 234–47; Dwight L. Dumond, ed., *Letters of James G. Birney 1831–1857* (2 vols.: New York, 1937), I, ix–x, II, 733, 1009. Cf. Joseph G. Rayback, "The Liberty Party Leaders of Ohio: Exponents of Antislavery Coalition," *OAHQ*, LVII (1948), 174; William Goodell, *Slavery and Antislavery* (New York, 1855), 472; John R. Hendricks, "The Liberty Party in New York State, 1838–1848" (unpublished doctoral dissertation, Fordham University, 1959), 118–48.

lay at the root of his anti-slavery convictions, and in the 1850's, like other radicals, he strove to keep the moral wrong of slavery a leading concern of the Republican party. It was Chase who added the final clauses to Lincoln's Emancipation Proclamation, asking the blessing of God for the great enterprise.[16] But Chase was also a shrewd politician. He realized that to win votes, the Liberty party would have to speak in political terms to the northern electorate and propose a program more precise than an abstract commitment to abolition. He also knew that many northerners believed—as he himself did—that federal interference with slavery in the states would be entirely unconstitutional, and that the Liberty party would have to devise a constitutional way in which to attack slavery. Chase therefore deplored the resolution of a New York Liberty meeting urging the slaves to run away from their masters, taking with them what food and clothing they needed. He also criticized the resolution adopted by the national Liberty convention in 1843, declaring the fugitive slave clause of the Constitution null and void.[17] Such statements might have an appeal to religious abolitionists, but the mass of northern voters found them incendiary and the actions proposed illegal.

Because of his eagerness to work in the Liberty party and his legal ability and prominence, Chase was chosen to write most of the important Ohio and national Liberty platforms and addresses. Through them, he developed a purely political approach for the party to follow. Without abandoning the goal of eventual abolition, Chase shifted the immediate attention of the Liberty party to all the places where slavery could constitutionally be reached and challenged by the federal government—the District of Columbia, the territories, the interstate slave trade, and the fugitive slave law. He coined the phrase "the absolute and unconditional divorce of the Government from slavery," which meant abolition wherever the federal government had the power to accomplish it, the admission of no more slave states, and the expulsion

16. Schuckers, *Chase*, 595–99, 610, Warden, *Chase*, 118, 188–90, 206, 279, 288–90; Chase Diary, February 21, 1836, April 30, 1843, and 1840 *passim*, Chase Papers, LC; Donn Piatt, *Memories of Men Who Saved the Union* (New York, 1887), 99; Albert B. Hart, *Salmon Portland Chase* (Boston, 1899), 53; N. S. Townshend, "Salmon P. Chase," *OAHQ*, I (June 1887), 116.

17. "Diary and Correspondence," 463; Kirk H. Porter and Donald B. Johnson, comps., *National Party Platforms 1840–1856* (Urbana, 1956), 8; *Congressional Globe*, 31 Congress, 1 Session, Appendix, 83; unidentified news clipping, October, 1848, Scrapbook, Chase Papers, LC; Margaret L. Plunkett, "A History of the Liberty Party With Emphasis on Its Activities in the Northeastern States" (unpublished doctoral dissertation, Cornell University, 1930), 123–24.

of slaveholders from control of the government. As this had been the intention of the founding fathers, it became the political program of the Liberty party. "It was his pen and influence," an anti-slavery newspaper said of Chase, "which gave body and popular consistency to the doctrines of the Liberty party." [18]

Chase also did what he could to cleanse the Liberty party of the taint of extremism. Though he never denied that the party's ultimate goal was the extinction of slavery, he took great pains to differentiate between moral and political anti-slavery action—or, more precisely, between abolition and anti-slavery. "Abolition," he wrote to Thaddeus Stevens in 1842, "seeks to abolish slavery everywhere. The means which it employs correspond with the object to be effected—they are of a moral nature—argument, persuasion, remonstrance and the like." Abolitionists' aims "cannot be effected by political power." But anti-slavery aimed at the separation of the federal government from slavery, and its deliverance from control by the Slave Power. As a result, "while abolition is not properly speaking a political object, antislavery is." Chase even suggested that the Liberty party publicly disown the label abolitionist, but eastern leaders would not hear of it. "In the first place," Joshua Leavitt complained to Chase, "I *am* an abolitionist, and expect to be one . . . until slavery is actually abolished." He went on to point out that there would be more abolitionists alienated by such a disavowal than non-abolitionists who would be convinced.[19]

As part of his efforts to broaden the Liberty party's political base, Chase tried to attract anti-slavery men from the two major parties to the Liberty standard. William H. Seward, Joshua Giddings, Thaddeus Stevens and others were approached, but all held aloof. Chase was also behind the unsuccessful attempt to substitute Seward or John Quincy Adams for Birney as the party's presidential candidate in 1844. But he did succeed in organizing the Southern and Western Liberty

18. Hart, *Chase,* 66; Theodore C. Smith, *The Liberty and Free Soil Parties in the Northwest* (New York, 1897), 88; Wm. G. Lewis, *Biography of Samuel Lewis* (Cincinnati, 1857), 286, 311; Chase and Cleveland, *Antislavery Addresses,* 96, 100; Porter and Johnson, comps., *Party Platforms,* 4–5; "Diary and Correspondence," 184–85; Bangor *Platform,* March 6, 1849, clipping, Scrapbook, Chase Papers, LC. Cf. Henry Wilson, *History of the Rise and Fall of the Slave Power in America* (3 vols.: Boston, 1875–77), II, 167.

19. Chase and Cleveland, *Antislavery Addresses,* 108; Chase Diary, June 26, 1843, Chase to H. B. Stanton and Elizur Wright, September 23, 1845, news clipping, Scrapbook, Chase to Charles D. Cleveland, October 22, 1841, Chase Papers, LC; Chase to Thaddeus Stevens, April 8, 1842, Thaddeus Stevens Papers, LC; Joshua Leavitt to Chase, December 6, 1841, Chase Papers, HSPa.

Convention, which met in Cincinnati in 1845 and attracted anti-slavery Whigs and Democrats as well as Liberty men. Chase was looking forward to a new anti-slavery coalition, such as that created in the Free Soil party in 1848, and he continued to urge that the Liberty party not demand that all its members adhere to the doctrine of immediate emancipation.[20]

Chase's efforts to have the Liberty party "disengage itself from the narrower ground it has occupied in some of the states" met with derision from most of the older Liberty leaders. True, Lewis Tappan assured the Ohioan that his program was "an improvement on the principles of the Eastern Liberty Parties," and said he hoped the whole party could adopt them. Seward expressed his pleasure that the address of the Ohio Liberty party had placed anti-slavery on "popular ground" and told Thurlow Weed that Chase was "the one wise man of his faction," adding, "We must cherish him." [21] But Birney complained that Chase's addresses dealt with the slavery issue "so little as a matter of religious duty," and Birney's son and Tappan both charged that Chase valued immediate success more than the principles of the movement. Chase's efforts to displace Birney struck eastern leaders as an insult to a seasoned anti-slavery veteran by a "raw recruit" and like Birney, they insisted that moral issues and not political arguments remain paramount in the party's addresses. Gerrit Smith advised Chase to spend more time informing the public about "the horrors of the great Southern Prison House," and said he would feel distinctly out of place in an Ohio Liberty Convention. "In this section," he observed, "a Liberty party convention is an abolition convention, and an Abolition convention a Liberty party convention." [22]

In state campaigns in the 1840's, eastern Liberty parties continued

20. Chase to Giddings, December 30, 1841, Joshua Reed Giddings Papers, OHS; George W. Julian, *The Life of Joshua R. Giddings* (Chicago, 1892), 131; Fladeland, *Birney*, 216–17; Raybeck, "Ohio Liberty Leaders," 170, 173; Dumond, ed., *Birney Letters*, II, 661, 756; H. W. King to Chase, April 26, 1845, Chase Papers, HSPa; Joel Goldfarb, "The Life of Gamaliel Bailey Prior to the Founding of the *National Era*; the orientation of a Practical Abolitionist" (unpublished doctoral dissertation, University of California at Los Angeles, 1958), 260, 268–77.
21. Chase to Lewis Tappan, September 15, 1842, Chase Papers, LC; Lewis Tappan to Chase, March 18, June 7, 1842, Chase Papers, HSPa; William H. Seward to Thurlow Weed, September 8, 1846, Thurlow Weed Papers, Rush Rhees Library, University of Rochester.
22. "Diary and Correspondence," 470; Dumond, ed., *Birney*, II, 673, 699, 732, 877, 892; Leavitt to Chase, January 29, 1842, February 16, 1843, December 31, 1844, Chase Papers, HSPa; Gerrit Smith to Chase, May 31, 1842, Letterbook, Gerrit Smith Papers; Syracuse University.

to stress moral appeals and full abolition. Perhaps this was why, as Lee Benson suggests, the party succeeded only in enticing abolitionists out of the major parties, rather than convincing those who were mildly anti-slavery to become abolitionists. But in the West the party generally adopted Chase's program, and its national platforms of 1844 and 1847, written largely by him, stressed the return of national policy to that of the founders—the divorce of the federal government from slavery and an end to the rule of the Slave Power—as the party's goals.[23] Moreover, as the slavery controversy was injected into politics in the 1840's, more and more anti-slavery men in the major parties adopted Chase's constitutional outlook. Joshua Giddings was expelled from the House of Representatives in 1842 for suggesting that slavery was a local institution with which the federal government could have no connection. He then published an influential series of articles analyzing the political aspects of slavery which stressed the local-law constitutional interpretation.[24] At the same time, the Conscience Whigs of Massachusetts, led by Charles Francis Adams, were developing the same legal position. Adams's report to the state legislature in the Latimer fugitive slave case called for the passage of legislation separating the people of Massachusetts from all connection with slavery. Chase also helped convince other anti-slavery leaders of the correctness of his legal views. John P. Hale, for example, was assured by Chase of the legality of abolition in the District of Columbia, and Sumner, who considered Chase's argument in the Van Zandt fugitive slave case the ablest legal brief ever prepared in the country, took from Chase's writings the arguments with which he condemned the fugitive slave law a few years later in the Senate.[25]

23. Hendricks, "Liberty Party," 118, 148; Lee Benson, The Concept of Jacksonian Democracy (Princeton, 1961), 113; Dumond, Birney Letters, II, 794, Plunkett, "Liberty Party," 157; Letter of Gerrit Smith to S. P. Chase on the Unconstitutionality of Every Part of American Slavery (Albany, 1847), 2; Rice, "Stanton," 279–80; Porter and Johnson, comps., Party Platforms, 4–8; Chase and Cleveland, Antislavery Addresses, 99; National Era, November 4, 1847.
24. Julian, Giddings, 118–19, 134, 417, 421–23; Dumond, ed., Birney Letters, II, 688; Richard W. Solberg, "Joshua Giddings, Politician and Idealist" (unpublished doctoral dissertation, University of Chicago, 1952), 151–52, 157, 174–75, 189–94. Cf. Chase to Giddings, February 9, 1843, Giddings-Julian Papers, LC; Giddings to Chase, October 30, 1846, Chase Papers, HSPa.
25. Wilson, Slave Power, I, 481; Martin B. Duberman. Charles Francis Adams 1807–1886 (Boston, 1961), 81–82; Charles Francis Adams to Chase, March 4, 1847, Lewis Tappan to Chase, October 6, 1847, John P. Hale to Chase, June 7, 1848, Theodore Parker to Chase, March 16, 1854, Chase Papers, HSPa; Chase to John P. Hale, June 15, 1848, Hale Papers, NHHS; "Diary and Correspondence,"

Despite his sanguine expectations, no federal court adopted Chase's constitutional interpretation in the ante-bellum years. Nor did Chase ever complete the comprehensive book on the Constitution which he began in 1847.[26] But through his briefs for fugitive slaves and the Liberty and Free Soil platforms and addresses he penned, the basic points of his political outlook became familiar throughout the North. When the major parties divided over the slavery issue in 1847 and 1848, many Conscience Whigs and Barnburner Democrats called for the divorce of the federal government from slavery. Even crusty old John McLean, Chase's choice for the Free Soil nomination in 1848, declared that slavery was a creature of local law, which could not legally exist in the territories, and that therefore the Wilmot Proviso was either unnecessary or redundant—it was already in the Constitution.[27] The Buffalo Free Soil platform of 1848, composed by Chase, restated his constitutional-historical argument that the founders had intended to make slavery a local institution, and that the federal government was barred by the Fifth Amendment from creating the condition of bondage anywhere in its jurisdiction. In the next decade these ideas became standard elements in northern political rhetoric. Chase declared in the Senate, "Freedom is national; slavery only is local and sectional," and "freedom national" became the rallying cry of the Republican party.[28] The slogan expressed the hope of anti-slavery men that the government would once again devote its efforts toward encouraging freedom, both at home and abroad.

Chase's position that Congress lacked constitutional authority to recognize or create slavery anywhere in its jurisdiction was endorsed by the Republican platforms of 1856 and 1860. To be sure, only radical Republicans accepted the full implications of Chase's position

---

134-36; Charles Sumner to Giddings, December 21, 30, 1846, Giddings Papers; David Donald, *Charles Sumner and the Coming of the Civil War* (New York, 1961), 233. Cf. Sumner to Chase, May 4, 1850, Chase Papers, LC; *The Law Reporter*, IX (April 1847), 553.

26. Seward to Smith, March 24, 1847, Smith Papers; Lewis Tappan to Chase, February 24, June 10, 1847, Chase Papers, HSPa; Chase to Tappan, March 4, 1847, Letterbook, Chase Papers, LC.

27. Donald, *Sumner*, 147, 155; "Diary and Correspondence," 130-31; Preston King to Chase, August 16, 1847, John McLean to Chase, December 22, 1847, February 7, 1848, Chase Papers, HSPa; Chase to McLean, January 10, August 2, 3, 4, 1848, John McLean Papers, LC.

28. Porter and Johnson, comps., *Party Platforms*, 13-14; *Congressional Globe*, 31 Congress, 1 Session, Appendix, 474. Cf. Andrew W. Crandall, *The Early History of the Republican Party* (Boston, 1930), 86.

demanding immediate abolition in the District of Columbia, an end
to the interstate slave trade, and condemning the fugitive slave law as
not only unwise, but unconstitutional.[29] Most Republicans held the view
of New York's Hamilton Fish, who said he would not endorse all of
Chase's legal interpretations, especially his denial that Congress was
competent to pass a fugitive slave law. But even these Republicans
adopted Chase's basic views. Almost every Republican believed that it
had been the intention of the founding fathers to restrict slavery and
divorce the federal government from all connection with it. Countless
Republicans cited statements by Washington, Jefferson, and others to
prove that the founders had been abolitionists. By 1860 Charles Sumner
could tell a New York audience that the views of the founders regarding slavery were so well known that he would not bother to quote them.[30]
Indeed, a major reason so many Republicans during the secession crisis
were against the proposed constitutional amendment which would have
guaranteed slavery in the states against federal interference, was their
conviction that it would be unwise to reverse the policy of the founders
and put an explicit recognition of slavery into the Constitution. E. L.
Pierce of Massachusetts declared that the amendment "would introduce
the word *slave* into the Constitution which Mr. Madison would not do,"
and a Vermont Republican said the amendment would "involve a
direct constitutional recognition of slavery for the first time." [31] Finally,
it was an article of faith for Republicans that slavery was a local institution, which could not exist anywhere without positive enabling legislation. At the same time southern spokesmen were claiming that the
Constitution carried slavery into the territories and that only positive
law could *exclude* slavery from a state, Republicans read Justice Mc-
Lean's dissent in the Dred Scott case, stressing the local character of
the peculiar institution, and heard men like John Sherman of Ohio and
Oliver Morton of Indiana declare that this idea was the underlying
principle of the Republican party.[32]

29. Porter and Johnson, comps., *Party Platforms*, 27–28, 32–33; tenBroek, *Anti-
slavery Origins*, 116.
30. E. L. Pierce to Chase, August 3, 1857, Chase Papers, LC; New York *Tribune*,
July 12, 1860; *Congressional Globe*, 34 Congress, 1 Session, Appendix, 470, 1078,
35 Congress, 1 Session, 342–44, Appendix, 274, 36 Congress, 1 Session, 731,
1855, 1871, 1905.
31. E. L. Pierce to Charles Sumner, December 31, 1860, Charles Sumner
Papers, Houghton Library, Harvard University; Chittenden, ed., *Peace Conference
Proceedings*, 255. Cf. Charles Francis Adams Diary, December 12, 1860, Adams
Papers, MHS.
32. Arthur E. Bestor, "The American Civil War as a Constitutional Crisis," *AHR*.

Recent interpretations of the intentions of the founding fathers regarding slavery have lent support to many of Chase's ideas. There is no question that the founders abhorred slavery, and intentionally avoided using the words "slave" and "slavery" when they drew up the Constitution. At the same time, most of the founders were unwilling to disturb property rights in slaves, and could not envision a society in which blacks and whites lived together as equals. Their commitment to emancipation was a hesitant and ambiguous one, not the out-and-out abolitionism which Chase described.[33] And there is no evidence that the Fifth Amendment was intended as a prohibition of the existence of slavery anywhere within the national jurisdiction. The flaws in Chase's reasoning were certainly as apparent in the 1840's and 1850's as they are today, yet his views received wide acceptance in the North. For if his arguments were legally less convincing than the southern and Garrisonian view that the Constitution recognized slavery, they were politically and tactically far superior. "The constitution," Chase wrote to Giddings in 1842, "must be vindicated from the reproach of sanctioning the doctrine of property in men." For this was an age which cared deeply about constitutional interpretation, and regarded the Constitution as the embodiment of legal wisdom. Congressman Jonathan Bingham later recalled that "everything was reduced to a Constitutional question, in those days," and the journalist Donn Piatt observed that northerners had to be convinced that the "guarantees" of the Constitution were "for freedom and not for slavery" before they would support the anti-slavery cause.[34] This made all the more important Chase's efforts to replace the Garrisonian concept of a pro-slavery Constitution with that of a document which, when

LXIX (January 1964), 350–51; Cincinnati *Gazette*, March 6, 1857; William M. French, ed., *Life, Speeches, State Papers, and Public Services of Gov. Oliver P. Morton* (Cincinnati, 1866), 83; *The Republican Party—Its History and Policy. A Speech by Hon. John Sherman of Ohio* (np, 1860), 1–2. Cf. *Congressional Globe*, 34 Congress, 1 Session, Appendix, 378, 938, 35 Congress, 1 Session, Appendix, 87–89, 36 Congress, 1 Session, 39; New York *Tribune*, January 7, 1857; New York *Times*, July 11, 1860.

33. Don B. Kates, Jr., "Abolition, Deportation, Integration: Attitudes Toward Slavery in the Early Republic," *JNH*, LIII (January 1968), 33–40; Staughton Lynd, "The Abolitionist Critique of the United States Constitution," in Martin Duberman, ed., *The Antislavery Vanguard* (Princeton, 1965), 215, 238; Winthrop D. Jordan, *White Over Black* (Chapel Hill, 1968), chs. 8, 12.

34. Chase to Giddings, May 19, 1842, Giddings Papers; Walter G. Shotwell, *Driftwood* (Freeport, N.Y., 1966), 81; Piatt, *Memories*, 136; Robert B. Russel, "Constitutional Doctrines with Regard to Slavery in the Territories," *JSH*, XXXII (November 1966), 486.

properly interpreted, was anti-slavery. The Garrisonian view played right into the hands of the slaveholders; indeed, one Alabama politician advised John C. Calhoun that an abolitionist pamphlet by Wendell Phillips outlining the Garrisonian view of the Constitution could be circulated in the South "to great advantage" if a few paragraphs were left out.[35]

Chase's political program also drew strength and effectiveness from identifying the anti-slavery North with the ideals and sentiments of the founding fathers, and charging the South with a betrayal of these ideals. David B. Davis and Marvin Meyers have pointed out how widespread in mid-nineteenth century America was the sense of reform as a conservative venture, an effort to restore an America which had somehow been lost or subverted. Anti-slavery politicians, even the most moderate, could say with Indiana's Oliver P. Morton, "We want no new views of the Constitution," and could describe their goal as the "historical and conservative" one of restoring the founders' policies. The Cincinnati *Gazette* could assure its readers after one of Chase's speeches: "There is nothing ultra or radical in the speech. Mr. Chase has selected for his exemplars upon the slavery question such men as Washington, Jefferson, Henry and Pinckney." [36]

If the American Civil War can be described in part as a "constitutional crisis," Chase played a leading role in shaping the constitutional position of the anti-slavery North. As George Boutwell later recalled of Chase's interpretation of the fugitive slave law, it was effective because "it satisfied many who wished to oppose the Fugitive Slave Law, and sustain the Constitution at the same time." Those Republicans who viewed the slavery controversy in constitutional terms would agree with Chase that there were "two opposite theories of the constitution" abroad in the land. "Does [the Constitution]," Chase asked, "establish slavery everywhere, outside of Free States, or Liberty everywhere, outside of Slave States? Shall the power it confers be used for the ex-

35. J. Franklin Jameson, ed., "Correspondence of John C. Calhoun," *Annual Report* of AHA, 1899, II, 1143. Cf. Walter M. Merrill, *Against Wind and Tide* (Cambridge, 1963), 206; Irving H. Bartlett, *Wendell Phillips, Brahmin Radical* (Boston, 1961), 119–20.
36. David Brion Davis, "Some Themes of Counter-Subversion: An Analysis of Anti-Masonic, Anti-Catholic, and Anti-Mormon Literature," *MVHR*, XLVII (September 1960), 209; Marvin Meyers, *The Jacksonian Persuasion* (New York, 1960 ed.), 16–17; French, ed., *Morton*, 36, 87; Cincinnati *Gazette*, August 7, 1855. Cf. *Speech of Hon. Salmon P. Chase, Delivered at the Republican Mass Meeting in Cincinnati, August 21, 1855* (Columbus, 1855), 8.

tension and perpetuation, everywhere, of human bondage, or of human freedom?" In a sense, Chase and other Republicans viewed the elections of 1856 and 1860 as constitutional referenda. As Richard Yates, the newly elected governor of Illinois, declared soon after the election of Lincoln, "this verdict has decided that a construction which is favorable to the idea of freedom shall be given to the Constitution, and not a construction favorable to human bondage." [37]

II

Chase's interpretation of the Constitution thus formed the legal basis for the political program which was created by the Liberty party and inherited in large part by the Free Soilers and Republicans. This in itself makes it vital to an understanding of the anti-slavery mind before the Civil War. But Chase's ideas were also intimately linked with another concept, which expressed the fears and resentments of the North toward southern intentions for the nation's future. In 1850, Chase wrote to Charles Sumner that his political outlook could be summarized in three ideas: [38]

> 1. That the original policy of the Government was that of slavery restriction. 2. That under the Constitution Congress cannot establish or maintain slavery in the territories. 3. That the original policy of the Government has been subverted and the Constitution violated for the extension of slavery, and the establishment of the political supremacy of the Slave Power.

Once anti-slavery men accepted the view that the original policy of the government had been overturned, it was an easy step to blame this reversal on a conspiracy of slaveholders, who had captured control of the national government and were determined to use federal power to foster the institution's growth. In order to restore the founders' policies, the Slave Power's hold on the federal government would have to be broken.

According to Chase and other anti-slavery spokesmen, the Slave Power consisted of the 350,000 or so slaveholders of the South—about

37. Bestor, "American Civil War," 327–52; George S. Boutwell, *Reminiscences of Sixty Years in Public Affairs* (2 vols.: New York, 1902), I, 119; *Message of the Governor of Ohio to the Fifty-Third General Assembly* . . . (Columbus, 1858), 38; *Speech of Hon. Richard Yates, Delivered in the Wigwam, at the Springfield Jubilee, November 20, 1860* (np, nd), 3.
38. "Diary and Correspondence," 205.

one per cent of the nation's population and five per cent of the South's. In the words of Charles Sumner, the "animating principle" of the Slave Power was "the perpetuation and extension of Slavery and the advancement of Slaveholders." [39] Within the slave states, these men totally dominated political and social life. Non-slaveholding whites, according to the Republicans, were barred from important offices and opportunities for social advancement, and were deprived of the civil liberties taken for granted in the North. Cassius M. Clay, who had seen his anti-slavery press burned in Kentucky, complained to Chase that the 800,000 non-slaveholders of his native state were "prostrated in all respects" before the 31,000 owners of slaves. And in a widely reprinted speech in 1858, Carl Schurz voiced the opinion that southern white society was divided into two classes: "One class of citizens is accustomed to rule, and the other to obey." [40]

Even worse than its complete domination of southern life, in the eyes of anti-slavery men, was the way in which the Slave Power had gained control of the federal government. George Julian, Gamaliel Bailey and other Republicans pointed out that a large majority of the Presidents, Secretaries of State, Chief Justices, and Congressional committee chairmen since 1789 had been southerners. Chase declared in 1855 that no one in Washington could "fail to observe the immense, not to say over-powering influence, which slavery exerts over almost every act of the Government," and four years later a Republican Congressman from Maine echoed, "The national Government, and every branch of the national Government, is as fully under the control of these few extreme men of the South, as are the slaves on their plantations." [41] Chase explained the pattern of southern control by the fact that southern politicians, whatever their differences on other

39. New York *Times*, October 22, 1860; Julian, *Speeches*, 67–68; *Congressional Globe*, 34 Congress, 1 Session, Appendix, 699; *Summer Works*, II, 77. Horace Greeley limited the Slave Power to the 60,000 male owners of more than ten slaves. New York *Tribune*, June 25, July 1, 1856. Gamaliel Bailey included the families of slaveholders, and said the Slave Power consisted of about two million persons. G. Bailey, *The Record of Sectionalism* (Washington, 1856), 4.
40. Cassius M. Clary to Chase. February 26, 1844. Chase Papers, HSPa; David L. Smiley, *Lion of Whitehall, the Life of Cassius M. Clay* (Madison, 1962), 99; Horace Greeley, ed., *The Writings of Cassius Marcellus Clay* (New York, 1848), 129. Carl Schurz, *Speeches of Carl Schurz* (Philadelphia, 1865), 11–12. Cf. *Ohio State Journal*, May 18, 1854.
41. George Julian, *Speeches on Political Questions* (New York, 1872), 25, 70; Bailey, *Record*, 1–4; *Congressional Globe*, 33 Congress, 2 Session, 877, 34 Congress, 1 Session, Appendix, 700–1, 35 Congress, 2 Session, Appendix, 190, 36 Congress, 1 Session, 1036–37.

matters, were united in serving the interests of slavery. As the New York *Times* put it, they were "held together like the feudal barons of the middle ages by a community of interest and of sentiment, and [act] together always for the promotion of their common ends." The three-fifths clause of the Constitution had increased their power in Congress and the electoral college to the point where they could control the policies of the major parties on slavery. Northern sentiment, meanwhile, was weakened by disunity on the slavery issue and cowardice in the face of southern threats of disunion. The three-fifths clause, Chase wrote in 1845, "has virtually established in the country an aristocracy of slaveholders," so complete had been their success in dominating the government.[42]

In Chase's view, the departure from the founders' policy toward slavery had begun in the earliest years of the republic. The very first Congress altered a report dealing with slavery to suit the South, and before the 1790's had passed, the Constitution had been violated by the passage of a fugitive slave law and by Congressional acceptance of a territorial cession from North Carolina which stipulated that slavery be allowed to exist in the area. Thus slavery and slaveholding were created in areas of national jurisdiction, and the policy of restricting and denationalizing slavery had begun to collapse. This pattern continued in the early years of the nineteenth century, with similar land cessions from other southern states, the purchase of Louisiana and Florida without prohibition of slavery, and finally the Missouri Compromise, which allowed slavery to cross the Mississippi River. The annexation of Texas and the compromise measures of 1850 only compounded these aggressions and solidified the Slave Power's domination.[43] Other Republicans had their own lists of the steps by which the Slave Power had overturned the constitutional limitations on slavery. Giddings stressed that the treaty of 1790 with the Creek Indians involved the government for the first time in the business of catching fugitive slaves, while the Address of the Republican Convention at Pittsburgh in February, 1856, dated the overthrow of the

42. *Congressional Globe*, 31 Congress, 1 Session, Appendix, 473, 479, *Liberty or Slavery?* 12; New York *Times*, June 10, 1856; Chase and Cleveland, *Antislavery Addresses*, 96–97.
43. *Liberty or Slavery?* 12; *Inaugural of Governor Chase*, 12; *Congressional Globe*, 31 Congress, 1 Session, Appendix, 472–73, 33 Congress, 1 Session, Appendix, 138; Chase to ?, March 12, 1854, "Lecture on Slavery—Delivered in Boston winter 1854–5," Manuscript, Box 17, Chase Papers, HSPa.

original policy from the administration of John Tyler. But Republicans agreed that by the 1850's the Slave Power dominated the government and was using it to extend the peculiar institution and impose a new and alien interpretation of the Constitution on the American people.[44]

As is the case with most political slogans, it is difficult to find the first use of the term "Slave Power." The essence of the concept was present in the Missouri debates of 1820, but the term itself and its widespread acceptance seem to have been products of the 1830's. Abolitionists found it effective to blame the South for mob violence directed against their freedom of speech and for Congressional restrictions on the right of petition. It was an easy transition to the idea that the South was plotting to subvert the liberties of northerners, and that either liberty or slavery must perish in the nation. In 1839, the Albany Convention which launched the Liberty party warned that there was no doubt that "the Slave Power is now waging a deliberate and determined war against the liberties of the free states," and a few months later an abolitionist newspaper noted that the term "slaveocracy," which was used as a synonym for "Slave Power," had come into wide use in anti-slavery circles.[45]

Whatever the origin of the phrase, it appears certain that it was Senator Thomas Morris of Ohio who made the idea of a Slave Power familiar to thousands of northerners. Morris was a typical Jacksonian Democrat—a foe of banks, monopolies, and paper money, and a loyal supporter of his party. He was unusual only in his tendency to apply Democratic principles to the slavery issue. In 1838 and 1839, Morris, who had been active in the fight against the Bank and the "Money Power," astounded the Senate and electrified anti-slavery northerners by declaring that a new power, based on slavery, was threatening the liberties of the nation. In January, 1839, Morris wrote an associate that, having fought the battle "in opposition to the power of concentrated wealth," he was ready to oppose slavery, "an interest which . . . is more powerful and dangerous to the peace and prosperity of the country than Banks or any other interest, that has ever existed among

44. Nye, *Fettered Freedom*, 230–31; Julian, *Giddings*, 432; *Official Proceedings of the Republican Convention Convened in the City of Pittsburgh, Pennsylvania, On the 22nd of February, 1856* (Washington, 1856), 14–15.
45. Nye, *Fettered Freedom*, 218–25; Plunkett, "Liberty Party," 46; Julian P. Bretz, "The Economic Background of the Liberty Party," *AHR*, XXXIV (January 1929), 251n.

us." In the next month, Morris rose in the Senate to defend abolitionists against Henry Clay's assaults. He pledged to devote his energies to the cause of emancipation, "and against the power of these two great interests—the slave power of the South, and banking power of the North—which are now uniting to rule this country." Both banking and slavery were based on "the unrequited labor of others," and both constituted dangers to republican institutions because of their aristocratic character and concentrated power. Morris declared that the slave interest had succeeded in obtaining control of the government, but he warned that, just as with the Bank, the people would mobilize against the Slave Power—"this goliath of all monopolies." [46]

The influence of Morris on the development of political anti-slavery was far more significant than most historians have recognized. He became the first political martyr of the anti-slavery cause when he was denied re-election to the Senate because of his abolitionist convictions. Chase later wrote that Morris had awakened him to the character of the Slave Power and to the need for political organization to combat its influences. Morris's speech in reply to Clay was widely read in the North, and helped put the phrase "Slave Power" into the jargon of politics. If, as Marvin Meyers suggests, the Money Power was the "master symbol" for the Age of Jackson, the Slave Power was equally effective as a symbol for all the fears and hostilities harbored by northerners toward slavery and the South. Morris and the countless Jacksonians who later joined the Republican party showed how easily one could jump from one master symbol to the next. The fight against the Bank, Meyers points out, represented for the Jacksonians "equality against privilege, liberty against domination, honest work against dead precedent." [47] An even greater complex of fears and associations was symbolized by the Slave Power. "The same men," said Senator James Doolittle, a Democrat who joined the Republican party, "who, when the United States bank undertook to enforce its recharter, organized to put it down, are organizing to put down a similar despotism which seeks today to control the administration of this federal government." [48]

46. Morris, Morris, 32–34, 119–20, 181, 217. Cf. 115, 127–29, 154, 180.
47. Morris, Morris, xi; Meyers, Jacksonian Persuasion, 10, 254.
48. Congressional Globe, 35 Congress, 2 Session, 1267. The Free Soil party of 1848 also made this identification in its appeals to Democratic voters. One pamphlet said, "Was any one apprehensive of the great monied power . . . who is not afraid of this monstrous, organized, active and pervading interest, based

Once it was accepted that slaveholders had organized as a political power, the logical next step for anti-slavery northerners was to create a countervailing political force committed to freedom. Chase later recalled that it was a conviction of the "absolute necessity of organized resistance to the extension of Slavery and the domination of the Slave Power" which led him into anti-slavery politics, and in 1841 he explained that anti-slavery—as opposed to abolitionism—meant "a hostility to slavery *as a power antagonist to free labor,* as an influence perverting the government from its true end and scope. . . ." The reason political organization against other evils, such as liquor, was not necessary, he explained, was that "there is no organized, law-sustained, compact, and efficient Rum Power," while the Slave Power was a full reality. Moreover, the Slave Power idea explained why northerners could not accept the assurances of men like Webster and Clay that slavery was barred from the western territories by climate and geography. "So long as a powerful and active political interest is concerned in the extension of slavery into new territories," Chase told the Senate, "it is vain to look for its exclusion from them, except by positive law." [49]

During the 1840's the Slave Power idea became a standard part of Liberty party rhetoric. In accepting the first Liberty nomination, Birney declared that the national government was in the hands of the Slave Power, and dated its ascendancy from the Missouri Compromise. Chase's local Liberty addresses and his national platforms of 1844 and 1847 charged the Slave Power with responsibility for transforming the Constitution from "the safeguard of Liberty . . . into a bulwark of slavery." [50] As the issue of slavery extension emerged, the idea of a slaveholders' conspiracy became more and more common in anti-slavery talk. The annexation of Texas and the Mexican War led many northern Whigs to complain that the government was acting merely to extend the peculiar institution. In Massachusetts, John G. Palfrey outlined the South's offenses in a series of articles entitled "Papers on the Slave Power." Many northern Democrats echoed his

upon the ownership of slaves?" *The Free Soil Question and its Importance to the Voters of the Free States* (New York, 1848), 15.

49. Untitled manuscript address, 1860, Box 17, Chase to Charles D. Cleveland, October 22, 1841, Chase Papers, HSPa, italics added; Chase to ?, August 1, 1851, Chase Papers, LC; *Congressional Globe,* 31 Congress, 1 Session, Appendix, 478.

50. Dumond, ed., *Birney Letters,* I, 567–68; "Liberty Address to People of Cincinnati," undated manuscript, Box 17, Chase Papers, HSPa; Porter and Johnson, comps., *Party Platforms,* 6.

charges.[51] And, as anti-slavery leaders realized how effective a political symbol the Slave Power could be, they intentionally stressed its evils in their speeches and platforms. A revealing letter by the Liberty party leader Joshua Leavitt to Chase demonstrates that the emphasis on the Slave Power was hardly an accident. In advising Chase on the platform of the forthcoming Buffalo Free Soil Convention, Leavitt wrote: [52]

> I believe now there is a general preparation in the minds of the people to look to "the overthrow of the Slave Power" as the ultimate result of our movement. I am struck with the facility with which this word has come into use in the documents of both Democrats and Whigs. The *Slave Power* is now indissolubly incorporated in the political nomenclature of the country, and will be inscribed indelibly upon the historical page. We must make the most of that word. It is not necessary that they who use it should ever know who taught it to them—the name and the thing—but the incessant use of the term will do much to open the eyes and arouse the energies of the people. . . . Let it appear that it is the *Slave Power* which we wish to restrict and curtail; that it is the *Slave Power* whose demands we resist, whose growth we will put down.

As Leavitt intended, the Slave Power idea was emphasized in the Free Soil campaign of 1848 as never before. "Much information with regard to the Slave Power has been diffused in quarters heretofore ignorant of this enormous tyranny," was Sumner's comment to Chase on the campaign. But two years later, the free-soil political activity of thousands of northern Democrats and Whigs was silenced by the Compromise of 1850, and anti-slavery men like Schuyler Colfax of Indiana could only hope that "new slavery aggressions may again awaken the North and cause them to stand fast for Freedom." [53] Within a few years Colfax's hope had been fulfilled. In the aftermath of the Kansas-Nebraska Act, political anti-slavery rose to heights never before achieved. No one played a greater role than Chase in convinc-

51. Joshua Giddings to Lura Maria Giddings, April 19, 1844, Giddings Papers; *Congressional Globe*, 29 Congress, 1 Session, Appendix, 826–27, 2 Session, Appendix, 332; Allan Nevins and Milton H. Thomas, eds., *The Diary of George Templeton Strong* (4 vols.: New York, 1952), I, 250; John G. Palfrey, *Papers on the Slave Power* (Boston, 1846); Avery Craven, *The Coming of the Civil War* (New York, 1942), 227; Chaplain W. Morrison, *Democratic Politics and Sectionalism* (Chapel Hill, 1967), 13–15; Silas Wright to John A. Dix, January 19, 1847, John A. Dix Papers, Columbia University.
52. Joshua Leavitt to Chase, July 7, 1848, Chase Papers, HSPa.
53. Sumner to Chase, November 16, 1848, Chase Papers, LC; Schuyler Colfax to William H. Seward, December 20, 1850, William H. Seward Papers, Rush Rhees Library, University of Rochester.

ing northerners that the repeal of the Missouri Compromise and the opening of Kansas and Nebraska to slavery was only one more example of the Slave Power's determination to dominate national life and to extend the peculiar institution everywhere.

"At last," an associate wrote Chase soon after the introduction of the Kansas-Nebraska bill, "the opportunity of your life has crossed your path," and Chase made the most of it. The "Appeal of the Independent Democrats," written by Chase in conjunction with Giddings, became the textbook of the conspiracy theory of the repeal of the Missouri Compromise.[54] In language reprinted in newspapers throughout the nation, the "Appeal" condemned the bill as "a criminal betrayal of precious rights; as part and parcel of an atrocious plot" to extend slavery into the West, creating there "a dreary region of despotism, inhabited by masters and slaves." Chase reiterated his position that the founding fathers had inaugurated a policy of restricting slavery; he reviewed the legislative history of the Missouri Compromise, arguing that its departure from the original policy had been achieved only by the pledge that most of the Louisiana Purchase would be forever free. The "Appeal" closed with a warning that "the dearest interests of freedom and the Union are in imminent peril," and called for religious and political organization to defeat the bill.[55]

Chase always regarded the "Appeal of the Independent Democrats" as "the *most valuable* of my works." As soon as it was written, he sent a copy to his friend Edward L. Pierce in Cincinnati, with instructions to have it printed in the Cincinnati *Gazette* at once and distributed to other newspapers. Later he claimed that the "Appeal" was "the first decisive step in opposition" to the Nebraska bill, and that it "aroused the Country. . . . It was reprinted and read everywhere." [56] Historians have tended to agree that the "Appeal" was one of the most effective pieces of political propaganda in our history. Chase may be charged

54. J. W. Taylor to Chase, February 7, 1854, Chase Papers, LC. On the authorship of the "Appeal," see Warden, *Chase*, 338; Giddings, *History of the Rebellion*, 366n.
55. Schuckers, *Chase*, 141–47.
56. "Diary and Correspondence," 263; Chase to E. L. Pierce, January 21, 1854, in Sumner Papers; Chase to Sidney H. Gay, March 14, 1854, Sidney Howard Gay Papers, Columbia University; "Mr. Seward and the Repeal of the Missouri Compromise," undated manuscript, Box 19, Chase Papers, HSPa. This last document, in Chase's handwriting, was probably composed in 1860. It attempts to downgrade Seward's role in the opposition to the Kansas-Nebraska bill, and credits Chase with arousing the North, through the "Appeal."

with inconsistency for glorifying the Missouri Compromise, which he had previously regarded as a surrender of the interests of freedom; but he recognized—as Stephen A. Douglas, the author of the Kansas-Nebraska bill, pointed out some years earlier—that the Compromise had been "canonized in the hearts of the American people," and could be disturbed only at the greatest peril.[57] Chase also realized that defending free territory against the encroachments of slavery had a far wider political appeal than any other anti-slavery program. In 1849 he had written that the Slave Power, once content to "retain slave territory as slave territory," had embarked on the new aggressive course of seeking to convert free territory into slave. Now, in 1854, Chase pointed out that once again freedom was on the defensive, and his interpretation of the Kansas-Nebraska Act was widely accepted in the North.[58] Israel Washburn of Maine told the House that the bill proved what abolitionists had long claimed to be true—"that slavery is aggressive . . . slavery must be crippled, or freedom go to the wall." Even the usually sedate New York *Times* said the bill was "part of this great scheme for extending and perpetuating the supremacy of the Slave Power." Despite Douglas's denials, thousands of northerners were convinced that the sole purpose of the bill was to ensure that slavery would enter Kansas and Nebraska.[59]

The repeal of the Missouri Compromise and the political campaigns which followed led many northerners finally to accept as a fact the existence of an aggressive Slave Power. Lewis Tappan even suggested that the mission of his abolition society was just about ended, since the entire North seemed to be awakening to the evils and encroachments of slavery. Many northerners, long uneasy about the existence of slavery but prepared to subordinate their feelings in the interests of national and party harmony, agreed with the Cincinnati *Gazette* that "it is impossible to satisfy the South," and that the time had come

57. Frederic Bancroft, *The Life of William H. Seward* (2 vols.: New York, 1899), I, 339; Wilfred E. Binkley, *American Political Parties* (New York, 1947 ed.), 192; Roy F. Nichols, "The Kansas-Nebraska Act: A Century of Historiography," *MVHR*, XLIII (September 1956), 205–7.

58. *Congressional Globe*, 31 Congress, 1 Session, 135, 33 Congress, 1 Session, Appendix, 134. Cf. New York *Tribune*, January 11, 1854.

59. *Congressional Globe*, 33 Congress, 1 Session, Appendix, 499; New York *Times*, May 19, 1854; *Ohio State Journal*, February 15, 1854; William Stocking, ed., *Under the Oaks* (Detroit, 1904), 47–48; Joseph P. Smith, ed., *History of the Republican Party in Ohio* (2 vols.: Chicago, 1898), I, 13.

to take a firm stand. Then in 1855 and 1856 came events in Kansas which appeared to justify the accusation that the Slave Power was using its control of the Democratic party and the federal government to force slavery into the territories. In the campaign of 1856, Republicans stressed the Kansas issue and linked it with the existence of a Slave Power. "Sir," said Henry Wilson at the national Republican convention, "our object is to overthrow the Slave Power of the country. . . ." [60]

When the idea of the Slave Power originated in the 1830's, abolitionists, whose basic liberties were under attack, insisted that the ultimate aim of the South was to destroy liberty in the free states. Two decades later, Lincoln, Seward, and many other Republicans agreed that freedom and slavery were incompatible, and that eventually the nation would become all free or all slave. Yet in early Republican statements and writings on the aims of the Slave Power, a more political—and realizable—objective was stressed. As Ben Wade wrote to an Ohio anti-Nebraska convention, "no doubt, this is but the first of a series of measures having for their object the *nationalization of* slavery, and its legalization and extension into every region protected by the American flag." Similarly, Richard Yates declared in 1855 that the issue between the sections was "whether slavery is to be nationalized; whether the spread of slavery is to be the chief concern and leading policy of this Government; whether it is to have the political ascendency in the government. . . ." [61] If the intent of the Republican party was to limit slavery to the slave states, that of the Slave Power was to confine freedom to the free states. Instead of the local, temporary institution which the founders had intended slavery to be, the Slave Power was striving to create an institution which would exist everywhere the federal government had exclusive jurisdiction, and whose interests dictated national policy. As the first Republican governor of Illinois, William Bissell, charged, "Slavery is no longer to be considered or treated as anomalous in our system, but is rather . . . to be a lead-

60. Annie H. Abel and Frank J. Klingberg, *A Side-Light on Anglo-American Relations, 1839–1858* (Lancaster, 1927), 347; Cincinnati *Gazette*, June 13, 1854; *Proceedings of the First Three Republican National Conventions* (np, nd), 30. Cf. Crandall, *Republican Party*, 77; Don E. Fehrenbacher, *Prelude to Greatness. Lincoln in the 1850's* (New York, 1964), 23; New York *Tribune*, June 12, August 27, October 29, 1856, May 2, 1857.
61. Smith, ed., *Ohio Republican Party*, I, 17; *Congressional Globe*, 33 Congress, 2 Session, Appendix, 252.

ing and favorite element of society . . . to which all else must bend and conform." [62]

Republicans did not generally adopt the argument that there was a danger of slavery spreading into the North until after the Dred Scott decision of 1857. Republicans agreed that, as the *Ohio State Journal* charged, the decision was one of the final acts of the Slave Power conspiracy, for it declared that slavery must be protected by the national government in the territories. "It is now demonstrated," announced the moderate Cincinnati *Commercial*, "that there is such a thing as the Slave Power. . . ," and Republicans who had not already seen the wisdom of Chase's constitutional arguments quickly adopted them.[63] "Freedom national" became the party's answer to Dred Scott. But many Republicans went even further, and claimed that according to the logic of the Dred Scott decision slavery could not be barred from a state any more than from a territory. If slavery were protected by the Constitution, they asked, how could a state, without violating the Constitution, exclude it? "Does the Constitution make slaves property?" asked one Republican speaker. "If so, slavery exists in Ohio today, for the Constitution extends over Ohio, doesn't it?" Lincoln, Trumbull, and countless other Republicans predicted—in what Simon Cameron called "the next step after the Dred Scott decision"—that the Court would deny the power of a state to exclude slavery.[64]

Many Republicans believed that slavery would be established in the North, not by a direct Supreme Court decision but by a ruling on the right of slaveholders to bring slaves into and out of free states without

62. D. W. Lusk, *Eighty Years of Illinois* (Springfield, 1889), 40; *Official Proceedings, Republicans Convention, February, 1856*, 22; Louis Pelzer, "The Origin and Organization of the Republican Party in Iowa," *IJHP*, IV (October 1906), 514. Cf. Chicago *Press and Tribune*, October 7, August 23, 1858; New York *Tribune*, May 6, 1856.

63. *Ohio State Journal*, March 11, 1857; Helen M. Cavenaugh, "Anti-Slavery Sentiment and Politics in the Northwest, 1844–1860' (unpublished doctoral dissertation, University of Chicago, 1938), 133. Cf. Springfield *Republican*, March 7, 9, 11, 1857; Milwaukee *Sentinel*, March 14, 19, 1857; New York *Tribune*, March 9, 11, 1857; Fehrenbacher, *Prelude*, 79–80.

64. Cincinnati *Gazette*, September 3, 1860; Roy P. Basler *et al.*, eds., *The Collected Works of Abraham Lincoln* (9 vols.: New Brunswick, 1953–55). II, 466–67; *Great Speech of Hon. Lyman Trumbull, on the Issues of the Day* (Chicago, 1858), 7, 10; *Ohio State Journal*, February 15, August 29, 1859; Simon Cameron to George Bergner, March 28, 1858 (draft), Simon Cameron Papers, LC. Cf. Chicago *Tribune*, March 13, 16, 1857; James R. Doolittle to Moses Davis, March 9, 1860, Moses Davis Papers, WisHS.

forfeiting their property rights. In the Lemmon case, which was pending before the Supreme Court at the outbreak of the Civil War, eight slaves brought from Virginia to New York for shipment to Texas sued for their freedom. The highest court in the state affirmed that on being brought to free soil a slave automatically became free, but Republicans were apprehensive that the Supreme Court would overturn this decision and establish the right of transit of slaves through the free states.[65] One New York politician expected the Lemmon case to furnish "the material for agitation through the whole of the next Presidential campaign, from 1860 to 1864." Others insisted that once the right of transit has been won, southerners would set up slave markets in the North. "We shall see men buying slaves for the New-York market," predicted Horace Greeley's New York *Tribune*. "There will be no legal power to prevent it." [66]

In the years before the Civil War, Republicans expanded the list of aggressions they charged the Slave Power was preparing. The Republican press often accused the South of plotting to reopen the African slave trade as a prelude to spreading slavery throughout the West. It also spoke of southern designs on Latin American territory.[67] Most heinous of all the Slave Power's aims was its plot to break up the Union if ever the North won control of the federal government. "They care nothing for the Union," said the Ohio Congressman James Ashley, "except so far as it subserves their purpose of building up and extending their peculiar institution, and perpetuating their own political power." When secession finally came, Republicans insisted that it was the final fruit of a conspiracy which had been germinating for thirty years. Even moderates like John Sherman of Ohio concluded that "these men have for years desired disunion; they have plotted for it." [68]

65. On the Lemmon case, see Chester L. Barrows, *William M. Evarts* (Chapel Hill, 1941), 83–87; New York *Tribune*, September 25, October 1–6, December 6, 1857, April 21, 1860; *Ohio State Journal*, May 17, 22, 1858, August 29, 1859; New York *Times*, November 15, 1852.
66. E. Pershine Smith to Henry C. Carey, January 15, 1860, Henry C. Carey Papers, HSPa; New York *Tribune*, March 8, 1857. Cf. John Appleton to William Pitt Fessenden, March 10, 1858, William Pitt Fessenden Papers, WRHS; Chicago *Tribune*, May 12, 1858; Springfield *Republican*, October 12, 1857; New York *Evening Post*, August 31, 1859.
67. Cavenaugh, "Anti-Slavery," 144–45; Cincinnati *Gazette*, February 3, March 18, 19, 1858, July 16, 30, 1859; New York *Tribune*, March 5, 1858, May 21, 1859, Chicago *Press and Tribune* July 19, 1859, *National Era*, March 24, 1859.
68. *Congressional Globe*, 36 Congress, 1 Session, Appendix, 365; Rachel Sherman Thorndike, *The Sherman Letters* (New York, 1894), 86. Cf. Cincinnati *Enquirer*, cited in New York *Tribune*, May 12, 1860.

III

In 1843, Joshua Giddings observed to Chase that the principal cause of the slow growth of anti-slavery politics in the North was "ignorance in regard to the encroachments of the Slave Power upon our rights." In the next twenty years, the Slave Power idea came to symbolize for northerners all the fears and resentments they felt toward slavery and the South. There were many reasons why the Slave Power was such an effective political symbol. For one thing, Americans of the mid-nineteenth century retained the distrust of centralized power which had characterized the revolutionary period. In addition, the idea of a Slave Power emphasized the southern threat to the interests and rights of northern white men, and thus had a far greater appeal than arguments focusing on the wrongs done the slave. Finally, its widespread acceptance was aided by the American penchant for viewing historical events in conspiratorial terms. David B. Davis has shown how counter-subversive movements in ante-bellum America, such as nativist and anti-masonic outbursts, helped to clarify democratic ideals and intensify group solidarity by conceiving a conspiratorial enemy which plotted the destruction of cherished values. The Slave Power certainly fits this tradition.[69]

Davis also points out, however, that the Slave Power idea enjoyed far greater acceptance than any of the other "enemies" against which political action was directed before the Civil War. And one important reason for this was that there was much truth in Republican charges that slavery had become the ruling interest of the national government and that southerners were bent on dominating the western territories. Of course many Republican leaders realized there was little chance of slavery being forced upon the North. They also knew, or should have known, that the South was seriously divided on such issues as the Mexican War, the Compromise of 1850, and events in Kansas.[70] Yet there is no question that slaveholders did dominate the political and social life of the South, and used their political power to protect their class interests, the greatest of which was slavery itself.

69. Davis Brion Davis, "Some Ideological Functions of Prejudice in Ante-Bellum America," *AmQ*, XV (Summer 1963), 116; Davis, "Counter-Subversion," 215, 224; Richard Hofstadter, *The Paranoid Style in American Politics* (New York, 1965).
70. Nye, *Fettered Freedom*, 249; Chauncey S. Boucher, "*In Re* That Aggressive Slaveocracy," *MVHR*, VIII (June-September 1921), 13-79.

Two judicious observers of the politics of the 1850's, Roy F. Nichols and Allan Nevins, agree that during the Buchanan administration southern control of all branches of the federal government was virtually complete. Nevins, indeed, declares that during the Lecompton controversy, the president was "obedient to the voice of his masters" —his masters being a directory of southern statesmen. Southern politicians had been instrumental in the repeal of the Missouri Compromise, and their constitutional position was accepted by the Supreme Court in the Dred Scott decision.[71]

By the late 1850's, with the disappearance of the southern Whig party, slave-state Congressmen did seem to have a unified program, which the North found extremely threatening. As Arthur Bestor points out, the demands of southern Congressmen in 1860 were quite extreme—they insisted that slavery was recognized by the Constitution and automatically existed wherever the federal government held exclusive jurisdiction, and they demanded a Congressional slave code for the territories to enforce this right. No matter that in the minds of some southern leaders this program was meant to defend an institution increasingly beleaguered in the nineteenth-century world, not to undermine northern liberties. It was not a Republican but Stephen A. Douglas who said that not one northern Congressman would ever endorse such proposals.[72] Southerners rarely claimed that they wanted slavery to go into the North—Jefferson Davis said the idea was "absurd"—but they did demand that it be treated as a national institution in the same way that Republicans insisted freedom was national.[73]

Perhaps the most puzzling part of the Slave Power idea was the firm belief of many Republicans that the ultimate intention of the South was to spread slavery into the North, and to destroy civil liberties in the free states. This charge owed a great deal to the fact that the idea

71. Roy F. Nichols, *The Stakes of Power 1845–1877* (New York, 1961), 76; Allan Nevins, *The Emergence of Lincoln* (2 vols.: New York, 1950), II, 269; Eugene D. Genovese, *The Political Economy of Slavery* (New York, 1965), 4.
72. Bestor, "American Civil War," 351; Arthur E. Bestor, "State Sovereignty and Slavery," *Journal of IllSHS*, LIV (Summer 1961), 162 165, 173; George H. Knoles, ed., *The Crisis of the Union* (Baton Rouge, 1965), 55, 86–89; Genovese, *Political Economy*, 260–62; Springfield *Republican*, September 22, 1858; *Congressional Globe*, 35 Congress, 1 Session, 1244.
73. Rowland Dunbar, ed., *Jefferson Davis, Constitutionalist, His Letters, Papers and Speeches* (10 vols.: Jackson, 1923), III, 32; *Congressional Globe*, 34 Congress, 1 Session, 857, 35 Congress, 1 Session, 925, 36 Congress, 1 Session, Appendix, 78, 2 Session, 203.

of the Slave Power originated in the 1830's, at a time when the civil liberties of abolitionists were indeed under attack. Chase himself, as we have seen, was drawn into the anti-slavery movement because of a mob attack on an abolitionist press, and many other northerners first came to sympathize with the abolitionists because of their travails, or because of the struggle led by John Quincy Adams and Joshua Giddings to permit the reception of abolitionist petitions in the House of Representatives. "The injudicious legislation in this Hall in reference to slavery," Galusha Grow told the House in 1854, "is the origin of political Abolitionism. . . . Previous to the passage of the [gag] rule, Abolitionism was but a sentiment, and a mere sentiment is not a sufficient basis for a formidable political organization. But when great principles of constitutional right are violated, . . . enduring political organizations [may be created]." [74] Moreover, the Slave Power threatened a principle which Republicans viewed as the essence of democracy—rule by majorities. The domination of both the South and the federal government by the Slave Power violated this basic democratic belief.

Nevertheless, the Republicans' fears of the Slave Power often had an apocalyptic quality which it is necessary to recognize. Some Republicans, to be sure, ridiculed what Congressman Eli Thayer called the "political Cassandras" of their party, "who are continually saying that slavery has always had its own way, and always will have it; that slavery under the Dred Scott decision, will yet be established in Massachusetts and New Hampshire." [75] Yet these "Cassandras" included some of the most respected members of the Republican party. Both Lincoln and Seward stated publicly in 1858 that unless the spread of slavery were halted, the institution would spread to the free states. And one Connecticut Congressman told the House that the South desired "the complete overthrow of democratic institutions, and the establishment of an aristocratic, or even monarchial government." [76] The same fears appear in the private correspondence of Republican leaders.

74. *Congressional Globe*, 33 Congress, 1 Session, Appendix, 976.
75. *Congressional Globe*, 35 Congress, 2 Session, Appendix, 236. Cf. the exchange of letters, Lyman Trumbull to John D. Caton, March 2, 1858, John D. Caton Papers, LC, Caton to Trumbull, March 6, 1857, Trumbull Papers; New York *Times*, November 24, 1858.
76. Basler, ed., *Lincoln Works*, II, 461; George E. Baker, ed., *The Works of William H. Seward* (5 vols.: Boston, 1853-84), IV, 292-94; Harry Jaffa, *Crisis of the House Divided* (Garden City, 1959), 371; *Congressional Globe*, 36 Congress, 2 Session, 551.

Joshua Giddings, for example, wrote to Chase in 1856 that he was certain "that northern liberty or southern slavery must fall," and in the same year Lafayette Foster, the conservative Senator from Connecticut, wrote that he viewed the presidential election as the last opportunity for the North *to save our liberties*." [77] These Republicans may be charged with overreacting to the events of the 1850's, but they were articulating fears which ran deep in the northern mind on the eve of the Civil War.

When Salmon Chase died in 1873, he was eulogized as the man who had set the tone and program of the political anti-slavery movement. "That slavery was sectional and freedom national," the New York *Tribune* observed, "is a phrase afterward so familiar to our ears that we hardly appreciate the courage it needed in a young lawyer to enunciate such a doctrine thirty-five years ago. . . ." Chase lived to see his political approach to the slavery issue spread from a handful of abolitionists to become the rallying-cry of a victorious political party. His interpretation of the Constitution and the founders' intentions, coupled with the Slave Power idea, expressed the conviction of the North that it, not the South, was on the defensive. As one Congressman expressed it in 1860, "Your aggressions forced the North into this contest—to defend the liberty of speech and of the press; to maintain the right of petition; . . . to defend the Territories from the curse of slavery." [78] The Slave Power idea, moreover, provided the link between the Republican view of the South as an alien society, and their belief in the necessity of political organization to combat southern influence. Two antagonistic societies, Republicans believed, were contesting for control of a single political system. As they viewed the events of the 1850's, Republicans could not but feel that the issue of the first Lincoln campaign was whether freedom or slavery would henceforth be the predominant interest in the national government. "Freedom national" expressed their hope, and their purpose; the idea of the Slave Power expressed their fears.

77. Giddings to Chase, December 18, 1856, Chase Papers, HSPa; Lafayette Foster to James F. Babcock, June 2, 1856, Miscellaneous Manuscripts, Connecticut State Library. Cf. Sarah J. Day, *The Man on a Hill Top* (Philadelphia, 1931), 168; William Dennison to Francis P. Blair, December 5, 1857, Blair-Lee Papers, Princeton University; William Dennison to Giddings, August 4, 1858, Giddings Papers.
78. New York *Tribune*, May 8, 1873; *Congressional Globe*, 36 Congress, 1 Session, Appendix, 180.

4

The Radicals:

ANTI-SLAVERY POLITICS AND
THE MORAL IMPERATIVE

"Our party in this, as in every other state, has its conservative and radical elements." So wrote the newly elected Republican Governor of Ohio, William Dennison in November, 1860. But Dennison would probably have found it difficult to define precisely what differentiated radicals from conservatives. The same problem has plagued historians of the entire Civil War era. Everyone knows that there were radical Republicans before, during, and after the war, and the names of the leading radicals—Charles Sumner, Thaddeus Stevens, Benjamin F. Wade, Joshua Giddings, and a few others—are readily agreed upon. But historians have differed in their definitions of what constituted radicalism. The radicals were once seen as agents of the northern capitalist class, whose anti-slavery professions were primarily a mask for a commitment to economic measures which would stimulate the growth of industry and enlarge the profits of businessmen. Recent studies, however, have tended to take the radicals at their word. Margaret Shortreed, in an influential article covering the years from 1840 to 1868, argued that the radicals were those Republicans who embraced a program of comprehensive political, economic, and social change. More recently, David Montgomery defined radicalism as an entrepreneurial orientation, coupled with a strong belief in nationalism and utilitarianism. He further observed that the radical areas of the North were rural counties experiencing substantial economic growth. And the latest study, by Hans L. Trefousse, sees the radicals as principled opponents of slavery, who had a number of differences but one basic quality: the determination not to compromise the issue of non-

extension before the Civil War, or of emancipation and civil rights
during the war and Reconstruction.[1]

One of the difficulties in arriving at a definition of radicalism is that
some individuals, like William H. Seward, were radicals during the
1850's and moderates or conservatives in the next decade. Moreover,
there was a substantial group of influential Republicans who defy exact
classification. Republican leaders like James Grimes of Iowa, William
Pitt Fessenden of Maine, Lyman Trumbull and Richard Yates of
Illinois, and the leading Republican editor, Horace Greeley, often
worked closely with the radicals, but at the same time exhibited conservative tendencies. Trumbull's most recent biographer calls him a
"conservative radical." Nevertheless, it is possible to list the most
prominent Republican radicals of the 1850's using as a criterion of
radicalism a persistent refusal to compromise with the South on any
question involving slavery. In New England, the leading radical group
was that wing of the Massachusetts party led by Charles Sumner,
Henry Wilson, and John Andrew, which also included Congressmen
John Z. Goodrich, John Alley, and Charles Francis Adams. These men
had been known as Conscience Whigs during the 1840's because of
their insistence that the Whig party make anti-slavery its major political issue. They had joined the Free Soil party in 1848 and had entered
the Republican party through it, although some dallied for a time with
Know-Nothingism.[2] Other New England radical leaders included
Israel Washburn of Maine, John P. Hale of New Hampshire and
Francis Gillette of Connecticut, all of whom served in Congress in
the 1850's.

In New York, William H. Seward was usually on the radical side
in the 1850's, although the ambitions of Seward and his political
mentor Thurlow Weed led them away from the radicals in the late
1850's. The former Barnburner-Democrat element of the New York
party, led by Preston King, was more consistently radical before the

1. William Dennison to Francis Preston Blair, November 10, 1860, Blair-Lee
Papers, Princeton University; Margaret Shortreed, "The Antislavery Radicals:
From Crusade to Revolution 1840–1868," *Past and Present,* XVI (November
1959), 66; David Montgomery, *Beyond Equality* (New York, 1967), 78; Hans
L. Trefousse, *The Radical Republicans, Lincoln's Vanguard for Racial Justice*
(New York, 1969), 4–5. For a short summary of the historiography of radicalism,
see Edward L. Gambill, "Who Were the Senate Radicals?" *CWH,* XI (September
1965), 237–38.
2. Mark M. Krug, *Lyman Trumbull, Conservative Radical* (New York, 1965);
Frank O. Gatell, " 'Conscience and Judgment;' The Bolt of the Massachusetts
Conscience Whigs," *Historian,* XXI (November 1958), 18–45.

Civil War than Seward and Weed. Pennsylvania and Indiana had only a few radical leaders, including Thaddeus Stevens, David Wilmot, and Galusha Grow in the former state and George Julian in the latter. The leaders of Ohio's substantial radical element included Governor Salmon P. Chase, Senator Benjamin F. Wade, and Congressmen Joshua Giddings, Edward Wade, and James Ashley. The Illinois radicals were led by Owen Lovejoy, Elihu Washburne, and the influential editors Charles Ray and Joseph Medill, while both Michigan and Wisconsin had large radical elements, among whom were Zachariah Chandler and Austin Blair in Michigan and John F. Potter, Charles Durkee, and Carl Schurz in Wisconsin. Of the Republican press, Greeley's *Tribune* often spoke for the radicals, as did Medill's Chicago *Tribune* and many newspapers of lesser influence. The most consistently radical paper was the *National Era.* Established in Washington in 1847 by the abolitionist American and Foreign Antislavery Society, the *Era* had supported the Liberty and Free Soil parties before joining the Republican. Elihu Washburne wrote in 1859 that the *Era* was "the best representative of the living and genuine principles of the Republican party. . . ." [3]

These radical Republicans certainly did not think alike on all matters. It is now well established, for example, that they did not share any unified economic policy or purpose. Seward, Chandler, Wade, and Stevens were firm Whiggish adherents of protection and government aid to business, but Chase, Julian, Lovejoy, Potter, and most of the Massachusetts radicals were free-traders who tended to oppose pro-business measures. [4] But one of the things the radicals did have in common was that the slavery issue had shaped their political careers. Most of the pre-war radical leaders came to the Republican party from

3. Phyllis M. Bannan, "Arthur and Lewis Tappan: A Study in New York Religious and Reform Movements" (unpublished doctoral dissertation, Columbia University, 1950), 143; Gaillard Hunt, *Israel, Elihu, and Cadwallader Washburn, A Chapter in American Biography* (New York, 1925), 185; Trefousse, *Radical Republicans,* 5–15.
4. Trefousse, *Radical Republicans,* 25–26; Louis M. Filler, *The Crusade Against Slavery* (New York, 1960), 181; W. R. Brock, *An American Crisis* (London, 1963), 236; *Congressional Globe,* 33 Congress, 2 Session, 885, Appendix, 302, 35 Congress, 1 Session, 130, 36 Congress, 1 Session, 174; George Julian to G. C. Starbuck, June, 1849, George W. Julian Papers, Indiana State Library; Horace Greeley to Schuyler Colfax, February 4, 1859, Greeley-Colfax Papers, NYPL; Charles A. Dana to Henry C. Carey, February 23, 1855, Henry C. Carey Papers, HSPa; *National Era,* June 28, 1855; Arthur M. Lee, "The Development of an Economic Policy in the Early Republican Party" (unpublished doctoral dissertation, Syracuse University, 1953), 7–8.

the Free Soil party. A few, like Chase, Lovejoy, Edward Wade, and Hale had been Liberty men, while others, like the Conscience Whigs and the New York Barnburners, had struggled to commit the major parties to anti-slavery views.[5] At the Buffalo Free Soil Convention of 1848, Charles Francis Adams listened to "a rather long but interesting history of the trials of the Barnburners" delivered by Benjamin Butler, and was struck by "the similarity of the details with those which we on the Whig side had experienced." The political careers of Liberty Men, Barnburners, and Conscience Whigs were shaped during the 1840's in the struggles over the annexation of Texas and the Wilmot Proviso. Even the radical leaders like Seward, Wade, and Stevens, who eschewed the Free Soil party in 1848 and did not break with the Whigs until 1854 or 1855, had tied their political fortunes to the slavery issue. As Giddings said of Stevens, he was more of a free-soiler than a Whig. The radicals' leadership in the anti-slavery crusade of the Republican party therefore had its roots in earlier political contests—indeed, they considered the Republican party the culmination of years of anti-slavery effort. As Adams put it when his town elected two Republicans to the Massachusetts legislature in 1856, "the labors of ten years are now visible." [6]

In general, radical Republican districts were concentrated in rural and small town New England, and in the areas of rural New York, Pennsylvania, and the West settled by New England migrants. It is well known that a steady stream of migrants spread out from New England throughout the nineteenth century, settling along a line almost due westward from their starting places, and bringing with them their churches, schools, and puritan culture. Long after New England itself was deluged by immigrants, who wrested a good portion of political power from the native inhabitants, centers of pure New England culture existed in the Northwest.[7] "Almost every free

5. Such future radical Republican leaders as Chase, Edward Wade, Charles Durkee, Francis Gillette, and Russell Errett either attended the 1847 National Liberty Convention, or were on the party's national committee. *National Era*, November 11, 1847.
6. Charles Francis Adams Diary, August 10, 1848, November 4, 1856, Adams Papers, MHS; Joshua Giddings to Molly Giddings, February 15, 1852, Giddings-Julian Papers, LC. Cf. George W. Julian, *The Life of Joshua R. Giddings* (Chicago, 1892), 382; Salmon P. Chase to Israel Washburn, March 13, 1858, Israel Washburn Papers, LC.
7. Lois K. Mathews, *The Expansion of New England* (Boston and New York, 1909), 160, 247–50; W. Dean Burnham, *Presidential Ballots 1836–1892* (Baltimore, 1955), 11–12; Charrie P. Koford, "Puritan Influences in Illinois Before

state has its New England within its border," Justin Morrill observed on the eve of the Civil War, and throughout the North these little New Englands, with their small towns and independent farmers, were not only centers of literacy, religion, and economic progress, but of Republican radicalism—and heavy Republican electoral majorities—as well.[8]

In New England itself, the rural areas and small towns were the most radical. The cities, with their commercial ties to the South and large numbers of immigrants, tended to be more conservative, and gave Republican candidates substantially fewer votes than did the countryside. Vermont, a state almost entirely rural, was generally considered to be the most radical in the North. It gave Lincoln 76 per cent of its vote in 1860.[9] In New York, New Englanders had settled heavily in the northern and western parts of the state, while the southern and eastern areas were inhabited by descendants of the Dutch, and increasingly by immigrants. Buchanan carried the city by a wide margin in 1856, but upstate, as one Democratic chieftain wrote, "beyond the cities, wherever the New England people have sway, they came down like an avalanche" for Frémont. St. Lawrence county, called "little Vermont" because of the origin of its inhabitants, gave Buchanan only 15 per cent of its vote in 1856. Some of the upstate New England areas had been strongly Whig before the advent of Republicanism, while some had been strongholds of locofoco Democracy. But all became centers of radical Republicanism in the 1850's.[10]

Farther west, the same pattern was evident. The "Northern Tier" counties of Pennsylvania sent David Wilmot and Galusha Grow to Congress. The area had been settled by New Englanders between 1810 and 1830, and in the 1850's it gave heavy majorities to Republican

1860," *Transactions* of the IllSHS, X (1905), 315; Frank H. Littell, *From State Church to Pluralism* (Garden City, 1962), 59, 71; *Congressional Globe,* 36 Congress, 2 Session, 663; Charles Francis Adams Diary, September 8, 1860, Adams Papers.
8. *Congressional Globe,* 36 Congress, 2 Session, 1007.
9. Reinhard H. Luthin, *The First Lincoln Campaign* (Cambridge, 1944), 191; Ollinger Crenshaw, "Urban and Rural Voting in the Election of 1860," in Eric Goldman, ed., *Historiography and Urbanization* (Baltimore, 1941), 54–55.
10. Alexander C. Flick, ed., *History of the State of New York* (10 vols.: New York, 1933–37), VII, 86–87; Walter Dean Burnham, "American Voting Behavior and the 1964 Election," *Midwest Journal of Political Science,* XII (February 1968), 21–22; Frederick W. Seward, ed., *Seward at Washington* (2 vols.: New York, 1891), I, 258; Philip S. Foner, *Business and Slavery* (Chapel Hill, 1941), 137.

candidates.[11] The center of Ohio radicalism was the Western Reserve, which again was almost completely of New England extraction. The inhabitants, said Congressman Edward Wade, were "a phalanx of emancipationists," and in 1856, the Reserve elected Congressmen Giddings and Wade by better than two to one, and gave Frémont 67 per cent of the vote. More often than not in the 1850's heavy Republican majorities in the Reserve were the key to Republican success in the state. In Indiana, George Julian's Congressional district gave Frémont 62 per cent of the vote in 1856, in a state carried easily by Buchanan. It was "one of the strongest anti-slavery districts in the Union," and its inhabitants were primarily Quakers and New Englanders.[12] In Illinois, according to the Republican leader Norman B. Judd, "the Northern one third of the state is Frémont all over—out of the cities and towns the Buchaneers have hardly enough to count." Again, this was an area settled almost exclusively by New Englanders. Frémont carried the three northernmost Congressional districts by better than two to one, polling almost 90 per cent in Winnebago and Boone counties. Elihu Washburne's Congressional district gave him the largest majority of any Congressman in the country. Finally, the rural areas of Wisconsin and Michigan were heavily Republican, and these states, where New England and New York migrants predominated in the population, were among the most radical in the North.[13]

A few of the radical Republican leaders, like Thaddeus Stevens, who candidly admitted that his views were far in advance of those of his constituents, represented areas outside the belt of heavy New England migration.[14] (Though it might be worth noting that Stevens

11. Lee F. Crippen, *Simon Cameron, Ante-Bellum Years* (Oxford, Ohio, 1942), 154–55; C. Maxwell Myers, "The Rise of the Republican Party in Pennsylvania, 1854–1860" (unpublished doctoral dissertation, University of Pittsburgh, 1940), 137; John A. Krout, *The Origins of Prohibition* (New York, 1925), 129–30; Alexander K. McClure to Abraham Lincoln, June 16, 1860, Robert Todd Lincoln Papers, LC; *Tribune Almanac*, 1857, 48–49.
12. *Congressional Globe*, 31 Congress, 1 Session, Appendix, 573, 33 Congress, 1 Session, Appendix, 667; *Ohio State Journal*, November 10, 1856; Eugene H. Roseboom, *The Civil War Era 1850–1873* (Columbus, 1944), 323, 371; *Tribune Almanac*, 1857, 56–58.
13. Norman B. Judd to Edwin D. Morgan, September 18, 1856, in Thurlow Weed Papers, Rush Rhees Library, University of Rochester; *Tribune Almanac*, 1857, 59–63; Floyd B. Streeter, *Political Parties in Michigan 1837–1860* (Lansing, 1918), 199, 256; Joseph Schafer, "Know-Nothingism in Wisconsin," *WisMH*, VIII (September 1924), 8.
14. Thaddeus Stevens to Salmon P. Chase, September 25, 1858, Salmon P. Chase Papers, HSPa.

himself had grown up in New England.) But New England and the Yankee West seem to have been particularly fertile soil for reform movements of all kinds, including radical Republicanism. As one Republican said of the Western Reserve, it "was for many years seemingly the residence—the home of the various *isms*. . . ." It is well known that the areas of New England settlement were swept in the 1820's and 1830's by a series of religious revivals, which strongly influenced the reformism of the ensuing years. The "burned-over" districts of upstate New York, the Western Reserve, and other areas became centers of abolitionism in the 1830's, and of radical Republicanism in the 1850's. The evangelical revivalists instilled in them a commitment to reform the evils they saw in society, and fostered a view of the world in which compromise with sin was itself a sin.[15]

The religiously oriented abolitionism of the 1830's, represented in different ways by Theodore Weld and William Lloyd Garrison, had a profound influence on many radical leaders. Both Weld and Garrison, whatever their differences, stressed that slavery must be opposed primarily because it was a sin, and that it must be immediately abolished, not reformed or compromised with. When Weld toured the Western Reserve in the 1830's, he converted Joshua Giddings, Ben Wade, and Edward Wade to abolitionism. Thaddeus Stevens, Owen Lovejoy, and the Illinois radical leader Ichabod Codding were also strongly influenced by Weld. Similarly, eastern radicals like Sumner, Andrew, and Wilson freely acknowledged their debt to William Lloyd Garrison. All were readers of the *Liberator* in the formative years of their political careers.[16] It is not surprising that these radicals grounded their anti-slavery convictions on religious belief. Edward Wade told Congress that the Bible was "the supreme authority in every moral

15. A. G. Riddle, "The Rise of Antislavery Sentiment on the Western Reserve," *Magazine of Western History*, VI (June 1887), 145; John L. Thomas, "Antislavery and Utopia," in Martin Duberman, ed., *The Antislavery Vanguard* (Princeton, 1965), 247–48; Charles C. Cole, *The Social Ideas of the Northern Evangelists 1826–1860* (New York, 1954), 4–5, 193, 217; Seymour M. Lipset, "Religion and Politics in the American Past and Present," in Robert Lee and Martin Marty, eds., *Religion and Social Conflict* (New York, 1964), 78–79; Gilbert H. Barnes, *The Anti-Slavery Impulse* (New York, 1933), 3–16.
16. Barnes, *Anti-Slavery Impulse*, 79–80. 122, 196–97; Theodore Clarke Smith, *The Liberty and Free Soil Parties in the Northwest* (New York, 1897), 13; *Congressional Globe*, 36 Congress, 1 Session, Appendix, 270; John L. Thomas, *The Liberator, William Lloyd Garrison* (Boston, 1963), 452–53; *Liberator*, June 24, 1853; January 31, 1851; Charles Sumner to George Putnam, April, 1848, Charles Sumner Papers, Houghton Library, Harvard University; William B. Hesseltine, *Lincoln and the War Governors* (New York, 1948), 19.

question," and proceeded to detail how slavery violated Scriptural injunctions. George Julian said political action was merely a subdivision of moral action, and wrote that "the great central truth of Christianity is the great central truth of our movement as a party." The uncompromising political stance of many radicals stemmed in large part from their conviction that slavery should be viewed primarily as a sin, that the anti-slavery movement had been ordained with what John Andrew called "the high and holy mission and duty to redeem America." [17]

Some historians have viewed radicalism as an expression of the political and economic interests of northern capitalism. Yet to most of the radicals—with the exception of such Whig spokesmen as Seward and Stevens—economic issues were only peripheral to the basically moral question of slavery. Like other Republicans, radicals did engage in elaborate statistical comparisons between North and South to prove the economic superiority of the free labor system, but what distinguished them from other Republicans was their determination to keep the moral side of the slavery issue from being obscured by any other aspect.[18] The New York *Tribune* expressed this well in 1859, when it declared that the aim of the Republican party was to prevent the extension of slavery, but added that "that purpose implies and involves a conviction that *slavery is wrong;* if not, the resistance to its extension would be unjustifiable." The emphasis of conservatives on economic issues and questions of political power seemed to the radicals to reveal in Giddings's words, "a cold atheism," which lacked "recognition of right, of enduring principle." James Russell Lowell summed up the radical view on the eve of the Civil War: [19]

> It is in a moral aversion to slavery as a great wrong that the chief strength of the Republican party lies. . . . It will not do for the Republicans to confine themselves to the mere political argument, for the matter then becomes one of expediency. . . . they must go deeper, to the radical question of Right and Wrong. . . .

17. *Congressional Globe,* 36 Congress, 1 Session, Appendix, 356; Julian to Committee of Invitation, April 29, 1853, Giddings-Julian Papers; Boston *Atlas and Daily Bee,* March 8, 1860.
18. *Congressional Globe,* 28 Congress, Appendix, 345, 35 Congress, 1 Session, Appendix, 171, 36 Congress, 1 Session, 1886–87; Boston *Commonwealth,* May 6, 1853; *The Works of Charles Sumner* (10 vols.: Boston, 1870–83), V, 32–46.
19. New York *Tribune,* December 12, 1859; Julian, *Giddings,* 383; James Russell Lowell, "The Election of November," *Atlantic Monthly,* VI (October 1860), 499–500. The source for Lowell's authorship of this article is Horace E. Scudder, *James Russell Lowell, A Biography* (2 vols.: Boston, 1901), II, 437.

As part of their insistence on the primacy of the moral issue in the anti-slavery movement, radicals consistently stressed the cruelties and injustices inflicted on the slave. Giddings was the leading exponent of this approach. Throughout his two decades in the Congress he spoke with compassion of the wrongs of "the suffering slave," of brutality and death and the horrors of the slave trade, always insisting that slavery was above all a sin, and that the North shared a portion of the guilt for its continued existence.[20] Other radical leaders and editors told of slaves being burned alive, of punishments for those whites who extended education or religion to slaves, and of the break-up of families. Slavery, Charles Francis Adams wrote, was "the greatest wrong now existing in the world," and the radicals were determined to keep the northern public fully aware of the extent of the institution's injustices.[21]

In the years immediately preceding the Civil War, as conservative tendencies appeared in the Republican party, radical leaders intentionally made inflammatory speeches in Congress, bringing out more forcefully than ever the religious and moral issues in the anti-slavery movement. In February, 1858, Giddings gave his "American Infidelity" speech which castigated all opponents of the Republican party as infidels, and spoke of the "wholesale murder" of slaves. Garrison gave him the rare compliment of reprinting the speech in the Liberator, and wrote Giddings that he was "highly gratified with its moral and religious tone, and its anti-slavery fidelity." [22] Two years later, as the Republican national convention approached, Owen Lovejoy gave an even more radical speech. He felt the "moral issue" had been slighted in the Congressional debates of that session, and wanted to see whether "the country is ripe for what has been thought radical doctrines." Lovejoy condemned slavery as "the sum of all villainy," an amalgam of every crime known to man. Garrison praised and reprinted his words, and Charles Francis Adams declared that "no

20. Concord *Democrat and Freeman*, July 8, 1847, clipping, Scrapbook, Joshua R. Giddings Papers, OHS; Julian, *Giddings*, 181–82, 236; *Congressional Globe*, 28 Congress, 2 Session, Appendix, 345–47; 30 Congress, 1 Session, Appendix, 522; 2 Session, 129–30; 32 Congress, 1 Session, Appendix, 738–39; 33 Congress, 1 Session, Appendix, 986–89; 35 Congress, 2 Session, 345–46.
21. Charles Francis Adams Diary, July 15, 1845. Cf. *Sumner Works*, II, 299; *Congressional Globe*, 34 Congress, 1 Session, Appendix, 636, 36 Congress, 1 Session, Appendix, 435–36; Giddings to Chase, October 16, 1855, Chase Papers, HSPa; New York *Tribune*, February 6, 1854.
22. *Congressional Globe*, 35 Congress, 1 Session, Appendix, 65–68; Byron R. Long, "Joshua Reed Giddings," *OAHQ*, XXVIII (1919), 40–41.

similar speech has ever before been made within these walls." [23] Then, two months later, came Charles Sumner's monumental "Barbarism of Slavery" speech, which again detailed the myriad abuses of the slave system. Like Giddings and Lovejoy, Sumner was motivated by concern over moderating tendencies within the party, and he hoped to give the coming campaign a moral tone. "The time has come when slavery must be exposed," he wrote to a colleague, "and I mean to do it." Abolitionists and radicals reacted with overwhelming favor to the speech, but the moderate press criticized it as inflammatory. In the end, it was widely distributed where its moral appeal would find its most receptive audience—in the rural North. The weekly edition of Greeley's *Tribune*, which circulated in the radical rural areas, printed the speech, although the daily edition did not, and many small town Republican papers gave it extensive coverage.[24]

As the actions of Giddings, Lovejoy, and Sumner make clear, the radicals believed that one of their primary functions was to influence northern public opinion. They readily admitted that they were political agitators; indeed, they were proud of the name. "Agitation," said Giddings, "is the great and mighty instrument for carrying forward . . . reforms. Agitation is necessary to purify the political atmosphere of this nation. . . ." John P. Hale told the Senate that everything of value in American institutions was the result of agitation. "I glory in the name of agitator," said Hale, "I wish the country could be agitated vastly more than it is." And when conservatives promised that they would end the protracted controversy over the slavery question, radicals replied that it was slavery itself which caused the agitation.[25]

In the radicals' view, agitation had a political as well as a moral function. For the radicals realized what historians have only recently pointed out—that the second American party system, the system of the Democratic and Whig parties, was artificial in that deeply divisive

23. *Congressional Globe*, 36 Congress, 1 Session, Appendix, 203–05; *Liberator*, April 20, 1860; Charles Francis Adams Diary, April 5, 1860, Adams Papers; J. Jeffrey Auer, ed., *Antislavery and Disunion, 1858–1861* (New York, 1963), 117–23.
24. *Sumner Works*, V, 20–24, 27–28, 50–61; Sumner to Henry L. Pierce, June 29, 1860, Miscellaneous Manuscripts, Houghton Library, Harvard University; David Donald, *Charles Sumner and the Coming of the Civil War* (New York, 1961), 352, 362; Edward L. Pierce, *Memoir and Letters of Charles Sumner* (4 vols.: Boston, 1877–93), III, 613.
25. *Congressional Globe*, 32 Congress, 1 Session, Appendix, 740; 31 Congress, 2 Session, 577. Cf. John Andrew to Sumner, February 9, 1858, Sumner Papers; *National Era*, February 3, 1859.

sectional issues were consciously kept out of politics. As Richard Mc-
Cormick observes, one reason for the prominence of the fiscal and
economic issues debated by the major parties was that they were
"sectionally innocuous." [26] This helps to explain the indifference of
many radicals to economic questions. Sumner, for instance, said he
knew "nothing, absolutely nothing" about the Independent Treasury.
But the radicals did know that if parties were debating economic
issues they would ignore the slavery question. So beginning with the
handful who worked with Giddings and John Quincy Adams against
the gag rule in the 1830's and early 1840's, they strove to introduce
the slavery question into political debate at every point they could.
They seized every opportunity to exacerbate the sectional cleavages
which lay beneath the placid surface of politics in the early 1840's,
and in the end played an important role in disrupting the party system.[27]

The radicals thus had a very expedient attitude toward political
parties—they viewed them as means, not as ends, and they were ready
to abandon a party if it would help further the anti-slavery cause. The
Massachusetts Conscience Whigs, for example, labored in the 1840's
to commit the Whig party of their state to an outright anti-slavery
position, with a pledge not to support any but anti-slavery men for
the presidency. This would have effectively severed the ties between
Massachusetts and southern Whigs, and the Conscience men were
defeated, whereupon they turned to the Free Soil party. Henry Wilson,
who said his only political affiliation was anti-slavery and that he would
work with "any set of men—Whigs, Democrats, Liberty men" to achieve
abolition, wrote that he would rather see the Whig party destroyed
than see it elect a slaveholder President.[28] The radicals repudiated the

26. Richard P. McCormick, *The Second American Party System* (Chapel Hill,
1966), 353; Thomas B. Alexander, *Sectional Stress and Party Strength* (Nashville,
1967), 112.
27. Sumner to John G. Palfrey, November 7, 1848, John G. Palfrey Papers,
Houghton Library, Harvard University; Barnes, *Anti-Slavery Impulse*, 180–89.
Cf. *National Era*, March 17, 1853, October 8, 1857; *Congressional Globe*, 36 Congress, 1 Session, Appendix, 178.
28. Thomas Russell and Elias Nason, *The Life and Public Services of Hon.
Henry Wilson* (Boston, 1872), 66–67; Henry Wilson to Giddings, February 6,
April 10, 1847, Giddings Papers; Martin B. Duberman, *Charles Francis Adams
1807–1886* (Boston, 1961), 116; Frank O. Gatell, *John Gorham Palfrey and the
New England Conscience* (Cambridge, 1963), 109; Kinley J. Brauer, *Cotton
Versus Conscience* (Lexington, 1967), 129. The Conservative Whig Robert Winthrop later recalled that the aim of the Conscience men was "the formation of a
party which should have no Southern wing." Robert C. Winthrop, Jr., *A Memoir
of Robert C. Winthrop* (Boston, 1897), 193.

principle of party loyalty if it meant that party members were bound
to support the policies and nominees of their party even when they
disagreed with them. "I care not one fig for any party as a 'party'
after it departs from correct principles," said an Iowa Republican.
And Carl Schurz agreed that "the mere machinery of the party" was
a matter of indifference to him, since "Parties, sir, are nothing but
arrangements by which principles are to be carried into effect." [29]

Principles, then, were what made the radicals adhere to the Republican party. Charles Sumner may have been typically self-righteous
when he wrote in 1860 that unlike most politicians he was motivated
solely by principles, but he was also close to the truth.[30] During the
1850's, the major effort of the radicals was to maintain anti-slavery as
the guiding principle of the Republican party. They constantly denounced what Gamaliel Bailey, editor of the *National Era*, called the
"passion for immediate success" which led some Republicans to try to
"trim and weaken our movement" merely to attract more votes. They
would rather see the party defeated but true to its principles, than
victorious on an innocuous platform. But the radicals were also convinced that adherence to principle was the surest way to political success, and in the districts they represented, this was in large measure
true. "The anti-slavery sentiment of the country is stronger than
political leaders suffer it to appear," said the radical Worcester *Spy* in
1859; in the same year, John Potter wrote that Republican victory in
1860 could only be assured if the party were "true, firm, and unflinching," and stood by its principles.[31] It was both politically and morally
necessary, therefore, for the Republican party to be unyielding in its
anti-slavery position. After the Civil War, Nathaniel Banks said of
Charles Sumner that he was "not a harmonizer." This was true of all
the radicals, for they rejected a cardinal principle of American politics,

29. *The Debates of the Constitutional Convention of the State of Iowa* (2 vols.:
Davenport, 1857), II, 679; "Speech at Republican Rally," Manuscript, March
1860, Carl Schurz Papers, LC. Cf. Cincinnati *Gazette*, September 3, 1860;
Boston *Commonwealth*, May 3, 1854; Carl Schurz, *Speeches of Carl Schurz*
(Philadelphia, 1865), 44.
30. Sumner to Henry L. Pierce, June 29, 1860, Miscellaneous Manuscripts,
Houghton Library, Harvard University.
31. Gamaliel Bailey to Chase, April 18, 1856, Chase Papers, HSPa; Godfrey T.
Anderson, "The Slavery Issue as a Factor in Massachusetts Politics from the Com-
promise of 1850 to the Outbreak of the Civil War" (unpublished doctoral disserta-
tion, University of Chicago, 1944), 250; John F. Potter to William Schouler,
October 27, 1859, William Schouler Papers, MHS. Cf. William Brisbane to Chase,
June 22, 1859, Letterbooks, William Brisbane Papers, WisHS.

that of compromise.[32] They were as much moralists as politicians, using political means to eradicate a sin from American society.

II

"He, who believes slavery to be a great wrong," Salmon P. Chase wrote in 1853, "and desires to promote its abolition by political action, is a political abolitionist." Chase's dictum is a useful definition of radical Republicanism, for during the 1840's and 1850's, the radicals developed a comprehensive program of political action against slavery, one which would not breach the constitutional barrier against direct federal interference with slavery in the states, but would nevertheless arrive at complete emancipation. Like other Republicans, the radicals did disavow any intention of promoting abolition by unconstitutional means. "I have never met the first man or woman who maintained that Congress had a right to interfere with slavery in any State in this Union," said John P. Hale in 1856. Thaddeus Stevens agreed that the Constitution barred Congressional interference, adding, "I greatly regret that it is so; for were it within our legitimate control, I would go, regardless of all threats, for . . . its final extinction." [33] Some historians have taken these assurances to mean that while Republicans hoped slavery could be abolished, they lacked "a long-range plan" for achieving it. According to John L. Thomas, this was the party's "most serious liability," and Charles and Mary Beard took Republican pledges of non-interference as proof that slavery had little if anything to do with the coming of the Civil War.[34]

Yet many Republicans believed that the abolition of slavery could be promoted by constitutional actions outside the slave states. It was

32. Fred H. Harrington, *Fighting Politican, Major General N. P. Banks* (Philadelphia, 1948), 11. Cf. *Congressional Globe*, 29 Congress, 2 Session, Appendix, 403; *Proceedings of the State Disunion Convention, Held at Worcester, Massachusetts, January 15, 1857* (Boston, 1857), 19.

33. *Politics in Ohio. Senator Chase's Letter to Hon. A. P. Edgerton* (np, 1853), 12; *Congressional Globe*, 34 Congress, 3 Session, 11; 31 Congress, 1 Session, Appendix, 142. Cf. Chicago *Press and Tribune*, October 21, 1858; New York *Times*, February 18, 1854; *Speeches of John A. Andrew at Higham and Boston* (Boston, 1860), 7; *How Ought Workingmen to Vote in the Coming Elections? Speech of Hon. Henry Wilson, at East Boston, Oct. 15, 1860* (Boston, 1860), 8; Charles Francis Adams to Ansel Bascomb, September 17, 1855, Letterbook, Adams Papers.

34. Thomas, "Antislavery and Utopia," 265; Charles A. Beard and Mary Beard, *The Rise of American Civilization* (New York, 1933 ed.), II, 39–40. Cf. Norman A. Graebner, ed., *Politics and the Crisis of 1860* (Urbana, 1961), 2, 7.

a commonly accepted axiom of political economy before the Civil War that slavery had to expand in order to survive. In the late 1840's David Wilmot made it quite clear that the proviso which bore his name was a step toward emancipation as much as a limitation on the extension of slavery. Wilmot explained the South's expansionism by pointing to the exhaustion of southern soil by slave labor. The ever-pressing need for new and fertile lands made the extension of slavery an economic necessity for the South. "Keep it within given limits," he told a New York audience in 1847, ". . . and in time it will wear itself out. Its existence can only be perpetuated by constant expansion. . . . Slavery has within itself the seeds of its own destruction." [35] This kind of argument was used constantly in the 1850's; by opposing slavery's extension, many Republicans hoped to strike a fatal blow at slavery in the states as well. "To restrict Slavery within its present limits," Horace Greeley informed his readers during the campaign of 1856, "is to secure its speedy decline and ultimate extinction." Thaddeus Stevens explained that he opposed "the diffusion of slavery" because to "surround it by a cordon of freemen" would lead to abolition within twenty-five years. And Carl Schurz stated this intention as explicitly as could be desired in his Chicago speech of September, 1858: "the clearest heads of the slaveholding States tell you openly that slavery cannot thrive, unless it be allowed to expand. . . . Well, then, . . . pent it up!" [36]

But the radicals' program went far beyond the view that non-extension would mean eventual abolition. For them, barring slavery from spreading was only one of a series of actions the federal government could take to secure emancipation, and they developed a program of constitutional political action which they were convinced would secure the speedy abolition of slavery throughout the country. This radical program was essentially the Liberty party policy which Chase had enunciated in the 1840's. It called for the "divorce of the federal

35. *Proceedings of the Herkimer Mass Convention of October 26, 1847* (Albany, 1847), 14; Charles B. Going, *David Wilmot Free-Soiler* (New York, 1924), 272; *Congressional Globe*, 31 Congress, 1 Session, Appendix, 943.
36. New York *Tribune*, October 15, 1856; *Congressional Globe*, 31 Congress, 1 Session, Appendix, 142; Schurz, *Speeches*, 26. Cf. *Proceedings of the Democratic and Free Democratic Conventions . . .* (Rome, 1849), 60; Cincinnati *Gazette*, July 27, 1860; Chicago *Press and Tribune*, August 23, 1859; William H. Freehling has made the suggestive point to me that the expand-or-die outlook was quite pervasive in mid-nineteenth-century American thought, and was applied to many other institutions and structures aside from slavery.

government from slavery" or "no slavery outside the slave states"—the abolition of the institution everywhere within the constitutional jurisdiction of Congress. This included action against slavery in the territories, the District of Columbia, and on American ships on the high seas; it meant absolutely prohibiting the admission of any more slave states, the strict enforcement of laws against the foreign slave trade, and the abolition of the interstate slave trade. In addition, the radical program called for the federal government to become what Sumner called "Freedom's open, active and perpetual ally," by refusing office to slaveholders, barring the use of slaves in federal construction projects, and in other ways exerting its influence against slavery. "With these principles established," Chase declared, "and an administration based upon them, Slavery would come to a speedy end." [37]

During the 1840's this program of "opposition to Slavery within the Constitution," as Sumner called it, was adopted by the men who would be radical Republican leaders a decade later. As we have seen, Chase's program was adopted by western state Liberty conventions and by that party's national gatherings. The policy of divorcing the federal government from slavery also became the rallying-cry of the Conscience Whigs of Massachusetts. Henry Wilson called for federal action "as far as we have the constitutional right, . . . in favor of emancipation," and Charles Sumner drew up the Conscience platform of 1847 which made clear that complete abolition was their ultimate political aim.[38] Barnburner leaders like Preston King echoed the call for the divorce of the government from any support of slavery. It cannot be overemphasized that the radicals adopted this program as a sure means toward abolition, and one which would command far more popular support than unconstitutional interference with slavery in the states. Giddings made this clear when he wrote to Chase in 1848

37. *Sumner Works*, II, 284; Chase to Editor of *American Citizen*, April 4, 1845, Salmon P. Chase Papers, LC. Arthur Bestor claims that "responsible political leaders" before the Civil War denied the power of Congress to interfere with the interstate slave trade. Bestor, "The American Civil War as a Constitutional Crisis," *AHR*, LXIX (January 1964), 342. But many radicals insisted the power existed and demanded it be exercised. See *Sumner Works*, I, 308; Chase to Sidney H. Gay, January 3, 1855, Sidney H. Gay Papers, Columbia University; John G. Palfrey, *Papers on the Slave Power* (Boston, 1846), 82–87; Edward Magdol, *Owen Lovejoy; Abolitionist in Congress* (New Brunswick, 1967), 85.
38. John Bigelow, *Retrospections of an Active Life* (5 vols.: New York, 1909–13), I, 126; Russell and Nason, *Wilson*, 64; Donald, *Sumner*, 147, 155. Cf. Pierce, *Sumner*, III, 139, 217; Russell and Nason, *Wilson*, 73–74; *National Era*, July 2, 9, 1857.

concerning proposed resolutions for the Ohio Free Territory Convention:

> I would say nothing about the *abolition* of slavery. This is misunderstood and frightens many. ~~I would go for the~~ *separaton of the federal government from all interference with that institution.* This in its effect and consequences is abolition, but in a much more acceptable form than the other.

Charles Sumner made the same point in speaking of the anti-slavery Democrats. He was sure that they would soon move from a simple opposition to the extension of slavery to a "broader conclusion . . . the duty of no longer allowing the *continuance* of the evil anywhere within our constitutional action." Then he added the revealing sentence: "They must become Abolitionists." The radicals thus considered their program a form of abolitionism. Though they differed with the Garrisons and Gerrit Smiths, the radicals would agree with Chase's political lieutenant, E. S. Hamlin, when he wrote in 1850: "our mission is to overthrow slavery *in the States,* as well as to keep it out of the territories." [39]

After they joined the Republican party, the radicals did not abandon their program of political action, nor did they seek to conceal that their ultimate objective was complete emancipation. Henry Wilson told a New York audience in 1855 that he favored immediate abolition "wherever [slavery] exists under the Constitution of the United States," and he told a Michigan convention in the same year that Republicans "mean to place the Government actively and fully on the side of Liberty. . . ." "Let it be distinctly understood," Wilson declared, "that our object is the emancipation of the bondsmen in America." The influential western editor John C. Vaughan informed Chase that the "one end" of political anti-slavery was *"the best means by Northern action of securing Southern Emancipation. . . ."* [40] During the 1856 campaign, Horace Greeley wrote a public letter which candidly acknowledged that ~~preventing the extension of slavery was only "the first practicable step" toward abolition, and that when the Republicans gained power, "other steps will naturally follow from which con-~~

---

39. Preston King to Chase, August 16, 1847, Giddings to Chase, June 17, 1848, E. S. Hamlin to Chase, March 11, 1850, Chase Papers, HSPa; Sumner to Giddings, January 21, 1847, Giddings Papers.
40. New York *Times,* May 9, 1855; New York *Tribune,* September 17, 1855; J. C. Vaughan to Chase, September 16, 1855, Chase Papers, HSPa. Cf. *Congressional Globe,* 33 Congress, 2 Session, Appendix, 238; New York *Tribune,* July 27, 1854; Boston *Commonwealth,* September 13, 1854.

servatives will probably recoil." After the defeat of Frémont, as conservatives sought to moderate Republican platforms in many states,
the radicals did not waver in their adherence to their program. The
radicals, Chase wrote Giddings in 1857, must insist upon the denationalization of slavery, not mere non-extension, as party policy, "boldly
avowing that we expect as the consequence of such action that slavery
will be abolished everywhere. . . ." In the same year George Julian
chided Republicans who were "ashamed to avow" that abolition was
"our ultimate purpose as members of the Republican party," and in
1858 the Chicago *Tribune* editorialized that complete abolition was a
goal "devoutly to be wished and earnestly to be labored for," but
that the party was committed to "*first* securing to freedom the new
and unoccupied Territories of the Union." [41] Nor did radicals moderate
their program during the presidential year of 1860. Charles Sedgwick
told the House in March that he wanted the government to go to "the
extreme verge of constitutional authority" against slavery, and a
former Congressman from Maine, Daniel Somes, declared in October
that a Republican victory would lead to abolition in the nation's
capital, an end to the use of slaves in federal employment, and eventually to emancipation in the South itself.[42] All in all, the radicals made
it quite plain that they would hardly be satisfied if a Republican
government merely prevented slavery from expanding. From first to
last, the stakes for which they aimed were far more comprehensive.

The radicals' conviction that their program would lead to abolition
was based on their analysis of the political situation within the South.
They were convinced that once slavery was confined to the slave states
and its extension forever prohibited, southerners themselves would
take up the work of abolition. As Chase put it in 1851, "Restrict slavery
in the slave States! prevent its ingress into territories! repeal the
Fugitive Slave law! put the general government on the side of freedom!
and emancipation will spring up in the Southern States!" [43] For it was
an axiom of radical policy that there existed a latent mass of anti-
slavery feeling within the South. The whole Slave Power idea was

41. Horace Greeley to William M. Chace, *et al.*, May 9, 1856, Horace Greeley
Papers, NYPL; Chase to Giddings, January 7, 1857, Giddings Papers; Grace Julian
Clarke, *George W. Julian* (Indianapolis, 1923), 185; Chicago *Tribune*, May 15,
1858. Cf. Chase to Gerrit Smith, February 16, 1857, Chase Papers (ser II), LC;
New York *Tribune*, February 6, 1858.
42. *Congressional Globe*, 36 Congress, 1 Session, Appendix, 175–76; *Liberator*,
October 5, 1860. Cf. July 13, 1860; Chicago *Democrat*, August 15, 1860.
43. New York *Times*, October 2, 1851. Cf. *Politics in Ohio*, 5–6; *Sumner Works*,
III, 458–59; *Wisconsin State Journal*, August 20, 1860.

based on the assumption that a small aristocracy of slaveholders controlled southern life and politics, effectively stifling the aspirations of the mass of poor non-slaveholders. The radicals expected to find numerous anti-slavery allies once the political strength of the Slave Power was broken by a Republican victory in a presidential election. "There is a vast amount of antislavery sentiment in the Slave States, which requires to be fostered and developed," Chase informed Giddings in 1846. One of the major goals of the radicals' anti-slavery activity was to give encouragement to this "dormant mass of anti-slavery feeling at the South." [44] It was an easy step from the conviction—shared by all adherents of the free labor ideology—that slavery was a curse to the poor whites of the South, to the assumption that the southern masses either desired or could be taught to desire abolition. "These poor white men of the South," Simon Cameron wrote in 1858, "who are our brothers, and our natural allies, must be taught . . . that we are battling for their rights. They will learn in time, that by acting with us, they will cease to be the 'mudsills of society.'" The radicals were convinced that the antagonism between the class interests of the slaveholders and non-slaveholders was, as James Ashley told Congress in 1860, "the real point of danger to the ruling class of the South." Once Republicans ended the Slave Power's control of the federal government, the slaveholders would find their power challenged at home as well. "We believe," wrote James Russell Lowell on the eve of Lincoln's election, "that the 'irrepressible conflict' . . . is to take place in the South itself." [45]

During the pre-war decades, the radicals seized upon every evidence of anti-slavery activity in the South as proof that emancipation could be achieved from within slave society. In the 1840's they hailed Cassius M. Clay's attempt to organize an anti-slavery political force in Kentucky as the harbinger of successful efforts throughout the South. [46] In the next decade they watched hopefully as anti-slavery

44. "Diary and Correspondence of Salmon P. Chase," Annual Report of AHA, 1902, II, 112; E. A. Stansbury to Charles Francis Adams, June 26, 1848, Adams Papers. Cf. Sumner Works, IV, 45; Congressional Globe, 35 Congress, 1 Session, 752, 36 Congress, 1 Session, Appendix, 49.
45. Simon Cameron to George Bergner, March 28, 1858 (draft), Simon Cameron Papers, LC; Congressional Globe, 36 Congress, 1 Session, Appendix, 374; Lowell, "Election," 498. Cf. New York Tribune, March 10, 1856, July 11, 1857, August 24, 1859; George W. Julian, Speeches on Political Questions (New York, 1872), 68.
46. David L. Smiley, Lion of Whitehall, the Life of Cassius M. Clay (Madison, 1962), 55, 107; Charles Francis Adams to Clay, May 2, 1845, Letterbook, Adams

politics developed throughout the border area. Republican newspapers printed reports of Republican meetings in Virginia, Delaware,
and other states, publishing letters from anti-slavery men in the Deep
South as well. When a Republican was elected to the Delaware legislature in 1860, Adams termed it the best news of the election aside from
Lincoln's success, and the New York *Tribune* gave prominence to the
election of a Republican from western Virginia to that state's Senate.
The fledgling Republican newspapers of western Virginia received
financial aid and advice from leading Republican radicals, and radical
and moderate Republicans alike encouraged the distribution of Hinton
Helper's appeal to non-slaveholders to rise against slavery and the
southern aristocracy.[47]

The most hopeful southern anti-slavery activity before the Civil
War was the Republican movement led by Francis P. Blair, Jr., in
Missouri. Seward called Blair "the man of the West, of the age," and
other radicals agreed that his was one of the most important movements in American politics. When Blair was elected to Congress from
St. Louis in 1856, the *National Era* declared that a new age in the
politics of the country had opened and predicted that Blair would
soon be joined by Republicans from Kentucky, Maryland, and other
border states. In the next year the election of a Republican mayor of
St. Louis was hailed by radicals as the first step toward anti-slavery
victory in Missouri and the entire border area. "Our principles have
become *aggressive*," said the *Era*. "We no longer stand upon the defensive. We have crossed the line, and are upon slaveholding
ground." [48]

The radicals made it quite clear throughout the 1850's that they
expected a Republican presidential victory to lead to the organization of Republican parties in almost every Southern state. At the
1856 Republican Convention, E. Rockwood Hoar of Massachusetts

Papers; Russell and Nason, *Wilson*, 82–83. Cf. Palfrey, *Slave Power*, 59–61.
47. New York *Times*, August 21, 1856; New York *Tribune*, September 3, 1856,
September 29, 1859; Charles Francis Adams Diary, November 8, 1860, Adams
Papers; Ralph G. Lowe, "Republican Newspapers in Antebellum Virginia," *WVaH*,
XXVIII (July, 1967), 282–84; Allan Nevins, *The Emergence of Lincoln* (2 vols.:
New York, 1950), I, 213–14.
48. William Seward to James Watson Webb, October 1, 1858, William H. Seward
Papers, Rush Rhees Library, University of Rochester; *National Era*, August 14,
1856, May 14, 1857. Cf. New York *Evening Post*, April 8, 1857; Springfield *Re-
publican*, February 10, 1857; Chicago *Press and Tribune*, April 6, 1859; Boston
Atlas and Daily Bee, June 13, 1859; Chase to Sumner, May 1, 1857, Sumner
Papers.

declared that if the Republicans won in November, the next national convention could be held in Virginia or Maryland. To the Democratic charge that their party was sectional, Republicans responded that once freedom of speech and of the press was restored to the South, "we will have more Republican votes, in proportion, in the slave States, than there are Democratic votes in the free states." [49] Throughout the presidential year 1860, radicals were quite explicit about the results they hoped for from a Republican victory. Benjamin Stanton of Ohio predicted that there would be a Republican organization in every southern state within six months of a Republican presidential victory, and Israel Washburn pledged that the party, after electing Lincoln, would "Lincoln one Slave State after another." And at the Chicago Convention, the delegates heard former governor Chauncey Cleveland of Connecticut explain that when the party spoke of overthrowing the Slave Power, it meant revolutionizing the politics of the slave states as well as that of the federal government. "Power," Cleveland asserted, "is to be changed from the hands of the slave oligarchy and placed in the hands of the friends of freedom. . . ." [50]

It is within the context of this over-all plan for the constitutional abolition of slavery that radical disavowals of any intention to interfere with slavery in the states must be viewed. As the *National Era* put it in 1855, "We should be far from countenancing any legislative interference with Slavery in the States, which we regard as unconstitutional; but the Government may legitimately use its patronage and influence to encourage the growth of principles congenial with its own." A Republican administration, in the radical view, would open the southern mails to anti-slavery literature and newspapers. "The postmasters of the Southern States," the Chicago *Democrat* declared on the eve of Lincoln's election, "will no longer be allowed to decide what

49. Moorfield Storey and Edward W. Emerson, *Ebenezer Rockwood Hoar. A Memoir* (Boston, 1911), 117; *Congressional Globe*, 35 Congress, 2 Session, Appendix, 197. Cf. New York *Tribune*, January 24, December 27, 1859; *National Era*, April 6, 20, 1854.

50. *Congressional Globe*, 36 Congress, 1 Session, 1913; New York *Tribune*, July 2, 1860; *Proceedings of the First Three Republican National Conventions* (np, nd), 110. Cf. *Wisconsin State Journal*, September 13, 1860; New York *Evening Post*, September 26, 1860; New York *Tribune*, October 20, 1860; Springfield *Republican*, November 3, 1860; C. H. Ray to E. L. Pierce, April, 1860, E. L. Pierce Papers, Houghton Library, Harvard University; John C. Underwood to Carey, November 6, 1860, Carey Papers; John Bigelow to Mr. Hargreaves, November 10, 1860, John Bigelow Papers, NPYL.

newspapers their neighbors may read." [51] But the most powerful weapon in the radicals' view was control of the patronage of the federal government. As early as 1846, Chase had taken the position that the government could "give a clear preference to antislavery men in public appointments," and in the 1850's the radicals believed that the patronage could be used to help build a strong Republican party in every southern state. The unanimity of southern politicians in defense of slavery, the radicals argued, stemmed from the fact that with the Slave Power in control of both national parties and the federal government, only pro-slavery men could expect patronage preferment. But the election of a Republican president, as Frank Blair put it, would introduce "a different political atmosphere," by demonstrating that "slavery propagandism is not the road to political elevation." The New York *Evening Post* agreed that the moment southerners discovered "that cabinet offices, foreign missions, clerkships, postmasterships, . . . etc., etc., are no longer to be the rewards to those who advocate the extension of slavery," not only would politicians whose sole interest was office rally to the Republican party, but the great mass of non-slaveholders would become active and influential in government.[52] And southern Republicans like Cassius Clay agreed that a "remorseless" exercise of the patronage power would "revolutionize the Slave States . . . in two administrations." Of course many moderate Republicans, including Greeley and Lincoln, insisted that slaveholders could and would hold office under a Republican administration. But if the radicals were to have a strong voice in a Republican government, the election of an anti-slavery president would indeed prove, in the words of the perennial historical debate, "an immediate menace to slavery in the states." [53]

51. *National Era*, August 30, 1855; Chicago *Democrat*, November 5, 1860. Cf. *National Era*, September 7, 1854, September 15, 1859; New York *Tribune* February 3, 1857.
52. Chase to Giddings, August 15, 1846, Chase Papers, LC; F. P. Blair, Jr. to F. P. Blair, February 10, 1856, Blair-Lee Papers; New York *Evening Post*, September 6, 1856. Cf. *National Era*, August 21, 1856; John Bigelow to William Cullen Bryant, March 20, 1860, Bigelow Papers; *Missouri Democrat*, cited in New York *Tribune*, February 28, 1857.
53. Wendell Phillips, *Speeches, Lectures, and Letters* (Boston, 1863), 363–64; *National Era*, May 5, 1859; Basler, ed., *Lincoln Works*, IV, 152; Arthur C. Cole, "Lincoln's Election an Immediate Menace to Slavery in the States?" *AHR*, XXXVI (July 1931), 740–67; J. G. de Roulhac Hamilton, "Lincoln's Election an Immediate Menace to Slavery in the States?" *AHR*, XXXVII (July 1932), 700–11.

III

Between the mid-1840's and 1860, the radicals took the lead in the movement to create a northern party with mass support, committed to opposing slavery in the way they desired. The first attempt to create such a party—the formation of the Free Soil Party in 1848—was the result of several years of planning by leading radicals, coupled with the fortuitous schism in the Democratic party of New York State. Salmon P. Chase had decided soon after the election of 1844 that the Liberty party could never aspire to mass support, so he and other western Liberty men began to work for a coalition between their party and the steadily increasing anti-slavery wings of the two major parties. Between 1846 and 1848, a stream of letters passed between Chase and the leading Conscience Whigs and Barnburner Democrats. Most prominent in the correspondence were Giddings, Sumner, Adams, Wilson, and Preston King, all of whom echoed Chase's call for united political action against slavery.[54]

By 1848, it was clear that some kind of political union was going to take place. But for the anti-slavery radicals, the platform of the new party was a question of primary importance. The key question was, as Giddings put it, "Will the Barnburners agree to and adopt a definite antislavery platform?" The radicals insisted that the platform go further than non-extension—they wanted a commitment to the divorce of the federal government from slavery.[55] But Martin Van Buren, the most likely Free Soil presidential candidate, declared in the summer of 1848 that he opposed abolition in the District of Columbia, a cardinal point in the radical program. Many radicals shared Liberty leader Joshua Leavitt's complaint that Van Buren's position "requires us not only to go into the canvass on the one narrow issue of non-extension, but to tie up our hands from every aggressive movement, however legal or constitutional, which tends to weaken the slave interest within its present bounds." Radical support for Van

---

54. "Diary and Correspondence," 109, 121, 123; Chase to Giddings, February 29, March 10, 1848, Sumner to Giddings, January 22, 1847, Giddings Papers; Sumner to Chase, December 12, 1846, Chase Papers, LC; Flamen Ball to Chase, September 1, 1847, Chase Papers, HSPa; Julian, *Giddings*, 212–13; Donald, *Sumner*, 155–56; Frederick J. Blue, "A History of the Free Soil Party" (unpublished doctoral dissertation, University of Wisconsin, 1966), 60.
55. Giddings to Joseph A. Giddings, July 30, 1848, Giddings Papers; Sumner to Chase, March 12, 1847, Chase Papers, LC; "Diary and Correspondence," 123.

Buren and the Free Soil party therefore hinged on the platform adopted by the Buffalo Convention.[56]

At Buffalo, of course, the radicals got what they wanted. In exchange for the nomination of Van Buren, the Barnburners gave the Liberty men carte blanche in writing the platform. Chase was, in the words of a Wisconsin newspaper, "the guiding spirit" of the convention. In the platform committee, he and Preston King expressed the opinion that the resolutions should demand the complete separation of the federal government from slavery, and Chase composed the resolutions, which the convention adopted by acclamation, restating the constitutional position he had been advocating for a decade. It was, Leavitt wrote, "a thorough Liberty platform," and it satisfied almost all the radicals. The *National Era* later declared that the position defined in the Buffalo platform was as far as a political party could go in opposing slavery by constitutional means.[57] Most state Free Soil platforms between 1848 and 1854 took this radical ground, and the 1852 national resolutions, which were taken primarily from a draft prepared by Chase, again stressed the denationalization of slavery as the party's goal.[58]

The Free Soil party, of course, never fulfilled the radicals' hopes that it would become the rallying point for all anti-slavery northerners and eventually become the major party of the North. After the Whig debacle of 1852, they again looked forward to a political reorganization, confident that the Whigs, unable to regain their lost power, would have to merge with the Free-Soilers. But it was not until 1854, in the aftermath of the Kansas-Nebraska Act, that a full political reorganization

56. Joshua Leavitt to Giddings, July 6, 1848, Giddings Papers; *National Era*, July 13, 1848; Charles Francis Adams to Van Buren, July 16, 1848, Gamaliel Bailey to Van Buren, August 2, 1848, Martin Van Buren Papers, LC; Samuel Lewis to John P. Hale, July 10, 1848, Lewis Tappan to Hale, July 8, 1848, Hale Papers, NHHS; Gamaliel Bailey to Adams, July 13, 1848, Adams Papers; Sumner to Giddings, July 15, 1848, Giddings Papers.
57. Milwaukee *Free Democrat*, February 28, 1849, Scrapbook, Chase Papers, LC; Chase to J. Taylor, August 15, 1848, Chase Papers, HSPa; Robert B. Warden, *An Account of the Private Life and Public Services of Salmon Portland Chase* (Cincinnati, 1874), 319; Kirk H. Porter and Donald B. Johnson, comps., *National Party Platforms 1840-1956* (Urbana, 1956), 13; Joshua Leavitt to Hale, August 23, 1848, Henry B. Stanton to Hale, August 20, 1848, Hale Papers; *National Era*, July 8, 1852.
58. Boston *Commonwealth*, July 7, 1852, September 16, 1853; Charles Francis Adams Diary, September 15, 1852, Adams Papers; *National Era*, November 8, 1849, June 16, 1853; Warden, *Chase*, 338; Porter and Johnson, comps. *Party Platforms*, 18-19.

took place and a mass anti-slavery party began to emerge. The decisive role of the radicals in organizing the initial northern reaction to Douglas's measure and in the formation of the Republican party has often been overlooked. Historians have agreed that the North instantly rose in protest against the plan to repeal the Missouri Compromise, opening the western territories to slavery, but in reality, for the first month after Douglas introduced his bill, radicals were worried by the lack of popular response. The radical press—the *National Era,* New York *Tribune,* and local free-soil journals—instantly condemned the bill, but other northern papers at first ignored it.[59] From Massachusetts, Charles Sumner received complaints about popular apathy, and Charles Francis Adams noted in his diary that despite the warnings of the anti-slavery press, "the mass of the community are cold and apathetic." Even in the West, a Cleveland free-soil paper asserted, "It is a matter of amazement to us that the Douglas bill does not startle the whole North as would the shock of an earthquake." Eventually, of course, the mass reaction did come, but the radicals had to take the lead. Chase's "Appeal of the Independent Democrats" did much to arouse popular opinion, and in New York, Seward finally took it upon himself to organize a rally against the Nebraska bill, since none had arisen spontaneously.[60]

Once the northern reaction against the Nebraska Act took place, the radicals swung into action to attempt another political reorganization. Henry Wilson declared the Whig party dead, and vowed to oppose any efforts to resurrect it. Greeley's *Tribune* called for the formation of a new northern party, and Wade, Chase, Sumner, and other radicals spoke out for the union of all opponents of the Nebraska act.[61] The *National Era* insisted that the old political parties had out-

59. Trefousse, *Radical Republicans,* 65; Giddings to Joseph A. Giddings, January 11, 1853, Giddings Papers, Boston *Commonwealth,* January 9, 1854; *National Era,* January 12, 19, 1854. Moderate and conservative papers of Massachusetts virtually ignored the Kansas-Nebraska bill until a good month after its introduction. Pierce, *Sumner,* III, 349.
60. Samuel Gridley Howe to Sumner, January 18, 25, 1854, Samuel Gridley Howe Papers, Houghton Library, Harvard University; Albert G. Browne to Sumner, February 22, 1854, Sumner Papers; Works Projects Administration, eds., *Annals of Cleveland, 1818–1935* (59 vols.: Cleveland, 1937–38), XXXVII, 438; New York *Herald,* February 1, 1854. For other radical complaints about initial popular apathy, see Hunt, *Washburn,* 29; John Jay to Richard Henry Dana, Jr., February 8, 1854, Richard Henry Dana, Jr. Papers, MHS; Charles Francis Adams Diary, February 16, 17, 1854; *National Era,* October 19, 1854.
61. Boston *Commonwealth,* June 1, 1854; Wilson to Israel Washburn, May 28, 1854, Israel Washburn Papers, LC; Wilson to Seward, May 28, 1854, Seward

lived their usefulness, and its editor, Gamaliel Bailey, played an important part in calling a caucus of anti-slavery Whig and Democratic Congressmen in May. Meeting in the rooms of Israel Washburn, some thirty opponents of the Nebraska act issued a call for the organization of a new political party and suggested that "Republican" would be the most appropriate name. The radicals also took a leading role in the creation of the Republican party in many northern states during the summer of 1854. But, as in 1848, the radicals refused to accept moderate anti-slavery demands as the platform of the new party. While conservatives and many moderates were content merely to call for the restoration of the Missouri Compromise or a prohibition of slavery extension, the radicals insisted that no further political compromise with slavery was possible.[62]

In almost every northern state, the radicals attempted to have a Republican party or an anti-Nebraska fusion movement organized in 1854. In areas where the radicals controlled the new organization, the comprehensive radical program became the party policy. The Michigan Republican Convention which met at Jackson on July 6th, for example, took the radical ground of demanding no further compromises with slavery, the repeal of the fugitive slave law, and abolition in the District of Columbia. Wisconsin Republicans, meeting in their first convention a week later, called for the restriction of slavery to the states in which it already existed. In New York and Illinois, radical leaders attempted to create state-wide Republican organizations, but the Whigs held aloof, and in Massachusetts, the Free Soilers created a Republican organization which was promptly swamped by the rise of Know-Nothingism. But Republican conventions in all these states adopted radical platforms.[63] Where the radicals could not

Papers; New York *Tribune*, March 17, May 24, June 17, 1854; *Congressional Globe*, 33 Congress, 1 Session, Appendix, 764; Chase to N.S. Townshend, February 10, 1854, Chase Papers, HSPa; Sumner to Amasa Walker, April 26, 1854, Amasa Walker Papers, MHS.

62. *National Era*, February 16, March 30, 1854; James S. Pike, *First Blows of the Civil War* (New York, 1879), 233, 237-38, 247; Francis Curtis, "The Birth of the Republican Party," *Munsey's Magazine*, XXX (March 1904), 806; Allan Nevins, *Ordeal of the Union* (2 vols.: New York, 1947), II, 322. Cf. *Boston Commonwealth*, June 1, 1854; George W. Julian, *Political Recollections* (Chicago, 1884), 137.

63. *National Era*, July 20, 1854; Racine *Weekly Advocate*, May 22, July 17, 1854; New York *Tribune*, August 18, 1854; Elihu Washburne to Zebina Eastman, July 5, 1854, James F. Aldrich Papers, ChicHS; Paul Selby, "The Genesis of the Republican Party in Illinois," *Transactions* of the IllSHS, XI (1904), 383; Don E. Fehrenbacher, *Prelude to Greatness, Lincoln in the 1850's* (New York, 1964

control the new party by themselves, they had to compromise on resolutions. Chase and Wade drew up the call for the Ohio Anti-Nebraska Convention of July 13, and included the demand for no slavery outside the slave states. But the convention adopted a platform merely opposing the extension of slavery—a compromise between the radical position and conservative demands that the restoration of the Missouri Compromise be made the main issue. Chase was disappointed by "the comparatively narrow basis" of the platform, but was consoled by the thought that the radicals would be able to "urge our larger and sounder views" on public opinion while working in the new party. In Indiana, where conservatives controlled the anti-Nebraska coalition, a radical minority platform proposed by George Julian was voted down.[64]

Between 1854 and 1860, radicals in every northern state fought to strengthen the Republican party, to give it a more comprehensive program than mere non-extension, and to keep the issue of slavery in the political forefront.[65] Republican platforms in such radical states as Wisconsin, Michigan, Maine, and Vermont usually called for the divorce of the government from slavery, the repeal of the fugitive slave law, and no more slave states, as did platforms in Pennsylvania, Minnesota, and Massachusetts when radical influence was high.[66] Because the radicals had a well-thought-out and comprehensive program for dealing with the slavery question, and had spokesmen who articulated it with clarity and persuasiveness, they were able to influence many of the new politicians who rose to power via the Republican

ed.), 35–36; Magdol, Lovejoy, 107–16; William G. Bean, "Party Transformation in Massachusetts With Special Reference to the Antecedents of Republicanism 1848–1860" (unpublished doctoral dissertation, Harvard University. 1922), 192–93; Springfield Republican, July 21, 1854; Charles Francis Adams Diary, July 7, 1854, Adams Papers; Boston Commonwealth, July 21, September 8, 1854.

64. Boston Commonwealth, June 21, 1854; Joseph P. Smith, ed., History of the Republican Party in Ohio (2 vols.: Chicago, 1898), I, 22; Chase to N. S. Townshend, July 22, 1854, Chase Papers, HSPa; "Diary and Correspondence," 262; Charles Zimmerman, "The Origin and Development of the Republican Party in Indiana," IndMH, XIII (September 1917), 236; Clarke, Julian, 153–55. On the general role of the radicals in 1854, see Trefousse, Radical Republicans, 76–81.

65. New York Tribune, May 7, June 28, 30, November 5, 1855; George Julian, Speeches on Political Questions (New York, 1872), 107–08; Myers, "Rise of Republican Party," 61; Congressional Globe, 35 Congress, 2 Session, 343; Charles Francis Adams to Francis Bird, October 16, 1854, Letterbook, Adams Papers; National Era, September 23, 1858, January 27, 1859.

66. National Era, July 12, September 20, 1855; New York Tribune, August 6, September 17, 1855; Chester V. Easum, The Americanization of Carl Schurz (Chicago, 1929), 141; Boston Atlas and Daily Bee, June 26, 1858.

movement. An interesting example of this was Chase's impact on the January, 1855 inaugural addresses of two new Republican governors, James Grimes of Iowa and Kinsley Bingham of Michigan. When Grimes was elected in April, 1854, Chase congratulated him and noted that "your message will be looked for with great interest." He urged Grimes to call for the complete separation of the federal government from slavery. Such a statement, Chase wrote, "will help shape the new movement." Grimes responded by sending Chase a copy of his inaugural before its delivery, and Chase was highly pleased by its radical tone. Bingham was also receptive to Chase's suggestions, and told the Ohioan that he had incorporated some of Chase's own words into his inaugural address. Men like Grimes and Bingham were powerful politicians, and their views had an important impact on the shaping of Republican platforms in their states.[67]

Just as they helped organize the Republican party in the summer of 1854, the radicals played an important role in the national organization of the party in 1856. Gamaliel Bailey had a key part in calling the Pittsburgh Convention of February, 1856, which launched the Republican party as a national organization. Other radicals like Chase, Sumner, John Z. Goodrich of Massachusetts, A. P. Stone of Ohio, Cassius Clay, and Lewis Clephane also participated in planning the gathering. But although many radical leaders attended the convention, Henry J. Raymond's moderate policy statement, focusing on non-extension and the Kansas controversy, was adopted. Just before the May Philadelphia Convention, the *National Era* reported that radicals in many states were becoming uneasy over attempts by moderates to soften the Republican platform.[68] As in 1848, the radicals approached the nominating convention of the new anti-slavery party in a suspicious mood, withholding their full endorsement until the platform was

67. Chase to James M. Grimes, April 24, 1854, Chase Papers, HSPa; William Salter, *The Life of James W. Grimes* (New York, 1876), 54–61, 63n.; Kinsley Bingham to Chase, January 8, 1855, Chase Papers, LC; George N. Fuller, ed., *Messages of the Governors of Michigan* (4 vols.: Lansing, 1925–27), II, 298–99; Louis Pelzer, "The Origin and Organization of the Republican Party in Iowa," *IJHP*, IV (October 1906), 493.
68. Lewis Clephane, *Birth of the Republican Party* (Washington, 1889), 8–12; George W. Julian, "The First Republican National Convention," *AHR*, IV (January 1899), 313–22; Seward, *Seward*, I, 264; Andrew W. Crandall, *The Early History of the Republican Party* (Boston, 1930), 50–51; Charles Francis Adams Diary, December 26, 1855, Gamaliel Bailey to Adams, January 20, 1856, Adams Papers; Trefousse, *Radical Republicans*, 98; *Official Proceedings of the Republican Convention Convened in the City of Pittsburgh, Pennsylvania On the 22nd of February, 1856* (Washington, 1856), 23; *National Era*, May 22, 1856.

adopted. And as in 1848, the platform turned out to be all that they desired. It linked slavery and polygamy as "twin relics of barbarism" (a phrase suggested by the Massachusetts radical E. R. Hoar), endorsed Chase's constitutional position that the federal government was bound to abolish slavery everywhere within its jurisdiction, and specifically denied the authority of either Congress or a territorial legislature to establish slavery in any territory. Giddings played an influential role on the platform committee, and was highly pleased with the result.[69] "I think it is ahead of all other platforms ever adopted," he informed Julian, and added that while he would have preferred one of the experienced radicals as the presidential candidate, the platform was so radical that "I am willing to let them [the moderates] have the offices to support our doctrines." Other radical leaders were equally exultant. Chase wrote that he could not believe the delegates understood the full implications of the platform, since the resolutions clearly demanded "the denationalization of slavery entire." Julian declared "I accept it, because I think I can stand upon it and preach from it the whole anti-slavery gospel." And other radicals pointed out that if a Republican administration felt bound to carry out the letter of the platform, it would have to abolish slavery in the District of Columbia and in the territories, bar any slave states from admission to the Union, and restrict the institution to the states where it already existed.[70]

The campaign of 1856 was waged almost exclusively on the slavery issue, focusing on the question of Kansas. The Republicans did remarkably well for a new party, carrying eleven states and polling 45 per cent of the northern vote. But the large vote cast for Know-Nothing candidate Millard Fillmore in such key states as Pennsylvania, Indiana, and Illinois prevented Frémont from capturing these states. It was obvious that in order to win in 1860, the Republicans would have to attract a large portion of this nativist and conservative vote, and many Republicans therefore felt it was essential to moderate the party's platform. The radicals were increasingly concerned by what Chase called "an obvious disposition among many to place our cause on the lowest possible ground—to connect it with the least possible advocacy of principle," and he wrote Sumner that if the conservatives

69. Storey and Emerson, *Hoar,* 116–17; Porter and Johnson, *Party Platforms,* 27; Julian, *Giddings,* 335–36, 382; *Congressional Globe,* 35 Congress, 2 Session, 345. 70. Giddings to Julian, June 24, 1856, Chase to Julian, July 17, 1856, Giddings-Julian Papers; Julian, *Speeches,* 151–52. Cf. *National Era,* June 26, 1856; Chase to John C. Frémont, June 27, 1856, in Diary, Chase Papers, LC.

succeeded, it might be necessary to re-create the Free Soil party. Chase was particularly disturbed by the tendency of many Republicans to eschew moral attacks on slavery for political and economic arguments. Soon after the 1856 election, he explained to Giddings the course which the radicals should pursue:[71]

> Let those of us who are prepared to do so take the ground of no slavery outside of Slave States. . . . Let us get rid of that cold indifference to Slavery as a system which some of our prominent men seem so anxious to display. Let us condemn it as it deserves to be condemned every where . . . [and] put our action upon the moral ground.

The movement to modify the Republican position on slavery reached its high point in 1858, when Stephen A. Douglas broke with the Buchanan administration over its attempt to force slavery into Kansas. Douglas's opposition to the Lecompton Constitution, and his demand that the people of Kansas be permitted to vote on whether or not to accept the pro-slavery document, placed many Republicans in a political dilemma. On the one hand, they knew that they would have to work with Douglas if they hoped to defeat Buchanan, but on the other, to endorse Douglas's policy would be a tacit admission that the people of a territory could introduce slavery if they saw fit. At first the radical Congressmen refused to support the Crittenden-Montgomery bill, which provided for a referendum on the Lecompton Constitution and promised the admission of Kansas as a slave state if the document were approved. But the pressure of their colleagues, the threat that the Douglasites would support the administration if the Crittenden bill failed, and fear of being responsible for the admission of Kansas as a slave state, caused the radicals to waver. In the end, they reluctantly yielded, and all ninety-two Republican Congressmen voted for the Crittenden bill, which passed the House but was defeated in the Senate.[72] But some radicals were appalled by what they considered a surrender of principle. Chase declared that the Republican party had

71. "Diary and Correspondence," 276; Chase to Sumner, March 30, 1858, Chase Papers, HSPa; Chase to Giddings, January 7, 1857, Giddings Papers. Cf. Chase to Sumner, May 1, 1857, Sumner Papers; Philemon Bliss to John C. Underwood, February 24, 1857, John C. Underwood Papers, LC.
72. Sarah J. Day, *The Man on a Hill Top* (Philadelphia, 1931), 215; William Schouler to Chase, March 28, 1858, Giddings to Chase, April 9, 1858, Chase Papers, HSPa; Giddings to Lura M. Giddings, April 30, 1858, Giddings-Julian Papers; Julian, *Giddings*, 345–49; Philemon Bliss to Chase, April 2, 1858, Chase Papers, LC; *Congressional Globe*, 35 Congress, 1 Session, 774, 1437, 1905–6, 1957.

in effect endorsed the principles of the Kansas-Nebraska Act, and expressed his astonishment that any radical could endorse the view "that a majority can enslave a minority rightfully, and that it is no objection to the admission of a state into the Union that her fundamental act—her constitution—provides for such enslavement." [73] Many radicals were highly embarrassed by the vote, and during the state campaigns of 1858 they resumed their struggle with the conservatives for control of party policy. A few radicals, like Henry Wilson and Seward, wanted to endorse Douglas's bid for re-election in Illinois, and perhaps attract him and his followers into the Republican party, but most opposed any idea of fusion, except on strictly Republican terms. Like Lincoln, they recognized that fusion with Douglas would have deflated the real energy of the growing Republican movement in Illinois, and completely undermined the moral aspect of the anti-slavery appeal. Chase was particularly adamant on this point, and almost alone among Republican leaders, he campaigned extensively for Lincoln in the campaign of 1858—a favor which earned Lincoln's everlasting gratitude. The radicals insisted that their party must be more than "a mere opposition"—that it must retain its distinctive and affirmative principles. [74]

Many historians have interpreted the 1860 Republican platform as a significant defeat for the radicals, as evidence of conversative trends within the party. Since Congressional legislation barring slavery from the territories was not specifically endorsed, they argue, the door was left open for co-operation with conservatives and even popular sovereignty men. More recently, Don E. Fehrenbacher and Robert Russel have questioned this traditional view, and pointed to the similarities between the platforms of 1856 and 1860. [75] It is true that many radicals would have been happy to see the Philadelphia resolutions adopted *in*

73. Chase to Sumner, March 30, 1858, Chase Papers, HSPa. Cf. Chase to John C. Crittenden, April 29, 1858, Chase Papers, HSPa; Chase to Hale, January 23, 1856, Hale Papers; Pike, *First Blows*, 419–20.
74. Trumbull to Lincoln, January 3, 1858, Lincoln Papers; Wade to Chase, December 25, 1857, Chase Papers, LC; Basler, ed., *Lincoln Works*, IV, 34; Samuel Gridley Howe to Sumner, July 27, 1858, Howe Papers; Chase to Henry Wilson, December 20, 1858, Chase Papers, HSPa.
75. Luthin, *First Lincoln Campaign*, 149; Cole, "Lincoln's Election," 754–55; Jeter A. Isely, *Horace Greeley and the Republican Party 1853–1861* (Princeton, 1947), 288; Fehrenbacher, *Prelude to Greatness*, 156–57n.; Robert R. Russel, "Constitutional Doctrines with Regard to Slavery in Territories," *JSH*, XXXII (November 1966), 469–70. Cf. Bestor, "American Civil War," 347n.; Jacobus tenBroek, *The Antislavery Origins of the Fourteenth Amendment* (Berkeley, 1951), 116.

toto by the Chicago Convention, and that the inflammatory description of slavery as a "relic of barbarism" was omitted. But the resolutions regarding slavery were fundamentally the same as they had been in 1856. Framed by John A. Kasson, the former Massachusetts Free Soiler who now lived in Iowa, the platform declared that slavery could not constitutionally exist in any territory because of the due process clause of the Fifth Amendment, and called for legislative action if it should be necessary to enforce this prohibition by statute. The platform committee rejected Horace Greeley's proposal that the resolutions merely declare that slavery could not exist except where it had been established by law. It did leave out the 1856 endorsement of the egalitarian sentiments of the Declaration of Independence, but this was reinserted after a dramatic protest on the convention floor by Giddings, who blamed Greeley for this "low insidious effort to leave out of our platform, the declaration of human rights." [76] Contemporaries recognized that the platform was by no means conservative. Henry Wilson said it was even more radical than the 1856 platform, and Carl Schurz, a member of the platform committee, told a Wisconsin audience that it raised "the creed of the party far above the level of a mere oppositional party." Conservatives at the Chicago Convention who opposed Seward's candidacy argued that the platform was so radical that a moderate candidate was needed to help capture the doubtful states. And in the following months, Republican conservatives like Tom Ewing and Edward Baker voiced public objections to the eighth resolution, which declared that the normal condition of territories was freedom.[77] All in all, the radicals had done an effective job of shaping the official policy of the Republican party.

IV

The struggle between radicals and conservatives for control of the Republican party was waged in almost every northern state between

76. Giddings to Chase, October 20, 1859, Chase Papers, HSPa; "John A. Kasson, An Autobiography," *Annals of Iowa,* 3rd ser, XII (July 1920), 347–49; Henry H. Smith, *All the Republican National Conventions* (Washington, 1896), 19; Edward Younger, *John A. Kasson* (Iowa City, 1955), 104; William M. Hesseltine, ed., *Three Against Lincoln* (Baton Rouge, 1960), 147; Porter and Johnson, *Party Platforms,* 32; Russel, "Constitutional Doctrines," 485; Julian, *Giddings,* 373; Giddings to Smith, May 24, 1860, Smith Papers.
77. *Liberator,* July 13, 1860; *Wisconsin State Journal,* June 4, 1860; New York *Tribune,* May 18, 1860; *Speech of the Hon. Thomas Ewing at Chillicothe, Ohio* (Cincinnati, 1860), 14–15; *Congressional Globe,* 36 Congress, 2 Session, 1385.

1856 and 1860. In several instances—most notably in Wisconsin and Ohio—the radicals used the issue of the fugitive slave law to further their cause. Many historians have commented ironically that the same radicals who became staunch defenders of national supremacy, taking an almost unlimited view of the powers of the federal government in the years after the Civil War, went to the verge of nullification in opposing the fugitive slave law in the 1850's. It is true that both the Liberty and Free Soil parties had taken an extremely limited view of the powers of the federal government. Few radicals would agree with Liberty party leader Gerrit Smith that not even the state governments should build public works or maintain public schools, but both state and national Liberty and Free Soil platforms espoused a belief in the sovereignty of the states and a strict interpretation of the Constitution.[78] Nonetheless, the radicals championed states rights during the 1850's primarily as a political tactic. It is, of course, customary for political minorities to attack the powers of the federal government, and during the 1840's and 1850's, when the radicals were out of power and believed the government to be controlled by the Slave Power, they espoused states rights views. As one astute southerner observed in 1856, the radicals were "driven to assert those doctrines, . . . as the only means of nullifying the Fugitive Slave Law in the free States."[79]

The radicals condemned the fugitive slave act from the moment of its passage in 1850. Many vowed that they would not obey it, and defended the right of slaves to escape if they could. Giddings went so far as to urge armed resistance to slave-catchers and federal marshals, and John Andrew praised the rescue of a fugitive from a Boston jail as "a noble thing—nobly done." But the radicals also used the issue of the fugitive slave law as a means of strengthening their position in the Republican party. This was illustrated by events in Wisconsin, where the Republican party took the most uncompromising position

78. Larry Gara, "The Fugitive Slave Law: A Double Paradox," *CWH*, X (September 1964), 229–33; Octavius B. Frothingham, *Gerrit Smith* (New York, 1878), 181–84; Smith to Beriah Green, January 5, 1850, Smith to W. L. Crandall, April 28, 1850, Letterbook, Smith Papers; Joel Goldfarb, 'The Life of Gamaliel Bailey Prior to the Founding of the *National Era;* the orientation of a Practical Abolitionist" (unpublished doctoral dissertation, University of California at Los Angeles, 1958), 294; *National Era*, February 10, 1853; Porter and Johnson, *Party Platforms*, 18; George W. Julian, "The Death-Struggle of the Republican Party," *North American Review*, CXXVI (1878), 263–64.
79. J. Daniel Loubert, 'The Orientation of Henry Wilson, 1812–1856" (unpublished doctoral dissertation, Boston University, 1952), 226.

on states rights. The Wisconsin controversy arose from the capture of a fugitive slave, Joshua Glover, in 1854, and his rescue a few days later by a group led by the radical editor, Sherman Booth. The legal controversies arising out of this case were not decided until the eve of the Civil War. By then, the Supreme Court of Wisconsin had declared the fugitive slave law unconstitutional, and the federal Supreme Court, in the landmark decision of *Ableman v. Booth,* vindicated the supremacy of the federal courts over state judiciaries, and upheld the law.[80] The radical wing of the Wisconsin party made Booth's cause their own, and insisted on fidelity to states rights as a test of Republican loyalty. In 1857, the Republican legislative caucus chose James R. Doolittle as its nominee for the Senate over Timothy Howe, because Howe, an old Whig, refused to affirm the right of state courts to final jurisdiction in all cases involving federal-state conflicts. Doolittle, a former Democrat, was much more at home in the states-rights position. The Republican legislators also endorsed the Virginia and Kentucky resolutions, and passed a personal liberty law which effectively nullified the fugitive slave law. In 1860, they denied renomination to Wisconsin Chief Justice Dixon because he had affirmed the appellate jurisdiction of the federal Supreme Court.[81] Out-of-state radicals like Chase and Sumner had high praise for Wisconsin's stand, and Carl Schurz and other radicals made extreme states-rights speeches which caused them considerable embarrassment later in their careers. Some, like the lawyer Byron Paine, admitted that their views had been strongly influenced "by the reasoning of Mr. Calhoun in his work on the constitution." For many radicals, however, the fugitive slave agitation itself was as important as the ultimate outcome. As the Wisconsin editor Rufus King wrote Seward in 1855: [82]

80. For summaries of the Glover-Booth cases, see Julius Yanuck, "The Fugitive Slave Law and the Constitution" (unpublished doctoral dissertation, Columbia University, 1953), 186–99; Vroman Mason, "The Fugitive Slave Law in Wisconsin, With Reference to Nullification Sentiment," *Proceedings* of State Historical Society of Wisconsin, XLIII (1895), 122–40.
81. Milwaukee *Sentinel,* January 19, 20, 1857; *Wisconsin State Journal,* January 20, 24, 1857, March 1, 1860; James L. Sellers, "Republicanism and State Rights in Wisconsin," *MVHR,* XVII (September 1930), 214–18, 228.
82. Mason, "Fugitive Slave Law," 133, 137, 140–44; Milwaukee *Free Democrat,* cited in New York *Tribune,* February 22, 1855; Milwaukee *Free Democrat,* cited in *Liberator,* June 17, 1859; *Wisconsin State Journal,* March 25, 1859; New York *Tribune,* April 1, 1859; Byron Paine to Sumner, January 12, 1856, A. D. Smith to Sumner, January 1, 1856, Sumner Papers; George Hoadley to Chase, April 9, 1859, Chase Papers, LC; Rufus King to Seward, February 11, 1855, Seward Papers.

You will see that Wisconsin is thoroughly waked up on the subject
of the Fugitive Slave Law. Our Supreme Court have taken a very
bold stand. I am not lawyer enough to decide whether it be tech-
nically right, but it must provoke, everywhere, discussion and agitation, and Liberty and Right must profit by these.

As in Wisconsin, the controversy over the fugitive slave law in Ohio
was brought to fever-pitch by attempted rescues of fugitives who had
been seized by federal marshals. But even before the series of cases
which aroused Ohio Republicans in 1857 and 1859, the party in that
state had taken a states-rights view. The Republican state convention
of 1855 called for the preservation of "the rights of the several States
as independent governments," and in 1856 the Republican legislature
enacted a series of personal liberty laws and called for the repeal of
the fugitive slave act. In his annual messages, Governor Chase condemned federal usurpations of states rights and warned of the dangers
of centralization of power.[83] Then in 1857 came the Margaret Garner
case, in which a captured fugitive woman killed her own daughter to
prevent her from being taken back to slavery. A few months later,
United States marshals seized four Ohio citizens for harboring fugitives, but the marshals were arrested for assault. In the litigation which
followed, the judicial supremacy of the federal courts again was
called into question as state and federal judges issued conflicting orders,
each voiding the writs of habeas corpus issued by the other. The net
result was to push the radicals further towards complete nullification.[84]

The issue came to a head in 1859, when several citizens of Oberlin
were imprisoned for attempting to rescue a fugitive. Radicals like
Giddings, Wade, and Ashley took part in mass meetings held in the
Western Reserve denouncing the fugitive slave law and the federal
courts, and calling for the preservation of the rights of the states.
Giddings said the prisoners should have killed the federal marshals
rather than allow themselves to be arrested. When the Republican
state convention met, the radicals insisted on making repeal of the

83. Smith, *Ohio Republican Party*, I, 35–36; David H. Bradford, "The Background and Formation of the Republican Party in Ohio, 1844–1861" (unpublished
doctoral dissertation, University of Chicago, 1947), 153; *Message of the Governor
of Ohio to the Fifty-Second General Assembly* . . . (Columbus, 1857), 27. Cf.
George H. Porter, *Ohio Politics During the Civil War Period* (New York, 1911),
20–21.
84. Julius Yanuck, "The Garner Fugitive Slave Case," *MVHR*, L (June, 1953),
47–66; Yanuck, "Fugitive Slave Law," 179–86; *Message of the Governor of Ohio
to the Fifty-Third General Assembly* . . . (Columbus, 1858), 34–35.

law the only issue in the campaign, and demanded that judge Joseph Swan, who had voted to sustain the constitutionality of the law, be denied renomination. "We do not recognize men to be Republicans here in northern Ohio," said one leading radical, "who will for a moment sustain this miserable enactment." [85] The party seemed about to split apart as conservative leaders Thomas Corwin, Benjamin Stanton, and Lewis Campbell insisted on an endorsement of Swan. In the end, a fragile compromise was reached. The platform made the fugitive slave law and federal-state relations the sole issues of the campaign, for the first time ignoring the Kansas question, and demanded repeal of the fugitive slave law, but it did not proclaim the law unconstitutional, a position the conservatives said they would never accept. Judge Swan was not renominated, but a moderate, whose views were unknown, was chosen over the radical candidate. Nonetheless, the radicals were satisfied. Giddings wrote Chase that if Swan had been selected, "we should have been disbanded." In 1860, conservative Republicans joined with Constitutional Unionists and Douglas supporters to endorse a single candidate against Judge Jacob Brinkerhoff, whom the Republicans had renominated and who had declared that the fugitive slave law was unconstitutional. But Brinkerhoff was elected with a majority of 20,000 votes.[86]

The effort to nullify the fugitive slave law, and to exalt the powers of the states at the expense of the federal government, was vigorously pursued by radicals in almost every northern state. In Massachusetts, they waged a successful struggle for the removal of a judge who as a federal commissioner had returned the fugitive Anthony Burns to slavery in 1854, and in several other states they succeeded in having Republican conventions either condemn the fugitive slave law or endorse the states-rights view of government.[87] All this is quite re-

85. Giddings to Ralph Plumb, May 4, 1859, news clipping, Scrapbook, Giddings Papers; William C. Cochran, "The Western Reserve and the Fugitive Slave Law," WRHS Collections, CI (1920), 172–86; Jacob R. Shipherd, comp., History of the Oberl'n-Well'ngton Rescue (Boston, 1859), 244, 253; Porter, Ohio Politics, 26.
86. Roeliff Brinkerhoff, Recollections of a Lifetime (Cincinnati, 1904), 109–13; Douglass' Monthly, August, 1859; Roseboom, Civil War Era, 351; Giddings to Chase, June 7, 1859, Chase Papers, HSPa; Chase to Lincoln, June 13, 1859, Lincoln Papers; Giddings to Adams, October 22, 1860, Adams Papers.
87. Robinson, "Warrington", 210; Henry G. Pearson, The Life of John Andrew (2 vols.: Boston, 1904), I, 80–83: Charles Franc s Adams D'ary, March 19, 1858, Adams Papers; E. L. Pierce to Sumner, April 8, 1858, Sumner Papers; Pelzer, "Origin of Republican Party in Iowa," 514; Boston Evening Traveller, June 27, 1857; Boston Atlas and Daily Bee, June 26, 1858; James S. Pike to Chase, February 27, May 23, 1858, Chase Papers, HSPa.

markable in view of the conduct of the radicals during Reconstruction.
But even more startling was the penchant of some radicals for making
statements in favor of disunion in the 1840's and 1850's. After almost
every anti-slavery defeat of these years, there was an upswing of disunionist sentiment in radical circles. Many radicals, including Joshua
Giddings, William Slade, and William Jay, felt in 1845 and 1846 that
the annexation of Texas justified northern secession, and Charles
Sumner reported from Boston that "a very respectable number" of
Conscience Whigs felt likewise. After the Free Soil defeat of 1848,
Charles Francis Adams took the position that southern secession should
not be opposed, since it would break the Slave Power's control of the
federal government and increase anti-slavery sentiment in the North.[88]
The passage of the fugitive slave law led many radicals to echo Sumner's view that if the survival of the Union were dependent on the
enforcement of the act, "then it ought not to exist." Similarly, the enactment of the Kansas-Nebraska bill was followed by a long series of
articles in the New York *Tribune* claiming to demonstrate that the
North would be far stronger economically if it were independent of
the South. The *Tribune* also carried a series of disunionist articles by
its iconoclastic editor James S. Pike in 1856 and 1857, although Greeley
vigorously condemned his colleague's views. And as late as January
1860, at a meeting in Gerrit Smith's home town of Peterboro, New
York protesting the execution of John Brown, a Republican member
of the state legislature urged anti-slavery men to "invite a free correspondence with the disunionists of the South. . . ."[89]

Most radicals, however, realized that to advocate disunion in most
parts of the North would be to court political disaster. They recognized
that northerners of all parties shared what Lovejoy called "a semi-
religious attachment" to the Union, and some of them were quite
bitter toward the Garrisonian disunionists who, they felt, injured

88. L. Belle Hamlin, ed., "Selections from the Follett Papers," *Quarterly Publica-
tions* of the Ohio Historical and Philosophical Society, XI (1916), 15–16, 21;
Congressional Globe, 29 Congress, 1 Session, Appendix, 72; William Slade to
Giddings, July 30, 1846, Giddings Papers; William Jay to Chase, March 24, May
5, April 22, 1845, Chase Papers, HSPa; Sumner to J. Storey, February 5, 1845,
Sumner Papers; Adams to Palfrey, December 10, 1849, Letterbook, Adams Papers.
89. Donald, *Sumner*, 263; New York *Tribune*, April 12, May 13, 1854, June 5,
December 20, 1856, January 30, 1857; Robert F. Durden, *James Shepherd Pike*
(Durham, 1957), 20–26; Pike, *First Blows*, 358–59; Lawrence T. Lowrey,
"Northern Opinion of Approaching Secession, October, 1859 – November, 1860,"
Smith College Studies in History, III (1918), 218–19.

the anti-slavery cause by associating it with disloyalty to the Union.[90] Sumner, Chase, and other radicals took great pains to dissociate themselves from the Garrisonians, and Henry Wilson later wrote that Garrisonian disunionism "was indeed a most potent weapon in the hands of the apologists, perpetualists, and propagandists of slavery." Wilson insisted that the Republican party was "the party of the constitution and the Union," and Chase made it clear on several occasions that while he agreed with Southern spokesmen on states rights, he could not accept their position that state sovereignty legitimized either nullification or disunion.[91]

Nonetheless, there was a marked difference between the radicals' attitude toward the Union, and that of moderate and conservative Republicans. For many conservatives, the preservation of the Union was an end in itself, and to maintain it they urged that the anti-slavery agitation be abandoned. But to the radicals, the Union was a means, not an end. They believed that the Union had been established for the noble purposes of securing the right of all Americans to life, liberty, and the pursuit of happiness, and that the founders had intended that slavery should one day cease to exist in the nation. Thus, just as the disunionism of the Garrisonians was as much an anti-slavery tactic as a deep philosophical conviction (for they believed that, as Wendell Phillips put it, "disunion is abolition"), the radicals' support of the Union hinged on the government's remaining true to the original goals of the founders.[92] They adopted Webster's motto, "Liberty and Union," at the same time making clear that if a conflict arose between the two, they would be found on the side of liberty. "Let me have liberty and Union, if we can"; said a Maine Congressman, "but liberty

90. *Congressional Globe*, 36 Congress, 2 Session, Appendix, 87; Goldfarb, "Bailey," 373; Pierce, *Sumner*, II, 196; Vincent Y. Bowditch, *Life and Correspondence of Henry Ingersoll Bowditch* (2 vols.: Boston, 1902), I, 170; W. L. Greene to Robert Carter, October 18, 1855, Robert Carter Papers, Houghton Library, Harvard University; Cleveland *Leader*, October 30, 1857.
91. Pierce, *Sumner*, III, 141; Chase to L. S. Abbott, March 6, 1850, Chase Papers, HSPa; *Chase Cincinnati Speech*, 7; *Congressional Globe*, 31 Congress, 1 Session, Appendix, 480, 32 Congress, 1 Session, 641; undated manuscript speech (1855 by internal evidence), Box 17, Chase Papers, HSPa; Wilson, *Slave Power*, I, 574–75. Cf. New York *Tribune*, October 10, 1855; Walter M. Merrill, *Against Wind and Tide* (Cambridge, 1963), 234.
92. Phillips, *Speeches*, 362. On Garrisonian disunionism, see James M. McPherson, *The Struggle for Equality* (Princeton, 1964), 32–34; Thomas, *The Liberator*, 329, 348–49; *Liberator*, January 30, 1857; Phillips, *Speeches*, 355; Lewis Tappan to George Thompson, December 8, 1856, Letterbook, Lewis Tappan Papers, LC.

without Union rather than Union without liberty." Edward Wade declared that the motto of the Western Reserve was "Liberty first and Union afterwards." And other radicals insisted that if the Union was to be what the Slave Power intended—merely an instrument for the protection and extension of slavery—then by all means it should be dissolved. The difference between the Unionists by principle, and the radicals, who saw Union as a means to liberty rather than as an end in itself, was graphically demonstrated by an exchange between Seward and Lovejoy a few days after Lincoln's inauguration. Addressing a delegation from Illinois, Seward implored them to remember "that the battle for Freedom has been fought and won," and that they should "exert [their] best influences now to save the Union." To this Lovejoy responded: "And remember that the Union is worth nothing except so long as there is Freedom in it." [93]

The most important attempt to unite radical Republicans and Garrisonian abolitionists in support of disunion was the Worcester Disunion Convention of January, 1857. The convention was organized by Thomas Wentworth Higginson, who was not a Garrisonian but who believed that the defeat of Frémont demonstrated that the Slave Power's control of the federal government was all but permanent. The invitation to the convention began with the assertion that the Union was "a failure, as being a hopeless attempt to unite under one government two antagonistic systems of society," and it was remarkable that a majority of the signers were not Garrisonians but Republicans, including such radical leaders as Francis Bird, Charles Allen, and Thomas Earle.[94] The response of radicals to Higginson's convention illustrated the complexities of the Union-disunion question. William H. Seward penned a strong rejoinder to Higginson's call, defending the Union and denouncing the convention, but then his political in-

93. *Congressional Globe*, 36 Congress, 2 Session, 969; Edward Wade to Giddings, February 21, 1850, Giddings Papers; New York *Tribune*, March 7, 1861. For other uses of the "liberty and Union" theme, see *Wisconsin State Journal*, March 25, 1859; Russell and Nason, *Wilson*, 76–77; Chase to Sidney H. Gay, April 28, 1847, Gay Papers; New York *Tribune*, September 17, 1855.
94. Thomas Wentworth Higginson, *Cheerful Yesterdays* (Boston, 1899), 236–38; Thomas Wentworth Higginson, *The New Revolution: A Speech Before the American Anti-Slavery Society* (Boston, 1857), 12; Higginson to Smith, November 22, 1856, Smith Papers, Syracuse University; Higginson to Seward, December 29, 1856, Seward Papers; Higginson to Sumner, December 31, 1856, Sumner Papers; *Liberator*, January 2, July 17, 1857; George F. Hoar, "Charles Allen of Worcester," *Proceedings* of the American Antiquarian Society, n.s., XIV (October 1901), 376–78.

stincts prevailed and he decided not to send it. Other Republicans were not so reticent. Edward Wade agreed with the invitation that slavery and freedom were irreconcilable, and even that, up to 1856, the Union had been a failure. He counseled waiting a while longer to see whether action against slavery could still be taken within the Union, but concluded: "rather than to give the strength, moral and political, of the people of the Free States, to the extension and perpetuity of slavery, *let the Union perish.*" Amasa Walker agreed with Wade, though in less fiery language, that the Union was "a *means* and not an *end,*" and that the question of Union or disunion should always be considered in light of tactics in the overriding contest against slavery. Joshua Giddings and Charles Francis Adams were more negative, both stressing that anti-slavery men had more hope of achieving their goals within the Union than outside it, but only Henry Wilson spoke out in really strong language against the whole purpose of the convention. He heaped scorn upon the gathering, damning it as a movement which was "impotent for good . . . [and] can only be productive of evil," because it would alienate the majority of northerners, with their intense nationalism, from all anti-slavery activity. He urged the delegates to "leave all the impotent and puerile threats against the Union to the Southern slave propagandists." In the end, of course, nothing came of the Worcester Convention, although Higginson thought it a great success. Most radicals agreed with George Julian, who wrote to Higginson later that year, "If we can breathe into the people a true anti-slavery life the Union, instead of being the prison-house of the slave will be the gateway of his escape." [95]

Unlike most Republicans, it was not until the secession crisis that the radicals adopted the full-fledged nationalism which would characterize their conduct during the Civil War and Reconstruction. And even during the winter of 1860–61, the radicals' main effort was directed not toward preserving the Union per se, but toward preventing any compromise with the South. Radical governors and Congressmen in-

---

95. Seward to Higginson, January 3, 1857 (draft), Seward Papers; *Liberator,* January 23, 30, 1857; Mary T. Higginson, ed., *Letters and Journals of Thomas Wentworth Higginson, 1846–1906* (Boston, 1921), 77; Julian to Higginson, October 24, 1857, Giddings-Julian Papers. Cf. Charles Francis Adams Diary, January 31, 1857; Giddings to Chase, January 14, 1857, Chase Papers, HSPa; Wilson to Sumner, January 19, 1857, Sumner Papers; George W. Curtis to Higginson, January 22, February 5, 1857, Thomas Wentworth Higginson Papers, Houghton Library, Harvard University.

sisted that secession was unconstitutional and should be met with
force if necessary, and contemporaries agreed that the radical areas of
the North were firm against concessions. Carl Schurz wrote Lincoln
after a quick tour of the free states that the cities were wavering, but
that the rural areas and small towns were firm, and Thurlow Weed
admitted that his calls for compromise were being harshly received
in the Republican countryside.[96] As the radicals saw it, the secession
crisis was a testing time for the Republican party. To give up the fruits
of years of anti-slavery labor by concessions under the threat of disunion would all but dissolve the Republican party, and some radicals
made it clear that they were ready to inaugurate a new party rather
than yield to compromise.[97] Too often in the past, southern threats of
secession had coerced the North into making political concessions—as
Stevens caustically put it, "We have saved this Union so often that I
am afraid we will save it to death." So the radicals stood firm, and
refused to bow to southern threats. "We all feel that Peace is a great
blessing—but that *War* is not the *worst* calamity," one wrote. It would
be worse for the Republican party to surrender its hard-won victory,
with its promise that the difficult task of achieving emancipation
would at last begin. They were particularly adamant against the proposed amendment to the Constitution which would have denied the
federal government any power to interfere with slavery in the states.
Although they admitted that direct federal intervention would be
unconstitutional even without the new measure, the radicals foresaw
the day when southern states might voluntarily ask for federal aid in
planning emancipation, and they wished to place no obstacle in the
path of such a development. As Charles Sedgwick of New York put it,
if the amendment made "the task of emancipating the slave in any

96. Schurz to Lincoln, December 18, 1860, Lincoln Papers; Sidney D. Brummer,
Political History of New York State During the Period of the Civil War (New
York, 1911), 101. For the views of radicals during the secession crisis, see
Trefousse, *Radical Republicans*, chapter 4; David Potter, *Lincoln and His Party
in the Secession Crisis* (New Haven, 1942), 176–77; *Congressional Globe*, 36
Congress, 2 Session, 99–104, 583–85, 621, 797, Appendix, 229; Giddings to Sumner,
December 3, 1860, Sumner Papers; Chase to Lincoln, January 20, 1861, Lincoln
Papers; Israel Washburn to Adams, January 4, 1861, Adams Papers; Russell Errett
to Cameron, January 23, 1861, Cameron Papers.
97. Laura A. White, "Charles Sumner and the Crisis of 1860–61," in Avery
Craven, ed., *Essays in Honor of William E. Dodd* (Chicago, 1935), 152; Kenneth
Stampp, *And the War Came* (Baton Rouge, 1950), 157; Russell K. Nelson, "The
Early Life and Congressional Career of Elihu B. Washburne" (unpublished
doctoral dissertation, University of North Dakota, 1953), 218; Washburne to
Lincoln, January 7, 1861, Lincoln Papers.

State harder and more difficult; if it protracts their bondage for one single day in any State of this confederacy; then I am opposed to it upon principle." [98] As always, even as the radicals fought the day-to-day battles of politics, the ultimate goal of abolition was never far from their minds.

In January, 1860, when the controversy over the fugitive slave law was still raging in Wisconsin, a German Republican newspaper shrewdly predicted that if the Republicans won control of the federal government, and the South attempted to defy federal authority, the northern states-rights radicals would probably conclude that the supremacy of the national government must be upheld. It is true that a few Wisconsin radicals, including Sherman Booth, whose arrest had triggered the prolonged legal controversies, insisted during the secession winter that the federal government could not force a state to remain in the Union, and that state sovereignty implied the right of secession. But Booth's Milwaukee *Free Democrat* was the only Republican journal in Wisconsin to take this ground. Indeed, radicals and conservatives buried their long-standing differences by electing Timothy Howe to the Senate in January, 1861. And the radical Racine *Advocate*, the organ of Senator James R. Doolittle, declared that the states rights issue was dead in Wisconsin. "When the National Government was in the hands of the Slaveocracy," it explained, "it was important to have in our national council, representatives who watched with zealous care every encroachment upon the reserved rights of the States," but with a Republican president, such vigilance was no longer necessary. Within a few years Doolittle would complain that the radicals now wanted to destroy "all the rights reserved to the States, and make this republic a consolidated empire." [99] The radicals' commitment to the Union and federal supremacy was born in the secession crisis, and once made, it was pursued in the same uncompromising spirit as characterized their every action.

98. *Congressional Globe,* 36 Congress, 2 Session, 796, 1332; Erastus Hopkins to Adams, January 21, 1861, Adams Papers. Cf. *Congressional Globe,* 36 Congress, 2 Session, Appendix, 83, 87; John A. Bingham to Giddings, January 14, 1861, Giddings Papers.
99. *Wisconsin Democrat,* cited in *Wisconsin State Journal,* January 31, 1860; Milwaukee *Free Democrat,* cited in *Wisconsin State Journal,* November 20, 1860; C. L. Sholer to John F. Potter, November 18, 1860, John F. Potter Papers, WisHS; Racine *Weekly Advocate,* January 9, 1861; Duane Mowry, "An Appreciation of James Rood Doolittle," *Proceedings* of the Historical Society of Wisconsin, 1909, 291.

V

It may well have been true that, as the Cincinnati *Gazette* observed in August, 1858, the radicals "constitute but a very small minority of the Republican party." Yet by the eve of the Civil War, the radicals had established themselves as a powerful influence within the party. Generally they were stronger in the "upper North"—New England, New York, Michigan and Wisconsin—than in the more southerly free states. This was evidenced by the solid support given by that section to Seward at the Chicago Convention, and by the election of such radical leaders as Israel Washburn of Maine, John Andrew of Massachusetts, Austin Blair of Michigan, and Alexander Randall of Wisconsin, to the governorships of their states in 1860. Even in the more moderate states, governors Oliver Morton of Indiana, William Dennison of Ohio, and Richard Yates of Illinois were closer to the radical than to the conservative wing of their party. A good indication of how far radicalism had gone among Congressional Republicans was the vote of December 4, 1860 on the proposal to establish the Committee of 33, whose purpose was to seek a compromise settlement of the secession crisis. The resolution passed by a vote of 145 to 38, with the Republicans splitting 59 in favor and 38 against. Although the vote is not an exact index of radicalism—since such radicals as John Alley, Francis Spinner, and Israel Washburn voted for the resolution, and the moderate John Sherman voted against it—it did indicate that about 40 per cent of the Republican Congressmen were not interested in any compromise with the South.[100]

One feature of the politics of the 1850's which enhanced the influence of the radicals was the fact that on most issues they saw eye-to-eye with the ex-Democrats in the party. We have already seen that a large number of radicals were free-traders and foes of government aid to business, and that they supported a states-rights interpretation of the Constitution before the Civil War. For their part, the ex-Democrats were known for their uncompromsing attitude towards the South. To some extent this reflected the fact that the largest number of Democratic defections occurred in areas like the old Free-Soil strongholds of upstate New York and northern Illinois, which had a strong concentration of New England population and were fertile fields for

---

100. Cincinnati *Gazette*, cited in *Liberator*, September 3, 1858; Fehrenbacher, *Prelude*, 158n.; *Congressional Globe*, 36 Congress, 2 Session, 6.

political radicalism. In addition, as David Potter points out, Democrats who left their party over the slavery issue must have been "of stout conscience" to begin with. Finally, the radicals and the ex-Democrats shared a common political enemy in the 1850's—the conservatives who wished to commit the party to a Whiggish economic program and a moderate approach to the slavery question. Charles Francis Adams spoke for all the radicals when he inveighed against "the old rump of the Whig party," who wanted "to make us all so very conservative that we should be hardly distinguishable from our old friends the Whigs." And he found that ex-Democrats with whom he came in contact shared his feelings. As the former Democrat Montgomery Blair wrote to the radical leader John Andrew in 1859, "I have the same disgust for Corwinism that you feel." [101]

The radicals' influence in the Republican leadership did undergo a decline in the aftermath of the election of 1856, when it became clear that victory in 1860 depended upon carrying the doubtful states. But there is convincing evidence that the mass of Republican voters responded more favorably to radical speeches and policies than to conservative ones. Charles Sumner, for example, received almost no correspondence from leading Republican figures, aside from a few radical friends, but contemporaries agreed that Sumner had an enormous impact on northern public opinion. George Boutwell may have exaggerated when he later claimed that Sumner "was able to affect and perhaps even to control the opinions of the country upon the slavery question," but Wendell Phillips, himself an expert practitioner of the art of political agitation, wrote the Massachusetts Senator in 1853, "you are read by a million—and shape their conduct." Similarly, Ben Wade's scorching attacks on slavery and southerners during the 1850's were enthusiastically received by his constituents. William Dennison explained to Wade that the people of Ohio wanted to hear bold, firm speeches from their representatives, and that was why they liked Wade.[102]

If the Republican electorate wanted strong talk from their repre-

101. Potter, *Lincoln and His Party*, 22; Charles Francis Adams Diary, December 30, August 4, 1859; Montgomery Blair to John Andrew, November 23, 1859, John Andrew Papers, MHS. The reference is to Thomas Corwin, the former Whig leader and conservative Republican Congressman from Ohio. Cf. Adams to E. L. Pierce, February 8, 1860, E. L. Pierce Papers, Houghton Library, Harvard University. 102. George S. Boutwell, *Reminiscences of Sixty Years in Public Affairs* (2 vols.: New York, 1902), I, 228; Wendell Phillips to Sumner, March 7, 1853, Sumner Papers; Dennison to Wade, March 12, 1860, Wade Papers.

sentatives, the radicals did their best to satisfy them. Wade was the master of what one reporter called "scorching sarcasms." When it seemed that the Senate was more interested in discussing the acquisition of Cuba than the homestead bill, Wade told the southerners, "The question will be, shall we give niggers to the niggerless, or land to the landless?" And after a slaveholding Senator described with tenderness his relationship with an old house servant, Wade retorted, "nobody wished to forbid his taking his old mammy with him to Kansas—we only sought to forbid his selling her after he got her there." [103] Other radicals were equally famous for their blunt sayings. Henry Wilson informed the Senate in 1855 that the Republicans would abolish slavery in the District of Columbia "by securing a majority in this Senate and in the House of Representatives, and voting you gentlemen of the South down." And after John Brown's raid, when most Republican leaders were frantically trying to dissociate their party from the venture, John Andrew insisted that "whether the enterprise itself was [right or wrong], John Brown himself is right." [104]

The northern public also responded warmly to the radicals' physical courage in the face of southern threats. "We do not like to have our representatives catechised by Southern Disunionists," wrote a constituent of Elihu Washburne, and the Republicans liked even less physical assaults on their leaders. After the beating of Senator Sumner, Ben Wade announced in the Senate that he was ready to come "armed for the combat" to future sessions, and he meant it. Wade, Zachariah Chandler, and Simon Cameron made a secret agreement to fight to the death, if necessary, to prevent any repetition of the assault. In 1860, after a dispute over where Owen Lovejoy was standing while delivering his most radical anti-slavery speech erupted into violence, with John Potter pitted against Roger Pryor of Virginia, Potter received scores of congratulatory letters. As one Republican wrote, "the Northwest likes *pluck*, and after so much bullying as we have been treated to in Congressional proceedings it is really refreshing to have such an episode." [105]

103. Pike, *First Blows*, 219; *Congressional Globe*, 35 Congress, 2 Session, 1354; New York *Tribune*, September 6, 1854.
104. *Congressional Globe*, 33 Congress, 2 Session, Appendix, 238; Pearson, *Andrew*, I, 100. Cf. *Congressional Globe*, 33 Congress, 1 Session, 339, 34 Congress, 1 Session, 856, 35 Congress, 1 Session, 1254, 36 Congress, 1 Session, 1887.
105. Benjamin W. Porter to Elihu Washburne, December 31, 1859, Washburne Papers; *Congressional Globe*, 34 Congress, 1 Session, 1305; A. G. Riddle, *The Life of Benjamin F. Wade* (Cleveland, 1888), 250; letters in Potter Papers, April, 1860; N. Vose to Washburne, April 21, 1860, Washburne Papers.

All these factors, as well as the strong cohesion of the radical group developed over long years of personal friendship and political association, help explain the strong influence the radicals had on the pre-war Republican party. And there was one other fact of political life of which most Republican leaders were aware—if their party ever became too conservative, the radicals would be ready to bolt and form a new organization, as they had done so many times in the past. Party loyalty, as we have seen, was not the radicals' forte. Although the radical leaders would not be able to carry a majority of Republican voters with them, they would certainly be able to ensure the defeat of the regular candidates. Thus Murat Halstead reported from the Philadelphia Convention of 1856 that one strong argument against the nomination of the conservative candidate John McLean was that the Western Reserve would not vote for him, and that without the Reserve the Republicans could not carry Ohio. Two years later, a correspondent of the New York *Tribune* declared that if conservative attempts to "lower" the Republican platform succeeded, "a new Liberty or a new Free Soil Party would be formed," which would destroy the Republican party in New England, New York, and Ohio. This aspect of the radicals' power was summarized in 1858 by the *Ohio State Journal* in explaining why the conservative movement to transform the Republicans into an "Opposition" party could not succeed. "It is simply impossible," declared the *Journal*, "to gain as many adherents to a new party from the ranks of Americanism and of the Administration as would be lost from the ranks of Republicanism by any compromise of position or organization." [106]

On the eve of Lincoln's election, the Springfield *Republican* paid tribute to the special role the radicals had played:

We congratulate the "old guard" of anti-slavery, who have labored, prayed, and suffered for so many years, and have been strong and persistent under defeats and discouragements that would have disheartened other men, that they are about to see the reward of their labors in the inauguration of an administration of the government whose influence shall be positively and effectively on the side of human freedom. . . .

Chase, who was more responsible than any other individual for the development of the radical program, took particular pleasure in the

106. William B. Hesseltine and Rex G. Fisher, eds., *Trimmers, Trucklers, and Temporizers* (Madison, 1961), 85; New York *Tribune*, November 9, 1858; *Ohio State Journal*, May 27, 1858.

result. "At length the first of the great wishes of my life is accomplished," he wrote Edward L. Pierce.[107]

But a few weeks later Chase observed that it was not yet clear what the Republicans would make of their victory. Other radicals were also apprehensive, for they were not sure that Lincoln would inaugurate what they considered "an affirmative policy." Giddings informed Chase that the latter should go into the new cabinet because "it is important that Lincoln's administration should take radical grounds."[108] But the prospective struggle for control of the administration was submerged in the secession crisis. With secession and the beginning of Civil War, a new dimension was added to the radical program. John Quincy Adams had long ago declared that under the war power the president would be entitled to abolish slavery if civil conflict broke out. In July, 1860, the moderate Henry J. Raymond warned secessionists that "it is the Constitution which converts the extreme Anti-Slavery men into talkers instead of actors." With the firing on Fort Sumter, the radicals recognized that constitutional limitations on direct action against slavery were things of the past. "We have entered upon a struggle," one wrote, "which ought not to be allowed to end until the Slave Power is completely subjugated, and *emancipation made certain*."[109] The radicals had embarked on the final phase of the struggle to destroy slavery.

107. Springfield *Repuublican,* November 3, 1860; Chase to E. L. Pierce, November 7, 1860, in Sumner Papers.
108. John Albree, ed., *Whittier Correspondence From the Oak Knoll Collection 1830–1892* (Salem, 1911), 136; Thurlow Weed Barnes, *Memoir of Thurlow Weed* (Boston, 1884), 310; Giddings to Chase, December 7, 1860, Chase Papers, HSPa.
109. Solberg, "Giddings," 455; Carl F. Krummel, "Henry J. Raymond and the New York Times in the Secession Crisis 1860–61," *NYH,* XXXII (October 1951), 387; Samuel Gridley Howe to Sumner, April 16, 1861, Howe Papers.

5

The Democratic-Republicans

The decade of the 1850's witnessed one of the few fundamental re-organizations of the American political system. For the last time in American history, one of the two major parties was disbanded, and a new organization captured the presidency in its second national campaign. The Democratic party, which had swept to an unprecedented victory in 1852, was reduced to a minority throughout the North, and in several states all but obliterated. Because the bulk of the votes for the Republican party came from Whigs, it has been easy to ignore or underestimate the contributions of former Democrats to the party's early success. Few historians would go as far as William B. Hesseltine, who described the Republicans as "little more than an enlarged Whig party disguised in a new vocabulary," and it is well known that half the members of Lincoln's first cabinet had once been Democrats.[1] But the Democratic element in the Republican party went far beyond this. During the 1850's, at least eight former Democrats served as Republican governors, seven as Republican Senators, and each Congress from 1854 to 1860 had a contingent of "Democratic-Republicans."[2] The fact that a sizable portion of the party's leader-

1. William B. Hesseltine, *Lincoln and the War Governors* (New York, 1948), 18. Montgomery Blair, Simon Cameron, Salmon P. Chase and Gideon Welles were the ex-Democrats in Lincoln's first cabinet.
2. Democratic-Republican governors in the 1850's were: Nathaniel P. Banks of Massachusetts, Kinsley Bingham of Michigan, William H. Bissell of Illinois, Salmon P. Chase of Ohio, Hannibal Hamlin of Maine, Samuel J. Kirkwood of Iowa, Ralph Metcalf of New Hampshire, Lot Morrill of Maine, and Alexander Randall of Wisconsin. Bingham and Hamlin also served as Senators, along with James R. Doolittle of Wisconsin, John P. Hale of New Hampshire, Preston King of New York, Lyman Trumbull of Illinois, and David Wilmot of Pennsylvania.

ship and mass support was composed of former Democrats had considerable impact on the emergence of a distinctive Republican political program and ideology. We have already seen how the ex-Democrats' ideas influenced the free labor ideology of the Republican party. Equally important were their contributions to the party's anti-southern and pro-unionist outlook and to the way in which it dealt with economic issues in the 1850's.

The largest and most influential group of Democrats who entered the Republican party were the self-styled "heirs of Jackson," close friends and advisors of Old Hickory who felt they had been displaced in the Democratic leadership during the 1840's. Though most Jacksonians could not bring themselves to abandon their party in the 1850's, the presence among Republican leaders of Jackson's trusted associate Francis P. Blair, his cabinet member Benjamin F. Butler, and the organizers of the Connecticut Democracy, Gideon Welles and John M. Niles, was proof enough of a serious schism in the Jacksonian ranks. These men did not abandon their party and personal friends lightly; it was only after a prolonged struggle against southern domination of the Democracy that they felt the time had come to leave. As one Iowan described his feelings: [3]

> I was educated a Democrat from my boyhood. Faithfully did I adhere to that party until I could no longer act wth it. Many things did I condemn ere I left that party, for my love of party was strong. And when I did, at last, feel compelled to separate from my old Democratic friends, it was like tearing myself away from old home associations.

For the Jacksonians who left their party, and for many who remained in it, 1844 was a turning point of critical importance. In that year, Martin Van Buren, who was universally expected to be the Democratic candidate for president, was deprived of the nomination because of his opposition to the immediate annexation of Texas as a slave state. Tension had always existed between the northern and southern wings of the Democracy, but Van Buren's defeat instilled in his supporters a hatred for southern political power which was never completely eradicated.[4] Van Buren's friends were convinced he had been sacrificed

---

3. Roy F. Nichols, *The Democratic Machine 1850–1854* (New York, 1923), 79; *The Debates of the Constitutional Convention of the State of Iowa* (2 vols.: Davenport, 1857), II, 701.
4. The most recent and thorough treatment of the events of 1844 is Charles Sellers, *James K. Polk Continentalist 1843–1846* (Princeton, 1966), 32–162. Cf. James C. N. Paul, *Rift in the Democracy* (Philadelphia, 1951).

to the interests of slavery; over twenty years later, Gideon Welles still believed that 1844 had marked the beginning of the "ultimate downfall of the Democratic party." After that year, he said, "confidence and united zeal never again prevailed, and parties subsequently took a sectional or personal character." [5]

It would be a serious mistake to dismiss the bitterness of the Van Burenites as merely the normal complaints of political losers. The Van Burenites were convinced that Polk's nomination was not the result of open deliberations by party leaders, but of "the most stupendous intrigue that has ever been successful in this country, the strongest exhibition of contempt and disregard of the popular will that has ever yet been manifested." Though Senator Robert Walker of Mississippi was the man who engineered Van Buren's defeat, the ex-president's followers thought they discerned a far more sinister hand directing the intrigue—that of Jackson's arch-enemy, John C. Calhoun.[6] To the Van Burenites, the history of the Democratic party was something of a morality play, with a hero, Jackson, the defender of the party and the Union, and a villain, Calhoun, the plotter of disunion. They believed that Calhoun had long conspired to take control of the Democratic party or, should he be unsuccessful, to form a southern party with himself at the head, as a prelude to secession. Calhoun had raised the cry of nullification over the tariff during Jackson's presidency, but had been defeated by the forceful action of Old Hickory. Now he had seized upon the slavery issue as a new instrument for his designs, and this would either give him control of the Democracy or unite the South in defense of slavery and in willingness to secede.[7]

5. Howard K. Beale, ed., *Diary of Gideon Welles* (3 vols.: New York, 1960), II, 387. Cf. James S. Wadsworth to Martin Van Buren, June 1, 1844, Martin Van Buren Papers, LC; *Oliver Dyer's Phonographic Report of the Proceedings of the National Free Soil Convention at Buffalo, N.Y., August 9th and 10th, 1848* (Buffalo, 1848), 3.
6. "Tyler's Break with the Whig Party; Polk's Nomination and Election," undated manuscript [written in 1849], Gideon Welles Papers, NYPL. On Walker's role, see Welles to ?, January 24, 1849 (draft), "Events Leading to the Nomination of Polk and Dallas, 1844," undated manuscript, Welles Papers, NYPL; Welles to Azariah C. Flagg, February 4, 1848, Azariah C. Flagg Papers, Columbia University; James P. Shenton, *Robert John Walker, A Politician From Jackson to Lincoln* (New York, 1961), 42–45.
7. Francis P. Blair to Andrew Jackson, May 2, 19, July 7, 1844, Andrew Jackson Papers, LC; William N. Chambers, *Old Bullion Benton, Senator from the New West* (Boston, 1956), 276; Thomas Hart Benton, *Thirty Years' View* (2 vols.: New York, 1856), II, 582–83; "Review of Calhoun's Career," undated manuscript, Gideon Welles Papers, ConnHS; John R. Dickinson, ed., *Speeches, Correspondence, Etc., of the Late Daniel S. Dickinson of New York* (2 vols.: New York, 1867), II, 421–22.

The injection of the slavery issue into national politics in the form
of the Texas question violated an unspoken but well-understood agreement between the northern and southern wings of the Democratic
party. Fourteen years later, Preston King, a Van Burenite who became
a leading Republican, wrote that 1844 had marked the end of the
traditional politics of the Jacksonian era, because "Slavery upon which
by common consent no party issue had been made was then obtruded
upon the field of party action." Throughout the stormy years which
followed the nomination and election of Polk, despite the fact that
Van Burenites championed the Wilmot Proviso barring slavery from
territories acquired during the Mexican War, they insisted that they
did not wish to make any position on slavery a test of party loyalty.
They were quite willing to tolerate disagreements within the national
party over the peculiar institution, but they resented what they considered southern efforts to force pro-slavery views upon the party as
a whole. Welles wrote that it was absurd to attempt "to make Connecticut conform to the views of South Carolina on the subject of permitting or excluding slavery in the territories." David Wilmot agreed
that the South was wholly responsible for party divisions, because
"It is the South, that has attempted to make this question of the extension of slavery into free territory, a party test." The Van Burenites
believed that a national party could only exist if its members agreed
to permit disagreement about slavery.[8]

Coupled with their resentment against the South for introducing the
slavery question into national politics was a jealousy of southern
political power. If the Baltimore Convention of 1844 represented an
attempt by the South to take control of the Democracy, the events of
Polk's administration convinced many northern Democrats that the
attempt had succeeded. The story of how the Van Burenites broke with
Polk over such matters as patronage and the Wilmot Proviso has often
been told.[9] By 1847, the New York Van Burenites, or Barnburners as they were called, walked out of the Democratic state
convention when the pro-administration Hunkers refused to endorse

8. Preston King to Gideon Welles, September 16, 1858; Welles to ? (draft), July
20, 1849, Gideon Welles Papers, LC; *Proceedings of the Herkimer Mass Convention of October 26, 1847* (Albany, 1847), 15; Eric Foner, "The Wilmot Proviso
Revisited," *JAH*, LVI (September 1969), 262–79.
9. Herbert D. A. Donovan, *The Barnburners* (New York, 1925); Sellers, *Polk*,
162–213; Joseph G. Rayback, "Martin Van Buren's Break with James K. Polk: The
Record," *NYH*, XXXVI (January 1955), 51–62.

the principle of the non-extension of slavery, and in the next year they helped organize the Free Soil party, with Van Buren as its presidential nominee. Historians have traditionally divided the Barnburners into two groups. Some, like Preston King, William Cullen Bryant—the editor of the New York *Evening Post*—and David Dudley Field were motivated by sincere anti-slavery convictions. Most of the older Van Burenites—including the ex-president himself, John A. Dix, and Azariah Flagg—entered the free-soil movement reluctantly. They deplored the schism in the New York Democracy and opposed a third party movement until the last moment. To some extent, they were motivated by simple revenge. Gideon Welles, for example, described the Free Soilers as "the democrats disposed to *right, in 1848, the wrongs* of 1844. . . ." [10] Primarily, however, they were interested in challenging southern domination of the Democratic party. As John M. Niles put it, "I wish to see restored to the free States that influence, that equality, that control in the affairs of the Government, to which they are entitled." The Barnburners felt that the Democratic nominee, Lewis Cass, was a prime example of the northerner who cravenly submitted to southern dictates in order to gain political advancement, and they hoped to prevent his election as a lesson to the party. If the party was to survive on the old basis as a national organization with no test on the slavery question, Cass would have to be defeated. As David Wilmot later explained, "the ambitious and aspiring must learn that they cannot reach the Presidency by a base bowing down to the power of slavery." [11]

The election of 1848 did not work out exactly as the more optimistic Free Soilers had hoped. True, Cass was defeated, but Van Buren failed to carry a single state. Yet contemporaries agreed that one reason for this disappointing showing was that throughout the North, all parties claimed the cause of free soil as their own. "During the last Presidential canvass," said Salmon Chase in 1850, "it was hard to find

10. Chaplain Morrison, *Democratic Politics and Sectionalism* (Chapel Hill, 1967), 25, 127; Arthur M. Schlesinger, Jr., *The Age of Jackson* (Boston, 1945), 463; Flagg to Van Buren, October 13, 1847, June 19, 1848, Van Buren Papers; Dix to Flagg, June 5, 1848, Welles to Flagg, February 4, 1848, Flagg Papers.
11. *Congressional Globe*, 30 Congress, 1 Session, Appendix, 698; 31 Congress, 1 Session, Appendix, 942; Welles to ?, October 21, 1848, Welles Papers, ConnHS; Marcus Morton to John A. Dix, March 2, 1848, Letterbook, Marcus Morton Papers, MHS; Benjamin F. Butler to Van Buren, June 1, 1848, Blair to Van Buren, August 13, 1848, Van Buren Papers; Max M. Mintz, "The Political Ideas of Martin Van Buren," *NYH*, XXX (October 1949), 440–41.

in the free States an opponent of slavery prohibition."[12] The Free Soil party thus played an important role in the spread of anti-slavery sentiments. In addition, the spectacle of a founder of the Democratic party and an ex-president repudiating the regular nominee of his party and running on an independent ticket "totally dispelled the prestige, sanctity, and domination of 'regular' nominations," in the words of one disgruntled Hunker. The experience of 1848 must have made the mass defections from the Democracy a few years later much easier for many Democrats. But perhaps the most important consequence of the campaign of 1848 was its effect on intraparty sectional relations. A campaign run on the basis of opposition to the spread of slavery and the domination of the Slave Power in party and nation could not help but strain what Dix called "the bond of confidence . . . the current of reciprocal kindness . . ." between northern and southern Democrats. As Van Buren observed to Dix, the events of 1848 "have produced impressions which neither you nor I will live to see eradicated."[13]

The Compromise of 1850 reflected the recognition by most Democrats, North and South, that sectional strife over slavery had gone far enough to endanger both the party and the Union. In the slavery debates of that year, northern Democrats tended to adopt a more moderate position than their Whig counterparts, and throughout the North, state Democratic parties endorsed the Compromise as the final settlement of the slavery controversy, although there were some reservations about the fugitive slave law. The older Barnburners—Van Buren, Dix, Flagg, and others—were quite willing to accept the settlement, and even the younger and more radical Van Burenites made their peace with the party. The Van Burenites, of course, did not abandon their ambition to regain control of the Democracy. They unsuccessfully pushed William O. Butler of Kentucky for the presidential nomination in 1852, but were not displeased with the choice of Franklin Pierce.[14]

12. *Congressional Globe,* 31 Congress, 1 Session, Appendix, 477. Cf. Theodore C. Smith, *The Liberty and Free Soil Parties in the Northwest* (New York, 1897), 148, 189, 221; John Van Buren to Joshua Giddings, December 11, 1848, Giddings-Julian Papers, LC; N. Dwight Harris, *The History of Negro Servitude in Illinois* (Chicago, 1904), 177.

13. Walter L. Ferree, "The New York Democracy: Division and Reunion, 1847–1852" (unpublished doctoral dissertation, University of Pennsylvania, 1953), 404; *Congressional Globe,* 30 Congress, 1 Session, Appendix, 1183; Martin Van Buren to John A. Dix, July 14, 1848, John A. Dix Papers, Columbia University. Cf. John Van Buren to Giddings, May 26, 1849, Giddings-Julian Papers.

14. Joel H. Silbey, *The Shrine of Party* (Pittsburgh, 1967), 110; John Bigelow to Charles Sumner, undated, 1851, Charles Sumner Papers, Houghton Library,

In fact, some Barnburners had proposed Pierce as Butler's running mate. But the selection of the new cabinet indicated that the Van Burenites were not in favor with the administration. Pierce himself wanted to give Dix a post in the cabinet but southern pressure forced him to withdraw the offer. Then the French mission was promised him and similarly withdrawn. "I do not know a man of the Jackson Van Buren stripe who has any weight in the administration," Blair complained. As they had once become increasingly disillusioned with Polk, the Van Burenites slowly lost their trust in Pierce. "He is not Jackson, that is certain," wrote Welles in October, 1853. "If he does not prove a Tyler I shall be thankful." 15

II

The year 1854 opened with the northern Democracy still suffering from the schisms and divisions which had plagued it for years. Indeed, in many states, factional bitterness over issues other than slavery—internal improvements, temperance, nativism, and the perennial disputes over patronage—were slowly tearing the party apart.[16] The stage was therefore set for the mass defections which took place between 1854 and 1856; yet it is difficult to imagine the party chaos and reorganization which marked these years having occurred without the introduction of the Kansas-Nebraska bill in January, 1854 and the subsequent warfare in Kansas. The motives behind Stephen A. Douglas's measure, amended in mid-January, 1854, to repeal the Missouri Compromise barring slavery from most of the Louisiana Purchase territory, are still somewhat obscure. But Roy F. Nichols has demonstrated convincingly that a group of southern Democrats, annoyed because

Harvard University; Preston King to Welles, June 12, July 3, November 19, 1852, Welles Papers, LC; Welles to C. F. Cleveland, June 14, 1852, Welles Papers, ConnHS; William E. Smith, *The Francis Preston Blair Family in Politics* (2 vols.: New York, 1933), I, 281.

15. Horace Greeley to Thurlow Weed, December 1, 1851, Miscellaneous Manuscripts, NYHS; Roy F. Nichols, *Franklin Pierce* (Philadelphia, 1958 ed.), 227, 287–88; Nichols, *Democratic Machine*, 178–81, 208–13; Martin Lichterman, "John Adams Dix: 1798–1879" (unpublished doctoral dissertation, Columbia University, 1952), 243; Blair to Van Buren, November 27, 1853, Van Buren Papers; Welles to ?, October, 1853 (draft), Welles Papers, LC.

16. Mildred C. Stoler, "The Influence of the Democratic Element in the Republican Party of Illinois and Indiana, 1854–1860" (unpublished doctoral dissertation, Indiana University, 1938), 26–28; David S. Sparks, "The Decline of the Democratic Party in Iowa, 1850–1860," *IJH*, LIII (January 1955), 2.

Pierce had been attempting to win the favor of northern free-soil Democrats by patronage offers, decided to make a new Nebraska measure a test of the free-soilers' loyalty to the party. They told Douglas they would support no bill for organizing Nebraska with slavery barred from the territory. Douglas's original bill side-stepped the Missouri Compromise issue by merely providing that the inhabitants of the territory had full power over their domestic institutions, but when a Whig Senator from the South moved to insert an outright repeal of the Compromise, Douglas acquiesced, and used his influence to obtain administration support. On January 24, the administration's organ, the Washington *Union*, declared the bill "a test of Democratic orthodoxy." [17]

Seven years before the introduction of the Kansas-Nebraska Act, a close associate of Calhoun wrote him that "the Anti-Slavery Democrats, Butler of New York, Hamlin etc. must be driven off to the Whigs." Political observers in 1854 agreed that for southern Democrats, the purpose of the Nebraska bill was to drive off a portion of the northern free-soilers and to subordinate the rest even further to southern control.[18] Reuben Fenton, a Democratic Congressman from upstate New York who had supported the Free Soil party and who would soon become a Republican, complained in February 1854 of the southern demand for "ostracising a portion of the Democratic party. . . ." The free-soilers were once again embittered by the imposition of a new party test on slavery, and by the administration's ruthless manipulation of the patronage to ensure the bill's passage. "The administration," Welles complained, "has identified itself with this new test and, wielding the power and patronage of the government, it assumes an attitude of open hostility to any democrat who does not conform to its views." To Blair, the repeal of the Missouri Compromise was a perfect example of how the South always got its way in party and national affairs. The slaveholders planned to obtain northern votes, not by virtue of any popular support for the Nebraska bill, but by compelling northern presidential aspirants—Douglas, Pierce, Cass, and Buchanan—to bid for

17. Roy F. Nichols, "The Kansas-Nebraska Act: A Century of Historiography," *MVHR*, XLIII (September 1956), 201–4; Nichols, *Pierce*, 303–4, 320–21; Theodore Clarke Smith, *Parties and Slavery* (New York, 1906), 98.
18. J. Franklin Jameson, ed., "Correspondence of John C. Calhoun," *Annual Report of AHA*, 1899, II, 1132; New York *Herald*, January 11, 1854; Jabez D. Hammond to William H. Seward, February 28, 1854, William H. Seward Papers, Rush Rhees Library, University of Rochester; Frederick W. Seward, *Seward at Washington* (2 vols.: New York, 1891), I, 216.

southern friendship, by forcing "jobbers and plunderers" to purchase southern votes for their pet schemes, and by packing northern party conventions with paid administration functionaries and party hacks. "We are to have a renewed contest for the ascendency of slavery over freedom," Blair wrote, adding that he would rather see Whig victories, North and South, than the success of the Nebraska scheme.[19]

Many of the anti-southern themes which had marked Van Burenite campaigns in the 1840's were reasserted in the Nebraska debate. One Pennsylvania Democrat wrote indignantly, "I have suffered more (as a politician), for my opposition to abolitionism and anti-masonry, than from any other cause. Some of the southern men have neither discretion, heart or consideration! They require and exact too much of us!" And at an anti-Nebraska convention in Ohio, a Democrat who would later serve as a Republican Congressman expressed the bitterness of thousands against the demands and ingratitude of the South: "We have submitted to slavery long enough, and must not stand it any longer. . . . I am done catching negroes for the South." [20] In states where anti-Nebraska coalitions were created in the summer of 1854, Democrats often played leading roles. "Radical and Jackson Democrats," a Republican Congressman later claimed, ". . . were the first to aid in organizing the Republican party, especially in the West." Many Democrats who deserted their party in 1854 had long histories of opposition to slavery and southern domination—men like Wilmot, who had supported Pierce in 1852 but now denounced him as "the mere tool and puppet of the Slave power." But the revolt of 1854 went far beyond anything that had been seen before—and far beyond the ranks of the chronically disaffected Van Burenites. "I voted for Franklin Pierce in 1852, for Cass in '48, and for Polk in '44," wrote a Democrat to the New York *Tribune* who went on to call for a fusion of all elements opposed to the Nebraska bill. He was only one of countless Democrats, previously regular supporters of party platforms and nominations, who could not swallow Douglas's bill. The schism in the

19. *Congressional Globe*, 33 Congress, 1 Session, 156; "Lessons of the recent Elections," manuscript, 1854, Welles Papers, ConnHS; Reginald C. McGrane, *William Allen, A Study in Western Democracy* (Columbus, 1925), 136–37; Morgan Dix, comp., *Memoirs of John Adams Dix* (2 vols.: New York, 1883), I, 283–84; Blair to Van Buren, August 24, 1854, Van Buren Papers.
20. John M. Butler to Simon Cameron, June 10, 1854, Simon Cameron Papers, LC; Joseph P. Smith, ed., *History of the Republican Party in Ohio* (2 vols.: Chicago, 1898), I, 15–16. Cf. Hannibal Hamlin to William P. Haines, January 25, 1854, Hannibal Hamlin Papers, University of Maine, Orono.

northern Democracy was made clear by the House vote on the Nebraska bill—forty-four free-state Democrats favored the bill, and forty-three voted against.[21]

Just as the administration had wielded the patronage to force wavering Congressmen into line, so in state after northern state the party hierarchy demanded obedience to the Douglas measure. In Indiana, Senator Jesse Bright, the party dictator, had opponents of the bill expelled from the state convention and from local conclaves. In New York, where free-soil Democracy was strongest and where twelve of twenty-one Democratic Congressmen had opposed the bill, the state convention of the "soft" faction of the Democracy did call the Nebraska act inexpedient, but condemned agitation for its repeal. When the majority, including many federal officeholders, voted down an anti-Nebraska plank, Preston King led over one hundred delegates in a walkout.[22] The party's lack of willingness to accommodate differences of opinion on the Nebraska act converted some wavering Democrats into supporters of Douglas, but it also forced many out of the party for good. Nowhere was this better demonstrated than in Douglas's home state of Illinois. If Abraham Lincoln is to be believed, only three Democratic legislators in Illinois favored the bill in February, 1854— but when orders came from Douglas to pass resolutions supporting him the party swung into line. Douglas insisted that "the principle of this bill will form the test of Parties," and threatened to "shoot the deserters." Eventually, only five Democratic legislators, all from northern Illinois, continued their opposition to the bill.[23] Throughout the summer and fall of 1854, Douglas and his supporters denounced the anti-Nebraska Democrats with extreme venom, and used control of federal patronage to force waverers into line. "I am astonished at their bitterness," wrote Lyman Trumbull, adding, "there is no making

21. James M. Ashley to Horace Greeley, April 26, 1859, Horace Greeley Papers, NYPL; Charles B. Going, *David Wilmot Free-Soiler* (New York, 1924), 460; New York *Tribune*, February 10, 1854; *National Era*, June 1, 1854.

22. Roger H. Van Bolt, "The Rise of the Republican Party in Indiana, 1840–1856" (unpublished doctoral dissertation, University of Chicago, 1950), 206–8; New York *Evening Post*, September 8, 1854; New York *Tribune*, September 8, 1854; Allan Nevins, *Ordeal of the Union* (2 vols.: New York, 1947), II, 148.

23. Roy F. Basler *et al.*, eds., *The Collected Works of Abraham Lincoln* (9 vols.: New Brunswick, 1953–55), II, 322; Robert W. Johannsen, ed., *The Letters of Stephen A. Douglas* (Urbana, 1961), 283; John M. Palmer, *Personal Recollections of John M. Palmer* (Cincinnati, 1901), 64; George F. Milton, *The Eve of Conflict* (Cambridge, 1934), 171–72; George T. Palmer, *A Conscientious Turncoat. The Story of John M. Palmer 1817–1900* (New Haven, 1941), 27.

terms or getting along in harmoney with such men." [24] Trumbull, whose election to the Senate in 1855 sent the Douglasites into spasms of rage (they would have much preferred to see the Whig candidate, Abraham Lincoln, chosen),[25] later said he had no intention of leaving the Democratic party when he first voiced his opposition to the Nebraska act. "But, sir," he added, "then was inaugurated that test of Democracy which had never before obtained in this country." The Douglasites' bitter attacks on anti-Nebraska Democrats, and their attempts to defeat them in the fall elections, made future party unity all but impossible. As a friend of Lincoln wrote of an anti-Nebraska legislative candidate, "He *was* a Democrat—in the canvass was abandoned and vilified by his party and elected by whigs—never hopes for a restoration . . . to his first love." [26]

As early as May, 1854, Preston King was convinced "that past lines of party will be obliterated with the Missouri line." His prediction was accurate, but the break-up of the northern Democracy, the demise of the Whigs, the rise and fall of Know-Nothingism, and the formation of the Republican party, did not take place overnight. Many Democrats did not cast their lot with the new party until the middle of 1856. The Van Burenites, for example, split into three groups. The younger, more radical ones led by Wilmot and King, left the Demorcratic party for good in 1854 or 1855. A second group, including Welles and Blair, repudiated the Nebraska act but still hoped the old Van Burenite group could regain control of the Democratic party, and did not abandon it until 1856. And many older Van Burenites, including Samuel J. Tilden, Azariah Flagg, and Martin Van Buren himself, could not overcome their loyalty to the party and their fear of disunion if parties were divided along sectional lines.[27] They stayed with the party,

24. George T. Palmer, ed., "A Collection of Letters From Lyman Trumbull to John M. Palmer, 1854–1858," *Journal* of the IllSHS, XVI (April–July 1923), 20–22. Cf. Mark M. Krug, *Lyman Trumbull, Conservative Radical* (New York, 1965), 84; Arthur C. Cole, *The Era of the Civil War 1848–1870* (Springfield, 1919), 125–26.
25. Basler, ed., *Lincoln Works*, II, 306; Richard Yates and Catherine P. Yates, *Richard Yates*, ed., John Krenkel (Danville, Ill., 1966), 115; George T. Allen to Lyman Trumbull, January 19, 1856, Lyman Trumbull Papers, LC.
26. *Congressional Globe*, 35 Congress, 1 Session, 1164; Leonard Swett to Abraham Lincoln, December 22, 1854, Robert Todd Lincoln Papers, LC. Cf. James Knox to Richard Yates, September 4, 1854, in Logan U. Reavis Papers, ChicHS.
27. Preston King to Flagg, May 20, 1854, Flagg Papers; Donovan, *Barnburners*, 112–18; Dix, comp., *Memoirs*, I, 285; Samuel J. Tilden to ?, August 26, 1854, Samuel J. Tilden Papers, NYPL.

though it is important to remember that they opposed the Nebraska act and sincerely hoped to counteract southern influence in the Democracy. Van Buren felt "indignant against the repeal of the Missouri Compromise," and at first was determined to fight for its restoration, while Azariah Flagg signed a call for an anti-Nebraska rally.[28] But Van Buren also believed that the only way to prevent disunion was to preserve "party cohesions between men of the free and slave states," and Tilden and Dix had "not a particle of faith in the Whigs," who they feared would dominate a fusion party. All agreed, moreover, that the experiment of 1848, which "gave power to inferior men by weakening our hold upon the party," should not be repeated.[29]

Welles, Blair, and their group of Van Burenites were willing to break with the Democratic party as a last resort, but first wanted to make a last effort to regain control. Welles, who insisted, "I have no faith in the democratic organization as it is called, for it is hostile to the principles of democracy," had believed for several years that a re-organization of the party system was necessary. The political alignments of the Jacksonian era, Welles felt, had been forged over financial issues which were no longer matters of controversy. Both parties had long since abandoned their distinctive principles and were interested solely in patronage and power.[30] Along with Blair, Welles hoped to infuse principles back into the Democratic party, and to attract support from anti-slavery Whigs, by putting Thomas Hart Benton forward as an "anti-convention" candidate for President. Benton would have to be nominated by local mass meetings rather than by a national convention, for the Van Burenites had learned by bitter experience that "the old managing intrigues of the South . . . have

28. Martin Van Buren to Moses Tilden, September 1, 1856, in Samuel J. Tilden Papers; Martin Van Buren, *Inquiry into the Orig'n and Course of Political Parties in the United States* (New York, 1867), 354–55; New York *Evening Post*, August 4, 1854. Cf. "Letter of John Van Buren to ex-Senator Chalmers," clipping, February 3, 1854, Salmon P. Chase Papers, HSPa.
29. Van Buren to Moses Tilden, September 1, 1856. in Samuel J. Tilden Papers; Dix to Francis P. Blair, October 19, 1848, Blair-Lee Papers, Princeton University; Tilden to ?. August 12, 1854, Tilden Papers. Cf. John Van Buren to Blair, January 26, 1855, Blair Family Papers, LC; New York *Times*, February 10, 1952.
30. Welles to Blair, May, 1854, Welles Papers ConnHS; "Comment upon the Election of Zachary Taylor as Marking the Close of the Second Party Dynasty in U.S.," undated manuscript, Welles Papers, NYPL; Welles to ?, November 11, 1848, March 1, 1852, March 13, 1858, Welles to King, April 23, 1855, Welles Papers, ConnHS; Welles to ?, September 18, 1848 (copy), Welles to James F. Babcock, March 14, 1855 (copy), Welles Papers, LC.

control of democratic national conventions." [31] Benton, however, sharing Van Buren's fear that a sectional party division would endanger
the Union, rejected the proposal. The failure of the Benton movement
led Blair to identify himself with the Republican party late in 1855,
and his role as presiding officer at the February, 1856 convention which
officially launched the party as a national organization, symbolized the
decision of an important group of Van Buren Democrats to cast their
lot with the Republicans.[32]

In September, 1855, the New York *Tribune* informed its readers
that "a large mass of the Democratic vote is afloat." Throughout the
North in that year, anti-Nebraska Democrats struggled to make up
their minds. In New York, for instance, the editors of the New York
Evening Post, Bryant and John Bigelow, endorsed no gubernatorial
candidate in 1854, although a sizable number of Barnburners supported
the anti-Nebraska Whig candidate. Bryant and Bigelow believed that a
party based on only one issue could not be permanent, and feared Whig
domination of an anti-Nebraska coalition. The crushing Democratic
defeats of 1854, they insisted, proved that the party would have to
abandon its pro-slavery position. As late as April, 1855, they confessed
that they were "drifting along the stream of events," and not until the
fall did they endorse the new Republican party.[33]

Similar confusion prevailed among Illinois Democrats opposed to
the Nebraska act. In 1854, the Chicago *Democratic Press* strongly
condemned the bill but at the same time warned Democrats to beware
of sectional parties and to work from within the Democracy for the
restoration of the Missouri Compromise. The bitter attacks of Douglas
and his followers slowly forced the *Press* out of the Democratic fold,
but in July, 1855 it still insisted that once Douglas was "thrown over-

31. Welles to ?, undated, 1856, Welles Papers, ConnHS; King to Welles, October
21, 1854, Welles Papers, LC; Welles to Blair, July 8, 1854, King to Blair, October
14, 1854, Blair-Lee Papers; Blair to Van Buren, August 24, 1854, Van Buren
Papers; New York *Evening Post*, November 30, December 15, 28, 1855.
32. Andrew W. Crandall, *The Early History of the Republican Party* (Boston,
1930), 46–47, 53; Welles to John Bigelow, May 3, 1858, Welles Papers,
ConnHS; New York *Evening Post*, December 10, 1855.
33. New York *Tribune*, September 5, 1855; New York *Evening Post*, April 21,
June 8, September 8, October 30, November 16, 1854; May 4, September 7, 29,
1855; Ernest P. Muller, "Preston King: A Political Biography" (unpublished
doctoral dissertation, Columbia University, 1957), 552–53; Bigelow to Blair, August
30, 1854, Blair-Lee Papers; Margaret Clapp, *Forgotten First Citizen: John Bigelow*
(Boston, 1947), 98.

board" the party would be all right.[34] By 1856, however, the Illinois anti-Nebraska Democrats were convinced that the Slave Power's control of the Democracy was complete. They played a leading role in the formation of the Republican party in Illinois in 1856, and one of their own, William Bissell, was elected the state's first Republican governor.[35]

Even in 1856, many northern Democrats clung to the hope that the party's national convention would repudiate the Kansas-Nebraska Act and Pierce's Kansas policy, or at least not make support of them a measure of party loyalty. In May, 1856 all eyes turned to Cincinnati, where the Democratic party assembled for one of its most momentous decisions. But the result was a foregone conclusion—the platform emphatically endorsed the Kansas-Nebraska Act, and the convention nominated a candidate whom anti-Nebraska Democrats believed to be pro-slavery. "Southern politicians," the *Evening Post* complained, controlled the convention.[36] Lot Morrill of Maine considered the platform "an insult to the North," and abandoned the Democracy. He was later elected governor by the Republicans. Maine's Democratic Senator, Hannibal Hamlin, who had maintained cordial relations with Pierce despite his opposition to the Nebraska act and had supported the administration on other issues, was convinced that "The old Dem. party is now the party of slavery. It has no other issue in fact and this is the standard on which [it] measures every thing and every man." A few days after the convention he rose in the Senate to announce that he could no longer count himself a Democrat. His decision mirrored that of countless less exalted northern Democrats. "When the Democratic convention, in 1856, indorsed the policy of Franklin Pierce," a Democrat who became a Republican Congressman later recalled, ". . . I became satisfied that its organization was in the hands of the slave power. . . . With many Democrats throughout the Union, I could no longer worship the divinity when the spirit had fled. . . .

34. Chicago *Democratic Press*, February 2, 3, March 1, 21, May 19, 24, 30, June 7, July 22, August 17, 1854, January 13, February 12, 21, July 17, August 27, 1855.

35. Palmer, ed., "Trumbull-Palmer Letters," 28; Harris, *Negro Servitude*, 200–1; J. Rutherford to Trumbull, January 15, 1856, A. J. Ashton to Trumbull, June 10, 1855; D. Phillips to Trumbull, January 18, 1856; W. H. Bissell to Trumbull, May 5, 1856, Trumbull Papers.

36. Isaac Sherman to Nathaniel P. Banks, March 5, 1856, Nathaniel P. Banks Papers, LC; Kirk H. Porter and Donald B. Johnson, comps., *National Party Platforms 1840–1956* (Urbana, 1956), 23–26; New York *Evening Post*, July 7, 1856.

Sir, I would rather desert a political organization than turn traitor to my own conscience." [37]

The campaign and election of 1856 revealed the extent of defections from the northern Democracy. Frémont swept large areas of the North previously unshakable in their loyalty to the Democratic party, and carried states like Maine, New Hampshire, and Michigan which had been Democratic strongholds. In such states as Ohio and Indiana, the political geography remained fairly stable, with relatively few Democrats joining the Republicans. In Pennsylvania, large defections from the Democracy were concentrated in the northern and western part of the state. David Wilmot's Congressional district, now represented by Galusha Grow, had given Pierce a majority of 2,500 votes in 1852; it gave Frémont over 70 per cent of the vote with a majority of over 9,000. In Michigan, the entire Democratic organization in some counties came out for Frémont, and Kinsley Bingham, the Democrat elected Governor as a Republican in 1854, said Frémont's majority of 21,000 "are all democrats of the best kind." A local Republican paper in 1858 estimated that 40 per cent of the Michigan Republicans came from "the old Jackson party." Similar wholesale defections took place in northern Illinois. The northeastern corner of the state—Chicago and the surrounding counties—gave Pierce 48.8 per cent of the vote, and a 2,618 plurality in 1852. Two years later, anti-Nebraska fusion candidates received a 5,265 majority, and in 1856, Frémont received almost 70 per cent of the vote and a majority of over 12,000. With Democrats like Lyman Trumbull, William Bissell, Gustav Koerner, John M. Palmer, and Norman Judd supporting Frémont, a leading Whig could exult, "The men here who have been regarded as the *elite* of the Democratic party are now with us for the Republican ticket." [38]

37. George F. Talbot, "Lot M. Morrill, Sketch of his Life and Public Services," *Collections* of Maine Historical Society, 2 ser., V (1894), 232; Harry Draper Hunt III, *Hannibal Hamlin of Maine* (Syracuse, 1969), 84, 236n.; Hamlin to Leander Valentine, June 6, 1856, Hamlin Papers; *Congressional Globe*, 34 Congress, 1 Session, 1396–97, 36 Congress, 1 Session, 1027.
38. Thomas A. Flinn, "Continuity and Change in Ohio Politics," *Journal of Politics*, XXIV (August 1962), 529; David H. Bradford, "The Background and Formation of the Republican Party in Ohio, 1844–1861" (unpublished doctoral dissertation, University of Chicago, 1947), 165; *Tribune Almanac*, 1855, 62; 1857, 48–49, 60–61; Kinsley S. Bingham to Blair, October 6, November 14, 1856, Blair-Lee Papers; Thomas M. Pitkin, "Western Republicans and the Tariff in 1860," *MVHR*, XXVII (December 1940), 405; Richard Yates to Trumbull, August 3, 1856, Trumbull Papers.

The largest withdrawals from the Democratic party came, as expected, in New York state. The historian William O. Lynch estimates that over 100,000 Democrats—a large majority of the Barnburner wing —voted for Frémont. Although older Barnburners like Van Buren, Flagg, Tilden, and Dix remained in their party, scores of important Barnburner leaders joined the Republicans. Among them were ex-Congressmen Preston King, Timothy Jenkins, George Rathbun and Martin Grover; James R. Doolittle (now living in Wisconsin), who had drafted the Wilmot Proviso plank for the 1847 state Democratic convention, and David Dudley Field, who had introduced it; [39] the editors of the *Evening Post*, Bryant, Bigelow, and Parke Godwin; and a long list of others, long active in party affairs, including James S. Wadsworth, George Opdyke, Abijah Mann, James Nye, and Reuben Fenton. Benjamin F. Butler's support of Frémont demonstrated that even the older Jacksonian group was not unanimous in remaining in the Democracy. In other states the same thing was seen in the actions of Francis P. Blair, Jackson's Secretary of the Treasury, S. D. Ingham, ex-Senator Benjamin Tappan, Gideon Welles, and John M. Niles.[40] The largest defections in New York were in the upstate counties which had long been Barnburner strongholds. Oneida county, which had always been Democratic, gave Frémont a 4,700 majority; Herkimer, which Pierce had carried by over 1,000 votes, and which had gone to a Democrat in 1854, gave Frémont 63 per cent of the vote. Preston King's St. Lawrence county, where Pierce had a plurality of 1,000 over Scott, gave Frémont 7,748 more votes than Buchanan, with over 75 per cent of the vote. Francis E. Spinner, who had been elected to Congress from King's district as a Democrat in 1854 but had voted for the Republican candidate for Speaker of the House, was re-elected as a Republican with one of the largest majorities in the nation. Frémont's majority in the sixteen New York counties in which Van Buren had run either first or second in 1848—the counties of Barnburner strength—was more than 56,000.[41]

Other northern states with large Democratic elements in the Republican party included Massachusetts, Wisconsin, and Maine. Even

39. James L. Sellers, "James Rood Doolittle," *WisMH*, XVII (1923–34), 172–73.
40. New York *Tribune*, October 10, 1855, September 2, October 16, 1856.
41. *Tribune Almanac*, 1849, 49; 1855, 54; 1857, 46; F. G. Barry, "General F. E. Spinner," *College and School*, I (April 1890), 104; Spinner to Lincoln, July 23, 1860, Lincoln Papers. Cf. Timothy Jenkins to Hamlin, November 7, 1856, Hamlin Papers; New York *Evening Post*, November 21, 1856.

before the defection of the popular Senator Hamlin, many Maine Democrats had abandoned their party. "In this vicinity," a friend wrote Hamlin in 1856, "a majority of those who have, since Jackson's time, been Democrats, are now in the Republican ranks." Hamlin's candidacy for governor, along with the addition of the temperance Democrats, meant that almost all the prominent politicians in the state were in the Republican fold in 1856. Taking the North as a whole, the ex-Democratic portion of the Republican vote in 1856 may have been as much as 25 per cent.[42]

Even these statistics do not suggest the full extent of the influence of ex-Democrats in the early Republican party, for their representation in leadership positions was far greater than the proportion of votes they supplied. The reason for this was simple—the Republicans could not hope to succeed without defections from the Democracy, and anti-slavery Democrats were more likely to abandon party allegiance if the Republican candidate was also a Democrat. In Maine in 1856, for example, Republican leaders felt Hannibal Hamlin would run six to eight thousand votes better than any ex-Whig candidate. "Many Democrats," one wrote, "are wavering and would be induced to join the Republicans if a man was nominated whose antecedents had been Democratic." The arch-Whig Horace Greeley suggested in 1855 that William Cullen Bryant, with whom he had long been at odds politically, head the Republican state ticket. "I suppose, that I don't like B. personally, and he certainly never wasted any civility on me;" Greeley observed, "so my judgment is at least disinterested." Bryant declined the invitation, but another leading Barnburner, Preston King, was chosen to head the ticket, which consisted of three former Whigs and six Democrats. This kind of division persisted in the New York party down to the Civil War. About half the Republican state candidates from 1855 to 1861 were ex-Democrats, as were at least eleven of the twenty-six Republican Congressmen elected in 1858.[43] In the West,

42. Josiah Drummond to Hamlin, April 9, 1856, Hamlin Papers; R. Michael Fosburg, "The Formation of the Republican Party in Maine: A Study of Hannibal Hamlin's Change in Party Affiliations" (unpublished master's essay, Columbia University, 1967), 65; William O. Lynch, "The Convergence of Lincoln and Douglas," Transactions of the IllSHS, XXXII (1925), 157. Lynch's estimate of the Democratic element in the Republican party is probably low, because it is based on the assumption that no Whigs voted for Buchanan, and it ignores the Free Soil vote of 1852.
43. Gaillard Hunt, Israel, Elihu, and Cadwallader Washburn, A Chapter in American Biography (New York, 1925), 50; Fosburg, "Hamlin," 2; Josiah Drummond

Kinsley Bingham, the first Republican Governor of Michigan, has already been noted. In Indiana, Whigs opposed to the Nebraska act intentionally remained in the background in the call for a fusion convention in 1854. They desired to avoid its being "set down as a Whig movement." Indiana's first Republican gubernatorial candidate was Oliver P. Morton, an ex-Democrat. The Anti-Nebraska state ticket in Ohio in 1854 was headed by a Democrat, Joseph Swan, and in Illinois, the first action of the new anti-Nebraska legislature in 1855 was to send Lyman Trumbull to the Senate.[44]

Similar considerations helped determine the choice of John C. Frémont as Republican presidential candidate in 1856. The ex-Democrats wanted one of their own as the standard-bearer and Frémont's candidacy was masterminded by Blair, Bigelow, and Nathaniel Banks. At the Philadelphia Convention which nominated Frémont, David Wilmot was chairman of the platform committee, and one newsman reported that a majority of the delegates were "men with Democratic antecedents." [45] Former Democrats played a major role in organizing the 1856 campaign. In part, this was an attempt to dispel fears that the Republican party was simply "the old Whig party in disguise," but it also was a recognition of the talent, experience, and fighting spirit of the Democratic-Republicans. As an Illinois Whig wrote Trumbull, "My observation is that we old line whigs in the Republican ranks are not worth a curse to carry on a campaign and its only life is in the Democratic part of the ranks." And years later, the ex-Whig James G. Blaine recalled that the Democrats "infused into the ranks of the new organization a spirit and an energy which Whig tradition could never inspire." [46]

to Hamlin, April 9, 1856, Hamlin Papers; Horace Greeley to E. A. Stansbury, August 3, 1855, Horace Greeley Papers, NHHS; New York *Times*, September 28, 1855, September 15, 1856, September 13, 1859; Greeley to B. Brockway, November 14, 1858, Horace Greeley Papers, LC.

44. O. J. Hollister, *Life of Schuyler Colfax* (New York, 1886), 73n.; Walter R. Sharp, "Henry S. Lane and the Formation of the Republican Party in Indiana," *MVHR*, VII (September 1920), 108; Palmer to Trumbull, May 25, 1858, Trumbull Papers.

45. Banks to Bigelow, March 24, 1856, Bigelow Papers; Schuyler Colfax to H. Wheeler, January 13, 1856, Schuyler Colfax Papers, LC; New York *Tribune*, June 6, 1856; Greeley to Israel Washburn, June 13, 1856, Israel Washburn Papers, LC; Samuel Bowles to Henry L. Dawes, April 19, 1856, Henry L. Dawes Papers, LC; William B. Hesseltine and Rex. G. Fisher, eds., *Trimmers, Trucklers, and Temporizers* (Madison, 1961), 90.

46. James M. Ashley to Greeley, April 26, 1859, Greeley Papers, NYPL; Jesse K. DuBois to Trumbull, July 17, 1858, Trumbull Papers; James G. Blaine, *Twenty Years of Congress* (2 vols.: Norwich, 1884), I, 117.

Throughout the early history of the Republican party, the ex-Democrats formed a self-conscious faction, proud of their antecedents, insistent on proper recognition in offices and patronage, and above all, determined that the party not become a mere reconstruction of Whiggery. In most states, Republican tickets and appointments were carefully balanced between Whigs and Democrats, and sometimes Liberty men as well. Occasionally former Democrats voted as a bloc in party conventions to ensure that some of their number received offices. The Democratic-Republicans regarded the anti-slavery convictions of their Whig colleagues as suspect, and they feared that the Whigs were plotting to gain complete control of the Republican party.[47] "A Democrat myself until 1854," one Minnesota Republican wrote Salmon Chase, ". . . I have nothing in common with those of our party who can see nothing in it but the party that furnished a Webster, a Fillmore, and an Everett." From Michigan, Chase received a complaint that "the old Whig element" was "determined to have matters their own way, and deal out rewards and punishments to individuals according to their antecedents." And as former Whigs joined the party in increasing numbers in the late 1850's, an Ohio Democratic-Republican complained that the party's growth was only "an increase of enemies." [48]

The leaders of the Democratic element co-operated with each other in combating Whig influence and ideology. Francis P. Blair sought aid from other ex-Democrats in financing a daily newspaper in Washington, the *Republic,* whose purpose was to help *"democratize* our party." Edited by a former Democrat from Maine, George Weston, the paper lasted from 1857 to 1859, when financial pressures forced its suspension. In Connecticut, John M. Niles, former governor Chauncy Cleveland, and especially Gideon Welles, struggled to prevent the party from becoming "but another phase of Whiggery." [49] Democratic-Republicans

47. C. H. Ray to Elihu Washburne, December 16, 24, 1854, Elihu B. Washburne Papers, LC; New York *Evening Post,* September 13, 18, 1856, May 22, 1858; "Letters of Gideon Welles," *Magazine of History,* Extra Number, No. 105, XXVII (1924), 20; Joshua Leavitt to Chase, May 2, 1856, Chase Papers, HSPa: B. R. Wood to Chase, May 21, 1856, Salmon P. Chase Papers, LC; New York *Tribune,* September 21, 1857.
48. George A. Nourse to Chase, September 8, 1860, J. H. Maye to Chase, June 18, 1860, Ralston Skinner to Chase, June 7, 1860, Chase Papers, LC. Cf. George A. Nourse to Trumbull, November 13, 1859, John Olney to Trumbull, March 12, 1860, Trumbull Papers.
49. Blair to Chase, October 26, 1857, Chase Papers, HSPa; Preston King to Seward, June 27, 1857, Seward Papers; Day, *Hill Top,* 147; George M. Weston to Trumbull, December 7, 1859, Trumbull Papers; Welles to ?, June 4, 1856, Welles to James F. Babcock, December 21, 1857, Welles Papers, ConnHS.

tended to downgrade the ability of the Whigs and to take credit themselves for Republican triumphs, maintaining that their faction was "the
mainstay of the Republican organization." It is also clear that there was
no love lost between the ex-Whigs and their Democratic allies. David
Davis of Illinois considered the Democratic element "a perfect oligarchy
with a maw ready to swallow everything." And an Ohio Whig-Republican complained that while the Democrats amounted to perhaps
10 per cent of the party in that state, "Old Whigs have no chance" for
patronage. One prominent Maine Whig-Republican questioned the
whole purpose of dividing offices in the way the Democrats demanded.
"If we are to continue to balance and adjust all offices with reference
to old party names—and have in view the equal distribution among
those old parties," former Governor Edward Kent wrote, "—then we
are a coalition and not a party." [50]

III

The fact that a sizable portion of its leadership and mass support
was composed of former Democrats was of the greatest importance
in the emergence of a distinctive Republican policy and ideology, as
well as in the selection of issues with which to appeal for mass support.
Perhaps the most important result was the virtual elimination from
national party politics of the financial issues which had formed the core
of Jacksonian political campaigns. This was absolutely essential if the
Republican party were to remain united, for while the party's Whig
majority believed in positive government action in support of economic
development, including protective tariffs, aid to internal improvements,
and federal regulation of the currency, most Democratic-Republicans
came from a tradition of strict construction of the Constitution, rigid
governmental economy, and hostility to tariffs, corporations, banks,
and monopolies. The Barnburners of New York had long feuded with
their Hunker opponents, as well as with the Whigs, over financial
policy. During the 1830's and 1840's, they fought for a limitation to the
state's canal program, urged direct taxation instead of borrowing to

50. Simon Cameron to Thurlow Weed, November 9. 1856, Thurlow Weed Papers,
Rush Rhees Library, University of Rochester; Rufus P. Spaulding to Chase, May
8, 1858, Chase Papers, HSPa; David Davis to Weed, February 2, 1861, Weed
Papers; R. W. Corwine to William Schouler, September 30, 1856, William Schouler
Papers, MHS; Edward Kent to Fessenden, November 22, 1856, Fessenden Papers,
WRHS.

pay for state expenses, opposed the suspension of specie payments by New York banks during the Panic of 1837, and generally held to the hard money, anti-bank views which had characterized the fiscal policies of Presidents Jackson and Van Buren. The Whigs and Hunkers found there were large areas in financial affairs on which they agreed, yet it was the Barnburners who joined the Whigs in the Republican party during the 1850's.[51]

A similar situation prevailed outside of New York State. Democratic defections in the 1850's tended to come from the "radical" wing of the party, which followed the Barnburners in their strict economic outlook. Hannibal Hamlin and his followers in Maine supported hard-money measures in the 1830's and 1840's. In Pennsylvania, David Wilmot described his district as "the most radical, thorough, inflexible Democratic district in the State; . . . opposed to a high protective tariff, to a national bank, to extravagant schemes of internal improvement by the General Government." The radical Democrats of Ohio demanded a specie currency, strict regulation of banks, individual liability of bank directors, and unlimited liability of corporation stockholders. At the Ohio constitutional convention of 1850, Democratic delegates who later joined the Republican party condemned corporations and banks of issue. And in Michigan, Kinsley Bingham had been the leader in the 1830's and 1840's of the anti-bank, anti-monopoly faction of the Democratic party.[52]

Differences on economic policy had long been a stumbling block to the union of anti-slavery Whigs and Democrats. One of the reasons many Democratic Free Soilers of 1848 supported Pierce four years later was their fear that Whig victory would result in mistaken economic policies. Preston King said that "the profligacy of the Whigs" was "the worst of all evils that threaten," and William Cullen Bryant felt that a Democratic victory was "the only certainty we have of safety" in financial matters. When the Republican party

51. Donovan, *Barnburners*, 15–16, 20–26; Muller, "King," 56–61, 100–01; John Bigelow to Charles Sumner, April 23, 1851, Sumner Papers; Frederick W. Seward, ed., *William H. Seward: An Autobiography* (New York, 1891), 764; Harriet A. Weed, ed., *Autobiography of Thurlow Weed* (Boston, 1883), 471.
52. Hunt, *Hamlin*, 17; *Congressional Globe*, 31 Congress, 1 Session, Appendix, 941; Benjamin P. Thomas and Harold Hyman, *Stanton, The Life and Times of Lincoln's Secretary of War* (New York, 1962), 23–28; *Report of the Debates and Proceedings of the Convention for the Revision of the Constitution of the State of Ohio, 1850–51* (2 vols.: Columbus, 1851), I, 402–7, 420, II, 800; Floyd B. Streeter, *Political Parties in Michigan 1837–1860* (Lansing, 1918), 31–33.

was created, many anti-slavery Democrats held aloof for a time because of "fear of the financial policy of the Republicans." [53] As a
result, the new party consciously avoided economic issues during the
first years of its existence. Most early state platforms dealt exclusively
with the slavery issue, and some, like Michigan's platform of 1854,
explicitly stated that Republicans were "postponing and suspending
all differences with regard to political or administrative policy." Anti-
slavery Democrats were quite pleased, as a Barnburner leader wrote,
that the call for the first Republican nominating convention "tolerates
as I understand it differences on all subjects—the purpose being to
combine men of all single creeds for one single purpose—to oppose
aggressions of slavery." During the 1856 campaign, Republican orators
insisted that the old issues of party politics were obsolete—that, as
Hamlin said, "Questions of commercial considerations now pass away
before the rising of the dark issue of slavery." [54]

Many of the financial issues over which Republicans disagreed
were, indeed, obsolete. Marvin Meyers has pointed out that the 1846
New York Constitutional Convention demonstrated that, despite differences of rhetoric, Empire State politicians had drawn much closer
together on economic issues since the 1830's. Anti-internal improvements Democrats had no wish to dismantle the state's canal system,
their differences with the Whigs being confined to specific questions
of operation and expansion. Similarly, both parties accepted the existence of the corporation, with the Barnburners insisting only that the
right to form corporations be open to all, through a general incorpora-
tion act. Moreover, Whig-Republicans recognized that the Whig party
had suffered from being identified as the party of business and wealth.
Thurlow Weed, the astute Whig leader in New York, said that though
he personally favored a national bank, any party identifying itself
with such a proposal was sure to be branded as a supporter of aristocracy and privilege. When a bill came up in Ohio in 1858 for a

53. King to Flagg, September 30, 1852, Flagg Papers; Parke Godwin, A Biography
of William Cullen Bryant (2 vols.: New York, 1883), II, 63; Hiram Barney to
Chase, October 11, 1855, Chase Papers, HSPa. Cf. Dix, comp., Memoirs, I, 239;
New York Evening Post, September 20, 1852.
54. Stephen M. Allen, Origin and Early Progress of the Republican Party in the
United States . . . (Boston, 1879), 34; Arthur M. Lee, "The Development of an
Economic Policy in the Early Republican Party" (unpublished doctoral disserta-
tion, Syracuse University, 1953), 22–26; Isaac Sherman to Banks, April 3, 1856,
Banks Papers; Charles E. Hamlin, The Life and Times of Hannibal Hamlin (Cam-
bridge, 1899), 299.

"Sub-Treasury law," and state bankers wanted the Republican state convention to oppose it, Democratic-Republicans warned that such a step would mark the Republicans as the party of the "Bank interest." Not only would this alienate radical Democrats in the party, but "it will place us where the Whigs were in relation to the U. S. Sub-Treasury —and prove as injurious to us as it did to them." The Republican convention avoided the question.[55]

Democratic-Republicans retained their hard-money views in principle, but in Chase's words, as "practical men" they recognized that a mixed currency of coin and paper would certainly exist "for an indefinite period."[56] Most Democratic-Republicans called for stricter regulation of the currency, and the prohibition of bank notes of small denominations, rather than an exclusively specie currency. After the Panic of 1857, many Whig-Republicans agreed with the ex-Democrats that the banks had been guilty of abuses, that too much paper had been issued, and that a better regulated currency was required. They dissented from the tendency of former Democrats to agree with President Buchanan in blaming the panic exclusively on the banks, but at the same time they insisted that banking policy formed no part of the Republican creed. "Some of us are Bank men, others for Hard Money," said the New York *Tribune*, "but neither Banks nor Hard Money have any place in our platform, and any Republican is at perfect liberty to cherish and maintain his own theory with regard to the currency."[57]

It is true that in states where Whigs predominated in the Republican party, the party tended to take a friendly attitude towards banks and corporations. In Ohio, for instance, the first anti-Nebraska legislature exempted some banks from taxation, and passed a general banking law which was later rejected in a popular referendum. But Governor

55. Marvin Meyers, *The Jacksonian Persuasion* (New York, 1960 ed.), 256, 262–70; Horace Greeley, *Recollections of a Busy Life* (New York, 1868), 314; James S. Pike, *First Blows of the Civil War* (New York, 1879), 174–75; Thomas Bolton to Chase, July 12, 1858, Chase Papers, HSPa.

56. *Message of the Governor of Ohio to the Fifty-Second General Assembly* . . . (Columbus, 1857), 7. Cf. *Address of His Excellency Nathaniel P. Banks to the Two Branches of the Legislature of Massachusetts, January 7, 1858* (Boston, 1858), 13; George N. Fuller, ed., *Messages of the Governors of Michigan* (4 vols.: Lansing, 1925–27), II, 291; Chicago *Press*, October 7, 1857; New York *Evening Post*, November 2, 20, 1857.

57. Chicago *Tribune*, November 12, December 7, 1857; Cincinnati *Gazette*, December 11, 12, 1857, January 5, 1858; Pike, *First Blows*, 378; New York *Tribune*, November 16, 1857.

Chase supported both these measures, and the leading Whig-Republican paper wrote that the party "has no duty or mission in defense of the treasury or the banks." The state parties usually sought to compromise differences on financial matters within the party. In New York the Whigs' demand for the completion of a proposed series of extensions to the state canal system was combined with the Barnburners' insistence that the money be raised by direct taxation rather than by loan. Barnburners were nominated for the state's financial offices in 1856 and 1857 to assure former Democrats that the canal completion would be pursued as economically as possible, and Republicans insisted that "there is no longer a real difference" concerning the state's system of public works.[58]

The Iowa Constitutional Convention of 1857, in which Republicans had a majority of the delegates, provided a good test of the party's position on banking. The Constitution of 1846, written by the Democrats, had barred banks from the state altogether, but this had led to the state's being flooded with worthless paper from other states. The Republicans went into the convention pledged to allow some kind of banking system, but their delegates divided on the merits of free banking as opposed to a state bank. The convention finally passed the issue along to the legislature, by allowing it to enact a general law for corporations, to be approved by popular vote, or to set up a state bank, though only "on an actual specie basis." The Constitution also barred special legislation granting corporate charters, and subjected all corporate property to taxation. And a section allowing the legislature to repeal grants of corporate charter was favored by ten Republicans, while nine opposed it. Since the Democratic minority wanted to continue the ban on banks and corporations, the Republicans could be considered more favorable to business than their opponents; yet with all its restrictions, the Constitution was hardly the kind that a Whig convention would have adopted fifteen or twenty years before.[59]

58. Bradford, "Ohio Republican Party," 153–54; Eugene H. Roseboom, The Civil War Era 1850–1873 (Columbus, 1944), 314–15; Cincinnati Gazette, October 20, 1857; New York Tribune, September 28, 29, October 25, 1855, September 26, 1856, July 25, September 28, 1857, September 11, 1858; New York Evening Post, September 24, 1857, September 8, 1859; Samuel A. Foot, Reasons for Joining the Republican Party (Washington, 1856), 2.
59. Russell M. Ross, "The Development of the Iowa Constitution of 1857," IJH, LV (April 1957), 105–6; "Contemporary Editorial Opinion of the 1857 Constitution," IJH, LV (April 1957), 115, 122, 133; Benjamin F. Shambaugh, History of the Constitutions of Iowa (Des Moines, 1902), 339–42; Iowa Constitutional Convention, I, 106–7, 113–14, 174, 345–46, 364, 381

Perhaps the greatest threat to co-operation between Democrats and Whigs within the Republican party was the tariff issue. Indeed, this had been a problem for anti-slavery politics for years before the formation of the Republican party. One of the few discordant notes at the Buffalo Free Soil Convention of 1848 was a dispute over the tariff in the platform committee. Like other economic issues, the tariff was ignored in most of the early state Republican platforms, and the national convention of 1856 did not mention it.[60]

It was the Panic of 1857 which brought the tariff issue back into the political spotlight. Horace Greeley's New York *Tribune*, which was strongly influenced by the views of the Pennsylvania protectionist economist Henry C. Carey, blamed the financial crisis on the low tariff of 1857, and demanded a return to a protective policy. Carey and his disciples hoped to make the Republicans "a protective party *en bloc*," but they recognized that they would have to move carefully because of rising opposition from Democratic-Republicans. Some of the latter were still doctrinaire free-traders in the 1850's; more recognized that direct taxation to finance the government was politically impossible, but they wanted a low tariff with uniform rates which would bring in only the revenue required by the government. William Cullen Bryant, who had written that free trade was "a part of the grand movement of mankind toward a nobler condition of social existence," lashed out at the rising protectionism among Whig-Republicans. The *Evening Post* ridiculed Carey's economic views, pointing out that the Pennsylvanian had once believed in free trade himself and seemed now to be "suffering under a sort of monomania" regarding the tariff. The alarm of former Democrats was well expressed by a constituent of Lyman Trumbull: "I regret to see an indication in Philadelphia, and in other parts of the East, of an effort on the part of many heretofore (and perhaps yet) earnest Republicans, . . . to 'revive' as they call it, a *Protective* party." [61]

Yet here, as with other financial issues, there was more room for

60. E. S. Hamlin to Chase, May 14, 1848, Chase Papers, HSPa; E. S. Hamlin to John McLean, August 17, 1848, John McLean Papers, LC; Charles Francis Adams Diary, August 9, 1848, Adams Papers, MHS; New York *Evening Post*, August 18, 1848; Chase to Butler, July 26, 1849, Butler Papers.
61. Arthur M. Lee, "Henry C. Carey and the Republican Tariff," *PaMHB*, LXXI (July 1957), 285–90; E. Pershine Smith to Carey, February 6, 1859, Carey Papers; Godwin, *Bryant*, I, 388; New York *Evening Post*, January 14, 1860; Sarah J. Day, *The Man on a Hill Top* (Philadelphia, 1931), 214; Thomas Allen to Trumbull, July 1, 1858, Trumbull Papers.

agreement within the party than at first seemed apparent. For many politicians had long been willing to modify their positions on the tariff to achieve political ends. In 1844, for example, Silas Wright had pointed out that the parties were closer together on the tariff than their rhetoric would imply, and in that year Polk, supposedly an advocate of free trade, had judiciously written a campaign letter to a Pennsylvania friend, supporting incidental protection for that state's iron interests.[62] Moreover, aside from Carey and some of his followers, there were few unqualified protectionists in the Republican party. That is, few wanted the tariff to be higher than was necessary to raise the revenue needed by the government. On the other hand, as we have seen, few ex-Democrats wanted an immediate adoption of free trade and direct taxation. And once they agreed that some kind of tariff was necessary for revenue, it was not difficult to convince them that some form of "incidental protection" was in order, especially for the iron industry of Pennsylvania, a pivotal state in the coming presidential election. After 1857, as Republicans hoped to woo votes in Pennsylvania, the party tended to coalesce behind the proposed Morrill tariff, with only a few doctrinaire free-traders like Francis Spinner of New York (who represented the Barnburner stronghold, St. Lawrence county), opposing any increase in rates. Morrill insisted that his bill was primarily intended to raise revenue and that "no prohibitory duties have been aimed at," though a few industrial interests, particularly iron and wool, were protected.[63]

That there was a basis for agreement on the tariff within the Republican party was demonstrated by the position taken by leading former Democrats between 1857 and 1860. They recognized that Pennsylvania was demanding protection and that the demand would have to be satisfied in some way if the Republicans were to carry the state. They therefore adopted the policy which Doolittle called "some incidental protection to the iron interest, avoiding, nevertheless, the idea of a high tariff." [64] Chase, who had been an advocate of free trade for most

62. Silas Wright to Martin Van Buren, January 8, 1844, Van Buren Papers; Sellers, Polk, 119.

63. Richard Hofstadter, "The Tariff Issue on the Eve of the Civil War," AHR, XLIV (October 1938), 50–54; Congressional Globe, 35 Congress, 2 Session, Appendix, 117, 226, 241, 36 Congress, 1 Session, 1832, 2 Session, 1023, 1026; New York Tribune, September 26, 1856; Pitkin, "Western Republicans," 401–2. Robert Sharkey characterizes Morrill as "at heart only a moderate protectionist." Sharkey, Money, Class, and Party (Baltimore, 1959), 77n.

64. James R. Doolittle to John F. Potter, November 7, 1860, John F. Potter Papers, WisHS. Cf. New York Tribune, October 2, 1857; Concord Independent Democrat, June 19, 1858, clipping, John P. Hale Scrapbook, NHHS.

of his career, was forced to modify his position because of his candidacy for the presidential nomination in 1860. He received information from many states that ex-Whigs were reluctant to support him because of his free trade reputation, but his advisers also informed him, "nobody is in favor of a high protective tariff or prohibitive tariff." Chase perceived very clearly the basis for a compromise on the tariff: all "extreme positions" would have to be avoided, and he announced his willingness to accept a revenue tariff with "incidental protection." [65]

The Republican Convention of 1860, which adopted planks calling for a tariff, internal improvements, a Pacific railroad and a homestead law, is sometimes seen as a symbol of Whig triumph within the party. A closer look, however, indicates that the Whig victory, if it was that, was of a very tentative nature. It is true that economic issues were playing a larger role in Republican state platforms in 1859 and 1860 than in previous years, and that this reflected in part the increasing influence of former Whigs in the party's councils. But former Democrats also recognized that in the wake of the Panic of 1857 the party would have to broaden its platforms. "I do not see what we are to do without some financial policy" was the way John Wentworth put it. Moreover, many of the economic planks in the 1860 platform concerned matters which had not been in dispute between Democrats and Whigs. Both parties in the West had favored government aid to internal improvements and the construction of a Pacific railroad, and these planks had been included in the 1856 Republican platform when a protest from the ex-Democrats would surely have excluded them. The homestead was primarily a sectional, not a party issue, with both parties in the North affirming their support in 1859 and 1860.[66]

The main problem was the tariff plank. Bryant, who took a more uncompromising line on the tariff than did most former Democrats, charged two months before the convention that there was a "conspiracy . . . to pervert the Republican party to the purposes of the

65. Joseph Medill to Chase, July 27, 1859, Chase to Israel Green, March 16, 1859, HSPa; James A. Briggs to Chase, May 2, 1859, Ralph Lowe to Chase, December 12, 1859, Chase Papers, LC; Chase to James A. Briggs, April 19, 1859, Chase Papers (ser II), LC. Cf. "Diary and Correspondence," 282; New York *Tribune*, October 20, 1860; Chase to Lewis Campbell, June 2, 1855, Chase Papers, LC; Chase to Briggs, April 7, 1859, Chase Papers, HSPa.
66. Lee, "Economic Policy," 36, 128; John Wentworth to Lincoln, November 28, 1859, Lincoln Papers; Porter and Johnson, *Party Platforms*, 28; "Gov. Chase's Speech at Toledo, May 30, 1851," manuscript, Box 17, Chase Papers, HSPa. Cf. Allan Nevins, *The Emergence of Lincoln* (2 vols.: New York, 1950), I, 197.

owners of coal and iron mines." Many politicians, including Lincoln,
felt the tariff issue to be so divisive that it should be avoided altogether
at Chicago. At the convention, however, Pennsylvania delegates demanded some kind of tariff plank, and the resolutions committee split
on the issue. Horace Greeley insisted on a strong protectionist plank;
Austin Blair, the radical from Michigan, called for a more moderate
resolution; and John A. Kasson, a free-soil Democrat, took an even
more moderate position. In light of the traditional view that the Republican party of 1860 was "a homestead and high tariff party" which
adopted "a magnificent Whig economic program," it is interesting that
the tariff plank was written not by Greeley or Blair, but by Kasson.[67]
Its chief characteristic was ambiguity. The word "protection" was not
mentioned at all; the resolution called only for "an adjustment of . . .
imports . . . to encourage the development of the industrial interests
of the whole country." The Pennsylvania delegation cheered the plank
heartily, but privately they voiced their disappointment. So vague was
its wording that the *Evening Post* could claim that the party had come
out in favor of free trade. Nonetheless, the Republican party was presented as the party of protection in Pennsylvania during the 1860
campaign, although the Democrats in that state took the same position. Elsewhere in the North, however, the tariff played a minor role
in the election. It seems that Carey's disciple, E. Pershine Smith of
New York, was right when he wrote his mentor in 1859: "As to the
tariff, the fact is that our people do not care—I and you know that they
ought to, but the fact is that they *don't*." [68]

IV

In spite of Democratic-Whig disagreements over economic matters—
which required the avoidance or compromise of such issues as the

67. New York *Evening Post*, March 1, April 16, 1860; Basler, ed., *Lincoln Works*,
IV, 49, Chicago *Press and Tribune*, May 2, 1860; R. Hosea to Chase, May 16,
1860, Chase Papers, LC; Henry H. Smith, *All the Republican National Conventions* (Washington, 1896), 19; Younger, *Kasson*, 103; New York *Tribune*, May 27,
1860; Elbert B. Smith, *The Death of Slavery* (Chicago, 1967), 165; Charles A.
Beard and Mary R. Beard, *The Rise of American Civilization* (New York, 1933
ed.), II, 39.
68. Porter and Johnson, *Party Platforms*, 33; Nevins, *Emergence*, II, 253;
William H. Russell, "A. K. McClure and the People's Party in the Campaign of
1860," *PaH*, XXVIII (October 1961), 337–38; William B. Hesseltine, ed., *Three
Against Lincoln* (Baton Rouge, 1960), 152; New York *Evening Post*, May 18,
1860; Emerson D. Fite, *The Presidential Campaign of 1860* (New York, 1911),
197; E. Pershine Smith to Carey, January 16, 1859, Carey Papers.

tariff—the influence of the Democratic-Republicans on the development of Republican policy and ideology was by no means wholly negative. For the presence of ex-Democrats among Republican leaders, as well as among the rank and file, reinforced and lent plausibility to beliefs which were widely accepted by former Whigs, Democrats, and Liberty men alike. Their defection from the Democracy lent credence to the charge that the regular Democratic party was no longer the champion of popular rights that it had been in Jackson's day, for these men could testify from personal experience that the Slave Power had taken control of the party and was pressing forward with plans for the expansion of slavery. Their attacks on the government for fiscal extravagance carried far greater weight than did those of former Whigs, who were known for their belief in an active government. And above all, the inflexible Jacksonian Unionism of the ex-Democrats made certain that when the secession crisis arrived, there would be a large body of Republicans who viewed secession as treason, and who were unalterably opposed to any concessions to the South.

The bitterness against the South which had marked the free-soil campaigns of the Van Burenite Democrats in the 1840's also characterized the participation of Democratic-Republicans in campaigns of the 1850's. Indeed, it would not be inaccurate to say that many of these ex-Democrats were more anti-southern than they were anti-slavery. Blair wrote Van Buren that he was incensed by "the triumph of every rogue in power who reached it by betraying you and who now pander to your enemies and the enemies of the Union," and added that he viewed Buchanan as "the tool of the black oligarchy of slave holders." Charges that the Democratic party had become, as David Dudley Field said, the "tool of a slaveholding oligarchy," were standard fare in the rhetoric of the former Democrats. Timothy Day, a Republican Congressman from Ohio who said he had voted for every Democratic presidential candidate from Jefferson to Pierce, told the House that "the lion of Democracy has become the jackal of slavery." [69]

Republican speakers often charged that the Democratic party of the 1830's and 1840's no longer existed. The "wild absurdities" of Calhoun regarding slavery and nullification, which had been repudiated by the Democracy in Jackson's time, had finally, according to Gideon Welles, become the official doctrines of the Democratic party.

69. Blair to Van Buren, February 6, 1858, Van Buren Papers; Blair to Cameron, October 20, 1858, Cameron Papers; New York *Tribune*, July 25, 1856; *Congressional Globe*, 34 Congress, 1 Session, Appendix, 414.

"Democracy in 1858 means the nullification doctrines of South Carolina in times gone by," Hannibal Hamlin declared, and one Republican Congressman, formerly a Democrat, went so far as to say that in
1854 the Democratic party had been disbanded "and is now known as
the Republican party." That the Republicans were the real heirs of
the tradition of Jacksonian democracy was constantly reiterated by
the ex-Democrats, and they therefore denied that they were guilty
of disloyalty to their former party. Rather, it was the leaders of the
Democracy who had changed. "To occupy its present ground," King
wrote, "the democratic party has changed its members, its principles,
its purposes, its character. Everything but its name is changed." And
Timothy Day, after listing the various sins committed by the Pierce
administration in Kansas, asked his "old Democratic co-workers. . . .
if this is the party we once considered honored in being attached
to?" [70]

The former Democrats felt that just as they remained true to the
heritage of Jackson in their opposition to southern control of the
Democratic party, so also were they faithful to Old Hickory's fierce
Unionism. During the nullification crisis of 1832–33, Jackson had denounced Calhoun's position that a state could nullify an act of Congress and could secede from the Union as a last resort to protect its
rights. Jackson's view was simple: nullification was treason and secession was insurrection. Both would be met, if necessary, with force.
Jackson's close adviser Francis P. Blair strongly defended the President's actions during the crisis and remained a firm Unionist throughout his life.[71] During the 1840's and 1850's Blair and his sons Frank
and Montgomery insisted that the Republicans were "the party of the
Union" and charged southern Democrats with being "the progeny of
Calhoun doctrines." During the secession crisis they used all their
influence to urge a strong stand against the South. While some Republicans argued that offers of compromise would conciliate the Border
states, Frank Blair insisted that only uncompromising firmness would

70. "Dissertation on Current Political Matters," undated manuscript, Welles Papers,
ConnHS; *Congressional Globe*, 35 Congress, 1 Session, 1005; 34 Congress, 1
Session, Appendix, 1269; King to Welles, September 16, 1858, Welles Papers,
LC; Timothy Day, *The Humbug and the Reality* (Washington, 1856), 5. Cf.
Chicago *Press*, October 10, 1857.
71. Marquis James, *The Life of Andrew Jackson* (New York, 1938), 610–17;
James D. Richardson, ed., *A Compilation of the Messages and Papers of the Presi-
dents* (10 vols.: Washington, 1896–99), II, 648–50, 1218–19; Blair to Jackson,
September 9, 1844, Jackson Papers; Smith, *Blair Family*, I, 53–55.

force those states to stay in the Union. Montgomery wrote that the South needed to be taught a lesson, and advocated the use of force to preserve the Union.[72]

The Blairs and the New York Barnburners had been warning about southern disunion conspiracies since the 1840's, consistently arguing that the only way to meet such threats was by the willingness to suppress treason with force. Other northern Democrats first came to take southern threats seriously during the crisis which preceded the Compromise of 1850. A good example of the latter group was William H. Bissell; in 1850, a Democratic Congressman from Illinois and later the state's Republican Governor. Bissell was genuinely alarmed by southern bluster. He was amazed to find that southern Congressmen were "as unreasonable, impracticable, insane, and reckless as the most fanatical abolitionist ever was charged with being," and that many "are in favour of disunion *for the sake of* disunion." In order to prevent disunion and preserve the Democratic party, Bissell was willing to support the Compromise measures, but not before he had issued a stern warning to the South:

> I know the people of my state. I know the people of the Great West and Northwest; and I know their devotion to the American Union. And I feel warranted in saying in my place here, that when you talk to them of destroying this Union, there is not a man throughout that vast region who will not raise his hand and swear by the Eternal God, as I do now it shall never be done, if our arms can save it.

Bissell's speech caused a sensation. It was widely circulated in 1850, and again as a Republican campaign document in 1856, 1858, and 1860. Better than any other statement, it expressed the unflinching devotion to the Union which characterized the Democratic-Republicans.[73]

72. New York *Tribune*, January 26, 1860; Francis P. Blair to Lincoln, January 15, 1861, Lincoln Papers; F. P. Blair, Jr., to Dawes, December 15, 1860, Dawes Papers; Robert M. Thompson and Richard Wainwright, eds., *Confidential Correspondence of Gustavus V. Fox* (2 vols.: New York, 1918), I, 4–5. Cf. "Selected Letters, 1846–1856, from the Donelson Papers," *Tennessee Historical Magazine*, III (December 1917), 291.
73. William H. Bissell to William Martin, February 5, 1850 (photostat copy), William H. Bissell Papers, ChicHS; *Congressional Globe*, 31 Congress, 1 Session, Appendix, 228; Frank Elliot, "Governor William H. Bissell," *Transactions* of the McLean County Historical Society, III (1900), 137; Chicago *Democratic Press*, July 24, 1856.

During 1860, and in the secession winter of 1860–61, virtually all the leading ex-Democrats in the Republican party insisted that disunion was treason, to be met with force if necessary, and opposed all compromise measures. When the House, early in December 1860, voted to set up a committee to look into the causes of the crisis, at least eleven Democratic-Republicans opposed the measure, while only four favored it (and one of these, Francis Spinner, said he only voted for it because "I knew it could effect nothing").[74] In addresses in 1860 and 1861, Governors Randall of Wisconsin, Kirkwood of Iowa, and Morton of Indiana, all ex-Democrats, threw their influence against concession. Morton warned the South in November, "if it was worth a bloody struggle to establish this nation, it is worth one to preserve it."[75] Spokesmen for the New York Barnburner-Republicans likewise denounced secession as treason, as did Vice-President-elect Hamlin and Gideon Welles. In urging Welles's appointment to Lincoln's cabinet, one former Democrat wrote in December, "In these trying times, there is need of Jacksonism. . . . Welles, of Connecticut, is Jacksonism."[76]

Their support of Wisconsin Republicans' efforts to nullify the fugitive slave law only a few years earlier did not prevent Welles, Randall, and Senator James R. Doolittle from taking strong Unionist positions. The former Democrats came from a tradition which viewed the states as the locus of most governmental action, and they were extremely fearful of centralized power in Washington. Welles, for instance, described himself as a Republican "of the old Jefferson and Jackson kind, having none of the centralism or loose latitudinous notions of federalism or Whiggery." He believed Whig Republicans had no comprehension of the basic constitutional issues involved in the slavery controversy, because they believed that the nation was "a consolidated empire" rather than a federation of "sovereign communities." Many

74. *Congressional Globe*, 36 Congress, 2 Session, 6; Day, *Hill Top*, 235–36.
75. *Annual Message of Alexander W. Randall, Governor of the State of Wisconsin, and Accompanying Documents* (Madison, 1860), 27; Benjamin F. Shambaugh, ed., *The Messages and Proclamations of the Governors of Iowa* (7 vols.: Iowa City, 1903–05), II, 247; William M. French, ed., *Life, Speeches, State Papers, and Public Services of Gov. Oliver P. Morton* (Cincinnati, 1866), 130. Cf. Henry C. Hubbart, *The Older Middle West 1840–1880* (New York, 1936), 172–73.
76. Hamlin, *Hamlin*, 383; New York *Evening Post*, November 12, 1860; Bigelow to Mr. Hargreaves, December 12, 1860, Bigelow Papers, NYPL; Muller, "King," 653; *Congressional Globe*, 36 Congress, 2 Session, 1157; George G. Fogg to William Butler, December 28, 1860, William Butler Papers, ChicHS.

Democratic-Republicans viewed the southern contention that the Constitution carried slavery into all the territories as the height of "centralism" and a complete abandonment of traditional Democratic doctrines.[77] They also vehemently denied the right of the Supreme Court to impose its constitutional views on the state judiciaries—as it did in the Wisconsin fugitive slave law case—or to "control the political destiny of the people by obiter dicta," as in the Dred Scott decision. But despite their states-rights position—which some Whig-Republicans feared bordered on nullification doctrines—the ex-Democrats never contemplated disunion. At the very time he was endorsing the Virginia and Kentucky resolutions and helping to bring Wisconsin to the verge of nullifying the fugitive slave law, James R. Doolittle took pains to make clear that "we stand upon our rights as a sovereign State *in the Union,* and do not seek our redress by going *out of the Union.*"[78]

V

The influence of the former Democrats in the Republican party on the eve of the Civil War was demonstrated both in the selection of a presidential candidate and in the choice of the first Republican cabinet. Most leading former Democrats—including governors Randall, Bissell, and Bingham, and all the leading New York Barnburners except Preston King—would have preferred the nomination of Salmon P. Chase.[79] Primarily, however, they were concerned with blocking the nomination of William H. Seward, and former Democrats played an important part in Seward's defeat at the Chicago Convention. Strict constructionists like Gideon Welles objected strongly to Seward's Whiggish belief "that the federal government is imperial—that it is

77. Welles to J. R. Rean, May 25, 1858, Welles Papers, ConnHS; Welles to ?, (draft), December 28, 1855, Welles Papers, LC; New York *Tribune,* August 26, 1857; Welles to Cleveland, April 27, 1857, Welles Papers, LC; Albert Mordell, ed., *Lincoln's Administration, Selected Essays by Gideon Welles* (New York, 1960), 24, 47–50.
78. Blair to John A. King, October 27, 1857, in Weed Papers; *Wisconsin State Journal,* January 22, 1857; James R. Doolittle to Moses Davis, March 9, 1860, Moses Davis Papers, WisHS; *Congressional Globe,* 35 Congress, 1 Session, 962, 36 Congress, 1 Session, Appendix, 125–27.
79. W. H. Brisbane to Chase, July 13, 1859, W. H. Bissell to Chase, February 4, 1860, George Opdyke to Chase, May 11, 1860, D. Taylor to Chase, May 22, 1860, Chase Papers, LC; David Wilmot to ?, May 29, 1859, Simon Gratz Collection, HSPa; King to Welles, June 17, July 30, September 16, 1858, Welles Papers, LC.

the source of all power." Welles wrote a long article for the *Evening Post* criticizing Seward's "Irrepressible Conflict" speech, not because of its radical statements on slavery but because Seward had declared that the states of the Union must ultimately have the same social system.[80] The former Democrats also feared that a Seward administration would be marked by the most reckless government spending and aid to all kinds of special economic interests. They were well aware of Seward's support in the Senate of government aid to the Collins steamship line, his advocacy of a a protective tariff, and other acts they considered extravagant. "He gives his countenance and vote to almost every appropriation of land or money asked for," one complained, and from New York, Barnburner Republicans reported that Seward's supporters in the New York legislature were guilty of fiscal recklessness and corruption.[81]

There were, of course, many factors responsible for Seward's defeat at the Chicago Convention, but important among them were the activities of former Democrats. New York Barnburners like George Opdyke, James Wadsworth, Hiram Barney, and William Cullen Bryant spread the word among wavering delegates that Seward's nomination would alienate many New York Republicans and possibly cause the loss of the state. The Blairs and Gideon Welles, also delegates, exerted their own influence against the New Yorker.[82] Though their first choice, Chase, never had a chance, the ex-Democrats were quite pleased with the Republican ticket of Lincoln and Hamlin. The choice of Hamlin for the vice-presidency was a recognition of the importance of the Democratic element; indeed, of the five leading candidates for second place on the ticket, only one, Cassius M. Clay, was a former Whig. Lincoln's cabinet selections also more than satisfied the ex-Democrats, although the final list was not settled upon until after an acrimonious dispute between Democratic and Whig elements in the party. Seward and his followers hoped to dominate the Cabinet, and objected to the

80. Welles to Blair, 1859 (draft), Welles Papers, ConnHS; New York *Evening Post*, November 15, 1858; James Dixon to Welles, December 2, 1858, Welles Papers, LC; Welles to King, August, 1858, Welles Papers, ConnHS.

81. Jacob Brinkerhoff to Hamlin, May 25, 1858, Hamlin Papers. Cf. Bingham to Chase, July 7, 1855, C. Robinson to Chase, February 3, 1860, Chase Papers, LC; Hiram Barney to Chase, April 3, 1860, Chase Papers, HSPa.

82. Henry B. Stanton, *Random Recollections* (New York, 1887), 214; Henry M. Field, *The Life of David Dudley Field* (New York, 1898), 136–40; George Opdyke to Blair, May 10, 1860, Blair-Lee Papers; Field to Lincoln, January 3, 1861, Lincoln Papers.

inclusion of too many former Democrats, particularly "such ultra democrats as Welles and Blair." [83] For their part, the ex-Democrats wanted Seward excluded from the cabinet entirely, and exerted strong pressure on Lincoln to include Chase and other ex-Democrats. Lincoln himself took great care in drawing up his cabinet to strike a balance between men of Democratic and Whig antecedents. He was determined to give the former Democrats their "fair share" of the posts, and finally selected Montgomery Blair, Welles, Chase, and Simon Cameron.[84] Lincoln was sagacious enough to realize that the former Democrats were quite right in warning that the Republicans must avoid appearing to be "only the old Whig party, under a new name." [85]

In retrospect, it is clear that with the firing on Fort Sumter the influence of Democratic-Republicans within the party began to wane. What the exertions of former Whigs had been unable to accomplish— the adoption of an essentially Whig economic program as Republican national policy—was achieved because of the exigencies of the Civil War. Without the financial crisis created by the war, it is very doubtful whether the very high tariffs, national banking system, and paper money of the war years could have been adopted. It is true that the Republican economic policy which finally crystallized during these years combined aspects of pre-war Democratic as well as Whig economic programs. But it cannot be doubted that such measures as the national banking act, land grants to colleges, and a high tariff were based on a conception of the federal government and its role which had previously been associated with Whiggery. The anomalous position in which many ex-Democrats were placed by these financial measures was symbolized by the fact that Salmon P. Chase, an advo-

83. Hesseltine, ed., *Three Against Lincoln,* 174–75; Palmer, *Recollections,* 81; George A. Nourse to Hamlin, May 28, 1860, Hamlin Papers; "Comment upon the Autobiographical Sketch of Thurlow Weed Relating to the Formation of Lincoln's Cabinet," undated manuscript, Welles Papers, NYPL. Cf. "Letters of Welles," 25, 32.

84. "Diary and Correspondence," 485–90; Bryant to Lincoln, November 10, December 29, 1860, January 22, 1861; Field to Lincoln, January 3, 1861, Doolittle to Lincoln, January 10, 1860, Lincoln Papers; Trumbull to Hamlin, January 2, 1861, Hamlin Papers; Fogg to William Butler, December 13, 1860, William Butler Papers; Henry B. Stanton to Chase, November 13, 1860, Chase Papers, LC; Weed, ed., *Weed Autobiography,* 606–7; Basler, ed., *Lincoln Works,* IV, 161, 171; Hiram Barney to Bryant, January 17, 1861, Bryant-Godwin Papers; "Letters of Welles," 24.

85. William Endicott to Chase, January 17, 1861, Chase Papers, LC. Cf. Bryant to Lincoln, December 25, 1860, Lincoln Papers; "Diary and Correspondence," 483.

cate of specie currency, directed the same Treasury Department which
issued millions of dollars in paper greenbacks, while each note was
adorned with the signature of Francis E. Spinner, Treasurer of the
United States and former hard-money Barnburner.[86]

During the 1860's, Republican economic policy would lead some
former Democrats to return to the Democracy. One later remarked that
"the Republican Party ought to have resolved itself into its original
elements instead of foisting old Whiggery upon the Democratic adherents." Even more disturbing to many former Democrats, however,
was the vast expansion of federal power which took place during the
war, and the virtual abandonment of states rights as a philosophy of
government. Even while he worked in Lincoln's cabinet directing the
Navy Department, Gideon Welles complained bitterly about the
trend toward "centralism." To a large degree, it was the inability to
accept this growth of national power which led many Democratic-
Republicans back into the Democracy after the Civil War. The actions of such ex-Democrats as the Blairs, Welles, Doolittle, Field,
Trumbull, Randall, Chase, and other former Democrats who deserted
the Republican party were forecast by Welles in his 1858 reply to
Seward's "Irrepressible Conflict" speech: [87]

> I can most cheerfully cooperate with Senator Seward, in opposing
> the aggressions of slavery, although we belong to entirely different
> schools of politics. . . . Strict constructionists of the school of Jef-
> ferson opposed the centralizing policy in regard to slavery, as they
> did in regard to banking, because they would restrain the action of
> the federal government within its constitutional limitations, and
> maintain for the states all reserved rights. . . . [But] there is
> no disposition on the part of the [states rights men] to be carried
> . . . into the whirlpool of consolidation.

86. Lee, "Economic Policy," 304–9; Blaine, *Twenty Years*, I, 198–99; Margaret
G. Meyers, *The New York Money Market* (New York, 1931), 218; Beale, ed.,
Welles Diary, I, 168, 525, II, 12, 180; Irwin Unger, *The Greenback Era* (Prince-
ton, 1964), 18; Sharkey, *Money, Class, and Party*, 221–22.
87. Roeliff Brinkerhoff, *Recollections of a Lifetime* (Cincinnati, 1904), 126; Beale,
ed., *Welles Diary*, II, 197–98; New York *Evening Post*, November 15, 1858. As
the Coxes show, however, the race issue was also crucial in the return of ex-
Democrats to the Democracy after the Civil War. See Lawanda and John H. Cox,
Politics, Principle, and Prejudice, 1865–1866 (Glencoe, Ill., 1963), 54–55, 214–19;
Smith, *Blair Family*, II, 462, and chapter eight below, for the racial attitudes of
the Democratic-Republicans. On the general question of the return of the Democratic-Republicans, see Albert Cole, Jr., "The Barnburner Element in the Republican Party" (unpublished master's essay, University of Wisconsin, 1951),
71–114, 122.

The Democratic-Republicans had not wanted slavery to be the basis of political divisions; witness their denunciations of southerners for having made it a national question. Once the issues of slavery and disunion had been settled by the Civil War, many were prepared to abandon the Republican party rather than be swept up in the "whirlpool" of federal centralization. But during the 1850's these same men, who strongly influenced the policies and ideology of the Republican party, were a major force behind the submergence of divisive economic issues and the emergence of a coherent anti-southern, pro-Unionist Republican outlook. And while many Whig-Republicans were willing to compromise on the slavery issue, contemporaries noted that the ex-Democrats insisted on remaining true to "genuine Republican principles" even if this should postpone success.[88] "The warmest defenders of the church are said to be the new converts," observed a Kansas Republican, and a Democratic-Republican from Minnesota explained his uncompromising anti-slavery position by saying, "I am so ashamed of staying so long in the Democratic party that I admire especially the *early* anti-Slavery men." If the former Whigs could sometimes be charged with lack of principle, their wavering inclinations were counterbalanced by radical Republicans and former Democrats. Along with the radicals, as one Connecticut Republican put it, the ex-Democrats were "the soul of the Republicans." [89]

88. Trumbull to Sumner, April 22, 1859, Sumner Papers; New York *Times*, August 30, 1859.
89. G. W. Brown to Chase, April 6, 1857, Chase Papers, LC; George A. Nourse to Trumbull, April 27, 1858, Trumbull Papers; Lawrence Bruser, "Slavery and the Northern Mind: A Case Study of Free-Soil Sentiment, 1846–1850" (unpublished master's essay, Columbia University, 1967), 57.

6

Conservatives and Moderates

Among the political facts of life in the 1850's which helped shape the Republican party's policy and program was the distinct difference between the politics of the upper and lower North. The former area, as we have seen, was the home of radical Republicanism; the latter, consisting of a belt stretching from lower New York State through Pennsylvania and the southern parts of Indiana, Ohio, Illinois, and Iowa, constituted, as one Republican wrote, "a sort of belt or breakwater between the extremes of North and South." [1] The political conservatism of this area is explained partly by geographical proximity to the South and by the southern ancestry of many inhabitants of the lower West, and also by the influence of the large urban centers of New York and Philadelphia. These cities, with their large immigrant populations and close economic and social ties with the South, were usually carried by the Democrats, and urban Republicans tended to take a more conciliatory attitude toward slavery and the South than their rural allies. Surrounding areas like the counties of southern New York and eastern Long Island, western Connecticut and southeastern Pennsylvania, all followed the cities in their politics.[2] Some states, as Don E. Fehrenbacher points out with reference to Illinois, were

1. J. L. Balen to Justin S. Morrill, March 11, 1859, Justin S. Morrill Papers, LC. Cf. George W. Julian *Political Recollections, 1840–1872* (Chicago, 1884), 177; *National Era*, May 9, 1850; *The Debates of the Constitutional Convention of the State of Iowa* (2 vols.: Davenport, 1857), II, 834.
2. Cassius M. Clay to William H. Seward, July 10, 1858, William H. Seward Papers, Rush Rhees Library, University of Rochester; Elmer D. Elbert, "Southern Indiana Politics on the Eve of the Civil War 1858–1861" (unpublished doctoral dissertation, Indiana University, 1967), 1–7, 203–10; Philip S. Foner, *Business and Slavery* (Chapel Hill, 1941); Springfield *Republican*, December 29, 1858.

microcosms of the national political scene: the areas settled by New Englanders being staunchly Republican, those settled from the South as firmly devoted to the Democracy, and a belt of border counties, whose people were known for their political moderation, holding the balance of power.[3] Lincoln's victory in 1860 was accomplished primarily by attracting to the Republican standard enough of those moderates and conservatives who had failed to support Frémont in 1856 to carry the "doubtful states" of Illinois, Indiana, and Pennsylvania.

The Republican conservatives were representatives of a political tradition which was already growing old in the 1850's. Devotion to the Union was the cornerstone of their political outlook, and they were willing to sacrifice more immediate political goals to preserve national harmony. Most of the conservatives were "Old Line" or "national" Whigs, who deplored the repeal of the Missouri Compromise in 1854, yet dreaded the sectional strife which it aroused. Daniel Webster and Henry Clay were the conservatives' ideal statesmen, firmly committed to the preservation of the Union but willing to conciliate the South to avoid sectional antagonism. Webster struck the keynote of their politics during the nullification controversy of the 1830's. By insisting that the Union was the creation of the people and that the idea of state sovereignty was a fallacy, and by suspending political hostilities to work with Jackson in suppressing nullification, Webster taught the Old Line Whigs that party and sectional considerations must give way if the integrity of the Union were in danger.[4]

In the two decades preceding the Civil War, Webster, Clay, and their political disciples viewed the slavery controversy as the major threat to national unity. For this reason they strove to keep the issue of slavery out of national politics and expressed extreme bitterness toward abolitionists, whom they viewed as irresponsible fanatics bent on disrupting that unity. Webster and his political allies in

3. Don E. Fehrenbacher, *Prelude to Greatness, Lincoln in the 1850's* (New York, 1964 ed.), 47; Don E. Fehrenbacher, *Chicago Giant, A Biography of "Long John" Wentworth* (Madison, 1957), 130.
4. Theodore Clarke Smith, *Parties and Slavery* (New York, 1906), 40–42; Major L. Wilson, "An Analysis of the Ideas of Liberty and Union as Used by Members of Congress and the Presidents from 1828 to 1861" (unpublished doctoral dissertation, University of Kansas, 1964), 4; Richard N. Current, *Daniel Webster and the Rise of National Conservatism* (Boston, 1955), 66, 78; *The Writings and Speeches of Daniel Webster* (18 vols.: Boston, 1903), VI, 197–98; Claude M. Feuss, *Daniel Webster* (2 vols.: Boston, 1930), I, 379, 394–95, II, 4, 219. Cf. Thomas H. O'Connor, *Lords of the Loom* (New York, 1968), 161.

Massachusetts did oppose the annexation of Texas and did support the Wilmot Proviso when it was first introduced. But when these policies threatened to sever their ties with southern Whigs and plunge national politics into the maelstrom of sectional controversy, they drew back, while the more radical Conscience Whigs pursued the anti-slavery policy and eventually left the Whig party.[5] Conservative Whigs like Webster and Tom Corwin of Ohio tried in 1847 to forestall the whole Proviso question by demanding that the Mexican War be ended without any territorial acquisitions.[6] They supported the non-extension principle in 1848, but two years later took the lead in convincing the North that the Compromise of 1850 was a final adjustment of sectional differences. The endorsement which Webster and Henry Clay gave to the compromise measures helped persuade many northern Whigs to support them. As one anti-slavery Whig complained, "the great reverence, almost adoration, felt by many northern Whigs for Mr. Clay blinds them to the path of safety." In the aftermath of the compromise, Webster considered the possibility of creating a new national party of Unionists North and South, excluding anti-slavery radicals and southern fire-eaters, a dream which would continue to appeal to conservative Republicans during the pre-war decade.[7]

The antipathy of Webster and Clay toward anti-slavery agitation was reflected in conservative Republican thought throughout the 1850's. As the New York *Times* put it in 1859, the best thing to do about slavery "would be *for the North to stop talking about it*." What conservatives found particularly offensive was the constant moralizing of abolitionists and radicals about the peculiar institution. "I deny,

5. *Webster Writings*, X, 89; Charles Roll, *Colonel Dick Thompson, The Persistent Whig* (Indianapolis, 1948), 140; *Congressional Globe*, 30 Congress, 2 Session, Appendix, 185–86; Charles Francis Adams Diary, March 21, 1844, Adams Papers, MHS; David Donald, *Charles Sumner and the Coming of the Civil War* (New York, 1961), 136; Kinley J. Brauer, *Cotton Versus Conscience* (Lexington, 1967), 17–18, 129; William S. Appleton, "The Whigs of Massachusetts," *Proceedings* of MHS, 2 ser., XI (March 1897), 280.

6. Edward L. Pierce, *Memoir and Letters of Charles Sumner* (4 vols.: Boston, 1877–93), III, 159–60; *Webster Writings*, X, 12; Charles Sumner to Thomas Corwin, September 7, 1847, Corwin to Sumner, October 25, 1847, E. S. Hamlin to Sumner, October 26, 1847, Charles Sumner Papers, Houghton Library, Harvard University; Corwin to Joshua Giddings, August 18, 1847, Joshua R. Giddings Papers, OHS.

7. Schuyler Colfax to William H. Seward, April 27, 1850, Seward Papers; Current, *Webster*, 198; C. N. Van Tyne, ed., *The Letters of Daniel Webster* (New York, 1902), 433.

at the outset," said Richard Thompson, the Old Line Whig of Indiana, "that slavery, as it exists in this country, presents a *moral* question for our consideration, or that we of the *free* States have any just right to discuss it as a *moral* question." Not that conservatives felt slavery should not be discussed at all—this was clearly unavoidable in the 1850's—but they insisted that any discussions "be conducted with . . . soberness and moderation of temper," that the South not be insulted, and that slavery be treated as a problem in political economy, not as a moral abstraction.[8] "With the South," argued the New York *Times,* "the question is mainly one of *Social and Industrial Economy,* to be canvassed as involving the material interests of the slave-holding class themselves." William Evarts insisted that he never had condemned slaveholders as sinners or discussed "the oppression of the slave," and that his sole concern was with "*the system of slavery.*" Radical Republicans, who, as one conservative wrote, saw "nothing but the moral evil of Slavery in the abstract," injured both the cause of emancipation and the Union itself by their reckless assaults on the peculiar institution.[9] And even conservatives like Orville Browning of Illinois, who acknowledged "the abstract injustice of human slavery," thought the slaves were tolerably well treated, and did not believe the two races could live peaceably together unless the blacks were enslaved.[10]

But there was another side to the political outlook of the Old Line Whigs, one which disposed them to act with the Republican party in spite of their dislike of anti-slavery agitation. Webster, Clay, and most northern Whigs intensely disliked slavery. Clay, though himself a slaveholder, had long advocated gradual emancipation, strongly supporting the American Colonization Society's efforts to free and deport the slaves. In 1833 he told the Senate that slavery was "the darkest spot in the map of our country," and four years later termed the institution "a curse to the master; a wrong, a grievous wrong, to the slave." Clay was also well aware of the South's isolation in the world of the nine-

8. New York *Times,* January 19 1859; *Speech of R. W. Thompson, Upon the Political Aspects of the Slavery Question* (Terre Haute, 1855), 6; Philadelphia *North American and United States Gazette,* August 3, 1855.

9. New York *Times,* April 7, 1854, October 25, 1856; Reuben Chapman to Henry L. Dawes, January 27, 1860, Henry L. Dawes Papers, LC.

10. Theodore C. Pease and James G. Randall, eds., *The Diary of Orville Hickman Browning* (2 vols.: Springfield, 1927–33), I, 138–39; Allan Nevins and Milton H. Thomas, eds., *The Diary of George Templeton Strong* (4 vols.: New York, 1952), II, 22, 287; Frederick Law Olmsted, *A Journey in the Back Country* (New York, 1863), vi–viii.

teenth century. If the calamity of civil war should ever come, he told the Senate in 1850, all mankind would side with the North. Many western Whig-Republican leaders, including Henry Lane and Abraham Lincoln, learned their anti-slavery convictions as well as their staunch Unionism from Clay.[11] Webster, too, often spoke out against slavery. He had fought against the admission of Missouri in 1819, and in 1844 said that one major reason for his opposing the annexation of Texas was "that it is a scheme for the extension of the slavery of the African race." In 1847, he supported the Wilmot Proviso so vehemently that Joshua Giddings was willing to support him for president. Webster's faction of Massachusetts Whiggery abhorred slavery almost as much as the Conscience element, although they refused to place the slavery question above party loyalty and sectional harmony. When the Massachusetts Whigs split in two in 1848, with the Conscience wing joining the Free Soil party, Webster remained with the Whigs but privately noted his unhappiness in having to differ "from Whig friends whom I know to be as much attached to universal liberty as I am, and they cannot be more so." [12]

In the 1840's northern Whigs generally had a much more anti-slavery outlook than their Democratic opponents, and as Thomas Alexander points out, the Congressional Whigs were polarized along sectional lines every time an issue involving slavery came up for consideration. Indeed, one Whig-Republican could say with much truth in 1855 that the party's opposition to the extension of slavery was "the principle for which we so earnestly contended in 1844," when northern Whigs opposed the annexation of Texas. It was not a free-soil radical, but the conservative New York Whig Washington Hunt, who wrote Salmon P. Chase in 1846 that there was little difference between the two men's views on slavery, since "we both regard it as a crime and a curse, and I do not think your desire to see it eradicated is stronger than mine." And two years later, Hunt reminded

---

11. Calvin Colton, ed., *The Life, Correspondence, and Speeches of Henry Clay* (6 vols.: New York, 1857), I, 186–209, III, 309; Glyndon G. Van Deusen, *The Life of Henry Clay* (New York, 1937), 311–14; Clement Eaton, *Henry Clay and the Art of American Politics* (Boston, 1957), 93, 118, 126–34; Walter R. Sharp, "Henry S. Lane and the Formation of the Republican Party in Indiana," *MVHR*, VII (September 1920), 111–12.
12. Feuss, *Webster*, I, 270–71, 377; *Webster Writings*, VI, 11–12, XIII, 245; Van Tyne, ed., *Webster Letters*, 364, 372. Cf. *Webster Writings*, XIII, 359; Martin B. Duberman, *Charles Francis Adams 1807–1886* (Boston, 1961), 114, 140.

Thurlow Weed, "we must not forget that the mass of our northern Whigs are deeply imbued with anti-slavery sentiments, and thousands of them are immovably fixed." [13]

In their own way, therefore, even Old Line Whigs were free soil in sentiment. Indeed, the very fact that so many of them finally joined the Republicans showed that they could live with a party whose main principle was anti-slavery. Where they differed from the radicals was that anti-slavery was not the end-all and be-all of their politics. The federal government, they believed, had more important things to do than direct its energies toward the eradication of slavery. They viewed the government as an active agent in the improvement of the country, and accepted Clay's picture of a nation bound together through economic development. It was in these very terms that Webster explained his decision not to join the Free Soilers in 1848. He could not support Van Buren merely because he agreed with him about slavery, he explained to a Conscience Whig, because "there are other great interests of the country in which you and I hold Mr. Van Buren to be essentially wrong." [14]

In 1857, the Springfield *Republican* thus defined the difference between radical and conservative Republicans: "There are two classes in the party—first a class of philanthropists—men who . . . engage in the republican party for the overthrow of a great moral wrong. Another class are purely politicians—men who seek the overthrow of a despotic interest in the administration of the government." The idea of combating southern political power and its economic consequences was the key to conservative support for the Republican party. Such measures as a Pacific railroad, a homestead act, a protective tariff, and government aid to internal improvements had been blocked time and again by the Democratic party, at the dictation, it seemed, of the South. [15] The conservatives hoped to use the Republican party to

13. Thomas B. Alexander, *Sectional Stress and Party Strength* (Nashville, 1967), 111; Samuel A. Foot, *Reasons for Joining the Republican Party* (Washington, 1856), 2; Washington Hunt to Salmon P. Chase, March 18, 1846, Salmon P. Chase Papers, HSPa; Thurlow Weed Barnes, *Memoir of Thurlow Weed* (Boston, 1884), 165.
14. Van Tyne, ed., *Webster Letters*, 372; Eaton, *Clay*, 44; Current, *Webster*, 105.
15. Springfield *Republican*, August 8, 1857; New York *Tribune*, February 14, 1854; Philadelphia *North American*, cited in *National Era*, June 10, 1847; *Congressional Globe*, 29 Congress, 1 Session, Appendix, 72; Michael F. Holt, "Forging a Majority: The Formation of the Republican Party in Pittsburgh, Pennsylvania, 1848–1860" (unpublished doctoral dissertation, Johns Hopkins University, 1967), 71–75.

wrest control of the federal government away from the slaveholders, and they viewed the sectional struggle as primarily a contest for political power. While many radicals viewed the demand for slavery extension as inherent in the very logic of the slave system—slavery, they argued, must expand in order to survive because it exhausted the southern soil [16]—conservatives explained it in political terms. "It is not room that you are anxious to obtain," said an Indiana Congressman, "but *power—political power.*" The New York *Times* went so far as to claim that slavery itself was "merely an incident of the real controversy," since "possession of the Federal Government is what both North and South are striving for." In this it was only echoing the views of Webster and other northern Whigs of the 1840's who had opposed the annexation of Texas and the Mexican War on the grounds that any addition of slavery territory and subsequent admission of slave states would upset the balance of sectional power in the South's favor.[17]

Both radical and conservative Republicans therefore hoped to drive the Slave Power from control of the national government. But while radicals saw a national Republican victory as only the first step in a relentless crusade to eradicate the peculiar institution, for conservatives the election of a Republican President would end the slavery controversy and allow the federal government to turn its attention to the more important problem of national economic development. Many Old Line Whigs were appalled that the slavery controversy was diverting the attention of the federal government from its more enduring concerns. "The slavery question is still the order of the day at Washington," Illinois Whig David Davis wrote in 1850. "Will anything else be done during the session of Congress?" A year later, Hamilton Fish of New York complained to Washington Hunt of the "dismal discord and sectional strife" which darkened the political landscape. What Fish wanted was that "the great interests of the country may be looked [to] —Protection to domestic industry, Rivers and Harbors, and the development of the wealth and power and resources of our great Confederacy

16. *Congressional Globe*, 33 Congress, 1 Session, Appendix, 664, 34 Congress, 1 Session, Appendix, 148, 971, 36 Congress, 1 Session, 1914; New York *Tribune*, April 19, 1854; *National Era*, March 2, 1854.
17. *Congressional Globe*, 34 Congress, 3 Session, Appendix, 91; New York *Times*, February 18, 1854, May 30, July 4, 1860; *Webster Writings*, IX, 57–58; Wilson, "Ideas of Liberty and Union," 142; "The Diaries of Sidney George Fisher, 1844–1849," *PaMHB*, LXXXVI (January 1962), 80–81.

—but all these things are overlayed by the incubus resting upon us." [18]
The incubus was the slavery controversy, which not only diverted
attention and energy from economic legislation, but unsettled private
development plans as well. During the 1850's, after much soul-searching, enough Old Line Whigs like Fish turned to the Republican party
to provide the margin of victory in 1860. They came to accept the
timetable laid down by the New York politician E. Pershine Smith.
"The first thing," Smith wrote Henry Carey, "is to destroy the Southern domination" by electing a Republican president and Congress.
"That done, . . . we shall begin to think of our bread and butter—
and not before." [19]

II

Between 1850 and 1854, northern Whigs believed that the slavery
question had truly been driven from national politics. And despite the
disastrous defeat of their presidential candidate Winfield Scott and
the deaths of Clay and Webster, they clung to the hope that their
party could once again become the broadly based national coalition
it had been in the 1840's. These hopes were rudely shattered in the
storm aroused by the Kansas-Nebraska Act in 1854. Not that the Old
Line Whigs did not wish to see Douglas's bill defeated. Senator Truman Smith of Connecticut viewed it as an "atrocious proposition,"
and his colleague Hamilton Fish of New York urged his own state's
Whig boss Thurlow Weed to organize popular opposition to the measure, as the only way to prevent its passage. Smith and Fish sincerely
desired to prevent the spread of slavery into free territory, but they
also feared that the bill would thrust the slavery question back into
the center of national politics. "The Repeal of the Missouri Compromise," warned the conservative New York *Courier and Enquirer*, "will
surely produce an immense agitation throughout the North." [20] For

18. David Davis to Julius Rockwell, July 7, 1850 (copy), David Davis Papers,
ChicHS; Hamilton Fish to Washington Hunt, December 20, 1851, Letterbook,
Hamilton Fish Papers, LC.
19. E. Pershine Smith to Henry C. Carey, June 20, 1858, January 15, 1860, Henry
C. Carey Papers, HSPa. Cf. the statement of one New York Whig that until
the slavery question was settled, "questions of the greatest moment to our country's
welfare," would not "receive any attention whatever, much less that attention
which their importance demands," [George Scroggs], *The Duty of Americans*
(Buffalo, 1860), 4.
20. Truman Smith to Roger S. Baldwin, January 28, 1854, Baldwin Family

the sake of the Union and the Whigs' survival as a national party, northern Whigs pleaded with their southern colleagues to oppose the bill. But they were in for a rude awakening. Soon after the debate began, a secret caucus of southern Whig Senators and Representatives agreed to support the measure. Northern Old Line Whigs, who had risked their political careers in 1850 to support the compromise measures, were deeply shocked. "I have not believed till within a few days," Washington Hunt wrote bitterly, "that the moderate and honest members from the South would consent to accept the dishonorable advantage which Douglas offers them. But it seems now that the slave states are to give a compact vote." By April, 1854, the *Ohio State Journal* could declare that the Kansas-Nebraska bill had resulted in "the ultimate disruption and *denationalization* of the Whig party." [21]

Despite the political chaos of 1854, most of the northern national Whigs hoped that their party could be reconstructed. In the states where the party was strongest—Pennsylvania, New York, and Massachusetts—they resisted the attempts of anti-slavery men to create fusion anti-Nebraska movements, and the Whig party did survive into 1855. The New York *Times* conceded that there was an urgent need to drive from power all politicians associated with the repeal of the Missouri Compromise but since in the free states the guilty parties were Democrats, the Whig party could easily be the vehicle for anti-Nebraska action.[22] Where the Whig party was weaker, particularly in the West, fusion took place almost immediately, but the Old Line Whigs worked to moderate the demands of the new coalition. In Ohio, R. M. Corwine, Thomas Ewing, and other national Whigs insisted that the restoration of the Missouri Compromise, not the prohibition of slavery in all the territories, be made the major issue of the 1854

Papers, Yale University; Hamilton Fish to Thurlow Weed, January 25, 1854, Thurlow Weed Papers, Rush Rhees Library, University of Rochester; New York *Courier and Enquirer*, cited in *Ohio State Journal*, February 8, 1854.
21. Alvah Hunt to Weed, March 12, 1854, Weed Papers; Roger S. Baldwin to Truman Smith, February 18, 1854, Baldwin Family Papers; [James M. Ashley], *Reminiscences of the Great Rebellion* (np, 1890), 17; Arthur C. Cole, *The Whig Party in the South* (Washington, 1913), 286; Washington Hunt to Fish, February 7, 1854, Fish Papers; *Ohio State Journal*, April 19, 1854. "The violation of faith on the part of the South," wrote a New York Whig, ". . . I feel has released me from whatever responsibility I owed under existing compacts to the 'peculiar institution.'" B. Arnold to Daniel Ullmann, June 8, 1854, Daniel Ullmann Papers, NYHS.
22. Allan Nevins, *Ordeal of the Union* (2 vols.: New York, 1947), II, 317-18; New York *Times*, May 29, June 10, 1854.

campaign. They were disappointed when the fusion convention of
July 13 made non-extension its rallying cry. In Illinois, fusion took
place in Congressional elections in the northern part of the state, but in
the Whig strongholds of central Illinois the party maintained its identity. "Try to save the Whig party," the Whig leader David Davis
wrote a Massachusetts friend. "I don't fancy its being abolitionized—
although no one can be more opposed to Nebraska than I am." In
general, national Whigs in the 1854 elections fought to make the
Kansas-Nebraska Act, not the entire question of slavery in the territories, the key issue, and as late as 1860 some conservatives still wanted
the Republican party to be content with demanding the restoration
of the Missouri Compromise. As George Julian later recalled, "they
talked far more eloquently about the duty of keeping covenants, and
the wickedness of reviving slavery agitation, than the evils of slavery,
and the cold-blooded conspiracy to spread it over an empire of free
soil." [23]

Between 1854 and 1856 the Old Line Whigs of the North were
faced with an acute political dilemma. Their position was forcefully
expressed by Robert Winthrop of Massachusetts, a conservative cast
in the mold of Webster. "What can be done by a man who feels as I
do?" wrote Winthrop in 1855. "I voted against the Fugitive Bill . . .
I deplore the passage of the Nebraska Act . . . I am for resisting the
aggressions of slavery, but I cannot unite in taking the first great step
for ending the Union by the formation of a sectional party." Winthrop
held aloof from the Republican party when it was organized in Massachusetts, and in New York, Hamilton Fish and Washington Hunt
severed their long political association with William Seward and refused to join the new party. Hunt objected not only to the sectional
nature of the party but to the strong influence of the Barnburner
Democrats. The conservative Whig merchant Daniel P. Barnard
echoed the fears and hopes of many of his political associates when
he condemned the organization of the Republican party "with no
principle to stand on, but that of eternal hatred and eternal war
against the South," but expressed confidence that "the sentiment of

23. Joseph P. Smith, ed., *History of the Republican Party in Ohio* (2 vols.:
Chicago, 1898), I, 17; *Speech of the Hon. Thomas Ewing at Chillicothe, Ohio*
(Cincinnati, 1860), 7–8; Cincinnati *Gazette*, July 8, 1854; R. M. Corwine to
William Schouler, February 24, 1856, William Schouler Papers, MHS; David
Davis to Julius Rockwell, July 15, 1854 (copy), Davis Papers; Julian, *Political
Recollections*, 136–37; New York *Times*, March 13, 1860.

Nationality" would again make itself felt, in the emergence of a new "conservative and national party." [24]

Especially in the eastern states, many conservative Whigs hoped that the Know-Nothing organization could provide the basis for the Unionist party of which Barnard spoke. The nativist movements of the 1850's were both an expression of the ethnic tensions inherent in mid-century American society, and an attempt by political conservatives to smother the slavery question with a new issue, which could unite Americans of all sections. Many Whigs found the transition to Know-Nothingism an easy one, for their party had always had an undertone of anti-foreign sentiment. In many states, Whig leaders blamed the increasing immigrant population, and its tendency to cast solidly Democratic ballots, for their party's perennial defeats. Conservative Whigs in New York City and Philadelphia had worked hand in glove with nativists in local elections, and the Whigs' vice-presidential candidate of 1844, Theodore Frelinghuysen, and their presidential nominee of 1852, Winfield Scott, both had reputations for anti-foreign, anti-Catholic prejudices. "It is not to be denied, or disguised," wrote one conservative Whig in 1855, "that the great body of genuine Whigs have a strong odor of Americanism about them." [25]

Know-Nothingism thus had an intrinsic appeal to conservative Whigs, but they were even more attracted to the movement's Unionism. One leading New York merchant endorsed Know-Nothingism in 1855 as "the only means for preserving a great Union party in opposition to abolitionism and sectional names," and an Indiana nativist described the cardinal principles of the party as peace, prosperity, and a desire to overcome issues which disturbed national harmony.[26] In Michigan and Illinois, the Know-Nothing party was composed mostly of con-

24. Robert C. Winthrop, Jr., *A Memoir of Robert C. Winthrop* (Boston, 1897), 181; Washington Hunt to Fish, October 7, 1855, Daniel P. Barnard to Fish, July 9, 1855, Fish Papers; Hunt to Weed, August 10, 1855, Weed Papers; Allan Nevins, *Hamilton Fish* (New York, 1936), 55–56; New York *Tribune*, August 16, 1855.

25. Robert D. Parmet, "The Know-Nothings in Connecticut" (unpublished doctoral dissertation, Columbia University, 1966), 52–53; Sister M. Evangeline Thomas, *Nativism in the Old Northwest, 1850–1860* (Washington, 1936), 60, 69, 77; Clifford S. Griffin, *Their Brothers' Keepers: Moral Stewardship in the United States, 1800–1865* (New Brunswick, 1960), 57, 122, 164; Benjamin F. Wade to Schouler, May 3, 1855, Schouler Papers; Robert A. West to Fish, December 15, 1855, Fish Papers.

26. Foner, *Business and Slavery*, 113; Carl F. Brand, "History of the Know-Nothing Party in Indiana." *IndMH*, XVIII (1922), 183.

servative Whigs who clung to the hope that the Whig party could be revived, while in Ohio the nativists joined the fusion movement and attempted to make its platform more moderate. In Massachusetts, where the Know-Nothings achieved their most striking success, the Boston aristocrat and friend of Webster, Henry Gardner, was elected governor, supported, according to Samuel Bowles, "by some of the most old-fogy and conservative Whigs." [27] And in New York, whose Whig party had for years been divided into the anti-slavery Seward faction and the conservative Silver-Greys, the conservatives seized control of the Know-Nothing movement, hoping to use it to destroy Seward's political career. Not all the Old Line Whigs were happy about the rise of Know-Nothingism—Washington Hunt and Hamilton Fish had long fought nativist trends in the Whig party and now wanted nothing to do with either Know-Nothings or Republicans. But the selection of Daniel Ullmann, a leading Silver-Grey, as the nativist gubernatorial candidate in 1854, revealed the Old Line Whigs' control of the new party. That National Whiggery and Know-Nothingism were more or less interchangeable so far as the conservatives were concerned was made clear by Alexander Mann, the influential editor of the Rochester *Daily American*. "If a judicious course is pursued," Mann wrote to Daniel Ullmann, "we may sweep the Union in '56. We may carry 25 states at least. But shall we fight as 'National Whigs' or as the 'American Party?' " [28]

In the western states, conservatives were more likely to join the

27. Floyd B. Streeter, *Political Parties in Michigan, 1837–1860* (Lansing, 1918), 39; Don E. Fehrenbacher, "Illinois Political Attitudes, 1854–1861" (unpublished doctoral dissertation, University of Chicago, 1951), 273; Roy F. Basler *et al.*, eds., *The Collected Works of Abraham Lincoln* (9 vols.: New Brunswick, 1953–55), II, 316; Eugene H. Roseboom, "Salmon P. Chase and the Know-Nothings," *MVHR*, XXV (December, 1938), 335–50; William G. Bean, "Party Transformation in Massachusetts With Special Reference to the Antecedents of Republicanism 1848–1860" (unpublished doctoral dissertation, Harvard University, 1922), 250–52; George S. Merriam, *The Life and .Times of Samuel Bowles* (2 vols.: New York, 1885), I, 173–74.

28. Aida D. Donald, "Prelude to Civil War: The Decline of the Whig Party in New York, 1848–1852" (unpublished doctoral dissertation, University of Rochester, 1961), 280–88; Thomas J. Curran, "Know-Nothings of New York State" (unpublished doctoral dissertation, Columbia University, 1963), 174–75; Robert J. Rayback, *Millard Fillmore, Biography of a President* (Buffalo, 1959), 381–84, 391; Louis D. Scisco, *Political Nativism in New York State* (New York, 1901), 111, 116–21; Horace Greeley to Schuyler Colfax, July 26, August 20, September 7, 1854, Greeley-Colfax Papers, NYPL; Robert A. West to Fish, November 7, 1855; Fish to J. B. Gibson, February 21, 1854, Letterbook, Fish Papers; Barnes, *Weed Memoir*, 121; Alexander Mann to Daniel Ullmann, November 16, 1854, Ullmann Papers.

new fusion parties than the Know-Nothings, and where their influence
was strong, they attempted to make Republicanism a reincarnation of
Whiggery. In Indiana and Illinois, the states which George Julian
called "outlying provinces of the empire of slavery" because of their
large southern-born populations, Old Line Whigs had become powerful
influences in the Republican party by 1856. Indiana's fusion platform
of 1854 focused on the repeal of the Missouri Compromise rather than
the denationalization of slavery as Julian demanded in a minority platform. The radical leader complained in October that the new party's
leaders were "not anti-slavery men, but some of them even pro-slavery
Democrats, who merely regret that equilibrium has been disturbed.
They recoil from abolitionism and do their best to keep Free Soil
men in the background." [29] In Illinois, moderate and conservative
Whigs held aloof when radicals tried to create a Republican organization in 1854, and it was not until two years later that a viable Republican party finally emerged. The resolutions of the Bloomington Convention which launched the party were composed by Old Line Whig
Orville H. Browning, and the original Republicans—radicals like Owen
Lovejoy and Ichabod Codding—were entirely left off the state ticket.
"We wish, if possible," Browning observed to Lyman Trumbull, "to
keep the party in this State under the control of moderate men, and
conservative influences." For the time being, he had been successful.[30]

During the presidential campaign of 1856, northern national Whigs
remained divided in their political loyalties. The selection of Millard
Fillmore as the Know-Nothing candidate was a triumph of conservatives over the original nativists, and ensured that the party would stress
national unity and conservatism more than anti-foreign and anti-
Catholic sentiments. Those Old Line Whigs who cast their lots with the
Republicans worked for the nomination of John McLean for president,
on the theory that the selection of the well-known Ohio conservative

29. Julian, *Political Recollections*, 115, 154; *National Era*, October 5, 1854, May
22, 1856; Grace Julian Clarke, *George W. Julian* (Indianapolis, 1923), 151–53;
Russell M. Seeds, *History of the Republican Party in Indiana* (Indianapolis, 1899),
21, 25; Julian to Smith, November 16, 1854, Smith Papers, Syracuse University.
30. Mildred C. Stoler, "The Influence of the Democratic Element in the Republican Party of Illinois and Indiana, 1854–1860" (unpublished doctoral dissertation, Indiana University, 1938), 101–6, 116; Edward Magdol, *Owen Lovejoy:
Abolitionist in Congress* (New Brunswick, 1967), 135–36, 145; Paul Selby, "The
Editorial Convention of 1856," *Journal* of the IllSHS, V (July 1912), 343–49;
O. H. Browning to Lyman Trumbull, May 19, 1856, Lyman Trumbull Papers, LC.

would lead to Fillmore's withdrawal and an alliance between southern Know-Nothings and northern Republicans. From the Philadelphia Convention, Murat Halstead reported that the McLean movement was "an attempt made by the antediluvian Whigs . . . to reorganize the defunct Whig Party under a thin disguise of Republicanism, to consist solely of talk about the Missouri Compromise." McLean's rejection and the nomination of Frémont convinced many conservatives that the Republican party was too radical and sectional to be trusted, although Republican spokesmen worked diligently to counteract this impression. "Above all stick to the Union and deny that we are disunionists," a Whig leader of Maine advised Israel Washburn, and throughout the North Republican orators stressed their party's devotion to the Union, particularly in areas where the votes of conservatives were crucial.[31]

The results of the 1856 election revealed that thousands of conservative Whigs had not been won over to the Republican party. It is true that many influential conservatives did support Frémont. After much soul-searching, Hamilton Fish of New York declared for the Republicans, explaining that while he had no sympathy with abolitionism, he believed the extension of slavery to be wrong, and besides, "in a political view I do not wish to increase . . . the slave power in the general government." Similarly, Tom Corwin of Ohio cast his vote for Frémont, on the grounds that a party which opposed the repeal of the Missouri Compromise was more likely to govern effectively and wisely than the one responsible for that disastrous measure.[32] The assault on Charles Sumner in the United States Senate chambers in late May 1856, had an important psychological impact on many conservatives, and helped swing their support to the Republicans. David Davis wrote that Sumner's injuries, along with the conflict in Kansas, "have made Abolitionists of those who never dreamed they were drifting into it," and in Boston and New York, substantial citizens,

31. Scisco, *Political Nativism*, 172; William B. Hesseltine and Rex G. Fisher, eds., *Trimmers, Trucklers, and Temporizers* (Madison, 1961), 89–90; O. H. Browning to Trumbull, May 19, 1856, Trumbull Papers; Gaillard Hunt, *Israel, Elihu, and Cadwallader Washburn, A Chapter in American Biography* (New York 1925), 39, 43.
32. Nevins, *Fish*, 58–61; Fish to Sidney Lawrence, November 22, 1856, Letterbook, Fish Papers; Daryl Prendergaft, "Thomas Corwin and the Conservative Republican Reaction, 1858–61," *OAHQ*, LVII (January 1948), 2–3. Cf. Samuel F. Vinton to Fish, September 27, 1856, Weed to Fish, September 27, 1856, Fish Papers.

usually the pillars of conservatism, joined with radicals in denouncing the outrage.[33] Nevertheless, Fillmore and Buchanan received enough votes from conservative Whigs to ensure Frémont's defeat. The situation in Illinois was typical, Norman B. Judd reporting in September that in central Illinois the Clay Whigs were equally divided between Fillmore and Frémont, while in the southern part of the state Frémont had little support. In many states, the Know-Nothing party was sundered in 1856, the more radical element entering the Republican party, while conservatives stayed with Fillmore. This was the case in New York, where Old Line Whigs like Washington Hunt and Samuel Ruggles endorsed the Know-Nothings, and in Indiana, where Know-Nothings turned Republican in the northern part of the state, while the old Whig counties of the south gave Fillmore heavy support.[34] And some conservative Whigs, including a number of business and commercial leaders in the northern cities, even turned to the Democrats to ensure the defeat of the sectional candidate Frémont.[35]

In its election post-mortem of November 15, 1856, the Chicago *Democratic Press*, a Frémont journal, attributed Buchanan's victory to southern threats that the election of a Republican president would lead to the dissolution of the Union. The most cursory analysis of the election returns bears out the implication that it was the conservative Whigs who defeated Frémont. National Whigs held the balance of power in the lower North, and it was abundantly clear that to win in 1860 the Republicans would have to select a candidate capable of attracting their support. The election returns only increased the efforts of conservatives within the Republican party to moderate the party's program. From Vermont, a radical Republican reported to Salmon P. Chase that there was "a strong rallying of the 'Whig element,' on the basis of a virtual ignoring of all Slavery issues." Similarly in Indiana

33. Isabel Wallace, *Life and Letters of General W. H. L. Wallace* (Chicago, 1909), 74; Winthrop, *Memoir*, 184; Nevins and Thomas, eds., *Strong Diary*, II, 273–76; James A. Rawley, *Edwin D. Morgan 1811–1883; Merchant in Politics* (New York, 1955), 54; Foner, *Business and Slavery*, 104; John P. Hale to Theodore Parker, May 25, 1856, John P. Hale Papers, NHHS.
34. Norman B. Judd to Edwin D. Morgan, September 18, 1856, in Weed Papers; D. G. Brinton Thompson, *Ruggles of New York* (New York, 1946), 121–24; Emma Lou Thornbrough, *Indiana in the Civil War Era 1850–1880* (Indianapolis, 1965), 74.
35. Foner, *Business and Slavery*, 120; Daniel P. Barnard to Fish, September 23, 1856, Fish Papers; Francis Curtis, *The Republican Party* (2 vols.: New York, 1904), I, 229; Willard L. King, *Lincoln's Manager David Davis* (Cambridge, 1960), 113; Holt, "Forging a Majority," 326–27.

the conservative leader Henry Lane declared that he wanted to see
the party platform "so constructed as to embrace all the Old Whigs
if it can be done without any sacrifice of principle, and I have no doubt
it can be." As late as 1858, the name "Republican" was not used in
states like Indiana, Pennsylvania, Massachusetts, and Rhode Island,
in order not to antagonize conservatives who associated Republicanism
with radical policies. ("Think of a baby going three years without a
name," protested one radical journalist.) [36]

The conflict between conservatives and radicals in the Republican
party focused on different issues in different states, but the most
strident controversies arose in Massachusetts, Ohio, and Wisconsin
over radical efforts to commit the Republican party to nullification or
repeal of the fugitive slave law. Many conservatives felt that the
radicals were less interested in the issue of states rights and fugitive
slaves than in preventing the accession of too many conservatives to
the party. Moreover, the idea of nullification utterly contradicted
their heritage of nationalistic Whiggery. Massachusetts conservatives
were outraged at the radicals' demand for the dismissal of a judge
who had returned a fugitive to slavery, but they were unable to prevent
the dismissal from taking place. The New York *Times* called the action
"the grossest attack upon the independence of the judiciary ever
witnessed in the United States." [37] In Ohio, Tom Corwin, Lewis
Campbell, Samuel Galloway, and other Old Line Whigs led the fight
against nullification. [38]

In Wisconsin, former Whigs Timothy Howe and George Rublee
—the latter the editor of the *Wisconsin State Journal*—insisted that
nullification was not only unconstitutional but politically suicidal.
There was a great difference, Howe declared, between repeal of the
fugitive slave law, which he favored, and nullification. "Almost the
whole country," he wrote in 1859, "has declared *nullification* to be an

36. Chicago *Democratic Press*, November 15, 1856; Joseph H. Barrett to Chase,
November 30, 1858, Chase Papers, LC; Roll, *Thompson*, 156; Mrs. W. S. Robinson,
ed., *"Warrington" Pen-Portraits* (Boston, 1877), 234.
37. Montgomery Blair to Trumbull, March 11, 1859, Trumbull Papers; Boston
Atlas, March 23, 1855; Fred Harvey Harrington, *Fighting Politician, Major-General
N. P. Banks* (Philadelphia, 1948), 46; New York *Times*, March 20, 1858. Cf.
Philadelphia *North American and United States Gazette*, May 14, 1855.
38. Samuel Galloway to Lincoln, July 23, 1859, Robert Todd Lincoln Papers,
LC; Cincinnati *Gazette*, November 17, 1859; New York *Times*, June 7, 1859;
Josiah Morrow, ed., *Life and Speeches of Thomas Corwin* (Cincinnati, 1896),
380–81; *Congressional Globe*, 34 Congress, 1 Session, Appendix, 549, 36 Congress,
1 Session, 73–75.

unconstitutional remedy. . . . Do you think it wise to discard all those
who will go for repeal but who will not go for nullification?"[39] The
bitter opposition of Wisconsin's moderate and conservative Republicans to the nullification policy eventually forced its abandonment. The
Old Line Whig element deserted the party in the judicial election of
April, 1860, causing the defeat of the radical candidate for the state
supreme court. Moreover, William Seward, Wisconsin's choice for
the presidential nomination, urged the radicals to drop the fugitive
slave law as an issue. In 1861, Howe received the election to the Senate
which had been denied him four years earlier because of his nationalistic views.[40]

Even in a radical state, therefore, conservatives were able to exert
some influence on the Republican platform. In the states where they
controlled the Republican party between 1856 and 1860, conservatives
sought to refashion the party platform entirely by downgrading the
slavery issue and introducing other questions which would attract the
votes of Old Line Whigs and Know-Nothings. One such effort to
broaden the party's appeal occurred in Pennsylvania, where conservatives attempted to substitute protection for anti-slavery as the leading
Republican principle. The tariff, of course, had always been an important issue in Pennsylvania politics, but between 1851 and 1857
it was more or less ignored by politicians. Buchanan carried Pennsylvania in 1856, while Frémont trailed far behind. It was clear that in
order to win, Republicans would have to conciliate conservative and
nativist voters, and in 1858, after David Wilmot's unsuccessful gubernatorial campaign of the year before, a new organization, the People's
Party, was created, a coalition of Republicans and Know-Nothings.
The platform reduced anti-slavery to a minimum—merely opposing the
administration's Kansas policy—and added nativist planks and the
potent demand for a protective tariff. The Panic of 1857 had refocused
national attention on economic issues, and in Pennsylvania, the pro-

39. Timothy Howe to George Rublee, April 3, 1859, Timothy Howe Papers,
WisHS; Wisconsin State Journal, January 19, March 12, 1857, June 7, 1859, Jan-
uary 27, 1860; Racine Weekly Advocate, January 18, 1860; H. S. Paine to John
F. Potter, March 12, 1860, John F. Potter Papers, WisHS; J. Pearse to Gideon
Welles, January 26, 1861, Gideon Welles Papers, LC.
40. Wisconsin State Journal, January 27, March 1, 7, 17, April 5, 18, 1860;
Sherman Booth to Smith, March 21, 1860, Smith Papers; Frederic Bancroft, ed.,
Speeches, Correspondence, and Political Papers of Carl Schurz (6 vols.: New York,
1913), I, 111–12; Aaron M. Boom, "The Development of Sectional Attitudes in
Wisconsin, 1848–1861" (unpublished doctoral dissertation, University of Chicago,
1948), 198–203.

tectionists, led by Henry Carey, took up the argument that protection was the cure for the nation's economic ills.[41] He was joined by conservatives who saw in the tariff issue not only an answer to the depression, but a way of reuniting northern and southern Whigs on the basis of the old American system of Henry Clay. The Philadelphia *North American*, long a national Whig organ, declared that the slavery question was losing its hold on the public mind, and that the tariff would soon take its place. Making national economic development and protection the major features of the Republican appeal, the *North American* argued, would dispel the party's image of sectionalism and attract former Whigs in the border states, making the Republican party a truly national organization.[42]

"An attempt is making from the old Whig side to stuff in the protective tariff as a substitute for the slave question," Charles Francis Adams reported to Charles Sumner in August 1858, and in Pennsylvania the attempt met with much success. In both the 1858 and 1860 elections, the slavery question was stressed by the Republicans in the radical northern and western counties of the state, while the tariff became a major issue in conservative areas. The protection issue was attractive to nativists as well as Old Line Whigs, because it was phrased in terms of protecting American free labor against foreign competition. "Let our motto," said a Pennsylvania Congressman in 1860, "be, protection to *everything American against everything foreign.*" The tariff issue was one cause of the stunning Republican victories in the Keystone state after 1857, although the *North American* no doubt exaggerated when it claimed in 1860 that Lincoln's triumph had nothing to do with "any sectional aspect of the slavery question."[43]

Another means by which conservatives hoped to broaden the base of Republican support was the pressure they exerted for a moderation

41. Malcolm R. Eiselen, *The Rise of Pennsylvania Protectionism* (Philadelphia, 1932), 230–45; Arthur M. Lee, "Henry C. Carey and the Republican Tariff," *PaMHB*, LXXXI (July 1957), 280–302; Elwyn B. Robinson, "The 'North American': Advocate of Protection," *PaMHB*, LXIV (July 1940), 347; Philadelphia *North American and United States Gazette*, July 16, 1858; William Dusinberre, *Civil War Issues in Philadelphia* (Philadelphia, 1965), 77–78.

42. George W. Smith, *Henry C. Carey and American Sectional Conflict* (Albuquerque, 1951), 65–66; Philadelphia *North American and United States Gazette*, October 22, 1857, August 14, September 2, 13, October 30, 1858, November 5, 1859.

43. Adams to Sumner, August 1, 1858, Letterbook, Adams Papers; *Congressional Globe*, 36 Congress, 1 Session, 1844; Philadelphia *North American and United States Gazette*, April 26, 1858; November 7, 1860; A. K. McClure to Lincoln, June 16, 1860, Lincoln Papers.

of the party's stand on slavery in the territories. If Republicans would adopt the policy of popular sovereignty, it was argued, they could form an alliance with anti-administration southerners and create a national "Opposition" party. The controversy over the Lecompton constitution in 1858 offered the best opportunity for such a political realignment. Southern Know-Nothings like John Bell and John C. Crittenden opposed the administration's attempt to force the pro-slavery constitution upon Kansas, and conservatives argued that Republicans should take up the demand that the people of each territory be given the power to accept or reject slavery. Among the spokesmen for this position was the New York *Times*, which urged the party to substitute popular sovereignty for the policy of "no more slave states" as a means of finally settling the slavery question. The *Times* insisted that to stand a chance of victory in 1860, the Republicans would have to appeal to all those voters who for one reason or another were disenchanted with the Buchanan administration. "It is as a national organization, not as a sectional organization, that the Republicans must look for victory in 1860," the *Times* declared, and it urged that an alliance be forged with the budding opposition movements which were challenging Democratic control of the border states. Such an alliance would make the Republicans "the national, conservative, Union party of the country" —that is, a resurrection of Whiggery.[44]

But although the Indiana Republican party endorsed popular sovereignty in 1858, and a number of influential Republicans even supported Stephen A. Douglas's bid for re-election to the Senate in that year, the movement to form an opposition party never approached success. The opposition movement of the Upper South, which looked so promising in 1858, was snuffed out in the hysteria that followed John Brown's raid of December 1859.[45] And although many conservatives still clung to the hope that the party would abandon the demand for non-extension in favor of popular sovereignty, Eli Thayer, the Republican Congressman most closely associated with this view, was denied renomination in 1860 by the Republican convention in his Massachusetts Con-

44. New York *Times*, April 7, 1858, August 22, 1859, April 1, 1858. Cf. March 1, October 15, 30, November 16, December 1, 3, 1858; William Schouler to Chase, March 26, 1858, Chase Papers, HSPa.

45. Julian, *Political Recollections*, 167; Albert K. Beveridge, *Abraham Lincoln 1809–1858* (2 vols.: Boston, 1928), II, 47, 55; Joseph Medill to Chase, October 30, 1859, Chase Papers, HSPa; Cole, *Whig Party in the South*, 331–36

gressional district, and was defeated when he ran as an independent candidate supported by Democrats and Constitutional Unionists.[46]

The failure of the Opposition movement reveals the limitations of conservative influence in the Republican party. For despite their crucial role as a balance-of-power segment of the electorate, the conservatives for the most part could succeed in determining Republican policy only when they won a significant portion of the moderate Republicans to their position. The moderates included men like William Pitt Fessenden of Maine, James W. Grimes of Iowa, John Sherman of Ohio, Schuyler Colfax of Indiana, Samuel Bowles of Massachusetts, and Richard Yates and Abraham Lincoln of Illinois. Like the conservatives, they were usually former Whigs who revered the Union, disliked sectional antagonism, and believed that the government had interests and purposes which transcended the slavery controversy. But like the radicals, they were nonetheless convinced of the central importance of the slavery question and were determined to meet it head-on, not by expedients and compromises, but with a firm adherence to the principle of non-extension. By the late 1850's, the moderates were firmly committed to the Republican party, and had rejected the conservative dream of a resurrection of Whiggery.

III

Between 1856 and 1860, the moderate Republicans held the balance of power within the Republican party, and they used it to maintain the party's integrity and purpose against attacks from both the right and left. On the one hand, they upheld the ideal of party regularity against radicals who sometimes threatened to desert conservative Republican nominees at the polls. In Massachusetts, for example, although several leading radicals refused to support Nathaniel Banks for governor in 1857 because of his close ties with the Know-Nothings, the influential spokesman for the moderates, Samuel Bowles, defended Banks and supported his candidacy in spite of Bowles's own dislike of nativism.[47] In many states, moderates worked to confine the Re-

---

46. Springfield *Republican*, September 20, 28, 1860; J. D. Baldwin to John Sherman, August 4, 1860, John Sherman Papers, LC; P. Emory Aldrich to Dawes, October 18, 1860, Dawes Papers.
47. Robinson, *Warrington*, 221; Harrington, *Banks*, 44; Springfield *Republican*, August 21, 1857; Boston *Evening Traveller*, August 20, 1857.

publican platform to the simple principle of non-extension, instead of
the radicals' denationalization of slavery or the conservatives' restoration of the Missouri Compromise. But when, on the other hand, conservatives tried to transform the party into a mere opposition organization, moderates worked with the radicals to maintain the party's
identity. Not that moderates objected to soliciting support from southern oppositionists and northern Old Line Whigs. They insisted, however, that the Republican principle of non-extension, rather than
popular sovereignty or an anti-Lecompton stand, be the basis of any
such union.[48]

Like the conservatives, moderate Republicans disliked the slavery
controversy and resented the doctrinaire morality of the Sumners,
Lovejoys, and Julians, whose speeches, they felt, did the Republican
party more harm than good. But their hatred for slavery was too deep
to disguise. Timothy Howe, who battled Wisconsin radicals over
nullification, privately conceded that he abhorred slavery as much as
any of them, and Godlove S. Orth of Indiana said he regarded slavery
as "an evil which all good men should desire to see totally eradicated."
One of the more conservative Republicans, William T. Sherman, reacted to a speech of his brother, a leading moderate, by observing that
while John Sherman disavowed any intention of interfering with
slavery in the states, "still, you hit the system as though you had feeling
against it." William Sherman preferred an attitude of "perfect im-
partiality" toward the peculiar institution, and like most conservatives
hoped the slavery question could somehow be ignored. But the moderates were aware of the depth of northern feeling, and recognized that
the question could not be artificially kept out of national politics. "What
else but the system and question of human slavery is there, at this time,
which divides the people of this country, politically," the former
governor of New York, Myron Clark, inquired of William Seward in
1858, and an Illinois moderate declared in 1861 that the basis of the
sectional impasse was "a conflict of opinion between the people of the
South and the people of the North in relation to the institution of
slavery. . . ."[49]

48. William Schouler to Chase, March 27, 1858, William Schouler Papers; Springfield *Republican*, January 2, 1857, May 4, 1858; *Ohio State Journal*, March 12,
1858.
49. William Salter, *The Life of James W. Grimes* (New York, 1876), 127; David
M. Potter, *Lincoln and His Party in the Secession Crisis* (New Haven, 1942), 24;
Howe to George Rublee, May 17, 1857, Howe Papers; L. E. Chittenden, *A Report*

Perhaps the most striking similarity between the political outlook of the moderates and that of the radicals lay in their expectations regarding the national future. For the moderates were convinced that a Republican victory, by removing the Slave Power from control of the federal government and ensuring that slavery would be prohibited from entering the territories, would be a large first step on the path to complete abolition. The moderates accepted the radical view that there was a large body of anti-slavery sentiment among southern non-slaveholders. Even the New York *Times*, commented on the "general desire" in the South to overthrow the political ascendancy of the slaveholders, and added, "We have little doubt that a large portion of the people of the Southern States still adhere to the doctrines of the founders of the Republic concerning slavery." The Boston *Atlas and Daily Bee*, one of the more moderate voices of Massachusetts Republicanism, agreed that "throughout the slave states are multitudes of thinking men who are opposed to the institution." And John Sherman predicted in 1860 that within two years after the election of Lincoln there would be a Republican party in every southern state, and he explained to the abolitionist Lydia Maria Child that while he disagreed with radicals who would use federal power to destroy slavery in the states, the inevitable result of a Republican victory would be to encourage emancipation by the slave states themselves.[50]

Moderates and radicals thus agreed that the effect of a national Republican victory would be to inaugurate an "irrepressible conflict" within the slave states themselves. However, they parted company over timing: whether to use federal power to attack slavery, or allow events to take a slower natural course. To the radicals, slavery was so immense an evil that a Republican administration would be morally delinquent if it did not use all its constitutional powers to eradicate the institution. The moderates were willing to wait. "Let us withdraw from it the protection of our federal government," said the Boston *Atlas and Daily Bee*, "leave it to itself, and it will at once decline and

---

of the Debates and Proceedings in the Secret Sessions of the Conference Convention . . . Held at Washington, D.C., in February, A.D. 1861 (New York, 1864), 263–64; Rachel Sherman Thorndike, *The Sherman Letters* (New York, 1894), 83; Myron H. Clark to Seward, November 30, 1858, Miscellaneous Manuscripts, NYHS; *Congressional Globe*, 36 Congress, 2 Session, Appendix, 193.
50 New York *Times*, July 23, 24, 1856; Boston *Atlas and Daily Bee*, July 23, 1858; Cincinnati *Gazette*, September 29, 1860; John Sherman to Lydia Maria Child, February 8, 1860 (copy), Sherman Papers. Cf. *Wisconsin State Journal*, October 22, 1860; New York *Evening Post*, April 30, 1856.

at length die." Sherman believed that the eventual extinction of slavery
was certain, but that "a chronic disease, which has been the growth of
centuries, cannot be cured in a day or a generation." Even Henry
Carey believed that if the federal government adopted economic
policies which would stimulate the development and diversification of
the southern economy, slavery would be doomed. Abolition would be
a long-drawn-out process, he warned, but in an economy of modern
agriculture and expanding industry, blacks would be more valuable
as freemen than as slaves, and their emancipation would eventually
come about.[51]

The moderates thus shared the radicals' sublime confidence that
they were on the side of history, but they were willing to let historical
processes take their natural course. As Bowles wrote, the end of slavery
would not come for some years, "long after the question has been completely removed from national politics." Yet while they did not favor
such drastic federal action as the radicals proposed—abolishing the
interstate slave trade, repealing the fugitive slave law, and the like—
the moderates did not expect a Republican administration to be entirely
inactive. The Boston *Atlas and Daily Bee* spoke vaguely of the "aid
and encouragement" the federal government could give southern anti-
slavery men; the Springfield *Republican* insisted that the major obstacle
to emancipation in the border states was "the malign influence of the
national administration." Bowles's journal was quick to disavow any
direct federal interference with slavery in the states, but it went on to
declare, "But we are not saying that when the general government
comes into the hands of the republican party . . . its influence will not
be felt in the slave states, as well as the free, in the support of its own
principles." And on the eve of Lincoln's election, Bowles predicted that
northern opponents of slavery would soon find "an army of vigorous
allies springing up on the soil cursed by the unnatural institution."
The moderates were no doubt intentionally vague as to exactly what
kind of assistance the federal government could offer slave state Republicans—probably, they thought primarily in terms of patronage and
colonization which, as we shall see, was supported by many Re-

51. Boston *Atlas and Daily Bee*, July 22, 1858; Sherman to Lydia Maria Child,
February 8, 1860 (copy), Sherman Papers; Henry C. Carey, *The Harmony of
Interests, Agricultural, Manufacturing, and Commercial* (New York, 1856), 163–
65; Henry C. Carey, *Principles of Social Science* (3 vols.: Philadelphia, 1858–59),
III, 470; Carey to Sumner, May 4, July 24, 1852, Sumner Papers, Carey to Sher-
man, December 21, 1860, Sherman Papers.

publicans precisely because their border state allies deemed it essential for the progress of anti-slavery in the South. They also believed that a Republican victory would inaugurate a new political atmosphere throughout the nation, one in which the question of emancipation could be discussed openly and without fear. With a little encouragement from the federal government, the moderates were convinced, "the seat of war is to be transferred to the locality where the evil exists and can be most effectively reached"—the slave states themselves.[52]

On the eve of Lincoln's nomination in 1860, Charles Ballance, an Old Line Whig from central Illinois, gave Lyman Trumbull a summary of the politics of that pivotal area:

> With regard to general politics, our people are generally moderate men—opposed to extremes . . . and are willing to be foiled in our projects, provided the union is safe—provided the country is quiet and prosperous. The majority of us are opposed to the fugitive slave law, but for the sake of peace we say let it be enforced; but when an attempt is made to open up the slave trade, or force slavery into the territories . . . there is no difference of opinion here.

It was the course of events in the 1850's rather than firm ideological commitments which led moderate Republicans to side more often with radicals than conservatives. Men like Sherman, Bowles, and Grimes were radicalized by what they considered the aggressions of the Slave Power. We have already seen that the Kansas-Nebraska Act, the Dred Scott decision, and the Lecompton controversy convinced many moderates that radical claims regarding the Slave Power's intentions were fully justified. The moderates' concern over the trend of national politics was well expressed by former Senator Roger Baldwin of Connecticut. Though he had been out of office for seven years, Baldwin wrote Chase in 1858, he had been an attentive observer "of the progress of events tending to the centralization of the powers of the government in the Executive, while he, himself, [the Executive] has been but the chosen instrument of an irresponsible and unscrupulous oligarchy." It was this kind of concern which led many moderates to support resistance to the fugitive slave law, although they refused to endorse

52. Springfield *Republican*, October 20, 1860; Boston *Atlas and Daily Bee*, July 23, 1858; Springfield *Republican*, March 2, 1858, November 3, 1860; New York *Times*, September 27, 1860.

the idea of nullification. Bowles, for example, supported the radicals'
demand for the removal of Judge Loring, the man who had ordered
a fugitive slave returned to his owner, on the grounds that it would
demonstrate that Massachusetts "will neither obey nor resist the
Fugitive Slave Law," and he urged the national administration to
abandon any idea of enforcing the hated measure.[53] The Ohio moderate
Caleb B. Smith denounced federal usurpations of the rights of the
states, and even the sedate New York *Commercial Advertiser* remarked
that while all laws must be enforced, the federal government could
not expect to ride roughshod over states rights without encountering
resistance.[54]

The moderates' concern over the trend of events in the 1850's also
led them to agree with the radicals on the importance of encouraging
the moral aversion to slavery among northern voters. When the
National Era was in financial difficulty in 1859, radicals like Elihu
Washburne, Owen Lovejoy, and Henry Wilson contributed money,
but so did Edwin Morgan, John Sherman, Nathaniel Banks, William
Pitt Fessenden, and even old John McLean. These moderates did not
agree with the politics of the *Era's* editor, Gamaliel Bailey, but they
recognized the paper's value in spreading anti-slavery views. For the
same reason, Samuel Bowles called John Brown "the bravest man of
this generation," and "a true man and a Christian." Bowles disapproved
of Brown's raid, but he believed that the event itself and Brown's
execution had deeply strengthened "the moral hostility of the people
of the free states to slavery." The similarity of the aims of these two
wings of the party, despite their many political differences, was made
clear by Caleb Smith. On returning to Indiana after several years of
work in Ohio politics, Smith wrote the Hoosier radical leader George
Julian: [55]

> Our paths have diverged not from a difference of opinion upon
> public measures, but upon the expedience of effecting the same
> object. You are regarded as ultra in your anti-slavery notions, yet

53. Charles Ballance to Trumbull, May 7, 1860, Trumbull Papers; Baldwin to
Chase, April 5, 1858 (copy), Baldwin Family Papers; Springfield *Republican*,
February 17, 1855; Boston *Evening Traveller*, June 4, 1857.
54. Cincinnati *Gazette*, August 13, 1857; New York *Commercial Advertiser*, cited
in New York *Tribune*, June 2, 1857. Cf. Boston *Atlas and Daily Bee*, March 14,
1859; New York *Times*, August 30, September 12, 1855; Philadelphia *North
American*, September 12, 1855.
55. Gamaliel Bailey to Chase, May 10, 19, 1859, Chase Papers, HSPa; Springfield
Republican, November 12, December 3, 5, 7, 1860; Caleb B. Smith to George W.
Julian, February 13, 1859, Giddings-Julian Papers, LC.

I do not know that you have advanced an opinion in regard to slavery, or the legislation of the government concerning it, that I cannot endorse. There is nothing that I so much desire as to see the insolence of the slave power rebuked and its pride and arrogance humbled.

Perhaps the best illustration of the power of the moderates in the Republican party was the nomination of one of their own, Abraham Lincoln, in 1860. Lincoln's selection was the result of a combination of factors, but one of the most important was the party's recognition that it needed to be unified to succeed in the presidential canvass. William Seward and Salmon Chase, the radical candidates, and Edward Bates, the choice of the conservatives, were each objectionable to a sizable number of Republicans, and thus the nomination of any of them would place the party's success in jeopardy. As the Chicago convention approached, Seward was the leading contender, but political observers were well aware of his liabilities as a candidate. The nativist element in the Republican party, recalling Seward's advocacy of equal rights for foreigners and his campaign as governor of New York for public appropriations to Catholic parochial schools, plainly declared that they would not support him. Former Democrats charged that Seward was surrounded by a band of political corruptionists who would loot the national treasury. They also objected to his latitudinarian construction of the Constitution and his attachment to all kinds of schemes for government aid to business. Most serious was Seward's reputation—not altogether deserved—for radicalism.[56]

Seward's difficulties, however, did not enhance the chances of his two most prominent rivals, Chase and Bates. As a leading radical, Chase was as unacceptable to the doubtful states as Seward. Carl Schurz frankly told him early in 1860 that if the convention were disposed to radicalism, it would select Seward, and if not, it could not accept Chase.[57] Chase, indeed, because of his reputation as a free-

56. Glyndon G. Van Deusen, *William Henry Seward* (New York, 1967), 226; Rodney B. Field to Morrill, May 20, 1856, Morrill Papers; James Dixon to Welles, April 26, 1860, Welles Papers, LC; James S. Pike to William P. Fessenden, April 8, 1858, James S. Pike Papers, LC; George Rathbun to Hannibal Hamlin, June 4, 1860, Hannibal Hamlin Papers, University of Maine, Orono; George C. McRed to Elihu B. Washburne, April 15, 1860, Elihu B. Washburne Papers, LC; A. K. McClure, *Abraham Lincoln and Men of War-Times* (Philadelphia, 1892), 24–29.
57. Schurz's remark is in Carl Schurz, *Reminiscences of Carl Schurz* (3 vols.: New York, 1907–08), II, 171, and is confirmed in Chase to William G. Hosea, March 18, 1860, Commission on Western History, Miscellaneous Manuscripts, Houghton Library, Harvard University.

trader, was even less acceptable to the key state of Pennsylvania than Seward. Then, too, Chase had still not overcome the animosity of Ohio's Whig-Republicans over the circumstances of his first election to the Senate by a Free Soil-Democratic coalition in 1849. Finally, Chase's ambition to be President—having reached inordinate proportions by 1860—had already somewhat tarnished his reputation. "If S. P. Chase weren't in quite so big a hurry to be President," Horace Greeley observed in 1858, "he would stand a much better chance." [58]

Despite Seward's and Chase's lack of political availability, the conservative candidacy of Edward Bates never generated much enthusiasm among Republicans. Bates's supporters hoped that his nomination would attract not only northern Whigs who, like Bates himself, had supported Fillmore in 1856, but border state Unionists and Know-Nothings as well. But the radicals made it clear that they would bolt the party if Bates were chosen. As Congressmen DeWitt Leach explained it, they did not insist that the party accept their first choice—Seward—but they did demand that "a *Republican* candidate" be chosen, one who had supported Frémont in 1856. Moreover, Bates's nativist views made him anathema to the influential German-born western Republicans, whose spokesmen were Carl Schurz and Gustav Koerner. [59] The strength of the Bates movement was always more apparent than real, and was due more to Horace Greeley's energetic support in the New York *Tribune* than any real swing of Republican sentiment. And it was not ideological conservatism, but political pessimism, that led the New York editor to favor Bates. In the pages of the *Tribune*, Greeley boasted that free-soil sentiment dominated northern public opinion, but privately he was less sanguine. Early in 1860, he explained his support of Bates by arguing: "I want to succeed this time, yet I *know* the country is not Anti-Slavery. It will only swallow

58. R. G. Hazard to Chase, January 15, 1859, James A. Gurley to Chase, April 13, 1860, James Elliot to Chase, May 21, 1860, R. Brinkerhoff to Chase, June 19, 1860, Chase Papers, LC; Samuel Galloway to John McLean, April 20, 1860, John McLean Papers, LC; Ben Wade to Israel Washburn, October 13, 1855, Israel Washburn Papers, LC; Greeley to Colfax, April 11, 1858, Greeley-Colfax Papers.
59. Pease and Randall, eds., *Browning Diary*, I, 407; William E. Smith, *The Francis Preston Blair Family in Politics* (2 vols.: New York, 1933), I, 462; Reinhard H. Luthin, "Organizing the Republican Party in the 'Border-Slave' Regions: Edward Bates's Presidential Candidacy in 1860," *MoHR*, XXXVIII, (January 1944), 145; *Congressional Globe*, 36 Congress, 1 Session, 1166; Chicago *Press and Tribune*, March 15, 1860; F. I. Herriot, "The Germans of Davenport and the Chicago Convention of 1860," *Deutsch-Amerikanische Geschichtsblätter*, X (1910), 156–63.

a little Anti-Slavery in a great deal of sweetening." [60] But there was so little anti-slavery in Bates's record that he was unacceptable to all but the most conservative of Republicans.

Thus even before the opening of the Chicago Convention Republican moderates, who wished to see the party both united and victorious, were looking about for another possibility. As early as December 1858, William Pitt Fessenden had shrewdly forecast the Republicans' situation. "I think it pretty evident," he wrote Hamilton Fish, ". . . that our candidate will either be Seward or some one not yet named, who has no particular following, and, while a decided Republican, would not be obnoxious to any branch of the party—provided such a man can be found." As the convention approached, the name of Abraham Lincoln was discussed more and more by Republican leaders. Germans, who were aware of his anti-nativist sentiments, found Lincoln eminently acceptable, while nativist leaders would support him as an alternative to the hated Seward. In the doubtful states, political leaders agreed that Lincoln stood a much better chance of victory than Seward.[61] When the convention opened, the Associated Press reported that Lincoln and Ben Wade of Ohio were the two most likely possibilities after Seward, and when the doubtful states settled upon Lincoln as their choice, his nomination was assured. But while the key to his selection lay in the areas of conservative strength, it would not be accurate to say that he was nominated because he was a conservative. Actually, Lincoln's acceptability to all wings of the party was the basis of his availability—as one of his ardent supporters noted, he was "the second choice of everybody." In part, this was due to his lack of national prominence. (The official organ of the Wisconsin Republican party carried the name of "Abram Lincoln" on its masthead for two weeks after the nomination, scolding all who printed

60. New York *Tribune*, January 26, 1854; Greeley to Mrs. R. M. Whipple, undated, 1860, Horace Greeley Papers, LC. Cf. Greeley to Chase, September 28, 1858, Chase Papers, HSPa; Barnes, *Weed Memoir*, 255. Bates's biographer exaggerates the extent of Bates's support, in my opinion. Marvin R. Cain, *Lincoln's Attorney General, Edward Bates of Missouri* (Columbia, Mo., 1965), 105–6.

61. William Pitt Fessenden to Fish, December 18, 1858, Fish Papers; F. I. Herriot, "The Germans of Iowa and the 'Two Year' Amendment of Massachusetts," *Deutsch-Amerikanische Geschichtsblätter*, XIII (1913), 203–4; J. G. Randall, *Lincoln the President, Springfield to Gettysburg* (2 vols.: New York, 1945), I, 161; Holt, "Forging a Majority," 444; Harry J. Carman and Reinhard H. Luthin, "Some Aspects of Know-Nothingism Reconsidered," *SAQ*, XXXIX (April 1940), 230–31; J. P. Sanderson to Edward McPherson, March 20, 1860, Edward McPherson Papers, LC; David Wilmot to Joseph Casey, March 10, 1860, in Simon Cameron Papers, LC.

his name as "Abraham.") Henry Wilson had written a month before
the Chicago Convention that the nominee must be a man "not so mixed
up in the conflicts as to lose the support of the more moderate men."
Lincoln filled the prescription exactly.[62]

Despite some historians' tendency to see Lincoln's nomination as
a triumph of conservatism, the Republican party was actually more
radical in 1860 than it had been in 1857 and 1858. The year 1860 saw
a definite swing towards radicalism on the part of Republican Congressmen. One index of this trend was the vote on March 26, 1860, on a
resolution instructing the House judiciary committee to inquire into
the expediency of a bill freeing every human being and barring slavery
wherever Congress had jurisdiction to act. In effect, this resolution
would have put into operation the radicals' demand for abolition in
the territories, the District of Columbia, and all other areas of federal
jurisdiction. The House defeated it 109 to 60, but fifty-nine Republicans
supported the resolution and thirteen were paired in favor, while only
eleven opposed and twenty-six abstained. Only in Indiana, Pennsylvania, and New York were there sizable negative votes or abstentions.
The moderates had sided with the radicals, and two months later, as
we have seen, the Republican convention approved a radical platform.
"The Republicans," a New York *Times* correspondent reported from
Chicago, "are perfectly ready to take Mr. Seward's measures without
Mr. Seward." [63]

It is too often forgotten that in 1860 Lincoln was considered by
political observers to be closer to the radical than to the conservative
wing of the Republican party. In April, 1860, for example, Lyman
Trumbull was anything but optimistic about his friend's chances. He
wrote Lincoln candidly that many Republicans linked him and Seward
together as radicals inasmuch as both had forecast that the nation
would become either all free or all slave—Lincoln in the "House
Divided" speech, and Seward in his "Irrepressible Conflict" argument. Conservatives like Senator James Dixon of Connecticut and
William T. Sherman had the same estimate of Lincoln's views. Indeed,
a recent student of southern Indiana politics concludes that before his

62. Springfield *Republican*, May 16, 1860; Weed to Seward, May 20, 1860,
Seward Papers; Fehrenbacher, *Prelude*, 155–59; Charles Francis Adams Diary,
May 18, 1860, Adams Papers; John Farnsworth to Elihu B. Washburne, May 18,
1860, Washburne Papers; *Wisconsin State Journal*, May 22, 1860, Henry Wilson
to Carey, April 16, 1860, Carey Papers.
63. Alexander, *Sectional Stress*, 106; *Congressional Globe*, 36 Congress, 1 Session,
1359–60; New York *Times*, May 17, 1860.

nomination, Lincoln enjoyed little support in that bastion of conservatism because of his radical reputation.[64] The other side of this coin was that radicals were quite pleased with the nomination. Giddings, with whom Lincoln had discussed his proposal for emancipation in the District of Columbia when both were in Congress in 1849, declared that he would as soon trust Lincoln on the slavery question as Chase and Seward. The influential Chicago editor Charles Ray wrote that Lincoln was "intensely radical in fundamental principles," and the Boston correspondent of Greeley's *Tribune* asserted that the nominee was "ahead of the anti-slavery sentiment of the Republican party, rather than behind it. . . ."[65]

Despite the enthusiasm of Giddings and other radicals, Lincoln was hardly a doctrinaire on the order of Sumner, Julian, or Lovejoy. Yet he did share the radicals' moral abhorrence of slavery, and was fully committed to its eventual eradication. "I have always hated slavery, I think as much as any Abolitionist," Lincoln said in a Chicago speech of 1858, and according to a Wisconsin newspaper, he told an audience in that state in 1859 that the underlying principle of the Republican party was "hatred to the institution of slavery; hatred to it in all its aspects, moral, social and political." [66] In the Lincoln-Douglas debates of 1858, and again in his Cooper Union speech of 1860, Lincoln stressed the moral basis of Republicanism, and pointed to divergent attitudes on the morality of slavery as the essential point of conflict between North and South. Moreover, Lincoln made clear that his ultimate goal was not merely the non-extension of slavery—although he was inflexible in his adherence to this objective—but its "ultimate extinction." [67] Like other moderates, he was unwilling to jeopardize the Union by interfering directly with slavery in the states, but he was

64. Trumbull to Lincoln, April 24, 1860, Lincoln Papers; James Dixon to Welles, May 1, 1860, Welles Papers, LC; Walter L. Fleming, ed., *General W. T. Sherman As College President* (Cleveland, 1912), 232; Elbert, "Southern Indiana," 104.
65. Giddings to Julian, May 25, 1860, Giddings-Julian Papers; Giddings Diary, January 8, 19, 1849, Giddings Papers; C. H. Ray to E. L. Pierce, April, 1860, E. L. Pierce Papers, Houghton Library, Harvard University; New York *Tribune*, July 9, 1860. Cf. Frederick Douglass' analysis: "He is a radical Republican, and is fully committed to the doctrine of the 'irrepressible conflict.' . . . He is not a compromise candidate by any means." *Douglass' Monthly*, June, 1860.
66. Basler, ed., *Lincoln Works*, II, 492, III, 482. Cf. II, 255, 316, 320.
67. Harry Jaffa, *Crisis of the House Divided* (Garden City, 1959), 276; Basler, ed., *Lincoln Works*, II, 461, 498, III, 225–26, 312, 549–50. This pleased the radicals no end. Lovejoy closed a letter to Lincoln with the words, "Yours for the 'ultimate extinction of slavery.'" Lovejoy to Lincoln, August 4, 1858, Lincoln Papers.

convinced that once the spread of slavery had been halted, the long process of its decline would begin.

In politics as well as ideology, Lincoln represented a middle ground between conservatism and radicalism. He held aloof from the abortive Republican organization created by the Illinois radicals in 1854, but, as Don E. Fehrenbacher shows, took a leading part in organizing the party in 1856. Although many of his friends and advisers were central Illinois Old Line Whigs, he was also on good terms with Owen Lovejoy and other radical spokesmen, and he vetoed a conservative effort in 1858 to deprive Lovejoy of his district's Congressional nomination. Lincoln's support of Lovejoy reflected the determination of the moderates to place party unity above factional squabbling, and on the same ground Lincoln criticized out-of-state Republicans for embarrassing the party in more moderate areas by adding to Republican state platforms such issues as repeal of the fugitive slave law or restriction of the rights of foreign-born citizens. By the same token, he vehemently opposed efforts to modify the party's position on slavery to attract either Douglas Democrats or southern oppositionists. If, Lincoln wrote, the party gave up the object for which it had been formed—preventing the extension of slavery—it would go to pieces.[68] At the time of his nomination, Lincoln's political outlook more closely resembled that of the radicals than of the conservatives in his party. In this, he reflected the position of most Republican moderates in 1860.

The election of 1860, as we have seen, hinged on the states which Frémont had failed to carry—New Jersey, Pennsylvania, Indiana, and Illinois. In order to attract the votes of Old Line Whigs, particularly the Fillmore supporters of 1856 in these and other states, the Republican party utilized the services of its conservative members. In southern Ohio, for example, Tom Corwin, a reluctant Frémont supporter in 1856, and Tom Ewing, who had not voted at all in that year, played key roles in winning over Old Line Whigs. They minimized the slavery issue and insisted that the Republican platform was really nothing more than the old Whig program of Henry Clay—devotion to the Union, national economic development, and the non-extension of slavery, in that order of importance.[69] Corwin credited his own speeches

68. Fehrenbacher, *Prelude*, 33–47; Magdol, *Lovejoy*, 189–91; Edward Magdol, "Owen Lovejoy's Role in the Campaign of 1858," *Journal* of the IllSHS, LI (Winter 1958), 412–14; Basler, ed., *Lincoln Works*, III, 379, 384, 387–88, 390–91, 394.
69. Mrs. Ellen Ewing Sherman, comp., *Memorial of Thomas Ewing of Ohio* (New York, 1873), 265; *Speech of Ewing at Chillicothe, passim*; Morrow, ed., *Corwin*,

with bringing thousands of Fillmore Whigs into the Republican organization, and Ewing's insistence that Lincoln was "a sound conservative man," whose election would silence the slavery controversy forever, gave reassurance to conservatives like William T. Sherman. While radical Republicans could hardly agree with their interpretation of Republicanism (Ewing even said the party's aim was merely to restore the Missouri Compromise), they recognized the political effectiveness of their speeches. Joseph Medill, the radical Chicago editor, for example, urged that copies of a Corwin speech be sent to the southernmost area of Illinois, though he could not resist remarking, "It is well suited for that latitude." [70]

The use of former conservative Whig leaders to convince Fillmore men to vote for Lincoln was not confined to Ohio. Richard Thompson of Indiana, for example, although originally a supporter of the Constitutional Union ticket, not only switched to Lincoln in August but also influenced Old Line Whigs to support the Republican gubernatorial candidate Henry Lane. Thompson, who had known Lincoln in Congress in the late 1840's, wrote him that he was trying to persuade conservatives "that you would select your cabinet jointly from the North and the South and then inaugurate a conservative and national administration which, the slavery question out of the way, should bring about the restoration of *Whiggery*." [71] In New York, where Fillmore had polled over 20 per cent of the vote in 1856, Daniel Ullmann spoke for Lincoln to conservative audiences, while the influential Buffalo *Commercial Advertiser*, a Fillmore journal in 1856, assured its readers that the Republican platform had committed the party to dealing properly with the economic affairs of the nation once the slavery issue was settled. The importance of the support which men like Corwin, Ewing, Thompson, and Ullmann gave Lincoln was attested to by the conservative New York businessman Daniel P. Barnard, when he wrote Hamilton Fish early in 1861: [72]

61–62, 363–64, 369, 382–83; Prendergaft, "Corwin," 4–5, 9–12; Cincinnati *Gazette*, August 7, 1858, August 23, 1859; John W. Jones to Benjamin F. Wade, September 16, 1858, Benjamin F. Wade Papers, LC.

70. James S. Pike, *First Blows of the Civil War* (New York, 1879), 427; *Speech of Ewing at Chillicothe*, 13, 20–21; Thorndike, *Sherman Letters*, 84; Joseph Medill to Trumbull, April 16, 1860, Trumbull Papers; George W. Julian, *The Life of Joshua R. Giddings* (Chicago, 1892), 377.

71. Roll, *Thompson*, 163–65; R. H. Thompson to Lincoln, June 12, 1860, Lincoln Papers; New York *Times*, August 31, 1860.

72. *Speech of Daniel Ullmann, of New York, at the Lincoln and Hamlin Ratification Meeting in Newark, N.J., June 12, 1860* (np, nd); New York *Tribune*, May 21, 1860; Daniel P. Barnard to Fish, January 15, 1861, Fish Papers.

> I doubt if you are really aware of the extent of influence which your quiet and unobtrusive support of Mr. Lincoln carried with it. It was just the example of such men as yourself, and of none more than your own, which finally brought in so much conservative strength to swell his majorities in the Northern States.

In his letter to Fish, Barnard estimated that of Lincoln's 1.8 million votes in the free states, 300,000 to 400,000—or roughly 20 per cent— came from conservatives. This estimate is no doubt high; in addition, it is important to remember that Republican majorities in the doubtful states were created not in 1860 but in 1858, when many conservatives voted with the party to protest both the administration's attempt to force slavery into Kansas and its mishandling of economic affairs. The Republicans in 1858 raised their percentage of the vote in Illinois from 40.2 per cent in 1856 to 50.8 per cent, in Indiana from 40.1 per cent in 1856 to 49.4 per cent, and in Pennsylvania from 32 per cent in 1856 to 53.7 per cent. Two years later, Lincoln held or expanded these Republican gains, even though the Kansas controversy had subsided. In southern Indiana, for example, Lincoln ran only two hundred votes behind Douglas, and the Constitutional Unionist, Bell—representing the same political forces as had Fillmore in 1856—received only three thousand votes. Frémont had received only 18,000 votes in southern Indiana in 1856; Lincoln gathered over 54,000. In the crucial state of New York, moreover, where many conservatives supported a fusion electoral ticket agreed upon by all the anti-Republican candidates, Lincoln won enough of the Fillmore-Old Line Whig votes to give him a comfortable majority.[73]

IV

In April, 1858, Cassius M. Clay offered William Seward an analysis of border state politics which proved applicable to areas of conservative strength in the free states as well. "I have long foreseen," Clay wrote, "that the moderate whigs (Americans) would be forced to act directly or indirectly with the Republican party. Because whatever might be their attachment to slavery and the status quo, the Propagandists would by threatening the Union force them into opposition."

73. *Tribune Almanac*, 1859, 52, 59–61; 1861, 47, 56, 62; Elbert "Southern Indiana," 152; Jaffa, *Crisis of House Divided*, 73; Reinhard H. Luthin, *The First Lincoln Campaign* (Cambridge, 1944), 211; Eugene H. Roseboom, *The Civil War Era 1850–1873* (Columbus, 1944), 371.

One of the major reasons many conservatives supported Lincoln in 1860 was their belief that his election would preserve the Union by finally ending the slavery controversy. But when Lincoln's success plunged the nation into what one Republican Senator called "the first great crisis since the adoption of the Constitution," conservative Republicans turned back to the Clay-Webster tradition of concession and compromise to dispel southern fears and deal with southern threats.[74] Yet in the secession crisis the moderates once again held the balance of power within the party. While the conservatives would sacrifice anti-slavery to save the Union, and the radicals would endanger the Union to attack slavery, the moderates, with Lincoln at their head, refused to abandon either of their twin goals—free soil and the Union.

How extensive desire for compromise was in Republican ranks has long been a subject of controversy among historians. Concession found strong support among Old Line Whigs like Ewing, Corwin, and Fish, in urban centers like New York and Boston, and in the conservative belt of the lower North. James Dixon of Connecticut explained the conservatives' priorities when he wrote early in 1861 that while he hated slavery, "now in this hour of dreadful danger, slavery sinks into insignificance compared to that great danger to which we are exposed." Yet after studying the correspondence of Republican Congressmen and the files of the leading newspapers, one finds it difficult to disagree with Kenneth Stampp's conclusion that only a small minority of Republicans were willing to recede in any significant way from the Chicago platform.[75] The moderates' perception of the nature of the crisis was strikingly similar to that of the radicals. Justin Morrill considered the crisis the culmination of "a deep laid, long-pondered plot to break up the Government," and James Grimes wrote that the South was calling upon the free states "to surrender all our cherished ideas on the subject of slavery, and agree, . . . [to] change the Constitution into a genuine pro-slavery document, and to convert the Government into a great slave-breeding, slavery-extending empire."

74. Clay to Seward, April 18, 1858, Seward Papers; Foner, *Business and Slavery*, 189; New York *Times*, July 17, 1860; James F. Dixon to Mark Howard, December 4, 1860, Mark Howard Papers, ConnHS.
75. Fish to Thomas Turner, December 7, 1860, Letterbook, Fish Papers; O'Connor, *Lords of the Loom*, 145–49; Foner, *Business and Slavery*, 229; *Congressional Globe*, 36 Congress, 2 Session, 494; James Dixon to Greeley, undated [early 1861], Greeley Papers, LC; Kenneth Stampp, *And the War Came* (Baton Rouge, 1950), 87n., 125, 136–41.

Even Richard Henry Dana of Massachusetts, who described himself as "a Whig of the old school; . . . a highly conservative Whig," insisted that the North could not "buy the right to carry on the government, by any concession to slavery." [76] Men like Morrill, Grimes, and Dana were willing to make some concessions to the South—the first two voted for a constitutional amendment guaranteeing slavery in the states against federal interference, and Dana favored the repeal of northern personal liberty laws—but their conviction that southern fears and demands were essentially insatiable restricted the distance they would go to conciliate the South.[77]

The position of the moderate Republicans in the secession crisis was defined by president-elect Lincoln when he wrote to Seward that, while he was willing to satisfy southern demands regarding the fugitive slave law, slavery in the District of Columbia, and the internal slave trade, he was inflexible regarding the extension of slavery. Radical Republicans found this position unacceptable, for they rejected any and all concessions, but, as Stampp points out, the moderates came no nearer to satisfying the South than the radical position did. Indeed, many of the moderate "conciliators" were not interested in compromise at all. In order to play for time, satisfy northern compromisers, and give southern Unionists a chance to make themselves felt in the slave states, particularly the border region, they made proposals which they knew would be rejected. For example, Governor Buckingham of Connecticut seemed to favor conciliation when he approved the sending of delegates to the Washington Peace Conference of February, 1861. But he instructed Connecticut's representatives to oppose all proposals for "new guarantees for the protection of property in man," although he must have known that some such guarantee would be necessary to conciliate the South. And Thurlow Weed explained to Lincoln that his controversial compromise plan, which included the restoration of the Missouri Compromise, was

76. William B. Parker, *The Life and Public Services of Justin Smith Morrill* (Boston, 1924), 121; Salter, *Grimes*, 133–34; Richard Henry Dana, Jr., *Speeches in Stirring Times*, ed. Richard Henry Dana, 3rd, (Boston, 1910), 145; Dana to Adams, January 22, 1861, Adams Papers. Cf. Fessenden to Fish, December 15, 1860, Fish Papers; Dawes to Mrs. Ella Dawes, December 14, 1860, Dawes Papers; Morrill to Ruth Morrill, January 13, 1861, Morrill Papers; A. K. McLure to Edward McPherson, December 14, 1860, McPherson Papers.
77. *Congressional Globe*, 36 Congress, 2 Session, 1264, 1403; Morrill to ?, December 11, 1860, Morrill Papers; Samuel Shapiro, *Richard Henry Dana, Jr. 1815–1882* (East Lansing, 1961), 114–15.

an attempt to alleviate northern Democratic suspicion of Republican intentions, and to unite the North "to meet Disunion as patriots rather than as partizans." [78]

The varied considerations which motivated the conciliatory moderate Republicans, and their underlying refusal to compromise on what they considered essentials, are illustrated by the policies of Charles Francis Adams and William Seward in the secession winter. Both had been considered radicals up to the election of 1860, but they shared a perception of the seriousness of the crisis and a devotion to the Union which immediately separated them from their erstwhile radical associates. Adams abandoned the Chicago platform by proposing the admission of New Mexico as a slave state, ostensibly as a conciliatory gesture, and in the House Committee of 33 he proposed that the North revise its personal liberty laws, guarantee slavery in the states against outside interference, and allow territories south of the old Missouri Compromise line to choose whether they wanted free or slave institutions. Yet when Massachusetts radicals criticized his course, Adams assured them that his concessions really amounted to very little. "I think I know the difference between surrendering unimportant points and sacrificing principles," he wrote to E. L. Pierce, explaining that he was confident slavery could never go into New Mexico and the neighboring territories because of climatic conditions.[79] Other moderates who supported the New Mexico proposal, including John Sherman, William Kellogg of Illinois, and John Killinger of Pennsylvania, had the same expectation regarding the future of the territories. Adams believed that his offer had stripped away the pretense from southern complaints and revealed the reality of the secessionists' demands.[80] The fact that his concessions did not satisfy

78. Basler, ed., *Lincoln Works*, IV, 183; Stampp, *And the War Came*, 165, 173–75; William A. Buckingham to Roger S. Baldwin, February 4, 1861 (draft), William A. Buckingham Papers, Connecticut State Library; Weed to Lincoln, December 11, 1860, Lincoln Papers. Cf. Kenneth M. Stampp, ed., "Letters From the Washington Peace Conference of 1861." *JSH*, IX (August 1943), 394–403; Carl F. Krummel, "Henry J. Raymond and the New York Times in the Secession Crisis 1860–61," *NYH*, XXXII (October 1951), 385–95.

79. Adams to E. L. Pierce, January 1, 1861, Adams to W. S. Robinson, January 5, 1861, Adams to E. C. Banfield, January 13, 1861, Adams to F. W. Bird, February 16, 1861, Letterbook, Charles Francis Adams Diary, December 25, 1860, Adams Papers; E. L. Pierce to Sumner, January 8, 1861, Sumner Papers.

80. *Congressional Globe*, 36 Congress, 2 Session, 126, 194, 658, 696; Thorndike, *Sherman Letters*, 97; Duberman, *Adams*, 242–43; Adams to John A. Dix, January 6, 1861, John A. Dix Papers, Columbia University; Adams to Dana, December 23, 1860, Letterbook, Adams Papers.

the South proved that "the question is one of power, and nothing short of surrender of everything gained by the election will avail. They want to continue to rule." As Adams saw it, the only thing which would satisfy the South would be an abdication by the Republicans of control of the national administration. On this point, he wrote, there could be no compromise, "even at the hazard of a permanent disruption of the Union." [81]

The course of William Seward during the secession winter, even more disappointing to the radicals, has proved to be something of a puzzle for historians. It is easy to show, as David Potter makes clear, that Seward's efforts towards conciliation were motivated in large part by a desire to delay a confrontation until Lincoln had been inaugurated and southern Unionism had begun to assert itself, particularly in the upper South. But it must also be remembered that Seward's reputation for radicalism was in large measure undeserved. His devotion to the Union had always been far deeper than that of the radicals with whom he had been associated in the 1850's. Because of his faith in the power and integrity of the Union and his intense nationalism, one recent writer has said that more than any of his contemporaries, Seward represented the nineteenth-century idea of "Union absolute." [82] He was never comfortable in the doctrinaire circles of Giddings, Chase, and Lovejoy, and his perception of the slavery controversy was always more political than theirs. Seward had scandalized the radicals in 1858 when he declared in the Senate that since the main object of the Republican party was to make the North the dominant sectional power by securing the admission of new free states, he regarded the sectional battle "as already fought; it is over." [83] Indeed, he went so far as to say that the election of a Republican president would for all practical purposes end the irrepressible conflict, since "free states will henceforth be organized without resistance. All that has been gained by the slave power, in violation of the Constitu-

81. Adams to E. Farnsworth, December 9, 1860, Letterbook, Adams to Charles Francis Adams, Jr., December 30, 1860, Adams Papers. Cf. Adams to George Mirey, December 26, 1860, Letterbook, Adams Papers.
82. Potter, *Lincoln*, 240; Paul C. Nagel, *One Nation Indivisible* (New York, 1964), 105, 108.
83. *Congressional Globe*, 35 Congress, 1 Session, 521. Cf. New York *Tribune*, February 6, 1858; Sumner to Samuel Gridley Howe, July 26, 1859, Samuel Gridley Howe Papers, Houghton Library, Harvard University; Chase to ?, March 30, 1858, Chase Papers, HSPa.

tion, will be relinquished . . . and this great problem of the removal of slavery from our land will abide its solution in a constitutional way." Seward had an abiding faith in laws of historical progress, and was serenely confident that slavery was doomed. As we have seen, he was also confident of the future development of American imperial power, and his brand of anti-slavery was based in large measure in his belief that slavery was an obstacle to this destiny. In the secession crisis, therefore, once the slaveholders had been removed from national power, his attention turned to the preservation of national unity and he was willing to make concessions which might prolong the life of the peculiar institution for a time, but would not alter the inevitability of its demise. His attitude during the winter of 1860–61 was not inconsistent with his later conduct during Reconstruction.[84]

In the eyes of the moderates, including Lincoln, Adams, and Seward, the election of 1860 marked an irreversible turning point in the nation's history. "There is now," Adams wrote on November 7, "scarcely a shadow of a doubt that the great revolution has actually taken place, and that the country has once and for all thrown off the domination of the Slaveholders." We have already seen how the moderates expected a Republican victory to inaugurate an era of the gradual decline of slavery, the admission of new free states, progress toward emancipation in the border area, and eventual abolition throughout the nation. Lincoln in the "House Divided" speech had expressed his belief that the nation would have to reach and pass a "crisis" before the policy of non-extension could be implemented, the first step toward the goal of "ultimate extinction." For this reason, while they were willing to make concessions on such issues as the fugitive slave law and even the status of New Mexico, moderates like Lincoln would not accept proposals like the Crittenden Compromise, which they considered tantamount to a commitment to extend slavery throughout Central America. Such a course would reverse the result of the election of 1860, jeopardize the major achievement of that election, the Republicans' capture of national power, surrender the cardinal principle

84. New York *Tribune*, November 6, 1858; Frederick W. Seward, ed., *Seward at Washington* (2 vols.: New York, 1891), II, 495–96; William H. Seward, *The Elements of Empire in America* (New York, 1844), 21–22; George E. Baker, ed., *The Works of William H. Seward* (5 vols.: Boston, 1853–84), I, 87; New York *Tribune*, March 7, 1861. For Seward during Reconstruction, see Van Deusen, *Seward*, chapters 29–32.

of majority rule to coercion by a minority, and betray the election's character as a turning point in American history.[85]

In the end, the Republican party rejected compromise during the secession winter. A majority of the party's Congressmen voted against the only measure which stood any chance of conciliating the South, the Crittenden Compromise, and they also opposed the Adams-Seward plan for the immediate admission of New Mexico. Even the proposed constitutional amendment guaranteeing slavery in the states against federal interference (a guarantee included in the Chicago platform) received only eight of twenty votes by Republican Senators, and was rejected by House Republicans, 64 to 45. Only in Indiana, Pennsylvania, and Minnesota did a majority of Republican Congressmen favor the amendment, although it received large minority support in Ohio, New York, and Massachusetts. The defeat of this, perhaps the conciliatory proposal least offensive to the mass of Republicans, demonstrated that the moderates had cast their lot against compromise.[86]

Although conservative Republicans failed to commit the Republican party to a conciliatory course in the secession winter, they could take some solace from the party's emergence during the crisis as a united defender of the Union. We have already seen how the radicals abandoned their commitment to states rights and adopted an unqualified Unionism, once it became apparent that this would further the anti-slavery cause. For their part, even as they urged the party to make vital concessions to the South, conservatives like Hamilton Fish insisted that the right of secession could not be recognized, because it was inconsistent with the "nationality" of the United States. The conservative conciliators agreed with the radicals that if compromise failed and secession became a reality, armed resistance by the North would be preferable to peaceful submission.[87] Republicans of all factions of the party came to agree that the United States was a nation, not a

85. Charles Francis Adams Diary, November 7, 1860, Adams Papers; Basler, ed., *Lincoln Works*, II, 461; IV, 151; George G. Fogg to Greeley, December 1, 1860, Greeley Papers; Seward to Mrs. Elizabeth Schuyler, January 26, 1858, Seward Papers; Fehrenbacher, *Prelude to Greatness*, 95.
86. Potter, *Lincoln and His Party*, 302; *Congressional Globe*, 36 Congress, 2 Session, 1264, 1403.
87. Fish to Thomas Turner, December 7, 1860, Letterbook, Fish Papers; Stampp, *And the War Came*, 25, 90, 111; Pease and Randall. eds., *Browning Diary*, I, xx; Thorndike, *Sherman Letters*, 102; *Congressional Globe*, 36 Congress, 1 Session, 1167.

league of sovereign states, and that, as James Grimes put it, one of the cardinal issues of the crisis was "whether we have a country, whether or not this is a nation." [88]

In a sense, the nationalism which the Republican party embraced during that secession winter was a synthesis of the previous views of the conservatives and radicals, and as usual, this was the ground occupied by the moderates and their spokesman, Lincoln. That Lincoln's Unionism combined a number of strands of ante-bellum thought was illustrated by the fact that before his inaugural address he consulted Clay's compromise speech of 1850, Jackson's proclamation against nullification, and Webster's reply to Hayne. Lincoln agreed with the Webster-Clay tradition when he insisted that the Union preceded the Constitution and was a creation of the American people, not a compact between states. But to their unqualified devotion to the Union as the paramount end of politics, he added the radical conception of the Union as a means to freedom.[89] The Republican position on the Union as it emerged in the secession crisis was that the Union should be revered and defended not only for itself, but also because of the purposes for which it had been created. High among these purposes was the spread of freedom, which, in the 1850's, meant the confinement of slavery. To preserve the Union by undermining this purpose would be to subvert the foundations of the Union itself. The goals of Union and free soil were intertwined, and neither could be sacrificed without endangering the other.

88. Salter, *Grimes*, 136; *Congressional Globe*, 36 Congress, 1 Session, 1035, Appendix, 279; 2 Session, 910, 941, Appendix, 243; Chittenden, *Peace Conference Debates*, 61, 203; William H. Egle, *Life and Times of Andrew Gregg Curtin* (Philadelphia, 1896), 120.
89. Paul M. Angle, ed., *Herndon's Life of Lincoln* (Cleveland, 1965), 386; Basler, ed., *Lincoln Works*, IV, 264-65 Cf. James A. Rawley, "The Nationalism of Abraham Lincoln," *CWH*, IX (September 1963), 283–98; Erastus Hopkins to Adams, January 14, 1861, Adams Papers.

7

The Republicans and Nativism

Although the United States has long pictured itself as an asylum for the oppressed peoples of the world, anti-immigrant movements have displayed a striking tenacity in American politics. The nativist outbreaks of the 1790's, 1850's, and 1920's were but extreme versions of a recurrent pattern, which reflects the underlying tensions of a heterogeneous society. In recent years, a growing number of historians have become convinced that the ethnic and cultural diversity of American society, and not the differing ideologies or platforms of the major parties, have been the major determinants of American political alignments. Studies of modern state and presidential elections have demonstrated that immigrants and Catholics are much more likely to vote Democratic than native-born Protestants, and such findings have also appeared in analyses of nineteenth century voting behavior.[1] Of course astute political observers in the 1850's were hardly unaware of the ethnic dimensions of northern politics. Even Carl Schurz, who hoped to attract German voters to Republicanism, acknowledged that his party was composed "chiefly of . . . the native American farmers,"

1. Walter Dean Burnham, "Party Systems and the Political Process," in *The American Party Systems,* eds., William N. Chambers and Walter Dean Burnham (New York 1967), 285; Lee Benson, *The Concept of Jacksonian Democracy* (Princeton, 1961), 165ff.; Paul Lazarsfeld, Bernard Berelson, and Hazel Gaudet, *The People's Choice* (2nd ed.: New York, 1948), 22; David S. Sparks, "The Birth of the Republican Party in Iowa, 1854–1856," *IJH,* LIV (April 1956), 19; Michael F. Holt, "Forging a Majority: The Formation of the Republican Party in Pittsburgh, Pennsylvania, 1848–1860" (unpublished doctoral dissertation, Johns Hopkins University, 1967), 464–65; Thomas A. Flinn, "Continuity and Change in Ohio Politics," *Journal of Politics,* XXIV (August 1962), 542; Walter Dean Burnham, "American Voting Behavior and the 1964 Election," *Midwest Journal of Political Science,* XII (February 1968), 25–26.

while "the strength of our opponents lies mainly in the populous cities, and consists largely of the Irish and uneducated mass of German immigrants. . . ." [2]

Some historians have taken these ethno-political divisions to mean that party programs and ideologies are largely political window-dressing, having little to do with the way people vote. Samuel P. Hays, for example, argues that party ideologies never reflect the major concerns of grass-roots voters, and that on the local level ethno-cultural issues are much more effective in mobilizing electoral support than such national questions as the tariff and trusts (and presumably, slavery). Similarly, Lee Benson's pioneering study of New York voting behavior in the Jacksonian era, while by no means minimizing the role of ideology, concludes that such ethnic groups as native-born Protestants and immigrant Irish Catholics voted in different parties as one expression of the deep antipathy they felt for one another in view of their antithetical systems of value and ways of life. According to the ethnic analysis of politics, nativism and temperance, not anti-slavery, were responsible for the political upheaval of the 1850's. Or, as Hays puts it, all three movements were outgrowths of the same cultural impulse, evangelical Protestantism, and all reflected the cultural consciousness of native-born Protestant voters. Together, Hays says, they "produced both a sharp realignment of voting behavior and a cultural unity for the Republican party." [3] The implication is that the Republican party was as much a vehicle for anti-Catholic and anti-foreign sentiment as for anti-slavery.

There is no question that Republicanism was in part an expression of the hopes and fears of northern native-born Protestants. As Benson points out, the Whig-Republican view that the state should have broad powers to regulate the economic life of the nation had important moral implications as well. Reform movements such as temperance and anti-slavery, which proposed to use state power to attack moral evils, appealed to New England Protestants because of their tradition of "moral stewardship," what one historian calls their "zeal for making

2. Joseph Schafer, ed., *Intimate Letters of Carl Schurz, 1841–69* (Madison, 1928), 180.
3. Samuel P. Hays, "Political Parties and the Community-Society Continuum," in *The American Party Systems*, eds., Chambers and Burnham, 155, 158, 161–62; Samuel P. Hays, "History as Human Behavior," *IJH*, LVII (July 1960), 195–97; Benson, *Concept*, 165–78, 322–23. Cf. Joel H. Silbey, ed., *The Transformation of American Politics, 1840–1860* (Englewood Cliffs, 1967), 3–4.

others act correctly." According to Clifford S. Griffin, this attitude
stemmed from the Calvinist tradition that there was a moral aristocracy
on earth, whose duty it was to oversee the moral conduct of others
and remove sin from the world. The Yankee followers of the Republican
party felt this mission particularly threatened by the waves of immigrants, mostly Catholics, who poured into the country in the 1840's
and 1850's. Moreover, as Will Herberg has observed, perhaps the only
cement which has bound American Protestants together has been their
fear and hatred of Rome.[4] Many Republicans made it clear that they
shared this traditional feeling and considered the United States a part
of the world Protestant community. "American civilization," said
George William Curtis, "in its idea, is historically, the political aspect
of the Reformation. America is a permanent protest against absolutism. . . ." The Catholic Church to these Republicans represented
tyranny, while Protestantism meant liberty. Anti-slavery, said the
Massachusetts radical E. L. Pierce, was merely a reflection of the
general principle of liberty and equal rights expressed in the Declaration of Independence. "It is the principle," he continued, "which sus-
tained the States of Holland, when they bade defiance to the tides of
the ocean, the rage of the Inquisition, and the colonial power of Spain."
Similarly, John P. Hale and other Republicans opposed the annexation
of Cuba not only on anti-slavery grounds, but because the Cuban
population was largely Catholic and the American system of government could "only be maintained . . . on the principle of Protestant
liberty." For men like Hale, American democracy was not a historical
accident—it sprang logically from the fact that the early settlers had
been Anglo-Saxon Protestants. "The people made this government,
and not the government the people," wrote Charles Francis Adams,
and he believed that an influx of a different people, schooled in the
traditions of absolutism, would undermine American institutions.[5]
Many Republicans shared the nativist outlook which Milton Gordon

4. Benson, *Concept*, 180, 199–200, 206; Clifford S. Griffin, *Their Brothers'
Keepers: Moral Stewardship in the United States, 1800–1865* (New Brunswick,
1960), x–xiii, 5, 21; Seymour M. Lipset, "Religion and Politics in the American
Past and Present," in *Religion and Social Conflict*, eds., Robert Lee and Martin E.
Marty (New York, 1964), 75, 108.
5. Charles E. Norton, ed., *Orations and Addresses of George William Curtis* (3
vols.: New York, 1894), I, 51; Boston *Daily Traveller*, in Charles Francis Adams
Diary, October 28, 1858, Adams Papers, MHS; *Congressional Globe*, 35 Congress,
2 Session, Appendix, 165–66; [Charles Francis Adams], "The Reign of King
Cotton," *Atlantic Monthly*, VII (April 1861), 453. Cf. Boston *Evening Telegraph*,
October 3, 1854, January 23, 1855; *Ohio State Journal*, November 14, 1856.

has termed "Anglo-conformity," and which demands the complete renunciation by immigrant groups of their Old World cultural ancestry, and an unqualified commitment to assimilation into the dominant Anglo-Saxon culture of the United States. Its ideal of American society is the melting pot, rather than a pluralist culture in which divergent ethnic groups live in more or less segregated enclaves. Ante-bellum American society, however, was far from reflecting the melting pot ideal. Studies of a number of northern cities have concluded that immigrants tended to live in their own communities, and instead of desiring assimilation, they consciously strove to re-establish European traditions and values in the United States.[6] The refusal of immigrants to give up their cultural ancestry was a major complaint of nativists, shared by many Republicans who opposed the more extreme anti-foreign program. The Springfield *Republican*, for example, explained in 1854 that while it opposed "organized opposition to any portion of our population," it agreed that "it is good policy to Americanize everything resident in America." The New York *Times* put it more bluntly. The way for immigrants to escape nativist attacks, it declared, was to assimilate fully into American culture: [7]

> There is one duty we would earnestly urge upon the plain good sense and just feeling of our adopted citizens. It is the duty of thoroughly *Americanizing* themselves. . . . They should imbue themselves with American feelings. They should not herd themselves together for the preservation of the customs, habits, and languages of the countries from which they came.

These Republicans did not demand that immigrants give up all their values and beliefs as the price for acceptance in America. They believed that a "protestant toleration of all creeds and opinions" ought to be observed. But they did insist that the clannishness and self-segregation of immigrant groups come to an end, so that the United States could be "one harmonious and homogeneous people." [8]

6. Milton M. Gordon, *Assimilation in American Life* (New York, 1964), 85–98; Oscar Handlin, *Boston's Immigrants* (Cambridge, 1959), 161–76; Oscar Handlin, "Immigration in American Life: A Reappraisal," in *Immigration and American History*, ed., Henry Steele Commager (Minneapolis, 1961), 13; Holt, "Forging a Majority," 22–24; Joseph Schafer, "The Yankee and the Teuton in Wisconsin," *WisMH*, VII (1923–24), 156–58.
7. Springfield *Republican*, March 31, 1854; New York *Times*, June 23, 1854. Cf. *Liberator*, August 31, 1860; New York *Times*, April 7, 1852, December 6, 1854; Maldwyn A. Jones, *American Immigration* (Chicago, 1960), 156.
8. Boston *Atlas and Daily Bee*, July 15, 1858; Philadelphia *North American and United States Gazette*, June 5, 1857.

There were several other reasons, however, why many Republicans found nativist ideas attractive. Political nativism gave expression to the widespread concern among native-born citizens about the increasing political participation and power of foreigners. It was only natural that such feelings were especially pronounced among Whigs and, later, Republicans, because immigrants were generally absorbed into the urban political machines of the Democratic party and voted over-whelmingly for Democratic candidates. Federal law prescribed a five-year naturalization period before immigrants could attain citizen-ship, but in some Democratic states even this waiting period was waived, and resident aliens who declared their intention to become citizens were given the vote.[9] Whigs and Republicans strongly believed that the immigrants' increasing political power was being wielded by the Catholic Church and the Democratic bosses, especially since they thought foreigners were "by education and custom . . . more sub-missive to the voice of authority" than native-born Americans. Nativists charged that unscrupulous Democratic politicians obtained fraudulent naturalization papers for foreigners, and then herded them to the polls to vote the straight Democratic ticket. It was a major demand of the Know-Nothing party, and of many Republicans as well, that a system of voter registration be established to prevent these frauds and "secure the purification of the ballot-box."[10]

Because the political power of the immigrants was concentrated in the large towns and cities, the nativist reaction was most pronounced there. But rural anti-slavery men had their own reasons for resenting the political power of foreigners. Many Republicans were advocates of temperance legislation, while German and Irish immigrants were known to enjoy a good drink, and regularly voted against prohibition legisla-tion. Even more important, anti-slavery men were outraged by immi-

9. Carl F. Brand, "History of the Know-Nothing Party in Indiana," *IndMH*, XVIII (1922), 56–57; Jones, *American Immigration*, 141–43, 153–55; Holt, "Forging a Majority," 213–14; Schafer, "Yankee and Teuton," 159–61; Thomas J. Curran, "Know-Nothings of New York State" (unpublished doctoral dissertation, Columbia University, 1963), 97; Kenneth Stampp, *Indiana Politics During the Civil War* (Indianapolis, 1949), 9.
10. *Address of His Excellency Nathaniel P. Banks, to the Two Branches of the Legislature of Massachusetts, January 7, 1859* (Boston, 1859), 9; "Speech of Daniel Ullmann, Esq.," news clipping, August, 1858, Daniel Ullmann Papers, NYHS. Cf. C. Maxwell Myers, "The Rise of the Republican Party in Pennsylvania, 1854–1860" (unpublished doctoral dissertation, University of Pittsburgh, 1940), 30.

grant opposition to the anti-slavery movement. Nowhere was this more apparent than in Massachusetts, whose Irish immigrants were products of a culture characterized by hostility to reformism and deep respect for class distinctions. The pro-slavery atttudes of Boston's Irish were notorious, and Free Soilers attributed their electoral defeats in large measure to the Irish vote. Then in 1853, after the anti-slavery men had succeeded in drafting a new constitution substantially reducing the political power of conservative Boston, the document was defeated at the polls by the Irish vote.[11] When the Know-Nothing movement emerged in 1854, one political observer declared that it was "controlled in great measure by Free Soilers, who have been much outraged by the movement of the Catholics against the Constitution." "The Catholic press upholds the slave power," declared a Boston Free Soil organ. "These two malign powers have a natural affinity for each other." [12]

Another cause of Republican resentment against immigrants was that many blamed the newcomers for the social ills of the large cities. In the 1850's, large numbers of immigrants were dependent on local and state authorities for relief—in New York City in 1860, 80 per cent of the paupers were foreign-born—and immigrants were disproportionately represented in crime statistics. In view of the free labor attitude towards the native-born poor, it is hardly surprising that Republican spokesmen exhibited a lack of compassion for the poverty of immigrants. Most of them, said the Philadelphia *North American,* were unwilling to work and had come to this country "to steal or beg a living" as best they could.[13] In an era when eastern cities were plagued by expanding slums, increasing poverty, and rising crime rates, many Republicans feared that the influx of immigrants was threatening to

11. Benjamin F. Wade to William Schouler, May 3, 1855, William Schouler Papers, MHS; William G. Bean, "Party Transformation in Massachusetts with Special Reference to the Antecedents of Republicanism 1848–1860" (unpublished doctoral dissertation, Harvard University, 1922), 174–79, 195–223; William G. Bean, "An Aspect of Know-Nothingism—The Immigrant and Slavery," *SAQ,* XXIII (October 1924), 319–24; Boston *Commonwealth,* November 22, 1853; Handlin, *Boston's Immigrants,* 125–41; Joseph R. Gusfield, *Symbolic Crusade: Status Politics and the American Temperance Movement* (Urbana, 1963), 6, 55–56.
12. James W. Stone to Charles Sumner, March 15, 1854, Charles Sumner Papers, Houghton Library, Harvard University; Boston *Commonwealth,* June 24, 1854.
13. Jones, *American Immigration,* 133; Philadelphia *North American and United States Gazette,* November 20, 1855. Cf. New York *Times,* March 20, 1852, January 20, 1858; *Congressional Globe,* 35 Congress, 1 Session, 1005, 36 Congress, 1 Session, Appendix, 174; New York *Tribune,* March 16, 1853; Cleveland *Leader,* November 16, 1857.

destroy the free labor ideal of an open society. Frederick Law Olmsted, for example, concluded after visiting the South that economic opportunity was far greater for the northern poor than for the southern, but he warned that in its large cities the North seemed to be "taking some pains to form a permanent lower class"—exactly the class which Republicans claimed did not exist in free labor society. In terms of the free labor outlook, the poverty of the immigrants marked them as somehow inferior to the Yankees, who dominated the economic life of the North even in areas where immigrants were preponderant. George R. Taylor has commented upon the "discipline, sobriety, and reliability," which Yankees—both factory workers and business leaders—displayed, and on their "spirit of achievement." These qualities, many Republicans believed, were sorely needed by the immigrants, particularly the Irish. As E. Pershine Smith, a New York politician and disciple of Henry Carey, wrote, he preferred German immigrants to the Irish, because the Irish tended to be employed as wage earners while the Germans "become either artisans or cultivators of their own land at once." [14]

There were thus several areas of convergence between the Republican free labor outlook and nativism. Yet in assessing the political impact of nativism, one must also recall that many Republicans who shared nativist suspicions regarding Catholics and immigrants, and who supported the temperance cause, strenuously opposed the emergence of nativism as a political movement. Two powerful elements in the Republican party, the radicals and the followers of William H. Seward, had compelling ideological reasons for combating nativist influence. The radical Republicans viewed the upsurge of nativism exactly as they viewed other political events of the 1840's and 1850's; their first concern was how it would affect the anti-slavery cause. In one respect they did welcome the new movement, for the nativist upsurge of 1854–55 helped accomplish what the radicals themselves had long desired—the break-up of one or both of the major national parties. Samuel Gridley Howe, for example, declared that "the demolition of the two corrupt old organizations is a great good," in spite of the

14. Douglas T. Miller, *Jacksonian Aristocracy: Class and Democracy in New York, 1830–1860* (New York, 1967), 128–54; Frederick Law Olmsted, *A Journey in the Back Country* (New York, 1863), 416; George R. Taylor, "The National Economy Before and After the Civil War," in *Economic Change in the Civil War Era*, eds., David T. Gilchrist and W. David Lewis (Greenville, Del., 1965), 18–19; E. Pershine Smith to Henry C. Carey, March 11, 1858, Carey Papers, HSPa.

"selfish, narrow, and inhumane" nature of the nativist program.[15] Yet few radicals had even this much to say for the Know-Nothings. Those who had participated in the Liberty and Free Soil parties had long believed that the nation should cordially welcome immigrants and had always opposed efforts to abridge their rights.[16] Gamaliel Bailey, editor of the radical *National Era,* was merciless in his condemnation of nativism in 1854 and 1855, even though it cost him many subscribers, particularly in Massachusetts and Connecticut. Know-Nothingism, he declared, was "inconsistent with the fundamental principles of civil and religious liberty, as embodied in our free institutions." In 1854 all the leading Senate radicals voted in favor of Salmon P. Chase's motion allowing immigrants to benefit from the homestead act.[17]

Equally important in the radicals' opposition to nativism was their calculation of the movement's effect on the political fortunes of anti-slavery. Basically, anti-slavery men considered Know-Nothingism an unfortunate aberration which diverted attention from the anti-slavery cause and divided its adherents. "But for this ill-timed and distracting crusade against the Pope and the foreigners," said George Julian in 1855, "Freedom was bound to have taken possession of the government at the close of this execrable administration." In Illinois, Lyman Trumbull, not a radical but a sincere anti-slavery man, agreed that Know-Nothingism and temperance were irritating "side issues," preventing the formation of a united anti-administration party based on the slavery question.[18] The radicals believed that despite abuses of immigrants' political power, the demands of the Know-Nothings were excessive and unjustified, while the real danger to liberty—the Slave Power—

15. Samuel Gridley Howe to Horace Mann, November 14, 1854, Samuel Gridley Howe Papers, Houghton Library, Harvard University. Cf. John G. Palfrey to Giddings, December 20, 1854, Giddings Papers; Giddings to Palfrey, November 27, 1854, John G. Palfrey Papers, Houghton Library, Harvard University.
16. Joel Goldfarb, "The Life of Gamaliel Bailey Prior to the Founding of the *National Era;* the orientation of a Practical Abolitionist" (unpublished doctoral dissertation, University of California at Los Angeles, 1958), 309–11; *National Era,* February 8, 1849, April 1, 1852; Kirk Porter and Donald B. Johnson, comps., *National Party Platforms 1840–1956* (Urbana, 1956), 19.
17. Gamaliel Bailey to Charles Francis Adams, January 23, 1855, Adams Papers; *National Era,* November 30, 1854; *Congressional Globe,* 33 Congress, 1 Session, 1740.
18. George W. Julian to E. A. Stansbury, September 14, 1855, Giddings-Julian Papers, LC; Mildred C. Stoler, "The Influence of the Democratic Element in the Republican Party of Illinois and Indiana, 1854–1860'" (unpublished doctoral dissertation, Indiana University, 1938), 98. Cf. Sumner to Howe, January 13, 1855, Sumner Papers; George W. Julian, *Speeches on Political Questions* (New York, 1872), 122.

was ignored by them. "Neither the Pope nor the foreigners ever can govern the country or endanger its liberties," wrote Charles A. Dana of the New York *Tribune* after the election of 1856, "but the slave-breeders and slavetraders *do* govern it. . . ." Indeed, some radicals went so far as to describe the whole Know-Nothing movement as a southern plot to cripple the anti-slavery movement just at the moment of its greatest chance for success. The goal of the radicals for over a decade had been to make anti-slavery the focal point of national politics. They were not willing to let Know-Nothingism stand in their way.[19]

The struggle against nativism within the Republican party also drew strength from the position of William H. Seward, perhaps the party's single most popular leader. Seward had long been involved in a bitter struggle with New York nativists, dating from his proposal as governor of New York to appropriate public money for Catholic parochial schools. There have been many interpretations of Seward's motives, some historians viewing his plan as merely an effort to attract Catholic voters to the Whig party, and others crediting him with purely humanitarian motives.[20] There is no question that Seward had long believed that a major weakness of the Whig party had been its overt or covert hostility to foreigners, and that he did hope the school plan would gain support among immigrant voters. But the conservative Whigs of New York City rejected Seward's plans, and many refused to vote for him in 1840 because of his association with the Catholics. In 1844, Seward blamed Henry Clay's loss of New York on "the jealousy of the Whig party or a portion of it, against foreigners and Catholics. . . ."[21] And in the 1850's he bitterly attacked the Know-Nothing party, and sought to dissociate the Republican movement from nativ-

19. Charles A. Dana to Henry C. Carey, November 27, 1856, Carey Papers; New York *Tribune*, September 3, 1856; J. Robert Lane, *A Political History of Connecticut During the Civil War* (Washington, 1941), 46.
20. For various interpretations, see John W. Pratt, "Governor Seward and the New York City School Controversy, 1840–1842," *NYH*, XLII (October 1961), 351–64; Vincent P. Lannie, "William Seward and Common School Education," *HEdQ*, IV (September 1964), 181–92; Vincent P. Lannie, "William Seward and the New York School Controversy, 1840–1842: A Problem in Historical Motivation," *HEdQ*, VI (Spring 1966), 52–71; Glyndon G. Van Deusen, "Seward and the School Question Reconsidered," *JAH*, LII (September 1965), 313–19.
21. Allan Nevins, ed., *The Diary of Philip Hone* (2 vols.: New York, 1927), I, 509; George E. Baker, ed., *The Works of William H. Seward* (5 vols.: Boston, 1853–84), III, 389; William H. Seward to Henry Clay, November 7, 1844, Seward to Christopher Morgan, June 12, 1843, William H. Seward Papers, Rush Rhees Library, University of Rochester.

ism. For their part, the nativists opposed Seward at every point of his career, although the political magician Thurlow Weed was able to engineer Seward's re-election to the Senate in 1855 by a legislature with a large Know-Nothing contingent. Seward, of course, was quite willing to see the Republican party accept the votes of nativists, but he insisted that no concessions on either anti-slavery or the rights of foreigners be made to attract their support.[22]

Yet even more important than these political considerations was the fact that the encouragement of immigration and the widest possible dispersal of public education were vital parts of Seward's outlook on American society. Seward believed that the combined influences of universal public education, economic expansion, and the influx of immigrant labor would help secure the free labor ideal of social mobility and a steadily improving standard of living for Americans. He also viewed rapid expansion of the labor force as a necessary ingredient in his plans for an American empire. Seward's attitude toward immigrants was purely assimilationist—he accepted the image of America as both a melting pot and an asylum for the oppressed of the Old World, and believed that nativism would only delay social integration. His program of aid to Catholic education, he explained, was intended to facilitate assimilation. "I desire to see the children of Catholics educated as well as those of Protestants," he wrote in 1840, "not because I want them Catholics, but because I want them to become good citizens." Moreover, Seward believed that nativism was incompatible with the essential principles of democracy, which demanded that all subjects of a government be treated equally by the laws. American government, he declared, was founded upon "the rightful political equality of all the members of the state," but the Know-Nothings rejected this principle by attempting "to exclude a large and considerable portion of the members of the state from participation in the conduct of its affairs." [23] Seward's instinct for political

22. Baker, ed., *Seward Works*, II, 267, IV, 244, 284; Frederick Seward, ed., *Seward at Washington* (2 vols.: New York, 1891), I, 264, 269; E. Pershine Smith to Carey, June 14, 1854, Carey Papers. Cf. Thomas J. Curran, "Seward and the Know-Nothings," *NYHSQ*, LI (April 1967), 141–59, and the comment of the New York *Evening Post* when Seward was reelected to the Senate with Know-Nothing votes: "With the example of Seward's re-election, one need not be surprised if the vote of the Know-Nothings is cast for Pope Pius at the next election." (February 3, 1855).
23. Baker, ed., *Seward Works*, I, 56, 198–99, 322; III, 14, 480, 489–99; IV, 284; Benson, *Concept*, 104; New York *Tribune*, June 7, 1853; Glyndon G. Van Deusen, *William Henry Seward* (New York, 1967), 205–06.

power and the problems of governance led him to perceive the essential weakness of nativism in a democracy. No party, he recognized, could govern successfully if it excluded an important segment of the citizenry from meaningful participation in the processes of government.

Seward's attitude toward Know-Nothingism points up the fact that the nativist goal of restricting immigration ran counter to two cardinal objectives of the free labor ideology—free labor control of the western territories, and continuing northern economic expansion. The first consideration was illustrated by the steady southern opposition to homestead legislation in the 1850's and by the South's insistence that such legislation be limited to citizens. For both northerners and southerners believed that the settlement of immigrants in the West would erect an effective barrier against the extension of slavery. Immigrants of all political affiliations demonstrated their preference for life in a free labor society by refusing to settle in the South. When Seward hurled his famous challenge to the South on the eve of the passage of the Kansas-Nebraska bill, forecasting a contest between free and slave labor for control of the territories, he based his confidence in northern victory on the steady stream of immigrants who were making their way westward.[24]

The second contradiction between free labor and nativism was summed up by the New York *Tribune* in 1853: "We have five million acres and need at least one thousand million inhabitants to cultivate them. So we need not dread immigration, but may freely welcome its increasing influx." Economic development, so vital an element of the free labor social outlook, was in large measure dependent upon the continued availability of immigrant labor. "Strike out what the Irishman has done for America," said the Springfield *Republican*, "and the country would be set back fifty years in the path of progress."[25] Indeed, during the Civil War, when the manpower needs of the Union army created a labor shortage in the North, Seward used all the resources of the State Department to induce unemployed European

24. Baker, ed., *Seward Works*, IV, 471. Cf. Boston *Commonwealth*, June 24, 1854; *Congressional Globe*, 35 Congress, 1 Session, 1044, 1980; New York *Evening Post*, November 15, 1858; Roy M. Robbins, *Our Landed Heritage, The Public Domain, 1776-1936* (Princeton, 1942), 176.
25. New York *Tribune*, September 29, 1853; Springfield *Republican*, July 10, 1857. Cf. Arnold W. Green, *Henry Charles Carey, Nineteenth Century Sociologist* (Philadelphia, 1951), 127; Henry C. Carey, *The Harmony of Interests, Agricultural, Manufacturing, and Commercial* (New York, 1856), 229.

THE REPUBLICANS AND NATIVISM

workmen to emigrate to the United States, and the Republican Congress passed an act encouraging immigration. The Republican national
platform of 1864 went so far as to extol immigrants for their previous
contributions to the nation's economic growth, reaffirmed the historic
role of the United States as an asylum for the oppressed of all nations,
and endorsed a "liberal and just naturalization policy, which would
encourage foreign immigration." [26] The needs of the Union and the
northern economy thus took precedence over any lingering nativist
sentiments. The conflict over nativism in the Republican party was a
prolonged and sometimes bitter one, but in a sense, the Republican
party's rejection of nativism during the 1850's and 1860's was inherent
in its free labor ideology.

II

The complex story of the contest between nativism and Republicanism for ascendancy as the major opponent of the Democratic party in
the North begins with the collapse of the second American party system between 1854 and 1856. Ethnic issues, particularly temperance,
had been growing in importance in northern politics during the early
1850's,[27] and when the potent slavery question was reintroduced into
the political scene in 1854, traditional party alignments all but col-
lapsed. In most northern states, it was a combination of issues, not any
one of them, which led to the Democratic debacle in the elections of
1854. The situation in Connecticut was fairly typical. According to
Roger Baldwin, the spring election there led to a "political revolution
. . . growing out of the excitement in relation to the Kansas-Nebraska
outrage, and the Maine Law question."

The Know-Nothings scored striking successes in New York, Massachusetts, and Pennsylvania, where they organized as a separate party.
They carried virtually the entire Massachusetts legislature and elected

26. 37 Congress, 3 Session, Executive Document No. 1, 172; Arthur C. Cole,
The Irrepressible Conflict (New York, 1934), 360–61; David Montgomery, *Beyond
Equality* (New York, 1967), 22; Porter and Johnson, *Party Platforms*, 35–36.
27. Griffin, *Brothers' Keepers*, 150–51, 223–25; John Marsh, *Temperance Recollections* (New York, 1866), 255–58; Eugene H. Roseboom, *The Civil War Era
1850–1873* (Columbus, 1944), 220–26; Arthur C. Cole, *The Era of the Civil
War 1848–1870* (Springfield, 1919), 207–08; Aaron M. Boom, "The Development
of Sectional Attitudes in Wisconsin, 1848–1861" (unpublished doctoral dissertation, University of Chicago, 1948), 78–87; New York *Tribune*, May 13, August
15, October 26, 1853.

all of that state's Congressmen, made a strong showing in New York, and controlled over a third of the vote in the Keystone State.[28] In the Northwest, nativists took part in the fusion anti-Democratic movements, and in several states exerted a strong influence on the candidates and platforms of the new organizations. Their control was most secure in Indiana, where a secret Know-Nothing conclave a few days before the fusion convention decided in advance who the party's nominees would be. The People's Party platform combined the demand for the restoration of the Missouri Compromise with support for a prohibition law, a defense of the Protestant ministry against "abusive attacks," presumably by Catholics, and a demand for a five-year residence before foreigners could vote. In other western states, antislavery dominated the campaign, and even in Indiana its importance should not be minimized. As one Know-Nothing leader put it, the election returns revealed "a deep seated feeling in favor of human Freedom . . . and . . . also a fine determination that hereafter none but Americans in principle as well as by birth, shall rule America." [29]

In sum, a combination of nativism, temperance, and anti-slavery, with the proportions of the mixture varying from state to state and locality to locality, was responsible for the political upheaval of 1854. Stephen A. Douglas recognized this when he declared early in 1855 that the "anti-Nebraska movement" had actually been "a crucible into which [was] poured Abolitionism, Maine liquor law-ism, and what there was left of northern Whiggism, and then the Protestant feeling against the Catholic and the native feeling against the foreigner." The political confusion of 1854–55 was indicated by the fact that of the fusion candidates elected from the Northwest, the *Tribune*

28. Roger S. Baldwin to Roger S. Baldwin, Jr., May 18, 1854, Baldwin Family Papers, Yale University; Roger D. Parmet, "The Know-Nothings in Connecticut" (unpublished doctoral dissertation, Columbia University, 1966), 83–90; Bean, "Party Transformation in Massachusetts," 220–36; Louis D. Scisco, *Political Nativism in New York* (New York, 1901), 109–27; A. K. McClure, *Old Time Notes of Pennsylvania* (2 vols.: Philadelphia, 1905), I, 208–13.

29. Brand, "Know-Nothing Party in Indiana," 62–65, 69–76; Charles Zimmerman, "The Origin and Development of the Republican Party in Indiana," *IndMH*, XIII (1917), 236n.; J. Herman Schauinger, ed., "The Letters of Godlove S. Orth, Hoosier American," *IndMH*, XL (March 1944), 55–59; Roseboom, *Civil War Era*, 293, 336–37; Frank L. Byrne, "Maine Law Versus Lager Beer: A Dilemma of Wisconsin's Young Republican Party," *WisMH*, XLII (Winter 1958–59), 115–18; Sparks, "Republican Party in Iowa," 3–5, 11–18.

Almanac classified four as Know-Nothings and thirty-five as Republicans, while the *Congressional Globe* listed only ten Republicans and twenty-nine Know-Nothings. But in a sense, this confusion was only to be expected. A major political realignment like that which began in 1854 can only be the result of a combination of influences. The election returns in the western states are especially revealing in this regard. The fusionists received 63.1 per cent of the vote in Ohio, 53.4 in Indiana and 56.4 in Illinois, heights they would not again achieve in the 1850's.[30] The combination of anti-slavery, nativism, and temperance had produced a political revolution which no one of them could have achieved by itself.

Despite the smashing anti-Democratic victories of 1854, the formation of state Republican parties was a prolonged and often difficult process. But by 1856, the Republicans were clearly established as the first or second party in most northern states. One reason for the decline of Know-Nothingism was that, despite the party's electoral successes in New England and New York in 1855, the internal divisions in the nativist movement were beginning to manifest themselves. In 1855, a southern Know-Nothing leader wrote the New Yorker Daniel Ullmann, of the utter necessity of avoiding "that dangerous rock of slavery" if the party was to survive as a national institution. But before the year had ended, it was already clear that both the national and state Know-Nothing organizations were imperiled by the same perennial issue which had helped splinter Whiggery. The Know-Nothings' problem with the slavery question was based on the fact that while many of the party's leaders hoped to make it a national organization which could save the Union by diverting public attention from slavery to immigration, nativism and anti-slavery had worked hand in hand in many northern states in the election of 1854. In New England, where the Know-Nothings had become the leading party, their anti-slavery sentiments were also quite pronounced. The New Hampshire Know-Nothing party was controlled by anti-slavery Whigs and Free Soilers and the nativist legislature elected John P. Hale to the Senate and adopted resolutions condemning the Kansas-Nebraska Act and fugitive slave law. And the Massachusetts legislature of 1855

30. *Congressional Globe*, 33 Congress, 2 Session, Appendix, 216; Sister M. Evangeline Thomas, *Nativism in the Old Northwest, 1850–1860* (Washington, 1936), 180–82; *Tribune Almanac*, 1855, 59–62.

elected the Free Soil radical Henry Wilson to the Senate, passed a personal liberty law, and attempted to remove Judge Loring for his role in the rendition of a fugitive slave. Although Old Line Whigs like Governor Henry Gardner held most of the important positions in the state Know-Nothing party, many Free Soilers gained important posts. Of the eleven Massachusetts Congressmen elected by the Know-Nothing party, seven had been Free Soilers before 1854.[31]

In June, 1855 the national convention of the Know-Nothing party witnessed the most determined attempt to unite all segments of the party on a single platform, an effort which ended in the most singular failure. Led by Henry Wilson, and with Samuel P. Bowles of Massachusetts organizing their moves behind the scenes, fifty-three northern delegates withdrew from the convention when a resolution was adopted disparaging any agitation of the slavery question, and by implication approving the Kansas-Nebraska Act. Among the seceders were moderate former Whigs like Gardner, Thomas Ford of Ohio, and Godlove Orth of Indiana. They all believed that their party would disintegrate in the North if it did not take some anti-slavery stand. "If our delegates had pursued any other course," wrote the Know-Nothing Governor of Connecticut, ". . . the American party would have been blown to atoms in every northern state." A New York Know-Nothing leader agreed. "With the slavery clause in the platform," he wrote Daniel Ullmann, "I doubt very much whether a single county in the State can be carried. . . ."[32] The Philadelphia convention was a major turning point in the history of political nativism. The split within the national party was repeated in state after northern state, as anti-slavery nativists deserted Know-Nothingism for Republicanism, and the Know-Nothing party increasingly came under the control of Silver-Grey Whigs more interested in Unionism than nativism. Five years later, in a campaign speech for Abraham Lincoln, Daniel Ull-

31. Kenneth Raynor to Ullmann, August 21, 1855, Ullmann Papers; James O. Lyford, *Life of Edward H. Rollins* (Boston, 1906), 39; John P. Hale to Thurlow Weed, February 2, 1855, Weed Papers; Bean, "Party Transformation," 272–78; John R. Mulkern, "The Know-Nothing Party in Massachusetts" (unpublished doctoral dissertation, Boston University, 1963), 135; George W. Haynes, "The Causes of Know-Nothing Success in Massachusetts," AHR, III (October 1897), 81n.

32. Henry Wilson to Samuel Bowles, June 23, 1855, in Samuel Bowles II Papers, Yale University; New York *Tribune*, June 12–15, 1855; Thomas, *Nativism*, 176; Parmet, "Know-Nothings in Connecticut," 145; K. Miller to Ullmann, June 24, 1855, Ullmann Papers. Cf. B. Thompson to Ullmann, August 14, 1855, Ullmann Papers.

mann declared that because of its attempt to straddle or ignore the slavery issue, the American party had "gradually melted away." [33]

III

At the same time that the national Know-Nothing movement was experiencing difficulties, state Republican parties were beginning to dissociate themselves from "ethnic" issues. First to be jettisoned was the temperance question. In Maine, where the first prohibition law had been passed in 1851, the Democrats regained control of the legislature in 1855 by capitalizing on the ethnic antagonisms created by a new temperance act passed by the Republican legislature elected the previous year. Republicans vowed to keep the liquor question out of politics in the future. They ignored the Maine law in the 1856 campaign, and the party's platform in 1857 called for a popular referendum on any new laws dealing with liquor. A weak prohibitory measure, hardly satisfactory to ardent temperance advocates, was enacted and approved by the voters in 1858.[34] In New York, the Republicans ignored the liquor issue at their inaugural convention in September, 1855, partly because of the insistence of former Democrats like Abijah Mann and William Cullen Bryant that private conduct was not a proper subject for legislative control. Governor Myron H. Clark was denied renomination in 1856 because of his close association with temperance, and when the state's prohibition law was ruled unconstitutional in that year, Republicans took no steps to enact a new measure. A temperance leader later explained why his movement had been eased out of Republican politics: "Thousands of men, we were told, there were in the state, who would vote for an anti-slavery Governor, who would not vote for prohibition." [35]

33. Andrew W. Crandall, *The Early History of the Republican Party* (Boston. 1930), 59; Bean, "Party Transformation," 295; *Speech of Daniel Ullmann of New York, at the Lincoln and Hamlin Ratification Meeting in Newark, N.J., June 12, 1860* (np, nd), 1–2.
34. *The Reminiscences of Neal Dow* (Portland, 1890), 554–63; Frank L. Byrne, *Prophet of Prohibition: Neal Dow and His Crusade* (Madison, 1961), 67–69, 78; James G. Blaine to Hannibal Hamlin, December 27, 1856, "A Maine Law Man" to Hamlin, August 3, 1856, Hannibal Hamlin Papers, University of Maine, Orono. 35. John A. Krout, "The Maine Law in New York Politics," *NYH*, XVII (July 1936), 270–71; New York *Times*, September 29, 1855; Abijah Mann to Weed, September 29, 1855, Weed Papers; New York *Evening Post*, April 3, 27, 1855; Thurlow Weed Barnes, *Memoir of Thurlow Weed* (Boston, 1884), 247; Marsh, *Temperance Recollections*, 297.

The Maine law was also removed from western Republican politics. The Indiana People's Party legislature of 1855 passed a Maine law, but the State Supreme Court ruled it unconstitutional, and the Democrats made effective use of it in the fall campaign. The People's Party adopted a Maine law resolution in 1856, but the issue played little part in the politics of that year. "It was not once mentioned in the discussions of the campaign," a temperance leader later complained. "No preachers were invited to address political meetings. Temperance . . . was denominated a 'side issue,' not to be tolerated in a national party, such as the Republican Party had become." In Illinois, the anti-Nebraska legislature of 1855 passed a prohibitory law, but it went down to defeat in a referendum. The measure received its strongest support in the Yankee anti-slavery areas of the northern part of the state, but the German voters, particularly in Chicago, turned out against the measure overwhelmingly. Since their votes were crucial for Republican success, the temperance issue was ignored when the new party was organized in 1856.[36] The same consideration influenced the abandonment of prohibition by the Wisconsin Republicans. The Republican legislature of 1855 passed a Maine law, exempting beer, wine, and cider to appease the Germans. But the Democratic governor vetoed the measure, and his party ran an anti-Maine law campaign which brought it within a few votes of victory. The Republicans dropped the prohibition question in 1856, and in the state legislature they voted to postpone indefinitely the question of a new Maine law. The Republicans' reluctance to become involved in the temperance question was symbolized when the party's members in the Ohio legislature of 1859 intentionally voted on both sides of the prohibition issue, "so it cannot be made a party issue," the editor of the *Ohio State Journal* explained.[37]

At the same time they were abandoning temperance, Republicans in many states were combating nativist influence within and outside the Republican organization. One of the most prolonged struggles oc-

36. Griffin, *Brothers' Keepers*, 231; Rev. T. A. Goodwin, *Seventy-Six Years' Tussle With the Traffic* (Indianapolis, 1883), 22–23; Thomas J. McCormack, ed., *Memoirs of Gustav Koerner 1809–1896* (2 vols.: Cedar Rapids, 1909), I, 622–23; David Davis to Julius Rockwell, December 27, 1855 (copy), David Davis Papers, ChicHS; Cole, *Civil War Era*, 210; Albert J. Beveridge, *Abraham Lincoln 1809–1858* (2 vols.: Boston, 1928), II, 293–96.
37. Byrne, "Maine Law," 118–20; Boom, "Sectional Attitudes in Wisconsin," 98–105, 117–19; H. D. Cooke to John Sherman, February 19, 1859, John Sherman Papers, LC.

curred in Massachusetts, where a group of anti-slavery radicals who had refused to join the nativists in 1854 led the movement to organize a separate Republican party in 1855. Former Conscience Whig leaders Charles Francis Adams, Stephen C. Phillips, Edward L. Pierce, Samuel Gridley Howe, and Francis Bird, with encouragement from out-of-state radicals like Giddings, met soon after the Know-Nothing success of November 1854, to plan an anti-nativist strategy. Their efforts culminated in the Chapman Hall meeting of August 1855, in which the Free Soilers and a group of influential moderate Whigs agreed on the necessity for a new party based on anti-slavery principles. The Know-Nothings soon joined in the fusion movement, hoping to control it, but at the September Worcester Convention, the Republican Julius Rockwell narrowly defeated Know-Nothing Governor Henry Gardner for the party's gubernatorial nomination, and a strong anti-slavery platform was adopted.[38] "The incubus of Know-Nothingism is thrown off," wrote Adams, who had played a crucial role in drafting the resolutions and in engineering Rockwell's nomination. But the Know-Nothings, unwilling to accept defeat, renominated Gardner at their own convention. Despite the radicals' hopes, Gardner was re-elected, but the split of the nativists on the slavery issue had begun. Of the eleven Know-Nothing Congressmen elected in 1854, seven demonstrated that they put anti-slavery above nativism by supporting Rockwell.[39]

The political pattern in New York was strikingly similar to that of Massachusetts. Here, too, a separate Republican organization was created in 1855, only to be defeated by the nativists. Along with the Seward Whigs, the party had a sizable anti-nativist contingent in the Barnburner Democrats, who had long worked with immigrant voters, and still believed that, as Timothy Jenkins put it, "the foreigners are our natural allies." [40] The Republican platform condemned secret political organizations—a direct slap at the Know-Nothings—and the

38. Charles Francis Adams Diary, December 27, 1854, January 6, 10, 13, 17, August 16, 22, 1855, Adams Papers; James M. Stone to Sumner, December 29, 1854, Sumner Papers; Howe to Sumner, January 19, 1855, Howe Papers; Richard Henry Dana, Jr. to Mrs. Arnold, October 8, 1855, Richard Henry Dana, Jr. Papers, MHS; Bean, "Party Transformation," 314–21.

39. Charles Francis Adams Diary, September 21, 1855, Adams Papers; Bean, "Party Transformation," 322–24; Boston Evening Telegraph, December 5, 1856; Martin B. Duberman, "Some Notes on the Beginnings of the Republican Party in Massachusetts," NEQ, XXXIV (September 1961), 364–70.

40. Timothy Jenkins to Hamlin, November 7, 1856, Hamlin Papers. Cf. Isaac Sherman to Nathaniel P. Banks, March 5, 1856, Nathaniel P. Banks Papers, LC; New York Evening Post, January 13, 19, 1855.

party carried the radical areas of western New York and the Barn-burner strongholds of the northeast. Anti-slavery nativists were ob-viously leaving the Know-Nothing party for the Republican, while the nativists' strength was increasingly concentrated in the conserva-tive areas surrounding New York City. The 1855 campaign set the basis for a successful Republican party in New York State, combining Seward Whigs and radical Democrats on an anti-slavery platform.[41]

As in New York, nativism reached the peak of its influence in the Northwest during 1855, but its decline was much more dramatic here, where the foreign-born population ranged from 9 per cent in Indiana to over 33 per cent in Wisconsin. The pivotal struggle between na-tivists and anti-slavery men for control of the western fusion move-ments took place in Ohio in 1855. As soon as the election of 1854 had been decided, anti-slavery radicals, led by Chase and Giddings, began to prepare for the next campaign, insisting that the slavery question be, as Giddings put it, "the issue and the sole issue" of 1855. Giddings and the Western Reserve radicals were averse to any co-operation with the nativists—they insisted that the Know-Nothings abandon their lodges and join the Republican organization without any concessions from the anti-slavery forces. They demanded that Chase be the Republican nominee for governor, and threatened to form an independent party if he were not selected.[42] Chase himself took a flexible stand, working for his own nomination while attempting to moderate the sometimes bitter radical attacks on the nativists. But he did insist that the Know-Nothings continue to work as one element of the Republican coalition, rather than attempting to make it "an exclusively K. N. assocation." And Chase steadfastly refused to join the secret order, despite the Know-Nothings' insistence that such a

41. Ernest R. Muller, "Preston King: A Political Biography" (unpublished doc-toral dissertation, Columbia University, 1957), 559–64; Scisco, Political Nativism, 153, 168; Curran, "Know-Nothings of New York," 197–98; New York Evening Post, December 18, 1855; E. Pershine Smith to Carey, November 13, 1855, Carey Papers; Francis E. Spinner to John C. Underwood, October 9, 1856, John C. Underwood Papers, LC.
42. Thomas, Nativism, 101; Giddings to Palfrey, December 30, 1854, Palfrey Papers; Eugene H. Roseboom, "Salmon P. Chase and the Know-Nothings," MVHR, XXV (December 1938), 337–39; David H. Bradford, "The Background and Formation of the Republican Party in Ohio, 1844–1861" (unpublished doctoral dissertation, University of Chicago, 1947), 145n.; Giddings to Salmon P. Chase, May 1, 1855, Salmon P. Chase Papers, HSPa; Giddings to Julian, May 30, 1855, Giddings-Julian Papers, LC; M. H. Nichols to Salmon P. Chase, April 14, 1855, Salmon P. Chase Papers, LC.

move must precede his nomination. He had long courted the Ohio German vote, and now declared that he could not "proscribe men on account of their birth" or "make religious faith a political test." Chase was assisted in his efforts by the influential Whig editor Oran Follett, who believed that if properly coaxed the Know-Nothings would gradually abandon nativism for anti-slavery, while an open split between the two elements of the fusion movement would do the anti-slavery cause irreparable harm.[43]

The Republican Convention of July 1855 nominated Chase on a purely anti-slavery platform, while it chose a ticket of Know-Nothings to run with him. Though Chase openly declared during the campaign of 1855 that he was not a member of the order, the Know-Nothings still provided him with his margin of victory, since an independent nativist nominee received only 8 per cent of the vote. Chase used his influence as governor to erase the vestiges of nativism in the Ohio Republican party. He nominated Germans and anti-slavery nativists for public offices, and insisted that his choices be approved by the Republican legislature. The Ohio Republican platform of 1856 invited "all citizens, whether of foreign or of native birth" to join the party, and in 1857, none of the Know-Nothings who had run with Chase was renominated on his ticket. The nativists had been absorbed into the Republican party without being able to commit the party to an anti-Catholic or anti-foreign platform. "Ohio," Chase wrote, "has been the theatre of a trial of strength between the Anti-Nebraska principle and the Know-Nothing idea," and he and the other radicals were quite pleased with the outcome.[44]

The only western state in which the Know-Nothings continued to dominate the fusion movement after 1854 was Indiana, but even here nativist influence was on the decline by 1856. At the state People's Party Convention a prior agreement for a split Republican-American ticket was rejected in favor of a ticket with only one nativist, and the

43. L. Belle Hamlin, ed., "Selections from the Follett Papers," *Quarterly Publications* of the Ohio Historical and Philosophical Society, XIII (1918), 64; Chase to E. L. Pierce, May 14, 1855, in Sumner Papers; Annie A. Nunns, "Some Letters of Salmon P. Chase 1848–1865," *AHR*, XXXIV (April 1929), 551; J. W. Schuckers, *The Life and Public Services of Salmon Portland Chase* (New York, 1874), 158; Oran Follett to Chase, January 7, May 2, 1855, Chase Papers, LC.
44. Roseboom, "Chase and the Know-Nothings," 341–49; *National Era*, July 26, 1855; Chase to E. L. Pierce, April 15, 1856, in Sumner Papers; Joseph P. Smith, *History of the Republican Party in Ohio* (2 vols.: Chicago, 1898), I, 62; Chase to James Grimes, June 27, 1855, Chase Papers, HSPa.

platform did not go beyond condemning immigrant voting before the five-year naturalization period had expired.[45] The nativist decline was even swifter in Illinois, Wisconsin, and Iowa, all of which had substantial German populations whom the Republicans hoped to attract. As in Ohio, Illinois radicals insisted that the platform be free from nativism. A strong anti-Know-Nothing resolution, according to the Chicago editor Charles H. Ray, would attract "the Germans, English, Protestant Irish, Scotch, and Scandinavian vote—in all about 30,000—more than double the K. N. strength." The German leaders of Illinois, most notably Gustav Koerner, held aloof from the new party until they received assurances that no nativist resolutions would be included in its platform. There was "considerable difficulty" over the platform at the Bloomington Convention of May 1856, but an anti-nativist resolution was finally adopted. The German leader Francis A. Hoffman was nominated for lieutenant-governor.[46]

Wisconsin had the largest proportion of foreign-born residents of any northern state—over one-third in 1860. Too close an identification with nativism was thought to be suicidal by both Republicans and Democrats, and each tried to pin the Know-Nothing label on the other. At the Republican Convention of 1855, the radical leaders Byron Paine and Sherman Booth insisted that the party repudiate nativism and nominate no candidates offensive to foreign voters. Paine's resolution condemning secret societies was adopted, as was an invitation to all persons, native or foreign, to join the party. Nevertheless, most Know-Nothings went into the Republican party, and the Republican ticket was given an official nativist endorsement—a favor which greatly embarrassed the Republican gubernatorial candidate, who was already burdened with his party's identification with temperance. Some nativists did scratch from the Republican ticket the name of Carl Roeser, the party's German-born candidate for state treasurer, but he ran only 3,500 votes behind the gubernatorial candidate. In Iowa, finally, the

45. Brand, "Know-Nothing Party in Indiana," 273–74, 285–86, 299–300; Russel M. Seeds, *History of the Republican Party in Indiana* (Indianapolis, 1899), 25; Willard H. Smith, "Schuyler Colfax and the Political Upheaval of 1854–1855," *MVHR*, XXVIII (December 1941), 397–98.
46. C. H. Ray to Elihu Washburne, May 4, 1856 (misfiled, 1855), Elihu B. Washburne Papers, LC; Ray to Lyman Trumbull, March 21, 1856, Lyman Trumbull Papers, LC; McCormack, ed., *Koerner Memoirs*, II, 4, 34–35; Theodore C. Pease and James G. Randall, eds., *The Diary of Orville Hickman Browning* (2 vols.: Springfield, 1927–33), I, 237–38; Edward Magdol, *Owen Lovejoy: Abolitionist in Congress* (New Brunswick, 1967), 144–47.

Know-Nothing movement became a major political force in 1855, but when the Republican party was officially organized early in 1856, both temperance and nativism were avoided in order not to offend either Know-Nothings or Germans. A resolution favoring retention of the existing naturalization laws was adopted despite Know-Nothing opposition, and the rest of the platform dealt entirely with the slavery question. Governor Grimes went so far as to declare that the two major principles of Republicanism in Iowa were "Anti-Know-Nothingism and anti-slavery extension." [47]

While the Know-Nothing party was disintegrating in the states under the impact of the slavery issue, a battle was taking place in Congress which had a crucial bearing on the emergence of the national Republican party. Over thirty years ago, Fred H. Harrington showed how the long contest which resulted in the election of Nathaniel P. Banks as Speaker of the House helped to stir anti-slavery feeling in the North, forged a strong organization of Republican Congressmen, and prevented the Know-Nothing Congressmen from forming a national party organization. Although Banks was himself a member of the order, his candidacy was pushed by the anti-slavery radicals in order to destroy national Know-Nothingism and build a Congressional Republican party. By January 1856, Gamaliel Bailey, the radical editor who played a leading role in the day-to-day maneuverings, reported that of the anti-Nebraska Congressmen, thirty-five were opposed to nativism altogether, thirty to forty had some connection with the order but wished to subordinate nativism to anti-slavery, and the rest were found over the remainder of the political spectrum, all the way to bigoted xenophobia. Bailey put his finger on the main consequence of the speakership fight when he noted, "Some who came here more 'American' than Republican are now more Republican than American." Northern Silver-Greys like Congressman G. G. Haven of New York, who hoped to create a national Know-Nothing party for 1856, were dismayed by the course of events. The controversy over Kansas, Haven complained to Daniel Ullmann, had irrevocably split northern from southern nativists, and many Know-Nothing Congressmen were acting as if they were Republicans. Haven himself refused

47. Joseph Schafer, "Know-Nothingism in Wisconsin," *WisMH*, VIII (September 1924), 12–20; Chester V. Easum, *The Americanization of Carl Schurz* (Chicago, 1929), 141–43; Sparks, "Republican Party in Iowa," 19–32; Salter, *Grimes*, 79–80; Louis Pelzer, "The Origin and Organization of the Republican Party in Iowa," IJHP (October 1906), 503–4.

to support Banks, vowing that he would "stand upon purely conservative middle ground, making the American question subordinate to no other and fighting extreme men North and South." But most northern Know-Nothings finally supported Banks, and Samuel Bowles was not far wrong when he wrote that the Speaker fight was "settling the . . . new order of things, politically, for the next generation." [48] The Speakership contest helped make the Republicans a sectional and anti-slavery, not a national and nativist party.

The month of February, 1856 in which Banks's election was secured was a pivotal one in the development of the Republican party. The first national Republican gathering took place in Pittsburgh on Washington's birthday, with radicals in conspicuous attendance, and nativists either absent or silent. Several speakers denounced the order, and when a committee reported that it had been unable to agree on terms of co-operation with a committee of "North Americans," the convention applauded vehemently. A few days later came the break-up of yet another national Know-Nothing convention when seventy-three northern delegates walked out after Millard Fillmore was nominated for President. The North Americans, as the seceders called themselves, hoped to force the June Republican convention to nominate Nathaniel P. Banks for President. But Banks had already arranged to withdraw in favor of John C. Frémont when the Pathfinder was selected by the Republicans. The North Americans anticipated that their vice presidential nominee, William Johnson, would be adopted by the Republicans, but because of the insistence of Horace Greeley and others that the foreign vote not be alienated, William Dayton of New Jersey was chosen instead and the North Americans reluctantly accepted him.[49]

The Republican platform of 1856 was a signal defeat for the nativists. Before the convention, the North Americans indicated that they

48. Fred H. Harrington, " 'The First Northern Victory,' " *JSH*, V (May 1939), 186–205; Gamaliel Bailey to Adams, January 20, 1856, Adams Papers; S. G. Haven to Ullmann, December 13, 16, 1855, Ullmann Papers; O. J. Hollister, *Life of Schuyler Colfax* (New York, 1886), 86; Fred Harvey Harrington, *Fighting Politician, Major General N. P. Banks* (Philadelphia, 1948), 30–31.
49. William B. Hesseltine and Rex C. Fisher, eds., *Trimmers, Trucklers, and Temporizers* (Madison, 1961), 102–3; Clarke, *Julian*, 169–70; New York *Tribune*, February 27, 1856; Harrington, *Banks*, 36–38; Fred H. Harrington, "Frémont and the North-Americans," *AHR*, XLIV (July 1939), 842–48; Seward, ed., *Seward at Washington*, I, 283; Roy F. Nichols, "Some Problems of the First Republican Presidential Campaign," *AHR*, XXVIII (April 1923), 492–94.

would prefer the campaign to turn on the repeal of the Missouri Compromise and the admission of Kansas as a free state, rather than on the question of slavery in all the territories. But a radical platform was adopted. A dispute arose on the platform committee about a proposed plank disavowing any intention to proscribe foreign-born citizens, but after the wording was modified by Charles Francis Adams the resolution was adopted. German Republicans had made such a statement a condition of their support, and as one of them wrote, it was "a pretty hard pill for the Native Americans to swallow." [50] Moreover, although Seward was eliminated from contention by the unmitigated hostility of the nativists, Frémont was considered by the Germans to be the least offensive of the other Republican aspirants.[51]

The electoral strategy of the Republican party in 1856 varied from state to state, but almost everywhere the campaign was dominated by the issue of slavery extension. Soon after his election as Ohio's governor in 1855, Salmon Chase had outlined a program for national victory in 1856. "It seems to me," he wrote Governor Kinsley Bingham of Michigan, "that we can only carry the next Presidential election by making the simple issue of Slavery or Freedom. We shall need the liberal Americans and we shall also need the antislavery adopted citizens." But the foreign vote remained with the Democrats—Republicanism being still too closely identified with nativism and prohibition —and enough Know-Nothings voted for Fillmore to give the election to Buchanan.[52] One potent charge which the Fillmore men and Democrats used against the Republicans was the accusation that Frémont was a Catholic. Republican leaders and candidates in areas of nativist

50. A. P. Stone to Chase, March 30, 1856, Chase Papers, LC; Charles Francis Adams Diary, June 18, 1856, Adams Papers; McCormack, ed., *Koerner Memoirs*, II, 15, Cf. Seward, ed., *Seward at Washington*, I, 279; H. Kreismann to Banks, June 9, 1856, Banks Papers.
51. New York *Times*, April 18, 1856; Allan Nevins, *Frémont, Pathfinder of the West* (New York, 1955), 428. A short debate at the Philadelphia Convention illuminated the divergent Republican attitudes toward nativism in 1856. A motion was made to receive a communication from a committee of North Americans, but Giddings, speaking for the radicals, urged its rejection. The motion was voted down, but soon a number of eastern Republicans urged its reconsideration, arguing that precipitous action would injure the party, particularly in New England. The convention then reversed its original decision, although Giddings and Owen Lovejoy made it clear that the radicals had not changed their minds. *Proceedings of the First Three Republican National Conventions* (np, nd), 50–55.
52. Chase to Kinsley S. Bingham, October 19, 1855, Chase Papers, HSPa; Hollister, *Colfax*, 104; New York *Times*, November 6, 1856; Elmer D. Elbert, "Southern Indiana Politics on the Eve of the Civil War 1858–1861," (unpublished doctoral dissertation, Indiana University, 1967), 216–17.

strength said that the charge did their cause real damage; Thaddeus Stevens went so far as to blame it for the Republican defeat. Seward almost enjoyed the irony that "Frémont, who was preferred over me because I was not a bigoted Protestant, is nearly convicted of being a Catholic." [53] The election of 1856 proved both that nativism was still a potent force in many areas of the North, and that most northern Know-Nothings had already abandoned that party for the Republicans.

IV

The years 1856 to 1860 witnessed the climax of the struggle in New England between Know-Nothings and Republicans for control of the anti-Democratic movement, while further west the influence of nativism in the Republican movement continued to decline. The party's attitude toward nativism became an issue of national concern with the controversy over the amendment to the Massachusetts Constitution imposing a two-year waiting period after naturalization before foreign-born citizens could vote. Although historians who emphasize the influence of nativism in the Republican movement view the amendment as "a climactic example of the association of nativist sentiment with the Republican party," [54] the circumstances of its passage actually revealed how weak nativism had become in the state where it had been all-powerful just a few years before, and the reaction to it in the western states led the party to dissociate itself entirely from any designs on the rights of foreign-born Americans.

The issue of immigrant voting had held an important place in Massachusetts politics since 1854, when the Know-Nothings swept the state. The extreme nativists in the legislature of 1855 wanted to exclude foreigners from voting and office-holding completely, and Governor Gardner proposed an amendment requiring a twenty-one-year waiting period after naturalization before foreign-born citizens could vote. The measure was strenuously opposed by the anti-slavery Know-

53. Charles T. Congdon, *Reminiscences of a Journalist* (Boston, 1880), 154; Schuyler Colfax to John Bigelow, August 29, 1856, John Bigelow Papers, NYPL; Colfax to Francis P. Blair, July 17, August 15, 1856, Blair-Lee Papers, Princeton University; Samuel Galloway to Solomon Foot, October 23, 1856, Manuscript 2175, WRHS; Thaddeus Stevens to E. D. Gazzam, August 24, 1856, in Edward McPherson Papers, LC; Seward, ed., *Seward*, I, 287.
54. Silbey, *Transformation*, 14–15.

Nothings, led by Henry Wilson, who considered it "disgraceful to the party and the state" (although he felt a ten-year waiting period was acceptable). But it was adopted by the legislature, along with a literacy test for voting and a disbandment of foreign militia companies. Two successive passages were necessary for constitutional amendments, but the 1856 legislature reduced the twenty-one-year waiting period to fourteen. In the 1857 Republican legislature, nativists pressed for a second approval, but the radicals—along with moderate Republican leaders like Samuel Bowles—were able to defeat the fourteen-year period, and substitute a two-year one. Many radicals felt that this too was unacceptable, but others saw it as the only way "to quiet honest nativism." [55]

With a second approval of the two-year amendment by the Republican legislature of 1858, the stage was set for a popular referendum on immigrant voting. In 1859, when the vote took place, Massachusetts Republican leaders were deluged by complaints from party leaders in the West. Adoption of the amendment in a Republican state, they insisted, would seriously impair efforts of western Republicans to attract foreign voters, particularly Germans. The most prominent western Republicans, including Abraham Lincoln, Salmon P. Chase, Lyman Trumbull, James Harlan, and James Grimes, and newspapers like the Detroit *Advertiser*, Chicago *Tribune*, and *Ohio State Journal*, all urged Massachusetts Republicans to defeat the measure. They were joined by German spokesmen like Schurz and Koerner, and such eastern newspapers as the New York *Tribune* and *Evening Post* and Philadelphia *North American*. The protests made a deep impact upon Massachusetts Republicans. Wilson, Bowles, Sumner, and Rockwell all campaigned against the amendment, as did most Republican newspapers in the western part of the state.[56] In eastern Massachusetts,

55. Bean, "Party Transformation," 265, 280–82, 330–31; Henry Wilson to William Schouler, April 16, 1855, Schouler Papers; Wilson to Chase, November 17, 1855, Chase Papers, HSPa; Boston *Evening Traveller*, April 4, 1857; E. L. Pierce to Sumner, March 29, May 10, 1857, Sumner Papers; Springfield *Republican*, February 21, 1857. Cf. Wilson to E. L. Pierce, March 12, April 23, 1857, E. L. Pierce Papers, Houghton Library, Harvard University.
56. E. L. Pierce to Sumner, April 17, May 31, 1859; Frederic Bancroft, ed., *Speeches, Correspondence, and Political Papers of Carl Schurz* (6 vols.: New York, 1913), I, 41–43; McCormack, ed., *Koerner Memoirs*, II, 74–76; Boston *Atlas and Daily Bee*, April 28, May 4, 1859; Springfield *Republican*, March 27, 1860; Samuel Bowles to Henry L. Dawes, April 20, 1859, Henry L. Dawes Papers, LC; Bean, "Party Transformation," 366–72.

however, where Know-Nothing influence was still strong, the Republican press supported the amendment and denounced westerners for interfering in the affairs of Massachusetts. The Boston *Atlas and Daily Bee* said that approval of the amendment was the least Republicans could do to conciliate nativist sentiments, and its editor, William Schouler, remarked that Massachusetts Republicans "might as well find fault with Western Republicans for disfranchising colored men as they to find fault with us for the two years amendment." [57]

The two-year amendment was approved by the voters of Massachusetts in the spring of 1859. But in a year in which over 100,000 persons cast ballots for governor in November, only about 36,000 bothered to vote in the referendum. This is particularly interesting in light of Samuel Hays's insistence that ethnic issues mobilize voters on the local level far more effectively than national questions. If the referendum indicated anything, it was that the citizens of Massachusetts were losing their interest in nativism. When the two-year amendment was adopted for the second time by the legislature in 1858, E. L. Pierce, noting that there was almost no discussion of it, concluded that "the question has evidently lost its interest." Before the 1859 referendum, friends of the amendment had predicted its passage by a majority of over 100,000. But the actual vote was only 20,753 to 15,129. In the solid Republican areas of western Massachusetts the amendment was voted down, its majority coming from the Boston area where the Republican party was weakest, and the Know-Nothings still clung to life. Even if we agree with Congressman Henry L. Dawes that Democrats stayed away from the polls entirely, the result of the referendum indicated, first, that at least half the Republicans were not especially interested in the issue of alien voting, and second, that if Know-Nothing votes are subtracted, Republicans who did vote were probably equally divided on the question. [58] Moreover, as the Springfield *Republican* hastened to point out, although Republicans had held power in almost every northern state by 1859, "no similar enactment has been adopted or even seriously proposed in any other

57. E. L. Pierce to Carl Schurz, May 5, 1859, Carl Schurz Papers, LC; Boston *Atlas and Daily Bee*, May 3, 1859; William Schouler to Chase, May 3, 1859, Chase Papers, HSPa. Cf. Boston *Atlas and Daily Bee*, April 12, 25, 28, 1859; Charles Francis Adams Diary, May 9, 1859, Adams Papers.

58. E. L. Pierce to Sumner, February 25, 1858, Sumner Papers; Boston *Atlas and Daily Bee*, February 9, 1859; *Address of His Excellency John A. Andrew, to the Two Branches of the Legislature of Massachusetts, January 5, 1861* (Boston, 1861), 23; *Congressional Globe*, 36 Congress, 1 Session, 335.

state." [59] Far from demonstrating the connection between Republican-ism and nativism, the two-year amendment indicated that even in Massachusetts nativism was dying out as a political force.

The two-year amendment and the controversy it aroused played an important role in determining the relationship between Republicans and nativism in 1859 and 1860. Republican state conventions in Ohio and Iowa adopted resolutions affirming the equal rights of all citizens and opposing changes in the naturalization laws or legal discrimination between foreign and native-born Americans. In Wisconsin, Carl Schurz demonstrated that an articulate anti-slavery German could rise to a position of state-wide leadership. And in Illinois, Governor William Bissell insisted on appointing immigrants to office. "The Republicans of Wisconsin, Illinois, and some other sections if not states," a New York nativist complained in 1859, "are almost completely Abolitionized and Foreignized." [60] Even in Indiana, the 1858 state convention nomi-nated a German for state treasurer, and also included an Irish Protes-tant on the ticket. Two years later, Indiana Republicans rebuffed Know-Nothing efforts to form a fusion party, and the convention adopted a resolution indirectly criticizing the troublesome two-year amendment by supporting equal rights for all citizens "without refer-ence to their place of nativity," and opposing any changes in the natu-ralization laws. A number of nativist Republicans walked out of the Republican state convention when this resolution was adopted, and a German was again put on the state ticket. [61]

The nativists made their strongest efforts to influence the Republi-can party in the eastern states of Connecticut, New York, and Pennsyl-vania, and though their success was greater there than it had been in

59. Springfield *Republican*, March 27, 1860. This was not quite accurate, since Maine Republicans passed a three-month law in 1855, and the New York Repub-lican platform of 1858 called for an extension of the time between naturalization and suffrage. Byrne, *Dow*, 58; New York *Tribune*, September 11, 1858.

60. Smith, *Ohio Republican Party*, I, 91; Chase to Sumner, June 20, 1859, Sumner Papers; John A. Bingham to Chase, May 12, 1859, Chase Papers; F. I. Herriot, "The Germans of Iowa and the 'Two-Year' Amendment of Massachusetts," *Deutsch-Amerikanische Geschichtsblätter*, XIII (1913), 202–308; Morton M. Rosenberg, "The Election of 1859 in Iowa," *IJH*, LVII (January 1959), 3–19; Thomas, *Nativism*, 228; Koerner to Abraham Lincoln, April 4, 1859, Robert Todd Lincoln Papers, LC; C. H. Ray to Banks, April 2, 1859, H. Kreismann to Banks, April 2, 1859, Banks Papers; L. L. Pratt to Ullmann, May 31, 1859, Ullmann Papers.

61. Seeds, *Republican Party in Indiana*, 27–30; Elbert, "Southern Indiana Politics," 68, 76, 109–10; Zimmerman, "Republican Party in Indiana," 356, 385; Stampp, *Indiana Politics*, 29.

the West, the end result was more or less the same. Nativism posed a formidable dilemma for the Republican organization of New York, the free state in which Fillmore polled his highest percentage of the vote in 1856. Many Republicans, particularly the more conservative group wishing to oust Seward and Weed from the party leadership, urged that a formal fusion between the Republican and American parties take place. But Seward was dead set against any concessions. His position was explained by his political lieutenant, E. Pershine Smith:

> For my part I don't want *any* of them in the Republican party—it was a great blessing to get rid of them, getting as we did in their stead the best part of the Democrats of this state . . . As to Seward, those who come into the party in this state as a matter of course have got to support him . . . the Republican party would, but for him, have lost the German strength which they have since gotten and which is increasing and will increase if we only leave the damned Know-Nothings alone.

The movement for fusion, reaching a head in 1858, was blocked by Weed and Seward. Weed was looking to 1860, and hoped to prove that nativist hostility to Seward was not a serious liability by engineering a Republican victory in 1858 without Know-Nothing votes. The Republican platform did support a registry law and an extension of the time between naturalization and voting, but its address to the voters ignored nativism entirely. The decline of the Know-Nothing vote to 11.2 per cent from 20.9 in 1856 indicates that an increasing number of nativists were being absorbed into the Republican party, despite the refusal of Weed and Seward to make concessions to Know-Nothing feeling.[62]

It was in Pennsylvania that the influence of nativism on the Republican party was most prolonged. The election of 1856, in which Frémont received only 32 per cent of the state's vote and Fillmore 17.8, demonstrated the imperative need for some kind of co-operation between the anti-Democratic parties. An attempt was made to create

---

62. E. Pershine Smith to Carey, July 25, 1858, Carey Papers; Glyndon G. Van Deusen, *Thurlow Weed: Wizard of the Lobby* (Boston, 1947), 235–37; Curran, "Know-Nothings of New York," 269–75; New York *Times*, May 26, September 8–14, 1858; New York *Tribune*, September 11, 1858; *Tribune Almanac*, 1859, 45. For developments in Connecticut, see Parmet, "Know-Nothings in Connecticut," 250–52, 271–337; Alfred C. O'Connell, "The Birth of the G. O. P. in Connecticut," ConnHS *Bulletin*, XXVI (April 1961), 37–38, and for Massachusetts, Bean, "Party Transformation," 344–64.

such a coalition in the Union party of 1857. David Wilmot was nominated for governor, and two of the four places on the Union ticket were given to Know-Nothings. Nonetheless, the nativists were hardly satisfied with either the party's candidate—whose very name insured that slavery would be the focus of the campaign—or the platform, which endorsed the national Republican resolutions of 1856 and conceded to nativism only a statement opposing the naturalization of any immigrants owing allegiance "to any foreign potentate"—i.e. the Pope. Wilmot's defeat proved that anti-slavery alone could not carry Pennsylvania, but he did improve on Frémont's showing by 25 per cent, and the independent nativist ticket received only 28,000 votes, half of them in Philadelphia.[63] In 1858 a new organization, the People's Party, was created, stressing the tariff issue to appeal to the conservative Whig Know-Nothings of southeastern Pennsylvania and the iron manufacturers of the west. The party's platform included moderate nativist demands, such as a ban on the immigration of paupers and criminals, and a call for legislation against voting frauds and for strict enforcement of the naturalization laws. The planks were repeated in the 1859 and 1860 platforms, but the tariff and slavery issues played a larger part in Pennsylvania politics of the pre-war years than outright nativism. However, as we have seen, the demand for a tariff was couched in such a way as to appeal to both anti-slavery advocates and nativists. The defense of northern free labor against competition from foreign cheap labor was a goal both groups could and did support.[64]

Just as nativism was being eased out of the Republican platform in most northern states, Republican Congressmen were having to deal with troublesome questions involving immigrants. As we have seen, the election of 1854 placed a large number of northerners in Congress who owed their seats to Know-Nothing ballots. The strength of nativism in the anti-Democratic northern forces was indicated in a vote of December 22, 1856 on a Know-Nothing resolution asking that the rules be suspended in order to take up a bill repealing the naturalization laws and establishing a uniform code of naturalization. Pre-

63. Warren F. Hewitt, "The Know-Nothing Party in Pennsylvania," *PaH*, II (April 1935), 84–85; Myers, "Rise of Republican Party," 161–62; Holt, "Forging a Majority," 371–72; Washington *Republic*, October 2, 1857.
64. Myers, "Rise of Republican Party," 198–99, 210, 261; Thaddeus Stevens to Chase, September 25, 1858, Chase Papers, HSPa; Holt, "Forging a Majority," 395; *Congressional Globe*, 36 Congress, 1 Session, 1844.

sumably the new code would be harsher than the existing one, which imposed a five-year residence requirement on aliens who wished to become citizens. Needing a two-thirds vote to pass, the resolution failed to obtain even a simple majority, receiving 89 votes to 92 against. Analysis of the Republican vote is difficult, since party affiliations were so confused. But excluding a few Know-Nothings who had defeated fusion anti-Nebraska candidates, the northern anti-Democratic Congressmen elected in 1854 divided 62 in favor and 35 against, with 16 abstentions. But it is revealing that most of the Republican Congressmen who were to go on to positions of state and national leadership, including Schuyler Colfax, Galusha Grow, Jacob Howard, Edwin Morgan, Elihu Washburne, and Israel Washburn opposed the resolution as did the leading Congressional radicals, Giddings, Edward Wade, Francis Spinner, and others. Moreover, outside of New England, the nativist element in the anti-Democratic coalition came from areas where Republicanism was weakest. Thus, of the thirteen Pennsylvania Congressmen who voted for the measure, eight had already been replaced by Democrats in the elections of October and November 1856. Three of the five Indiana Congressmen who supported the nativists had also been replaced by Democrats, while the two Indiana fusionists who opposed the resolution had been re-elected.[65]

The same lame-duck session of the Thirty-fourth Congress also approved an act authorizing Minnesota to draft a constitution as a preliminary to admission as a state. Some Republican Congressmen objected to the measure because it allowed aliens who declared their intention of becoming citizens to vote before naturalization was completed. The provision was denounced by Know-Nothing journals, and twenty-five Republican and fusion Congressmen voted against the act because of it. But they failed to prevent the bill's passage because sixty-seven fusionists voted in the affirmative. The vote indicated that most northern anti-Democratic Congressmen were willing to forego nativism to secure the admission of another free state to the Union, although abstentions were heavy in Massachusetts, New York, and Pennsylvania. And in 1860, Republican Congressmen coalesced behind Galusha Grow's homestead bill, which allowed aliens to claim free land, in preference to the Senate version limiting benefits to citizens.[66]

65. *Congressional Globe*, 34 Conugress, 3 Session, 180; *Tribune Almanac*, 1857, 48–49, 57–58.
66. *Congressional Globe*, 34 Congress, 3 Session, 519, 36 Congress, 1 Session, Appendix, 123. Cf. New York *Evening Post*, February 26, 1857; New York *Tribune*, February 3, 1857.

V

As the Republican Convention of 1860 approached, the party's German-Republican leadership insisted that an anti-nativist plank be incorporated in the national platform. Late in February, the Wisconsin Republican convention, where Carl Schurz's influence ran high, condemned the Massachusetts two-year amendment and called upon the Chicago Convention to repudiate "all violations of equal rights among citizens, without regard to creed or birthplace." Just before the national convention opened, German leaders from throughout the North met at the Deutches Haus in Chicago, and demanded that the party completely dissociate itself from nativism and nominate a candidate acceptable to foreign voters.[67] At the convention itself, Schurz and Gustav Koerner served on the platform committee and exerted their influence in favor of the Deutches Haus resolutions. After a dispute in the full committee, the five-man sub-committee which actually drafted the resolutions decided to accept the German leaders' demands. The fourteenth plank of the platform made it official that the Republicans were more interested in conciliating immigrant voters than in issuing nativist appeals:

> The Republican party is opposed to any change in our naturalization laws, or any state legislation by which the rights of citizens hitherto accorded to immigrants from foreign lands shall be abridged or impaired; and in favor of giving a full and efficient protection to the rights of all classes of citizens, whether native or naturalized, both at home or abroad.

In a debate on the convention floor, Schurz insisted upon the disavowal of state as well as federal legislation, pointing out that the party's pledge of 1856 to oppose national legislation impairing the rights of immigrants had not protected them from injustices imposed by the states—a clear reference to Massachusetts.[68]

The German leaders were quite satisfied with both the nominee and platform of the Republican party in 1860. As might be expected, nativists were disappointed. Both the *Times* and *Tribune* of New York reported from Chicago that there was strong opposition on some

67. *Wisconsin State Journal*, March 1, 1860; J. G. Randall, *Lincoln the President. Springfield to Gettysburg* (2 vols.: New York, 1945), I, 161.
68. *Wisconsin State Journal*, June 4, 1860; McCormack, *Koerner Memoirs*, II, 87; Jones, *American Immigration*, 162; Henry H. Smith, *All the Republican National Conventions* (Washington, 1896), 19; Porter and Johnson, *Party Platforms*, 33; *Proceedings of First Three Republican Conventions*, 127–29.

delegations to the fourteenth plank. Nativist Republicans, Horace
Greeley wrote, regarded it as "an undue pandering to German fanati-
cism." A few days after the convention adjourned, the Boston *Daily
Atlas and Bee* repudiated the plank entirely, and by the end of May,
Lincoln had received reports from Schuyler Colfax and Lyman Trumbull about resentment in nativist areas. Northern Know-Nothings
faced a difficult electoral decision in 1860. Few were enthusiastic
about the Constitutional Union ticket of Bell and Everett, and most
were pleased by the rejection of Seward at Chicago. But as one
nativist leader wrote: [69]

> The Americans feel humiliated by a section of [the Republican]
> platform, because it strikes directly at them, yet they have reluc-
> tantly swallowed the pill. They know too that Lincoln and Hamlin
> are exclusively Republican.

In the campaign of 1860, nativist voters were wooed by such former
Know-Nothing leaders as Daniel Ullmann, whose services were in great
demand in areas like eastern Pennsylvania and New York City. In
some areas Republican spokesmen appealed to nativist voters by
attacking the Pope and Catholic Church, although they carefully
avoided expressing hostility to all foreigners.[70] Lincoln's victory, as
we have seen, was based on holding the former Fillmore supporters
who had been won to the party in 1858 in the doubtful states of
Pennsylvania, Illinois, and Indiana. But while most nativists eventually
cast their lot with the Republicans, they were absorbed into a party
which had made no concessions to them in its platform, and which
viewed their support as a distinct political liability in spite of the
necessity of obtaining their votes. And the election of such anti-
nativist governors as Washburn in Maine, Andrew in Massachusetts,
Yates in Illinois, Blair in Michigan, and Kirkwood in Iowa indicated
that in state after state the struggle for control of the Republican party
was being won by the anti-nativists.

There were many political reasons why nativism became more of a

69. New York *Tribune*, May 18, 1860; New York *Times*, May 18, 1860; Boston
Daily Atlas and Bee, May 23, June 4, 1860; Colfax to Lincoln, May 26, 1860,
Trumbull to Lincoln, May 22, 1860, Lincoln Papers; James F. Babcock to Mark
Howard, August 4, 1860, Mark Howard Papers, ConnHS.
70. New York *Tribune*, July 17, 1860; A. K. McClure to Ullmann, July 18, 1860,
James G. Graham to Ullmann, August 28, 1860, George William Curtis to Ullmann,
September 23, 1860, Ullmann Papers; Holt, "Forging a Majority," 445–46; S. D.
Carpenter, *Logic of History* (Madison, 1864), 27.

liability than an asset for the Republican party. The crucial one was the necessity for attracting part of the foreign vote, particularly the Protestant Germans. If German support for the Republican party was less extensive than historians once believed, it is nonetheless true that many Republicans believed that foreign voters held the balance of power in the western states. This basic political reality was also recognized by the Democrats, and they strove to keep ethnic issues at the center of the political stage, while Republicans increasingly sought to relegate them to the wings. So long as the Republican party was identified with nativism, the Democrats were able to retain their strangle hold on the immigrant vote. After 1856, as anti-slavery supplanted nativism in the Republican program, the Protestant foreign vote began to shift away from the Democrats.[71]

Yet it is too simple to say, as one historian does, that "Republican leaders speedily deserted temperance and anti-foreignism as soon as they realized that anti-slavery was even more popular." [72] This formulation ignores the struggle which radicals, Sewardites, and many Barnburners waged against nativist influence, even when the popularity of Know-Nothingism was at its height. It also fails to note that even in states where Republicans adopted nativist appeals and enacted nativist legislation, what is striking is how mild even these measures were compared with Know-Nothing demands for a twenty-one-year naturalization period and the restriction of office-holding to native-born citizens. These demands never became Republican policy in any state, nor did they come close to being enacted into law.[73] And both ante-

71. Until recently, historians assumed that German voters provided Lincoln's margin of victory in the Northwest in 1860. This view was challenged many years ago by Joseph Schafer, and a number of recent studies correlating local ethnic composition and voting patterns have thrown considerable doubt on the traditional view. Yet it is also clear that after 1856, the Republicans did make inroads into Democratic German strength, and in Illinois it is possible that the traditional interpretation was correct. See Donnal V. Smith, "The Influence of the Foreign-Born of the Northwest in the Election of 1860," *MVHR*, XXIX (September 1932), 192–204; Joseph Schafer, *Four Wisconsin Counties* (Madison, 1927), 140–58; Joseph Schafer, "Who Elected Lincoln?" *AHR*, XLVII (October 1941), 58–59; Robert P. Swierenga, "The Ethnic Voter and the First Lincoln Election," *CWH*, XI (March 1965), 27–44; George H. Daniels, "Immigrant Vote in the 1860 Election: The Case of Iowa," *Mid-America*, LXIV (July 1962), 146–62; Bradford, "Republican Party in Ohio," 218n.; Elbert, "Southern Indiana Politics," 216–17; Donald E. Simon, "Brooklyn in the Election of 1860," *NYHSQ*, LI (July 1967), 260; Jones, *American Immigration*, 161–62; C. H. Ray to Banks, April 2, 1859, Banks Papers.
72. Griffin, *Brothers' Keepers*, 237.
73. The historian of naturalization policies points out that despite the large num-

bellum Republican platforms specifically repudiated nativist appeals
and reaffirmed the right of foreign-born citizens to full equality before
the law.

In discussing the rise and fall of nativism, it is essential to distinguish
sharply between nativism as a cultural impulse, which many Republicans found attractive, and nativism as a force in politics. Although
it was not confined to the Know-Nothing party, the swift rise and
equally sharp decline of Know-Nothingism serve as a useful index to
the fortunes of political nativism. Political nativism reached its peak
in 1854 and 1855, partly because it was able to fill the political vacuum
left by the dissolution of the Whigs, partly because it was in some respects a genuine reform movement, attacking real abuses, and partly because of fears aroused by the great influx of European immigrants. But
almost immediately, the party began to break up under the impact of
the slavery issue, and as anti-slavery men abandoned it, political nativism increasingly was confined to Old Line Whigs who were much more
concerned, with nationalism than Know-Nothingism. The events of
the 1850's clearly demonstrated that the Republican ideology, which
identified the South and slavery as the enemies of northern "free
labor" and which offered immigrants a place in the economic development of the nation, had a far broader appeal to the native-born
Protestants who made up the bulk of the northern population than
did anti-foreign and anti-Catholic animus.

---

ber of Congressmen with Know-Nothing leanings, particularly in the Thirty-
fourth Congress, the naturalization laws were not altered during the 1850's. Frank
G. Franklin, *The Legislative History of Naturalization in the United States*
(Chicago, 1906), 295–300.

8

The Republicans and Race

On his visit to the United States in the 1830's, Alexis de Tocqueville made his justly famous observation that racial prejudice seemed to be stronger in the North than in the South, and was most intense in the western states which had never known slavery. Several recent historical studies have shown that racial prejudice was all but universal in ante-bellum northern society. Only five states, all in New England, allowed the black man equal suffrage, and even there he was confined to menial occupations and subjected to constant discrimination. In the West, Negroes were often excluded from the public schools, and four states—Indiana, Illinois, Iowa, and Oregon—even barred them from entering their territory.[1] This pervasive prejudice made the question of the proper place of the black man in American society the most troublesome and perplexing one the Republicans faced before the Civil War. Like the Democrats, Republicans often made use of electoral appeals which smacked of racism, and some historians have interpreted this as proof that there existed no fundamental differences between the two parties' racial attitudes. Yet the Republicans did develop a policy which recognized the essential humanity of the Negro, and demanded protection for certain basic rights which the Democrats denied him. Although deeply flawed by an acceptance of many racial stereotypes, and limited by the free labor ideology's assumption that the major responsibility for

1. Alexis de Tocqueville, *Democracy in America*, eds., J. P. Mayer and Max Lerner (New York, 1966), 315; Eugene H. Berwanger, *The Frontier Against Slavery* (Urbana, 1967); Leon F. Litwack, *North of Slavery* (Chicago, 1961), esp. chapters 1, 3–5; Charles H. Wesley, "Negro Suffrage in the Period of Constitution-Making," *JNH*, XXXII (April 1947), 166.

a person's success or failure rested with himself, not society, the Republican stand on race relations went against the prevailing opinion of the 1850's, and proved a distinct political liability in a racist society.

Nowhere did race present more political difficulties than in the Northwest. Why was this area, which some historians have seen as the very breeding ground of democracy and egalitarian individualism, marked by such intense racial prejudice? [2] Clearly one important reason was the large population of southern origin—men and women who had migrated to escape the influences of slavery, but had brought with them the anti-Negro outlook of slave society. As one Republican of southern background put it, "It is not probable, sir, with the prejudices of my early education, that I would be likely to have too great sympathy for negroes." However, states like Michigan and Wisconsin, whose population came largely from the East, also revealed racial prejudice, although to a lesser degree than Indiana, Illinois, and Ohio. It may be that the greater social mobility of western society helped make fear of the Negro—and therefore prejudice—more severe. In the East, no one questioned that the free black should occupy a subordinate position in society, even where he had substantial legal equality. In the more fluid social structure of the West, however, free Negroes might be able to rise socially and economically. This fear had an especially potent appeal in the lower West, which foresaw an influx of freedmen, ready to challenge the status and prerogatives of white men, should emancipation take place. Where the social order was least stratified—as in the frontier states of Kansas, California, and Oregon—legal discrimination was most severe. [3] Thus, paradoxically, the very social mobility for which the West has been celebrated may have tended to exaggerate racial prejudice.

Although many Republicans agreed with the black abolitionist Frederick Douglass that racism was "the greatest of all obstacles in the way of the anti-slavery cause," they also knew that advocacy of the free Negro's rights might prove politically disastrous. Horace Greeley, for example, explained in 1846 that though he favored equal suffrage for New York Negroes, a proposal to establish it would certainly be

2. On western prejudice, see Berwanger, *Frontier Against Slavery*; V. Jacque Voegeli, *Free But Not Equal* (Chicago, 1967); and V. Jacque Voegeli, "The Northwest and the Race Issue, 1861–1862," *MVHR*, L (September 1963), 235–51.
3. *Congressional Globe*, 36 Congress, 1 Session, 1903; Berwanger, *Frontier Against Slavery*, chapters 3–5; "Diary and Correspondence of Salmon P. Chase," *Annual Report* of American Historical Association, 1902, II, 479–80.

defeated in a popular referendum. Prejudiced voters were to blame, Greeley wrote: "You know how numerous and potent this class is." When Democrats charged in the 1850's that the Republicans favored Negro equality, an Indianan informed Salmon P. Chase that unless the claim were refuted, "we shall be beaten not only in Ind. but in the Union from this time forward." [4] Those Republicans who defended the rights of black men found themselves subjected to ridicule and insult. "I know, sir, it is an ungracious task," Henry Wilson told the Senate, ". . . to maintain even the legal rights of a proscribed race; I am not insensible to the gibes and jeers, the taunts and misrepresentations of a corrupted public opinion. . . ." And Oliver Morton said that the reason the Republicans did not carry every township in the North in 1860 was that many voters associated anti-slavery with the prospect of "turning the negroes loose among us." [5]

At times during the 1850's it seemed that the only weapon in the Democrats' political arsenal was the charge that the Republicans were pro-Negro. "Whenever we resist the expansion of slavery into the territories," Wilson complained, "we have a lecture about the equality of the races. When we propose the homestead policy . . . we have lectures about the equality of the races." Such attacks had always been a problem for anti-slavery men, but in the 1850's they were greatly increased. In the Lincoln-Douglas campaign of 1858, the organ of the Democratic party urged readers to "Keep it before the people of Illinois that the Abolition-Republican party headed by Abraham Lincoln are in favor of negro equality. . . ." Francis P. Blair later described this charge as the "incessant theme" of Douglas's campaign. The Wisconsin Democracy labeled the Republicans the "Nigger party," and in Indiana, a Democratic parade featured a group of young ladies carrying the banner, "Fathers, save us from nigger husbands." [6] Though

4. Philip S. Foner, ed., *The Life and Writings of Frederick Douglass* (4 vols.: New York, 1950–55), II, 127; Horace Greeley to Schuyler Colfax, April 22, 1846, Greeley-Colfax Papers, NYPL; A. L. Robinson to Salmon P. Chase, November 30, 1857, Salmon P. Chase Papers, LC. Cf. New York *Evening Post*, April 14, 1857.
5. *Congressional Globe*, 36 Congress, 2 Session, 1093; William M. French, ed., *Life, Speeches, State Papers, and Public Services of Gov. Oliver P. Morton* (Cincinnati, 1866), 90–91.
6. *Congressional Globe*, 36 Congress, 1 Session, 1684; Arthur C. Cole, *The Era of the Civil War 1848–1870* (Springfield, 1919), 175; Francis P. Blair to Abraham Lincoln, May 26, 1860, Robert Todd Lincoln Papers, LC; Aaron M. Boom, "The Development of Sectional Attitudes in Wisconsin, 1848–1861" (unpublished doctoral dissertation, University of Chicago, 1948), 134; J. A. Lemcke, *Reminiscences of an Indianan* (Indianapolis, 1905), 196.

most frequent in the West, such charges were not confined to that section. The New York Democratic platform of 1857, for example, charged the Republicans with favoring Negro suffrage. During the campaign of 1860, Democrats spread the rumor that the Republican vice-presidential candidate, Hannibal Hamlin, was a mulatto.[7] The most intense Democratic attacks were reserved for Republicans who had records of support for Negro rights. When Salmon P. Chase ran for Governor of Ohio in 1855, he was accused of believing that "one negro of the South was of more importance to our state government, than all the white people of the State." Two years later, a Republican reporting on a speech by Chase's Democratic opponent concluded, "this part of the speech was an appeal to the lowest prejudices of caste." It is not surprising that Chase complained that Democrats had little interest in any issue but race. All they wanted, he said, was "simply to talk about the universal nigger question, as they call it. All that they seem to say is 'nigger, nigger, nigger.' "[8]

Republicans revealed the variety of their racial attitudes in the ways in which they responded to these Democratic charges. Some Republicans denounced appeals to prejudice on principled grounds. One Ohio Congressman dismissed Democratic charges as "an appeal to that low, vulgar prejudice which wages war against the negroes because the lowest man in society is always anxious to find some one lower than himself. . . ." Others felt the Democrats could best be answered by ridicule. Democrats, the Cincinnati *Gazette* observed, seemed to fear that "the Caucasian type of manhood" was "in imminent danger of disappearing from this continent." And at the Iowa Constitutional Convention of 1857, the prolonged debates about the rights of free Negroes led a Republican delegate to remark, "The gentlemen over the way are more sensitive in regard to the negro than any men I have ever seen in my life."[9] More often, however, Republicans took the approach that

7. New York *Tribune*, September 18, 1858; Harry D. Hunt III, *Hannibal Hamlin of Maine* (Syracuse, 1969), 121–22. Cf. New York *Tribune*, September 5, 1857; Donald E. Simon, "Brooklyn in the Election of 1860," *New-York Historical Society Quarterly*, LI (July 1967), 257–59.

8. J. R. Meredith to Chase, September 1, 1855, E. B. Andrews to Chase, August 20, 1857, Chase Papers, LC; "Speech of Gov. Chase at Sandusky, Ohio, August 25, 1859," newspaper clipping, Box 17, Chase Papers, HSPa. Cf. Columbus *Ohio Statesman*, August 10, 22, September 5, 18, 1857; Cincinnati *Gazette*, September 7, 1855, September 26, 1857.

9. *Congressional Globe*, 36 Congress, 1 Session, 1910; Cincinnati *Gazette*, September 22, 1857; *The Debates of the Constitutional Convention of the State of Iowa* (2 vols.: Davenport, 1857), II, 835.

the question of Negro rights was irrelevant to their party's policies. The *National Era*—the organ of the Liberty and Free Soil parties which later served as a spokesman for radical Republicans—pointed out that many Americans opposed the extension of slavery out of concern for "the national honor and prosperity," rather than an interest in Negro rights. A man who advocated abolition in the District of Columbia, the *Era* observed, was not bound "to admit a black man to his table for the sake of consistency." The editor of the Chicago *Evening Journal*, Charles Wilson, said much the same thing. "It [does not] necessarily follow," he wrote, "that we should fellowship with the negroes because our policy shakes off their shackles." Often, Republican politicians tried to keep the race issue out of politics altogether. As Lyman Trumbull warned Lincoln when the Republican state platform was under consideration in Illinois, "It will not do, of course, to get mixed up with the free negro question. . . ." [10]

The use of the race issue as a potent political weapon by the Democrats led many Republicans to reply in kind. Especially in the West, Republican spokesmen insisted that they, not the Democrats, were the real "white man's party," and they often vehemently denied any intention of giving legal or social equality to free Negroes. [11] The astute politician David Davis, Lincoln's friend and adviser, insisted during the 1858 campaign that Republican orators "distinctly and emphatically disavow *negro suffrage*, negroes holding office, serving on juries and the like." When Democrats charged that anti-slavery spokesmen subordinated the rights of whites to those of Negroes, Republicans responded that they hoped to keep the territories open to free white settlers by barring slavery. It required no effort to show, an Iowa Congressman wrote, that the Democratic, not the Republican party, "exalts and spreads Africans at the expense of the white race." Because they opposed Democratic plans to "flood Kansas and the other Territories with negro slaves," Republicans claimed "that we are the only white man's party in the country." And when Democrats ac-

10. *National Era*, August 12, 1852; Charles S. Wilson to Lyman Trumbull, May 12, 1858, Lyman Trumbull Papers, LC; Lyman Trumbull to Lincoln, June 12, 1858, Lincoln Papers.
11. *Congressional Globe*, 34 Congress, 3 Session, Appendix, 91, 35 Congress, 1 Session, 774, 2 Session, 986; *Speech of O. H. Browning, Delivered at the Republican Mass Meeting, Springfield, Ill., August 8th, 1860* (Quincy, 1860), 14; Emma Lou Thornbrough, "The Race Issue in Indiana Politics during the Civil War," *IndMH* LXVII (June 1951), 167–68; Berwanger, *Frontier Against Slavery*, 132–34.

cused them of favoring the intermixing of the races, Republicans responded that keeping the races separate by barring slavery from the territories would prevent this very intermixing. Said a leading Iowa Republican, "It is the institution of slavery which is the great parent of amalgamation. Gentlemen need not fear it from those opposed to that institution." [12]

To a large extent, these expressions of racism were political replies to Democratic accusations rather than gratuitous insults to the black race. Few Republicans were as blatantly prejudiced as the New York *Tribune*'s associate editor James S. Pike, who so despised the Negro race that he hoped the South would secede, taking its black population with it. Some Republicans who insisted they were advocating the rights of the white race made sure to add that they did not wish "to disclaim any sympathy" for Negroes.[13] Yet inherent in the anti-slavery outlook of many Republicans was a strong overtone of racism. For the whole free labor argument against the extension of slavery contained a crucial ambiguity. Was it the institution of slavery, or the presence of the Negro, which degraded the white laborer? Sometimes Republicans clearly stated that the institution itself, not the race of the slave, was to blame. An Ohio Congressman declared that while he agreed that a black population represented a nuisance, "a free white man could live where there are negroes, and maintain his freedom; but no white non-slaveholder can live where slave laws, customs, and habits pertain, and retain [his] rights. . . ." The radical *National Era* informed the South, "We are not opposed to the extension of either class of your population, provided it be *free*, but to the existence of slavery and migration of *slaves*." More often, however, Republicans indicated that they made little distinction between free Negroes and slaves, and felt that association with any black degraded the white race. "I want to have nothing to do, either with the free negro or the slave negro . . . ," said Lyman Trumbull. "We wish to settle the Territories with free white men." And Simon Cameron of Pennsylvania stated that he

12. David Davis to Lincoln, August 3, 1858, Lincoln Papers; Samuel R. Curtis to George G. Fogg, September 9, 1860, George G. Fogg Papers, NHHS; *Congressional Globe*, 35 Congress, 1 Session, 1042; *Debates of Iowa Convention*, II, 829. Cf. Chicago *Tribune*, July 1, September 1, 1857; Cleveland *Leader*, July 21, 1857; New York *Tribune*, June 8, 1854.
13. Robert F. Durden, *James Shepherd Pike* (Durham, 1957); New York *Tribune*, January 9, 1857, March 13, 1860; *Congressional Globe*, 34 Congress, 1 Session, 1520. Cf. Sherman Evarts, ed., *Arguments and Speeches of William Maxwell Evarts* (3 vols.: New York, 1919), II, 508-9.

wished to keep Negroes out of the territories, because the white laborer "must be depressed wherever the Negro is his competitor in the field or the workshop." [14]

Although this kind of argument was resorted to throughout the Republican party, it was used most frequently by the former Democrats. These men, particularly the New York Barnburners and their followers like Wilmot and the Blairs, came from a political tradition hostile to Negro rights and accustomed to the use of race prejudice as a political weapon. During the fight for free soil in the 1840's, they had linked racism and anti-slavery in a way which was repeated in the pre-war decade.[15] David Wilmot, for example, insisted that his Proviso of 1846 was the "White Man's Proviso," and he told the House that by barring slavery from the Mexican Cession he intended to preserve the area for "the sons of toil, of my own race and own color." An astute abolitionist observer noted that Wilmot's speeches often contrasted "black labor" and "free labor," "as though it were the negro and not slavery which degraded labor." Similarly, the *National Era* pointed out that the New York Barnburners tended to place their opposition to slavery extension "on the ground of an abhorrence of 'black slaves,'" rather than of slavery itself. And during the 1850's, the former Democrats took the lead in racist appeals. They represented in the most extreme degree the racism from which no portion of the Republican party could claim total freedom.[16]

II

Another index of the scope of racism within the Republican party was the wide acceptance of plans for colonizing blacks outside the

14. *Congressional Globe*, 36 Congress, 1 Session, 1857; *National Era*, May 3, 1849; *Great Speech of Hon. Lyman Trumbull, on the Issues of the Day* (Chicago, 1858), 13; Simon Cameron to George Bergner, March 28, 1858 (draft), Simon Cameron Papers, LC. Cf. New York *Times*, August 21, 1856; New York *Tribune*, March 22, 1854.
15. Eric Foner, "Racial Attitudes of the New York Free Soilers," *New York History*, XLVI (October 1965), 311–29; Chaplain W. Morrison, *Democratic Politics and Sectionalism* (Chapel Hill, 1967), 73.
16. *Proceedings of the Herkimer Mass Convention of October 26, 1847* (Albany, 1847), 14; Charles B. Going, *David Wilmot Free-Soiler* (New York, 1924), 174; *Pennsylvania Freeman*, December 7, 1848; *National Era*, June 15, 1848; Berwanger, *Frontier Against Slavery*, 133–34. Cf. letters to Trumbull by John M. Palmer, December 8, 1858, A. Ballinger, December 18, 1860, and W. Kitchell, December 18, 1860, Trumbull Papers.

United States. Colonization as a solution to the race problem and as an adjunct of gradual emancipation had been advocated for many years. Many of the founding fathers, including Jefferson, Madison, and Henry, had been opposed to slavery but had believed in coupling emancipation with deportation of the freedmen. Later, the American Colonization Society attempted to establish colonies in Africa, but the fact that both free Negroes and abolitionists viewed the plan as an attempt to strengthen the slave system, by removing free blacks from the country, prevented its ever being put in full operation. One Republican Congressman expressed the typical anti-slavery view of the Society when he said, "at the South it meant new and increased guarantees for the perpetuation of slavery, while at the North it was held out to the rich and philanthropic as a means for the ultimate extinction of slavery." [17] Some politicians, including a group of conservative Whigs, lent their support to the Colonization Society during the 1850's. Most prominent among them were Daniel Webster, Washington Hunt, Millard Fillmore, Edward Everett, and Hamilton Fish. But by the late 1850's the failure of attempts at African colonization was apparent. The idea of removing the nation's black population persisted, but most Republicans contemplated an area closer to home. [18]

The authors of the Republican colonization plan were Francis P. Blair and his sons Frank and Montgomery. The Blairs proposed that the United States arrange for the settlement of colonies of Negroes in Central America, either by the outright acquisition of land there or through the co-operation of the local governments. They hoped that free transportation, free homesteads, and financial aid in establishing farms and businesses would make the colony attractive enough to induce a sizable number of free blacks to settle there. Under the protection of the American government, the pioneer colony would flourish, and later new ones would be planted. As slaves were freed

17. Walter L. Fleming, "Deportation and Colonization: An Attempted Solution of the Race Problem," *Studies in Southern History and Politics* (New York, 1914), 3–4; Don B. Kates, Jr., "Abolition, Deportation, Integration: Attitudes Towards Slavery in the Early Republic," *JNH*, LIII (January 1968), 45–47; *Congressional Globe*, 36 Congress, 1 Session, Appendix, 178.
18. Frederic Bancroft, "The Colonization of American Negroes, 1801–1865," in Jacob E. Cooke, ed., *Frederic Bancroft, Historian* (Norman, Okla., 1957), 185–86; *The Writings and Speeches of Daniel Webster* (18 vols.: Boston, 1903), X, 96; New York *Times*, January 7, 1852, January 19, 1853; Benjamin J. Haight to Hamilton Fish, January 9, 1855, Hamilton Fish Papers, LC; Allan Nevins, *Ordeal of the Union* (2 vols.: New York, 1947), I, 511; Francis P. Blair, Jr., *The Destiny of the Races of this Continent* (Washington, 1859), 32; *Congressional Globe*, 35 Congress, 1 Session, 294, 2207; Francis P. Blair to Gerrit Smith, April 9, 1858, Smith Papers, Syracuse University.

in the southern states, they would be transported to the black colonies, until eventually the vast bulk of the Negro population of the United States would be removed.

At the root of all colonization plans, including the Republican one, was the assumption that the United States was, or should be, a nation of white men. "It is certainly the wish of every patriot," Francis P. Blair wrote in 1858, "that all within the limits of our Union should be homogeneous in race and of our own blood." Another colonizationist, Senator James R. Doolittle of Wisconsin, said the plan would "keep our Anglo-Saxon institutions as well as our Anglo-Saxon blood pure and uncontaminated." Some supporters frankly expressed their conviction that free Negroes were "a grievous nuisance to every State of the Union," and that colonization "would relieve us from the curse of free blacks." [19] They were convinced that these were the views of a majority of Americans. "The great mass of white men," said Preston King, desired the separation of the two races, and even a lukewarm supporter of colonization like Salmon P. Chase admitted that his state desired "a homogeneous population." The strong element of racism in the colonization idea was candidly acknowledged by an Iowa Republican. Speaking of free Negroes and slaves, he declared, "I have my prejudices against them. My prejudice is such as to lead me to desire that they shall not be left in this country. . . . I am, therefore, a colonizationist." [20]

But there was much more than simple racism to the Republican colonization plan. It is significant that its leading advocates, the Blairs, were deeply involved in the politics of Missouri and Maryland. In these border states the slave system seemed weak, and emancipation sentiment was rising. The Blairs were anti-slavery slaveholders who shared the assumptions of their class regarding race, and who attacked slavery primarily because of its effect upon southern white labor.[21] The Blairs

19. Blair to Smith, April 9, 1858, Smith Papers; James R. Doolittle to Hannibal Hamlin, September 18, 1859, Hannibal Hamlin Papers, University of Maine, Orono; St. Louis *Evening News,* cited in Cincinnati *Gazette,* November 10, 1859; *Congressional Globe,* 30 Congress, 2 Session, 208.
20. *Congressional Globe,* 35 Congress, 1 Session, 2207; 31 Congress, 1 Session, 136; *National Era,* February 8, 1859; Chase to Mrs. Chase, December 30, 1848, Chase Papers, LC; *Debates of Iowa Convention,* II, 700.
21. Frank Blair, the eldest son of Francis P. Blair, was a Republican leader in Missouri. He inherited slaves from his father's and mother's families, but began to free them in 1858. He once met a slave who had run away from him, in Illinois, and let him remain free. E. L. Pierce to Charles Sumner, June 3, 1853, Charles Sumner Papers, Houghton Library, Harvard University; William E. Smith, *The Francis Preston Blair Family in Politics* (2 vols.: New York, 1933), I, 443.

hoped to build up a Republican party in the South, based on the poor whites, which would gradually abolish slavery. The one great obstacle, as they saw it, was the antipathy of the non-slaveholding whites toward the Negro, and their fear that emancipation would lead to equality and intermixing of the races. "It is this compounding of the races," Blair explained to a northern anti-slavery leader, "which is supposed to be the aim of abolitionism, that enables slaveholders to excite such abhorrence against abolitionists throughout the South." Blair's son Frank, the first Republican Congressman from a slave state, agreed. "The idea of liberating the slaves and allowing them to remain in the country," he told a New England audience, "is one that never will be tolerated." [22] Only when the non-slaveholders of the South were convinced that the removal of the black population would go hand in hand with emancipation, would their latent anti-slavery inclinations find political expression.

To the Blairs, therefore, colonization was an essential part of a larger plan to destroy slavery from within the southern states. Endorsement of colonization by the Republican party would be "an enabling act to the emancipationists of the South," for it would effectively rebut the slaveholders' charges that abolition meant Negro equality. "This is the only point needing elucidation and comprehension by the southern people," Montgomery Blair wrote, "to make us as strong at the South as at the North." This analysis was endorsed by other slave state Republicans, including Cassius M. Clay of Kentucky and Edward Bates of Missouri. The Maryland and Missouri Republican platforms, which were dictated by the Blairs and their friends, endorsed colonization, denounced racial amalgamation and "free negro equality," and declared that the party's objective was "Missouri for white men and white men for Missouri." [23]

22. Francis P. Blair to H. Beecher, January 15, 1857 (draft), Blair-Lee Papers, Princeton University; Springfield *Republican*, September 22, 1858. Cf. Blair, *Destiny of Races*, 22; Francis P. Blair, Jr., *Colonization and Commerce* (Cincinnati, 1859), 1–2.

23. F. P. Blair to Cameron, March 22, 1859, Cameron Papers; Montgomery Blair to James R. Doolittle, November 11, 1859, Miscellaneous Manuscripts, WisHS; David L. Smiley, "Cassius M. Clay and John G. Fee: A Study in Southern Anti-Slavery Thought," *JNH*, XLII (July 1957), 204; *Missouri Democrat*, cited in New York *Tribune*, July 3, 1858; Cincinnati *Gazette*, March 13, 1860; F. P. Blair, Jr. to F. P. Blair, March 25, 1857, Blair-Lee Papers; *Address of Montgomery Blair, Before the Maryland State Republican Convention* (Washington, 1860), 3, 7; Reinhard H. Luthin, "Organizing the Republican Party in the 'Border-Slave' Regions: Edward Bates's Presidential Candidacy in 1860," *MoHR*, XXXVIII (January 1944), 153–54.

The wide acceptance of colonization among border state Republicans led many northerners to suspend some of their doubts about its practicability. After all, these southerners were the men who were counted on to achieve the eventual abolition of slavery. Charles Francis Adams, for one, doubted that the Blairs' plan could be put into effect, but he noted in his diary, "Whatever may be thought of his plan in its application we must respect it as coming from an earnest and sincere emancipationist in a slave state." The *National Era* carried a letter from a northern man in Kentucky reporting that the strongest single objection to emancipation in that state was not the monetary value of the slaves, "but their presence after liberation." Frederick Law Olmsted's widely read reports of his journey through the South said much the same thing. It is thus not surprising that many northern Republicans came to support the idea of colonization. It seemed to them the only way in which "our friends in Missouri, Maryland, Delaware, Kentucky, and Virginia, who are emancipationists, can fight the battle and win the victory there, and Republicanize these states." [24]

Colonization would aid southern Republicans, and it would, at the same time, enhance the prospects of the party in the North. According to Doolittle, Republicans in the doubtful states of Illinois, Indiana, and Pennsylvania "must first answer the question, what are you Republicans going to do *with* and for the negroes *when emancipated* before they will be prepared to *go with us*." He suggested that the party's rallying cry for 1860 be "down with amalgamation" or "separate the races," and Blair assured Lincoln that a public endorsement of colonization would "ward off the attacks made upon us about negro equality." When Trumbull of Illinois endorsed the plan in the Senate, he received enthusiastic letters from his constituents. One declared that the proposal, if incorporated into the Republican platform, would "be of immense advantage to us," and "would be a complete stopper to all the nonsensical talk about 'wooly heads,' etc." From Minnesota, Frank Blair reported that his speeches favoring colonization were well received by Republican leaders there. "They say I relieved them of the slang about negro equality," he informed his father.[25]

24. Charles Francis Adams Diary, January 26, 1859, Adams Papers, MHS; *National Era*, July 8, 1847; Frederick Law Olmsted, *A Journey in the Seaboard Slave States* (New York, 1856), 44, 94–97; Frederick Law Olmsted, *A Journey in the Back Country* (New York, 1863), viii, 203; James R. Doolittle to John F. Potter, November 7, 1860, John F. Potter Papers, WisHS.
25. James R. Doolittle to Thurlow Weed, August 23, September 6, 1859, Thurlow Weed Papers, Rush Rhees Library, University of Rochester; Doolittle to Hamlin,

To many of the earlier colonizationists, whose interest centered on Africa, the plan would not only solve the race problem in the United States but would fulfill a great religious end. American Negroes would serve as Christian missionaries, bringing the gospel to the Dark Continent. In the eyes of Republican colonizationists, however, the Negroes were to be emissaries of a different kind; as black agents of the American Empire, they would help establish the commercial and political hegemony of the United States in Latin America. It is important to remember that during the 1850's much of the attention of American foreign policy was focused on Central America. That area was a hotbed of international conflict, with the United States and Britain vying for dominance and southern expansionists and filibusters eyeing it as part of a future slave empire. The Blairs argued that the establishment of Negro colonies there would ensure American dominance. Colonization, the elder Blair wrote, would create "rich colonies under our protection, likely in the end, to appropriate the whole region to our use." [26] Many New York and New England merchants were already interested in commerce with Central America, and Frank Blair made two of his most important speeches on colonization before influential mercantile audiences in Boston and New York. He described the great mineral wealth and trade possibilities of the region, and offered colonization and the Pacific railroad as twin measures which would expand America's commerce and empire. Central America, Blair declared, "would, in fact, become our India." [27]

Not only would colonization enable the United States to outflank the British in Central America, but it would also effectively block southern plans to expand the slave system southward. The elder Blair wrote in 1859 that his plan would "build up a free black power, which will counteract the design of making all south of Mason and Dixon's line to Brazil a slave empire. . . ." Doolittle drew the analogy between Kansas, where the settlement of white laborers had

August 20, 1859, Hamlin Papers; H. Wing to Trumbull, May 4, 1860, T. McKibben to Trumbull, December 29, 1859, A. Ballinger to Trumbull, February 16, 1860, Trumbull Papers; F. P. Blair, Jr. to F. P. Blair, October 6, 1859, Blair-Lee Papers.
26. Bancroft, "Colonization," 162; Nevins, Ordeal, I, 550, II, 368ff., 405ff.; Francis P. Blair to Martin Van Buren, February 13, 1860, Martin Van Buren Papers, LC. 27. Eli Thayer to Amos A. Lawrence, January 23, 1858, Amos A. Lawrence Papers, MHS; Blair, Destiny of the Races, 23; Blair, Colonization and Commerce, 2–4. Cf. F. P. Blair, Jr. to F. P. Blair, undated, 1858, Blair-Lee Papers; F. P. Blair to Cameron, March 22, 1859, Cameron Papers.

prevented slavery from establishing a foothold, and Central America, where a free black colony would bar slavery. The peculiar institution and the slave trade, he wrote, could "no more go there than they could go through a wall of fire." [28]

It was highly ironic that Negroes were considered capable of becoming the agents of American empire in the Caribbean while they were being viewed at the same time as an undesirable population at home. Republicans tried to justify this contradiction by appealing to the widely accepted belief that the white and black races were suited to different climates.[29] Only the blacks could establish American influence in the tropics, because in that climate, as Doolittle put it, "the white race is doomed." "It is by this race alone," Frank Blair told his New York audience, "that those regions are to be regenerated, and brought within the circle of civilization." Nevertheless, the praise which colonizationists heaped upon the Negro sometimes seemed quite extravagant. American Negroes, they said, were far superior to the races which inhabited Central America. "The infusion of American negro blood," one colonizationist newspaper declared, "would . . . make an actual improvement in the civilization of Mexico." The Albany *Evening Journal* agreed that the American Negro was "a race vastly superior, physically and in intellect, to the dwarfed and imbecile natives" of Latin America.[30] These statements illustrated the crowning irony of the colonization enterprise. While the African colonizationists continued to look upon the black as an African transported to the United States (Lincoln, for instance, spoke of sending the Negroes "to Liberia —to their own native land"), the Blairs and their followers recognized

28. F. P. Blair to Pierce, April 9, 1859, Pierce Papers; Doolittle to Potter, July 25, 1859, Potter Papers. Cf. Doolittle to Edwin Morgan, January 29, 1860, in Weed Papers; *National Era,* February 24, 1859; *Wisconsin State Journal,* September 2, 1859.

29. Chase, for example, believed that the two races, "adapted to different latitudes and countries by the influences of climate," would never have come together except by the use of force. He and other western Republicans used this idea to counter Democratic charges that emancipation would cause an influx of freedmen into the Northwest. In fact, they insisted, quite the reverse was true. It was slavery which forced blacks to escape to the North; with emancipation, "our colored population would begin to retire southward." Chase to ? December 13, 1850, Chase to Frederick Douglass, May 4, 1850, Chase Papers, HSPa; Chase to C. H. and J. M. Langston, November 11, 1850, Chase Papers (ser II), LC; *Ohio State Journal,* December 19, 1859.

30. *Congressional Globe,* 37 Congress, 2 Session, Appendix, 83; Blair, *Colonization and Commerce,* 4; Washington *Republic,* October 6, 1857; Albany *Evening Journal,* August 29, 1859.

that the Negro had become an American. Even as they prepared to
expel him from the country, the colonizationists spoke of how the
Negro would carry with him "the intelligence, the industry, the Progressive impulse" of all labor in the United States. "It is this race of
men," said Frank Blair, "christianized in our churches, civilized by
our firesides, and educated in government by hearing our political
discussions," who could establish the laws, customs, and power of the
United States in Central America. "They have in fact ceased to be
Africans," said the New York *Tribune* in 1857. "Just as our native-born
white population have ceased to be Englishmen, Irishmen, or Germans,
they are becoming black Americans just as we have become white
Americans." [31]

Paradoxically, while white colonizationists saw the Negro as a suit-
able emissary of empire because of his Americanization, blacks who
supported the plan did so because of the conviction that their race
needed a nationality and culture of their own. Traditionally, abolitionists and black leaders had staunchly opposed any plan of colonization. But as the 1850's witnessed an increase in anti-Negro legislation,
with some southern states moving to expel or enslave free Negroes, and
some western states barring them from entering their territory, the
hope of interracial justice seemed increasingly untenable. As a result, a
number of important black spokesmen—including Henry Garnet, H.
Ford Douglass, Martin Delany, and William H. Day—supported the
Blair plan. They echoed the assertion of one delegate to an Ohio
colored convention: "I for one, sir, am willing, dearly as I love my
native land, . . . to leave it, and go wherever I can be free." [32]

Black support for colonization was part of a growing Negro militancy
and racial consciousness. The passage of the fugitive slave law and
other pro-slavery measures of the 1850's led many blacks, along with
many white abolitionists, to abandon their faith in moral suasion as a
means of achieving emancipation. In some areas, clandestine black

31. Roy F. Basler *et al.*, eds., *The Collected Works of Abraham Lincoln* (9 vols.:
New Brunswick, 1953–55), II, 255, 409; Blair, *Destiny of the Races*, 23; Blair,
Colonization and Commerce, 4–5; New York *Tribune*, May 9, 1857.
32. *State Convention of the Colored Citizens of Ohio, Convened at Columbus,
Jan. 10–13, 1849* (Oberlin, 1849), 8; Howard H. Bell, "A Survey of the Negro
Convention Movement, 1830–1861" (unpublished doctoral dissertation, North-
western University, 1953), 209–15; Blair, *Destiny of the Races*, 33–38; *Liberator*,
May 21, 1852; *Proceedings of the National Emigration Convention of Colored
People* (Pittsburgh, 1854).

militia companies were formed to prevent the rendition of fugitive slaves. Even Douglass wrote in 1860 that he had lost faith in the peaceful extinction of slavery.[33] The rise in Negro nationalism went hand in hand with increasing militancy. Some Negroes began to eschew the aid of white anti-slavery men and to insist that blacks had to rely on their own efforts to deliver their race from oppression.[34] Even the more conservative, established Negro leadership, which opposed emigrationist plans, advocated the creation of separate black institutions, including schools and businesses. The more militant black nationalists tended to favor emigration, arguing that Negroes were a distinct race, and needed a separate existence from the whites. As one expressed it, "We must have a nationality. I am for going anywhere, so we can be an independent people."[35]

The most influential black leader, Frederick Douglass, remained skeptical about colonization. He realized that the Negroes who chafed the most at unequal treatment—the best educated and most talented— were also those whose services were most needed in this country. "It would seem," he wrote in 1853, "that education and emigration go together with us; for as soon as a man rises amongst us, capable, by his genius and learning, to do us great service, just so soon he finds that he can serve himself better by going elsewhere." Douglass feared that colonization would remove only these talented and educated blacks, leaving behind "the degraded and worthless . . . to help bind us to our present debasement." But the very fact that colonization was most appealing to the educated minority prevented it from gaining much mass support.[36] Only during the Civil War did colonization plans have any chance of succeeding. Yet by then, as Negroes joined in the Union

33. John Demos, "The Antislavery Movement and the Problem of Violent 'Means,'" *NEQ*, XXXVII (December 1964), 501–26; *Douglass' Monthly,* January, 1860; Foner, ed., *Douglass,* II, 51, 487.
34. Such statements were profoundly disturbing to some white abolitionists, who were used to working closely with blacks, usually with the whites in positions of leadership. One abolitionist wrote, in a letter strongly reminiscent of modern-day reactions to black militancy, that Negroes should not alienate their white supporters, and should recognize how much they owed to white philanthropy. *Liberator,* October 1, 1858.
35. *Ohio Colored Convention, 1849,* 8. On this subject, see also Bell, "Negro Convention Movement," 111–31; Howard H. Bell, "Negro Nationalism: A Factor in Emigration Projects, 1858–1861," *JNH,* XLVII (January 1962), 42–53.
36. Foner, ed., *Douglass,* II, 231, 151; *Liberator,* August 26, 1859, March 18, 1860; *Weekly Anglo-African,* March 17, 1860; *Proceedings of a Convention of the Colored Men of Ohio* (Cincinnati, 1858), 7.

war effort and as emancipation became a reality, the prospect of racial justice at home seemed real enough to most blacks to kill any desire they may have had to emigrate.

Colonization did not become a major political issue until after the 1856 election, although the elder Blair had referred to the idea in an influential pamphlet of the Frémont campaign. Between 1857 and 1860, the Blairs and Doolittle engaged in an extensive propaganda campaign within the party on behalf of their proposal. They wrote letters soliciting support from leading Republican editors and politicians, and Frank Blair gave public addresses on colonization in New England, New York, and the Northwest. Doolittle spread the idea in campaign speeches in Wisconsin and Iowa, and worked to convince western governors to endorse the plan.[37] By early 1860, Governors Kirkwood of Iowa, Randall of Wisconsin, Bissell of Illinois, and Dennison of Ohio had come out for colonization, as had an impressive list of Republican Congressional leaders, including Preston King, Henry Wilson, Lyman Trumbull, Hannibal Hamlin, James Harlan, Ben Wade, C. C. Washburn, Charles Sedgwick, and James Ashley.[38] Among the leading Republican newspapers which spoke approvingly of the proposal were the *Times* and *Evening Post* of New York, the Chicago *Press and Tribune*, the Cleveland *Leader*, the *Wisconsin State Journal*, the Boston *Atlas and Daily Bee*, and the Albany *Evening Journal*.[39]

Many political observers expected colonization to be adopted as part of the national Republican platform. Frank Blair wrote in 1859 that

37. *National Era*, October 2, 1856; Smith, *Blair Family*, I, 446–47; F. P. Blair, Jr. to Montgomery Blair, October 20, 1859, Blair Family Papers, LC; F. P. Blair, Jr. to James R. Doolittle, October 15, November 3, 1859, James R. Doolittle Papers, LC; F. P. Blair, Jr. to F. P. Blair, November 2, 1859, Blair-Lee Papers; James R. Doolittle to Samuel J. Kirkwood, November 9, 1859 (xerox copy), James R. Doolittle Papers, WisHS.

38. Dan E. Clark, *Samuel Jordan Kirkwood* (Iowa City, 1917), 145; *Annual Message of Alexander W. Randall, Governor of the State of Wisconsin, and Accompany Documents* (Madison, 1860), 26; William Dennison to Benjamin F. Wade, November 30, 1859, February 6, 21, 1860, Benjamin F. Wade Papers, LC. F. P. Blair, Jr. to F. P. Blair, undated, 1858, Blair-Lee Papers, lists King, Trumbull, Doolittle, and Bissell among the supporters of colonization, and F. P. Blair to Van Buren, March 26, 1859, Van Buren Papers, lists Hamlin and Wade. For Sedgwick, see Earle Field, "Charles B. Sedgwick's Letters from Washington, 1859–1861," *Mid-America*, LXIX (April 1987), 136, and for Wilson, Harlan, Washburn, and Ashley, see *Congressional Globe*, 35 Congress, 1 Session, Appendix, 172–73; 36 Congress, 1 Session, Appendix, 57, 265, 373–76.

39. New York *Times*, July 9, 1859; New York *Evening Post*, February 17, 1859; Chicago *Press and Tribune*, August 16, 1859, February 11, 1860; Cleveland *Leader*, March 19, 1859; *Wisconsin State Journal*, September 3, 1859; Boston *Atlas and Daily Bee*, August 26, 1858; Albany *Evening Journal*, August 29, 1859.

it was "now likely to be adopted as the programme of the Republican Party in the contest of 1860," and Dennison, Trumbull, Doolittle, and Wade were equally sanguine. Two weeks before the convention opened, the *Wisconsin State Journal* reported that the subject would "undoubtedly be brought forward," and that no significant opposition was foreseen.[40] But the Republican platform of 1860 did not mention colonization. This could hardly have been an oversight, since the three Blairs were at Chicago, and their close associate, John A. Kasson, was an influential member of the platform committee. Francis P. Blair explained the lack of a colonization plank by writing Lincoln that it was "too large a scheme and involved too many details to be introduced into our party platform at Chicago." This explanation has a certain validity, but it is very probable that the Blairs, fearing a floor fight over the colonization plank, decided in the end not to press it. The whole political effect of the plank would be lost if it were adopted only after a protracted intraparty dispute.[41]

It seems quite improbable that a plank on colonization satisfactory to all elements of the party could have been adopted at Chicago. Even among supporters, there were significant differences of emphasis and program. Some, for example, seemed to want the Central American colonies to become parts of the Union, presumably as states. This raised the prospect of black Senators and Representatives sitting in the halls of Congress. Most, however, wanted Central America to be, as the elder Blair put it, "*free* yet subject to our influence." [42] More important was the question whether colonization should be voluntary or compulsory. The Blairs insisted that their plan provided for voluntary emigration only, but Edward Bates felt compulsion should be used as a last resort. Most colonizationists hoped that the offer of free transportation and homesteads would make the colonies so

40. F. P. Blair, Jr. to Dana, March 1, 1859, Dana Papers; Dennison to Wade, March 12, 1860, Wade Papers; *Congressional Globe*, 36 Congress, 1 Session, 60, 1633, Appendix, 154–55; Doolittle to Weed, January 23, 1860, Weed Papers; *Wisconsin State Journal*, May 8, 1860.

41. Smith, *Blair Family*, I, 474–84; Edward Younger, *John A. Kasson* (Iowa City, 1955), 65; Blair to Lincoln, May 26, 1860, Lincoln Papers. One Illinois Republican wrote Trumbull, "it is highly important that the adoption of the principle should *be without objection*." H. Wing to Trumbull, May 4, 1860, Trumbull Papers.

42. F. P. Blair to Cameron, March 22, 1859, Cameron Papers; Doolittle to Hamlin, August 20, 1859, Hamlin Papers; F. P. Blair, Jr. to F. P. Blair, September 10, 1858, Blair-Lee Papers; *Congressional Globe*, 36 Congress, 1 Session, 102; Blair, *Colonization and Commerce*, 8.

attractive that compulsory deportation would be unnecessary. But they also wanted emancipation to be contingent upon a commitment to emigrate. This aspect of the proposal worried many Republicans. Chase, for example, was cool to the Blair plan, although he wrote that were he a black man, "I would gather a colony—go to Jamaica—buy one of the deserted plantations." He insisted, however, that "no man, native or naturalized, . . . be driven forth from his country." Many Republicans, particularly easterners and radicals, shared Chase's reservations.[43]

Charles Sumner called attention to another aspect of the colonization plan which bothered many Republicans when he wrote during the Civil War that the deportation of three million slaves "will deprive the country of what it most needs, which is labor." Many Republicans expected the slaves, once freed, to become the free labor force of the South. The radical Congressman Owen Lovejoy spoke of emancipation as a transformation of the blacks "from slaves into serfs." Seward discouraged Lincoln's colonization plans during the war, saying, "I am always for bringing men and States *into* this Union, never for taking any out."[44] Pro-colonization Republicans countered by suggesting that deportation be a gradual process, and that free white labor, from Europe and the North, could take the place of the slaves. The New York *Times* even suggested importing Chinese laborers, although it was not clear how this would serve one of the major aims of colonization, the separation of races. But to Republicans concerned with the nation's economic development, the idea of transporting out of the country "the whole labor-power of the south" seemed fantastic.[45]

The failure of the Chicago Convention to endorse their plan did not discourage the colonizationists. They resumed their propaganda efforts, and were heartened by the sympathy of both Republican nominees to their proposal. The story of Lincoln's unsuccessful attempt to put the

43. Howard K. Beale, ed., *Diary of Gideon Welles* (3 vols.: New York, 1960), I, 152; Chase to ?, December 13, 1850, Chase Papers, HSPa; *Congressional Globe*, 32 Congress, 2 Session, 1064. Cf. *National Era*, November 28, 1850; *Wisconsin State Journal*, May 8, 1860.

44. Charles H. Wesley, "Lincoln's Plan for Colonizing the Emancipated Negroes," *JNH*, IV (January 1919), 11–12n.; *Congressional Globe*, 36 Congress, 1 Session, Appendix, 206; Frederick W. Seward, *Seward at Washington* (2 vols.: New York, 1891), II, 227; "Diary and Correspondence of Chase," 93. Cf. Fawn M. Brodie, *Thaddeus Stevens* (New York, 1959), 161.

45. New York *Times*, May 15, 1852; H. C. Carey, *Principles of Political Economy* (3 vols.: Philadelphia, 1837–40), III, 197.

Blair plan into operation during the Civil War has often been told. After the war, Doolittle, Greeley, and others still clung to the plan, and even in the twentieth century, there would be suggestions that the federal government buy property abroad for settlement by American Negroes.[46] That the idea of colonization has been so persistent is due, in large part, to its appeal either to prejudice or to a desire to escape from the whole problem of an interracial society. That most of the strong supporters of colonization were former Democrats—the Blairs, Doolittle, Trumbull, King, Randall, Kirkwood, and others—shows how the plan appealed most strongly to those who came from a political tradition of opposition to Negro rights. Yet it must be remembered that, even on the eve of the Civil War, Republicans believed the end of slavery would come gradually and peacefully. And colonization seemed to be the only way to convince southern non-slaveholders as well as northwestern racists to support eventual emancipation. Adoption of colonization as a federal policy would "put an end to the agitation of the slavery question," Doolittle said, by providing a peaceful road to emancipation. This link with emancipation led many Republicans who resolutely opposed colonization plans limited to free blacks, to support the Blair proposal.[47]

The Republican colonizationists also recognized that lying deeper than the issue of slavery was the dark question of race. Even with its racism, colonization included a genuine humanitarian element, for many Republicans sincerely believed racial prejudice in the United States was so powerful that the Negro could never attain any kind of legal or social equality. "In this country," said the New York *Evening Post*, "the colored man has no future to which he can look forward, with hope of pleasure." Ben Wade agreed that free Negroes were "despised by all, repudiated by all; outcasts upon the face of the earth,

---

46. Wesley, "Lincoln's Plan," 7–21; Warren A. Beck, "Lincoln and Negro Colonization in Central America," *Abraham Lincoln Quarterly*, VI (September 1950), 162–83; Bancroft, "Colonization," 196–258; Lawanda and John H. Cox, *Politics, Principle, and Prejudice 1865–1866* (Glencoe, 1963), 215; Jeter A. Isely, *Horace Greeley and the Republican Party 1853–1861* (Princeton, 1947), 299n.; Brainerd Dyer, "The Persistence of the Idea of Negro Colonization," *Pacific Historical Review*, XII (March 1943), 53–66.

47. Racine *Weekly Advocate*, August 3, 1859. Cf. Doolittle to Weed, January 23, 1860, Weed Papers; Blair to Lincoln, May 26, 1860, Lincoln Papers; *Congressional Globe*, 36 Congress, 1 Session, 1632; Benjamin F. Shambaugh, ed., *The Messages and Proclamations of the Governors of Iowa* (7 vols.: Iowa City, 1903–05), II, 243–44.

without any fault of theirs that I know of." He deplored the prejudice, but believed it "perfectly impossible that these two races can inhabit the same place and be prosperous and happy." [48] Many Republicans believed that racial prejudice did not exist in the Central American states. Governor Randall of Wisconsin, for instance, in urging his legislature to endorse colonization, spoke of Latin America as an area "where color is no degradation," and where Negro colonists would enjoy "all the rights of settlement and citizenship." The Blairs may be charged with insincerity in extolling the prospects for free Negroes in Central America, but when men like Chase and Samuel C. Pomeroy despaired of the chances for racial justice in the United States, they reflected the genuine disillusionment of many Republicans who had long fought for Negro rights. [49]

In an age which witnessed the voluntary emigration of millions of Europeans to the United States and the constant flow westward of the American population, the idea that black Americans would wish to seek a better life in other lands did not seem as impractical as it does today. The radical Senator John P. Hale said colonization was "one of the most absurd ideas that ever entered into the head of man or woman," but Doolittle countered by pointing out that between 1847 and 1860 over three and a half million Europeans had arrived in the United States. "Colonization," said George Julian, "is one of the great tidal forces of modern civilization." [50] In many ways, therefore, the Blair plan was a logical product of its times, and in its strange mixture of racism and humanitarianism, imperialism and missionary zeal, it reflected many aspects of the Republican ideology as a whole. But in the end, though the colonizationists must be given credit for their awareness of the immense difficulties of achieving racial justice in this country, their proposal was an attempt to escape from the problem, not to solve it.

48. Racine *Weekly Advocate*, September 19, 1860; *National Intelligencer*, January 21, 1860, clipping in Doolittle to Weed, January 23, 1860, Weed Papers; New York *Evening Post*, September 8, 1851; *Congressional Globe*, 36 Congress, 1 Session, Appendix, 154–55.
49. *Annual Message of Alexander W. Randall*, 24–25; Chase to C. H. and J. M. Langston, November 11, 1850, Chase Papers (ser II), LC; Duane Mowry, ed., "Negro Colonization. From Doolittle Correspondence," *Publications* of the Southern Historical Association, IX (November 1905), 401–02; Theodore C. Pease and James G. Randall, eds., *The Diary of James G. Randall* (2 vols.: Springfield, 1927–33), I, 577.
50. *Congressional Globe*, 37 Congress, 2 Session, 332, 1605, Appendix, 97–98.

III

While racism and colonization were important elements of the Republican attitude toward the Negro, they were by no means the entire story. Many men entered the Republican party with long histories of support for Negro rights, and many of the areas of the North which gave the Republicans their largest majorities had distinguished themselves in the past by their endorsement of Negro suffrage and opposition to Negro exclusion laws. Most Liberty party voters went into the Republican party in the 1850's, for example, and in the preceding decades these men had fought long and hard for the repeal of western black laws and for full legal equality for black citizens.[51] Thousands of Whig voters who became Republicans had supported Negro suffrage in the 1840's because Negro rights had been largely a party issue, especially in the East. And in the West, the areas known as centers of radical Republicanism in the 1850's had long defended Negro rights. The Western Reserve of Ohio always elected legislators who opposed the state's black laws, and in Illinois, fourteen northern counties voted in favor of a Negro suffrage provision in 1848, although it went down to defeat in the state as a whole. These same counties strenuously opposed the Negro exclusion law of 1853, and would soon roll up overwhelming Republican majorities.[52]

Even more striking was the large number of Republican leaders who had taken pro-Negro positions earlier in their political careers, sometimes at the cost of their own political advancement. John P. Hale of New Hampshire, for instance, defended fugitive slaves in court and received a testimonial from Boston Negroes. In Connecticut, Francis Gillette, Republican Senator in the 1850's, played an important role

51. Edgar A. Holt, "Party Politics in Ohio, 1840–50," *OAHQ*, XXXVIII (1929), 134–35; N. Dwight Harris, *The History of Negro Servitude in Illinois* (Chicago, 1904), 148, 161; William H. Seward to Chase, December 6, 1846, Chase Papers, LC. When Connecticut voters defeated a Negro suffrage proposal in 1847, a Liberty party newspaper declared, "There is not, we venture to affirm, a Liberty man in Connecticut who did not desire that the amendment should prevail." Hartford *Charter Oak*, October 28, 1847.

52. Foner, "Racial Attitudes," 311–14; Dixon Ryan Fox, *The Decline of Aristocracy in the Politics of New York* (New York, 1919), 269n.; Emil Olbrich, "The Development of Sentiment on Negro Suffrage to 1860," *Bulletin* of the University of Wisconsin, III (1912), 90, 105; Albert G. Riddle to Joshua Giddings, July 4, 1846, Joshua Reed Giddings Papers, OHS; New York *Tribune*, March 7, 1853; Theodore C. Smith, *The Liberty and Free Soil Parties in the Northwest* (New York, 1897), 284.

in the Liberty party's fight for equal suffrage. Massachusetts Conscience Whig leaders like Charles Francis Adams, Stephen C. Phillips, Henry Wilson, John Andrew, and Charles Sumner fought legal discrimination in the 1830's and 40's.[53] Andrew, the Republican Civil War governor, defended so many fugitives that he became known as "the Attorney-General of the Negroes." He helped buy slaves out of bondage, and took a close interest in their progress as free men.[54] The most prominent Republican of New York, William H. Seward, had long advocated political rights for free Negroes. In 1846 he supported Negro suffrage proposals considered by the state constitutional convention, and he braved popular abuse to defend an insane Negro, William Freeman, who had murdered four members of a New York family. Seward's political partner, Thurlow Weed, was a friend of Frederick Douglass and a supporter of Negro suffrage, and Charles B. Sedgwick, later a Republican Congressman, defended fugitive slaves free of charge. "Although I do not suppose that kind of business is likely to bring many friends about a stranger here or much money to his purse," he wrote in 1854, "yet my principles and feelings will not permit me to decline rendering all the aid in my power in any such case." In Pennsylvania, Thaddeus Stevens had long fought for Negro suffrage, and he and John B. Read, a Democrat who became a Republican, defended the Negroes accused of murder in the famous Christiana case.[55]

Further west, the same pattern was evident. Chase, Wade, and Giddings of Ohio were long-time supporters of Negro rights. In a famous address in 1845, Chase demanded equal suffrage for black

53. Congressional Globe, 35 Congress, 1 Session, 1970; Hartford Charter Oak, September 30, 1847; Eric Foner, "Politics and Prejudice: The Free Soil Party and the Negro, 1849–1852," JNH, L (October 1965), 244–46; Martin B. Duberman, Charles Francis Adams 1807–1886 (Boston, 1961), 74; Henry Wilson, History of the Rise and Fall of the Slave Power in America (3 vols.: Boston, 1875–77), I, 495–97; Louis Ruchames, "Jim Crow Railroads in Massachusetts," AmQ, VIII (Spring 1956), 61–75.

54. John Andrew to Sumner, January 22, 31, February 2, 26, March 3, 1855, Sumner Papers; E. L. Pierce to Chase, September 21, 1859, Chase Papers, LC; James Freeman Clarke, Anti-Slavery Days (New York, 1883), 170–72; George G. Shackelford, ed., "Attorneys Andrew of Boston and Green of Richmond Consider the John Brown Raid," Virginia Magazine of History and Biography, LX (January 1952), 113.

55. George E. Baker, ed., The Works of William Seward (5 vols.: Boston, 1853–84), III, 370; Seward to Weed, May 28, 1846, Weed Papers; Frederick W. Seward, ed., William Seward: An Autobiography (New York, 1891), 759, 764, 810; Thurlow Weed to Horace Greeley, June 10, 1847, Miscellaneous Manuscripts, NYHS; Charles B. Sedgwick to John Jay, December 1, 1854, John Jay Papers, Columbia University; Brodie, Stevens, 63, 66, 117.

citizens and denounced "the whole policy of our legislation in relation to our colored population." Four years later he drafted the bill repealing Ohio's black laws. Giddings and Wade also advocated Negro suffrage, and in 1849 Giddings scandalized Congress—including many anti-slavery men—by introducing a bill for a referendum on slavery in the District of Columbia, with both black and white residents voting. He and James M. Ashley, a Republican Congressman in the 1850's and 1860's, assisted runaway slaves.[56] In Indiana, perhaps the most anti-Negro state of the North, three delegates to the constitutional convention of 1850 soon became Republican Congressmen—Schuyler Colfax, William Dunn, and David Kilgore. All opposed the Negro exclusion measure adopted by the convention, and while none endorsed black suffrage, Kilgore and Colfax supported an unsuccessful motion to allow a popular referendum on the issue. Colfax condemned the anti-Negro sentiments which dominated the convention, and when he ran unsuccessfully for Congress in 1851, his position was used against him by his Democratic opponent. Lucien Barbour, a Democrat who served as Republican Congressman in the 1850's, defended a fugitive slave in 1853, and George Julian, leader of Indiana radicals, had long opposed legal discrimination.[57]

The story in other western states was similar. Jacob Howard and Zachariah Chandler, two powerful Michigan politicians, aided the underground railroad, and DeWitt Leach, elected Republican Congressman in 1858, had been one of the few delegates to favor equal suffrage at the constitutional convention of 1850. Austin Blair, the state's Civil War governor, presented a report favoring Negro suffrage to the Michigan legislature in 1846. "This, however, displeased a large

56. Foner, "Politics and Prejudice," 240–42; *The Address and Reply on the Presentation of a Testimonial to S. P. Chase, by the Colored People of Cincinnati* (Cincinnati, 1845), 27; Chase Diary, January 7, 1849, Chase Papers, LC; *Congressional Globe*, 30 Congress, 2 Session, 55; Giddings Diary, 1848–1849, December 19, 25, 1848, Giddings Papers; Berwanger, *Frontier*, 40; Hans L. Trefousse, *Benjamin Franklin Wade* (New York, 1963), 46; Charles S. Ashley, "Governor Ashley's Biography and Messages," *Contributions* to the Historical Society of Montana, VI (1907), 148.
57. *Report of the Debates and Proceedings of the Convention for the Revision of the Constitution of the State of Indiana* (2 vols.: Indianapolis, 1850), I, 228–34, 252–54, 455–57, 617, 956, II, 1787–88; New York *Tribune*, December 13, 1850; Schuyler Colfax to Seward, December 6, 20, 1850, Seward Papers; O. J. Hollister, *Life of Schuyler Colfax* (New York, 1886), 63; Emma Lou Thornbrough, *The Negro in Indiana* (Indianapolis, 1957), 116; George Julian to Convention of Colored Citizens of Illinois, September 17, 1853, George W. Julian Papers, Indiana State Library.

section of the Whig party," he later wrote, "and occasioned my defeat in the next election. . . ." [58] In Wisconsin, Alexander Randall and Louis Harvey, later Republican governors, advocated Negro suffrage in the 1840's, and the Democrat Randall's position was so unpopular with his constituents that it kept him out of politics for several years. Charles Durkee, Republican Senator in the 1850's also distinguished himself by his support of Negro rights. And in Illinois, David Davis, John M. Palmer, Jesse O. Norton, and James Knox—the last two of whom were Republican Congressmen in the 1850's—opposed Negro exclusion at the constitutional convention of 1847. In the Illinois legislature, Civil War governor Richard Yates favored repeal of the black laws.[59] Lyman Trumbull and Gustav Koerner were leaders in the legal contests which invalidated the state's indenture system for Negroes in the 1840's, and Koerner bought and freed a Negro who had entered the state in violation of the exclusion law of 1853 and was to be sold into slavery. Radicals Owen Lovejoy and Zebina Eastman assisted fugitive slaves, and had long fought for legal equality for Negroes.[60]

The fact that so many Republican leaders had defended the rights of free Negroes and fugitive slaves in the 1840's and early 1850's should be proof that there was more to Republican attitudes than mere racism. Most Republicans, of course, shared the prevalent prejudices of their times, and were by no means ready to afford complete equality to black citizens. But by their actions in state legislatures and in Congress in the ante-bellum decade, the Republicans demonstrated

58. Detroit *Post and Tribune, Zachariah Chandler: An Outline Sketch of His Life and Public Services* (Detroit, 1880), 75; Floyd B. Streeter, *Political Parties in Michigan 1837–1860* (Lansing, 1918), 191; *Report of the Proceedings and Debates in the Convention to Revise the Constitution of the State of Michigan, 1850* (Lansing, 1850), 758; Austin Blair Autobiographical Sketch, Austin Blair Papers, Burton Historical Collection, Detroit Public Library.
59. Milo M. Quaife, ed., *The Attainment of Statehood* (Madison, 1928), 384–86; Milo M. Quaife, ed., *The Convention of 1846* (Madison, 1919), 241–48; Cox and Cox, *Politics, Principle, Prejudice*, 219; *Proceedings of the Convention of the Colored Freemen of Ohio* (Cincinnati, 1852), 23; *Journal of the Convention, Assembled at Springfield, . . . for the Purpose of . . . Revising the Constitution of the State of Illinois* (Springfield, 1847), 76; Chicago *Democrat*, July 23, 1860; D. W. Lusk, *Eighty Years of Illinois* (Springfield, 1889), 109–10.
60. Harris, *History of Negro Servitude*, 108–9, 122–23; Mark M. Krug, *Lyman Trumbull, Conservative Radical* (New York, 1965), 61–64; Thomas J. McCormack, ed., *Memoirs of Gustav Koerner 1809–1896* (2 vols.: Cedar Rapids, 1909), I, 487, II, 30–31; Chicago *Journal*, undated clipping, 1857, Box 19, Chase Papers, HSPa; *A Memorial of Zebina Eastman by His Family* (np, nd), 15–16; Edward Magdol, *Owen Lovejoy: Abolitionist in Congress* (New Brunswick, 1967), 36.

that they were willing to guarantee Negroes certain basic rights, and they consistently fought Democratic attempts to make the legal and social position of black citizens even worse than it was.

The issue of race was much less important in New England in the 1850's than in the West, primarily because far fewer legal disabilities were imposed on the Negro. Nevertheless, Massachusetts Republicans took an active part in broadening the rights of colored citizens. The Know-Nothing legislature of 1855 opened the state's schools to all children regardless of race, and two Republican leaders, John Andrew and Henry Wilson, were instrumental in the measure's passage.[61] Four years later, the Republican legislature voted to allow Negroes to enroll in the militia, but the bill was vetoed by Governor Banks, a former Democrat and member of the party's conservative wing. A similar law enacted by New Hampshire Republicans in 1857, however, was put into effect.[62] In New York, the 1857 legislature by a strict party vote enacted a constitutional amendment providing for equal suffrage, but because of a legal technicality no referendum was held on the issue. Three years later the measure was re-enacted, with only five of eighty-nine Republicans in the Assembly opposing it. The New York *Tribune* gave it a quiet endorsement, but most Republican papers ignored the referendum, fearing it would injure Lincoln's chances of carrying the state. Though Lincoln was successful, equal suffrage went down to defeat, 337,984 to 197,503. However, nineteen of the forty-six Republican counties voted in its favor, and the majorities in opposition were rolled up in the Democratic strongholds around New York City. A comparison of the presidential and Negro suffrage returns reveals that over half the Republican voters cast ballots in favor of equal suffrage, while almost all the Democrats opposed it, and a sizable number of Republicans abstained. In addition, some of the Republican counties which had previously been Democratic showed a marked change since the referendum of 1846. St. Lawrence county, for instance, had gone two to one against equal suffrage in 1846; now it went two to

61. Dwight L. Dumond, *Antislavery, The Crusade for Freedom in America* (Ann Arbor, 1961), 121; *Liberator*, December 28, 1855; Wilson, *Slave Power*, II, 640; James M. Bugbee, "Memoir of Henry Lillie Pierce," *Proceedings* of MHS, 2nd ser., XI (May 1897), 394.
62. New York *Tribune*, October 7, 1859; Fred Harvey Harrington, "Nathaniel Prentiss Banks, A Study in Anti-Slavery Politics," *NEQ*, IX (December 1936), 651; F. W. Bird, *Review of Gov. Banks' Veto of the Revised Code* (Boston, 1860).

one in favor. What all this adds up to is that Negro suffrage was to a large extent a party issue in New York, with all Democrats opposed and a majority of Republicans in favor.[63]

Even in the West, the stronghold of racism, a majority of Republicans were ready to give some recognition to Negro rights, and the party strenuously opposed Democratic efforts to enact new anti-black legislation. In 1858, 1859, and 1860, the Democrats tried unsuccessfully to get a Negro exclusion law through the Ohio legislature, but each time Republicans defeated it. In the 1860 vote, forty Republicans voted against thirty-one Democrats and four Republicans to kill the bill. The Democrats did manage to enact a law in 1859, barring anyone with a "visible admixture" of Negro blood from exercising the franchise. Governor Chase urged its repeal, but the Democratic minority was able to persuade a few conservative Republicans to ally with them to block it. The Republican-controlled Supreme Court, however, soon declared the law unconstitutional.[64] Some Republican legislators favored Negro suffrage, and the party's state organ, the *Ohio State Journal,* said the state would not suffer in the least from its adoption. But enough Republicans allied with the Democrats to prevent its enactment. The experience of Indiana Republicans was similar. The majority wanted to repeal the state's exclusion law, but they were frustrated by an alliance of conservative Republicans and Democrats. The same kind of alliance defeated an attempt by a majority of Illinois Republicans to repeal that state's black laws in 1857. Two years later, a majority of Republicans voted to allow Negroes to testify in court and attend the public schools, but the Democrats, who had won control of the legislature, defeated the bill.[65]

63. *Journal of the Assembly of New York,* 80 Session, 863–64, 83 Session, 332–33; *Journal of the Senate of New York,* 80 Session, 354; Olbrich, "Negro Suffrage," 126–28; *National Era,* April 9, 1857; New York *Tribune,* August 7, September 17, 1860; *Douglass' Monthly,* November, 1860; *Tribune Almanac,* 1861, 41. The most recent study of the 1860 referendum concludes that there was a very high correlation (+.91) between the pro-Negro suffrage vote and Republican voting. John L. Stanley, "Majority Tyranny in Tocqueville's America: The Failure of Negro Suffrage in 1846," *PSQ,* LXXIV (September 1969), 428.
64. *Journal of the House of Representatives of Ohio,* 54 General Assembly, 1 Session, 523, 542; *Ohio State Journal,* January 29, February 3, 1858; Berwanger, *Frontier,* 44; Cleveland *Leader,* February 8, March 24, 1858; George H. Porter, *Ohio Politics During the Civil War Period* (New York, 1911), 22–23, 30–34; *Message of the Governor of Ohio to the Fifty-Fourth General Assembly* (Columbus, 1860), 28.
65. *Ohio State Journal,* January 13, 23, 1857; *Journal of the House of Representatives of Indiana,* 38 Session, 785; *Congregational Herald,* cited in *National Era,*

In 1857, the Republican legislature of Wisconsin overcame Democratic opposition and authorized a referendum on Negro suffrage. The Republican state platform gave the proposal an ambiguous endorsement by stating its opposition to "the proscription of any man on account of birthplace, religion, or color." Negro suffrage received cautious approval from the Republican press, while the Democrats bitterly denounced it. The Republican organ, the *Wisconsin State Journal*, denied that Negro suffrage was a party issue but acknowledged that almost all the affirmative votes would come from Republicans. The proposal was defeated in the fall election, as the Republican gubernatorial candidate was winning a very narrow victory, but a majority of Republican voters cast affirmative ballots. All seventeen counties which gave it majority support had voted for Frémont in 1856.[66]

Perhaps the best illustration of the extent and limits of western Republicans' commitment to Negro rights was given at the Iowa Constitutional Convention of 1857. When they won control of the convention, Iowa Republicans had already repealed a law barring Negroes from testifying in court. The new constitution affirmed this right, together with the right of black men to hold property and send their children to public schools. All these clauses were adopted by fairly strict party votes, and a Democratic proposal for Negro exclusion was defeated. A minority of Republicans favored Negro suffrage, and the convention adopted a plan for a referendum on the subject over Democratic objections.[67] In the fall election, the Democratic press urged voters to oppose Negro suffrage and to defeat the constitution, in part because of its provisions for Negro education and testimony. The Republicans defended these clauses, but ignored the Negro suffrage issue. The constitution was adopted by Iowa voters, but Negro suffrage went down to a resounding defeat, 49,387 to 8,489. A majority of both party's voters opposed the measure, and some Re-

---

July 9, 1857; Lusk, *Eighty Years*, 41–42; *Tribune Almanac*, 1857, 61; *Congressional Globe*, 36 Congress, 1 Session, 239.

66. Milwaukee *Sentinel*, August 3, 21, September 7, 19, October 17, 1857; *Wisconsin State Journal*, August 1, October 21, 1857; Boom, "Development of Sectional Attitudes," 158–60; *Tribune Almanac*, 1858, 62–63; Olbrich, "Negro Suffrage," 119–21. Cf. Leslie H. Fishel, Jr., "Wisconsin and Negro Suffrage," *WisMH*, XLVI (Spring 1963), 186–88; John G. Gregory, "Negro Suffrage in Wisconsin," *Transactions* of the Wisconsin Academy of Sciences, Arts, and Letters, XI (1896–97), 94–101.

67. William Salter, *The Life of James W. Grimes* (New York, 1876), 98–99; Joel H. Silbey, "Proslavery Sentiment in Iowa 1838–1861," *IJH*, LX (October 1957), 313; *Iowa Constitutional Convention*, I, 172, 200, II, 735, 832, 913, 917.

publican convention delegates were later defeated for public office because they had favored equal suffrage. But the majorities in Democratic areas were larger than in Republican. In 1859, the Democrats renewed their attacks on the Negro education clause and again demanded the exclusion of free Negroes from the state, but Republicans prevented the enactment of such a measure.[68]

Republicans in Congress had few opportunities to vote on issues of Negro rights in the 1850's but in the instances which did come up, their differences with northern Democrats were clearly demonstrated. In 1854, an amendment barring blacks from participating in homestead benefits passed the House and Senate. Twenty-four Whig and Democratic Congressmen who later served in Congress as Republicans voted against the provision, and none favored it. Among the opponents of the restriction were Galusha Grow ("father of the homestead law"), Elihu Washburne, and four men who would soon serve as Republican governors—Nathaniel P. Banks, Richard Yates, Edwin Morgan, and Israel Washburn. In the Senate such Republican leaders as Chase, Seward, Hamlin, Sumner, Wade, and Fessenden opposed the amendment.[69] A few years later, Republican Senators Hale, Harlan, Clark, and Durkee attempted to have a provision for the education of black children included in the District of Columbia school bill.[70]

Only during the debates over the admission of Oregon in 1858 and 1859 did the rights of free Negroes become the subject of prolonged discussion in Congress. Ordinarily, Republicans would be expected to support enthusiastically the admission of a free state to the Union, but with Oregon, there were several complications. Some Republicans objected that Oregon was seeking admission with too small a population, while Kansas had been barred until she had 93,000 inhabitants. Others pointed to Democratic control of the territory as evidence that admission would merely add to their opponents' Congressional strength.

68. "Contemporary Editorial Opinion of the 1857 Constitution," *IJH*, LV (April 1957), 115–46; Carl H. Erbe, "Constitutional Provisions for the Suffrage in Iowa," *IJHP*, XXII (April 1924), 206; Chicago *Press*, September 7, 1857; Robert R. Dykstra and Harlan Hahn, "Northern Voters and Negro Suffrage: The Case of Iowa, 1868," *POQ*, XXXII (Summer 1968), 207; Louis Pelzer, "The History of Political Parties in Iowa from 1857 to 1860," *IJHP*, VII (April 1909), 208.

69. *Congressional Globe*, 33 Congress, 1 Session, 549, 1744, Appendix, 1121–22. Cf. 33 Congress, 1 Session, 529, 1072–73; *National Era*, March 16, 1854; James T. DuBois and Gertrude S. Matthews, *Galusha A. Grow, Father of the Homestead Law* (Boston, 1917), 103.

70. *Congressional Globe*, 35 Congress, 1 Session, Appendix, 371, 36 Congress, 1 Session, 1679–83; Wilson, *Slave Power*, II, 583.

Still others disliked the constitutional provision giving the suffrage to resident aliens. But the objection most frequently raised by Republicans concerned the treatment of free Negroes by the Oregon constitution. Not only were black men barred from entering the state, but the few already there were forbidden to testify in court, make contracts, or hold property. When the Oregon issue first came before the Senate in May, 1858, a number of influential Republicans declared they could not support admission with the proposed constitution. Henry Wilson called the constitution "unconstitutional, inhuman and unchristian," and Fessenden said he could never support a measure which would bar black citizens of Maine from entering another state. Others, however, felt they had to vote to admit a free state, regardless of the circumstances. Seward, for instance, said he regretted the Negro clauses, but voted for admission. And two ex-Democrats, Preston King and Lyman Trumbull, went out of their way to make clear that they did not object to the anti-Negro provisions, although Trumbull opposed admission for political reasons. In the end, the Republican Senators divided eleven to six in favor of admission.[71]

When the Oregon issue reached the House, however, Republican opposition to admission had mounted, and only fifteen Republicans voted in favor, while seventy-three opposed, and some of the fifteen said they regretted the Negro clauses. The motives of those who opposed admission are hard to fix with certainty, but many, especially from the East, sincerely objected to the treatment of free Negroes. Abbott of Maine, for example, denounced the constitution in the strongest terms. "You may go back to the earliest monuments of the human race," he said, ". . . you may search the journals of barbarians and pirates, . . . and you will find nothing that is more infamous and inhuman than the negro section of the Oregon constitution."[72] Mason Tappan of New Hampshire wrote to a political associate that he could not have voted for such a constitution, "though you, and every other

71. *Congressional Globe*, 35 Congress, 1 Session, 1964–66, 1970, 2205–07. On Trumbull's position, see Charles S. Wilson to Trumbull, May 12, 1858, Trumbull to "Editor, Times," May 21, 1858, Trumbull Papers; George T. Palmer, ed., "A Collection of Letters from Lyman Trumbull to John M. Palmer, 1854–1858," *Journal* of the IllSHS, XVI (April–July 1923), 37; Trumbull to Chase, February 7, 1859, Chase Papers, HSPa.
72. *Congressional Globe*, 35 Congress, 2 Session, 1011, 950–51, 974, Appendix, 228, 193. Cf. 2 Session, 987–88, 1006, Appendix, 108. For the various motives behind Republican opposition to the bill, see New York *Tribune*, January 11, 1859, and the slightly cynical account in Henry H. Simms, "The Controversy over the Admission of the State of Oregon," *MVHR*, XXXII (December 1945), 355–74.

voter in my District had appealed to me to do so," and Henry Dawes
of Massachusetts said the time had come to oppose the western
tendency to deny Negroes the basic rights of humanity. Dawes received
a letter from a constituent assuring him that nine-tenths "of our
people" agreed with him.[73]

Out of experiences in state legislatures, in constitutional conventions,
and in the Oregon debate, a distinctive Republican position on the
rights of free Negroes finally became clear. It was not accepted by
everyone in the party, but it did represent what may be called the
mainstream of Republican opinion. Fundamentally it asserted that free
Negroes were human beings and citizens of the United States, entitled
to the natural rights of humanity and to such civil rights as would
protect the natural rights of life, liberty, and property. Given the racism
which pervaded northern society, the Republicans' insistence on the
humanity of the Negro was more of a step forward than might appear.
In the Lincoln-Douglas debates, for example, Douglas continually
contended that the black man was not included in the Declaration of
Independence's proclamation of human equality. But Lincoln replied
that "all men are created equal" meant just what it said—all men, without distinction of race. Republicans insisted that so far as natural
rights were concerned, the question of Negro inferiority was irrelevant.
So long as he was a man, the Negro was entitled to his natural rights.
"It is a question," said Governor Randall of Wisconsin, "of manhood,
not of color."[74]

Some radical Republicans insisted that the Negroes' inclusion in
the Declaration of Independence automatically entitled them to full
legal and political equality with whites. As DeWitt Leach of Michigan
expressed it, "They, sir, are naturally entitled to all the rights which
you and I, as individuals of the white race, can claim." But most differentiated among natural rights, to which all men were entitled, civil
rights—legal enactments which protected natural rights—and political

73. Mason Tappan to George G. Fogg, February 13, 1859, Mason Tappan Papers,
NHHS; *Congressional Globe*, 35 Congress, 2 Session, 974–75, 36 Congress, 1
Session, 1904; J. T. Robinson to Henry L. Dawes, February 19, 1859, P. Emory
Aldrich to Dawes, February 19, 1859, David Lee Child to Dawes, February 20,
1859, Henry L. Dawes Papers, LC.
74. Basler, ed., *Lincoln Works*, III, 16, 249; Chicago *Press and Tribune*, October
4, 1859. Cf. New York *Tribune*, July 28, 1858; Don E. Fehrenbacher, *Prelude to
Greatness, Lincoln in the 1850's* (New York, 1964 ed.), 111; *Congressional Globe*,
33 Congress, 1 Session, 339.

rights, which could be regulated at the discretion of the majority. Giddings, for example, described the Republican position on Negro rights as follows: "We do not say the black man is, or shall be, the equal of the white man; or that he shall vote or hold office, however just such position may be; but we assert that he who murders a black man shall be hanged; that he who robs the black man of his liberty or his property shall be punished like other criminals." [75] This was the basis of many Republicans' objections to the Oregon constitution—that it denied Negroes the access to the courts which was essential for the protection of their lives and property. Most Republicans also opposed Negro exclusion laws, for it seemed a natural right for a man to live in the place where he was born, or move freely if he saw fit. [76]

Beyond the guarantee of these basic rights to free blacks, there were sharp differences within the party. Republicans from New England boasted that in their states there was little or no legal discrimination, and they said their goal was complete equality before the law. Henry Wilson, for example, declared that "wherever and whenever we have the power to do it, I would give to all men, of every clime and race, of every faith and creed, freedom and equality before the law." And the radical Chase insisted that the moment the law excluded a portion of the community from equal protection, caste and aristocracy were introduced, and democracy was endangered. [77] Most Republicans, however, were not prepared to insist on full legal equality, especially equality of political rights. The exclusion of Negroes from the suffrage, they argued, was not a violation of civil equality, just as women, children, and unnaturalized foreigners did not surrender their natural rights because they could not vote. This distinction between natural and civil rights on the one hand, and political rights on the other, was endorsed by most western Republicans. As a leading Iowa Republican editor explained it, Republicans were opposed to all legal disabilities which interfered with the exercise of the Negro's natural rights. "Or

75. *Michigan Constitutional Convention*, 289; *Congressional Globe*, 35 Congress, 2 Session, 346. Cf. 33 Congress, 1 Session, Appendix, 311, 35 Congress, 2 Session, Appendix, 199, 36 Congress, 1 Session, 921, 1910.
76. *Congressional Globe*, 33 Congress, 1 Session, Appendix, 224, 35 Congress, 1 Session, Appendix, 93, 2 Session, 947, 979–81, 987–88, Appendix, 108.
77. *Official Report of the Debates and Proceedings in the State Convention . . . to Revise and Amend the Constitution of the Commonwealth of Massachusetts* (3 vols.: Boston, 1853), II, 81; *Address and Reply on the Presentation of a Testimonial*, 20.

in other words, that the colored population, if they come here, shall have the right of protection under our laws, and shall be protected in the enjoyment of their rights of property." [78]

If the Negro's enjoyment of his natural and civil rights did not necessarily imply political equality with the white man, even less did it mean his race would enjoy social equality. The Republicans argued that the social relations between the races were regulated by custom and choice, not legislation. "Equality is one thing," said the New York *Tribune*, "familiarity another," and Governor Randall insisted in 1859 that the whole issue of social equality was a red herring. "It is not whether we want to associate with the black man," he said in a debate with his Democratic rival, ". . . sit by the fireside with them in the social circle, or intermarry with them. That is a question of taste." Most Republicans believed that even if the Negro did attain full equality before the law, social differences and distinctions would remain. "There is a natural antipathy between him and the white race," declared the *Wisconsin State Journal*, "that we do not profess to have overcome. This, however, has nothing to do with the question of suffrage." Black spokesmen tended to agree that political and legal equality was much more important than any social recognition. As one leading Negro newspaper put it, "When our political rights are acquired, the social will take care of themselves." [79]

In accordance with their conception of the civil rights of free Negroes, Republicans consistently attacked the policies of the federal government denying the citizenship of the black man. During the 1850's the government generally rejected passport applications from Negroes and denied them the right to benefits under pre-emption laws. Republicans criticized these policies, and reversed them early in Lincoln's presidency. They also bitterly denounced Chief Justice Taney's opinion in the Dred Scott case that Negroes could not be citizens of the United States, and had "no rights which the white man

---

78. *Iowa Constitutional Convention*, II, 675. Cf. *Congressional Globe*, 36 Congress, 1 Session, 102, 918, 1904; *Report of the Debates and Proceedings of the Convention for the Revision of the Constitution of the State of Ohio* (2 vols.: Columbus, 1851), II, 635. There are interesting parallels between the Republicans' distinction between different kinds of rights for blacks, and T. H. Marshall's discussion of the progression of the English working class from civil to political to social rights in the nineteenth and twentieth centuries. Marshall, *Citizenship and Social Class* (Cambridge, 1950), esp. 10–11.
79. New York *Tribune*, January 17, 1851; Chicago *Press and Tribune*, October 4, 1859; *Wisconsin State Journal*, August 1, 1857; *Weekly Anglo-African*, August 20, 1859.

was bound to respect." Throughout the North, the Republican press denounced this opinion, and several state conventions of the party in 1857 affirmed free Negro citizenship.[80] The Republican legislatures of New Hampshire, Vermont, New York, and Ohio passed resolutions stating that color did not disqualify a resident of the state from citizenship, and the Supreme Court of Maine took the same position, in reaffirming the right of free blacks to vote. Even in Indiana, Republicans defeated a Democratic attempt to have the legislature endorse Taney's views.[81] That a majority of the Republican party stood by the citizenship of the Negro on the eve of the Civil War was demonstrated at the ill-fated Peace Convention of February, 1861. When a resolution was proposed providing that Congress guarantee that citizens of each state have their rights recognized in all the states, an Illinois delegate moved to limit the provision to "free white citizens." The amendment was adopted, ten states to eight, but the Republican delegation from the six New England states, together with those of New York and Iowa, voted against it, while the only free states in favor were New Jersey, Pennsylvania, Indiana, and Illinois.[82]

Many Republicans insisted before the Civil War that their party had no position on the questions of race relations and Negro rights, and certainly the differences between easterners and westerners, and men of Whig, Democratic, and Liberty background made it extremely difficult to reach a consensus within the party. Chase discovered this in January, 1860, when he penned a few lines for his annual message to the Ohio legislature:

> A majority of the people of Ohio unquestionably desire a homogeneous population and would gladly see such provision made for the colored race in more congenial latitudes as would supersede the necessity of their emigration to northern states. They are also,

80. Litwack, North of Slavery, 50–57; National Era, April 22, 1858; Springfield Republican, April 13, 1858; New York Tribune, March 10, 12, 19, April 9, May 22, 1857; Boston Atlas and Daily Bee, July 1, August 26, 1858, March 25, 1859; Cincinnati Gazette, December 11, 1858; Wisconsin State Journal, August 4, 1857.
81. Dumond, Antislavery, 120; Message of His Excellency William Haile, Governor of the State of New Hampshire (Concord, 1857), 15; George S. Merriam, The Life and Times of Samuel Bowles (2 vols.: New York, 1885), I, 223, William C. Cochran, "The Western Reserve and the Fugitive Slave Law," Collections of WRHS, CI (1920), 116–17; Chicago Tribune, August 22, 1857; Congressional Globe, 35 Congress, 1 Session, 1964; Wilson, Slave Power, II, 641; Thornbrough, Negro in Indiana, 132.
82. L. E. Chittenden, A Report of the Debates and Proceedings in the Secret Sessions of the Conference Convention . . . Held at Washington, D.C., in February, A. D. 1861 (New York, 1864), 380–81.

no doubt, indisposed to admit any others than whites to a participation in their political power through the right of suffrage. But
they do not, in my judgment, desire any unjust or harsh legislation
against anybody, with intent either to exclude him from the State
or to oppress him in it.

In Chase's view, the position he outlined defined "exactly the right
view" of the race issue. But when he submitted the section to friends
for criticism, he was surprised by their reactions. Some criticized the
first part as conceding too much to "the spirit of caste," while others
felt the latter portion "savored too much of the spirit of negro equality."
Rather than exacerbate intraparty differences on race, Chase decided
to omit the whole subject from his message.[83]

Nevertheless, by the eve of the Civil War there had emerged a
distinctive Republican attitude towards the Negro. As on other
questions, it was well represented by Abraham Lincoln. Seward's
record of favoring Negro suffrage had been one of the reasons westerners felt he could not carry their states in 1860, and it therefore
contributed to his failure to receive the nomination.[84] Lincoln, coming
from Illinois, was well aware of the strength of racial prejudice, and
he knew too that "a universal feeling, whether well- or ill-founded, can
not be safely disregarded." Like most western Republicans, he opposed
Negro suffrage and was an ardent colonizationist, though he insisted
that emigration be voluntary. However, he never pandered to racial
prejudice, even when confronted with the racist attacks of Douglas.
And he consistently affirmed the basic humanity of the Negro and
his right to an economic livelihood. Just after his election, the New
York *Times* summed up Lincoln's position regarding the Negro: "He
declares his opposition to negro suffrage, and to everything looking
towards placing negroes upon a footing of political and social equality
with the whites;—but he asserts for them a perfect equality of civil
and personal rights under the Constitution." Many eastern Republicans
would go further than this; many westerners, on the other hand, felt
that Lincoln had gone too far; but Lincoln himself articulated a

83. "The Colored People," Manuscript in Box 17, Chase Papers, HSPa. This paper
is in Chase's handwriting, and includes the proposed section dealing with the
Negro, and the reaction of Republican leaders. On the other side is written:
"Colored population—views intended for message Jan'y 1860 but not used."
84. New York *Times*, August 28, 1860; Earl W. Wiley, " 'Governor' John Grenier
and Chase's Bid for the Presidency in 1860," *OAHQ*, LVIII (July 1949), 268; F. I.
Herriot, "Memories of the Chicago Convention of 1860," *Annals of Iowa*, 3rd
ser., XII (October 1920), 466.

shaky consensus within the party. On the eve of the Civil War, the Republican party had arrived at the position which John and LaWanda Cox have identified as their basic outlook when Reconstruction began— that the fundamental civil rights of the Negro, short of suffrage, deserved legal protection.[85]

IV

During the 1850's, a good number of abolitionists and black leaders remained aloof from the Republican party because of its racist elements. An influential Negro newspaper charged in 1860 that antislavery meant little more to the Republicans than "opposition to the black man," and the black orator H. Ford Douglass told a Massachusetts abolitionist audience that no party deserved their votes "unless that party is willing to extend to the black man all the rights of a citizen." On the other hand, prominent blacks like Frederick Douglass and Dr. John Rock actively supported Frémont and Lincoln, and colored conventions throughout the North endorsed Republican candidates.[86] These men recognized that the basic fault of the Republicans' racial attitude was not simple racism but ambivalence. Even Republicans who attacked racial prejudice and defended Negro rights were not free from prejudice, for almost all accepted in some degree the racial stereotypes of their time. Even Seward and Chase, with their long records of advocacy of Negro rights, had this problem. Seward could lecture a Michigan audience during the campaign of 1856 on the necessity for giving blacks the rights to vote—a position which could hardly be of political advantage—but at the same time, he viewed the Negro as a "foreign and feeble" element of the population which, unlike European immigrants, could never be assimilated and would eventually "altogether disappear." And Chase could insist during the gubernatorial campaign of 1857, at great political hazard, that one of his aims was to have it acknowledged "that colored people have rights

85. Basler, ed., *Lincoln Works*, II, 256; Fehrenbacher, *Prelude*, 111–12; New York *Times*, November 8, 1860; Cox and Cox, *Politics, Principle, Prejudice*, viii, 163–64.
86. *Weekly Anglo-African*, March 17, 1860; *Liberator*, July 13, 1860; Lewis Tappan to Frederick Douglass, November 27, 1856, Tappan to L. A. Chamerovzow, December 10, 1856, Letterbook, Tappan Papers; *Life and Times of Frederick Douglass* (Hartford, 1883), 399; Bell, "Negro Convention Movement," 193; New York *Times*, September 27, 1856, October 7, 1858; New York *Tribune*, November 3, 1857; *Liberator*, September 5, 1856; Foner, ed., *Douglass*, II, 396–98.

and privileges which they have not now." But he also believed that an eventual separation of the races was both inevitable and necessary.[87]

To a large extent, the ambivalence and contradictions in the Republican attitude towards the Negro stemmed from the fact that their racial outlook was part of their larger free labor ideology. The Republicans' affirmation of the Negro's natural rights included the right to participate as a free laborer in the marketplace, and, as we have seen, they demanded that he be protected in such legal rights as were essential to that participation, such as holding property and testifying in court. In 1857, Lincoln defined the irreducible minimum of the Negro's natural rights in economic terms. Speaking of a black woman, he declared, "In some respects she is certainly not my equal, but in her natural right to eat the bread she earns with her own hands without asking leave of anyone else, she is my equal, and the equal of all others." As a free laborer, moreover, the Negro was entitled to compete for economic advancement. "Give every man a fair and equal chance upon the arena of human endeavor," Chase demanded in 1853, and in the debate on education in the District of Columbia, Henry Wilson urged the Senate to "educate, if we can, these poor colored children, and enable them, as far as possible, to improve their condition in life." And Edward Wade of Ohio insisted that the free Negro be allowed to participate in the homestead bill's benefits, so he could "locate himself where he can have the opportunity to prove his equality with the whites, or make his inequality manifest beyond controversy." [88]

Wade's statement makes manifest the central ambiguity of the free labor attitude towards the Negro. On the one hand, it sought to strike down discriminatory legislation and provide an opportunity for economic advancement; on the other, there lingered the nagging doubt whether the Negro was indeed capable of making use of the opportunities offered him. Some Republicans, to be sure, thought the Negro "amenable to the Law of Progress," as the *National Era* put it, and they insisted that discrimination, not inferiority, was to blame for his lowly social position. "It is nonsense to talk about the inferiority of the negro race, whilst at the same time they are kept in a state of degrada-

87. *Speech of Hon. William H. Seward at Jackson, October 4, 1856* (np, nd), 12–14; Baker, ed., *Seward Works*, I, 56, III, 14, IV, 317; New York *Times*, August 29, 1857.
88. Basler, ed., *Lincoln Works*, II, 405; *Congressional Globe*, 32 Congress, 2 Session, 1064, 36 Congress, 1 Session, 1684, 33 Congress, 1 Session, 1072.

tion, which renders mental and moral improvement an impossibility," said a New York Congressman. And a Minnesotan agreed that "the temporary condition of a people" was a poor measure of what they might achieve in the future.[89] To most Republicans, however, the Negro, free or slave, was a poor prospect for social advancement. They accepted the stereotype of the black man which pictured him as lazy, unenterprising, and lacking in the middle-class, Puritan qualities of character so essential for economic success. "As a class," the New York *Tribune* complained in 1855, "the Blacks are indolent, improvident, servile, and licentious." Greeley argued that while black men, because of prejudice, could hardly be expected to gain economic parity with whites, they "ought to be more industrious, energetic, thrifty, independent, than a majority of them are." The Philadelphia *North American* agreed that the reason for the Negro's confinement in menial jobs was not merely discrimination but "something deeper . . . the constitution of the negro himself." [90]

Republican spokesmen also attributed the reluctance of free Negroes to take part in colonization projects to their lack of initiative. Negroes "must become possessed with the same spirit of self-relying enterprise" as the whites, the *National Era* complained. "Were we a colored man, we would never rest from our wanderings till we had found a place where our children might grow up into the dignity of a noble manhood." The influential Springfield *Republican* declared that a black colony would long since have been established in Central America, "if they had any pluck—if the best of them had a particle of spirit of the white man." Reports about southern slaves told the same story. Olmsted reported that the great majority of field hands appeared "very dull, idiotic, and brute-like," and lazy besides. Cassius M. Clay of Kentucky insisted that Negroes could never achieve anything in the South because they lacked self-reliance, and a visitor to the South from Vermont wrote his Republican Congressman that although slavery was an evil, the blacks would starve if set free, since "labor is not connected with their ideas of freedom." [91] In vain did some radicals

89. *National Era,* April 24, 1851; *Congressional Globe,* 36 Congress, 1 Session, Appendix, 232; *Debates and Proceedings of the Constitutional Convention for the Territory of Minnesota* (St. Paul, 1858), 351. Cf. New York *Tribune,* May 29, 1857.
90. New York *Tribune,* September 22, 26, 1855, August 3, September 26, 1857; Philadelphia *North American,* cited in *Weekly Anglo-African,* September 3, 1859.
91. *National Era,* March 13, 1851; Springfield *Republican,* cited in *Liberator,* August 31, 1860; Olmsted, *Seaboard Slave States,* 18; Olmsted, *Back Country,* 432;

argue that the free Negroes of New England and Western Reserve were industrious, intelligent, self-reliant, and literate. Most Republicans would agree with the *National Era* that "It is the real evil of the negro race that they are so fit for slavery as they are." [92]

A good number of the ambiguities in Republicans' racial attitudes stemmed from the contradiction between their political outlook, which stressed civil rights and some kind of legal equality, and the free labor ideology. For even those Republicans most active in efforts to extend the legal rights of free Negroes insisted that black men must prove themselves capable of economic advancement before they could expect full recognition of their equality. Greeley, for example, criticized black leaders for devoting their time to the struggle for political rights. Instead, he insisted, they should concern themselves with self-improvement and character-building, by having black men withdraw from menial trades, form separate communities, and prove that they could acquire wealth and manage business. "One negro on a farm which he has cleared or bought," the New York editor wrote, ". . . is worth more to the cause of Equal Suffrage than three in an Ethiopian (or any other) convention." The New York *Times* agreed. "It matters little," it advised colored citizens, "whether a man is black, white, or mingled. If he is respectable, he will be respected." Horace Mann, Ben Wade, and Cassius Clay gave the same answer to an Ohio colored convention which solicited their advice in 1852. Negroes should wait for political rights, and concentrate on learning trades, forming their own communities, and acquiring "habits of self-respect and independence." Just as the free labor ideology insisted that a white man must have an independent economic existence to be truly free, it demanded that blacks prove, by economic advancement, that they deserved legal equality. "White people," said Wade, "while poor and ignorant, are no more respected than you are. I say again, color is nothing. When you have attained intelligence and independence, you will soon be admitted to your social and political rights." [93]

David L. Smiley, *Lion of Whitehall, the Life of Cassius M. Clay* (Madison, 1962), 56–57; Rodney B. Field to Justin S. Morrill, October 18, 1859, Justin S. Morrill Papers, LC.

92. *Congressional Globe*, 35 Congress, 1 Session, 1970, 36 Congress, 1 Session, 1636, 1886; William B. Dodge to Elihu B. Washburne, January 13, 1860, Elihu B. Washburne Papers, LC; Cleveland *Leader*, September 5, 1857; *Ohio Constitutional Convention*, I, 337; *National Era*, June 2, 1853.

93. New York *Tribune*, September 22, 1855; New York *Times*, October 5, 1855; *Ohio Colored Convention, 1852*, 15–20, 24–25.

Many of the Republican criticisms of free Negroes were shared by black leaders. "The colored people," Frederick Douglass told Harriet Beecher Stowe, "are wanting in self-reliance," and he deplored their tendency to remain in menial occupations. Some colored conventions advised Negroes to leave the cities and take jobs on farms as a means of self-improvement, and other spokesmen insisted that frugality, self-reliance, and a "better regulation of our domestic habits," were essential preconditions to social advancement.[94] The black leaders insisted, however, that the Negro's deficiencies in character and achievement were wholly the result of prejudice and discrimination, and they objected to the "tone of assumed superiority and arrogant complacency," with which Republicans like Greeley criticized black citizens. But black spokesmen accepted the free labor idea that independence was the key to respectability, and that "to be dependent is to be degraded." And they insisted that they desired not any special privileges or aid, but merely equality of opportunity. "Remove all obstacles, and give the black man an equal chance," the black spokesmen said, ". . . and then should he not succeed, he will not ask you or anyone else to mourn over his failure." [95]

During the 1850's, Republicans accepted the idea that the Negro should be given an "equal chance" to prove himself capable of economic advancement, and their actions in state legislatures and in Congress had the effect of breaking down some of the legal inequalities which surrounded the black citizen. "I want every man to have the chance—and I believe a black man is entitled to it—in which he *can* better his condition . . . ," Lincoln insisted in 1860. The limitations of the Republican outlook did not become fully manifest until the tragic failure of Reconstruction. Given the long history of slavery and the continuing fact of discrimination, the mere granting of civil equality was not enough to guarantee real equality of opportunity for northern Negroes, much less for newly freed southern slaves. Many Republicans, of course, never expected the Negro to attain complete equality. Greeley had written before the war that, free or slave,

94. Foner, ed., *Douglass*, II, 232; *Proceedings of the Colored National Convention, Held in Rochester, July 6th, 7th, and 8th, 1853* (Rochester, 1853), 39; Litwack, *North of Slavery*, 174; *Ohio Colored Convention, 1852*, 6; *North Star*, September 29, 1848; *Liberator*, August 19, 1859; *Weekly Anglo-African*, July 23, 1859, March 10, 1860.
95. Foner, ed., *Douglass*, II, 370; *North Star*, September 22, 1848; *Weekly Anglo-African*, September 3, 1859. Cf. February 25, 1860; *Douglass' Monthly*, September, 1859.

Negroes would always occupy an inferior social position, and during
Reconstruction, Seward observed philosophically, "They are God's
poor; they always have been and always will be everywhere." But
even the more radical Republicans, who sincerely hoped that the
Negro could rise to economic and social equality, shrank from a long
period of federal protection of Negro rights and a redistribution of
southern property.[96] The free labor ideology, based on the premise that
all Americans, whatever their origins, could achieve social advancement if given equal protection of the law, was only an incomplete
version of the full commitment which would have been necessary to
make these hopes fully realized.

96. Basler, ed., *Lincoln Works*, IV, 24; New York *Tribune*, May 31, 1853, July
28, 1857; Rollo Ogden, ed., *Life and Letters of Edward Lawrence Godkin* (2 vols.:
New York, 1907), I, 261–63. Cf. W. R. Brock, *An American Crisis* (London,
1963), 286–87; Patrick W. Riddleberger, "The Radicals' Abandonment of the
Negro During Reconstruction," *JNH*, XLV (April 1960), 95; Glyndon G. Van
Deusen, *Horace Greeley, Nineteenth Century Reformer* (Philadelphia, 1953), 381.

9

Slavery and the
Republican Ideology

"Of the American Civil War," James Ford Rhodes wrote over a half a century ago, "it may safely be asserted that there was a single cause, slavery." In this opinion, Rhodes was merely echoing a view which seemed self-evident to Abraham Lincoln and many other participants in the sectional conflict. Their interpretation implicitly assumes that the ante-bellum Republican party was primarily a vehicle for anti-slavery sentiment. Yet partly because historians are skeptical of explanations made by participants of their own behavior, Rhodes' view quickly fell under attack. Even before Rhodes wrote, John R. Commons had characterized the Republicans as primarily a homestead party, and Charles and Mary Beard later added the tariff as one of its fundamental concerns. More recently, historians have stressed aversion to the presence of blacks—free or slave—in the western territories as the Republicans' motive for opposing the extension of slavery. Because the Republicans disavowed the intention of attacking slavery in states where it already existed by direct federal action, their anti-slavery declarations have been dismissed by some historians as hypocritical.[1] And recently, a political analyst, not a professional historian, revealed how commonplace a cynical attitude toward the early Repub-

1. James Ford Rhodes, *Lectures on the American Civil War* (New York, 1913), 2; Roy F. Basler *et al.*, eds., *The Collected Works of Abraham Lincoln* (9 vols.: New Brunswick, 1953–55), VII, 332; John R. Commons, "Horace Greeley and the Working Class Origins of the Republican Party," *PSQ*, XXIV (September 1909), 488; Charles A. Beard and Mary R. Beard, *The Rise of American Civilization* (2 vols.: New York, 1933 ed.), II, 39; Eugene H. Berwanger, *The Frontier Against Slavery* (Urbana, 1967); Milton Viorst, *Fall From Grace* (New York, 1968), 39; Bernard Mandel, *Labor: Free and Slave* (New York, 1955), 147.

lican party has become when he wrote: "The Republican Party succeeded by soft-pedalling the issue of slavery altogether and concentrating on economic issues which would attract Northern businessmen and Western farmers."[2]

Controversy over the proper place of anti-slavery in the Republican ideology is hardly new. During the 1850's, considerable debate occurred within abolitionist circles on the proper attitude toward Republicanism. In part, this was simply an extension of the traditional schism between political and non-political abolitionists, and it is not surprising that William Lloyd Garrison and his followers should have wasted little enthusiasm on the Republicans. Yet many abolitionists who had no objection on principle to political involvements considered the anti-slavery commitment of the Republican party insufficient to merit their support. Gerrit Smith and William Goodell, for example, who had been instrumental in organizing the Liberty party in New York State, declared that they could not support a party which recognized the constitutionality of slavery anywhere in the Union. The Republican party, Smith charged, "refuses to oppose slavery where it is, and opposes it only where it is not," and he continuously urged radicals like Chase and Giddings to take an abolitionist stance.[3] Theodore Parker made the same criticism. When Chase declared in the Senate that the federal government would not interfere with slavery in the states, Parker wrote that while he did not object to attacking slavery one step at a time, he "would not promise *not to take other steps.*"[4]

Yet it is important to remember that despite their criticisms of the Republican party, leading abolitionists maintained close personal relations with Republican leaders, particularly the radicals. The flow of letters between Chase and Smith, cordial even while each criticized the attitude of the other, is one example of this. Similarly, Parker kept up a correspondence with Henry Wilson, Charles Sumner, and William

2. I. F. Stone, "Party of the Rich and Well-Born," *New York Review of Books,* June 20, 1968, 34. Cf. George H. Mayer, *The Republican Party 1854–1966* (New York, 1967 ed.), 75.
3. Margaret L. Plunkett, "A History of the Liberty Party with Emphasis on Its Activities in the Northeastern States" (unpublished doctoral dissertation, Cornell University, 1930), 173n. Cf. Gerrit Smith to Salmon P. Chase, April 15, 1855, March 1, August 13, 1856, January 26, 1857, Salmon P. Chase Papers, HSPa; William Goodell to George W. Julian, June 18, 1857, Giddings-Julian Papers, LC.
4. John Weiss, *Life and Correspondence of Theodore Parker* (2 vols.: New York, 1864), II, 228. Cf. II, 208, 223.

Seward as well as Chase.[5] And he and Wendell Phillips, both experts at the art of political agitation, recognized the complex interrelationship between abolitionist attempts to create a public sentiment hostile to slavery, and the political anti-slavery espoused by Republicans. "Our agitation, you know, helps keep yours alive in the rank and file," was the way Wendell Phillips expressed it to Sumner. And Seward agreed that the abolitionists played a vital role in awakening the public conscience—"open[ing] the way where the masses can follow." For their part, abolitionists like Theodore Parker were happy to borrow statistics and arguments from the anti-slavery speeches of politicians.[6]

The evidence strongly suggests that outside of Garrison's immediate circle, most abolitionists voted with the Republican party despite their wish that the party adopt a more aggressive anti-slavery position. Indeed, abolitionist societies experienced financial difficulties in the late 1850's, as former contributors began giving their money to the Republicans. Even Gerrit Smith, who insisted he could "never vote for any person who recognizes a law for slavery," contributed five hundred dollars to the Frémont campaign. The attitude of many abolitionists was summed up by Elizur Wright, a proponent of Smith and Goodell's brand of political anti-slavery who nonetheless voted for Lincoln in 1860. While Wright criticized the Republicans for their shortcomings on slavery, he acknowledged that "the greatest recommendation of the Republican Party is, that its enemies do not quite believe its disclaimers, while they do believe that [it is] sincerely opposed to slavery as far as it goes." Prophetically, he added: "Woe to the slave power under a Republican President if it strikes the first blow." [7]

5. Hans L. Trefousse, *The Radical Republicans, Lincoln's Vanguard for Racial Justice* (New York, 1969), 15–19; Henry Steele Commager, *Theodore Parker* (Boston, 1936), 254–61. For Chase's high regard for Smith, see Chase to Smith, October 18, 1852, December 15, 1854, Salmon P. Chase Papers, LC; Chase to Charles D. Cleveland, May 27, 1853, Chase to Smith, March 4, 1857, Chase Papers, HSPa.
6. Wendell Phillips to Charles Sumner, March 7, 1853, Charles Sumner Papers, Houghton Library, Harvard University; Frederick W. Seward, ed., *Seward at Washington* (2 vols.: New York, 1891), I, 208. Parker is quoted in George Sumner to Chase, February 14, 1854, Chase Papers, HSPa.
7. Irving H. Bartlett, *Wendell Phillips, Brahmin Radical* (Boston, 1961), 206; Aileen S. Kraditor, "A Note on Elkins and the Abolitionists," *CWH*, XIII (December 1967), 333; Betty Fladeland, *James Gillespie Birney: Slaveholder to Abolitionist* (Ithaca, 1955), 292; H. Warren to Zebina Eastman, December 24, 1856, Zebina Eastman Papers, ChicHS; New York *Tribune,* February 25, 1857; Gerrit Smith to Horace Greeley, October 25, 1856, Horace Greeley Papers, LC; Ralph

The fact that so many abolitionists, not to mention radical Republicans, supported the Republican party, is an indication that anti-slavery formed no small part of the Republican ideology. Recent historians have concluded, moreover, that writers like Beard greatly overestimated the importance of economic issues in the elections of 1856, 1858, and 1860. We have already seen how tentative was the Republican commitment to the tariff. As for the homestead issue, Don E. Fehrenbacher has pointed out that the Republicans carried most of the Northwest in 1856 when free land was not a political issue, and that in 1860, Douglas Democrats supported the measure as ardently as Republicans.[8] More important, it would have been suicidal for the Republicans to have put their emphasis on economic policies, particularly the neo-Whiggism described by Beard. If one thing is evident after analyzing the various elements which made up the party, it is that anti-slavery was one of the few policies which united all Republican factions. For political reasons, if for no other, the Republicans were virtually obliged to make anti-slavery the main focus of their political appeal. Such questions as the tariff, nativism, and race were too divisive to be stressed, while the homestead issue could be advanced precisely because it was so non-controversial in the North.

Conservative Republicans and radicals, ex-Democrats and former Whigs, all agreed that slavery was the major issue of the 1850's. It was not surprising that Giddings should insist that "there is but one real issue between the Republican party and those factions that stand opposed to it. That is the question of slavery," or that Salmon P. Chase should declare that the election of 1860 had not turned on "subordinate questions of local and temporary character," but had vindicated the principle of "the restriction of slavery within State limits."[9] But Orville H. Browning, as conservative as Giddings and Chase were radical, appraised the politics of 1860 in much the same way. "It is manifest to all," he declared, "that there is an unusual degree of

V. Harlow, *Gerrit Smith, Philanthropist and Reformer* (New York, 1939), 364; Elizur Wright, *An Eye-Opener for the Wide Awakes* (Boston, 1860), 47, 53–54. 8. George H. Knoles, ed., *The Crisis of the Union* (Baton Rouge, 1965), 18, 27; Allan Nevins, *The Emergence of Lincoln* (2 vols.: New York, 1950), II, 302. 9. George W. Julian, *The Life of Joshua R. Giddings* (Chicago, 1892), 379; L. E. Chittenden, *A Report of the Debates and Proceedings in the Secret Sessions of the Conference Convention . . . Held at Washington, D.C., in February A.D. 1861* (New York, 1864), 428. Cf. 131–32, 327; [James Russell Lowell], "The Election of November," *Atlantic Monthly*, VI (October 1860), 499; Thomas Richmond to Lyman Trumbull, December 14, 1860, Lyman Trumbull Papers, LC.

political interest pervading the country—that the people, everywhere, are excited, . . . and yet, from one extremity of the Republic to the other, scarcely any other subject is mentioned, or any other question discussed . . . save the question of negro slavery. . . ." Ex-Democrats in the Republican party fully agreed. Both Francis Spinner and Preston King rejected suggestions that Democratic economic policies be engrafted onto the Republican platform, on the ground that these must await settlement until the slavery issue had been decided. As Spinner tersely put it, "Statesmen cannot make issues for the people. As live men we must take the issues as they present themselves." The potency of the slavery issue, and the way in which it subordinated or absorbed all other political questions, was noted by the anti-Lecompton Democrat from New York, Horace Clark, on the eve of the 1860 campaign: [10]

It is not to be controverted that the slavery agitation is not at rest. It has absorbed and destroyed our national politics. It has overrun State politics. It has even invaded our municipalities; and now, in some form or other, everywhere controls the elections of the people.

In a recent study of Civil War historiography, Roy F. Nichols observed that we still do not know whether either section had reached its own consensus on major issues by 1861. Some historians have interpreted the strong showing of Stephen A. Douglas in the free states as proof that a substantial portion of the electorate rejected the Republican brand of anti-slavery.[11] Though there is some truth in this view, it is important to remember that by 1860 the Douglas Democrats shared a good many of the Republicans' attitudes toward the South. One of the most striking aspects of the Democratic debate over the Lecompton constitution was the way in which the Douglasites echoed so many of the anti-southern views which anti-Nebraska Democrats had expressed only a few years earlier. There is a supreme irony in the fact that the same methods which Douglas had used against

10. *Speech of Hon. O. H. Browning, Delivered at the Republican Mass Meeting, Springfield, Ill., August 8th, 1860* (Quincy, 1860), 3; John Bigelow, *Retrospections of an Active Life* (5 vols.: New York, 1909–13), I, 179–80; Sarah J. Day, *The Man on a Hill Top* (Philadelphia, 1931), 223–24; *Congressional Globe*, 36 Congress, 1 Session, 23. Cf. 120; Robert L. Bloom, "Newspaper Opinion in the State Election of 1860," *PaH*, XXVIII (October 1961), 352–53; New York *Tribune*, November 9, 1860.
11. Roy F. Nichols, "A Hundred Years Later: Perspectives on the Civil War," *JSH*, XXXIII (May 1967), 157; Mary Scrugham, *The Peaceable Americans of 1860–1861* (New York, 1921), 23, 51, 69; Elbert B. Smith, *The Death of Slavery* (Chicago, 1967), 166.

dissident Democrats in 1854 were now turned against him and his supporters. Buchanan applied the patronage whip ruthlessly, and anti-Lecompton Democrats complained that a new, pro-slavery test had suddenly been imposed upon the party. And like the anti-Nebraska Democrats, who were now members of the Republican party, the Douglasites insisted that they commanded the support of most northern Democrats. Historians have tended to agree with them. Roy Nichols suggests that the enthusiasm Douglas's anti-southern stand aroused among rank and file Democrats was one reason why he refused to accept the compromise English bill to settle the Lecompton controversy, and recent students of Pennsylvania and Indiana politics agree that the vast majority of the Democracy in those states favored Douglas against the administration.[12]

The bitterness of Douglas Democrats against the South did not abate between 1858 and 1860. They believed that the South had embarked upon a crusade to force slavery into all the territories, and protested that endorsement of such a goal would destroy the northern Democracy. "We have confided in their honor, their love of justice, their detestation of what is wrong," Henry Payne, a prominent Ohio Democrat, said of his southern colleagues in 1858, *"but we can do it no more."*[13] And many Republicans believed that, even if Douglas made his peace with the Democratic organization, many of his followers had acquired "a feeling against Slavery and its arrogant de-

---

12. Roy F. Nichols, *The Disruption of American Democracy* (New York, 1948), 165, 173; *Congressional Globe*, 35 Congress, 1 Session, 1055, Appendix, 322, 2 Session, Appendix, 171, 36 Congress, 1 Session, 119; Philadelphia *Press*, cited in New York *Times*, March 15, 1858; Elmer D. Elbert, "Southern Indiana Politics on the Eve of the Civil War 1858–1861" (unpublished doctoral dissertation, Indiana University, 1967), 95; Michael F. Holt, "Forging a Majority: The Formation of the Republican Party in Pittsburgh, Pennsylvania, 1848–1860" (unpublished doctoral dissertation, Johns Hopkins University, 1967), 375. Cf. J. Robert Lane, *A Political History of Connecticut During the Civil War* (Washington, 1941), 98.

13. Cincinnati *Gazette*, March 3, 1858. Cf. Don E. Fehrenbacher, *Prelude to Greatness, Lincoln in the 1850's* (New York, 1964 ed.), 57; Howard C. Perkins, ed., *Northern Editorials on Secession* (2 vols.: New York, 1942), I, 47, 49; *Congressional Globe*, 35 Congress, 1 Session, 474, 1239, 1354, 1905, Appendix, 321. The resentment expressed by the anti-Lecompton Congressman from New York, Horace Clark, was typical: "I am one of that Democratic party of the North which has been often beaten and torn in its struggle for the maintenance of the constitutional rights of the South, until we have been, as it were, driven to take refuge within the walls of our northern cities." *Congressional Globe*, 35 Congress, 1 Session, 1307.

mands which *if cherished* will prevent their going back. . . ." A few Democrats did defect to the Republican party in 1858, 1859, and 1860, including a former chairman of the Iowa Democracy, several anti-Lecompton Congressmen, and F. P. Stanton, the former Democratic governor of Kansas.[14] That there were not more defections largely reflected the continuation into 1860 of Douglas's contest with the administration, which increasingly took on what one historian calls "a semi-free-soil" tone. And when the 1860 Democratic national convention broke up over the South's insistence on a platform guaranteeing slavery in the territories, the bitterness of the Douglasites knew no bounds. The reporter Murat Halstead observed that he had "never heard Abolitionists talk more rancorously of the people of the South than the Douglas men here." For their part, southerners insisted they would not accept popular sovereignty since this would be as effective as the Wilmot Proviso in barring slavery from the territories.[15]

There were, of course, many important differences between the Douglasites and Republicans. Douglas still insisted in 1860 that the slavery question was not important enough to risk the disruption of the Union, he was much more inclined to use racism as a political weapon, and, as one Republican newspaper put it, in words echoed by several recent scholars, Douglas "does not recognize the moral element in politics. . . ."[16] Yet in their devotion to the Union and their bitter opposition to southern domination of the government, Republicans and Douglasites stood close together in 1860. There was much truth in the observation of one Republican that "the rupture between

14. A. H. Reeder to Wayne MacVeagh, August 20, 1858, Wayne MacVeagh Papers, HSPa; Morton M. Rosenberg, "The Election of 1859 in Iowa," *IJH*, LVII (January 1959), 2–3; *Wisconsin State Journal*, July 28, 1860; Charles Francis Adams Diary, December 15, 1859, Adams Papers, MHS. Cf. Lyman Trumbull to Chase, June 17, 1858, Chase Papers, HSPa.

15. Henry C. Hubbart, *The Older Middle West 1840–1880* (New York, 1936), 133–38; Wilfred E. Binkley, *American Political Parties* (2nd ed.: New York, 1947), 203; Nevins, *Emergence of Lincoln*, II, 227; Knoles, ed., *Crisis of the Union*, 56–57.

Republicans were quite annoyed at the Douglas Democrats' attempts to portray themselves as the "real" anti-southern, anti-slavery party. Chicago *Press and Tribune*, August 12, 1858; James G. Blaine, *Political Discussions* (Norwich, Conn., 1887), 12; James R. Doolittle to Hannibal Hamlin, September 18, 1859, Hannibal Hamlin Papers, University of Maine, Orono; *Speech of Carl Schurz, of Wisconsin, at the Cooper Institute* . . . (Washington, 1860), 1.

16. Springfield *Republican*, April 14, 1860; *Congressional Globe*, 36 Congress, 1 Session, 733; Robert W. Johannsen, "Stephen A. Douglas, Popular Sovereignty and the Territories," *Historian*, XXII (August 1960), 379; Nevins, *Ordeal*, II, 107–9.

the northern and southern wing of the democracy, is permanent with
the masses . . . ," and the experiences of the Douglas Democrats in the
years preceding the Civil War go a long way toward explaining the
unanimity of the North's response to the attack on Fort Sumter.[17]

II

The attitude of the Douglasites toward the South on the eve of the
Civil War partially reflected their assessment of northern opinion regarding slavery. Politicians of all parties agreed that northerners opposed slavery as an abstract principle, although they disagreed on
the intensity of this sentiment. John C. Calhoun had estimated in 1847
that while only 5 per cent of northerners supported the abolitionists,
more than 66 per cent viewed slavery as an evil, and were willing to
oppose its extension constitutionally. Similarly, a conservative Republican declared in 1858, "There is no man [in the North] who is an
advocate of slavery. There is no man from that section of the country
who will go before his constituents and advocate the extension of
slavery." Northern Democrats had the same perception of northern
sentiments. Even the Hunkers of New York, who consistently opposed
the Wilmot Proviso, refused to say "that they are not opposed to
slavery." For as William L. Marcy declared in 1849, "In truth we all
are." [18]

Anti-slavery as an abstract feeling had long existed in the North. It
had not, however, prevented abolitionists from being mobbed, nor
anti-slavery parties from going down to defeat. Democrats and Whigs
had long been able to appeal to devotion to the Union, racism, and economic issues, to neutralize anti-slavery as a political force. "The anti-
slavery sentiment," Hamilton Fish explained in 1854, "is inborn, and
almost universal at the North . . . but it is only as a *sentiment* that it
generally pervades; it has not and cannot be inspired with the activity

---

17. Ralston Skinner to Chase, June 7, 1860, Chase Papers, LC; Robert W.
Johannsen, "The Douglas Democracy and the Crisis of Disunion," *CWH*, IX
(September 1963), 229–47. Cf. Preston King to Azariah C. Flagg, May 7, 1860,
Azariah C. Flagg Papers, Columbia University; Cincinnati *Gazette*, March 12, 1858.
18. Richard K. Crallé, ed., *The Works of John C. Calhoun* (6 vols.: Charleston
and New York, 1851–56), IV, 387–88; *Congressional Globe*, 35 Congress, 1
Session, 1312; Alto Lee Whitehurst, "Martin Van Buren and the Free Soil Movement" (unpublished doctoral dissertation, University of Chicago, 1932), 189.
Cf. J. Franklin Jameson, ed., "Correspondence of John C. Calhoun," *Annual Report* of AHA, 1899, II, 1143; Chicago *Democratic Press*, July 18, 1854; Chittenden, ed., *Peace Conference Proceedings*, 199–200.

that even a very slight interest excites." [19] But Fish failed to foresee the fundamental achievement of the Republican party before the Civil War: the creation and articulation of an ideology which blended personal and sectional interest with morality so perfectly that it became the most potent political force in the nation. The free labor assault upon slavery and southern society, coupled with the idea that an aggressive Slave Power was threatening the most fundamental values and interests of the free states, hammered the slavery issue home to the northern public more emphatically than an appeal to morality alone could ever have done.

To agree with Rhodes that slavery was ultimately the cause of the Civil War, therefore, is not to accept the corollary that the basis of the Republican opposition to slavery was simple moral fervor. In a speech to the Senate in 1848, John M. Niles listed a dozen different reasons for his support of the Wilmot Proviso—but only once did he mention his belief that slavery was morally repugnant. And thirteen years later, George William Curtis observed that "there is very little moral mixture in the 'Anti-Slavery' feeling of this country. A great deal is abstract philanthropy; part is hatred of slaveholders; a great part is jealousy for white labor, very little is consciousness of wrong done and the wish to right it." The Republican ideology included all these elements, and much more. Rhodes argued that northerners wished to preserve the Union as a first step toward abolition. A more accurate formulation would reverse the equation and say that many Republicans were anti-slavery from the conviction that slavery threatened the Union. Aside from some radicals, who occasionally flirted with disunion, most Republicans were united by the twin principles of free soil and Unionism. Cassius M. Clay even suggested that the Free-Soilers in 1851 adopt the name "Liberty and Union" party, in order to impress their essential goals upon the electorate. The New York *Times* emphasized this aspect of Republican thought in 1857: "The barbaric institution of slavery will become more and more odious to the northern people because it will become more and more plain . . . that the States which cling to Slavery thrust back the American idea, and reject the influences of the Union." [20]

19. Hamilton Fish to John M. Bradford, December 16, 1854, Letterbook, Hamilton Fish Papers, LC.
20. *Congressional Globe*, 30 Congress, 1 Session, 1199–1200; Gordon Milne, *George William Curtis and the Genteel Tradition* (Bloomington, 1956), 112; Rhodes, *Lectures*, 5–6; Cassius M. Clay to Chase, August 12, 1851, Chase Papers, HSPa; New York *Times*, May 16, 1857.

Still, Unionism, despite its importance to the mass of northerners, and obviously crucial to any explanation of the Republicans' decision to resist secession, was only one aspect of the Republican ideology. It would have been just as logical to compromise on the slavery question if the preservation of the Union were the paramount goal of Republican politics. Nor should Republicanism be seen merely as the expression of the northern drive toward political power. We have seen, to be sure, that resentment of southern power played its part, that many Democratic-Republicans had watched with growing jealousy the South's domination of the Democratic party and the national government, and that many former Whigs were convinced that the South was blocking economic programs essential for national economic development. But there is more to the coming of the Civil War than the rivalry of sections for political power. (New England, after all, could accept its own decline in political power without secession.)

In short, none of these elements can stand separately; they dissolve into one another, and the total product emerges as ideology. Resentment of southern political power, devotion to the Union, anti-slavery based upon the free labor argument, moral revulsion to the peculiar institution, racial prejudice, a commitment to the northern social order and its development and expansion—all these elements were intertwined in the Republican world-view. What they added up to was the conviction that North and South represented two social systems whose values, interests, and future prospects were in sharp, perhaps mortal, conflict with one another. The sense of difference, of estrangement, and of growing hostility with which Republicans viewed the South, cannot be overemphasized. Theodore Sedgwick of New York perhaps expressed it best when he declared during the secession crisis: "The policy and aims of slavery, its institutions and civilization, and the character of its people, are all at variance with the policy, aims, institutions, education, and character of the North. There is an irreconcilable difference in our interests, institutions, and pursuits; in our sentiments and feelings." Greeley's *Tribune* said the same thing more succinctly: "We are not one people. We are two peoples. We are a people for Freedom and a people for Slavery. Between the two, conflict is inevitable." An attack not simply on the institution of slavery, but upon southern society itself, was thus at the heart of the Republican mentality. Of all historians, I think Avery Craven caught this feature best: "By 1860, slavery had become the symbol and carrier of *all* sectional differences and conflicts." [21] Here and elsewhere, Craven describes the symbolic nature of the slavery controversy, reflected as it was in the widespread acceptance among Republicans of the Slave Power idea—a metaphor for all the fears and resentments they harbored toward the South. But Craven did leave out something crucial. Slavery was not only the symbol, but also the real basis of sectional conflict, for it was the foundation of the South's economy, social structure, aspirations, and ideology.

"Why do we Meddle with Slavery?" the New York *Times* asked in an 1857 editorial. The answer gives us a penetrating insight into the Republican mind on the eve of Civil War:

> The great States of the North are not peopled exclusively by quidnuncs and agitators. . . . Nevertheless, we do give ourselves great and increasing concern about the existence of Slavery in States over whose internal economy we have no right and no wish to exercise any control whatever. Nevertheless, we do feel, and the feeling is growing deeper in the northern heart with every passing year, that our character, our prosperity, and our destiny are most seriously involved in the question of the perpetuation or extinction of slavery in those States.

What is striking about this statement is a concern directed not only against the extension of slavery, but against its very existence. Lincoln put the same concern even more succinctly to a Chicago audience in 1859, "Never forget," he said, "that we have before us this whole matter of the right or wrong of slavery in this Union, though the immediate question is as to its spreading out into new Territories and States." [22]

Lincoln and the editors of the *Times* thus made explicit that there was more to the contest over the extension of slavery than whether the institution should spread to the West. As Don E. Fehrenbacher puts it, the territorial question was the "skirmish line of a more extensive struggle." [23] Only by a comprehension of this total conflict between North and South, between Republican and southern ideologies, can the meaning of the territorial issue be fully grasped. Its importance went even beyond the belief shared widely in both sections that slavery

21. *Congressional Globe*, 36 Congress, 2 Session, 797; New York *Tribune*, April 12, 1855; Avery Craven, *An Historian and the Civil War* (Chicago, 1964), 163. Cf. Avery Craven, *The Repressible Conflict* (Baton Rouge, 1939), 76.
22. New York *Times*, May 16, 1857; Basler, ed., *Lincoln Works*, III, 369.
23. Knoles, ed., *Crisis of the Union*, 22–23.

required expansion to survive, and that confinement to the states where it already existed would kill it. For in each ideology was the conviction that its own social system must expand, not only to insure its own survival but to prevent the expansion of all the evils the other represented. We have already seen how Republicans believed that free society, with its promise of social mobility for the laborer, required territorial expansion, and how this was combined with a messianic desire to spread the benefits of free society to other areas and peoples. Southerners had their own grandiose design. "They had a magnificent dream of empire," a Republican recalled after the war, and such recent writers as C. Stanley Urban and Eugene Genovese have emphasized how essential expansionism was in the southern ideology. The struggle for the West represented a contest between two expansive societies, only one of whose aspirations could prevail. The conflict was epitomized by two statements which appeared in the Philadelphia North American in 1856. Slavery, the North American argued, could not be allowed to expand, because it would bring upon the West "a blight whose fatal influence will be felt for centuries." Two weeks later the same paper quoted a southern journal, which, in urging slavery expansionism, used precisely this logic in reverse. Such expansion, the southern paper argued, would "forbid the extension of the evils of free society to new people and coming generations." [24]

Here then was a basic reason why the South could not accept the verdict of 1860. In 1848, Martin Van Buren had said that the South opposed the principle of free soil because "the prohibition carries with it a reproach to the slaveholding states, and . . . submission to it would degrade them." Eight years later, the Richmond Enquirer explained that for the South to abandon the idea of extending slavery while accepting Republican assurances of non-interference in the states would be "pregnant with the admission that slavery is wrong, and but for the constitution should be abolished." To agree to the containment of slavery, the South would have had to abandon its

---

24. Roeliff Brinkerhoff, Recollections of a Lifetime (Cincinnati, 1904), 42; C. Stanley Urban, "The Ideology of Southern Imperialism: New Orleans and the Caribbean, 1845–1860," Louisiana Historical Quarterly, XXXIX (January 1956), 48–73; Eugene D. Genovese, The Political Economy of Slavery (New York, 1965), 243–49; Philadelphia North American and United States Gazette, September 10, 1856; Richmond Enquirer, cited in Philadelphia North American and United States Gazette, September 25, 1856. Cf. National Era, March 10, 1859.

whole ideology, which had come to view the institution as a positive good, the basis of an enlightened form of social organization.[25]

III

Although it has not been the purpose of this study to examine in any detailed way the southern mind in 1860, what has been said about the Republican ideology does help to explain the rationale for secession. The political wars of the 1850's, centering on the issue of slavery extension, had done much to erode whatever good feeling existed between the sections. The abolitionist Elihu Burrit suggested in 1857 that a foreigner observing American politics would probably conclude "that the North and South were wholly occupied in gloating upon each others' faults and failings." During the 1856 campaign, Burrit went on, sectional antagonisms had been brought "to a pitch of rancor, never reached before" in American politics. This was precisely the reason that Union-loving conservatives like Hamilton Fish dreaded the mounting agitation. "I cannot close my eyes to the fact which all history shows," Fish wrote Thurlow Weed in 1855, "that every physical revolution (of governments) is preceded by a moral revolution. [Slavery agitation] leads to estrangement first, and next to hostility and hatred which end inevitably in separation." By the time of the secession crisis another former Whig could observe that "the people of the North and of the South have come to hate each other worse than the hatred between any two nations in the world. In a word the moral basis on which the government is founded is all destroyed." [26]

It is thus no mystery that southerners could not seriously entertain Republican assurances that they would not attack slavery in the states. For one thing, in opposing its extension, Republicans had been logically forced to attack the institution itself. This, indeed, was one of the reasons why radicals accepted the emphasis on non-extension. "We are disposed to select this single point," Sumner explained to Chase,

---

25. O. C. Gardiner, *The Great Issue* (New York, 1848), 146; Richmond *Enquirer,* June 16, 1856, clipping, scrapbook, Giddings Papers; Genovese, *Political Economy,* 250. Cf. Robert R. Russel, "The Issues in the Congressional Struggle Over the Kansas-Nebraska Bill, 1854," *JSH,* XXIX (May 1963), 190; Chaplain W. Morrison, *Democratic Politics and Sectionalism* (Chapel Hill, 1967), 65–66.

26. Cleveland *Leader,* August 27, 1857; Hamilton Fish to Thurlow Weed, November, 18, 1855, Letterbook, Fish Papers; L. B. Hamlin, ed., "Selections From the William Greene Papers, II," *Quarterly Publications* of Historical and Philosophical Society of Ohio, XIV (January–March 1919), 26.

"because it has a peculiar practical issue at the present moment, while its discussion would, of course, raise the whole question of slavery." Frederick Douglass agreed that agitation for the Wilmot Proviso served "to keep the subject before the people—to deepen their hatred of the system—and to break up the harmony between the Northern white people and the Southern slaveholders. . . ." [27] As we have seen, many Republicans, both radicals and moderates, explicitly stated that non-extension was simply the first step, that there would come a day when slavery would cease to exist.

As southerners viewed the Republican party's rise to power in one northern state after another, and witnessed the increasingly anti-southern tone of the northern Democrats, they could hardly be blamed for feeling apprehensive about the future. Late in 1859, after a long talk with the moderate Unionist Senator from Virginia, R. M. T. Hunter, Senator James Dixon of Connecticut reported that the Virginian was deeply worried. "What seems to alarm Hunter is the *growth* of the Anti-slavery feeling at the North." [28] Southerners did not believe that this anti-slavery sentiment would be satisfied with the prohibition of slavery in the territories, although even that would be bad enough. They also feared that a Republican administration would adopt the radicals' program of indirect action against slavery. This is why continued Democratic control of Congress was not very reassuring, for executive action could implement much of the radicals' program. Slavery was notoriously weak in the states of Missouri, Maryland, and Delaware. With federal patronage, a successful emancipation movement there might well be organized. And what was more dangerous, Lincoln might successfully arouse the poor whites in other states against the slaveholders. "Cohorts of Federal office-holders, Abolitionists, may be sent into [our] midst," a southern Senator warned in January 1861; ". . . Postmasters . . . controlling the mails, and loading them down with incendiary documents," would be appointed in every town. One southern newspaper declared that "the great lever

27. Sumner to Chase, February 7, 1848, Chase Papers, LC; Philip S. Foner, ed., *The Life and Writings of Frederick Douglass* (4 vols.: New York, 1950–55), II, 70. Cf. Craven, *Historian and the Civil War*, 41; Helen M. Cavenaugh, "Anti-Slavery Sentiment and Politics in the Northwest, 1844–1860," (unpublished doctoral dissertation, University of Chicago, 1938), 140–41; N. J. Tenney to Chase, July 28, 1848, Chase Papers, LC.
28. James Dixon to Gideon Welles, December 17, 1859, Gideon Welles Papers, LC. Cf. Chittenden, *Peace Conference Proceedings*, 93.

by which the abolitionists hope to extirpate slavery in the states, is the aid of the non-slaveholding citizens of the South." The reply of Republicans to these warnings was hardly reassuring. Commenting on one southern editorial, the Cincinnati *Commercial* declared that the spread of anti-slavery sentiment among southern poor whites was "an eventuality against which no precautions can avail." And by December 1860, Republican Congressmen were already receiving applications for office from within the slave states.[29]

For many reasons, therefore, southerners believed that slavery would not be permanently safe under a Republican administration. Had not William H. Seward announce in 1858, "I know, and you know, that a revolution has begun. I know, and all the world knows, that revolutions never go backward." Did not Republican Congressmen openly express their conviction that "slavery must die"? The Republican policy of preventing the spread of slavery, one southerner wrote to William T. Sherman, "was but the entering wedge to overthrow it in the States." [30]

The delegates to South Carolina's secession convention, in their address to the people of the state, explained why they had dissolved the state's connection with the Union:

> If it is right to preclude or abolish slavery in a Territory, why should it be allowed to remain in the States? . . . In spite of all disclaimers and professions, there can be but one end by the submission of the South to the rule of a sectional anti-slavery government at Washington; and that end, directly or indirectly, must be —the emancipation of the slaves of the South.

Emancipation might come in a decade, it might take fifty years. But North and South alike knew that the election of 1860 had marked a turning point in the history of slavery in the United States. To re-

29. Nevins, *Emergence of Lincoln*, II, 469; *Congressional Globe*, 36 Congress, 2 Session, 357; Dwight L. Dumond, ed., *Southern Editorials on Secession* (New York, 1931), 173–74; Perkins, ed., *Northern Editorials*, I, 55–56; Herman Cox to Trumbull, November 27, 1860, William Gayle to Trumbull, December 9, 1860, Trumbull Papers; Nichols, *Disruption*, 352–53. Cf. Robert R. Russel, "The Economic History of Negro Slavery," *AgH*, XI (October 1937), 320–21; *Congressional Globe*, 36 Congress, 2 Session, 49.
30. George E. Baker, ed., *The Works of William H. Seward* (5 vols.: Boston, 1853–84), IV, 302; *Congressional Globe*, 36 Congress, 2 Session, Appendix, 69; Walter L. Fleming, ed., *General W. T. Sherman As College President* (Cleveland, 1912), 287. Cf. Henry R. Selden to James R. Doolittle, May 14, 1858, James R. Doolittle Papers, NYPL.

main in the Union, the South would have had to accept the verdict of "ultimate extinction" which Lincoln and the Republicans had passed on the peculiar institution.[31]

The decision for civil war in 1860–61 can be resolved into two questions—why did the South secede, and why did the North refuse to let the South secede? As I have indicated, I believe secession should be viewed as a total and logical response by the South to the situation which confronted it in the election of Lincoln—logical in the sense that it was the only action consistent with its ideology. In the same way, the Republicans' decision to maintain the Union was inherent in their ideology. For the integrity of the Union, important as an end in itself, was also a prerequisite to the national greatness Republicans felt the United States was destined to achieve. With his faith in progress, material growth, and the spread of both democratic institutions and American influence throughout the world, William Seward brought the Republican ideology to a kind of culmination. Although few Republicans held as coherent and far-reaching a world view as he, most accepted Lincoln's more modest view that the American nation had a special place in the world, and a responsibility to prove that democratic institutions were self-sustaining. Much of the messianic zeal which characterized political anti-slavery derived from this faith in the superiority of the political, social, and economic institutions of the North, and a desire to spread these to their ultimate limits.

When a leading historian says, therefore, that the Republican party in 1860 was bound together "by a common enmity rather than a common loyalty," he is, I believe, only half right.[32] For the Republicans' enmity toward the South was intimately bound up with their loyalty to the society of small-scale capitalism which they perceived in the North. It was its identification with the aspirations of the farmers, small entrepreneurs, and craftsmen of northern society which gave the Republican ideology much of its dynamic, progressive, and optimistic quality. Yet paradoxically, at the time of its greatest success, the seeds of the later failure of that ideology were already present. Fundamental

31. John Amasa May and Joan Reynolds Faust, South Caroloina Secedes (Columbia, 1960), 88–89; Genovese, Political Economy, 266–69. I am greatly indebted in my understanding of the secession crisis to conversations with William H. Freehling of the University of Michigan. Professor Freehling's forthcoming study of the South in the 1850's will undoubtedly be a major contribution to Civil War historiography.
32. William B. Hesseltine, Lincoln and the War Governors (New York, 1948), 4

changes were at work in the social and economic structure of the North, transforming and undermining many of its free-labor assumptions. And the flawed attitude of the Republicans toward race, and the limitations of the free labor outlook in regard to the Negro, foreshadowed the mistakes and failures of the post-emancipation years.

Selected Bibliography

This bibliography does not attempt to list every source consulted in the preparation of this study, or even all those cited in the footnotes. Such a listing would be excessively long and would, I am sure, be of interest to only a relatively few scholars. Those who desire to examine such a list may consult my unpublished doctoral dissertation, "Free Soil, Free Labor and Free Men: The Ideology of the Republican Party Before the Civil War," (Columbia University, 1969), an earlier version of this work. In the belief that it may be of use to students of the ante-bellum period, I have included a full listing of manuscript collections cited in the footnotes, but elsewhere I have tried to confine myself to three kinds of works: those on which I relied most heavily for information, those which most influenced my interpretations, and the major sources in the various areas I have dealt with, to assist those interested in further reading or research.

Manuscript Collections
Adams Papers, Massachusetts Historical Society
James F. Aldrich Papers, Chicago Historical Society
American Missionary Association Archives, Fisk University
John Andrew Papers, Massachusetts Historical Society
Baldwin Family Papers, Yale University
Nathaniel P. Banks Papers, Library of Congress
Charles S. Benton Papers, State Historical Society of Wisconsin
John Bigelow Papers, New York Public Library
Francis W. Bird Papers, Houghton Library, Harvard University
William H. Bissell Papers, Chicago Historical Society
Austin Blair Papers, Burton Historical Collection, Detroit Public Library
Blair Family Papers, Library of Congress
Blair-Lee Papers, Princeton University
Samuel Bowles II Papers, Yale University
William H. Brisbane Papers, State Historical Society of Wisconsin

Orville H. Browning Papers, Illinois State Historical Library
Bryant-Godwin Papers, New York Public Library
Benjamin F. Butler Papers, Princeton University
William Butler Papers, Chicago Historical Society
William A. Buckingham Papers, Connecticut State Library
Simon Cameron Papers, Library of Congress
Henry C. Carey Papers, Edward Carey Gardiner Collection, Historical Society of Pennsylvania
Robert Carter Papers, Houghton Library, Harvard University
John D. Caton Papers, Library of Congress
Zachariah Chandler Papers, Library of Congress
Salmon P. Chase Papers, Library of Congress
Salmon P. Chase Papers, Historical Society of Pennsylvania
Schuyler Colfax Papers, Library of Congress
Commission on Western History, Miscellaneous Manuscripts, Houghton Library, Harvard University
Richard Henry Dana, Jr. Papers, Massachusetts Historical Society
David Davis Papers, Chicago Historical Society
Moses Davis Papers, State Historical Society of Wisconsin
Henry L. Dawes Papers, Library of Congress
John A. Dix Papers, Columbia University
James R. Doolittle Papers, Library of Congress
James R. Doolittle Papers, New York Public Library
James R. Doolittle Papers, State Historical Society of Wisconsin
Zebina Eastman Papers, Chicago Historical Society
William Pitt Fessenden Papers, Western Reserve Historical Society
Hamilton Fish Papers, Library of Congress
Azariah C. Flagg Papers, Columbia University
Azariah C. Flagg Papers, New York Public Library
George G. Fogg Papers, New Hampshire Historical Society
Sidney Howard Gay Papers, Columbia University
Joshua R. Giddings Papers, Ohio Historical Society
Giddings-Julian Papers, Library of Congress
Simon Gratz Collection, Historical Society of Pennsylvania
Horace Greeley Papers, Chicago Historical Society
Horace Greeley Papers, Library of Congress
Horace Greeley Papers, New Hampshire Historical Society
Horace Greeley Papers, New York Public Library
Greeley-Colfax Papers, New York Public Library
John P. Hale Papers, New Hampshire Historical Society
John P. Hale Scrapbook, New Hampshire Historical Society
Hannibal Hamlin Papers, University of Maine, Orono
Thomas Wentworth Higginson Papers, Houghton Library, Harvard University
Mark Howard Papers, Connecticut Historical Society

Samuel Gridley Howe Papers, Houghton Library, Harvard University
Timothy Howe Papers, State Historical Society of Wisconsin
Andrew Jackson Papers, Library of Congress
John Jay Papers, Columbia University
George W. Julian Papers, Indiana State Library
Amos A. Lawrence Papers, Massachusetts Historical Society
Joshua Leavitt Papers, Library of Congress
Charles G. Leland Papers, Historical Society of Pennsylvania
Robert Todd Lincoln Papers, Library of Congress
Logan Family Papers, Library of Congress
John McLean Papers, Library of Congress
Edward McPherson Papers, Library of Congress
Wayne MacVeagh Papers, Historical Society of Pennsylvania
Miscellaneous Manuscripts, Connecticut State Library
Miscellaneous Manuscripts, Houghton Library, Harvard University
Miscellaneous Manuscripts, New-York Historical Society
Miscellaneous Manuscripts, State Historical Society of Wisconsin
Miscellaneous Manuscripts, Western Reserve Historical Society
Edwin Morgan Papers, New York State Library
Justin S. Morrill Papers, Library of Congress
Marcus Morton Papers, Massachusetts Historical Society
John G. Palfrey Papers, Houghton Library, Harvard University
Edward L. Pierce Papers, Houghton Library, Harvard University
James S. Pike Papers, Library of Congress
John F. Potter Papers, State Historical Society of Wisconsin
Presidential Manuscripts, Pierpont Morgan Library, New York
Henry J. Raymond Papers, New York Public Library
Logan U. Reavis Papers, Chicago Historical Society
Albert G. Riddle Papers, Western Reserve Historical Society
F. B. Sanborn Papers, Library of Congress
William Schouler Papers, Massachusetts Historical Society
Carl Schurz Papers, Library of Congress
William H. Seward Papers, Rush Rhees Library, University of Rochester
John Sherman Papers, Library of Congress
Gerrit Smith Papers, Syracuse University
Thaddeus Stevens Papers, Library of Congress
Charles Sumner Papers, Houghton Library, Harvard University
Lewis Tappan Papers, Library of Congress
Mason W. Tappan Papers, New Hampshire Historical Society
Samuel J. Tilden Papers, New York Public Library
Lyman Trumbull Papers, Library of Congress
Trumbull Family Papers, Illinois State Historical Library
Daniel Ullmann Papers, New-York Historical Society
John C. Underwood Papers, Library of Congress
Martin Van Buren Papers, Library of Congress

Benjamin F. Wade Papers, Library of Congress
Amasa Walker Papers, Massachusetts Historical Society
Israel Washburn Papers, Library of Congress
Elihu B. Washburne Papers, Library of Congress
James Watson Webb Papers, Yale University
Thurlow Weed Papers, Rush Rhees Library, University of Rochester
Gideon Welles Papers, Connecticut Historical Society
Gideon Welles Papers, Library of Congress
Gideon Welles Papers, New York Public Library

Among these hundred-odd manuscript collections, only a minority were used extensively. The collections I found most useful were those of Salmon P. Chase and William H. Seward, for as the two most prominent Republican leaders of the 1850's, Chase and Seward wrote and received letters on every aspect of the party's politics and ideology. The Chase papers are especially important for understanding the evolution of Liberty, Free Soil, and Republican interpretations of the Constitution, the position of radicals and former Democrats within the Republican party, and the Republican response to the issue of race, while the papers of Seward and his political alter ego Thurlow Weed are equally revealing of the ideas of the Whig element in the party, as well as of general political developments throughout the North. Other collections which proved to be abundant sources of information on specific subjects were: on the radicals, the papers of Adams, Giddings, Julian, Pierce, Schurz, and Sumner; on the Democratic-Republicans, those of the Blairs, Doolittle, Hamlin, Trumbull, and Welles; on moderates and conservatives, those of Carey, Davis, Fish, and Lincoln; on nativism, the collections of Banks and Ullmann; and on race, particularly colonization plans, the papers of the Blairs, Doolittle, and Trumbull.

Published Collections of Writings, Speeches, Letters, and Documents
Unfortunately, the speeches of Salmon P. Chase have not been collected, but "Diary and Correspondence of Salmon P. Chase," *Annual Report* of AHA, 1902, II, is an extremely valuable edition of letters from the Chase Papers in the Library of Congress and the Historical Society of Pennsylvania. I also made extensive use of the excellent compilation, Roy F. Basle *et al.*, eds., *The Collected Works of Abraham Lincoln* (9 vols.: New Brunswick, 1953–55), as well as three collections of Carl Schurz's works: Frederic Bancroft, ed., *Speeches, Correspondence, and Political Papers of Carl Schurz* (6 vols.: New York, 1913); Joseph Schafer, ed., *Intimate Letters of Carl Schurz, 1841–69* (Madison, 1928); and Carl Schurz, *Speeches of Carl Schurz* (Philadelphia, 1865). William Seward's son, Frederick W. Seward, published in 1891 an invaluable three-volume collection of Seward's letters which, however, is marred by omissions and alterations in some letters. The first volume is entitled *William H. Seward: An Autobiography* (New York, 1891); the remaining volumes are *Seward at Washington* (2 vols.: New

York, 1891). I also used extensively George E. Baker's collection, *The Works of William H. Seward* (5 vols.: Boston, 1853–84). The most important speeches of Charles Sumner are included in *The Works of Charles Sumner* (10 vols.: Boston, 1870–83), and there are excerpts from Sumner's letters in Edward L. Pierce, *Memoir and Letters of Charles Sumner* (4 vols.: Boston, 1877–93).

Other useful, but less important collections of speeches and writings include Dwight L. Dumond, ed., *Letters of James G. Birney 1831–1857* (2 vols.: New York, 1938), which sheds considerable light on developments in the Liberty party; George S. Boutwell, *Speeches and Papers Relating to the Rebellion and the Overthrow of Slavery* (Boston, 1867); Josiah Morrow, ed., *Life and Speeches of Thomas Corwin* (Cincinnati, 1896); Richard Henry Dana, Jr., *Speeches in Stirring Times*, ed., Richard Henry Dana, 3rd (Boston, 1910); Duane Mowry, ed., "Negro Colonization. From Doolittle Correspondence," *Publications* of the Southern Historical Association, IX (November 1905), 401–10; and Theodore C. Pease and James G. Randall, eds., *The Diary of Orville Hickman Browning* (2 vols.: Springfield, 1927–33), which reveals the political outlook of an important Illinois conservative. The works of Cassius M. Clay are collected in Horace Greeley, ed., *The Writings of Cassius Marcellus Clay* (New York, 1848), and *The Life of Cassius Marcellus Clay. Memoirs, Writings, and Speeches* (Cincinnati, 1886). Philip S. Foner, ed., *The Life and Writings of Frederick Douglass* (4 vols.: New York, 1950–55) is invaluable for black reactions to the Republican party. Other helpful collections are Sherman Evarts, ed., *Arguments and Speeches of William Maxwell Evarts* (3 vols.: New York, 1919); Sarah Forbes Hughes, ed., *Letters and Recollections of John Murray Forbes* (2 vols.: Boston, 1899), and Hughes, ed., *Letters (Supplementary) of John Murray Forbes* (3 vols.: Boston, 1905); L. Belle Hamlin, ed., "Selections from the Follett Papers," a series in *Quarterly Publications* of the Ohio Historical and Philosophical Society, IX (1914) through XIII (1918), which includes letters from Chase, Wade, and other Ohio leaders; George W. Julian, *Speeches on Political Questions* (New York, 1872); and Horace Mann, *Slavery: Letters and Speeches* (Boston, 1851).

I also made use of William M. French, ed., *Life, Speeches, State Papers, and Public Services of Gov. Oliver P. Morton* (Cincinnati, 1866); two collections edited by J. Herman Schauinger, "The Letters of Godlove S. Orth, Hoosier Whig," *IndMH*, XXXIX (December 1943), 365–400, and "The Letters of Godlove S. Orth, Hoosier American," *IndMH*, XL (March 1944), 51–66; George T. Palmer, ed., "A Collection of Letters From Lyman Trumbull to John M. Palmer, 1854–1858," *Journal* of the IllSHS, XVI (April–July 1923), 20–41, which sheds light on the thinking of Democratic-Republicans; Rachel Sherman Thorndike, *The Sherman Letters* (New York, 1894); and Allan Nevins and Milton H. Thomas, eds., *The Diary of George Templeton Strong* (4 vols.: New York, 1952), in which one can trace the transformation of a conservative Whig into a Republican. James S. Pike,

First Blows of the Civil War (New York, 1879), is a collection of articles and correspondence of the New York *Tribune*'s Associate Editor, and Howard C. Perkins, ed., *Northern Editorials on Secession* (2 vols.: New York, 1942) is an excellent compilation of newspaper opinion of all parties. And I found Kirk H. Porter and Donald B. Johnson, comps., *National Party Platforms 1840–1956* (Urbana, 1956), extremely valuable.

Government Documents, Official and Semi-Official

Since the letters and speeches of Republican politicians were the basic source materials for this work, I made extensive use of the *Congressional Globe* from the mid-1840's to 1861. Unfortunately, state legislatures did not publish the speeches of legislators, but I did find the proceedings of state constitutional conventions and the messages of Republican governors very valuable sources. The most useful convention reports were *Report of the Debates and Proceedings of the Convention for the Revision of the Constitution of the State of Indiana* (2 vols.: Indianapolis, 1850); *The Debates of the Constitutional Convention of the State of Iowa* (2 vols.: Davenport, 1857); *Official Report of the Debates and Proceedings in the State Convention . . . to Revise and Amend the Constitution of the Commonwealth of Massachusetts* (3 vols.: Boston, 1853), a convention at which Charles Sumner and Henry Wilson were among the delegates; and *Report of the Debates and Proceedings of the Convention for the Revision of the Constitution of the State of Ohio* (2 vols.: Columbus, 1851). Benjamin F. Shambaugh, ed., *The Messages and Proclamations of the Governors of Iowa* (7 vols.: Iowa City, 1903–05), and George N. Fuller, ed., *Messages of the Governors of Michigan* (4 vols.: Lansing, 1925–27) are both useful collections which include the messages of Republican governors of the 1850's. Messages of other governors include *Address of His Excellency John A. Andrew, to the Two Branches of the Legislature of Massachusetts* (Boston, 1861); *Annual Message of Alexander Randall . . . and Accompanying Documents* (Madison, 1860); *Inaugural Address of Salmon P. Chase* (Columbus, 1856); *Message of the Governor of Ohio to the Fifty-Third General Assembly . . .* (Columbus, 1858); and *Message of the Governor of Ohio to the Fifty-Fourth General Assembly . . .* (Columbus, 1860). L. E. Chittenden, *A Report of the Debates and Proceedings in the Secret Sessions of the Conference Convention . . .* (New York, 1864), contains the speeches of Republican delegates to the ill-fated Peace Convention of February, 1861.

Newspapers and Periodicals

Republican newspapers were another invaluable source, not only because their editorials both reflected and helped shape the outlook of politicians and voters, but because the newspapers carried reports of Republican state conventions as well as of speeches by major and minor Republican leaders which are unavailable elsewhere. The politics of the leading Republican paper, the New York *Tribune*, are difficult to classify because of the vacillations of its idiosyncratic editor, Horace Greeley, but historians of the 1850's are agreed that a careful examination of the *Tribune's* pages is indispensable to an understanding of the Republican mind. The leading moderate Republican papers included Samuel Bowles's Springfield *Republican*, the (Columbus) *Ohio State Journal*, and the Cincinnati *Gazette*, while the *National Era*, edited by Gamaliel Bailey, expressed the views of the radicals. Democratic-Republicans were represented by William Cullen Bryant's New York *Evening Post*, John Wentworth's Chicago *Democrat*, and the Chicago *Democratic Press*, while Henry J. Raymond's New York *Times*, and the Philadelphia *North American and United States Gazette* reflected the outlook of Republican conservatives.

These were the newspapers of which I made the most extensive use. Others consulted included the Boston *Commonwealth*, organ of the Massachusetts Free Soilers; the Boston *Atlas and Daily Bee*, Chicago *Press and Tribune*, Cleveland *Leader*, Milwaukee *Sentinel*, Racine *Advocate*, Washington *Republic*, and (Madison) *Wisconsin State Journal*. *Douglass' Monthly* and the *Weekly Anglo-African* contain the comments of black leaders on the Republican party, while *The Liberator*, edited by William Lloyd Garrison, has more speeches and letters by and about Republicans than might be expected. The *Atlantic Monthly*, edited by James Russell Lowell, includes a number of articles by Republicans. The New York *Tribune's* yearly *Almanac* contains invaluable compilations of state and national election statistics.

Contemporary Speeches, Convention Proceedings, Books, and Pamphlets
A number of important speeches by Republican spokesmen are preserved in pamphlet form. The largest pamphlet collections are located in the Library of Congress, the New York Public Library, and the library of Harvard University. Speeches which I found most valuable include two statements by Francis P. Blair, Jr. on colonization, *Colonization and Commerce* (Cincinnati, 1859), and *The Destiny of the Races of This Continent* (Washington, 1859); *Speech of Hon. O. H. Browning, Delivered at the Republican Mass Meeting . . .* (Quincy, 1860); two important legal arguments by Salmon P. Chase, *An Argument for the Defendant . . . in the Case of Wharton Jones vs John Vanzandt* (Cincinnati, 1847), and *Speech of Salmon P. Chase in the Case of the Colored Woman, Matilda* (Cincinnati, 1837); and *Speech of the Hon. Thomas Ewing at Chillicothe, Ohio* (Cincinnati, 1860), and C. L. Martzo¹ff, ed., "Address at Marietta, Ohio, 1858. By Hon. Thomas Ewing," *OAHQ*, XXVIII (1919), 186–207, which are important statements of the conservative Republican out'ook. Three important speeches by William H. Seward which George Baker did not include in his edition of Seward's works are *The Elements of Empire in America* (New York, 1844); *Immigrant White Free Labor, or Imported Black African Slave Labor* (Washington, 1857); and *Speech of Hon. William H. Seward at Jackson, October 4, 1856* (np, nd). John Sherman's *The Republican Party—Its History and Policy* (np, 1860) is an extremely useful

statement by a leading moderate, while two speeches by Lyman Trumbull express the views of Democratic-Republicans: *Great Speech of Hon. Lyman Trumbull, on the Issues of the Day* (Chicago, 1858), and *Speech of Hon. Lyman Trumbull, on the Politics of the Day* (np, 1857).

The proceedings of Republican and other conventions during the 1850's also proved very useful, particularly *Proceedings of the First Three Republican National Conventions* (np, nd); *Proceedings of the State Disunion Convention, Held at Worcester* . . . (Boston, 1857); and *Proceedings of the Convention of the Colored Freemen of Ohio* (Cincinnati, 1852). Letters to this latter convention by Horace Mann, Benjamin Wade, and Cassius Clay are particularly revealing of Republicans' racial attitudes. Salmon P. Chase and Charles D. Cleveland, *Antislavery Addresses of 1844 and 1845* (London, 1867), includes the important address of the Southern and Western Liberty Convention of 1845.

Contemporary books of which I made considerable use include four works by Henry C. Carey: *Principles of Political Economy* (3 vols.: Philadelphia, 1837–40), *Principles of Social Science* (3 vols.: Philadelphia, 1858–59), *The Harmony of Interests, Agricultural, Manufacturing, and Commercial* (New York, 1856), and *The Past, the Present, and the Future* (Philadelphia, 1872). George Fitzhugh's *Cannibals All!*, ed., C. Vann Woodward (Cambridge, 1960) and *Sociology for the South: or the Failure of Free Society* (Richmond, 1854) are exemplary versions of pro-slavery thought. Among the writings of Horace Greeley, I found *Hints Towards Reforms* (New York, 1850) and *The Crystal Palace and Its Lessons* (New York, 1852) most useful. Frederick Law Olmsted's *A Journey in the Back Country* (New York, 1863), *A Journey in the Seaboard Slave States* (New York, 1856), and *A Journey Through Texas* (New York, 1861) were extremely influential descriptions of southern society and life.

Other important contemporary publications include O. C. Gardiner, *The Great Issue* (New York, 1848), a record of the Free Soil campaign of 1848; two pamphlets by John G. Palfrey, *Papers on the Slave Power* (Boston, 1846) and *Five Years' Progress of the Slave Power* (Boston, 1852); and George Weston's *The Poor Whites of the South* (Washington, 1856) and *The Progress of Slavery in the United States* (Washington, 1857).

Autobiographies, Memoirs, and Reminiscences
Although these works must be handled with considerable care, they often yield valuable insights and recollections. The most useful memoirs and reminiscences are John Bigelow, *Retrospections of an Active Life* (5 vols.: New York, 1909–13); *The Reminiscences of Neal Dow* (Portland, 1890); Horace Greeley, *Recollections of a Busy Life* (New York, 1868); George W. Julian, *Political Recollections, 1840–1872* (Chicago, 1884); "John A. Kasson, An Autobiography," *Annals of Iowa*, 3 ser., XII (July 1920), 346–58, which contains valuable information about the Chicago Convention of 1860; Thomas J. McCormack, ed., *Memoirs of Gustave Koerner 1809–1896*

(2 vols.: Cedar Rapids, 1909); A. K. McClure, *Old Time Notes of Pennsylvania* (2 vols.: Philadelphia, 1905); John M. Palmer, *Personal Recollections of John M. Palmer* (Cincinnati, 1901); Carl Schurz, *Reminiscences of Carl Schurz* (3 vols.: New York, 1907–08); and the two-volume set, Harriet A. Weed, ed., *Autobiography of Thurlow Weed* (Boston, 1883) and Thurlow Weed Barnes, *Memoir of Thurlow Weed* (Boston, 1884). Two classic histories of the sectional conflict are in the nature of reminiscences: Joshua Giddings, *History of the Rebellion* (New York, 1864); and Henry Wilson, *History of the Rise and Fall of the Slave Power in America* (3 vols.: Boston, 1875–77).

Biographies

Although a number of Republican leaders, particularly Chase, still need modern biographies, the careers of a large number of first- and second-line politicians have been adequately surveyed. Among the most useful biographies are Martin B. Duberman, *Charles Francis Adams 1807–1886* (Boston, 1961); Henry G. Pearson, *The Life of John Andrew* (2 vols.: Boston, 1904); Fred Harvey Harrington, *Fighting Politician, Major General N. P. Banks* (Philadelphia, 1948); William E. Smith, *The Francis Preston Blair Family in Politics* (2 vols.: New York, 1933); and George S. Merriam, *The Life and Times of Samuel Bowles* (2 vols.: New York, 1885), and Parke Godwin, *A Biography of William Cullen Bryant* (2 vols.: New York, 1883), both of which quote liberally from editorials and correspondence. Various aspects of Henry Carey's career are dealt with in George W. Smith, *Henry C. Carey and American Sectional Conflict* (Albuquerque, 1951), A. D. H. Kaplan, *Henry Charles Carey* (Baltimore, 1931), and Arnold W. Green, *Henry Charles Carey, Nineteenth Century Sociologist* (Philadelphia, 1951). On Chase, J. W. Schuckers, *The Life and Public Services of Salmon P. Chase* (New York, 1874) and Robert B. Warden, *An Account of the Private Life and Public Services of Salmon P. Chase* (Cincinnati, 1874) are long on selections from Chase's letters, but short on interpretation and criticism. Albert B. Hart, *Salmon P. Chase* (Boston, 1899), while good, is brief.

Other good biographies include David L. Smiley, *Lion of Whitehall, the Life of Cassius M. Clay* (Madison, 1962); O. J. Hollister, *Life of Schuyler Colfax* (New York, 1886); Samuel Shapiro, *Richard Henry Dana, Jr. 1815–1882* (East Lansing, 1961); Willard L. King, *Lincoln's Manager David Davis* (Cambridge, 1960); Sarah J. Day, *The Man on a Hill Top* (Philadelphia, 1931), a biography of Ohio Congressman Timothy Day which contains some surprisingly valuable correspondence; Frank L. Byrne, *Prophet of Prohibition: Neal Dow and His Crusade* (Madison, 1961); Charles A. Jellison, *Fessenden of Maine* (Syracuse, 1962); Allan Nevins, *Hamilton Fish* (New York, 1936); George W. Julian, *The Life of Joshua Giddings* (Chicago, 1892), which includes selections from Giddings's writings and speeches; Jeter A. Isely, *Horace Greeley and the Republican Party 1853–1861* (Princeton, 1947); Glyndon G. Van Deusen, *Horace Greeley,*

Nineteenth Century Crusader (Philadelphia, 1953); William Salter, *The Life of James W. Grimes* (New York, 1876), another of the old-style biographies with generous selections from Grimes's correspondence; and Richard Sewell, *John P. Hale and the Politics of Abolition* (Cambridge, 1965).

Harry Draper Hunt III, *Hannibal Hamlin of Maine: Lincoln's First Vice-President* (Syracuse, 1969) supersedes the older but still useful Charles E. Hamlin, *The Life and Times of Hannibal Hamlin* (Cambridge, 1899). The same cannot be said for Patrick W. Riddleberger, *George Washington Julian, Radical Republican* (Indianapolis, 1966), which is thin and superficial on the pre-war years, and forces one to refer to Grace Julian Clarke, *George W. Julian* (Indianapolis, 1923), which is not much better. Ernest P. Muller, "Preston King: A Political Biography" (unpublished doctoral dissertation, Columbia University, 1957), is an exhaustive and valuable study of a neglected figure. On Lincoln's career before the Civil War, see Don E. Fehrenbacher, *Prelude to Greatness, Lincoln in the 1850's* (New York, 1964 ed.), and Albert K. Beveridge, *Abraham Lincoln 1809–1858* (2 vols.: Boston, 1928).

Additional biographies are Edward Magdol, *Owen Lovejoy: Abolitionist in Congress* (New Brunswick, 1967); B. F. Morris, ed., *The Life of Thomas Morris* (Cincinnati, 1856), containing lengthy excerpts from Morris's speeches and letters; Robert F. Durden, *James Shepherd Pike* (Durham, 1957), a book which has played an important role in the recent reconsideration of Republican racial attitudes; Chester V. Easum, *The Americanization of Carl Schurz* (Chicago, 1929); Glyndon G. Van Deusen, *William Henry Seward* (New York, 1967); David Donald, *Charles Sumner and the Coming of the Civil War* (New York, 1961); Charles Roll, *Colonel Dick Thompson, The Persistent Whig* (Indianapolis, 1948); Mark M. Krug, *Lyman Trumbull, Conservative Radical* (New York, 1965); Hans L. Trefousse, *Benjamin Franklin Wade* (New York, 1963); Gaillard Hunt, *Israel, Elihu, and Cadwallader Washburn, A Chapter in American Biography* (New York, 1925); Glyndon G. Van Deusen, *Thurlow Weed: Wizard of the Lobby* (Boston, 1947); Don E. Fehrenbacher, *Chicago Giant, A Biography of 'Long John' Wentworth* (Madison, 1957); Charles B. Going, *David Wilmot Free-Soiler* (New York, 1924); Richard H. Abbott, "Cobbler in Congress: Life of Henry Wilson, 1812–1875" (unpublished doctoral dissertation, University of Wisconsin, 1965); and Thomas Russell and Elias Nason, *The Life and Public Services of Hon. Henry Wilson* (Boston, 1872).

Books and Articles

The historiography of the coming of the Civil War is, of course, a vast subject. In working my way through this body of literature, and trying to understand the various schools of interpretation, I found the following surveys very instructive: David Potter, *The South and the Sectional Conflict* (Baton Rouge, 1968); Thomas J. Pressly, *Americans Interpret Their Civil*

War (Princeton, 1954); Thomas N. Bonner, "Civil War Historians and the 'Needless War' Doctrine," *Journal of the History of Ideas,* XVII (April 1956), 193–216; and David Donald, "American Historians and the Causes of the Civil War," *SAQ,* LIX (Summer 1960), 351–55. John S. Rosenberg, "Toward a New Civil War Revisionism," *American Scholar,* XXXVIII (Spring 1969), 250–72 is an interesting article which concludes that the war was needless, not because it might have been avoided, but because its results did not justify so massive a loss of life. The best historical survey of the ante-bellum years is unquestionably Allan Nevins's *Ordeal of the Union* (2 vols.: New York, 1947) and *The Emergence of Lincoln* (2 vols.: New York, 1950), upon which I relied heavily. I was also strongly influenced by the writings of Avery Craven, although I disagree with many of his interpretations. See Craven's *The Repressible Conflict 1830–1861* (Baton Rouge, 1939), *The Coming of the Civil War* (New York, 1942), and *An Historian and the Civil War* (Chicago, 1964). Three other works with chapters on the coming of the Civil War which affected my outlook are Charles A. Beard and Mary R. Beard, *The Rise of American Civilization* (2 vols.: New York, 1933 ed.); William A. Williams, *The Contours of American History* (London, 1961 ed.); and Barrington Moore, Jr., *Social Origins of Dictatorship and Democracy* (Boston, 1966). Finally, Eugene D. Genovese, *The Political Economy of Slavery* (New York, 1965) strongly influenced my approach to the coming of the Civil War, and to the study of ideology.

On the anti-slavery movement in general, I found Louis Filler, *The Crusade Against Slavery* (New York, 1960) a very useful survey, with an excellent bibliography. Dwight L. Dumond, *Antislavery, The Crusade for Freedom in America* (Ann Arbor, 1961), although often, and rightly, criticized for its uncritical approach, still has many suggestive insights. Gilbert H. Barnes's classic, *The Anti-Slavery Impulse* (New York, 1933) and several essays in Martin Duberman, ed., *The Antislavery Vanguard* (Princeton, 1965), were also valuable. George H. Mayer, *The Republican Party 1854–1966* (New York, 1967 ed.) is a competent survey, which does not concern itself with ideology, while Andrew W. Crandall, *The Early History of the Republican Party 1854–1856* (Boston, 1930) covers political aspects of these early years in rich detail. On the 1856 election, see James A. Rawley, "Financing the Frémont Campaign," *PaMHB,* LXXV (January 1951), 25–35, Roy F. Nichols, "Some Problems of the First Republican Presidential Campaign," *AHR,* XXVIII (April 1923), 492–96, and Fred H. Harrington, "Frémont and the North-Americans," *AHR,* XLIV (July 1939), 842–48. Harrington's "'The First Northern Victory,'" *JSH,* V (May 1939), 186–205 covers the election of Nathaniel P. Banks as Speaker of the House. The most useful studies of Lincoln's election are Reinhard H. Luthin, *The First Lincoln Campaign* (Cambridge, 1944), and Ollinger Crenshaw, "Urban and Rural Voting in the Election of 1860," in Eric Goldman, ed., *Historiography and Urbanization* (Baltimore, 1941), 43–66. George H. Knoles, ed., *The Crisis of the Union* (Baton Rouge, 1965) and Norman A. Graebner, ed., *Politics and the Crisis of 1860* (Urbana, 1961) contain essays on the election of 1860 and its aftermath, while the secession crisis is examined in two excellent works, David M. Potter, *Lincoln and His Party in the Secession Crisis* (New Haven, 1942), and Kenneth Stampp, *And the War Came* (Baton Rouge, 1950). See also Robert W. Johannsen, "The Douglas Democracy and the Crisis of Disunion," *CWH*, IX (September 1963), 229–47. Other works which I found useful were Paul C. Nagel, *One Nation Indivisible* (New York, 1964), which contains abundant documentation on the development of northern Unionism, but does not do this important subject justice; Major L. Wilson, "An Analysis of the Ideas of Liberty and Union as Used by Members of Congress and the Presidents from 1828 to 1861" (unpublished doctoral dissertation, University of Kansas, 1964); Lois K. Mathews, *The Expansion of New England* (Boston and New York, 1909); Harry Jaffa, *Crisis of the House Divided* (Garden City, 1959), an analysis of the Lincoln-Douglas debates; Philip S. Foner, *Business and Slavery* (Chapel Hill, 1941); and Thomas B. Alexander, *Sectional Stress and Party Strength* (Nashville, 1967), a compilation and analysis of antebellum Congressional roll calls.

My understanding of the state of the northern economy in the 1840's and 1850's was influenced by Stuart Bruchey, *The Roots of American Economic Growth 1607–1861* (New York, 1965); Douglass C. North, *The Economic Growth of the United States 1790–1860* (New York, 1961); and two works by George R. Taylor, *The Transportation Revolution 1815–1860* (New York, 1951) and "The National Economy Before and After the Civil War," in David T. Gilchrist and W. David Lewis, eds., *Economic Change in the Civil War Era* (Greenville, Del., 1965), 1–22. Marvin Meyers, *The Jacksonian Persuasion* (New York, 1960 ed.) and Irwin Unger, *The Greenback Era* (Princeton, 1964) contain masterful analyses of American values before and after the Civil War, while attitudes toward labor are dealt with in Bernard Mandel, *Labor: Free and Slave* (New York, 1955) and David Montgomery, *Beyond Equality: Labor and the Radical Republicans, 1862–1872* (New York, 1967). Henry Nash Smith, *Virgin Land* (Cambridge, 1950), and Arthur E. Bestor, "Patent-Office Models of the Good Society: Some Relationships between Social Reform and Westward Expansion," *AHR*, LVIII (April 1953), 505–26, shed considerable light on the importance of the West in northern thought. See also George M. Stephenson, *The Political History of the Public Lands from 1840 to 1862* (Boston, 1917); Roy M. Robbins, *Our Landed Heritage, The Public Domain, 1776–1936* (Princeton, 1942); and Robbins, "Horace Greeley: Land Reform and Unemployment, 1837–1862," *AgH*, VII (January 1933), 18–41.

The best introduction to the tariff issue is F. W. Taussig, *The Tariff History of the United States* (7th ed., New York, 1923), while its importance in Republican thought is explained in Arthur M. Lee, "Henry C. Carey and the Republican Tariff," *PaMHB*, LXXXI (July 1957), 280–302, and Rodney J. Morrison, "Henry C. Carey and American Economic Development," *Ex-*

plorations in Entrepreneurial History, 2nd ser., V (Winter 1968), 132–44. See also Thomas M. Pitkin, "Western Republicans and the Tariff in 1860," *MVHR*, XXVII (December 1940), 401–20; and Arthur M. Lee's excellent unpublished doctoral dissertation, "The Development of an Economic Policy in the Early Republican Party" (Syracuse University, 1953). On the all-important subject of the Republican image of the South, there is unfortunately little to recommend. Two articles by George W. Smith are quite useful: "Ante-Bellum Attempts of Northern Business Interests to 'Redeem' the Upper South," *JSH*, XI (May 1945), 177–213, and "Some Northern Wartime Attitudes Toward the Post-Civil War South," *JSH*, X (August 1944), 253–74; and C. Vann Woodward has several valuable insights in "The Southern Ethic in a Puritan World," *William and Mary Quarterly*, 3 ser., XXV (July 1968), 343–70. Howard R. Floan, *The South in Northern Eyes 1831 to 1861* (Austin, 1958) is thin and inadequate.

Constitutional aspects of the sectional conflict are discussed in two articles by Arthur E. Bestor: "The American Civil War as a Constitutional Crisis," *AHR*, LXIX (January 1964), 327–52, and "State Sovereignty and Slavery," *Journal of IllSHS*, LIV (Summer 1961), 117–80; and in Robert R. Russel, "Constitutional Doctrines with Regard to Slavery in Territories," *JSH*, XXXII (November 1966), 466–86; Julius Yanuck, "The Fugitive Slave Law and the Constitution" (unpublished doctoral dissertation, Columbia University, 1953); and Jacobus tenBroek, *The Antislavery Origins of the Fourteenth Amendment* (Berkeley, 1951). On the Slave Power, there are important insights in Russell B. Nye, *Fettered Freedom, Civil Liberties and the Slavery Controversy 1830–1860* (East Lansing, 1949), and Larry Gara, "Slavery and the Slave Power: A Crucial Distinction," *CWH*, XV (March 1969), 5–18. Chauncey S. Boucher criticizes the Slave Power idea in "*In Re* That Aggressive Slaveocracy," *MVHR*, VIII (June–September 1921), 13–79; while David Brion Davis, "Some Themes of Counter-Subversion: An Analysis of Anti-Masonic, Anti-Catholic, and Anti-Morman Literature," *MVHR*, XLVII (September 1960), 205–24, helps explain why the idea was so widely accepted.

Hans L. Trefousse, *The Radical Republicans, Lincoln's Vanguard for Racial Justice* (New York, 1969) is the place to begin in examining the radicals. See also Margaret Shortreed's influential article, "The Antislavery Radicals: From Crusade to Revolution 1840–1868," *Past and Present*, XVI (November 1959), 65–89. Theodore C. Smith, *The Liberty and Free Soil Parties in the Northwest* (New York, 1897) is still the best treatment of its subject, but should be supplemented with Joseph G. Rayback, "The Liberty Party Leaders of Ohio: Exponents of Antislavery Coalition," *OAHQ*, LVII (1948), 165–78. John R. Hendricks, "The Liberty Party in New York State, 1838–1848" (unpublished doctoral dissertation, Fordham University, 1959) is quite useful. The phenomenon of free-soilism still needs study, as does the Free Soil party, one of the most successful third parties in American history. Frederick J. Blue, "A History of the Free Soil Party" (unpublished doctoral dissertation, University of Wisconsin, 1966) covers the political chronology well, but neither asks nor answers most of the important questions.

The role of Democrats in the Republican party is another area requiring further study. Albert J. Cole, Jr., "The Barnburner Element in the Republican Party" (unpublished master's essay, University of Wisconsin, 1951), and Mildred C. Sto'er, "The Influence of the Democratic Element in the Republican Party of Illinois and Indiana, 1854–1860" (unpublished doctoral dissertation, Indiana University, 1938) are the on'y works bearing directly on this subject. Herbert D. A. Donovan, *The Barnburners* (New York, 1925) is a valuable study of the New York Van Burenite Democrats. It should be supplemented with Max M. Mintz, "The Political Ideas of Martin Van Buren," *NYH*, XXX (October 1949), 422–48. Chaplain Morrison explains the genesis of the Wilmot Proviso and its effect on the Democratic party in *Democratic Politics and Sectionalism* (Chapel Hill, 1967). My own interpretation, "The Wilmot Proviso Revisited," *JAH*, LVI (September, 1969), 262–79, has a somewhat different emphasis. Three excellent works by Roy F. Nichols trace the disruption of the Democratic party in the 1850's: *The Democratic Machine 1850–1854* (New York, 1923), *The Disruption of American Democracy* (New York, 1948), and "The Kansas-Nebraska Act: A Century of Historiography," *MVHR*, XLIII (September 1956), 187–212.

My perception of the importance of nativism in the 1850's, and its relation to the Republican party, has been shaped by the following works: Oscar Handlin, *Boston's Immigrants* (Cambridge, 1959); Clifford S. Griffin, *Their Brothers' Keepers: Moral Stewardship in the United States, 1800–1865* (New Brunswick, 1960); John Higham, "Another Look at Nativism," *Catholic Historical Review,* XLIV (July 1958), 147–58; and Lee Benson, *The Concept of Jacksonian Democracy* (Princeton, 1961), a pioneering work from which I have profited immense'y, despite the fact that Professor Benson and I disagree on this subject. Ray A. Billington's *The Protestant Crusade 1800–1860* (New York, 1938) proved less helpful than I expected, whi!e Sister M. Evangeline Thomas, *Nativism in the Old Northwest, 1850–1860* (Washington, 1936) contains much useful information. Other interpretations include William G. Bean, "An Aspect of Know-Nothingism—The Immigrant and S'avery," *SAQ*, XXIII (October 1924), 319–34; Harry J. Carman and Reinhard H. Luthin, "Some Aspects of Know-Nothingism Reconsidered," *SAQ*, XXXIX (April 1940), 213–34; Seymour M. L'pset, "Religion and Politics in the American Past and Present," in Robert Lee and Martin E. Marty, eds., *Religion and Social Conflict* (New York, 1964), 69–126; and Samuel P. Hays, "Political Parties and the Community-Society Continuum," in William N. Chambers and Walter Dean Burnham, eds., *The American Party Systems* (New York, 1967), 152–81. On the temperance movement, see John A. Krout. *The Origins of Prohibition* (New York, 1925), and Joseph R. Gusfield, *Symbolic Crusade: Status Politics and the American*

Temperance Movement (Urbana, 1963). Three investigations of the foreign-born vote in the election of 1860 are Joseph Schafer, "Who Elected Lincoln?," *AHR*, XLVII (October 1941), 51–64; Robert P. Swierenga, "The Ethnic Voter and the First Lincoln Election," *CWH*, XI (March 1965), 27–44; and George H. Daniels, "Immigrant Vote in the 1860 Election: The Case of Iowa," *Mid-America*, XLIV (July 1962), 146–62. For further information on nativism and temperance in the 1850's, see the state studies listed below.

The standard study of the conditions of free blacks in the ante-bellum North is Leon F. Litwack, *North of Slavery* (Chicago, 1961). Litwack takes the Republicans to task for racial prejudice within their ranks, and several other recent writers have concurred, most notably Eugene H. Berwanger, in *The Frontier Against Slavery* (Urbana, 1967); V. Jacque Voegeli, in *Free But Not Equal: The Midwest and the Negro During the Civil War* (Chicago, 1967) and "The Northwest and the Race Issue, 1861–1862," *MVHR*, L (September 1963), 235–51; and Robert F. Durden, in his contribution to Duberman's *The Antislavery Vanguard*, and his biography of James Shepherd Pike. As I have indicated in the text, I believe that these writers have carried a good point too far, and have failed to make the necessary distinctions either within the Republican party or between Republicans and Democrats. I made an earlier attempt to deal with this question in "Racial Attitudes of the New York Free Soilers," *NYH*, XLVI (October 1965), 311–29, and "Politics and Prejudice: The Free Soil Party and the Negro, 1849–1852," *JNH*, L (October 1965), 232–56. Other important works on this subject include Emil Olbrich, "The Development of Sentiment on Negro Suffrage to 1860," *Bulletin* of the University of Wisconsin, III (1912), 1–135; Emma Lou Thornbrough, *The Negro in Indiana* (Indianapolis, 1957) and "The Race Issue in Indiana Politics during the Civil War," *IndMH*, XLVII (June 1951), 165–88; John L. Stanley, "Majority Tyranny in Tocqueville's America: The Failure of Negro Suffrage in 1846," *PSQ* LXXIV (September, 1969), 412–35; and Leslie H. Fishel, Jr., "Wisconsin and Negro Suffrage," *WisMH*, XLVI (Spring 1963), 180–96. The sensible approach of W. R. Brock in *An American Crisis* (London, 1963) strongly influenced my own thoughts on this subject.

There are treatments of Republican colonization plans in Walter L. Fleming, "Deportation and Colonization: An Attempted Solution of the Race Problem," in *Studies in Southern History and Politics* (New York, 1914), 3–30; Frederic Bancroft, "The Colonization of American Negroes, 1801–1865," in Jacob E. Cooke, *Frederic Bancroft, Historian* (Norman, Okla., 1957), 145–258; and Charles H. Wesley, "Lincoln's Plan for Colonizing the Emancipated Negroes," *JNH*, IV (January 1919), 7–21. For black reactions, see Howard H. Bell, "A Survey of the Negro Convention Movement, 1830–1861" (unpublished doctoral dissertation, Northwestern University, 1953), and "Negro Nationalism: A Factor in Emigration Projects, 1858–1861," *JNH*, XLVII (January 1962), 42–53. Benjamin Quarles,

Black Abolitionists (New York, 1969), contains disappointingly little on black reactions to the Republican party.

Because of the interest historians have traditionally had in the coming of the Civil War, there are studies of ante-bellum politics for almost every northern state. Although these works usually do not concern themselves with ideology, they provide essential information about the rise of the Republican party during the 1850's. For the New England states, the most useful of these state studies were: Richard R. Wescott, "A History of Maine Politics, 1840–1855: the Formation of the Republican Party" (unpublished doctoral dissertation, University of Maine, Orono, 1966); Frank O. Gatell, "'Conscience and Judgement'; The Bolt of the Massachusetts Conscience Whigs," *Historian*, XXI (November 1958), 18–45; Martin B. Duberman, "Some Notes on the Beginnings of the Republican Party in Massachusetts," *NEQ*, XXXIV (September 1961), 364–70; Thomas H. O'Connor, *Lords of the Loom* (New York, 1968); Kinley J. Brauer, *Cotton versus Conscience: Massachusetts Whig Politicians and Southwestern Expansion, 1843–1848* (Lexington, 1967); William G. Bean, "Party Transformation in Massachusetts With Special Reference to the Antecedents of Republicanism 1848–1860" (unpublished doctoral dissertation, Harvard University, 1922); Alfred C. O'Connell, "The Birth of the G.O.P. in Connecticut," ConnHS *Bulletin*, XXVI (April 1961), 33–39; J. Robert Lane, *A Political History of Connecticut During the Civil War* (Washington, 1941); Robert D. Parmet, The Know-Nothings in Connecticut" (unpublished doctoral dissertation, Columbia University, 1966); and Lawrence Bruser, "Slavery and the Northern Mind: A Case Study of Free-Soil Sentiment, 1846–1850" (unpublished master's essay, Columbia University, 1967), which deals with Connecticut free-soilism, but has implications for the entire North.

Valuable studies of New York politics include Sidney D. Brummer, *Political History of New York State During the Period of the Civil War* (New York, 1911); Thomas J. Curran, "Know-Nothings of New York State" (unpublished doctoral dissertation, Columbia University, 1963); John A. Krout, "The Maine Law in New York Politics," *NYH*, XVII (July 1936), 262–72; and Louis D. Scisco, *Political Nativism in New York State* (New York, 1901). There is great need for a detailed study of Pennsylvania's complicated politics in the 1850's, but each of the following tells part of the story: William Dusinberre, *Civil War Issues in Philadelphia 1856–1865* (Philadelphia, 1865); Michael F. Holt, "Forging a Majority: The Formation of the Republican Party in Pittsburgh, Pennsylvania, 1848–1860" (unpublished doctoral dissertation, Johns Hopkins University, 1967), an excellent study which stresses ethnic alignments in Pittsburgh politics; Henry R. Mueller, *The Whig Party in Pennsylvania* (New York, 1922); C. Maxwell Myers, "The Rise of the Republican Party in Pennsylvania, 1854–1860" (unpublished doctoral dissertation, University of Pittsburgh, 1940), a rather superficial survey; Asa E. Martin, "The Temperance Movement in Pennsylvania Prior to the Civil War," *PaMHB*, XLIX (1925), 195–230;

William H. Russell, "A. K. McClure and the People's Party in the Campaign of 1860," *PaH*, XXVIII (October 1961), 335–44; and Robert L. Bloom, "Newspaper Opinion in the State Election of 1860," *PaH*, XXVIII (October 1961), 346–64.

Eugene H. Roseboom, *The Civil War Era 1850–1873* (Columbus, 1944), is the standard history of Ohio during these years. Also valuable are George H. Porter, *Ohio Politics During the Civil War Period* (New York, 1911); David H. Bradford, "The Background and Formation of the Republican Party in Ohio, 1844–1861" (unpublished doctoral dissertation, University of Chicago, 1947); and Joseph P. Smith, ed., *History of the Republican Party in Ohio* (2 vols.: Chicago, 1898), which contains the platforms of Republican state conventions. Useful studies of specific aspects of Ohio politics are Emmett D. Preston, "The Fugitive Slave Acts in Ohio," *JNH*, XXVII (October 1943), 422–77; Eugene H. Roseboom, "Salmon P. Chase and the Know-Nothings," *MVHR*, XXV (December 1938), 335–50; Daryl Prendergaft, "Thomas Corwin and the Conservative Republican Reaction, 1858–61," *OAHQ*, LVII (January 1948), 1–23; and William E. Van Horne, "Lewis D. Campbell and the Know-Nothing Party in Ohio," *Ohio History*, LXXVI (1967), 202–21. Two good general works on Indiana are Kenneth Stampp, *Indiana Politics During the Civil War* (Indianapolis, 1949); and Emma Lou Thornbrough, *Indiana in the Civil War Era 1850–1880* (Indianapolis, 1965); while both Charles Zimmerman, "The Origin and Development of the Republican Party in Indiana," *IndMH*, XIII (1917), 211–69, 349–412, and Carl F. Brand, "History of the Know-Nothing Party in Indiana," *IndMH*, XVIII (1922), 47–81, 177–206, 266–80, are competent studies. See also Elmer D. Elbert's very informative doctoral dissertation, "Southern Indiana Politics on the Eve of the Civil War 1858–1861" (Indiana University, 1967); and Roger H. Van Bolt, "The Rise of the Republican Party in Indiana, 1840–1856" (unpublished doctoral dissertation, University of Chicago, 1950), which was also printed as a series in *IndMH* between 1951 and 1954; Walter R. Sharp, "Henry S. Lane and the Formation of the Republican Party in Indiana," *MVHR*, VII (September 1920), 93–112; Willard H. Smith, "Schuyler Colfax and the Political Upheaval of 1854–1855," *MVHR*, XXVIII (December 1941), 383–98; and Russel M. Seeds, *History of the Republican Party in Indiana* (Indianapolis, 1899), which contains Republican state platforms.

Don E. Fehrenbacher's unpublished doctoral dissertation, "Illinois Political Attitudes, 1854–1861" (University of Chicago, 1951), proved quite valuable, as did Arthur C. Cole's more comprehensive study, *The Era of the Civil War 1848–1870* (Springfield, 1919). Other useful works on Lincoln's home state include Paul Selby, "The Genesis of the Republican Party in Illinois," *Transactions* of IllSHS, XI (1906), 270–83; N. Dwight Harris, *The History of Negro Servitude in Illinois* (Chicago, 1904); and John S. Wright, "The Background and Formation of the Republican Party in Illinois, 1846–60" (unpublished doctoral dissertation, University of Chicago, 1946). On Michigan, see Floyd B. Streeter, *Political Parties in Michigan 1837–1860* (Lansing, 1918) and "History of Prohibition Legislation in Michigan," *Michigan History*, II (April 1918), 289–308; and Jean J. L. Fennimore, "Austin Blair: Political Idealist, 1845–1860," *Michigan History*, XLVIII (June 1964), 130–66. Aaron M. Boom, "The Development of Sectional Attitudes in Wisconsin, 1848–1861" (unpublished doctoral dissertation, University of Chicago, 1948), traces political developments in that state. On the states rights issue in Wisconsin, see James L. Sellers, "Republicanism and State Rights in Wisconsin," *MVHR*, XVII (September 1930), 213–29; and Vroman Mason, "The Fugitive Slave Law in Wisconsin, With Reference to Nullification Sentiment," *Proceedings* of the WisHS, XLIII (1895), 117–44; and on ethnic aspects of politics, Frank L. Byrne, "Maine Law Versus Lager Beer: A Dilemma of Wisconsin's Young Republican Party," *WisMH*, LII (Winter 1958–59), 115–20; and two articles by Joseph Schafer: "The Yankee and the Teuton in Wisconsin," *WisMH*, VI (1922–23), 125–44, 261–79, 386–402, VII (1923–24), 3–19, 148–71; and "Know-Nothingism in Wisconsin," *WisMH*, VIII (September 1924), 3–21.

For Iowa politics, the starting point is two articles by Louis Pelzer: "The Origin and Organization of the Republican Party in Iowa," *IJHP*, IV (October 1906), 487–525, and "The History of Political Parties in Iowa from 1857 to 1860," *IJHP*, VII (April 1909), 179–229. More recent works include David S. Sparks, "The Decline of the Democratic Party in Iowa, 1850–1860," *IJH*, LIII (January 1955), 1–31 and "The Birth of the Republican Party in Iowa, 1854–1856," *IJH*, LIV (April 1956), 1–30; and Morton M. Rosenberg, "The Election of 1859 in Iowa," *IJH*, LVII (January 1959), 1–22. On ethnic politics, see Dan E. Clark, "The History of Liquor Legislation in Iowa 1846–1861," *IJHP*, VI (January 1908), 55–87, and F. I. Herriot, "The Germans of Iowa and the 'Two Year' Amendment of Massachusetts," *Deutsch-Amerikanische Geschichtsblätter*, XIII (1913), 202–308. Border state Republicanism is a subject which badly needs examination, but two good articles are Reinhard H. Luthin, "Organizing the Republican Party in the 'Border-Slave' Regions: Edward Bates's Presidential Candidacy in 1860," *MoHR*, XXXVIII (January 1944), 138–61; and Patricia Hickin, "John C. Underwood and the Antislavery Movement in Virginia, 1847–1860," *VaMHB*, LXXIII (April 1965), 156–68.

Index

A

Abbot, Nehemiah, quoted, 289
Ableman v. Booth, 135
Abolition:
  anti-slavery distinguished from, 80
  conservative Republican view of, 187–89
  moderate Republican view of, 207
  in Republican platform of 1856, 130
  resolution on, in 1860, 214
Abolitionists:
  Garrisonian, 74, 85–86, 138–40
  in politics, 74, 101
    radicals, 115–19, 122
    see also Liberty party
  religion of, 109–10
  Republicanism and, 302–4
Adams, Charles Francis, 7, 57, 106, 121, 124, 126, 141
  as Conscience Whig, 82, 104
  nativism opposed, 243, 249
  and Negro rights, 282
  quoted, 111–12, 228
    on middle class, 17
    on Negro colonization, 271
    on Republicans and Democrats, 34
    on secession, 221–23
    on Whigs, 145, 203
  secession, opinion on, 138, 221–23
  in secession crisis, 221–23
Adams, Henry, 39

Adams, John Quincy, 80, 101, 113, 148
Africa, Negro colonization in, 189, 267–68, 272–73
Agriculture:
  economic independence and, 17
  labor and, 32–33
  mechanized, 32–33
  opportunities in, 35
  tariff as aid to, 21
  tenancy, 33
Albany *Evening Journal*, 273, 276
Allen, Charles, 140
Alley, John, 104, 144
American Colonization Society, 189, 268
American party, 240–41, 245–46, 254
  see also Know-Nothings
Andrew, John, 104, 109, 134, 144, 145, 258
  and Negro rights, 285
  Negroes defended, 282
  quoted, 110, 146
Anti-slavery movement:
  abolition distinguished from, 80
  conservative Republican attitude toward, 187–90
  historiography, 1–10
  immigrants opposed to, 230–31
  Know-Nothings and, 233–34, 239–40
  in politics, 73–75, 80–84, 86–87, 101, 113–14
    radical program, 115–118, 124–28

in election of 1860, 216–17
former, in Republican party, 19–
20, 145, 149, 166–68, 281
see also Conservatives, Republican
and Kansas-Nebraska Act, 166,
193–95
and Know-Nothings, 196–97
nativism, 196–97, 203, 230, 234,
260
new party planned, 196–98
Wilmot, David, 60, 105, 107, 149n.,
157, 159, 202
and Frémont's candidacy, 166
quoted, 116, 152, 153, 169
racial prejudice, 267
in Union party, 255
Wilmot, Proviso, 60, 83, 106, 116,
152, 164, 188, 190, 267, 308, 309,
314
Wilson, Charles, quoted, 265
Wilson, Henry, 16, 21, 30, 96, 133,
210, 240, 302
and immigrant voting question, 251
Negro colonization favored, 276
and Negro rights, 282, 285, 289,
291, 296
quoted, 118, 139, 146, 214

on Negroes, 263, 291, 296
on Worcester Disunion Convention, 141
as radical, 104, 109, 113, 117, 124,
126, 132
Winthrop, Robert, quoted, 43,
195
Wisconsin:
fugitive slave law opposed in, 135,
201–2
nativism opposed in, 246
Wisconsin State Journal, 201, 276,
277, 287
quoted, 292
Worcester Disunion Convention, 140–
41
Worcester *Spy*, 114
Wright, Elizur, quoted, 303
Wright, Silas, 174

Y

Yates, Richard, 87, 104, 144, 205,
258
and Negro rights, 284, 288
quoted, 11, 28, 96